HomilyGrits Daily Discipline of Appled Truth and Proactive Prayer
Copyright © 2004Robert W. VanHoose

Library of Congress Control Number: 2004103921

1. All Scripture quotations unless otherwise indicated are taken from the New King James Version. Copyright © 1982 by Thomas Nelson, Inc. Used by permission. All rights reserved
2. Scripture quotations marked (NIV) are taken from the HOLY BIBLE, NEW INTERNATIONAL VERSION® NIV®. Copyright©1973,1978,1984 by International Bible Society. Used by permission of Zondervan. All rights reserved
3. Scripture quotations marked NLT are taken from the HOLY BIBLE, NEW LIVING TRANSLATION Original work copyright © 1996 by Tyndale Charitable Trust. All rights reserved.
4. Scripture quotations marked MSG are taken from THE MESSAGE: The Bible in Contemporary Language Copyright © 2002 by Eugene H. Peterson. All rights reserved
5. The author gratefully acknowledges the teachings and influence of Bible Study Fellowship, Charles Spurgeon, Oswald Chambers, Rick Warren, Dr. Bruce Wilkinson, Dr. Charles Stanley, Charles Swindoll, Max Lucado, Henry Blackaby. Chip Ingram, and others who the Lord has used to guide me in His Word., and a greater understanding of His truth.
   It is not my intent to copy anyone, but I am sure that many of these truths I have appropriated have been from Scriptural understandings taught by some of these teachers.

ISBN: 0-9742612-3-8
Published by Homily Grits Publishing Co.
All rights reserved. Printed in the United States of America

HOMILY GRITS

Daily Discipline
of
Applied Truth and Proactive Prayer

*(This book includes some devotions
previously published
in
Homily Grits
and
Homily Grits 2)*

Homily Grits Publishing Co.
Ocala, Florida
www.homilygrits.com
RVanHoose@homilygrits.com

"If you believe, you will receive whatever you ask for in prayer."
(Matthew 21:22 NIV)

"Keep alert and pray. Otherwise temptation will overpower you.
For though the spirit is willing enough, the body is weak!"
(Matthew 26:4 NLT)

"And so I tell you, keep on asking, and you will be given what you ask for. Keep on looking, and you will find. Keep on knocking, and the door will be opened. For everyone who asks, receives. Everyone who seeks, finds. And the door is opened to everyone who knocks. You fathers—if your children ask for a fish, do you give them a snake instead? Or if they ask for an egg, do you give them a scorpion? Of course not! If you sinful people know how to give good gifts to your children, how much more will your heavenly Father give the Holy Spirit to those who ask him."
(Luke 11:9-13 NLT)

"But if you stay joined to me and my words remain in you, you may ask any request you like, and it will be granted!"
(John 15:7 NLT)

"You didn't choose me. I chose you. I appointed you to go and produce fruit that will last, so that the Father will give you whatever you ask for, using my name"
(John 15:16 NLT)

"The truth is, you can go directly to the Father and ask him, and he will grant your request because you use my name. You haven't done this before. Ask, using my name, and you will receive, and you will have abundant joy"
(John 16:23b,24

FOREWORD

About four years ago someone asked me to put into print a series that I had taught called *Holy Ambition – What it takes to Make a Difference for God.* I didn't know anything about publishing but I knew that I wanted this message to get out to people all over America and perhaps the world.

One man, in the sunset years of his life, read that book and dreamed a great dream for God. His name is Robert W. VanHoose and he has a holy ambition to help regular people like you and me drink deeply from God's word but in a way that we can digest it in a hurry.

I heartily recommend <u>"Homily Grits" Snack Food for the Soul.</u> Drawn from over fifty years of walking with God in a down-home style with great Biblical content, Robert VanHoose will allow you to experience that spiritual shot-in-the-arm that we all need on a regular basis."

Chip Ingram, President
Walk Thru the Bible©

(Chip is also featured on over 570 radio stations thoughout the World with his "Living on the Edge" Bible teaching ministry.)

"I pray that you will begin to understand the incredible greatness of his power for us who believe him. This is the same mighty power that raised Christ from the dead and seated him in the place of honor at God's right and in the heavenly realms.
(Ephesians 1:19,20 NLT)

"Now glory be to God! By his mighty power at work within us, he is able to accomplish infinitely more than we would ever dare to ask or hope."
(Ephesians 3:20 NLT)

"Pray at all times and on every occasion in the power of the Holy Spirit. Stay alert and be persistent in your prayers for all Christians everywhere."
(Ephesians 6:18 NLT)

"Don't worry about anything; instead, pray about everything. Tell God what you need, and thank him for all he has done. If you do this, you will experience God's peace, which is far more wonderful than the human mind can understand. His peace will guard your hearts and minds as you live in Christ Jesus"
(.Philippians 4:6,7 NLT)

"Devote yourselves to prayer with an alert mind and a thankful heart.."
(Colossians 4:2 NLT)

"For this reason we also, since the day we heard it, do not cease to pray for you, and to ask that you may be filled with the knowledge of His will in all wisdom and spiritual understanding; that you may walk worthy the Lord, fully pleasing Him, being fruitful in every good work increasing in the knowledge of God; strengthened with all might, according to His glorious power, for all patience and longsuffering with joy"
(Col 1:9-11)

"Are any among you suffering? They should keep on praying about it. And those who have reason to be thankful should continually sing praiises to the Lord, Are any among you sick? They should call for the elders of the church and have them pray over them, anointing them with oil in the name of the Lord. And their prayer offered in faith will heal the sick, and the Lord will make them well. And anyone who has committed sins will be forgiven. Confess your sins to each other and pray for each other so that you may be healed .The earnest prayer of a righteous person has great power and wonderful results.
(James 5:13-16 NLT)

Introduction

"Because the Teacher was wise, he taught the people everything he knew. He collected proverbs and classified them Indeed, the Teacher taught the plain truth, and he did so in an interesting way."

Ecclesiastes 12:9 NLT

I don't know how wise I am, but I know Someone who is! What a joy to share some of the wisdom He has imparted to me for over some sixty years. My fervent prayer is that you will be as blessed in reading these words as I have been in writing them, and that God will be glorified.

From the inmates at Florida's faith based Lawtey Correctional Institution to Salvation Army needy - - - from college students to nursing home residents to people just trying to grow in their relationship with the Lord, - - - a lot of people have been nourished through Homily Grits and Homily Grits 2. My greatest joy has been in feeding some of the troops in Iraq with a daily internet version downloaded, printed and distributed by a very special young guardsman.

I have tried my best to let the Scriptures speak and come to life in practical applications that anyone can understand and relate. I take very seriously James' admonishment that those who teach will be judged by God with greater strictness. (James 3:1) I lean solely on His grace that these meditations may be pleasing in His sight.

I want to thank the love of my life, my wife Lorna, and the great teachers who have fed me so well for so many years and especially Dr. Bruce Wilkinson and Chip Ingram, whose teachings have changed my life dramatically, and actually inspired these writings.

I realize that journaling is not for everyone. But I know that myself and hundreds of thousands (maybe millions) have found great joy and blessing in writing their prayers as a discipline. Please give it a fair try of at least 21 days and then ask if this is working for you.

May God Bless your reading and help you find the heart of God through this discipline. This really is what's important.

In His Love,

Robert W. VanHoose

Colossians 1:9-11

Dedication

To our children, who are trophies of God's grace to us,
and to our children's spouses all of whom we
dearly love.

Next to our Lord Jesus Christ, and each other they
are our best friends,
our reminders of God's faithfulness.

Amy VanHoose Butler
Robert W. VanHoose, Jr., and Sandy
William E. VanHoose
Ruth Hudson and David
Allison VanHoose Braun
Rebecca Puig and Rafael

*"If you obey all the laws and commands that I will give you today, all will be well
with you and your children. Then you will enjoy a long life in the land the
LORD your God is giving you for all time."
(Deuteronomy 4:40 NLT)*

Bright Hope for Tomorrow

"For I know the plans I have for you," says the LORD. "They are plans for good and not for disaster, to give you a future and a hope. Jeremiah 29:11 NLT

As we begin a New Year, it is good to turn our backs on a lot of yesterdays. We need to remember that God has forgotten our sins and remembers them no more when we have confessed and repented. We can't let the enjoyment we have in God's grace be diminished by our past failures.

> *"So be strong and take courage, all you who put your hope in the LORD!*
> *Psalm 31:24 NLT*

God will often bring to mind the memories of past sins and blunders as a means of growing to become more like Christ in the future by avoiding the mistakes of the past.

And what is our bright hope for the future. Short term, it is the confidence in knowing that God is going before us, working all things for our good and His glory as he continues to conform us into the image of Christ.

All of the lost opportunities of the past are gone. We have all missed out on many chances for fruitfulness, blessings, and to be all that we can and should be in Christ.

The bright hope for the future is in knowing that our God is not only the God of second chances, but that His mercies are renewed every day and that He continues to accept us and love us through the many conflicts, failures and doubts that we experience in the daily grind of life.

> *"When the Spirit of truth comes, he will guide you into all truth. He will not be presenting his own ideas; he will be telling you what he has heard. He will tell you about the future."*
> *John 16:13 NLT*

Long term, our "bright hope for tomorrow" is the blessed assurance that *"The One on the Throne will pitch his tent there for them: no more hunger, no more thirst, no more scorching heat. The Lamb on the Throne will shepherd them, will lead them to spring waters of Life. And God will wipe every last tear from their eyes."(Revelation 7:14 MSG).* No wonder we can face the future with such confidence,

Father, thank you for my bright hope for tomorrow. Amen

Taking it to the Lord...

How can I apply this truth?____

____

____

Father, I've come to worship and praise you! You are my:_________________________________

____

I give you all Glory, Honor, and Praise O Lord!

Father, I am sorry that I have sinned by:____

Help me to repent. Cleanse me, strengthen me, restore me.

Father, THANK YOU for all your love, grace, mercy and blessings of life that you continually shower down upon me. Thank you especially for:

1.____________________________________   2.____________________________________

3.____________________________________   4.____________________________________

5.____________________________________   6.____________________________________

THANK YOU for answered prayers:____

Father, I need:____

Father, I ask that YOU:____

____

____

Lord, bless me that I may be a blessing. Give me Your heart for loving and serving others. Keep Your hand upon me. Keep me from all evil and harm, and let me cause harm to no one. Bind Satan that he have no power over me. All this I pray in subjection to your will and in the strong name of my Lord and Savior, Jesus Christ. Amen.

Any Other Way

**"My Father, if it is not possible for this cup to be taken away unless I drink it, may your will be done."
Matthew 26:39**

Twice Jesus pled with His Father that His cup of suffering and sorrow be taken away, if possible. Both times He was in total submission to the good and gracious will of His Father. If God, who loved His only begotten Son so much, could have found another way to save the lost and restore our right standing with Him, it is hard to believe that He would not have done so.

> *"You will show me the way of life, granting me the joy of your presence and the pleasures of living with you" forever."*
> *Psalm 16:11*

Today, the world is full of people trying to find loopholes and short cuts to heaven and to the abundant life. We straddle fences; we pick and choose what parts of the Bible we will believe and what parts we will disregard.

Many denigrate the immensity of the sacrifice of Christ by thinking that it was not enough, and that the way of good works is what brings right standing with God. Others gloss over the clear teaching of Scripture regarding homosexuality, marriage, pride, etc., and try to find validity and respectability for life styles and conduct that God calls abominations.

Jesus said that He was the way, the truth and the life. Scripture says there is no other name under heaven through which men may be saved.

Jesus submitted to the will of His father and underwent the horrendous pain and suffering of the scourging, the humiliation, and the torment of hell because it was the only way we could be saved.

> *"You can enter God's Kingdom only through the narrow gate. The highway to hell is broad, and its gate is wide for the many who choose the easy way."*
> *Mathew 7:13*

The way of the cross is the narrow way, and many never find it. The way of the cross can be a very hard way, filled with a lot of pain and suffering.

It is also the way of peace with God and with man. It is a life of contentment and joy. Why in the world would we want to live any other way?

Father, you died to make the way, and you lived to show the way. Let me always follow the way. Amen

Taking it to the Lord...

How can I apply this truth?____

____

Father, I've come to worship and praise you! You are my:____________________

____

I give you all Glory, Honor, and Praise O Lord!

Father, I am sorry that I have sinned by:_________________________________

Help me to repent. Cleanse me, strengthen me, restore me.

Father, THANK YOU for all your love, grace, mercy and blessings of life that you continually shower down upon me. Thank you especially for:

1.____________________________   2.____________________________

3.____________________________   4.____________________________

5.____________________________   6.____________________________

THANK YOU for answered prayers:_________________________________

Father, I need:____

Father, I ask that YOU:____

____

____

Lord, bless me that I may be a blessing. Give me Your heart for loving and serving others. Keep Your hand upon me. Keep me from all evil and harm, and let me cause harm to no one. Bind Satan that he have no power over me. All this I pray in subjection to your will and in the strong name of my Lord and Savior, Jesus Christ. Amen.

Thank You, Mel Gibson

"But He was wounded for our transgressions, He was bruised for our iniquities; the chastisement for our peace was upon Him, and by His stripes we are healed." Isaiah 53:5

Thanks to "The Passion of Christ" movie, I can now say "yes" when I sing or when I hear "Were You There When They Crucified my Lord".

> *"Then I will punish their transgression with the rod and their iniquity with stripes."*
> *Psalm 89:32*

The searing brutality of this movie will leave the suffering of Christ embedded in my heart forever.

The Scripture verse that says: "by His stripes we are healed," takes on new meaning after seeing the brutal and barbarous mutilations of our Lord's body by the savage Roman soldiers.

I didn't think about the Jews or Romans as the killers of Jesus. I winced at the truth that it was for every sin that I have ever committed for He chose to die so that I might have forgiveness and eternal life.

That someone so kind, so compassionate and full of love would choose to suffer such brutality, humiliation, rejection, pain and suffering in order to reconcile me to God shames and humbles me. At the same time, it inspires me to remember the price that was paid for me and to respond by living for the glory of the One who bought me with His own blood.

> *"Then Jesus began to tell them that he, the Son of Man, would suffer many terrible things and be rejected by the leaders, the leading priests, and the teachers of religious law. He would be killed, and three days later he would rise again."*
> *Mark 8:31 NLT*

I will take this picture of the broken body and shed blood of Christ with me to every communion table at which I am ever privileged to worship.

Thank you, God, for using Mel and a much and deservedly maligned media to remind the world who you were, are, and evermore shall be! May this masterpiece be a pre-cursor of the spiritual revival that so many have been praying for so long.

Father, thank you for using this movie for your Glory and the upbuilding of Your kingdom on earth. Amen

Taking it to the Lord...

How can I apply this truth?____

____

____

Father, I've come to worship and praise you! You are my:_________________________

____

I give you all Glory, Honor, and Praise O Lord!

Father, I am sorry that I have sinned by:_____________________________________

Help me to repent. Cleanse me, strengthen me, restore me.

Father, THANK YOU for all your love, grace, mercy and blessings of life that you continually shower down upon me. Thank you especially for:

1.____________________________________ 2.____________________________________

3.____________________________________ 4.____________________________________

5.____________________________________ 6.____________________________________

THANK YOU for answered prayers:____

Father, I need:____

Father, I ask that YOU:____

____

____

Lord, bless me that I may be a blessing. Give me Your heart for loving and serving others. Keep Your hand upon me. Keep me from all evil and harm, and let me cause harm to no one. Bind Satan that he have no power over me. All this I pray in subjection to your will and in the strong name of my Lord and Savior, Jesus Christ. Amen.

The Ice Age

"Beware lest anyone cheat you through philosophy and empty deceit, according to the tradition of men, according to the basic principles of the world, and not according to Christ." Colossians 2:8

There are a few still around that remember the old refrigerators cooled by big chunks of ice delivered daily by the iceman. From carving out boulders of ice from frozen lakes and rivers and storing in large insulated storage rooms to moving into electrical freezing, the ice house and ice man were a daily staple of life like the milk man who delivered milk daily by horse drawn cart.

> *"Therefore the Lord said :Inasmuch as these people draw near with their mouths and honor Me with their lips, but have removed their hearts far from Me and their fear toward Me is taught by the commandment of men," Isaiah 29:13*

Some churches seem to be stuck in the ice age of tradition and old biases that are causing them to lose their saltiness and relevance.

While the Gospel of Jesus Christ is a timeless message that will never change, the means of delivering the Good News have changed dramatically and will continue to do so.

Thanks to some of the many wonders of the communications age, the gospel has now been proclaimed throughout the world."

The churches that have come out of the ice age and combined uncompromising truth with authentic Christianity and used all the wonderful tools available are live growing churches. The Churches that have remained legalistic and self-centered have died throughout the world and are continuing to do so.

The competition for hearts and souls is intense. The world seems to be winning this war as intra-denominational disputes distract, and tunnel vision blinds many churches.

> *"Making the word of God of no effect through your tradition which you have handed down. And many such things you do." Mark 7:13*

Ice is great for cooling and preserving freshness, but the ice age is over and the coolness of hearts need the warmth of God's love, and the fire of the Spirit to kindle revival and let the light shine in a real and meaningful way.

Father, help me to distinguish between truth and tradition. Amen

Taking it to the Lord...

How can I apply this truth?____

____

Father, I've come to worship and praise you! You are my:_______________________

____

I give you all Glory, Honor, and Praise O Lord!

Father, I am sorry that I have sinned by:_______________________________________

Help me to repent. Cleanse me, strengthen me, restore me.

Father, THANK YOU for all your love, grace, mercy and blessings of life that you continually shower down upon me.

Thank you especially for:

1.________________________________   2.________________________________

3.________________________________   4.________________________________

5.________________________________   6.________________________________

THANK YOU for answered prayers:____

Father, I need:____

Father, I ask that YOU:____

____

____

Lord, bless me that I may be a blessing. Give me Your heart for loving and serving others. Keep Your hand upon me. Keep me from all evil and harm, and let me cause harm to no one. Bind Satan that he have no power over me. All this I pray in subjection to your will and in the strong name of my Lord and Savior, Jesus Christ. Amen.

Synthetic Christianity

"For the weapons of our warfare *are* not carnal but mighty in God for pulling down strongholds, casting down arguments and every high thing that exalts itself against the knowledge of God, bringing every thought into captivity to the obedience of Christ," 2 Corinthians 10:4, 5

Synthetic diamonds are a multi-million dollar business. Some shine brighter than real diamonds. All have less flaws than real gems.

> *"Nor will I go in with hypocrites. I have hated the assembly of evildoers."*
> *Psalm 26:4a*

We have the synthetic religion called secular humanism, which worships intellect, embraces evolution, hedonism, and the glory of man. It is freely taught in schools, and has disciples sitting on high courts, in government, and even in some churches.

Unfortunately, we have a lot of, and all are in danger of becoming, synthetic Christians. Paul calls them carnal Christians. Jesus called them "brood of vipers," "white washed tombstones," who would not escape the judgment of hell.

The chameleon has been protected by the ability to change colors to blend in and hide in any background. This ability is fine for a lizard. Jesus warns about wolves that dress in sheep's clothing seeking to prey on the unwary.

> *"The greatest among you must be a servant. But those who exalt themselves will be humbled, and those who humble themselves will be exalted."*
> *Matthew 23:11,12 NLT*

As long as we persist in living self-centered lives controlled by the flesh instead of the Spirit, we are always going to be phony imitations rather than genuine imitators of Christ.   It is only when we are transformed by the power of the Holy Spirit living within us that we can ever know the joy of what genuine Christianity is all about.

Father, help me to be a genuine Christian. Amen

Taking it to the Lord...

How can I apply this truth?____

____

____

Father, I've come to worship and praise you! You are my:_____________________

____

I give you all Glory, Honor, and Praise O Lord!

Father, I am sorry that I have sinned by:__________________________________

Help me to repent. Cleanse me, strengthen me, restore me.

Father, THANK YOU for all your love, grace, mercy and blessings of life that you continually shower down upon me. Thank you especially for:

1.____________________________________   2.____________________________________

3.____________________________________   4.____________________________________

5.____________________________________   6.____________________________________

THANK YOU for answered prayers:____

Father, I need:____

Father, I ask that YOU:____

____

____

Lord, bless me that I may be a blessing. Give me Your heart for loving and serving others. Keep Your hand upon me. Keep me from all evil and harm, and let me cause harm to no one. Bind Satan that he have no power over me. All this I pray in subjection to your will and in the strong name of my Lord and Savior, Jesus Christ. Amen.

The Day of the Lord

"Being confident of this very thing, that He who has begun a good work in you will complete *it* until the day of Jesus Christ." 1 Corinthians 1:6

Often used to prophecy judgment and destruction, sometimes as a promise of blessing and fulfillment, "the day of the Lord" is always a day when the sovereignty God is manifested.

> *"Every day of my life was recorded in your book. Every moment was laid out before a single day had passed."*
> *Psalm 139:16*

The "day of the Lord" can be a few minutes, a few hours, or for years, depending on the event or manifestation. The 70-year Babylonian captivity was "a day of the Lord". The 40-year wandering in the desert by the Israelites was "a day of the Lord." The birth, death, and resurrection of Jesus Christ were all "days of the Lord."

There are personal "days of the Lord" in the lives of every Christian. These are spiritual markers that define our faith and often determine the lives we live.

The day that we receive Jesus Christ as our Lord and Savior is a great "day of the Lord." This becomes a day of great rejoicing in heaven as well as for us who have seen the light.

We experience days of the Lord's blessing and days of the Lord's chastening. Every day should be viewed as a "day of the Lord" in the lives of all believers. He made every day for us "to rejoice and be glad" and to grow into the fullness of His son.

Most major prophesies made referring to the "day of the Lord" have been fulfilled, save one. What a marvelous day it will be for all believers, when Christ returns to gather His church to Himself!

If we go to such great lengths to prepare for our wedding day or other celebrations, how much more should we be preparing for this greatest of all days by being ready by *"being filled with the fruits of righteousness which are by Jesus Christ, to the glory and praise of God." (Philippians 1:1)*

> *"But the day of the Lord will come as a thief in the night,"*
> *2 Peter 3:10a*

Father, help me to be ever ready! Amen

Taking it to the Lord...

How can I apply this truth?____

____

____

Father, I've come to worship and praise you! You are my:_____________________

____

I give you all Glory, Honor, and Praise O Lord!

Father, I am sorry that I have sinned by:___________________________________

Help me to repent. Cleanse me, strengthen me, restore me.

Father, THANK YOU for all your love, grace, mercy and blessings of life that you continually shower down upon me. Thank you especially for:

1.___________________________________   2.___________________________________

3.___________________________________   4.___________________________________

5.___________________________________   6.___________________________________

THANK YOU for answered prayers:____

Father, I need:____

Father, I ask that YOU:____

____

____

____

Lord, bless me that I may be a blessing. Give me Your heart for loving and serving others. Keep Your hand upon me. Keep me from all evil and harm, and let me cause harm to no one. Bind Satan that he have no power over me. All this I pray in subjection to your will and in the strong name of my Lord and Savior, Jesus Christ. Amen.

How to Win by Losing

"And how do you benefit if you gain the whole world but lose your own soul in the process? Is anything worth more than your soul?" Matthew 16:25 NLT

We are a win-oriented society. The world would define us as winners or losers based on our performance in life.

> *"They did not conquer the land with their swords; it was not their own strength that gave them victory."*
> *Psalm 44:3*

The obsession to win at any price has carried bigger price tags than could be foreseen in every area of life where it has been the core value. Winning at anything is sweet affirmation.

There are a lot of things that we can win only by losing. I just won a major battle of the bulge by losing 9 pounds last week.

The lessons of life are learned a lot more through losing than through winning. God's character building program for us is built upon seeing us through our mistakes, disappointments, and failures and growing us through them.

Our Lord himself came to demonstrate this. He didn't have to endure all of the ridicule and rejection, betrayal, persecution and loneliness for His sake. He did it to show us how to deal with it, and how to be blessed and grow stronger in the process.

> *"But what things were gain to me, these I have counted loss for Christ. Yet indeed I also count all things loss for the excellence of the knowledge of Christ Jesus my Lord,"*
> *Philippians 3:7, 8*

God's lost and found department is constantly at work seeking the lost and helping them find a new life in Christ by losing their old life in sin as they receive His wonderful gift of salvation.

We must all lose our lives controlled by the flesh if we are to live in the new life controlled by the Spirit.

When we lose our pride and self-worship, we win God's approval and strength that is made perfect in our weakness.

Father thank you for covering my losses through Your Son's "big win" on the Cross. Amen

Taking it to the Lord...

How can I apply this truth?____
____
____

Father, I've come to worship and praise you! You are my:_______________________
____

I give you all Glory, Honor, and Praise O Lord!

Father, I am sorry that I have sinned by:____________________________________

Help me to repent. Cleanse me, strengthen me, restore me.

Father, THANK YOU for all your love, grace, mercy and blessings of life that you continually shower down upon me. Thank you especially for:

1._____________________________   2._____________________________
3._____________________________   4._____________________________
5._____________________________   6._____________________________

THANK YOU for answered prayers:____

Father, I need:____

Father, I ask that YOU:____
____
____

Lord, bless me that I may be a blessing. Give me Your heart for loving and serving others. Keep Your hand upon me. Keep me from all evil and harm, and let me cause harm to no one. Bind Satan that he have no power over me. All this I pray in subjection to your will and in the strong name of my Lord and Savior, Jesus Christ. Amen.

Throw out the Money Changers!

"In the Temple area he saw merchants selling cattle, sheep, and doves for sacrifices; and he saw money changers behind their counters. Jesus made a whip from some ropes and chased them all out of the Temple." John 2:14 NLT

The moneychangers are taking over our temples! Yes, the moneychangers have invaded our temples of the Holy Spirit by taking over TV programming, advertising, and movies, and by operating porn businesses. The effects have been devastating.

> *"And you will say, "How I hated discipline! If only I had not demanded my own way! Oh, why didn't I listen to my teachers? Why didn't I pay attention to those who gave me instruction?"*
> *Proverbs 5:12,13 NLT*

We have nearly more or more illegitimate children than children born in wedlock, soaring divorce rates, adultery, AIDS and other sexually transmitted diseases, addictions to pornography and sexual dysfunction.

The reason the moneychangers are getting rich at the expense of all these problems is because we buy it. Our temples of the Holy Spirit have become temples of worship for what the world defines as pleasure and God defines as sin and abominations. We have become spiritual adulterers if not actually physical adulterers.

Just as the rulers of the past followed the prophets' advice and cleaned out the temples that had been desecrated by the same of idolatry and worship of false gods, we need to do the same thing.

> *"And what union can there be between God's temple and idols? For we are the temple of the living God."*
> *2 Corinthians 6:16 NLT*

When enough of us turn the off button on TV sleaze, the moneychangers will get the message. When we stay away from the bad movies, they will quit making them. The porn sites will dry up when the cash cow quits giving milk.

We need a new sexual revolution of purity through promoting God's purposes and plans for sex. Lets begin by throwing out the moneychangers who are doing business in our temples.

Father, by the power of your Spirit, help me to cleanse your temple within me. Amen

Taking it to the Lord...

How can I apply this truth?____

____

Father, I've come to worship and praise you! You are my:________________

____

I give you all Glory, Honor, and Praise O Lord!

Father, I am sorry that I have sinned by:________________________________

Help me to repent. Cleanse me, strengthen me, restore me.

Father, THANK YOU for all your love, grace, mercy and blessings of life that you continually shower down upon me. Thank you especially for:

1.____________________________   2.____________________________

3.____________________________   4.____________________________

5.____________________________   6.____________________________

THANK YOU for answered prayers:____________________________________

Father, I need:____

Father, I ask that YOU:____

____

____

Lord, bless me that I may be a blessing. Give me Your heart for loving and serving others. Keep Your hand upon me. Keep me from all evil and harm, and let me cause harm to no one. Bind Satan that he have no power over me. All this I pray in subjection to your will and in the strong name of my Lord and Savior, Jesus Christ. Amen.

Terms of Endearment

"But the people's minds were hardened, and even to this day whenever the old covenant is being read, a veil covers their minds so they cannot understand the truth. And this veil can be removed only by believing in Christ." 2 Corinthians 3:14 NLT

Since the beginning of mankind, God's "terms of endearment" for His children have been expressed as covenants, where in God makes promises to us. He Promised Noah that He would not repeat the flood.

> *"I have sworn an oath to David, and in my holiness I cannot lie: His dynasty will go on forever; his throne is as secure as the sun."*
> *Psalm 89:35,36 NLT*

He promised Abraham that He would always be His God and the God of all His descendants an after God's own heart, God promised that through his descendents He would reign forever. This covenant comes to fullness in the lordship of Jesus Christ, the mediator of a new covenant.

God has never broken any of His covenants. While obedience is always accompanied by blessings, disobedience brings on curses and punishment. Confession and true repentance are necessary for the restoration of all covenant relationships.

Believers in Christ are recipients of a new and better covenant promise. We have Holy Baptism and the Lord's Supper given as signs of our covenant relationship of grace. Forever and initiated circumcision as a sign   He gave circumcision as a sign of acceptance of this covenant.

> *"Once for all time he took blood into that Most Holy Place, but not the blood of goats and calves. He took his own blood, and with it he secured our salvation forever."*
> *Hebrews 9:12 NLT*

The children of Israel promised to do "everything the Lord asks of us," and received God's covenant of the law and became God's "special treasure".

We are "special treasures" of God who loves us with an everlasting love and will keep His covenant of grace with us no matter what. These are real terms of endearment!

Father, keep me ever mindful of my covenant relationship with You, and help me to enjoy the blessings of obedience. Amen

Taking it to the Lord...

How can I apply this truth?____

____

Father, I've come to worship and praise you! You are my:_________________________________

____

I give you all Glory, Honor, and Praise O Lord!

Father, I am sorry that I have sinned by:____

Help me to repent. Cleanse me, strengthen me, restore me.

Father, THANK YOU for all your love, grace, mercy and blessings of life that you continually shower down upon me. Thank you especially for:

1.__________________________________   2.__________________________________

3.__________________________________   4.__________________________________

5.__________________________________   6.__________________________________

THANK YOU for answered prayers:____

Father, I need:____

Father, I ask that YOU:____

____

____

Lord, bless me that I may be a blessing. Give me Your heart for loving and serving others. Keep Your hand upon me. Keep me from all evil and harm, and let me cause harm to no one. Bind Satan that he have no power over me. All this I pray in subjection to your will and in the strong name of my Lord and Savior, Jesus Christ. Amen.

Just Don't Go There!

"When you bow down before the Lord and admit your dependence on him, he will lift you up and give you honor." James 4:10

The mind is a beautiful thing. God gave us the best one He created so that we could long for Him, learn of Him, and have intimacy and fellowship with Him.

"Give your burdens to the LORD, and he will take care of you. He will not permit the godly to slip and fall."
Psalm 55:22 NLT

He also gave us a free will infected with a sin problem. Even after our sin condition is dealt with by receiving Jesus Christ as our Savior, sin acts of commission and omission are going to continue as long as we live in these earthly, physical bodies

Temptations come custom made to fit our particular weaknesses. We have a hard time identifying with people who succumb to temptations that don't tempt us.

God has promised an escape plan for every temptation that satan sends our way. It involves resisting, humbling, fighting, and avoiding.

When we stand firm and resist, satan will flee. When we humble ourselves and admit that we cannot resist in our own strength God will come with the power of His Spirit to help us win the war.

"An ounce of prevention is worth a pound of cure."   We can prevent so many of problems just by not going there. We shouldn't go to bars with a drinking problem or to an all you can eat buffet with an obesity problem. You don't go to the TV channels or Internet sites that trigger your weaknesses.

"For we are not fighting against people made of flesh and blood, but against the evil rulers and authorities of the unseen world, against those mighty powers of darkness who rule this world, and against wicked spirits in the heavenly realms."
Ephesians 6:12 NLT

When a temptation or unhealthy craving tries to enter our mind or our heart, we can choose not to go there, and instead, go to God, asking him to deliver us from temptation and the power of any sin to ensnare us physically, just as He has already done spiritually.

Father, just as you have set me free from bondage to sin spiritually, keep me free emotionally and physically. Amen

Taking it to the Lord...

How can I apply this truth?____

____

____

Father, I've come to worship and praise you! You are my:_______________________

____

I give you all Glory, Honor, and Praise O Lord!

Father, I am sorry that I have sinned by:____________________________________

Help me to repent. Cleanse me, strengthen me, restore me.

Father, THANK YOU for all your love, grace, mercy and blessings of life that you continually shower down upon me. Thank you especially for:

1.__________________________________   2.__________________________________

3.__________________________________   4.__________________________________

5.__________________________________   6.__________________________________

THANK YOU for answered prayers:____

Father, I need:____

Father, I ask that YOU:____

____

____

Lord, bless me that I may be a blessing. Give me Your heart for loving and serving others. Keep Your hand upon me. Keep me from all evil and harm, and let me cause harm to no one. Bind Satan that he have no power over me. All this I pray in subjection to your will and in the strong name of my Lord and Savior, Jesus Christ. Amen.

Selective Compassion

"Since God chose you to be the holy people whom he loves, you must clothe yourselves with tenderhearted mercy, kindness, humility, gentleness, and patience." Colossians 3:12 NLT

We can be very compassionate when we choose to be. It is very easy to feel sorry for and show kindness and mercy to our friends and loved ones. We are easily touched by appeals for funds for mercy ministries. We like to be compassionate to those who are deserving of it.

> *"Unto the upright there arises light in the darkness; He is gracious, and full of compassion, and righteous."*
> *Psalm 112:4 NLT*

Sooner or later our compassion and patience run out for the undeserving. We ignore the beggar on the street. We don't have time for the institutionalized or homeless. The pleas of the undeserving are disregarded. We feel and show disdain rather than compassion.

The priest and the Levite in today's story of the Good Samaritan show a side of most of us that is very unbecoming to a follower of Christ.

In my preoccupation with self and total disregard for the hurt or needs of another, I have failed miserably in some of the opportunities the Lord has sent my way to show compassion. I have rationalized not giving to the beggar because I would be buying him booze. I have rationalized not giving aid and comfort to someone because I was too busy doing the Lord's work.

The truth is that we are never going to see anyone who does not matter to God, and because they matter to Him, they must matter to us.

> *"By chance a Jewish priest came along; but when he saw the man lying there, he crossed to the other side of the road and passed him by. A Temple assistant walked over and looked at him lying there, but he also passed by on the other side."*
> *Luke 10:31,32 NLT*

Before we exercise selective compassion by deciding who is deserving and who isn't, we need to look in a mirror. When we are honest with ourselves and realize how undeserving of God's compassion and mercy we are; it will change our perspective on how undeserving they are.

I don't know about you, but I can't afford the risk of failing God's compassion tests. I need more compassion and mercy than I can ever deserve. God makes it very clear that we will not receive it for ourselves if we withhold it from others. Instead of being selective, we should be elective and act like one of God's elect.

Father, help me to be merciful and compassionate to all. Amen

Taking it to the Lord...

How can I apply this truth?____

____

____

Father, I've come to worship and praise you! You are my:_______________________

____

I give you all Glory, Honor, and Praise O Lord!

Father, I am sorry that I have sinned by:______________________________________

Help me to repent. Cleanse me, strengthen me, restore me.

Father, THANK YOU for all your love, grace, mercy and blessings of life that you continually shower down upon me. Thank you especially for:

1.________________________________   2.________________________________

3.________________________________   4.________________________________

5.________________________________   6.________________________________

THANK YOU for answered prayers:____

Father, I need:____

Father, I ask that YOU:____

____

Lord, bless me that I may be a blessing. Give me Your heart for loving and serving others. Keep Your hand upon me. Keep me from all evil and harm, and let me cause harm to no one. Bind Satan that he have no power over me. All this I pray in subjection to your will and in the strong name of my Lord and Savior, Jesus Christ. Amen.

Who Really Brings Good Things to Life?

"I have come that they may have life, and that they may have *it* more abundantly." John 10:10b

With all due respect to General Electric and their "We bring good things to life" award-winning advertising slogan, they can't hold a candle to Jesus when it comes to bringing good things to life.

> *"This is the LORD,*
> *in whom we trusted.*
> *Let us rejoice in the*
> *salvation He*
> *brings!"*
> *Isaiah 25:b NLT*

General Electric makes products that make our life more comfortable and convenient, but the really good things of life begin with what God brought to life in His Son, Jesus Christ.

GE does a good job of cleaning clothes, but Jesus did the great job of cleansing our souls. GE heat pumps warm our homes, but God gave the Holy Spirit to warm our hearts. GE jet engines might power us into the sky, but God's Spirit powers us up, up and away beyond the sky into eternal life. GE's bulbs may light up a room, but Jesus lights up the World!

God longs for us to have a relationship with Him through faith in Jesus Christ. *"And the Word became flesh and dwelt among us, and we beheld His glory, the glory as of the only begotten of the Father, full of grace and truth."* *(John 1:14)* God came to earth as Jesus Christ to bring us the good things of eternal life.

Jesus Christ fulfilled the righteous demands of the law for us and brought in a New Covenant of Grace. He brings forever forgiveness, total acceptance, unconditional love, security, and significance for now and forever to all who will receive Him by faith.

> *"For my eyes have seen*
> *Your salvation which*
> *You have prepared*
> *before the face of all*
> *peoples, a light to bring*
> *revelation to the Gentiles,*
> *and the glory of Your*
> *people of Israel."*
> *Luke 2:30-32*

Jesus brings Sonship with the father, peace that surpasses all understanding, and a life filled with the assurance of the bliss of heaven. He brings friendship, joy, and the love of others.

He brings the promise of working all things for our good. He brings the way, the truth, and the life into our lives when we enter into a personal relationship with Him.

Father, thank You for bringing the good things of life to me through Your Son and my Savior Jesus Christ. Amen

Taking it to the Lord...

How can I apply this truth?____

____

____

Father, I've come to worship and praise you! You are my:_______________________

____

I give you all Glory, Honor, and Praise O Lord!

Father, I am sorry that I have sinned by:__________________________________

Help me to repent. Cleanse me, strengthen me, restore me.

Father, THANK YOU for all your love, grace, mercy and blessings of life that you continually shower down upon me. Thank you especially for:

1.___________________________   2.___________________________

3.___________________________   4.___________________________

5.___________________________   6.___________________________

THANK YOU for answered prayers:_______________________________________

Father, I need:____

Father, I ask that YOU:____

____

____

Lord, bless me that I may be a blessing. Give me Your heart for loving and serving others. Keep Your hand upon me. Keep me from all evil and harm, and let me cause harm to no one. Bind Satan that he have no power over me. All this I pray in subjection to your will and in the strong name of my Lord and Savior, Jesus Christ. Amen.

Worth Repeating

"Take delight in the LORD, and he will give you your heart's desires." Psalm 37.4 NLT

Do you realize that you are really good at meditating? The only problem is meditating about the wrong things.

> *"I will meditate on your majestic, glorious splendor and your wonderful miracles." Psalm 145:5 NLT*

When we worry, we are meditating. We can really focus our thoughts meditating about worries, whether they be financial, relational, physical, emotional, or spiritual.

How much better to focus our thoughts on the One who lightens our load and gives us the strength and the grace to overcome problem--instead of worrying about them?

Like Mary we should quietly treasure the things of God in our hearts and think about them often. When we think about God's forgiveness, we are led to forgive others. When we think about God's mercy, we are inspired to show mercy to others.   When we think about God's kindness, we become kind. When we think about His humility, we become humbled.

Best of all, when we think about God's love, we are inspired to love others in response to Him who first loved us!

When we focus our thoughts on getting to know God through His Son we learn how to know and to do the will of God. We will know what Jesus did as he fulfilled His purpose in coming to live among us to model and follow the will of the Father Who sent Him.

> *"Fix your thoughts on what is true and honorable and right. Think about things that are pure and lovely and admirable. Think about things that are excellent and worthy of praise." Philippians 4:8b*

Oh that God would grant us all the grace to worry less and meditate more on the peace and joy that are ours in Christ!

(I am indebted to Rick Warren who drew the correlation between worry and meditation in his great "Purpose Driven Life.")

Father, forgive me for all the needless pain and grief I have suffered through worrying instead of through meditating upon You and Your Word. Amen.

Taking it to the Lord...

How can I apply this truth?____

____

____

Father, I've come to worship and praise you! You are my:_______________________

____

I give you all Glory, Honor, and Praise O Lord!

Father, I am sorry that I have sinned by:_______________________________________

Help me to repent. Cleanse me, strengthen me, restore me.

Father, THANK YOU for all your love, grace, mercy and blessings of life that you continually shower down upon me. Thank you especially for:

1.______________________________   2.______________________________

3.______________________________   4.______________________________

5.______________________________   6.______________________________

THANK YOU for answered prayers:______________________________________

Father, I need:____

Father, I ask that YOU:____

____

____

Lord, bless me that I may be a blessing. Give me Your heart for loving and serving others. Keep Your hand upon me. Keep me from all evil and harm, and let me cause harm to no one. Bind Satan that he have no power over me. All this I pray in subjection to your will and in the strong name of my Lord and Savior, Jesus Christ. Amen.

Choices

"Today I have given you the choice between life and death, between blessings and curses. I call on heaven and earth to witness the choice you make." Deuteronomy 30:19a

The exercise of our free will results in choices that greatly determine the quality of our life in this world and our destination in the next.

> *"Who are those who fear the LORD? He will show them the path they should choose."*
> *Psalm 25:12 NLT*

Many choose to reject God's call to faith and will spend eternity in hell. Others will choose to reject God's calls to holiness, to worship, to service, and into a close personal relationship and miss out on the blessings that God wants to pour out on all of us.

Before receiving Jesus Christ as Savior we live in bondage to the curse of a sin condition caused by Adam's disobedience. This is a condition, not a practice, and can only be cured by being replaced with the righteousness of Christ. When we receive Him as Savior, it is accounted to us as righteousness and we are no longer under the wrath of God because of our sin condition.

Even though we have been set free from the condemnation and dominion of our sin condition, we continue to co exist in the flesh with a mind and body that can and will commit actual sin as we choose to live lives controlled by our flesh instead of lives transformed by the Spirit.

> *"Don't you realize that whatever you choose to obey becomes your master? You can choose sin, which leads to death, or you can choose to obey God and receive his approval."*
> *Romans 6:16 NLT*

Bad consequences usually follow bad choices that lead to a harvest of curses that will fill us with guilt and rob us of joy and so many of the blessings that God wants to bestow upon us.

When we choose to live obedient lives in the freedom from bondage that we received when we received Jesus Christ as our Savior, we escape the consequences of so many of our bad choices. Why in the world would we choose anything less?

Father, by the power of Your Spirit help me choose to abide in you so that your blessings may abound in and through me. Amen

Taking it to the Lord...

How can I apply this truth?____

____

____

Father, I've come to worship and praise you! You are my:_______________________

____

I give you all Glory, Honor, and Praise O Lord!

Father, I am sorry that I have sinned by:_____________________________________

Help me to repent. Cleanse me, strengthen me, restore me.

Father, THANK YOU for all your love, grace, mercy and blessings of life that you continually shower down upon me. Thank you especially for:

1.___________________________   2.___________________________

3.___________________________   4.___________________________

5.___________________________   6.___________________________

THANK YOU for answered prayers:___________________________________

Father, I need:____

Father, I ask that YOU:____

____

____

____

Lord, bless me that I may be a blessing. Give me Your heart for loving and serving others. Keep Your hand upon me. Keep me from all evil and harm, and let me cause harm to no one. Bind Satan that he have no power over me. All this I pray in subjection to your will and in the strong name of my Lord and Savior, Jesus Christ. Amen.

How to be a Big Spender

**"To those who use well what they are given, even more will be given, and they will have an abundance."
Matthew 19:29 NLT**

There is an axiom in business that it takes money to make money. The more you invest your time, talents, and treasures, the more success you will have. Scripture seems to confirm this principle in the parable of the talents.   Whether time, talent, love or money, God calls us all to be "big spenders!"

> *"The steps of the godly are directed by the LORD. He delights in every detail of their lives."*
> *Psalm 37:23 NLT*

The story of the prodigal son shows what happens to "big squanderers." When we pursue fame, fortune, and pleasure for self-gratification instead of for glorifying God, we will always fall short of His Glory and we will never grow into the fullness of Christ.

Another axiom in business says that "time is money." The parable of the talents likens the time we have been given on this earth to money.
Just as in the case of the servants, we are going to be called to give an account of how we have spent our lives.

The older we get, the more we will realize how trivial many of the things we held so dear really were. When we look back upon all of the wasted hours, wasted talents, and wasted treasures we will suffer a godly sorrow that drives us to the throne of grace for forgiveness and comfort.

Big spenders find that they cannot out give God in any area. *"Give, and it will be given to you: good measure, pressed down, shaken together, and running over will be put into your bosom. For with the same measure that you use, it will be measured back to you." Luke 6:38 NLT*

> *"God has given gifts to each of you from his great variety of spiritual gifts. Manage them well so that God's generosity can flow through you."*
> *1 Peter 4:10 NLT*

When we spend the financial, relational, and spiritual gifts that God has given each and every one of us by being fruitful in every good work we are not only going to enjoy the temporal blessings of this life, but we are going to receive our Lord's "well done, thou good and faithful servant" when we stand before him on judgment day.

Father, by the power of Your Spirit, help me to be a "big spender" of my time, talents, and treasures in ways pleasing to you. Amen

Taking it to the Lord...

How can I apply this truth?____
____
____

Father, I've come to worship and praise you! You are my:_______________________________
____

I give you all Glory, Honor, and Praise O Lord!

Father, I am sorry that I have sinned by:____

Help me to repent. Cleanse me, strengthen me, restore me.

Father, THANK YOU for all your love, grace, mercy and blessings of life that you continually shower down upon me. Thank you especially for:

1.____________________________________   2.____________________________________
3.____________________________________   4.____________________________________
5.____________________________________   6.____________________________________

THANK YOU for answered prayers:____
Father, I need:____
Father, I ask that YOU:____
____
____

Lord, bless me that I may be a blessing. Give me Your heart for loving and serving others. Keep Your hand upon me. Keep me from all evil and harm, and let me cause harm to no one. Bind Satan that he have no power over me. All this I pray in subjection to your will and in the strong name of my Lord and Savior, Jesus Christ. Amen.

Empowering Love

"Behold, I send the Promise of My Father upon you; but tarry in the city of Jerusalem until you are endued with power from on high." *Luke 24:49*

God, in his love, sent us not only a Savior, but also a power source that He could accomplish His good and perfect will in us and through us. When He pours out the Holy Spirit upon us, He empowers us with sanctifying grace, all-sufficient strength, and love for God and for others.

> *"Now I know that the Lord saves His anointed: He answers them from His holy heaven with the saving power of His right hand."*
> *Psalm 20:6 (NIV)*

God knows our weaknesses and the power of our flesh, the world, and Satan to take control of our thoughts, words, and actions to cause us to live self-centered, self-gratifying lives outside of the will of God. We need to know that "He who is in you is greater than he who is in the world"

The same empowering love that allowed 12 rag tag disciples turn the world upside down is in us to enable us to walk in the freedom that Christ earned for us on the cross. Through this empowering love, God is able to use us to accomplish His purposes in our lives.

God's power is made perfect in our weaknesses. When we are running empty on our own, we need to plug into the power that God promises will supply our every need.

> *"For God has not given us a spirit of fear, but of power and of love and of a sound mind."*
> *2 Timothy 1:7*

He has given us His "belt of truth", "breastplate of righteousness", "feet fitted with readiness that comes from the gospel of peace," "shield of faith," "helmet of salvation," and "sword of the spirit" – the full armor to put on daily to keep us under the control of His Spirit that we might glorify Him by bearing the fruit of His Spirit. May we daily put on this armor through prayer.

Father, thank you for empowering me with the Holy Spirit to do and to be all that you purpose for me. Amen

Taking it to the Lord...

How can I apply this truth?____

____

Father, I've come to worship and praise you! You are my:_________________________

____

I give you all Glory, Honor, and Praise O Lord!

Father, I am sorry that I have sinned by:____________________________________

Help me to repent. Cleanse me, strengthen me, restore me.

Father, THANK YOU for all your love, grace, mercy and blessings of life that you continually shower down upon me. Thank you especially for:

1.____________________________________   2.____________________________________
3.____________________________________   4.____________________________________
5.____________________________________   6.____________________________________

THANK YOU for answered prayers:____

Father, I need:____

Father, I ask that YOU:____

____

____

____

Lord, bless me that I may be a blessing. Give me Your heart for loving and serving others. Keep Your hand upon me. Keep me from all evil and harm, and let me cause harm to no one. Bind Satan that he have no power over me. All this I pray in subjection to your will and in the strong name of my Lord and Savior, Jesus Christ. Amen.

"Stature Quo"

"May you experience the love of Christ, though it is so great you will never fully understand it. Then you will be filled with the fullness of life and power that comes from God. Ephesians 3:19 NLT

We all too often strive to maintain the "status quo" instead of seeking to grow into the "stature quo". When we become comfortable with things as they are, we are reluctant to change, and certainly do not want to "rock the boat" of our comfort zone.

> *"But the godly will flourish like palm trees and grow strong like the cedars of Lebanon."*
> *Psalm 92:12 NLT*

Business after business has disappeared trying to maintain the status quo instead of growing. In business, to stand still is to go backward. In life, to stand still often leads to letting the world pass us by.

While there are certainly a lot of things in this world that we hope will pass us by (i.e. illness, pain, suffering, temptation, failure, etc.), we dare not let our relationship with God end with receiving His wonderful gift of salvation through faith in Jesus Christ.

Receiving Christ and being baptized are not the end of anything except our separation from God. They should be the beginning of everything in the life of the believer. The blessings of abiding, growing into the fullness of Christ, and being fruitful in every good work are just too good to let pass us by.

> *"Until we come to such unity in our faith and knowledge of God's Son that we will be mature and full grown in the Lord, measuring up to the full stature of Christ."*
> *Ephesians 4:13 NLT*

When we shortchange God by stopping short of being conformed to the image of His Son, we shortchange ourselves by missing out on the blessings that a close personal relationship brings.

As sweet as mother's milk, or the milk of the Word may be, there comes a time when we need solid food. As Paul says: *"For everyone who partakes only of milk is unskilled in the word of righteousness, for he is a babe."* (Hebrews 5:13)

How's your "stature quo?"

Father, let me enjoy my life to the fullest by growing into your fullness. Amen

Taking it to the Lord...

How can I apply this truth?____

____

____

Father, I've come to worship and praise you! You are my:___________________

____

I give you all Glory, Honor, and Praise O Lord!

Father, I am sorry that I have sinned by:_________________________________

Help me to repent. Cleanse me, strengthen me, restore me.

Father, THANK YOU for all your love, grace, mercy and blessings of life that you continually shower down upon me. Thank you especially for:

1.___________________________________   2.___________________________________

3.___________________________________   4.___________________________________

5.___________________________________   6.___________________________________

THANK YOU for answered prayers:_______________________________________

Father, I need:____

Father, I ask that YOU:____

____

____

Lord, bless me that I may be a blessing. Give me Your heart for loving and serving others. Keep Your hand upon me. Keep me from all evil and harm, and let me cause harm to no one. Bind Satan that he have no power over me. All this I pray in subjection to your will and in the strong name of my Lord and Savior, Jesus Christ. Amen.

Moral Excellence

"But now you are free from the power of sin and have become slaves of God. Now you do those things that lead to holiness and result in eternal life." Romans 6:22 NLT

The very instant we receive Jesus Christ as our Savior receive moral excellence in the sight of God. When God sees us, He sees us clothed in the perfect righteousness of Christ and we become holy in His sight. We have been set free from the power of sin to destroy us and we are no longer condemned.

> *"Give honor to the LORD for the glory of His name.*
> *Worship the LORD in the splendor of His holiness."*
> *Psalm 29:2*

We are given a new life in the Spirit, and have paradise regained and holiness restored. We become members of the Royal priesthood of believers.

While our Spiritual position has been resolved by receiving the righteousness of Christ, the battles of the physical flesh goes on and the life long, on going process of being conformed into the image of Christ, (also known as sanctification) begins.

God equips us to fight these battles with His armor: He gives us a belt of truth, a breastplate of righteousness, the gospel of peace as sandals, the helmet of salvation, the sword of the Spirit, and the shield of faith. (Ephesians 6:11-17)

When we occasionally lose one of these battles, we should take heart in knowing that we have not lost the war, and that renewal and restoration are just a prayer of confession and true repentance away.

> *"So make every effort to apply the benefits of these promises to your life. Then your faith will produce a life of moral excellence."*
> *2 Peter 1:5 NLT*

As we empty our hearts of the baggage of sin we make room for the fruit of Christ's righteousness for which the Holy Spirit provides the strength and the power to become imitators of Christ.

By the grace of God, we can all achieve that moral excellence which is the mark of the true believer.

Father, by the power of Your Spirit help me to live a life of moral excellence worthy of my calling as a disciple of Christ. Amen

Taking it to the Lord...

How can I apply this truth?____

____

Father, I've come to worship and praise you! You are my:_________________________

____

I give you all Glory, Honor, and Praise O Lord!

Father, I am sorry that I have sinned by:_____________________________________

Help me to repent. Cleanse me, strengthen me, restore me.

Father, THANK YOU for all your love, grace, mercy and blessings of life that you continually shower down upon me. Thank you especially for:

1._________________________________   2._________________________________

3._________________________________   4._________________________________

5._________________________________   6._________________________________

THANK YOU for answered prayers:____

Father, I need:____

Father, I ask that YOU:____

____

Lord, bless me that I may be a blessing. Give me Your heart for loving and serving others. Keep Your hand upon me. Keep me from all evil and harm, and let me cause harm to no one. Bind Satan that he have no power over me. All this I pray in subjection to your will and in the strong name of my Lord and Savior, Jesus Christ. Amen.

The Great Commitment

"For the eyes of the LORD range throughout the earth to strengthen those whose hearts are fully committed to him." **2 Chronicles 16:9**

We hear a lot about the great commandment and the great commission but not enough about the great commitment that both of these require.

> *"Commit your work to the LORD, and then your plans will succeed."*
> *Proverbs 16:3*

We make a three or four year commitment to serve when we enlist in the Armed forces. We make a commitment to make so many payments for so many months for so many years when we buy a home or auto.

We are often better at fulfilling our commitment to the bank or finance company than to fulfilling our commitment to God or our spouses, even though both of these are supposed to be lifetime commitments.

The soaring divorce rate is a sad commentary on how relatively meaningless commitment to a marriage has become. The general decline in church membership and attendance is a barometer indicating that our commitment to Christ and His Church leave a lot to be desired.

Commitment to Christ is what discipleship is all about. When we commit to get to know Him through the study of His Word we learn what His will for our lives is, and how He can accomplish it through us. .

> *"He gave his life to free us from every kind of sin, to cleanse us, and to make us his very own people, totally committed to doing what is right."*
> *Titus 2:14*

Thank God that His commitment to us is so much stronger than ours to Him. His free gift of eternal life is unconditional and irrevocable. When we receive it by faith, we also receive the supernatural desire and enabling power to commit our ways to Him and receive the peace of fulfillment that only a committed relationship to Him can bring.

We become children of the promise, and by His grace, promise keepers instead of promise breakers. We find our lives abounding in the abundance of His love and the fullness of His joy.

Father, let me be not only a hearer of the Word, but also a doer, totally committed to living out my faith every day in every way. Amen

Taking it to the Lord...

How can I apply this truth?____

____

____

Father, I've come to worship and praise you! You are my:__________________

____

I give you all Glory, Honor, and Praise O Lord!

Father, I am sorry that I have sinned by:_________________________________

Help me to repent. Cleanse me, strengthen me, restore me.

Father, THANK YOU for all your love, grace, mercy and blessings of life that you continually shower down upon me. Thank you especially for:

1.______________________________   2.______________________________

3.______________________________   4.______________________________

5.______________________________   6.______________________________

THANK YOU for answered prayers:_______________________________________

Father, I need:____

Father, I ask that YOU:____

____

Lord, bless me that I may be a blessing. Give me Your heart for loving and serving others. Keep Your hand upon me. Keep me from all evil and harm, and let me cause harm to no one. Bind Satan that he have no power over me. All this I pray in subjection to your will and in the strong name of my Lord and Savior, Jesus Christ. Amen.

Famous Amos

"My people have forgotten what it means to do right," says the LORD." Amos 3:10,11 NLT

We are not talking about cookies (as good as Famous Amos cookies are), and we are not talking about the senior partner of the "Amos and Andy" radio show of the thirties!

> *"Truly, O God of Israel, our Savior, you work in strange and mysterious ways. All who make idols will be humiliated and disgraced."*
> *Isaiah 45:15,16 NLT*

The real "Famous Amos" was an uneducated herdsman and tree trimmer who was called by God to "go prophesy to my people Israel." Amos' response was: *"The lion has roared—tremble in fear! The Sovereign LORD has spoken—I dare not refuse to proclaim his message!" (Amos 3:8 NLT)*

The timelessness of God's Word is reflected in (Amos 3:10), *"My people have forgotten what it means to do right," says the LORD. "Their fortresses are filled with wealth taken by theft and violence."*

.   Today call after call for people to repent goes unheeded. Since history has a way of repeating itself, how can we expect anything but the judgment of God to fall upon our nation and all those who will not repent and receive the saving faith God offers through Jesus Christ.

The peoples hardened hearts and sell out to sin made them ripe for the punishment of God. God chose plagues, famines, captivity, and scattering to distant lands as punishment for the children of Israel. As we become riper and riper what punishment will God choose for us and for our nation?

> *"Live in such a way that God's love can bless you as you wait for the eternal life that our Lord Jesus Christ in his mercy is going to give you."*
> *Jude 1:21 NLT*

The Good News that we have to see us through all of the bad stuff in Amos that we see happening daily today is that God will restore. He is also full of mercy and grace and offers forgiveness to all who will heed His warnings and turn away from sin and into His everlasting arms of restoration and forgiveness.

Father, thank you for introducing me to the real "famous Amos" found in your Word and to the insight he brings. Amen

Taking it to the Lord...

How can I apply this truth?____

____

Father, I've come to worship and praise you! You are my:________________________________

____

I give you all Glory, Honor, and Praise O Lord!

Father, I am sorry that I have sinned by:____

Help me to repent. Cleanse me, strengthen me, restore me.

Father, THANK YOU for all your love, grace, mercy and blessings of life that you continually shower down upon me. Thank you especially for:

1.____________________________________   2.____________________________________

3.____________________________________   4.____________________________________

5.____________________________________   6.____________________________________

THANK YOU for answered prayers:____

Father, I need:____

Father, I ask that YOU:____

____

____

Lord, bless me that I may be a blessing. Give me Your heart for loving and serving others. Keep Your hand upon me. Keep me from all evil and harm, and let me cause harm to no one. Bind Satan that he have no power over me. All this I pray in subjection to your will and in the strong name of my Lord and Savior, Jesus Christ. Amen.

Find that "Sweet Spot"!

"And whatever you do, do it heartily, as to the Lord and not to men." Colossians 3:23 NLT

> *"Trust in the LORD, and do good; dwell in the land, and feed on His faithfulness."*
> *Psalm 37:3*

Is there anything that gives more joy than doing something that you really like and for which you have a real God given passion? When you have a job that you can't wait to get to and hate to leave, you are blessed far beyond material compensation.

In the stewardship of life there is no joy greater than knowing that you are abiding in Christ and using the time, talents, and resources that He has given you "for such a time as this".

God has equipped us all for different works that He prepared for us before we were born. He never calls on us to do things that He has not equipped us. He doesn't make square pegs for round holes, although sometimes He does get us "over our heads" in order to show how His strength covers our weaknesses, and to make us aware of our total dependency upon Him. The apostle Paul found his "sweet spot" in proclaiming salvation to the Gentiles. Nehemiah found his in rebuilding the wall. All of the heroes of the faith, past and present, were ordinary people used by God for extraordinary purposes.

> *"May you experience the love of Christ, though it is so great you will never fully understand it. Then you will be filled with the fullness of life and power that comes from God."*
> *Ephesians 3:19 NLT*

When we grow into the personal relationship of abiding in and with Christ, we receive all of the blessings of friendship with God, awareness of the love of others, awareness of God's love, answered prayers, Jesus' joy, and especially the blessing of being fruitful in glorifying God. These are all "sweet spots" worth finding.

Father, thank you for giving me the sacred delight of being about fulfilling your purpose for my life. Amen.

Taking it to the Lord...

How can I apply this truth?____

____

____

Father, I've come to worship and praise you! You are my:_______________________

____

I give you all Glory, Honor, and Praise O Lord!

Father, I am sorry that I have sinned by:_____________________________________

Help me to repent. Cleanse me, strengthen me, restore me.

Father, THANK YOU for all your love, grace, mercy and blessings of life that you continually shower down upon me.

Thank you especially for:

1.____________________________　　2.____________________________

3.____________________________　　4.____________________________

5.____________________________　　6.____________________________

THANK YOU for answered prayers:___________________________________

Father, I need:____

Father, I ask that YOU:____

____

____

Lord, bless me that I may be a blessing. Give me Your heart for loving and serving others. Keep Your hand upon me. Keep me from all evil and harm, and let me cause harm to no one. Bind Satan that he have no power over me. All this I pray in subjection to your will and in the strong name of my Lord and Savior, Jesus Christ. Amen.

Virtual Reality

"From the time the world was created, people have seen the earth and sky and all that God made. They can clearly see his invisible qualities—his eternal power and divine nature. So they have no excuse whatsoever for not knowing God." Romans 1:20 NLT

Computer generated artificial worlds of Virtual Reality have arrived! We see it in movies, video games, and TV shows. People are having no problem at all buying into this artificial world, and yet have a hard time relating to the absolute truth of the reality of God.

"Here is my final conclusion: Fear God and obey his commands, for this is the duty of every person. 14God will judge us for everything we do, including every secret thing, whether good or bad." Ecclesiastes 12:13 NLT

Hours and hours daily, weekly, yearly are being spent in fantasy while the realities of life and death are being ignored, undermined, and made fun of.

The reality of God is lost in the virtual reality of artificial man made gods of intellect, wealth, power, fame, and pleasure. We probably have more gods in the world today than even the ancient Greeks ever thought of, while a majority of the world has relegated the Great I AM, the one True God, the Creator and Sustainer of Life to irrelevancy and a myth.

"And by him God reconciled everything to himself. He made peace with everything in heaven and on earth by means of his blood on the cross." Colossians 1:20 NLT

Being created in the image of God, we were also given a soul that yearns for love, fellowship and intimacy with God.   All of the artificial virtual realities are never going to fulfill this yearning.

We are either going to go through life trying to fill this yearning in all the wrong places and reaping a whirlwind of consequences in the process, or we are going to accept the reality of our sinfulness and our need to be reconciled with God by receiving Jesus Christ as our forgiver and fulfiller of a New Covenant of Grace.

Father, may I never confuse reality with virtual reality, and never trade what I have in you for the false promises and temptations of false gods. Amen

Taking it to the Lord...

How can I apply this truth?____
____
____

Father, I've come to worship and praise you! You are my:________________________________
____

I give you all Glory, Honor, and Praise O Lord!

Father, I am sorry that I have sinned by:____

Help me to repent. Cleanse me, strengthen me, restore me.

Father, THANK YOU for all your love, grace, mercy and blessings of life that you continually shower down upon me. Thank you especially for:

1.__________________________________   2.__________________________________
3.__________________________________   4.__________________________________
5.__________________________________   6.__________________________________

THANK YOU for answered prayers:____
Father, I need:____
Father, I ask that YOU:____
____
____

Lord, bless me that I may be a blessing. Give me Your heart for loving and serving others. Keep Your hand upon me. Keep me from all evil and harm, and let me cause harm to no one. Bind Satan that he have no power over me. All this I pray in subjection to your will and in the strong name of my Lord and Savior, Jesus Christ. Amen.

Surge Protectors

"Jesus turned to Peter and said, "Get away from me, Satan! You are a dangerous trap to me. You are seeing things merely from a human point of view, and not from God's." Matthew 16:23 NLT

If you have never had the experience of a power surge wiping out hours of unsaved work on your computer, be

> *"Don't sin by letting anger gain control over you."*
> *Psalm 4:4 NLT*

thankful. We now have automatic surge back up protectors which will keep our computers working for up to several hours if the surge is accompanied by a power outage.

So what about us? What kind of protection do we have from surges of anger, lust, pride, envy and the other traps of satan that seem to come upon us from out of nowhere. We all know otherwise nice people with "short fuses" who can go absolutely bonkers over the slightest provocation. What hits your "hot" button?

The news media is full of "crimes of passion" where anger surges and tragedies result. The ever-increasing incidents of road rage, coupled with the number of guns carried in cars, is sometimes becoming a bigger hazard than the traffic accident itself.

The Holy Spirit comes to dwell in our temples, and is the best surge protector we can have. When we give up control of our flesh and submit to the control of the Spirit, we will be empowered to surge with love, joy, peace, longsuffering, kindness, goodness, faithfulness, gentleness, self-control, patience, kindness, and love.

> *"You used to live just like the rest of the world, full of sin, obeying Satan, the mighty prince of the power of the air. He is the spirit at work in the hearts of those who refuse to obey God."*
> *Ephesians 2:2 NLT*

Even when we momentarily revert to the surges of the flesh, the Holy Spirit will convict us of our mistake and lead us to confess, repent, and get back on the right track.

The next time you feel a surge coming on, take time to call upon your surge protector to rescue you. His power surges come to take over when you have a spiritual power failure

Father, thank you for giving me surge protector. Amen

Taking it to the Lord...

How can I apply this truth?____

____

Father, I've come to worship and praise you! You are my:__________________________

____

I give you all Glory, Honor, and Praise O Lord!

Father, I am sorry that I have sinned by:____

Help me to repent. Cleanse me, strengthen me, restore me.

Father, THANK YOU for all your love, grace, mercy and blessings of life that you continually shower down upon me. Thank you especially for:

1.________________________________   2.________________________________
3.________________________________   4.________________________________
5.________________________________   6.________________________________

THANK YOU for answered prayers:____

Father, I need:____

Father, I ask that YOU:____

____

____

Lord, bless me that I may be a blessing. Give me Your heart for loving and serving others. Keep Your hand upon me. Keep me from all evil and harm, and let me cause harm to no one. Bind Satan that he have no power over me. All this I pray in subjection to your will and in the strong name of my Lord and Savior, Jesus Christ. Amen.

Tilt!

"Here on earth you will have many trials and sorrows. But take heart, because I have overcome the world." John 16:33b NLT

This electronic age has made pinball machines virtually obsolete except as collector's items. Oh the joy of having a nickel to play that noisy, bright light, tricky machine and have 5 balls to make a high enough score to maybe win some free games! What fun to compete with buddies for high score, and what excitement when the soda shop would get in a new model.

> *"For You, O LORD, will bless the righteous; with favor You will surround him as with a shield."*
> *Psalm 5:12*

The challenge of helping the ball rack up score by a timely push or thump on the machine was formidable. Style points for slam dunks must have gotten their start from the art of getting that ball into the right hole in the pinball machine.

Thump or push too hard and the "tilt" light and "game over" light would flash and you had to put in another nickel to start a new game. The tilt mechanism was put in the pinball machine to reduce damage and prolong the life of the machine.

We also have a built in "lilt" mechanism. As believers, we receive the indwelling of the Holy Spirit to reduce damage and to help us sustain our new life in Christ.

> *"We are hard-pressed on every side, yet not crushed; we are perplexed, but not in despair; [9]persecuted, but not forsaken; struck down, but not destroyed—"*
> *2 Corinthians 4:8*

When we get shoved and pushed around by circumstances, the Holy Spirit is right with us giving us the all-sufficient grace needed. When we get tilted by sin, He is on hand to do damage control by convicting us of our sin, filling us with godly sorrow, and giving us cleansing thru confession and repentance.

He is continually making intercessory prayers for us to keep us safe in the arms of faith until the Lord returns to take us home to heaven.

Father, thank you for sustaining me through the thumps and shoves of life. Amen

Taking it to the Lord...

How can I apply this truth?____
____
____

Father, I've come to worship and praise you! You are my:_____________________________
____

I give you all Glory, Honor, and Praise O Lord!

Father, I am sorry that I have sinned by:____

Help me to repent. Cleanse me, strengthen me, restore me.

Father, THANK YOU for all your love, grace, mercy and blessings of life that you continually shower down upon me. Thank you especially for:

1.___________________________________   2.___________________________________
3.___________________________________   4.___________________________________
5.___________________________________   6.___________________________________

THANK YOU for answered prayers:____

Father, I need:____

Father, I ask that YOU:____
____
____

Lord, bless me that I may be a blessing. Give me Your heart for loving and serving others. Keep Your hand upon me. Keep me from all evil and harm, and let me cause harm to no one. Bind Satan that he have no power over me. All this I pray in subjection to your will and in the strong name of my Lord and Savior, Jesus Christ. Amen.

Tempus Fugit!

"Live in such a way that God's love can bless you as you wait for the eternal life that our Lord Jesus Christ in his mercy is going to give you." Jude 1:21 NLT

The reality that time flies becomes more real the older we get. When growing up, time seems to stand still. We can't wait for school to start, and then to end. It seems to take forever to get to be old enough to get a drivers license.

> *"LORD, remind me how brief my time on earth will be. Remind me that my days are numbered and that my life is fleeing away."*
> *Psalm 39:4 NLT*

Time seems to go all too fast when we are having fun, and to drag on forever when we are trying to persevere through illnesses and other set backs. The perspective of time is far different for the criminal serving time in prison than for those on the outside.

When we look back, events of years past seem like yesterday. It seems like only yesterday that our grandchildren's parents were children themselves.   Birthdays and wedding anniversaries come and go and we never cease to marvel that memories of yesterday were actually memories of years and years ago.

The reality of the quick passage of time, and how short our lives really are in relation to eternity is hard to fully comprehend. Job and James both refer to life as a mere breath.

> *"For you have been born again. Your new life did not come from your earthly parents because the life they gave you will end in death. But this new life will last forever because it comes from the eternal, living word of God."*
> *1 Peter 1:23 NLT*

As painful as the loss of a loved one may be to those left behind, as fearful as we may be in leaving the known for the unknown, the assurances we have as born again believers sustain us. Death is only the end of pain and suffering. It is the beginning of the rest of our forever lives in the perfect, sinless, bliss of heaven. Our time is in His hands! There is no better place to have it.

Father, forgive me all the time I have wasted in trivial pursuits. By the power of Your Spirit, enable me to live the rest of my life pleasing You. Amen

Taking it to the Lord...

How can I apply this truth?____
____
____

Father, I've come to worship and praise you! You are my:_________________________
____
I give you all Glory, Honor, and Praise O Lord!

Father, I am sorry that I have sinned by:_____________________________________
Help me to repent. Cleanse me, strengthen me, restore me.

Father, THANK YOU for all your love, grace, mercy and blessings of life that you continually shower down upon me. Thank you especially for:

1.______________________________   2.______________________________
3.______________________________   4.______________________________
5.______________________________   6.______________________________

THANK YOU for answered prayers:____
Father, I need:____
Father, I ask that YOU:____
____
____

Lord, bless me that I may be a blessing. Give me Your heart for loving and serving others. Keep Your hand upon me. Keep me from all evil and harm, and let me cause harm to no one. Bind Satan that he have no power over me. All this I pray in subjection to your will and in the strong name of my Lord and Savior, Jesus Christ. Amen.

Buyer's Remorse

"You have sorrow now, but I will see you again; then you will rejoice, and no one can rob you of that joy."
John 16:22 NLT

We've all been there and done that. We have been consumed by a desire to have that car, that house, that cruise, etc., only to be hit with that real sick feeling that only the awareness that we should not have bought it brings.

> *"How long must I struggle with anguish in my soul, with sorrow in my heart every day?"*
> *Psalm 13:2*

Laws have even been written over the past few years to help cure buyer's remorse. Many contracts for purchase now have 72-hour cancellation provisions so that if you wake up hung over you can have a way out. Contracts signed while intoxicated have long been held invalid in courts of law.

When we buy into sin, we are always going to suffer remorse that is hopefully going to convict us of our need for confession and repentance or sometimes utterly destroy us. Judas was "filled with remorse" and took the thirty pieces of silver back and then went out and hanged himself.

When our sorrow over sin does not lead to repentance, we harden our hearts and become numb to the godly restraints against sin.

There are some sins that we buy into for which we will bear the pain of godly sorrow and sadness for the rest of our lives. Even though we have forgiveness, we still bear the consequences that are painful and hard to live with.

Satan is one of the slickest salesmen who ever came down the pike. He can sift us and bewitch us into buying into some of the biggest lies ever told and empty promises ever made.

> *"Now I rejoice, not that you were made sorry, but that your sorrow led to repentance."*
> *2 Corinthians 7:9a*

When we get suckered in and taken out of communion with God through sin, we need to take advantage of His "sinner's remorse" provision of true contrition and true repentance ASAP.

Father, thank You for using my godly sorrow over sins of the past to praise you for your grace and mercy, and to strengthen me to help avoid these sins in the future. Amen

Taking it to the Lord...

How can I apply this truth?____

____

____

Father, I've come to worship and praise you! You are my:______________________

____

I give you all Glory, Honor, and Praise O Lord!

Father, I am sorry that I have sinned by:__________________________________

Help me to repent. Cleanse me, strengthen me, restore me.

Father, THANK YOU for all your love, grace, mercy and blessings of life that you continually shower down upon me. Thank you especially for:

1.____________________________   2.____________________________

3.____________________________   4.____________________________

5.____________________________   6.____________________________

THANK YOU for answered prayers:________________________________

Father, I need:____

Father, I ask that YOU:____

____

____

Lord, bless me that I may be a blessing. Give me Your heart for loving and serving others. Keep Your hand upon me. Keep me from all evil and harm, and let me cause harm to no one. Bind Satan that he have no power over me. All this I pray in subjection to your will and in the strong name of my Lord and Savior, Jesus Christ. Amen.

Something New Under the Sun

"What can we say about such wonderful things as these? If God is for us, who can ever be against us?" Romans 8:31 NLT

Contrary to the old saying that "there is nothing new under the sun", there are some new things that we need to

> *"He has given me a new song to sing, a hymn of praise to our God."*
> *Psalm 40:3*

be aware of. It can make all the difference in the world when we begin our day pondering the grace and mercy of God which He renews every day.

Just as He delivered just enough manna for each day to the children of Israel wandering in the desert, God delivers a daily supply of new grace and mercy sufficient for our every need.

The more we abide in Him and His Word, the more grace we will receive. This is a promise that we dare not overlook. Answered prayers, joy, the awareness of God's love and the love of others, fruitfulness, and friendship with God are all daily tokens of God's grace that are renewed every day as we abide in Him.

Norman Vincent Peale's now famous thought: "today is the first day of the rest of my life" is another affirming truth worth pondering daily. When we die daily to sin by confession and repentance, we rise each day in newness of life in Christ.

Nothing or nobody can fill our hearts like Jesus. When we *"lay aside every weight, and the sin which so easily ensnares us," (Hebrews 12:1b)* we make room for the all-sufficient, super abundant grace of God.

> *"As the Father loved Me, I also have loved you; abide in My love."*
> *John 15:9*

We are rested and refreshed. The burdens of the past have been left behind at the foot of the cross. We arise in the peace that surpasses all understanding, in the security and love of our bright hope for the future.

We are filled with the assurance that we "can do all things through Christ who strengthens us" daily, weekly, yearly and eternally. Yes, there is something new under the sun. Don't miss out on it!

Father, morning by morning, let me experience and praise you for the new mercies I see. Amen

Taking it to the Lord...

How can I apply this truth?____

____

____

Father, I've come to worship and praise you! You are my:_____________________

____

I give you all Glory, Honor, and Praise O Lord!

Father, I am sorry that I have sinned by:____

Help me to repent. Cleanse me, strengthen me, restore me.

Father, THANK YOU for all your love, grace, mercy and blessings of life that you continually shower down upon me. Thank you especially for:

1.___________________________   2.___________________________

3.___________________________   4.___________________________

5.___________________________   6.___________________________

THANK YOU for answered prayers:_____________________________________

Father, I need:____

Father, I ask that YOU:____

____

____

Lord, bless me that I may be a blessing. Give me Your heart for loving and serving others. Keep Your hand upon me. Keep me from all evil and harm, and let me cause harm to no one. Bind Satan that he have no power over me. All this I pray in subjection to your will and in the strong name of my Lord and Savior, Jesus Christ. Amen.

We Can Never Out Forgive God!

"But when you are praying, first forgive anyone you are holding a grudge against, so that your Father in heaven will forgive your sins, too." Mark 11:25 NLT

We can never out give, out live, out love, or out forgive God. Often we have a hard time forgiving at all. "But you don't know what he or she did to me, said about me, or what trouble he or she caused me" are the most common responses to why we don't forgive.

> *"Though our hearts are filled with sins, You forgive them all."*
> *Psalm 65:3 NLT*

"I forgive, but I won't forget" is another stock response we give in dealing with our resentment over a real or imagined offense. Many times we take offense when none is intended or even that the offender has any idea that he or she has offended.

Pride, fear, and anger are at the root of unforgiving. We like to feel the self-righteous pride of being better than someone else. We fear that if we forgive and forget, we will be hurt again and we don't like to be vulnerable. We are righteously indignant and have every reason to be.

There is more than a coincidental link between a lot of serious illnesses and the sin of unforgiving. The seeds of unforgiving become roots of resentment that poison relationships, rob us of our joy, and will actually ruin our health.

Worst of all, we abuse the grace of God and tempt His wrath and judgment when we will not forgive. *"But if you refuse to forgive others, your Father will not forgive your sins." (Matthew 6:15)* is Jesus' clear warning that forgiveness is not an option but a command.

> *"Then Peter came to Him and said, "Lord, how often shall my brother sin against me, and I forgive him? Up to seven times?"*
> *Matthew 18:21 NLT*

God never asks us to do something that He has not done or will not do Himself. He *"remembers our sins no more." (Isaiah 43:25 NIV) "As far as the east is from the west, So far has He removed our transgressions from us." (Psalm 103:12 NLT)*

Father, take away any resentments or roots of unforgiving that are poisoning me and hurting my relationship with You. Amen

Taking it to the Lord...

How can I apply this truth?____

____

____

Father, I've come to worship and praise you! You are my:______________________

____

I give you all Glory, Honor, and Praise O Lord!

Father, I am sorry that I have sinned by:__________________________________

Help me to repent. Cleanse me, strengthen me, restore me.

Father, THANK YOU for all your love, grace, mercy and blessings of life that you continually shower down upon me. Thank you especially for:

1.________________________________   2.________________________________

3.________________________________   4.________________________________

5.________________________________   6.________________________________

THANK YOU for answered prayers:____

Father, I need:____

Father, I ask that YOU:____

____

____

____

Lord, bless me that I may be a blessing. Give me Your heart for loving and serving others. Keep Your hand upon me. Keep me from all evil and harm, and let me cause harm to no one. Bind Satan that he have no power over me. All this I pray in subjection to your will and in the strong name of my Lord and Savior, Jesus Christ. Amen.

Our Overflowing Cup of Kindness

"And so God can always point to us as examples of the incredible wealth of his favor and kindness toward us, as shown in all he has done for us through Christ Jesus." Ephesians 2:9 NLT

Is your cup of kindness filled to overflowing? Are you being kind and helpful to others as a celebration of God's kindness to you? If we are not, we should be!

> *"Happy are those who deal justly with others and always do what is right." Psalm 106:3 NLT*

In the Old Testament, kindness was reciprocal. You showed kindness to receive kindness. We see this alive today in the saying "what goes around comes around", or "your good deeds will not go unrewarded."

Kindness usually also embodies mercy and grace. All of the covenants of the Old Testament originated from the kindness, grace and mercy of God.

It's not too hard to be kind reciprocally.   We tend to respond kindly to people who are kind to us. The real test of kindness is whether we can be kind to the unkind, forgive the unforgivable, and live out the kindness of God that "is slow to anger and abounding in love". When our cups are filled to overflowing, we are kind just for the joy of it, without expecting anything in return.

God told the Children of Israel through Isaiah *"With a little wrath I hid My face from you for a moment; but with everlasting kindness I will have mercy on you," (Isaiah 54:8)*

When we think of God's amazing grace and kindness to us and how undeserving we are, our cups should be filled to overflowing with thanksgiving and praise and spill over into our lives lived with kindness and love for everyone.

> *"Therefore, as the elect of God, holy and beloved, put on tender mercies, kindness, humility, meekness, longsuffering;" Colossians 3:12*

None of us are so perfect that we dare abuse the grace of God by not being kind. Kindness is a fruit that bears cultivating and practicing every day of our lives.

Father, thank You for my overflowing cup of Your kindness. Help me to pass it on. Amen

Taking it to the Lord...

How can I apply this truth?____

____

Father, I've come to worship and praise you! You are my:_____________________

____

I give you all Glory, Honor, and Praise O Lord!

Father, I am sorry that I have sinned by:___________________________________

Help me to repent. Cleanse me, strengthen me, restore me.

Father, THANK YOU for all your love, grace, mercy and blessings of life that you continually shower down upon me. Thank you especially for:

1.____________________________   2.____________________________
3.____________________________   4.____________________________
5.____________________________   6.____________________________

THANK YOU for answered prayers:____

Father, I need:____

Father, I ask that YOU:____

____

____

Lord, bless me that I may be a blessing. Give me Your heart for loving and serving others. Keep Your hand upon me. Keep me from all evil and harm, and let me cause harm to no one. Bind Satan that he have no power over me. All this I pray in subjection to your will and in the strong name of my Lord and Savior, Jesus Christ. Amen.

Where's Your Security Deposit?

"The Spirit is God's guarantee that he will give us everything he promised and that he has purchased us to be his own people." Ephesians 1:14 NLT

Whether leasing a house or apartment or a car, the lessor usually requires a deposit to secure the lease. Reservations are not held after a specified time unless they are guaranteed by a deposit. Most contracts of any kind require consideration and "earnest money" deposits to be binding.

> *"Be of good courage, and He shall strengthen your heart, all you who hope in the* LORD.*"*
> *Psalm 31:24 NLT*

   All this is being said to bring up the question of the security of our reservations for heaven. It is amazing that so many professing Christians questions are basing their security on their own goodness. "I have tried to live a good life", "I have helped others." "I have been a good wife or husband", "I have ___________________" . seems to be the answer of a majority of people asked why they are going to heaven.

When we consider that God's standard is perfect holiness, we can understand the danger of basing our assurance of heaven on our goodness is ludicrous. We have all sinned and fallen short of the perfect holiness of God. Our goodness is as "filthy rags" in the sight of God.

Our reservations for heaven are secured only by the blood of Jesus Christ, the perfect, unblemished Lamb of God who becomes our righteousness when we believe that He died on the cross for our sins.

> *"Now He who has prepared us for this very thing is God, who also has given us the Spirit as a guarantee."*
> *1 Corinthians 5:5 NLT*

God has even sent us the Holy Spirit as a security deposit guaranteeing that: *"He who has begun a good work in you will complete it until the day of Jesus Christ;"* (Philippians 1:6).

No wonder we should joyfully sing: "my hope is built on nothing less than Jesus blood and righteousness." if anyone should ever ask about the reason for our blessed assurance of going to heaven.

Father, thank you for confirming my reservations by the power of Your Spirit. Amen

Taking it to the Lord...

How can I apply this truth?____

____

Father, I've come to worship and praise you! You are my:________________________

____

I give you all Glory, Honor, and Praise O Lord!

Father, I am sorry that I have sinned by:______________________________________

Help me to repent. Cleanse me, strengthen me, restore me.

Father, THANK YOU for all your love, grace, mercy and blessings of life that you continually shower down upon me. Thank you especially for:

1.___________________________________   2.___________________________________

3.___________________________________   4.___________________________________

5.___________________________________   6.___________________________________

THANK YOU for answered prayers:____

Father, I need:____

Father, I ask that YOU:____

____

____

____

Lord, bless me that I may be a blessing. Give me Your heart for loving and serving others. Keep Your hand upon me. Keep me from all evil and harm, and let me cause harm to no one. Bind Satan that he have no power over me. All this I pray in subjection to your will and in the strong name of my Lord and Savior, Jesus Christ. Amen.

Anchors Away

"Therefore we also, since we are surrounded by so great a cloud of witnesses, let us lay aside every weight, and the sin which so easily ensnares *us,* and let us run with endurance the race that is set before us," Hebrews 12:1

Sometimes we seem so anchored in guilt and despair over our sins that we feel like we are drowning. This is a good thing when it is the Holy Spirit convicting us our sinfulness and our need for a Savior.

> *"Don't let the floods overwhelm me, or the deep waters swallow me, or the pit of death devour me."*
> *Psalm 69:15 NLT*

Other times, in spite of our saving faith and sincere desire to please God, we find ourselves being pulled under by the weight of our passion for pleasure, for possessions, or for power or the approval of others.

There is an ongoing spiritual battle raging within us. Our adversaries are cunning and relentless. They fill us with false promises of pleasure, security, and significance that they cannot deliver.   Just as the prodigal son ended up in the pigpen we end up drowning in sorrow and despair and often pull others down with us.

These are the times we need to remember that the chain that anchors us to our sins has been broken. We need to remember *Romans 6:14: "For sin shall not have dominion over you, for you are not under law but under grace."* Romans 8:1, tells us, *"There is therefore now no condemnation to those who are in Christ Jesus."*

> *"Who will also confirm you to the end, that you may be blameless in the day of our Lord Jesus Christ."*
> *1 Corinthians 1:8 NLT*

We should always feel godly sorrow for our sins, but never despair or defeat. When we seek the forgiveness that comes from true contrition and repentance the anchors of our sin will never drown us.

When we anchor deep into the Word and the promises of God we will receive the way of escape from every temptation.

Father, You are the anchor of my soul. Let me never be cast about by doubt or despair. Amen

Taking it to the Lord...

How can I apply this truth?____
____
____

Father, I've come to worship and praise you! You are my:_________________________________
____

I give you all Glory, Honor, and Praise O Lord!

Father, I am sorry that I have sinned by:____

Help me to repent. Cleanse me, strengthen me, restore me.

Father, THANK YOU for all your love, grace, mercy and blessings of life that you continually shower down upon me. Thank you especially for:

1.____________________________________   2.____________________________________
3.____________________________________   4.____________________________________
5.____________________________________   6.____________________________________

THANK YOU for answered prayers:____
Father, I need:____
Father, I ask that YOU:____
____
____
____

Lord, bless me that I may be a blessing. Give me Your heart for loving and serving others. Keep Your hand upon me. Keep me from all evil and harm, and let me cause harm to no one. Bind Satan that he have no power over me. All this I pray in subjection to your will and in the strong name of my Lord and Savior, Jesus Christ. Amen.

The Other "A" Word

"Behind closed doors, you have set up your idols and worship them instead of me. This is adultery, for you are loving these idols instead of loving me." Isaiah 57:8 NLT

We usually think of adultery as sexual sin. As bad as sexual sin is, it is minor compared to the sin of spiritual adultery. When we sell out to the gods of the flesh and of the world, we become spiritual prostitutes who sell our birthright for all that we have and all that we are in Christ. It is a bad bargain with eternally bad consequences.

> *"They defiled themselves by their evil deeds, and their love of idols was adultery in the LORD'S sight."*
> *Psalm 106:39 NLT*

Many who would never think of cheating on their mates, will cheat on God at the rattling of a few extra coins, at the altar of pleasure, and even by building a palace of pride.

Our lives are filled with tests in the form of daily choices in which we often make the wrong choice. From choosing to watch the wrong TV show to choosing to respond to others in anger, jealousy, or strife instead of with longsuffering, kindness and love – we fail miserably and become spiritual adulterers.

The seriousness with which God addresses the sin of spiritual adultery is shown by the way He equates it to sexual adultery in Scripture. He even had Hosea marry a prostitute and see her have children by other men as a means of illustrating the way that the children of Israel were openly committing adultery against the Lord by worshipping other Gods.

> *"It is a terrible thing to fall into the hands of the living God."*
> *Hebrews 10:31NLT*

God's judgment upon the spiritual adultery of the children of Israel was the Assyrian captivity. May we avoid the terrible judgment of God by daily contrition and true repentance. May the sin of spiritual adultery not be named among us.

Father, forgive me for consorting with gods of the world, the flesh, and satan. Let me never sell out all that I have in you. Amen

Taking it to the Lord...

How can I apply this truth?____

Father, I've come to worship and praise you! You are my:____

I give you all Glory, Honor, and Praise O Lord!

Father, I am sorry that I have sinned by:____

Help me to repent. Cleanse me, strengthen me, restore me.

Father, THANK YOU for all your love, grace, mercy and blessings of life that you continually shower down upon me. Thank you especially for:

1.______________________________________   2.______________________________________

3.______________________________________   4.______________________________________

5.______________________________________   6.______________________________________

THANK YOU for answered prayers:____

Father, I need:____

Father, I ask that YOU:____

Lord, bless me that I may be a blessing. Give me Your heart for loving and serving others. Keep Your hand upon me. Keep me from all evil and harm, and let me cause harm to no one. Bind Satan that he have no power over me. All this I pray in subjection to your will and in the strong name of my Lord and Savior, Jesus Christ. Amen.

Encouraging Love

"Therefore, encourage one another and build each other up, just as in fact you are doing."
1 Thessalonians 5:11 NIV

Positive re-enforcement is one of the most effective tools available for parenting, counseling, building

> *"I will bless the LORD who has given me counsel;"*
> *Psalm 16:7*

relationships, and Christian growth. The pain of a negative self-image is one of the leading causes of drug or alcohol abuse, immoral conduct, and even hypocrisy.

Without the encouraging love of God we have in Jesus Christ, many tend to look for love in all the wrong places only to find temporary satisfaction with a bitter harvest of consequences that destroys inner peace and security.

God's encouraging love continually reinforces the fact that He loves us unconditionally, forgives us forever, and gives us the righteousness of Jesus Christ. When we are secure in the everlasting arms of His love and grace, we are free to love ourselves and to love God and others because He first loved us.

> *"Now may our Lord Jesus Christ Himself, and our God and Father, who loved us and gave us eternal encouragement and good hope. Encourage your hearts and strengthen you in every good deed and word."*
> *1 Thessalonians 2:16 (NIV)*

The flesh, the world, and satan himself are continually seeking to tear down. Thanks be to God that he builds us up and gives us the power of his spirit, the encouragement of his word, the encouragement of the saints who have gone on before, and the encouragement of our brothers and sisters in Christ to help us grow into the fullness of Christ.

Father, thank you for your encouraging love that strengthens and sustains me. Help me to be an encourager and never a discourager of others. Amen

Taking it to the Lord...

How can I apply this truth?____

____

Father, I've come to worship and praise you! You are my:___________________________________

____

I give you all Glory, Honor, and Praise O Lord!

Father, I am sorry that I have sinned by:____

Help me to repent. Cleanse me, strengthen me, restore me.

Father, THANK YOU for all your love, grace, mercy and blessings of life that you continually shower down upon me. Thank you especially for:

1.____________________________________   2.____________________________________

3.____________________________________   4.____________________________________

5.____________________________________   6.____________________________________

THANK YOU for answered prayers:____

Father, I need:____

Father, I ask that YOU:____

____

____

Lord, bless me that I may be a blessing. Give me Your heart for loving and serving others. Keep Your hand upon me. Keep me from all evil and harm, and let me cause harm to no one. Bind Satan that he have no power over me. All this I pray in subjection to your will and in the strong name of my Lord and Savior, Jesus Christ. Amen.

The Missing Link

"But if you persist in your slanders against God's Holy Spirit, you are repudiating the very One who forgives, sawing off the branch on which you're sitting, severing by your own perversity all connection with the One who forgives." Mark 3:28

> *"Restore us, O God; cause Your face to shine, and we shall be saved!"*
> *Psalm 80:1*

Scientists have been looking for the "missing link" for all of my lifetime. They have searched all over the World on land and sea trying to give credit for my creation to an ape.

The Bible is the supreme authority on finding missing links. It found Adam and Eve as our link to the evolution of sin in our lives and in the World. Our problem was not the ape's fault, it was the fault of a couple of babes in the woods who didn't realize that they were living in heaven on earth, and who let a sweet talking snake talk them into thinking there was something better.

Oh that these poor doubters who have spent lifetimes proving the unproven spend as much time in searching for and finding the real "missing link"!

Jesus Christ is the "missing link" between God and man. Until we find Him, we will never find peace restored and eternal paradise regained. He is our bridge over troubled waters, the mediator of our new covenant, our Savior in whom we find God's favor.

> *"For there is only one God and one Mediator who can reconcile God and people. He is the man Christ Jesus."*
> *1 Timothy 2:5 NLT*

Without the "missing link" the world is experiencing reverse evolution. Without the "missing link" man is swiftly going back into the death and destruction of sin. All of the head knowledge and secular research into the origin of life rather than into knowledge of Who it is that gives eternal life is vain.

Oh that we may find the peace and joy that comes in finding the real "missing" link and evolving into His image as we live a life in Him!

Father, you are my "missing link" to the Father. Thank you for restoring my relationship with Him. Amen

Taking it to the Lord...

How can I apply this truth?____
____
____

Father, I've come to worship and praise you! You are my:__________________________________
____

I give you all Glory, Honor, and Praise O Lord!

Father, I am sorry that I have sinned by:____

Help me to repent. Cleanse me, strengthen me, restore me.

Father, THANK YOU for all your love, grace, mercy and blessings of life that you continually shower down upon me. Thank you especially for:

1.____________________________________   2.____________________________________
3.____________________________________   4.____________________________________
5.____________________________________   6.____________________________________

THANK YOU for answered prayers:____
Father, I need:____
Father, I ask that YOU:____
____
____
____

Lord, bless me that I may be a blessing. Give me Your heart for loving and serving others. Keep Your hand upon me. Keep me from all evil and harm, and let me cause harm to no one. Bind Satan that he have no power over me. All this I pray in subjection to your will and in the strong name of my Lord and Savior, Jesus Christ. Amen.

My Daddy Can!

"Jesus looked at them intently and said, 'With men this is impossible. But with God all things are possible.'" Matthew 19:26

There is a time in the life of every child, when fathers become god in their eyes. Their daddies are big and strong, protective, and provide for their every need. They crave their daddy's attention, love, and approval. They can't wait for him to come home and play with them. They think that their daddies can do anything!

> *"God's voice is glorious in the thunder. We cannot comprehend the greatness of his power."*
> *Job 37:5 NLT*

The older they get, the more they become aware that their daddies can't quite do everything.

They learn that their daddy's can't make the sunshine or the rain stop. They can't make pain go away. Unfortunately, many find that their daddies are promise breakers, deserters, and even big babies themselves.

The good news is that we have a heavenly father who can do anything! He made everything, owns everything, and is everywhere all at the same time. He will do whatever it takes except to bring us into His family, and once we let Him adopt us by faith, He will do whatever it takes to keep us there.

He will never forsake us or run out on us. He loves us with an everlasting love, and wants the absolute best for us. He picks us up when we fall, sustains us through our heartaches, illnesses, and failures and promises that He will work everything for our good.

He loves us so much that He will chasten and discipline us in love. He loved us so much that He sent his own Son to come die for our sins so that we wouldn't have to.

> *"And by that same mighty power, he has given us all of his rich and wonderful promises."*
> *1 Peter 1:4 NLT*

Not only does He promise, whatever He promises He can do! Aren't you glad you have a "daddy who can!"

Father, thank you for letting me know by experience that You can do anything! Amen

Taking it to the Lord...

How can I apply this truth?____

____

____

Father, I've come to worship and praise you! You are my:____________________________________

____

I give you all Glory, Honor, and Praise O Lord!

Father, I am sorry that I have sinned by:____

Help me to repent. Cleanse me, strengthen me, restore me.

Father, THANK YOU for all your love, grace, mercy and blessings of life that you continually shower down upon me. Thank you especially for:

1.___________________________________   2.___________________________________

3.___________________________________   4.___________________________________

5.___________________________________   6.___________________________________

THANK YOU for answered prayers:____

Father, I need:____

Father, I ask that YOU:____

____

____

Lord, bless me that I may be a blessing. Give me Your heart for loving and serving others. Keep Your hand upon me. Keep me from all evil and harm, and let me cause harm to no one. Bind Satan that he have no power over me. All this I pray in subjection to your will and in the strong name of my Lord and Savior, Jesus Christ. Amen.

How Great is Our Faithfulness?

"But without faith *it is* impossible to please *Him,* for he who comes to God must believe that He is, and *that* He is a rewarder of those who diligently seek Him." Hebrews 11:6

Faith is a very rare word in the Old Testament. Here, the concept is more often described as to fear, stand firm, or believe. The word only appears twice in the King James Version of the Old Testament.   These Old Testament concepts become New Testament realities that we understand as faith.

"My God will send forth his unfailing love and faithfulness." Psalm 57:3b NLT

When Lamentations extols the faithfulness of God, the writer is talking about the steadfast and dependable character of God and His unfailing love.

Our faith is really our confidence and hope in God and relationship with Him as mediated through Jesus. Jesus the mediator of the New Covenant where we receive God's righteousness through belief in Christ and what He did on the cross rather than trying to achieve it by our own efforts.

When our faith grows into the fullness of this relationship, not only do we have saving faith, but we are also sanctified, purified, justified, and adopted as sons and daughters of God and brothers and sisters of Christ by faith.

Trust and obedience are part of the faith package. The more faith we have, the more we will trust and obey.

Faith is also defined as a gift for doing great things for God, and as a fruit of the Spirit, which evidences God's faithfulness through us.

"God, who calls you, is faithful; he will do this." 1 Thessalonians 5:24 NLT

When we have the faith to believe in the absolute truth of God's Word and the truth of all of His wonderful promises we will be close to achieving great faithfulness. Who knows, we might even move a mountain or two!

Father, thank you for your faithfulness and my faith and total trust in you. Amen

Taking it to the Lord...

How can I apply this truth?____

____

____

Father, I've come to worship and praise you! You are my:_________________________

____

I give you all Glory, Honor, and Praise O Lord!

Father, I am sorry that I have sinned by:____

Help me to repent. Cleanse me, strengthen me, restore me.

Father, THANK YOU for all your love, grace, mercy and blessings of life that you continually shower down upon me. Thank you especially for:

1.________________________________   2.________________________________

3.________________________________   4.________________________________

5.________________________________   6.________________________________

THANK YOU for answered prayers:____

Father, I need:____

Father, I ask that YOU:____

____

____

Lord, bless me that I may be a blessing. Give me Your heart for loving and serving others. Keep Your hand upon me. Keep me from all evil and harm, and let me cause harm to no one. Bind Satan that he have no power over me. All this I pray in subjection to your will and in the strong name of my Lord and Savior, Jesus Christ. Amen.

Membership Has its Privileges

"Compared to the high privilege of knowing Christ Jesus as my Master, firsthand, everything I once thought I had going for me is insignificant—dog dung." Philippians 3:7 MSG

We live in an age of privileges. Many things that used to be privileges have become rights. We can buy all sorts of membership privileges.

6"I will also bless the Gentiles who commit themselves to the LORD and serve him and love his name, who worship him and do not desecrate the Sabbath day of rest, and who have accepted his covenant."
Isaiah 56:6 NLT

Sometimes we get a little mixed up about fellowship in a local body of believers. We can get very self-centered and demanding, as though we are doing the church a favor by belonging or attending.

Even worse, we tend to view church attendance as an obligation, rather than a privilege, and we need to be very careful. Whether it's in giving, loving, or attending church, God doesn't like anything that's done grudgingly or under compulsion.

Belonging to a fellowship of believers is not only a right and a command, but also a privilege. Jesus earned us the right to become His brothers and sisters by His death on the cross. We are commanded not only, not to forsake the assembling of ourselves together, but to: *"Think of ways to encourage one another to outbursts of love and good deeds." (Hebrews 10:24 NLT)*

"But if we are living in the light of God's presence, just as Christ is, then we have fellowship with each other, and the blood of Jesus, his Son, cleanses us from every sin."
1 John 7 NLT

God created us not only for fellowship with him, but for fellowship with each other. This can and should take place within the fellowship of believers. We share salvation and we share the Holy Spirit with other believers. There is a lot of joy to be found in growing in our relationship with each other as we grow in our relationship with the Lord together.

Father, thank you for the privilege of fellowship with other believers. May I never forsake it. Amen

Taking it to the Lord...

How can I apply this truth?____

____

Father, I've come to worship and praise you! You are my:____________________________

____

I give you all Glory, Honor, and Praise O Lord!

Father, I am sorry that I have sinned by:____

Help me to repent. Cleanse me, strengthen me, restore me.

Father, THANK YOU for all your love, grace, mercy and blessings of life that you continually shower down upon me. Thank you especially for:

1._________________________________   2._________________________________

3._________________________________   4._________________________________

5._________________________________   6._________________________________

THANK YOU for answered prayers:____

Father, I need:____

Father, I ask that YOU:____

____

____

Lord, bless me that I may be a blessing. Give me Your heart for loving and serving others. Keep Your hand upon me. Keep me from all evil and harm, and let me cause harm to no one. Bind Satan that he have no power over me. All this I pray in subjection to your will and in the strong name of my Lord and Savior, Jesus Christ. Amen.

Win-Wins are Best!

"A new commandment I give to you, that you love one another; as I have loved you, that you also love one another." John 13:34

We often hear of win-win trades by ball teams where both sides benefit. I have seen firings turn into win wins for both employer and employee. The secret of success for any business is to win by making customers winners and winning profits while doing it.

> *"For You, O LORD, will bless the righteous; with favor You will surround him as with a shield."*
> *Psalm 5:11*

Winning by taking advantage of someone, or at the expense of someone may result in ill gotten gains, but will never satisfy like winning the win-win way.

Most good relationships are built on the win-win principle. We win friends by being a blessing to them, and they in return become blessings to us.

Generally speaking, most everyone falls into one of two categories. We are either givers or takers and there seems to be a lot of both in all of us. Our self-centered flesh cries out to "take take take" while the Holy Spirit calls out to our spirit to "give give give".

The most amazing thing about the grace of God and the economy of God is that takers never really win and givers never lose. We have a God that we can't out love or out give. Jesus said: *"Give, and it will be given to you: good measure, pressed down, shaken together, and running over will be put into your bosom. For with the same measure that you use, it will be measured back to you." (Luke 6:38)*

> *"Yes, the way to identify a tree or a person is by the kind of fruit that is produced."*
> *Matthew 7:20*

God set the standard of conduct for win wins. It's called "The Golden Rule". One of these days, we are going to be welcomed to enter into "the winners circle" because someone met this standard for us on the cross of Calvary.

Father, help me to live in the win-win of Your will so that Your glory will shine through me. Amen.

Taking it to the Lord...

How can I apply this truth?____

____

____

Father, I've come to worship and praise you! You are my:___________________________________

____

I give you all Glory, Honor, and Praise O Lord!

Father, I am sorry that I have sinned by:____

Help me to repent. Cleanse me, strengthen me, restore me.

Father, THANK YOU for all your love, grace, mercy and blessings of life that you continually shower down upon me. Thank you especially for:

1.____________________________________   2.____________________________________

3.____________________________________   4.____________________________________

5.____________________________________   6.____________________________________

THANK YOU for answered prayers:____

Father, I need:____

Father, I ask that YOU:____

____

____

____

Lord, bless me that I may be a blessing. Give me Your heart for loving and serving others. Keep Your hand upon me. Keep me from all evil and harm, and let me cause harm to no one. Bind Satan that he have no power over me. All this I pray in subjection to your will and in the strong name of my Lord and Savior, Jesus Christ. Amen.

Are You Blessed?

"Blessed are those whose lawless deeds are forgiven, and whose sins are covered; Blessed is the man to whom the LORD shall not impute sin." Romans 4:7

What do you think about when you think of being blessed? We talk of being blessed with good health, good fortune, good friends, a good marriage, etc. These are all tangibles that we can readily sense.

> *"Blessed is the man who walks not in the counsel of the ungodly, nor stands in the path of sinners, nor sits in the seat of the scornful;"*
> *Psalm 1:1*

Jesus tells us that we will be blessed when we are humble, meek, poor in spirit, peacemakers, pure in heart, merciful, persecuted, and when we mourn and pursue righteousness. These blessings consist of inheriting the kingdom of God, being comforted, receiving mercy, filled with righteousness, inheriting the earth, and receiving great rewards in heaven.

Scripture also tells us that we are blessed to have our sins forgiven, we are blessed when we read the Word of God and keep it, and are blessed when we die in the Lord.

> *"Blessed be the God and Father of our Lord Jesus Christ, who according to His abundant mercy has begotten us again to a living hope through the resurrection of Jesus Christ from the dead,"*
> *1 Peter 1:1*

We might equate being blessed as being divinely favored, fortunate, and being filled with happiness and joy. The old hymn, "Come Thou Fount of Every Blessing" says a lot about being blessed very well: Jesus is the fount of every blessing. We need His Spirit to "Tune my heart to sing Thy grace" "Streams of mercy, never ceasing, Call for songs of loudest praise".

The greatest blessing of all is the peace and joy that we find in our salvation. It sustains us when everything else fails. It surpasses all our understanding. Our blessings come to life in the person of Jesus whose love fills us with this joy and peace that makes us truly blessed.

Father, let the blessings that come from you fill me with joy and thanksgiving. Amen

Taking it to the Lord...

How can I apply this truth?____

____

Father, I've come to worship and praise you! You are my:_______________________

____

I give you all Glory, Honor, and Praise O Lord!

Father, I am sorry that I have sinned by:____________________________________

Help me to repent. Cleanse me, strengthen me, restore me.

Father, THANK YOU for all your love, grace, mercy and blessings of life that you continually shower down upon me. Thank you especially for:

1._________________________________ 2._________________________________
3._________________________________ 4._________________________________
5._________________________________ 6._________________________________

THANK YOU for answered prayers:____

Father, I need:____

Father, I ask that YOU:____

____

____

Lord, bless me that I may be a blessing. Give me Your heart for loving and serving others. Keep Your hand upon me. Keep me from all evil and harm, and let me cause harm to no one. Bind Satan that he have no power over me. All this I pray in subjection to your will and in the strong name of my Lord and Savior, Jesus Christ. Amen.

God Doesn't Operate a Speed Trap

'*As* I live,' says the Lord GOD, 'I have no pleasure in the death of the wicked, but that the wicked turn from his way and live." Ezekial 33:11

> *"You cannot stay angry with your people forever, because you delight in showing mercy."*
> *Micah 7:18b NLT*

There is a wide place in the road in Florida that for years has paid its operating budget by handing out tickets to unsuspecting motorists who dare go a couple of miles over the limit. It got so bad that AAA started routing motorists miles out of their way to avoid it.

Some people seem to have the idea that God is operating a sin trap, just so that he can zap us when we go astray. We sometimes transfer the wrath of earthly fathers into our concept of a heavenly father as a stern disciplinarian and kill joy.

While God does chasten those He loves and hates sin, He also loves sinners and is longsuffering, patient, and kind. He even came down to pay the fine for every sin we have ever committed or will ever commit.

The father of the prodigal son is the self-portrait of our heavenly Father who does not wish that any should perish, but that all would inherit eternal life. Rather than waiting in ambush hoping we will fall; He even gives us a built in sin "detector" Who will sound the alarm to help us escape temptation and keep us in the fold through convicting us of our sins and working repentance in our hearts.

> *"But we are not of those who draw back to perdition, but of those who believe to the saving of the soul."*
> *Hebrews 10:39 NLT*

When we heed these warnings there is absolutely no reason to fear that the grace of God that brought us into faith is not sufficient to keep us in the faith that assures eternal life and all of the joy this brings now and forever.

Father, thank you for your tender mercy and loving kindness that you have given me rather than the punishment I deserve. Amen

Taking it to the Lord...

How can I apply this truth?____

____

____

Father, I've come to worship and praise you! You are my:_______________________

____

I give you all Glory, Honor, and Praise O Lord!

Father, I am sorry that I have sinned by:____________________________________

Help me to repent. Cleanse me, strengthen me, restore me.

Father, THANK YOU for all your love, grace, mercy and blessings of life that you continually shower down upon me. Thank you especially for:

1.______________________________   2.______________________________

3.______________________________   4.______________________________

5.______________________________   6.______________________________

THANK YOU for answered prayers:____

Father, I need:____

Father, I ask that YOU:____

____

____

____

Lord, bless me that I may be a blessing. Give me Your heart for loving and serving others. Keep Your hand upon me. Keep me from all evil and harm, and let me cause harm to no one. Bind Satan that he have no power over me. All this I pray in subjection to your will and in the strong name of my Lord and Savior, Jesus Christ. Amen.

Second Oldest Profession?

"Pay all your debts, except the debt of love for others. You can never finish paying that!" Romans 13:8

The renting of money and commercial transactions seems to have been a mainstay in ancient Israel. Some of today's laws regarding collecting and forgiving debts are based on some of the Levitical laws of the Old Testament. Bill collectors were forbidden to go into a home to "fetch a pledge", but had to stand outside the door.

> *"But as for me, I will walk in my integrity; redeem me and be merciful to me."*
> Psalm 26:11

Our modern day seven -ear limitation on how often one can file for bankruptcy is no doubt based on the 7-year "release of debts" provision of Deuteronomy 15.1.

Jesus' parables of the pounds in Matthew 25 and of the talents in Luke 19 mention 'putting money in the bank' and 'drawing interest.'

In many ways, life can be likened to banking. In this world and the next, we can invest our time, talents, and treasures and earn returns in the form of wages or dividends.

We can accumulate staggering financial debts that lead to bankruptcy Court. We can accumulate staggering sin debts that will lead to spiritual bankruptcy if we don't take them to God's bankruptcy court a/k/a the Throne of Grace where these debts are paid in full the blood of Jesus Christ shed in our behalf.

> *"But as he was not able to pay, his master commanded that he be sold, with his wife and children and all that he had, and that payment be made."*
> Matthew 18:25

We go from welfare recipients to investors when we respond to our freedom from the bondage of our sin debt by producing the fruits of righteousness that are fully pleasing to God.

We can mortgage our futures by seeking instant gratification now and paying later sometimes forever, or assure our futures by storing up treasures in heaven while we still have time to do so.

Father, help me to make regular deposits into my heavenly bank account by producing the fruit for which you created and gifted me. Amen

Taking it to the Lord...

How can I apply this truth?____

____

____

Father, I've come to worship and praise you! You are my:_____________________

____

I give you all Glory, Honor, and Praise O Lord!

Father, I am sorry that I have sinned by:________________________________

Help me to repent. Cleanse me, strengthen me, restore me.

Father, THANK YOU for all your love, grace, mercy and blessings of life that you continually shower down upon me. Thank you especially for:

1.________________________________   2.________________________________

3.________________________________   4.________________________________

5.________________________________   6.________________________________

THANK YOU for answered prayers:____

Father, I need:____

Father, I ask that YOU:____

____

____

Lord, bless me that I may be a blessing. Give me Your heart for loving and serving others. Keep Your hand upon me. Keep me from all evil and harm, and let me cause harm to no one. Bind Satan that he have no power over me. All this I pray in subjection to your will and in the strong name of my Lord and Savior, Jesus Christ. Amen.

Fly the Friendly Skies

"He will shield you with his wings. He will shelter you with his feathers. His faithful promises are your armor and protection." Psalm 91:4

Thousands of airplanes with millions of passengers take off every day throughout the world. It is possible to go anywhere in the world in a matter of hours.

> *"Yea, though I walk through the valley of the shadow of death, I will fear no evil; for You are with me; Your rod and Your staff, they comfort me."*
> *Psalm 23:4 NLT*

Sometimes the skies are not so friendly. Turbulence, equipment problems, poor visibility, pilot errors, and seemingly frequent and long delays turn friendly skies into skies filled with fear, frustration and potential disaster even before they became the missiles of choice by terrorists.

Every time we get on an airplane, we are putting our safety into the hands of pilots, mechanics, and flight controllers that we don't know just hoping and trusting that they know what they're doing, and will get us to our destination safely.

Sometimes life is not so friendly. We run into turbulence, poor visibility, and equipment problems, and seemingly endless delays. Without God as our pilot and the Holy Spirit as our built in navigator, we journey by the seat of our pants and continually come up short of God's glory and our eternal destination.

It is rather ironic that some seem willing to put their lives into the hands of total strangers when they travel through the skies, and yet seem so reluctant to put their lives into the hands of someone who knows them, loves them, and wants to guide them through life safely to an eternal destination.

> *"And Jesus answered, "Why are you afraid? You have so little faith!" Then he stood up and rebuked the wind and waves, and suddenly all was calm."*
> *Matthew 8:26 NLT*

The only reservation that guarantees a safe flight and guaranteed arrival is our reservation made by faith in our heavenly pilot, and confirmed by the presence of His Spirit living within us. There is joy and peace in this journey!

Father, as I go through the turbulence of life, keep me ever mindful of where I am going and with whom I am traveling. Amen

Taking it to the Lord...

How can I apply this truth?____

____

Father, I've come to worship and praise you! You are my:_________________________

____

I give you all Glory, Honor, and Praise O Lord!

Father, I am sorry that I have sinned by:____

Help me to repent. Cleanse me, strengthen me, restore me.

Father, THANK YOU for all your love, grace, mercy and blessings of life that you continually shower down upon me. Thank you especially for:

1.____________________________   2.____________________________

3.____________________________   4.____________________________

5.____________________________   6.____________________________

THANK YOU for answered prayers:____

Father, I need:____

Father, I ask that YOU:____

____

____

Lord, bless me that I may be a blessing. Give me Your heart for loving and serving others. Keep Your hand upon me. Keep me from all evil and harm, and let me cause harm to no one. Bind Satan that he have no power over me. All this I pray in subjection to your will and in the strong name of my Lord and Savior, Jesus Christ. Amen.

Darkened Understanding

"For You have hidden their heart from understanding; Therefore You will not exalt *them.*" *Job 17:4*

We see those walking "in the futility of the mind" all around us. It is heartbreaking to see that the understanding of the world is so darkened there is no longer truth, but "relative truth", no longer commandments, but "suggestions".

> *"Blessed is he whose transgression is forgiven, Whose sin is covered."*
> *Psalm 32:1*

Moral depravity is running rampant throughout the world. Sodom and Gomorrah might well be selected "All American Cities" today. Some blame it on poverty, others on drugs or our schools. Many people think we have been corrupted by TV and the Internet. These factors are all symptoms of the real problem, which is sin.

We are born with the darkened understanding of unbelief. We are born in bondage to the flesh that is devoid of spiritual understanding and discernment.

Until the world becomes convicted of its sin problem and need for a Savior, we will continue to live in darkness doing the deeds of darkness, and bearing the consequences of our sins.

> *"This I say, therefore, and testify in the Lord, that you should no longer walk as the rest of the Gentiles walk, in the futility of their mind, having their understanding darkened."*
> *Ephesians 4:17-18*

May we help others to heed the call of God out of darkness into light as we glorify God through our living witness of bearing the fruit of the Spirit, and by interceding with God on behalf of our unsaved friends and family members who are living with darkened understanding.

Father, keep me safe from the darkened understanding of the world around me lest I fall into the traps of the World, the flesh, and the devil. Bring light to the lost sheep of the world. Amen

Taking it to the Lord...

How can I apply this truth?____

____

Father, I've come to worship and praise you! You are my:___________________

____

I give you all Glory, Honor, and Praise O Lord!

Father, I am sorry that I have sinned by:________________________________

Help me to repent. Cleanse me, strengthen me, restore me.

Father, THANK YOU for all your love, grace, mercy and blessings of life that you continually shower down upon me. Thank you especially for:

1.___________________________   2.___________________________
3.___________________________   4.___________________________
5.___________________________   6.___________________________

THANK YOU for answered prayers:____

Father, I need:____

Father, I ask that YOU:____

____

____

Lord, bless me that I may be a blessing. Give me Your heart for loving and serving others. Keep Your hand upon me. Keep me from all evil and harm, and let me cause harm to no one. Bind Satan that he have no power over me. All this I pray in subjection to your will and in the strong name of my Lord and Savior, Jesus Christ. Amen.

Are You "Certified"?

"Do your best to present yourself to God as one approved, a workman who does not need to be ashamed and who correctly handles the word of truth." 2 Timothy 2:15 NIV

The same word used to denote insanity and incompetence is also used to denote expertise and validation.

> *"I relish everything you've told me of life, I won't forget a word of it."*
> *Psalm 119:16 NLT*

"People unable to manage their own affairs are "certified" or declared to be incompetent by a judge or jury.

We have "certified" public accountants, "certified" trial lawyers, "certified" mechanics and "certified" financial planners. This indicates that someone has met the requirements of education or training, experience, and successfully passing an examination.

We have "certified" used cars, "certified" checks, and even "certified" mattresses, diets and toothpastes. What about certified disciples? How do we become one?

It's easy to become a believer. We simply confess Jesus Christ as Savior, and our faith is the only requirement for us to be "certified" as righteous by Christ.

Submitting to the Lordship of Jesus Christ and giving Him control of every area of our life is another matter.

We love God because He first loved us. Because we love Him, we want to please Him by living lives that please Him.

This starts with getting to know Him and especially His Heart through studying His Word. As we grow in our knowledge of Him, we grow in our relationship with Him. He becomes alive in us by the power of the Holy Spirit living within us and helping us be conformed into the likeness of His Son, Who is the living Word.

> *"Examine yourselves as to whether you are in the faith. Test yourselves. Do you not know yourselves, that Jesus Christ is in you?—unless indeed you are disqualified."*
> *2 Corinthians 13:5*

Becoming certifiable disciples begins with becoming "learners or pupils" as followers of "the way, the truth, and the life". It is a discipline of living a life of obedience.

Lord, let your "well done" be the only certification I seek. Amen

Taking it to the Lord...

How can I apply this truth?____

____

____

Father, I've come to worship and praise you! You are my:____________________

____

I give you all Glory, Honor, and Praise O Lord!

Father, I am sorry that I have sinned by:_________________________________

Help me to repent. Cleanse me, strengthen me, restore me.

Father, THANK YOU for all your love, grace, mercy and blessings of life that you continually shower down upon me.

Thank you especially for:

1._________________________________   2._________________________________

3._________________________________   4._________________________________

5._________________________________   6._________________________________

THANK YOU for answered prayers:____

Father, I need:____

Father, I ask that YOU:____

____

____

Lord, bless me that I may be a blessing. Give me Your heart for loving and serving others. Keep Your hand upon me. Keep me from all evil and harm, and let me cause harm to no one. Bind Satan that he have no power over me. All this I pray in subjection to your will and in the strong name of my Lord and Savior, Jesus Christ. Amen.

The Good Housekeeping Seal of Approval

"Who dares accuse us whom God has chosen for His own? Will God? No! He is the one who has given us right standing with himself." Romans 8:33 NLT

Since 1909 "Good Housekeeping" magazine has guaranteed the satisfaction of their advertiser's products by giving them a seal of approval and allowing the seal to be displayed on their products. Advertiser's sought this seal because it instilled consumer confidence in their products and increased sales.

> *'They will receive the LORD'S blessing and have right standing with God their savior."*
> *Psalm 24:5 NLT*

Consumer's Union has for years rated everything from cars to pills and their top rating has increased sales for these products so rated.

John 6:27 tells us that God the Father has placed His seal of approval on Jesus. Paul described Abraham's circumcision as "a seal of righteousness".

All believer's carry a much more important seal of approval. It's the indwelling of the Holy Spirit through whom God *"set his seal of ownership on us, and put his Spirit in our hearts as a deposit, guaranteeing what is to come."* (Corinthians 1:22 NIV)

Evidence of God's seal of approval is the fruit of His Spirit in the lives of all believers. Love, joy, peace, patience, kindness, goodness, faithfulness, gentleness, and self-control are the products of a life transformed by the power of the Spirit and conformed to the image of Christ.

> *"Wait! Don't hurt the land or the sea or the trees until we have placed the seal of God on the foreheads of his servants."*
> *Revelation 7:3 NLT*

When we display God's seal of approval in our lives, others around us are encouraged and inspired to buy into the kingdom of God through faith in the advertisement that our lives reveal.

As today's scripture plainly teaches, there is a "seal of approval" awaiting all who "wash their robes in the blood of the Lamb."

Father, help me to show Your seal of ownership by "walking the walk" in the way that you have shown. Amen

Taking it to the Lord...

How can I apply this truth?____
____
____

Father, I've come to worship and praise you! You are my:_____________________________
____

I give you all Glory, Honor, and Praise O Lord!

Father, I am sorry that I have sinned by:____

Help me to repent. Cleanse me, strengthen me, restore me.

Father, THANK YOU for all your love, grace, mercy and blessings of life that you continually shower down upon me. Thank you especially for:

1._________________________________   2._________________________________
3._________________________________   4._________________________________
5._________________________________   6._________________________________

THANK YOU for answered prayers:____
Father, I need:____
Father, I ask that YOU:____
____
____
____

Lord, bless me that I may be a blessing. Give me Your heart for loving and serving others. Keep Your hand upon me. Keep me from all evil and harm, and let me cause harm to no one. Bind Satan that he have no power over me. All this I pray in subjection to your will and in the strong name of my Lord and Savior, Jesus Christ. Amen.

The "A" Word

"God alone made it possible for you to be in Christ Jesus. For our benefit God made Christ to be wisdom itself. He is the one who made us acceptable to God." 1 Corinthians 1:30 NLT

Acceptance is one of the basic motivators of life. In human terms, we will go to almost any extreme to be received with pleasure and approval by our parents, family, and peers.

> *"And may the Lord our God show us his approval."*
> *Psalm 90:17*

The positive reinforcement we receive from acceptance is a tonic that stimulates us to do more and more of the things that earn this approval, and hopefully, less and less of the things that are not acceptable to those whose acceptance we seek.

When the affirmation of acceptance is not received within the home, family, or friends through positive means we sometimes go seeking it in all the wrong places often with disastrous results.

A positive self-image is acquired by receiving ourselves with pleasure and approval. It is a good thing to feel good about ourselves and to be secure about who we are and where we are going--when it is from a Divine perspective.

Divine acceptance is another basic need of everyone. Like it or not, security and our peace is never going to be complete unless we receive the positive reinforcement from a right relationship with God through faith in Jesus Christ.

> *"And do not be conformed to this world, but be transformed by the renewing of your mind, that you may prove what is that good and acceptable and perfect will of God."*
> *Romans 12:2*

God *"desires all men to be saved and to come to the knowledge of the truth." (1 Timothy 2:4.)* God's acceptance is no longer based on our obedience to the law, but on the obedience of Jesus Christ.

By virtue of our faith in Jesus Christ, we become unconditionally loved, forever forgiven, and totally accepted by God. We receive the positive reinforcement of becoming joint heirs with Christ and receive the power of the indwelling Spirit of God. What a tonic this is!

Father, thank you for the acceptance I have in you and the peace and joy that this brings. Amen

Taking it to the Lord...

How can I apply this truth?____
____
____

Father, I've come to worship and praise you! You are my:__________________________
____

I give you all Glory, Honor, and Praise O Lord!

Father, I am sorry that I have sinned by:_______________________________________

Help me to repent. Cleanse me, strengthen me, restore me.

Father, THANK YOU for all your love, grace, mercy and blessings of life that you continually shower down upon me. Thank you especially for:

1._________________________________   2._________________________________
3._________________________________   4._________________________________
5._________________________________   6._________________________________

THANK YOU for answered prayers:____

Father, I need:____

Father, I ask that YOU:____
____
____

Lord, bless me that I may be a blessing. Give me Your heart for loving and serving others. Keep Your hand upon me. Keep me from all evil and harm, and let me cause harm to no one. Bind Satan that he have no power over me. All this I pray in subjection to your will and in the strong name of my Lord and Savior, Jesus Christ. Amen.

A Bad Neighborhood

"Trust in the LORD with all your heart, and lean not on your own understanding; In all your ways acknowledge Him, and He shall direct your paths." Proverbs 3:5

Assumption Avenue is just off Good Intention Drive right in the middle of the ghetto. The Heartbreak Hotel is on the corner, and the only latte available is the cup of sorrows at the Bad News café. We best not go there without the full armor of God!

> *"But blessed are those who trust in the LORD and have made the LORD their hope and confidence." Jeremiah 17:7*

We assume that we are never going to have to worry about the imperfections of our chosen mate or the trauma of divorce, and yet about half of marriages of believers end there.

We assume that people are honest and up front, only to find that they are dishonest and devious. We assume that justice will be served only to see injustice prevail.

There comes a point in life where we realize that we can take nothing for granted. The good health that we enjoy is just an accident or illness away. The job security we think we have can disappear overnight in a fast moving economy and corporate mergers and business failures.

We assume that we will be happy only if whatever false assumption we think will make us happy happens.

Out of all the heartbreaks and disappointments of false assumptions comes the question of what we can assume to be true and whom we can trust. From a worldly perspective it's almost impossible to assume anything except the reality of death and taxes or to trust anyone.

> *"Do not throw away this confident trust in the Lord, no matter what happens. Remember the great reward it brings you!" Hebrews 10:35 NLT*

Thanks be to God for the wisdom and spiritual discernment that He gives us to believe that He is, He lives, and that He is a rewarder of those who seek him. Only when we assume by faith the truth that He works all things for the good of those who love Him can we find the sustaining grace to persevere through disappointments of false assumptions.

Father, help me to take nothing for granted except the hope and faith I have in you and your promises. Amen

Taking it to the Lord...

How can I apply this truth?____

____

____

Father, I've come to worship and praise you! You are my:____________________

____

I give you all Glory, Honor, and Praise O Lord!

Father, I am sorry that I have sinned by:__________________________________

Help me to repent. Cleanse me, strengthen me, restore me.

Father, THANK YOU for all your love, grace, mercy and blessings of life that you continually shower down upon me. Thank you especially for:

1.____________________________   2.____________________________

3.____________________________   4.____________________________

5.____________________________   6.____________________________

THANK YOU for answered prayers:_______________________________________

Father, I need:____

Father, I ask that YOU:____

____

____

Lord, bless me that I may be a blessing. Give me Your heart for loving and serving others. Keep Your hand upon me. Keep me from all evil and harm, and let me cause harm to no one. Bind Satan that he have no power over me. All this I pray in subjection to your will and in the strong name of my Lord and Savior, Jesus Christ. Amen.

True Joy

"For the Kingdom of God is not a matter of what we eat or drink, but of living a life of goodness and peace and joy in the Holy Spirit." Romans 14:17 NLT

True joy is the joy that comes only as a fruit of our right relationship with God. It is the happy state or delight that comes from knowing and serving God. Jesus said: *"These things I have spoken to you, that My joy may remain in you, and that your joy may be full." (John 15:11 NLT)* and: *"I have told them many things while I was with them so they would be filled with my joy." (John 17:13b NLT)*

> *"In Your presence is fullness of joy; at Your right hand are pleasures forevermore."*
> *Psalm 16:11b*

True joy produces the peace that surpasses all understanding. It is sustaining and fulfilling. It is the joy of forgiveness, love, and mercy received. It is joy that is set before us in the assurance of an everlasting life in heaven that makes the temporary sufferings of this life bearable.

Joy was one of the distinguishing characteristics of the New Testament Christians. The book of acts reveals that "they shared their meals with great joy and generosity", "there was great joy in the city," "the believers were filled with joy and with the Holy Spirit," and that "there was great joy throughout the church that day as they read this encouraging message."

Many churches and Christians seem to have lost their joy and give the impression that God is a "kill-joy", when the truth is that God takes joy in us, wants joy for us, and that we are a joy to Him. The real "kill-joys" are the self-indulgent, self-seeking pursuits of fame, fortune, and pleasure apart from a right relationship with God through faith in Jesus Christ that continually seek to rob us.

> *"So be truly glad! There is wonderful joy ahead, even though it is necessary for you to endure many trials for a while."*
> *1 Peter 1:6 NLT*

True joy is the fruit of the Spirit that lets us *"count it all joy when we fall into various trials" (James 1:2)*, the fruit that gives us strength to: *"Rejoice always, pray without ceasing, in everything give thanks; for this is the will of God in Christ Jesus for you." (1 Thessalonians 5:16)*

Father, let nothing or nobody rob me of my joy that I have found in you. Amen

Taking it to the Lord...

How can I apply this truth?____

____

Father, I've come to worship and praise you! You are my:______________________

____

I give you all Glory, Honor, and Praise O Lord!

Father, I am sorry that I have sinned by:___________________________________

Help me to repent. Cleanse me, strengthen me, restore me.

Father, THANK YOU for all your love, grace, mercy and blessings of life that you continually shower down upon me. Thank you especially for:

1.______________________________   2.______________________________

3.______________________________   4.______________________________

5.______________________________   6.______________________________

THANK YOU for answered prayers:__________________________________

Father, I need:____

Father, I ask that YOU:____

____

____

Lord, bless me that I may be a blessing. Give me Your heart for loving and serving others. Keep Your hand upon me. Keep me from all evil and harm, and let me cause harm to no one. Bind Satan that he have no power over me. All this I pray in subjection to your will and in the strong name of my Lord and Savior, Jesus Christ. Amen.

The Jabez Blessing

"And Jabez called on the God of Israel saying, "Oh, that You would bless me indeed, and enlarge my territory, that Your hand would be with me, and that You would keep *me* from evil, that I may not cause pain!" So God granted him what he requested." Chronicles 4:10

I am only one of thousands of people whose lives have been profoundly impacted by Dr. Bruce Wilkinson's big little book "The Prayer of Jabez"₁ about this spiritual nugget nestled in the Chronicles of the history of Israel.

> *"May God be merciful and bless us. May his face shine with favor upon us."*
> *Psalm 67:1 NLT*

To pray that God would bless us according to His good and gracious will and not our own specified desires is a prayer that God loves to answer because God loves to bless, and He has promised to answer prayers prayed in accordance with His will.

God knows that it is virtually impossible for us to be a blessing to others unless we have been blessed. We cannot give material blessings if we don't receive them, we cannot love others if we have not been blessed with love. Financial, emotional and relational blessings are all blessings that we are given so that we can use them to bless others.

> *"For everyone who asks, receives. Everyone who seeks, finds and the door is opened to everyone who knocks."*
> *Matthew 7:8 NLT*

When we ask God to bless us from the God centered perspective of being a blessing to others, we are actually praying for help in being faithful to the great commandment and the great commission. We cannot fulfill the purposes for which God created us without God's blessing upon our lives.

We have a heavenly Father who loves to give good gifts to His children. He is the fount of every blessing, the giver of every good and perfect gift.

Father, thank you for continuing to answer this prayer for me and for so many others. Amen

₁ This snack has been inspired by the *"Prayer of Jabez"* ©2001 Bruce Wilkinson,   *Multnomah Books*. We highly recommend this book!

Taking it to the Lord...

How can I apply this truth?____

____

Father, I've come to worship and praise you! You are my:_____________________________________

____

I give you all Glory, Honor, and Praise O Lord!

Father, I am sorry that I have sinned by:____

Help me to repent. Cleanse me, strengthen me, restore me.

Father, THANK YOU for all your love, grace, mercy and blessings of life that you continually shower down upon me. Thank you especially for:

1.______________________________________   2.______________________________________
3.______________________________________   4.______________________________________
5.______________________________________   6.______________________________________

THANK YOU for answered prayers:____

Father, I need:____

Father, I ask that YOU:____

____

____

Lord, bless me that I may be a blessing. Give me Your heart for loving and serving others. Keep Your hand upon me. Keep me from all evil and harm, and let me cause harm to no one. Bind Satan that he have no power over me. All this I pray in subjection to your will and in the strong name of my Lord and Savior, Jesus Christ. Amen.

What Does God Require?

"He has shown you, O man, what *is* good; and what does the LORD require of you but to do justly, to love mercy, and to walk humbly with your God?" Micah 6:8

> *"The LORD is king forever and ever! Let those who worship other gods be swept from the land."*
> *Psalm 10:6*

"But without faith it is impossible to please Him, for he who comes to God must believe that He is, and that He is a rewarder of those who diligently seek Him." (Hebrews 6) What seems so simple and easy to understand has sometimes been made so complex and complicated, that many are left to wonder what is true faith.

The centrality of the Good News is that God came to save sinners, and that all who believe that Jesus Christ died on the cross for their sins meet the requirements for eternal life. Our faith in this fact is credited to us as righteousness in the sight of God and assures us a place in heaven.

While faith is not performance, it initiates a new life in us, whereby we become temples of the Holy Spirit and are empowered and motivated to do the things that please God as a response to our faith.

By faith, we are set free from our bondage to sin and given the privilege and power to be fruitful in every good work for which we were created. These fruits of our new righteousness in Christ are evidence of our faith and will determine whether we have been good stewards of the new life we have been given in Christ. *"Moreover it is required in stewards that one be found faithful." (1 Corinthians* 4:2)

> *"And so, dear friends, while you are waiting for these things to happen, make every effort to live a pure and blameless life. And be at peace with God."*
> *1 Peter 3:14 NLT*

Salvation is a gift, not a reward. The rewards of an abundant life here on earth and all that may accompany the Lord's "well done thou good and faithful servant", in heaven are the rewards we earn as we respond to God's wonderful gift of salvation by loving, obeying, and leading lives fully pleasing to Him.

Father, may I be found faithful. Amen

Taking it to the Lord...

How can I apply this truth?____

____

____

Father, I've come to worship and praise you! You are my:____________________

____

I give you all Glory, Honor, and Praise O Lord!

Father, I am sorry that I have sinned by:__________________________________

Help me to repent. Cleanse me, strengthen me, restore me.

Father, THANK YOU for all your love, grace, mercy and blessings of life that you continually shower down upon me. Thank you especially for:

1.___________________________ 2.___________________________

3.___________________________ 4.___________________________

5.___________________________ 6.___________________________

THANK YOU for answered prayers:_______________________________________

Father, I need:____

Father, I ask that YOU:____

____

____

Lord, bless me that I may be a blessing. Give me Your heart for loving and serving others. Keep Your hand upon me. Keep me from all evil and harm, and let me cause harm to no one. Bind Satan that he have no power over me. All this I pray in subjection to your will and in the strong name of my Lord and Savior, Jesus Christ. Amen.

So We Won't Have To

"When we were utterly helpless, Christ came at just the right time and died for us sinners." Romans 5:6 NLT

Have you ever gone to pay your check at a restaurant and found out that someone has already paid your bill? It doesn't happen very often, but it's a very pleasant surprise when it does.

'But God is my helper. The Lord is the one who keeps me alive!" Psalm 54:4 NLT

We sometimes receive free tickets to ball games, amusement parks, etc. All of these freebies are nothing compared to the free gift of eternal life that we receive when we receive Jesus Christ as our Savior. When we think of the fact that Jesus died on the cross so that we wouldn't have to, we are experiencing something beyond human understanding.

It is against human reasoning to accept the fact that someone would die for us for any reason, much less for our sins. This is one of the main reasons we have such a difficult time forgiving ourselves and accepting the unconditional love of God.

We add terms and conditions that diminish the magnitude of Christ's performance and try to magnify the importance of our own conduct or behavior. It is important to be mindful of our conduct and behavior. We need to live lives above reproach in keeping with the freedom Christ won for us to do so on the Cross. It's all about motive.

"And so we keep on praying for you, that our God will make you worthy of the life to which he called you. And we pray that God, by his power, will fulfill all your good intentions and faithful deeds." 2 Thessalonians 1:11 NLT

Our salvation was earned by Jesus' death on the cross. We can do nothing to earn our salvation. Any good we do, all of the God honoring fruit we produce should be from hearts overflowing with love and gratitude for what He has done. We can earn our Lord's "well done" by leading "lives fully pleasing to Him and fruitful in every good work."

Father, I can never be worthy, but I can always be thankful, and show my thanks by seeking to please you in all things. Amen

Taking it to the Lord...

How can I apply this truth?____

____

____

Father, I've come to worship and praise you! You are my:___________________________

____

I give you all Glory, Honor, and Praise O Lord!

Father, I am sorry that I have sinned by:____

Help me to repent. Cleanse me, strengthen me, restore me.

Father, THANK YOU for all your love, grace, mercy and blessings of life that you continually shower down upon me. Thank you especially for:

1._____________________________________   2._____________________________________

3._____________________________________   4._____________________________________

5._____________________________________   6._____________________________________

THANK YOU for answered prayers:____

Father, I need:____

Father, I ask that YOU:____

____

____

Lord, bless me that I may be a blessing. Give me Your heart for loving and serving others. Keep Your hand upon me. Keep me from all evil and harm, and let me cause harm to no one. Bind Satan that he have no power over me. All this I pray in subjection to your will and in the strong name of my Lord and Savior, Jesus Christ. Amen.

Truth or Consequences

"And since we are his children, we will share his treasures, for everything God gives to his Son, Christ, is ours, too. But if we are to share His glory, we must also share His suffering. Yet what we suffer now is nothing compared to the glory He will give us later." Romans 8:17,18 NLT

Among the many problems that sin brought into the world, suffering is one of the most universal and perplexing. While it is easy to understand the suffering of consequences as punishment for sin, the truth of other causes of suffering is not all that clear. The discourses on "why bad things happen to good people" that began in the book of Job have continued up to this very day, and will only be fully understood when we get to heaven.

> *"When I thought how to understand this, it was too painful for me—*
> *Psalm 73:16*

We do learn from Scripture that suffering can be a punishment for sin. God has also promised to visit the iniquity of the father upon the children to the third and fourth generation of those who hate Him.   This is another mystery that will only fully be understood when all truth is revealed.

We also learn that God allows suffering in order to get our attention, our obedience, and to develop our character. We need to also know that satan uses suffering as a means of defeating us and trying to make us turn our backs on God.

> *"And God will wipe away every tear from their eyes; there shall be no more death, nor sorrow, nor crying. There shall be no more pain, for the former things have passed away."*
> *Revelation 21:4*

While we may wonder why God allows so many to suffer as the consequences of someone else's sin, we should never forget the grace of God in allowing Jesus Christ to suffer as He did in order to pay our sin debt in full. Jesus was without sin of any kind, and yet he drank of a cup of sorrow worse than anything any of us will ever have to suffer. This truth should give us hope when we find ourselves suffering for any reason.

Father, help me to keep my eye on the prize that is mine in You as I endure any suffering that comes my way. Amen.

Taking it to the Lord...

How can I apply this truth?____

____

Father, I've come to worship and praise you! You are my:_____________________

____

I give you all Glory, Honor, and Praise O Lord!

Father, I am sorry that I have sinned by:_________________________________

Help me to repent. Cleanse me, strengthen me, restore me.

Father, THANK YOU for all your love, grace, mercy and blessings of life that you continually shower down upon me. Thank you especially for:

1.___________________________________   2.___________________________________

3.___________________________________   4.___________________________________

5.___________________________________   6.___________________________________

THANK YOU for answered prayers:____

Father, I need:____

Father, I ask that YOU:____

____

____

Lord, bless me that I may be a blessing. Give me Your heart for loving and serving others. Keep Your hand upon me. Keep me from all evil and harm, and let me cause harm to no one. Bind Satan that he have no power over me. All this I pray in subjection to your will and in the strong name of my Lord and Savior, Jesus Christ. Amen.

When Your Reality Check Bounces

"Now that we know what we have—Jesus, this great High Priest with ready access to God—let's not let it slip through our fingers. We don't have a priest who is out of touch with our reality. He's been through weakness and testing," Hebrews 4:4 MSG

Contrary to what some believe, denial is not a river in Egypt, but It is often a river of disappointment and despair. We tend to sugar coat sin, dismiss shortcomings and failures, and think more highly of ourselves than we ought.

> *"Who are those who fear the LORD? He will show them the path they should choose."*
> *Psalm 25:12 NLT*

We refuse to admit that we have an addiction problem, a problem forgiving others, or that we are not really the captains of our fate.

Trying to borrow money can be a real eye opener. Some even believe that they can borrow their way out of debt. When the cards are maxed out, and the repossessors and bill collectors start showing up, reality sets in too late for too many.

Psychologists tell us that we base our security on how well we live within our self-picture of expectations. We are happy when we live within these parameters and are miserable when we don't.

When the reality that our perfect mate is not so perfect after all, that our adorable children are not so adorable all the time, that people are often going to disappoint us; we begin to realize that the bank of reality also marks accounts "insufficient."

.   When we bank on anything other than saving faith in Jesus Christ and that He died on the cross in order that we might have eternal life… when we base our security on what the world thinks instead of the reality of who we are in Christ…. we are sooner or later going find that our reality check has bounced.

> *"It is by our actions that we know we are living in the truth, so we will be confident when we stand before the Lord."*
> *1 John 3:19a NLT*

The Good News is that God's love, forgiveness, and acceptance is real. God's promises are true. He will never bounce our checks.

Father, thank you for being the one sure foundation in a world filled with disappointment and shattered realities. Amen

Taking it to the Lord...

How can I apply this truth?____

____

____

Father, I've come to worship and praise you! You are my:_________________________________

____

I give you all Glory, Honor, and Praise O Lord!

Father, I am sorry that I have sinned by:____

Help me to repent. Cleanse me, strengthen me, restore me.

Father, THANK YOU for all your love, grace, mercy and blessings of life that you continually shower down upon me. Thank you especially for:

1.__________________________________ 2.__________________________________

3.__________________________________ 4.__________________________________

5.__________________________________ 6.__________________________________

THANK YOU for answered prayers:____

Father, I need:____

Father, I ask that YOU:____

____

____

Lord, bless me that I may be a blessing. Give me Your heart for loving and serving others. Keep Your hand upon me. Keep me from all evil and harm, and let me cause harm to no one. Bind Satan that he have no power over me. All this I pray in subjection to your will and in the strong name of my Lord and Savior, Jesus Christ. Amen.

When You Got it, Flaunt It

"Wise people don't make a show of their knowledge, but fools broadcast their folly." Proverbs 12:25 NLT

This advertising theme seemed to work well for a while for Braniff Airlines, but they have been out of business for a long, long time. Flaunting and taunting seemed to work well for Goliath for a while, until David put him out of business.

> *"Your favor, O LORD, made me as secure as a mountain. Then you turned away from me, and I was shattered."*
> *Psalm 30:7 NLT*

In sports, hardly a week goes by without someone's flaunting and taunting motivating their opponents to play harder and become twice as hard to defeat.

Even though "it ain't braggin if it's true," people are easily turned off by ostentatious shows or show offs of any kind. Our Lord made no bones about the hypocritical showing off of the scribes and Pharisees. Pride seems to be the only thing God hates worse than self-righteousness. He certainly has a way of dealing with both.

When it comes to selling a product or sharing our faith, there is nothing wrong with accentuating the positive as long as we do it in a gracious and pleasing manner.

No matter what the endeavor, when you're good at it people notice. Positive Christianity is contagious Christianity, and when you've got it you don't have to flaunt it for people to notice.

> *"Take heed that you do not do your charitable deeds before men, to be seen by them. Otherwise you have no reward."*
> *Matthew 6:1*

Why are you so happy all the time? How come you never fly off the handle? How can you stand that jerk? These are just a few of the questions that people who notice will ask. The only thing you need to do is be prepared to give an answer for the love, joy, peace, longsuffering, kindness, goodness, faithfulness, gentleness, or self-control that they might notice and ask about.

It's good to remember that there is a difference between seeking and receiving the praise of men and the approval of God.

Father, let me never get a swelled head from patting myself on the back. Amen

Taking it to the Lord...

How can I apply this truth?____

____

Father, I've come to worship and praise you! You are my:_____________________________

____

I give you all Glory, Honor, and Praise O Lord!

Father, I am sorry that I have sinned by:____

Help me to repent. Cleanse me, strengthen me, restore me.

Father, THANK YOU for all your love, grace, mercy and blessings of life that you continually shower down upon me. Thank you especially for:

1.__________________________________   2._________________________________

3.__________________________________   4._________________________________

5.__________________________________   6._________________________________

THANK YOU for answered prayers:____

Father, I need:____

Father, I ask that YOU:____

____

____

Lord, bless me that I may be a blessing. Give me Your heart for loving and serving others. Keep Your hand upon me. Keep me from all evil and harm, and let me cause harm to no one. Bind Satan that he have no power over me. All this I pray in subjection to your will and in the strong name of my Lord and Savior, Jesus Christ. Amen.

His Masters Voice

"For a shepherd enters through the gate. The gatekeeper opens the gate for him, and the sheep hear his voice and come to him. He calls his own sheep by name and leads them out." John 10:2 NLT

Some will still remember the old crank up Victrolas and the big records they played. Others may have seen the "old talking machines" in a museum somewhere. The original slogan and logo for the Victor talking machine, or "Victrola" showed a spotted dog sitting and listening to "His Masters Voice" from the Victrola.

> *"The voice of the LORD is powerful; the voice of the LORD is full of majesty."*
> *Psalm 29:4 NLT*

Today, my dog perks up, wags his tail, and looks in wonderment when he hears my voice from a VCR or tape playing. He knows my voice! Most of the time, he comes running when I call. Other times, He insists on paying no attention when I call and keeps on doing whatever it is that is competing for his attention.

My dog has a good excuse for not always heeding my voice - He's only a dog. When he is unleashed he becomes free to choose whether to obey or disobey when called and will respond according to the degree to which he has been trained. What excuse do we have for often doing the same thing?

.   There are other voices calling us. They are the voices of our self-centered nature calling for instant gratification of all our perceived needs. They are the voices of the world calling us to fit into the mold of living by worldly standards.

It is only through the getting to know our Master's voice through getting to know Him through His Word that we can receive the obedience training we need and the power that He will supply to keep us hearing and obeying His voice.

> *"But never forget the warning: Today you must listen to his voice. Don't harden your hearts against him as Israel did when they rebelled."*
> *Hebrews 3:15 NLT*

Father, by the power of Your Spirit, help me to hear and obey your voice. Amen.

Taking it to the Lord...

How can I apply this truth?____

____

Father, I've come to worship and praise you! You are my:_____________________

____

I give you all Glory, Honor, and Praise O Lord!

Father, I am sorry that I have sinned by:_________________________________

Help me to repent. Cleanse me, strengthen me, restore me.

Father, THANK YOU for all your love, grace, mercy and blessings of life that you continually shower down upon me. Thank you especially for:

1.____________________________   2.____________________________
3.____________________________   4.____________________________
5.____________________________   6.____________________________

THANK YOU for answered prayers:_______________________________________

Father, I need:____

Father, I ask that YOU:____

____

____

Lord, bless me that I may be a blessing. Give me Your heart for loving and serving others. Keep Your hand upon me. Keep me from all evil and harm, and let me cause harm to no one. Bind Satan that he have no power over me. All this I pray in subjection to your will and in the strong name of my Lord and Savior, Jesus Christ. Amen.

Reach Out and Touch Someone

**"The sick begged him to let them touch even the fringe of his robe, and all who touched it were healed."
Matthew 14:36 NLT**

The advertising agency that came up with AT&T's outstanding advertising campaign probably had no idea that they were paraphrasing our Lord's great commission to go out and make disciples, but this is what our Lord is commanding us to.

> *"The LORD reigns; let the peoples tremble!
> He dwells between the cherubim; let the earth be moved!
> Psalm 99:1*

Whether the physical touch of Jesus or the disciples which brought instant healing, or the emotional touch of being called into saving faith by the power of the Holy Spirit as the Word is shared; we are called to "reach out and touch someone"!

A mighty movement of God moving the earth to faith, repentance, and love of God and each other is the only hope for dealing with the problems of this evil world. He did this through a nondescript group of disciples yesterday, and He can do it through us His disciples today.

Revival can spread like wildfire when all of God's people unite in purpose and begin reaching out and touching others with the love of God that is ours in Christ Jesus.

We can reach out and touch someone by living out our faith in bringing the fruit of the Spirit to bear in our relationship with others. We can be ready to give an account for the hope that is within us whenever God provides a divine opportunity to do this.

It may be in reaching out with a word of encouragement, with help to someone in need, through prayer, or in supporting missions throughout the World.

> *"But the believers who had fled Jerusalem went everywhere preaching the Good News about Jesus."
> Acts 8:4 NLT*

We are in relationship with Jesus Christ because the Holy Spirit reached out and touched us through the love and witness of someone.

Can we do any less than be a conduit of God's love to others?

Father, by the power of Your Spirit, use me to reach out and touch someone for you. Amen.

Taking it to the Lord...

How can I apply this truth?____

____

____

Father, I've come to worship and praise you! You are my:_____________________

____

I give you all Glory, Honor, and Praise O Lord!

Father, I am sorry that I have sinned by:_________________________________

Help me to repent. Cleanse me, strengthen me, restore me.

Father, THANK YOU for all your love, grace, mercy and blessings of life that you continually shower down upon me.
Thank you especially for:

1._________________________________   2._________________________________

3._________________________________   4._________________________________

5._________________________________   6._________________________________

THANK YOU for answered prayers:_____________________________________

Father, I need:____

Father, I ask that YOU:____

____

____

Lord, bless me that I may be a blessing. Give me Your heart for loving and serving others. Keep Your hand upon me. Keep me from all evil and harm, and let me cause harm to no one. Bind Satan that he have no power over me. All this I pray in subjection to your will and in the strong name of my Lord and Savior, Jesus Christ. Amen.

The Darkness of Doubt

"I, *even* I, *am* He who blots out your transgressions for My own sake; and I will not remember your sins." Isaiah 43:25

Through the ongoing battles of life, frequent sins of omission and commission often take their toll on even the strongest of Christians.   Unless we are blinded by denial, we cannot escape the reality that we too often fall short of the Glory of God and either do and think things or don't do and think things that are not becoming to a disciple of Jesus Christ.

> *"My wayward children," says the LORD, "come back to me, and I will heal your wayward hearts."*
> *Jeremiah 3:22 NLT*

Satan takes advantage of these dark times to make us doubt the reality of our salvation and wonder if we are really saved. The good news is that our conviction of sin and concern for our salvation are proof in themselves that we do not have the sin hardened heart of unbelief, but rather that the Spirit of God is living in us.

We need to know that our salvation and right standing with God are not based on the merits of our conduct, but on the merits of the perfect conduct of Jesus Christ, Who filled the demands of conduct for us by living the perfect life and becoming the perfect, unblemished sacrifice for our sins.

By virtue of our faith in Jesus Christ and that He died on the cross to earn our righteousness in the sight of God, we have God's forgiveness for every sin that we have ever committed or will ever commit.

This forgiveness is not a license to keep on sinning, but a motive and supernatural empowerment to live in the light of God's love and freedom from the condemnation and dominion of sin.

> *"And now, all glory to God, who is able to keep you from stumbling, and who will bring you into his glorious presence innocent of sin and with great joy."*
> *Jude 1:23 NLT*

When the darkness of doubt encircles us, we need to seek the light of God's love and rekindle the fires of faith through daily confession and repentance and by putting on the full armor of God. The war has been won! We have the victory in Jesus! Let's celebrate by living victorious lives in the fullness of Christ.

Father, help me to exercise the power you have given me to overcome the dominion of sin in my life. Amen.

Taking it to the Lord...

How can I apply this truth?____

____

____

Father, I've come to worship and praise you! You are my:__________________________

____

I give you all Glory, Honor, and Praise O Lord!

Father, I am sorry that I have sinned by:____

Help me to repent. Cleanse me, strengthen me, restore me.

Father, THANK YOU for all your love, grace, mercy and blessings of life that you continually shower down upon me. Thank you especially for:

1.__________________________________   2.__________________________________

3.__________________________________   4.__________________________________

5.__________________________________   6.__________________________________

THANK YOU for answered prayers:____

Father, I need:____

Father, I ask that YOU:____

____

____

____

Lord, bless me that I may be a blessing. Give me Your heart for loving and serving others. Keep Your hand upon me. Keep me from all evil and harm, and let me cause harm to no one. Bind Satan that he have no power over me. All this I pray in subjection to your will and in the strong name of my Lord and Savior, Jesus Christ. Amen.

Circumstances Beyond Our Control

"Actually, I don't have a sense of needing anything personally. I've learned by now to be quite content whatever my circumstances." Philippians 4:10 MSG

There are a lot of circumstances in life over which we have absolutely no control. We can't control where and to which parents we will be born. We can't control "acts of God" and other calamities that often besiege us.

> *"The earth is the LORD's, and all its fullness, the world and those who dwell therein."*
> *Psalm 24:1*

The good life is not so much about the circumstances beyond our control, but how we choose to use our free will to control what we can. Scripture after Scripture tells of God accomplishing extraordinary things through very ordinary people who chose to let God have His way in their lives.

We see the consequences of sin having a devastating effect on the sinner and those around him because he chose to exercise sin control instead of God control.

It is inconceivable but true that many choose to reject friendship with the One Who has control of everything.

> *"We cannot imagine the power of the Almighty, yet he is so just and merciful that he does not oppress us. No wonder people everywhere fear him. People who are truly wise show him reverence."*
> *Job 37:23,24 NLT*

There is absolutely nothing beyond God's control! He is all-powerful, all knowing, and ever present. He controls the forces of nature, and the fate of man. He gives spiritual strength and resources to His own that we might persevere in circumstances beyond our control.

When we try to replace the wisdom of God with the wisdom of man and faith in God, with faith in ourselves or others, we are headed for big trouble. What is beyond the control of man is still under the control of Almighty, ever loving, and ever lasting God.

Father, help me to always remember that nothing is impossible for you. Amen.

Taking it to the Lord...

How can I apply this truth?____

____

____

Father, I've come to worship and praise you! You are my:_________________________________

____

I give you all Glory, Honor, and Praise O Lord!

Father, I am sorry that I have sinned by:____

Help me to repent. Cleanse me, strengthen me, restore me.

Father, THANK YOU for all your love, grace, mercy and blessings of life that you continually shower down upon me.

Thank you especially for:

1._________________________________   2._________________________________

3._________________________________   4._________________________________

5._________________________________   6._________________________________

THANK YOU for answered prayers:____

Father, I need:____

Father, I ask that YOU:____

____

____

____

Lord, bless me that I may be a blessing. Give me Your heart for loving and serving others. Keep Your hand upon me. Keep me from all evil and harm, and let me cause harm to no one. Bind Satan that he have no power over me. All this I pray in subjection to your will and in the strong name of my Lord and Savior, Jesus Christ. Amen.

The Discipline of Discipleship

"Because the Teacher was wise, he taught the people everything he knew. He collected proverbs and classified them. Indeed, the Teacher taught the plain truth, and he did so in an interesting way." Ecclesiastes 12:9,10 NLT

Discipline has to do with the way someone learns a way of life. We have a military discipline that trains soldiers, the academic disciplines that train scholars in various fields.

> *"So commit yourselves completely to these words of mine. Tie them to your hands as a reminder, and wear them on your forehead." Deuteronomy 11:18 NLT*

The discipline of being a disciple of Jesus Christ means learning His teachings, following His ways, and learning how to obey and serve Him so that we might know His heart. This process often involves correction by a loving and wise heavenly father who wants us to be imitators of Christ and live lives that are fully pleasing to Him and a blessing to others.

Jesus exhorts us *to "Take My yoke upon you and learn from Me, for I am gentle and lowly in heart, and you will find rest for your souls. For My yoke is easy and My burden is light." (Matthew 11:29-30)* He also oftentimes calls for extreme levels of renunciation of family, friends, and possessions in order that we not be distracted and put anything or anybody ahead of Him.

Eternal life is a new life in Christ whereby we enter into the discipline of getting to know Him personally through His Word, experiencing His love and His joy.

Like any other discipline, discipleship is something we need to train for. The spiritual disciplines of worship, prayer, praise, confession, repentance, and obedience are a great place to start.

> *"The decisive issue is whether they obey my Father in heaven." Matthew 7:21b NLT*

When we set aside daily time to be with God in His Word and in prayer, we will experience the blessing of growing in discipleship and finding the heart of God.

Father, help me to be a disciple so that I can disciple others. Amen

Taking it to the Lord...

How can I apply this truth?____

____

Father, I've come to worship and praise you! You are my:_________________________________

____

I give you all Glory, Honor, and Praise O Lord!

Father, I am sorry that I have sinned by:____

Help me to repent. Cleanse me, strengthen me, restore me.

Father, THANK YOU for all your love, grace, mercy and blessings of life that you continually shower down upon me. Thank you especially for:

1._________________________________   2._________________________________

3._________________________________   4._________________________________

5._________________________________   6._________________________________

THANK YOU for answered prayers:____

Father, I need:____

Father, I ask that YOU:____

____

____

Lord, bless me that I may be a blessing. Give me Your heart for loving and serving others. Keep Your hand upon me. Keep me from all evil and harm, and let me cause harm to no one. Bind Satan that he have no power over me. All this I pray in subjection to your will and in the strong name of my Lord and Savior, Jesus Christ. Amen.

Unlimited Access

"In whom we have boldness and access with confidence through faith in Him." Ephesians 3:12

Individuals, corporations, and special interest groups spend billions of dollars each year on lobbyists for access to government leaders and authorities on a local, regional, state and national basis.

> *"O You who hear prayer, to You all flesh will come." Psalm 65:2 NLT*

Many pay a premium to get unlimited access to the Internet. God paid a premium to give us unlimited access to Him through faith in His Son.

There seems to be a Scriptural correlation between fasting and better access to God. Our Lord Himself set an example by fasting. Whatever helps to give God our undivided attention when we seek access to Him through prayer is good.

It is comforting to know that we have four-way access to God. We have the Holy Spirit continually interceding on our behalf, praying for things that we don't even know how or what to pray for. We have friends and loved ones praying for us, as well as the infallible Word of God.

> *"Here's what I want you to do: Find a quiet, secluded place so you won't be tempted to role-play before God. Just be there as simply and honestly as you can manage. The focus will shift from you to God, and you will begin to sense his grace." Matthew 6:5 MSG*

As members of a Royal Priesthood, we have direct access to God ourselves. Best of all, we have God's Son and our brother, seated at the right hand of God keeping the doorway to heaven open for us.

The only limits to our access to God are the limits we place on ourselves. We sometimes pray too half-heartedly and with too little real faith that God will answer. We often pray selfish, self-centered prayers, instead of God centered prayers.

Unconfessed, unrepented sins--especially harbored resentments against others—can really short-circuit our access. The more we grow in Christ and abide in Him and His Word, the more unlimited our access becomes.

Father, thank You for the joy of answered prayers. Thank you for the giving unlimited access to Your throne of grace. Amen.

Taking it to the Lord...

How can I apply this truth?____

____

Father, I've come to worship and praise you! You are my:____________________

____

I give you all Glory, Honor, and Praise O Lord!

Father, I am sorry that I have sinned by:____

Help me to repent. Cleanse me, strengthen me, restore me.

Father, THANK YOU for all your love, grace, mercy and blessings of life that you continually shower down upon me. Thank you especially for:

1.__________________________________   2.__________________________________

3.__________________________________   4.__________________________________

5.__________________________________   6.__________________________________

THANK YOU for answered prayers:____

Father, I need:____

Father, I ask that YOU:____

____

____

____

Lord, bless me that I may be a blessing. Give me Your heart for loving and serving others. Keep Your hand upon me. Keep me from all evil and harm, and let me cause harm to no one. Bind Satan that he have no power over me. All this I pray in subjection to your will and in the strong name of my Lord and Savior, Jesus Christ. Amen.

Nothing More, Nothing Less

"Dear brothers and sisters, when I first came to you I didn't use lofty words and brilliant ideas to tell you God's message. For I decided to concentrate only on Jesus Christ and his death on the cross. I did this so that you might trust the power of God rather than human wisdom." 2 Corinthians 2:1,2,5

There is real danger in both extremes of living a life in Christ. We can become performance driven and feel compelled to do more and more to validate our faith on the basis of our performance instead of on the perfect sacrifice of Jesus Christ on the Cross of Calvary.

> *"Those who know your name trust in you, for you, O LORD, have never abandoned anyone who searches for you."*
> *Psalm 9:10 NLT*

Whenever anything else is added as a requirement for eternal life, we are, in effect, saying that Jesus' death on the cross was not good enough, and that we have to do more. This denigrates and insults the grace of God.

Whenever we base our salvation on our morality, our intellect, or our terms instead of Jesus' blood and righteousness, we really rob God of His power, His strength, and His glory. We are building our hope on less.

God has created each and every one of us for good works that He ordained even before we were born. When we learn to abide in Christ and want to do those things that Glorify Him in response to His love, we are where we need to be to be about our Father's business.

Financial gifts given under compulsion are not pleasing in God's sight. Good works done grudgingly as though we have to do something instead of joyfully and because we want to do something are also not pleasing to God.

> *"Who is wise and understanding among you? Let him show by good conduct that his works are done in the meekness of wisdom."*
> *James 3:13*

Let the anthem: "My hope is built on nothing less than Jesus' blood and righteousness" be the foundation on which we live our lives, and let God take control of our lives through the Holy Spirit.

Only when we become Christ centered instead of self-centered can God use us for His highest purposes.

Father, let me never trust in less than your blood and righteousness for my salvation. Amen

Taking it to the Lord...

How can I apply this truth?____

____

Father, I've come to worship and praise you! You are my:_______________________________

____

I give you all Glory, Honor, and Praise O Lord!

Father, I am sorry that I have sinned by:____

Help me to repent. Cleanse me, strengthen me, restore me.

Father, THANK YOU for all your love, grace, mercy and blessings of life that you continually shower down upon me. Thank you especially for:

1.__________________________________   2._________________________________

3.__________________________________   4._________________________________

5.__________________________________   6._________________________________

THANK YOU for answered prayers:____

Father, I need:____

Father, I ask that YOU:____

____

____

Lord, bless me that I may be a blessing. Give me Your heart for loving and serving others. Keep Your hand upon me. Keep me from all evil and harm, and let me cause harm to no one. Bind Satan that he have no power over me. All this I pray in subjection to your will and in the strong name of my Lord and Savior, Jesus Christ. Amen.

Sweet Hour of Prayer

"Ask, and it will be given to you; seek, and you will find; knock, and it will be opened to you. For everyone who asks receives, and he who seeks finds, and to him who knocks it will be opened." Matthew 7:7

Throughout the Old and New Testament, we see the power of prayer. God heard the cries of the children of Israel. Moses successfully interceded with God to turn his wrath away from the "stiff necked" Israelites. Jacob wrestled with God in prayer. Solomon received wisdom through prayer. God worked miracles through the prayers of Elijah and Elisha.

> *"Because Your loving kindness is better than life, My lips shall praise You."*
> *Psalm 63:3*

David's prayers in the Psalms show his understanding of the need for confession and repentance, and also that there is value in a great variety of honest prayers of praise, protection, redemption, or healing. Psalm 86 is regarded as one of the great model prayers for believers.

Our Lord Jesus Christ realized the importance of and set the standard for the prayers of believers. He prayed at all crucial moments, He prayed regularly and fervently.

Jesus warned about the danger of praying to impress others, or long winded attempts to manipulate God. Selfish motives, corrupted character, and injured relationships are frequent hindrances to getting prayers answered in the affirmative.

As we abide more and more in Christ, it is amazing how more and more of our prayers are answered.

> *"And shall God not avenge His own elect who cry out day and night to Him, though He bears long with them?"*
> *Luke 18:7*

As we live in the presence of the Holy Spirit living within us our "sweet hour of prayer" becomes an on going, around the clock dialog where practically every waking hour is filled with spoken and unspoken prayers of thanksgiving, praise, and peace. *"You will keep him in perfect peace, whose mind is stayed on You, because he trusts in You."* (Isaiah 26:3)

Father, help me to live in the awareness of your presence, so that every hour will be a "sweet hour of prayer" for me. Amen

Taking it to the Lord...

How can I apply this truth?____

____

Father, I've come to worship and praise you! You are my:_______________________

____

I give you all Glory, Honor, and Praise O Lord!

Father, I am sorry that I have sinned by:_______________________________________

Help me to repent. Cleanse me, strengthen me, restore me.

Father, THANK YOU for all your love, grace, mercy and blessings of life that you continually shower down upon me. Thank you especially for:

1.__________________________________   2.__________________________________

3.__________________________________   4.__________________________________

5.__________________________________   6.__________________________________

THANK YOU for answered prayers:______________________________________

Father, I need:____

Father, I ask that YOU:____

____

____

Lord, bless me that I may be a blessing. Give me Your heart for loving and serving others. Keep Your hand upon me. Keep me from all evil and harm, and let me cause harm to no one. Bind Satan that he have no power over me. All this I pray in subjection to your will and in the strong name of my Lord and Savior, Jesus Christ. Amen.

Blemished Offerings

"Whatever has a defect, you shall not offer, for it shall not be acceptable on your behalf." Leviticus 22:20

Few things reveal the condition of our hearts as does our giving. Scripture after Scripture attests to the fact blemished offerings are not acceptable in God's sight.

> *"Says the LORD of hosts, "and you bring the stolen, the lame, and the sick; thus you bring an offering! Should I accept this from your hand?" Says the LORD."*
> *Malachi 1:13 b*

David insisted on paying for the land that was offered to him for free because he would not offer God anything that cost him nothing. Just as without the sacrificing of blood there is no remission for sin, without sacrificial giving, there are no blessings in offerings.

God established the principle of proportionate giving, and expects more from those to whom much has been given. The widow's mite was much more acceptable than much larger gifts from others, because she gave all that she had and others can give large amounts without sacrificing anything.

Our offerings become blemished when we give of our leftovers instead of our first fruits. God loves a cheerful giver who gives from the heart. A gift given grudgingly or without joy is a blemished offering. A showy, self-righteous gift is an abomination to God.

God apparently challenges us to test him by giving. *"And try Me now in this," says the LORD of hosts, "If I will not open for you the windows of heaven And pour out for you such blessing that there will not be room enough to receive it". (Malachi 3:10)*

> *"And not only as we had hoped, but they first gave themselves to the Lord, and then to us by the will of God."*
> *2 Corinthians 8:5*

Any motive in giving other than responding to God's love and what He has given us is blemished giving. God wants our hearts and when we give to him cheerfully with hearts overflowing with love, we are giving that unblemished sacrifice of praise that is acceptable in God's sight.

Father, let me abound in the grace of giving by giving from the heart. Amen

Taking it to the Lord...

How can I apply this truth?____

____

Father, I've come to worship and praise you! You are my:_____________________

____

I give you all Glory, Honor, and Praise O Lord!

Father, I am sorry that I have sinned by:_________________________________

Help me to repent. Cleanse me, strengthen me, restore me.

Father, THANK YOU for all your love, grace, mercy and blessings of life that you continually shower down upon me. Thank you especially for:

1.____________________________   2.____________________________

3.____________________________   4.____________________________

5.____________________________   6.____________________________

THANK YOU for answered prayers:_____________________________________

Father, I need:____

Father, I ask that YOU:____

____

____

Lord, bless me that I may be a blessing. Give me Your heart for loving and serving others. Keep Your hand upon me. Keep me from all evil and harm, and let me cause harm to no one. Bind Satan that he have no power over me. All this I pray in subjection to your will and in the strong name of my Lord and Savior, Jesus Christ. Amen.

Diamonds are Forever?

"Those who are wise will shine as bright as the sky, and those who turn many to righteousness will shine like stars forever." Daniel 12:3 NLT

According to "Advertising Age" magazine, the number one advertising slogan of the past century was "Diamonds are forever" for de Beers diamonds.

> *"If you seek her as silver, and search for her as for hidden treasures; then you will understand the fear of the LORD, and find the knowledge of God."*
> *Proverbs 2:4,5 NLT*

As a youth, I heard the story of a disgruntled employee who switched the price tags between the costume jewelry with imitation jewels, and the real jewels. Customers unknowingly bought valuable pieces for practically nothing, and paid outlandish prices for mere trinkets.

Just as "all that glitters is not gold", so "all that sparkles is not forever." How many times do we get turned on by the fake jewels of the flesh and the world that promise pleasure and significance that deliver disappointment and insignificance.

> *"But there is going to come a time of testing at the judgment day to see what kind of work each builder has done. Everyone's work will be put through the fire to see whether or not it keeps its value."*
> *1 Corinthians 3:13 NLT*

When we consult our appraiser's guide, we find that the things that will last forever are the relationship we have with God through Jesus Christ, and those good works that He prepared for us before we were ever born. These will survive the test of fire when we stand before God to give an accounting of the stewardship of our lives.

The real "sparklers" that will shine forever and ever are those who have made disciples of Jesus and those who store up their real treasures in heaven.

May your crown of righteousness be adorned with lives that were changed and people who God chose to love through you as you lived faithful to the great commandment and great commission. These are the diamonds that are forever!

Father, help me to keep my price tags firmly attached to the things that bring glory to You and true joy and peace to me. Amen

Taking it to the Lord...

How can I apply this truth?____

Father, I've come to worship and praise you! You are my:____

I give you all Glory, Honor, and Praise O Lord!

Father, I am sorry that I have sinned by:____

Help me to repent. Cleanse me, strengthen me, restore me.

Father, THANK YOU for all your love, grace, mercy and blessings of life that you continually shower down upon me. Thank you especially for:

1.____________________________________   2.____________________________________

3.____________________________________   4.____________________________________

5.____________________________________   6.____________________________________

THANK YOU for answered prayers:____

Father, I need:____

Father, I ask that YOU:____

Lord, bless me that I may be a blessing. Give me Your heart for loving and serving others. Keep Your hand upon me. Keep me from all evil and harm, and let me cause harm to no one. Bind Satan that he have no power over me. All this I pray in subjection to your will and in the strong name of my Lord and Savior, Jesus Christ. Amen.

The Pearl of Great Price

"When he discovered a pearl of great value, he sold everything he owned and bought it!" Matthew 13:4 6 NLT

In some ways, life can be likened to one big treasure hunt. Since the beginning of time, man has been searching for the meaning and purposes of life with many not even coming close to the answer.

> *"I rejoice in your word like one who finds a great treasure."*
> *Psalm 119:162-175*

Although God has put it into the heart of every man to know Him, and fills all creation with evidence of His existence, man continues to look for treasure in all the wrong places and eventually comes up empty handed.

Whether seeking gratification and validation of ones self through the approval of others, power, fame or fortune; or through dancing to the world's tune we wander aimlessly lost until we find that real treasure.

In asking ourselves "what is my pearl of great price" just ask where or with whom do we spend the greatest amount of our time. How do we spend the greatest amount of our discretionary resources? How do we use our talents that are on loan from God? What do we possess and what possesses us?

> *"The ransom he paid was not mere gold or silver. He paid for you with the precious lifeblood of Christ, the sinless, spotless Lamb of God."*
> *1 Peter 1:18b,19*

The rich young ruler was at least honest enough to walk away because he was possessed by His riches.

When we leave this world, we are leaving just as we came in, naked as jaybirds and without any of the treasures we held so dear and qualities we treasured so much – unless we are leaving with that "pearl of great price" which is our salvation which is through faith in Jesus Christ.

Do you really dare to leave "Home" without this?

Father, Helping me to hold on to the real pearl of life by the power of Your Holy Spirit. Amen.

Taking it to the Lord...

How can I apply this truth?____

____

Father, I've come to worship and praise you! You are my:_______________________

____

I give you all Glory, Honor, and Praise O Lord!

Father, I am sorry that I have sinned by:____________________________________

Help me to repent. Cleanse me, strengthen me, restore me.

Father, THANK YOU for all your love, grace, mercy and blessings of life that you continually shower down upon me. Thank you especially for:

1.________________________________   2.________________________________

3.________________________________   4.________________________________

5.________________________________   6.________________________________

THANK YOU for answered prayers:____

Father, I need:____

Father, I ask that YOU:____

____

____

Lord, bless me that I may be a blessing. Give me Your heart for loving and serving others. Keep Your hand upon me. Keep me from all evil and harm, and let me cause harm to no one. Bind Satan that he have no power over me. All this I pray in subjection to your will and in the strong name of my Lord and Savior, Jesus Christ. Amen.

Are You Underinsured?

"Because He has appointed a day on which He will judge the world in righteousness by the Man whom He has ordained. He has given assurance of this to all by raising Him from the dead." Acts 17:31

You can insure about any possible risk. From the unlikely possibility that someone will make a hole in one in a contest, to death, policies are available.   Often we never know how good our insurance is until we have to use it. Some of those fine print "exceptions" make some policies virtually worthless.

> *"My God is my rock, in whom I find protection. He is my shield, the strength of my salvation, and my stronghold, my high tower, my savior, the one who saves me from violence."*
> *2 Samuel 22:3*

Sun Life Assurance of Canada is one of the giants of the insurance world, but even they cannot guarantee that losses and calamities will not happen, but only that they will reimburse you if they do.

There is only one insurer that has never failed to honor a claim, has no hidden exceptions and will even guarantee to cover pre existing conditions. I like to call this "Son Life".

"Son Life" is the only insurance available that does not pay death benefits because "Son Life" guarantees that you will never die! The lump sum one-time premium was paid for you on the Cross of Calvary when Jesus Christ gave up His life so that you could have one forever.

> *"Let us draw near with a true heart in full assurance of faith, having our hearts sprinkled from an evil conscience and our bodies washed with pure water."*
> *Hebrews 10:22*

The application for this eternal life insurance is as simple as **ABC**, and cannot be rejected or cancelled. All you have to do to become fully insured is **A**dmit that you are a sinner, **B**elieve in the life, death, and resurrection of Jesus Christ as payment and proof of payment for your sins, and **C**onfess this admission and belief to God and to others. If your confession is sincere and your faith is real, you receive the keys to the kingdom and forever life with God in Christ.

If you do not have this policy, you are seriously underinsured! Call "Son Life" or a designated representative today!

Father, thank you for the assurance of eternal life I have through faith in Jesus Christ. Amen

Taking it to the Lord...

How can I apply this truth?____

____

Father, I've come to worship and praise you! You are my:___________________

____

I give you all Glory, Honor, and Praise O Lord!

Father, I am sorry that I have sinned by:________________________________

Help me to repent. Cleanse me, strengthen me, restore me.

Father, THANK YOU for all your love, grace, mercy and blessings of life that you continually shower down upon me. Thank you especially for:

1._________________________________   2._________________________________

3._________________________________   4._________________________________

5._________________________________   6._________________________________

THANK YOU for answered prayers:____

Father, I need:____

Father, I ask that YOU:____

____

____

Lord, bless me that I may be a blessing. Give me Your heart for loving and serving others. Keep Your hand upon me. Keep me from all evil and harm, and let me cause harm to no one. Bind Satan that he have no power over me. All this I pray in subjection to your will and in the strong name of my Lord and Savior, Jesus Christ. Amen.

To God Be the Glory!

"But we all, with unveiled face, beholding as in a mirror the glory of the Lord, are being transformed into the same image from glory to glory, just as by the Spirit of the Lord." 2 Corinthians 3:18

"Glory" is an interesting word, appearing in Scripture well over 300 times. It is used to mean honor, dignity, splendor, brightness, majesty, adoration, praise, the bliss of heaven, and perhaps most importantly, the infinite perfections of God.

> *"Give to the LORD the glory he deserves!"*
> *1 Chronicles 16:19a*

God chose to be born in a stable instead of a palace in order to manifest His glory. He chose a rag tag group of men of low estate rather than kings or princes to spread the gospel as proof that this was the work of God and not men.

Today, God uses ordinary people to accomplish extraordinary tasks that only God can do, lest He be robbed of His glory.

We must never lose sight of the fact that God "humbles the proud and gives grace to the humble".

Few things corrupt as much as power or pride. When we get to thinking more highly of ourselves than we ought, we become virtually useless to God.

God requires a broken spirit and a contrite heart before He can fill it with His grace and power to accomplish His purposes. David, the prodigal son, and Peter personify this truth.

> *"I brought glory to you here on earth by doing everything you told me to do."*
> *John 17:4*

It is only when we become Christ centered instead of self centered, and focus on glorifying God instead of ourselves that God's glory for which he created us can be manifested in our lives.

Father, keep me ever mindful that it's not about glorifying me, but about glorifying you. To You, alone, be all glory. Amen.

Taking it to the Lord...

How can I apply this truth?____

____

Father, I've come to worship and praise you! You are my:___________________________

____

I give you all Glory, Honor, and Praise O Lord!

Father, I am sorry that I have sinned by:____

Help me to repent. Cleanse me, strengthen me, restore me.

Father, THANK YOU for all your love, grace, mercy and blessings of life that you continually shower down upon me. Thank you especially for:

1.________________________________   2.________________________________

3.________________________________   4.________________________________

5.________________________________   6.________________________________

THANK YOU for answered prayers:____

Father, I need:____

Father, I ask that YOU:____

____

____

Lord, bless me that I may be a blessing. Give me Your heart for loving and serving others. Keep Your hand upon me. Keep me from all evil and harm, and let me cause harm to no one. Bind Satan that he have no power over me. All this I pray in subjection to your will and in the strong name of my Lord and Savior, Jesus Christ. Amen.

Be Careful What You Pray

"Father, if you are willing, please take this cup of suffering away from me. Yet I want your will, not mine." Luke 22:40 NLT

If you're like me, you often forget about whose will you're praying to be done when you pray the Lord's Prayer. For me at least, it has for too long and too often been a self centered prayer more to grant me the desires of my heart and my will, rather than the good and gracious will of God. To pray that the Lord's will be done is one of the easiest prayers to pray and yet the hardest prayer to really mean.

> *"Listen to my cry for help, my King and my God, for I will never pray to anyone but you."*
> *Psalm 5:2*

We can have the joy of knowing that God really does answer prayers, because by His grace, we can learn the secret of abiding in Him and His Word. Then most every prayer we pray will be based on our understanding of His will and His purposes. We need to learn to submit our petitions by praying as our Lord Jesus did - that it might please God to grant our requests, but always that they be subject to His good and gracious will.

It is great to know that we have the Holy Spirit continually praying for us." *For we don't even know what we should pray for, nor how we should pray. But the Holy Spirit prays for us with groanings that cannot be expressed in words. And the Father who knows all hearts knows what the Spirit is saying, for the Spirit pleads for us believers in harmony with God's own will." (Romans 8:26,27) NLT*

I am forever grateful to Dr. Charles Stanley, who many years ago asked that we pray this prayer from Colossians for him. It has become the center point of all my prayers for all those I love and those I pray for. To me it is one of the best prayers in the Bible.

> *[9]For this reason we also, since the day we heard it, do not cease to pray for you, and to ask that you may be filled with the knowledge of His will in all wisdom and spiritual understanding; [10]that you may walk worthy of the Lord, fully pleasing Him, being fruitful in every good work and increasing in the knowledge of God; [11]strengthened with all might, according to His glorious power, for all patience and longsuffering with joy.*
> *Colossian 1:9-11*

Father, help me to pray not from repetition or habit, but with real sincerity and meaning what I pray. Amen

Taking it to the Lord...

How can I apply this truth?____

____

Father, I've come to worship and praise you! You are my:________________________

____

I give you all Glory, Honor, and Praise O Lord!

Father, I am sorry that I have sinned by:_____________________________________

Help me to repent. Cleanse me, strengthen me, restore me.

Father, THANK YOU for all your love, grace, mercy and blessings of life that you continually shower down upon me. Thank you especially for:

1.________________________________ 2.________________________________

3.________________________________ 4.________________________________

5.________________________________ 6.________________________________

THANK YOU for answered prayers:____

Father, I need:____

Father, I ask that YOU:____

____

Lord, bless me that I may be a blessing. Give me Your heart for loving and serving others. Keep Your hand upon me. Keep me from all evil and harm, and let me cause harm to no one. Bind Satan that he have no power over me. All this I pray in subjection to your will and in the strong name of my Lord and Savior, Jesus Christ. Amen.

Things God Can't Do

"Let no one say when he is tempted, "I am tempted by God"; for God cannot be tempted by evil, nor does He Himself tempt anyone. But each one is tempted when he is drawn away by his own desires and enticed." James 1:13

As we proclaim the sovereignty and power of God it is easy to lose sight of one of the great truths and great comforts of our faith. There are some things God can't do!

> *"I have known from my earliest days that your decrees never change."*
> *Psalm 119:152*

God cannot be tempted by evil. He is the only one who had the power to overcome evil not for Himself, but for us, that we might be conformed to the image of Christ.

God can't lie! His every Word is truth, and we can take whatever He says or promises to the bank. *"God is not a man, that He should lie. He is not a human, that He should change his mind."* (Numbers 23:19)

God can't trust us! *"If God cannot trust his own angels and has charged some of them with folly, how much less will he trust those made of clay" (Job 4:18)* God knows the weakness of our flesh and our inability to save ourselves. This is why He sent His Son to do for us what we could not do for ourselves - be our Savior.

> *"God also bound himself with an oath, so that those who received the promise could be perfectly sure that he would never change his mind."*
> *Hebrews 6:18*

God can't turn His back on us! *"But this is the LORD'S reply: I would no more reject my people than I would change my laws of night and day, of earth and sky."* (Jeremiah 33:25)

Isn't it thrilling to know that we have a God who is love, who cannot fail, and in whom we can trust in every area of our lives?   If you have not yet come to this realization, think about it, pray about it, and claim this reality by faith. It's true!

Father, I am so glad that you are my one constant in a sea of turmoil and change. Keep me anchored deep in you and your unfailing love. Amen

Taking it to the Lord...

How can I apply this truth?____

____

____

Father, I've come to worship and praise you! You are my:_________________________________

____

I give you all Glory, Honor, and Praise O Lord!

Father, I am sorry that I have sinned by:____

Help me to repent. Cleanse me, strengthen me, restore me.

Father, THANK YOU for all your love, grace, mercy and blessings of life that you continually shower down upon me. Thank you especially for:

1._________________________________   2._________________________________

3._________________________________   4._________________________________

5._________________________________   6._________________________________

THANK YOU for answered prayers:____

Father, I need:____

Father, I ask that YOU:____

____

____

Lord, bless me that I may be a blessing. Give me Your heart for loving and serving others. Keep Your hand upon me. Keep me from all evil and harm, and let me cause harm to no one. Bind Satan that he have no power over me. All this I pray in subjection to your will and in the strong name of my Lord and Savior, Jesus Christ. Amen.

Whose Shoes?

**"For shoes, put on the peace that comes from the Good News, so that you will be fully prepared."
Ephesians 6:15**

Athletic shoes are a multi-billion dollar business. Nike, Reebok, Addidas and others pay hundreds of millions of dollars just to get athletes to wear and endorse shoes when many wouldn't want to be caught dead in some of their shoes.

> *"How beautiful on the mountains are the feet of those who bring good news of peace and salvation, the news that the God of Israel reigns!"*
> *Isaiah 52:7*

John said that he was not worthy even to carry Jesus' shoes, much less walk in them. Children of very famous and successful parents, successors of legendary coaches, athletes, and even preachers are often reminded of the "big shoes" they have to fill. Often the burden of trying to "fill the shoes" is too great, and those who try end up defeated and destroyed in the process.

Sandals were the footwear of biblical days, and apparently socks had not been invented. This caused a lot of dust and dirt to accumulate on the feet as people walked and worked in sandals, necessitating the removing of sandals and washing of feet by the lowliest of servants when anyone entered the homes of the high and mighty of those days.

No wonder the disciples were taken back when their leader and the one they thought would be king and ruler of the world, stooped to perform the lowliest task of the lowliest of slaves or servants when he washed their feet.

> *"If I then, your Lord and Teacher, have washed your feet, you also ought to wash one another's feet."*
> *John 13:14*

Whether barefooted or walking in $200 Nike's, we need to walk in humility with the one who filled the shoes that we could never fill. He lived a perfect life for us that we could never live for ourselves in order to fill the demands of the law for us that we could never keep for ourselves. He washed and cleansed us forever in the sight of God with His own blood.

When we walk by faith in the good news, we are wearing the shoes of the real champion.

Father, keep my ever mindful to "walk the walk" of peace that comes from the "good news". Amen

Taking it to the Lord...

How can I apply this truth?____

____

____

Father, I've come to worship and praise you! You are my:__________________________

____

I give you all Glory, Honor, and Praise O Lord!

Father, I am sorry that I have sinned by:_______________________________________

Help me to repent. Cleanse me, strengthen me, restore me.

Father, THANK YOU for all your love, grace, mercy and blessings of life that you continually shower down upon me. Thank you especially for:

1.___________________________________   2.___________________________________

3.___________________________________   4.___________________________________

5.___________________________________   6.___________________________________

THANK YOU for answered prayers:____

Father, I need:____

Father, I ask that YOU:____

____

____

____

Lord, bless me that I may be a blessing. Give me Your heart for loving and serving others. Keep Your hand upon me. Keep me from all evil and harm, and let me cause harm to no one. Bind Satan that he have no power over me. All this I pray in subjection to your will and in the strong name of my Lord and Savior, Jesus Christ. Amen.

Are You Down?

"With my authority, take this message of repentance to all the nations, beginning in Jerusalem: 'there is forgiveness of sins for all who turn to me." Luke 24:47

You may have never tasted goose before. But, if you are like me, you have cooked plenty of them. I don't know where the expression "your goose is cooked" came from, but I know that the ones I have cooked sure left a bad after taste.

> *"For all this His anger is not turned away,*
> *But His hand is stretched out still."*
> *Isaiah 5:25b*

As Isaiah lists the sins of the children of Israel, he is hitting too close for comfort upon the sins of all of us today. Of all the things that never change, the sinful nature of man seems to repeat the same sins over and over, generation to generation.

The good news is that while we can never un-cook a goose, we can feather our guilt and sorrow with the "down" of God's grace and become "upward bound" through faith in the life, death, and resurrection of Jesus Christ.

Goose down is much more popular than goose meat. Down filled pillows, jackets, and comforters command a premium price, and at one time, goose down feather beds were prized for sleeping comfort.

> *"And do not bring sorrow to God's Holy Spirit by the way you live. Remember, he is the one who has identified you as his own, guaranteeing that you will be saved on the day of redemption."*
> *Ephesians 4:30 NLT*

The next time you feel like "your goose is cooked" be sorry, but not discouraged. Throw yourself upon the "featherbed" of God's throne of grace with Godly sorrow and true repentance, and remember that there is no condemnation for those who are in Christ, but only restoration and all sufficient grace and mercy which are renewed every day for those who come with a broken spirit and contrite heart. *"When you bow down before the Lord and admit your dependence on him, he will lift you up and give you honor." James 4:10*

Father, thank you for taking the cup of death for the wages of sin away from me by sending Jesus to die for my sins on the Cross at Calvary. Amen

Taking it to the Lord...

How can I apply this truth?____

____

Father, I've come to worship and praise you! You are my:___________________

____

I give you all Glory, Honor, and Praise O Lord!

Father, I am sorry that I have sinned by:_________________________________

Help me to repent. Cleanse me, strengthen me, restore me.

Father, THANK YOU for all your love, grace, mercy and blessings of life that you continually shower down upon me. Thank you especially for:

1.____________________________		2.____________________________
3.____________________________		4.____________________________
5.____________________________		6.____________________________

THANK YOU for answered prayers:_______________________________________

Father, I need:____

Father, I ask that YOU:____

____

____

Lord, bless me that I may be a blessing. Give me Your heart for loving and serving others. Keep Your hand upon me. Keep me from all evil and harm, and let me cause harm to no one. Bind Satan that he have no power over me. All this I pray in subjection to your will and in the strong name of my Lord and Savior, Jesus Christ. Amen.

The Fear is Gone

"And the fear of you and the dread of you shall be on every beast of the earth, on every bird of the air, on all that move *on* the earth, and on all the fish of the sea. They are given into your hand." Gen 9:2

Banff, British Columbia is an interesting place. It is moose infested!   Moose have taken over the parks and the streets. They have lost their fear of humans, but these big animals with gigantic horns can hurt people.

> *"But your iniquities have separated you from your God; And your sins have hidden His face from you, So that He will not hear."*
> *Isaiah 59:2*

Alligator attacks are on the increase in Florida. As residential developments gobble up land surrounding lakes and canals, and fisherman, water skiers, and swimmers abound in the water, there is no place for the gators to run and hide, so they lose their fear and humans as gator bait.

The main reason that rogue alligators, moose, dogs, and other animals that attack humans are hunted down and killed is that once they lose their fear of humans, they will always be extremely dangerous.

One of the biggest causes of moral degeneration and the ever-increasing problems that this causes in our society is that many people have lost their fear of God. As people willfully sin and seemingly get away with it, they become emboldened and throw off all restraints until their lives become walking cesspools of unrestrained evil.

God is mocked, treated irreverently and irrelevantly and the moral meltdown has become a river of horrors. From "sparing the rod and spoiling the child," to casting off all sexual morality and inhibitions, to promoting secular humanism that denies the reality of hell and the omnipotence of God; we are becoming a pagan society.

> *"But these, like natural brute beasts made to be caught and destroyed, speak evil of the things they do not understand, and will utterly perish in their own corruption."*
> *2 Peter 2:12*

Revival is our only hope of avoiding the fate of Sodom and Gomorrah. Let it begin within me!

Father, have mercy upon us. Let the fire of a great awakening and restoration spread throughout the World. Amen.

Taking it to the Lord...

How can I apply this truth?____

____

Father, I've come to worship and praise you! You are my:_____________________________________

____

I give you all Glory, Honor, and Praise O Lord!

Father, I am sorry that I have sinned by:____

Help me to repent. Cleanse me, strengthen me, restore me.

Father, THANK YOU for all your love, grace, mercy and blessings of life that you continually shower down upon me.

Thank you especially for:

1.______________________________________   2.______________________________________

3.______________________________________   4.______________________________________

5.______________________________________   6.______________________________________

THANK YOU for answered prayers:____

Father, I need:____

Father, I ask that YOU:____

____

____

Lord, bless me that I may be a blessing. Give me Your heart for loving and serving others. Keep Your hand upon me. Keep me from all evil and harm, and let me cause harm to no one. Bind Satan that he have no power over me. All this I pray in subjection to your will and in the strong name of my Lord and Savior, Jesus Christ. Amen.

Don't Shrink Wrap God!

"Ah, Lord GOD! Behold, You have made the heavens and the earth by Your great power and outstretched arm. There is nothing too hard for You." Jeremiah 32:17

Shrink-wrap packaging has become one of great minor irritations of my life. Whether to prevent tampering, or shrinking by theft, everything seems to come "shrink wrapped".

> *"And the LORD said to Moses, "Has the LORD's arm been shortened?"*
> *Numbers 11:23*

I have a college degree and at least normal intelligence, but to get that sack of candy open without tearing up the whole sack, to get that slice of ham out of that "new and improved" zip lock pack, continues to outsmart me. I just wish that whoever devised some of the packaging on CD wrappers, computer software, and those postage stamp sized items wrapped in a package too big to slip in your pocket would have to share my frustration in trying to get them open.

Unfortunately, most of us have the tendency to "shrink wrap" God by boxing Him in to only a small portion of our hearts, our minds and our wills so that we miss out on so many of the blessings and joy that He would like to give us.

> *"Do it with all the strength and energy that God supplies. Then God will be given glory in everything through Jesus Christ. All glory and power belong to him forever and ever."*
> *1 Peter 4:11*

We shrink Him by failing to grow in our knowledge and understanding of Him through studying His Word, by trusting Him with our salvation, but not with our pocketbooks; our time on Sunday mornings but not the rest of the week.

The Great I AM, who not only ordains but deserves to be the top priority in our lives, is thwarted in His desire to accomplish His purposes for us and through us as we continue to put ourselves and our desires ahead of Him.

It's time to "take off the wraps" and let God take complete control of our lives and grow into the fullness of His love and His power.

Father, give me a faith as big as your love and in the power of Your Spirit help me to find out what real living is all about. Amen

Taking it to the Lord...

How can I apply this truth?____

____

Father, I've come to worship and praise you! You are my:____________________________

____

I give you all Glory, Honor, and Praise O Lord!

Father, I am sorry that I have sinned by:____

Help me to repent. Cleanse me, strengthen me, restore me.

Father, THANK YOU for all your love, grace, mercy and blessings of life that you continually shower down upon me. Thank you especially for:

1.______________________________   2.______________________________
3.______________________________   4.______________________________
5.______________________________   6.______________________________

THANK YOU for answered prayers:____

Father, I need:____

Father, I ask that YOU:____

____

____

Lord, bless me that I may be a blessing. Give me Your heart for loving and serving others. Keep Your hand upon me. Keep me from all evil and harm, and let me cause harm to no one. Bind Satan that he have no power over me. All this I pray in subjection to your will and in the strong name of my Lord and Savior, Jesus Christ. Amen.

How's Your Credit Rating?

"The Spirit is God's guarantee that he will give us everything he promised and that he has purchased us to be his own people. This is just one more reason for us to praise our glorious God." Ephesians 1:14 NLT

The four rules of credit are Character, Credit Record, Capacity, and Security. Defects in any of these areas, can make it difficult to get a credit card or finance anything.

"This release from debt, however, applies only to your fellow Israelites— not to the foreigners living among you." Deuteronomy 15:3 NLT

The time-honored cure for these defects is to have a co-signor to guarantee payments in the event of default. You get someone with the qualification you are lacking, to loan you their qualifications by co-signing.

The practice of co-signing has been around for a long, long time. Solomon warns against it several times in Proverbs:– *"Guaranteeing a loan for a stranger is dangerous; it is better to refuse than to suffer later."- "Do not co-sign another person's note or put up a guarantee for someone else's loan. If you can't pay it, even your bed will be snatched from under you." (Proverbs 11:15, 22:26-27 NLT)*

Have you ever thought about your credit rating with God? What kind of credit score would you get if He took your credit application based on your holiness, your conduct history, your capacity, and your security? I don't know about you, but this is a scary thought for me.

If anyone ever needed a co-signer with God, we most certainly do. The Good News is that Jesus Christ became our purchaser and paid our account in full when He died on the Cross for our sins. Not only was His righteousness credited to our account by our faith, but the Holy Spirit has come as a co-signer of sorts guaranteeing the transaction.. We even received over draft protection to cover the defaults that we all too often seem to incur.

God himself has prepared us for this, and as a guarantee he has given us his Holy Spirit." 2 Corinthians 5:5 NLT

. Father, thank you for the assurance that I have in the blood of Jesus and the power of the Holy Spirit that my credit standing will always be good with You. Amen

Taking it to the Lord...

How can I apply this truth?____

____

____

Father, I've come to worship and praise you! You are my:_____________________

____

I give you all Glory, Honor, and Praise O Lord!

Father, I am sorry that I have sinned by:__________________________________

Help me to repent. Cleanse me, strengthen me, restore me.

Father, THANK YOU for all your love, grace, mercy and blessings of life that you continually shower down upon me. Thank you especially for:

1.__________________________ 2.__________________________

3.__________________________ 4.__________________________

5.__________________________ 6.__________________________

THANK YOU for answered prayers:_______________________________________

Father, I need:____

Father, I ask that YOU:____

____

____

____

Lord, bless me that I may be a blessing. Give me Your heart for loving and serving others. Keep Your hand upon me. Keep me from all evil and harm, and let me cause harm to no one. Bind Satan that he have no power over me. All this I pray in subjection to your will and in the strong name of my Lord and Savior, Jesus Christ. Amen.

World's Worst Motivational Word

"The sinful mind is hostile to God. It does not submit to God's law, nor can it do so. Those controlled by the sinful nature cannot please God." Romans 8:7,8

"Don't" is one of the first words we have trouble understanding as children. We usually have to get spanked, scolded, or hurt several times before we begin to realize that it means "do not" instead of do.

> *"But the man who looks intently into the perfect law that gives freedom, and continues to do this, not forgetting what he has heard, but doing it–he will be blessed in what he does."*
> *James 1:25*

When Eve was led by satan to "do" instead of "don't" in the garden of Eden she triggered a transmittable disease that is still being inherited by every child born of woman. "Don't" seems to fuel the fire of our inborn rebelliousness, causing us to want to "do" instead of "don't"

We feel compelled to walk on the grass, touch the wet paint, park, lust, envy, and respond by doing exactly what we are told or asked not to do. Getting a movie banned somewhere most always assures it being a big hit.

> *"But now, by dying to what once bound us, we have been released from the law so that we serve in the new way of the Spirit, and not in the old way of the written code."*
> *Romans 7:6*

God recognized our problem and has provided a cure. His name Jesus! It is only by the grace of God in sending His son to die on the cross for our sins, and through the power of the Holy Spirit that we can do the "do's" and don't the "don'ts". When we receive Jesus Christ as our Savior, we are "new creatures" and under new management.

Because of what He has done for us, we want to do the things He wants us to do, and we no longer are compelled to do the things He forbids. Although we may momentarily stumble and fall back into our old nature from time to time, we can be sure that God is at work in us through the indwelling presence of the Holy Spirit to cleanse and conform us into the mind of Christ on an ongoing, daily basis when we daily die to sin and become alive in Christ through daily confession and repentance.

Father, help me to do the "do's" and don't the "don'ts" by the power of Your Spirit living in me. Amen

Taking it to the Lord...

How can I apply this truth?____

____

____

Father, I've come to worship and praise you! You are my:_____________________________

____

I give you all Glory, Honor, and Praise O Lord!

Father, I am sorry that I have sinned by:____

Help me to repent. Cleanse me, strengthen me, restore me.

Father, THANK YOU for all your love, grace, mercy and blessings of life that you continually shower down upon me. Thank you especially for:

1.____________________________________   2.____________________________________

3.____________________________________   4.____________________________________

5.____________________________________   6.____________________________________

THANK YOU for answered prayers:____

Father, I need:____

Father, I ask that YOU:____

___________:____

____

Lord, bless me that I may be a blessing. Give me Your heart for loving and serving others. Keep Your hand upon me. Keep me from all evil and harm, and let me cause harm to no one. Bind Satan that he have no power over me. All this I pray in subjection to your will and in the strong name of my Lord and Savior, Jesus Christ. Amen.

You're a Winner!

"Therefore, as God's chosen people, holy and dearly loved, clothe yourselves with compassion, kindness, humility, gentleness and patience." Colossians 3:12

There is hardly a day goes by that I do not find that I have won something! My mail comes with envelopes proclaiming: "you're a winner." All I have to do is go down to the car dealer's and pick up one of 5 prizes.

> *"Now I know that the LORD saves his anointed; he answers him from his holy heaven*
> *with the saving power of his right hand."*
> *Psalm 20:9*

My Internet is filled with pop-ups declaring me a winner. I have won more "3 free nights for 2 in Orlando " than I can remember.

There has been quite a dialogue going on within the body of Christ for several centuries now about the sovereignty of God vs. the freedom of the will. One thing is certain. We were dead in trespasses and sin and dead men have no power or will to do anything. It takes the grace of God exercised through His sovereign will to give any of us our life in Christ.

As scripture plainly says: *"So I want you to know how to discern what is truly from God: No one speaking by the Spirit of God can curse Jesus, and no one is able to say, "Jesus is Lord," except by the Holy Spirit." (1 Corinthians 12:3)*

> *"Who will bring any charge against those whom God has chosen? It is God who justifies."*
> *Romans 8:33*

The bottom line is that if you truly believe in Jesus Christ as your Savior and Lord, you are one of God's elect. He has selected you, He will continually inspect you, correct you, protect you, and perfect you more and more into the image of His son. You're a winner! Start living and running the race of life like one!

Father, thank you for calling me by name and making me one of your very own by your grace. Amen.

Taking it to the Lord...

How can I apply this truth?____
____
____

Father, I've come to worship and praise you! You are my:_______________________________
____

I give you all Glory, Honor, and Praise O Lord!

Father, I am sorry that I have sinned by:____

Help me to repent. Cleanse me, strengthen me, restore me.

Father, THANK YOU for all your love, grace, mercy and blessings of life that you continually shower down upon me. Thank you especially for:

1._________________________________   2._________________________________
3._________________________________   4._________________________________
5._________________________________   6._________________________________

THANK YOU for answered prayers:____

Father, I need:____

Father, I ask that YOU:____
____
____

Lord, bless me that I may be a blessing. Give me Your heart for loving and serving others. Keep Your hand upon me. Keep me from all evil and harm, and let me cause harm to no one. Bind Satan that he have no power over me. All this I pray in subjection to your will and in the strong name of my Lord and Savior, Jesus Christ. Amen.

Trophies of God's Grace

"But you are a chosen people, a royal priesthood, a holy nation, a people belonging to God, that you may declare the praises of him who called you out of darkness into his wonderful light. "Peter 2:9

We are humbled when we think of all the hero's of the faith and saints who are the trophies of Gods grace. By faith Abraham was willing to kill his own son as a sacrifice to God, believing that God could raise him from the dead. Joseph overcame slavery and prison, and St Paul was determined to wipe out Christians from the face of the earth thinking he was in God's will.

> **"But the eyes of the LORD are on those who fear him, on those whose hope is in his unfailing love,"**
> **Psalm 33:8 NIV**

The truth that we too are trophies of God's Grace and priests may seem a frightening concept. We certainly don't always live like priests, and we surely don't look like a trophy.

When we consider whether we were worthy Jesus dying on the cross, we can begin to understand the magnitude of God's grace. We certainly were not worth anyone dying for.

As trophies of God's grace we have to consider whether we are mindful of the price that was paid for our sainthood, and whether we are living in a manner that reflects who we are in Christ.

Fortunately for us, our being trophies does not depend on our behavior, but on the behavior of Jesus Christ on the Cross at Calvary. But, at the very least, we should always seek God's power through the Holy Spirit to walk in the wonderful light of God's love, doing the good works that He prepared for us even before we were born.

> **"These were all commended for their faith, yet none of them received what had been promised. 40God had planned something better for us so that only together with us would they be made perfect."**
> **Hebrews 11:39**

When we consider the price that was paid for us, we should give even more thought to how we might respond to God's love and undeserved favor as trophies of His grace.

Father keep me ever mindful of who I am in You, and help me to live like it. Amen

Taking it to the Lord...

How can I apply this truth?____

____

Father, I've come to worship and praise you! You are my:_________________________________

____

I give you all Glory, Honor, and Praise O Lord!

Father, I am sorry that I have sinned by:____

Help me to repent. Cleanse me, strengthen me, restore me.

Father, THANK YOU for all your love, grace, mercy and blessings of life that you continually shower down upon me. Thank you especially for:

1.____________________________________   2.____________________________________

3.____________________________________   4.____________________________________

5.____________________________________   6.____________________________________

THANK YOU for answered prayers:____

Father, I need:____

Father, I ask that YOU:____

____

____

Lord, bless me that I may be a blessing. Give me Your heart for loving and serving others. Keep Your hand upon me. Keep me from all evil and harm, and let me cause harm to no one. Bind Satan that he have no power over me. All this I pray in subjection to your will and in the strong name of my Lord and Savior, Jesus Christ. Amen.

Take This Job and Love it!

"And whatever you do, whether in word or deed, do it all in the name of the Lord Jesus, giving thanks to God the Father through him." Colossians 3:17

Don't you just love to see people who love their work and are really good at it? Isn't it sad to see people trapped in jobs they hate and have no ability for? When possible, we should either love it, leave it, or ask God to give us the grace to cope with it from His perspective.

> *"May the favor of the Lord our God rest upon us; establish the work of our hands for us- yes, establish the work of our hands."*
> *Psalm 90:17*

As Christians we must understand *"For we are God's workmanship, created in Christ Jesus to do good works, which God prepared in advance for us to do."* *(Ephesians 2:10)* Good stewardship of the life we have been given demands that we devote our time, talents, and resources for God's purposes as well as for our own. God has equipped us all differently for different tasks. We need always to check our equipment and use our best talents in serving the Lord.

Especially in serving God with our time and talents, we need to know that serving under compulsion and guilt are not good enough. God not only loves a cheerful giver of money, but also expects our gift of time and talents to be given in the joy of the Lord without complaining or feeling put upon.

It is when we look at our jobs from God's perspective that we can learn to love them more. When we realize work is a blessing, and that we are actually working to please God, it can make a big difference on how much we love our jobs in the church and in the workplace. .

> *"Serve wholeheartedly, as if you were serving the Lord, not men."*
> *Ephesians 3:17*

Father, thank you for the talents you have given me. Help me to use them to glorify you in your church and in the workplace. Amen.

Taking it to the Lord...

How can I apply this truth?____

____

Father, I've come to worship and praise you! You are my:___________________

____

I give you all Glory, Honor, and Praise O Lord!

Father, I am sorry that I have sinned by:_________________________________

Help me to repent. Cleanse me, strengthen me, restore me.

Father, THANK YOU for all your love, grace, mercy and blessings of life that you continually shower down upon me. Thank you especially for:

1._________________________________   2._________________________________

3._________________________________   4._________________________________

5._________________________________   6._________________________________

THANK YOU for answered prayers:____

Father, I need:____

Father, I ask that YOU:____

____

____

Lord, bless me that I may be a blessing. Give me Your heart for loving and serving others. Keep Your hand upon me. Keep me from all evil and harm, and let me cause harm to no one. Bind Satan that he have no power over me. All this I pray in subjection to your will and in the strong name of my Lord and Savior, Jesus Christ. Amen.

World's Champion!

"Even youths will become exhausted, and young men will give up. But those who wait on the LORD will find new strength. They will fly high on wings like eagles. They will run and not grow weary. They will walk and not faint. Isaiah 30:40 NLT

It has just dawned upon me that I am probably a World's Champion! Good as it sounds, it is not always something to brag about. In my case, I have done it in Florida, North Carolina, South Carolina, Virginia, West Virginia, Maryland, Indiana and Kentucky. I have done it in Cadillacs, Lincolns, Volvo's, Dodges, Fords, and several other makes. I have usually had a few horses and a few friends with me to share the experience. I am here and now laying title for the dubious distinction of being the World's Champion gas "runner outer!"

> *"Think about all he endured when sinful people did such terrible things to him, so that you don't become weary and give up."*
> *Hebrews 12:3 NLT*

Like so many of God's admonitions, I don't know what part about "empty" on the gas gauge I don't seem to understand. (Of course the extra weight of a horse trailer and horses using up a lot more gas is partly to blame). (I think maybe that I will only fill up at a filling station on the side of the road I'm traveling has also been partly to blame.)

I have survived running out of gas literally, and by the grace of God, and by the power of the Holy Spirit have been protected from "running out of gas" spiritually for most of my life.

> *" We are pressed on every side by troubles, but we are not crushed and broken. We are perplexed, but we don't give up and quit."*
> *2 Corinthians 4:8 NLT*

Just as gasoline is fuel for the automobile, the Word of God is fuel for the soul. We are told to be filled with the Spirit, so we don't obey the lusts of the flesh. We are told that we have been given the indwelling of the Holy Spirit God's guarantee that He will give us everything He has promised (Ephesians 4:1), and, best of all: *"being confident of this very thing, that He who has begun a good work in you will complete it until the day of Jesus Christ;" (Philippians 1:6)* Need a fill up?

Father, thank you for Your promise that You will never run out of patience with me, even when I seem to be running out on you. Amen

Taking it to the Lord...

How can I apply this truth?____

____

____

Father, I've come to worship and praise you! You are my:_________________________

____

I give you all Glory, Honor, and Praise O Lord!

Father, I am sorry that I have sinned by:_______________________________________

Help me to repent. Cleanse me, strengthen me, restore me.

Father, THANK YOU for all your love, grace, mercy and blessings of life that you continually shower down upon me. Thank you especially for:

1._________________________________   2._________________________________

3._________________________________   4._________________________________

5._________________________________   6._________________________________

THANK YOU for answered prayers:____

Father, I need:____

Father, I ask that YOU:____

____

____

Lord, bless me that I may be a blessing. Give me Your heart for loving and serving others. Keep Your hand upon me. Keep me from all evil and harm, and let me cause harm to no one. Bind Satan that he have no power over me. All this I pray in subjection to your will and in the strong name of my Lord and Savior, Jesus Christ. Amen.

Can You Hear Me Now?

"And I will give you treasures hidden in the darkness – secret riches. I will do this so you may know that I am the LORD, the God of Israel, the one who calls you by name." Isaiah 45:3 NLT

If the theory of evolution were true, we would soon see babies being born with cell phones growing out of their ears. These instant communication tools are everywhere.

"Happy are those who hear the joyful call to worship, for they will walk in the light of your presence, Lord." Psalm 89:15 NLT

When the TV ad features "can you hear me now?" it is echoing God's cry since the beginning of time as He has softly and tenderly and loudly and angrily called His children to repentance and relationship.

The children of Israel were world-class hearing impaired rebels. God spoke to them through a burning bush, a pillar of clouds by day and a fire by night, but all his calls were soon forgotten by a bunch of spoiled brats who were hard to satisfy but easy to be lead astray by every self centered concern and distraction.

Before we become too critical of the Children of Israel, we need to ask ourselves whether we are hearing God today. He gives His call to salvation and many have to be flat on their backs looking up before they hear, and others remain deaf.

He calls all believers to the ongoing process of sanctification and many have a connection problem as to what holy living is all about.

"But even more blessed are all who hear the Word of God and put it into practice." Matthew 13:17 NLT

He calls all believers to service for which He has equipped us to accomplish His purposes that He planned for us even before we were born. Why oh why don't we have more passion to hear and be faithful to this calling, whatever it might be?

God calls all believers to worship individually and corporately so that the other calls may be manifested in us and in others through us. Can you hear Him now?

Father, help me to turn off my mute button so that I can hear all of your calls loud and clear. Amen

Taking it to the Lord...

How can I apply this truth?____

____

____

Father, I've come to worship and praise you! You are my:________________________

____

I give you all Glory, Honor, and Praise O Lord!

Father, I am sorry that I have sinned by:_______________________________________

Help me to repent. Cleanse me, strengthen me, restore me.

Father, THANK YOU for all your love, grace, mercy and blessings of life that you continually shower down upon me. Thank you especially for:

1.__________________________________   2.__________________________________

3.__________________________________   4.__________________________________

5.__________________________________   6.__________________________________

THANK YOU for answered prayers:____

Father, I need:____

Father, I ask that YOU:____

____

____

____

Lord, bless me that I may be a blessing. Give me Your heart for loving and serving others. Keep Your hand upon me. Keep me from all evil and harm, and let me cause harm to no one. Bind Satan that he have no power over me. All this I pray in subjection to your will and in the strong name of my Lord and Savior, Jesus Christ. Amen.

All Prisoners are not in Prison

"**Jesus answered them, "Most assuredly, I say to you, whoever commits sin is a slave of sin. And a slave does not abide in the house forever, *but* a son abides forever. Therefore if the Son makes you free, you shall be free indeed." John 8:34**

There are some convicted felons in prison freer than many people living in the outside world. They have that peace and joy that only comes to the truly free while many on the outside are in captivity to all sorts of things.

> *"The LORD frees the prisoners. The LORD opens the eyes of the blind."*
> **Psalm 146.7**

Sometimes the walls we build around us to keep others out seem to imprison us by keeping us withdrawn and missing out on so much of God's love that is all around us. There are denominational, racial, and relational walls that need to come down.

It is a terrible thing to be captured and held hostage by an addiction of any kind that takes control of our lives with often devastating consequences. Whether its guilt, addiction to drugs, alcohol, or pornography, the consequences can be crushing not only to us but to those around us we love.

When we are controlled by lust, greed, envy, anger, hatred, or unforgiving, we can be more imprisoned than some locked up in maximum security.

The good news is that there is a cure available. Jesus said*: ""The Spirit of the Lord is upon me, for He has appointed me to preach Good News to the poor. He has sent me to proclaim that captives will be released, that the blind will see, that the downtrodden will be freed from their oppressors, and that the time of the Lord's favor has come." (Luke 4:18)* Saint Paul tells us to bring every thought into captivity into obedience to Christ.

> *"Likewise you also, reckon yourselves to be dead indeed to sin, but alive to God in Christ Jesus our Lord."*
> **Romans 6"11**

Before coming to faith in Jesus Christ there was no cure for sin available. Now that we have been set free from the power of sin to destroy us spiritually, we need to allow the Holy Spirit to take control of our lives so that sin might have no dominion over us.

Father, come into my life and take charge that I no longer am a slave to sin, but to your righteousness. Amen.

Taking it to the Lord...

How can I apply this truth?____

____

____

Father, I've come to worship and praise you! You are my:_______________________________

____

I give you all Glory, Honor, and Praise O Lord!

Father, I am sorry that I have sinned by:____

Help me to repent. Cleanse me, strengthen me, restore me.

Father, THANK YOU for all your love, grace, mercy and blessings of life that you continually shower down upon me. Thank you especially for:

1.___________________________________   2.___________________________________

3.___________________________________   4.___________________________________

5.___________________________________   6.___________________________________

THANK YOU for answered prayers:____

Father, I need:____

Father, I ask that YOU:____

____

____

Lord, bless me that I may be a blessing. Give me Your heart for loving and serving others. Keep Your hand upon me. Keep me from all evil and harm, and let me cause harm to no one. Bind Satan that he have no power over me. All this I pray in subjection to your will and in the strong name of my Lord and Savior, Jesus Christ. Amen.

Who's in Your Closet?

"Those who worship false gods turn their backs on all God's mercies. But I will offer sacrifices to you with songs of praise, and I will fulfill all my vows. For my salvation comes from the LORD alone." Jonah 2:8

Worship is much, much more than a formal ceremony at some church on Sunday. Worship is the on going every day praise of God through the sacrifice of giving our time, talents, treasures, and submitting to His will for our lives.

> *"Sing to the LORD; bless his name. Each day proclaim the good news that he saves."*
> *Psalm 96:2*

Sometimes, in spite of our best intentions, we get so preoccupied with the cares of this world and other distractions we tend to put God in the closet every Sunday along with our "go to meeting clothes", and spend the rest of the week taking on the world, the flesh and the devil in our own strength. This is a recipe for disaster.

God doesn't belong in the closet in your house, He belongs in the closet of your heart, where He can "stick closer than a brother", guiding you into all righteousness and revealing all truth.

When the love of God and His Spirit fills your heart, your worship will flow like rivers of living water into the lives of those around you. You will be blessed and be a blessing to those around you. If He is left in the clothes closet, your heart has a tendency to be filled with the idols of your flesh and you are an easy prey for the evil one who is out to destroy you.

> *"But the time is coming and is already here when true worshipers will worship the Father in spirit and in truth. The Father is looking for anyone who will worship him that way."*
> *John 4:23*

There is also no room in the kingdom of God for "closet Christians" who hoard their faith and God's love and pass up every opportunity to confess Jesus to others. *"Therefore whoever confesses Me before men, him I will also confess before My Father who is in heaven.³But whoever denies Me before men, him I will also deny before My Father who is in heaven. "Matthew 10:32 NLT*

Father, forgive me for putting you in the wrong closet too many times. Help me to come out of the closet and bring you with me. Amen

Taking it to the Lord...

How can I apply this truth?____
____
____

Father, I've come to worship and praise you! You are my:_________________________________
____

I give you all Glory, Honor, and Praise O Lord!

Father, I am sorry that I have sinned by:____

Help me to repent. Cleanse me, strengthen me, restore me.

Father, THANK YOU for all your love, grace, mercy and blessings of life that you continually shower down upon me. Thank you especially for:

1._______________________________   2._______________________________
3._______________________________   4._______________________________
5._______________________________   6._______________________________

THANK YOU for answered prayers:____

Father, I need:____

Father, I ask that YOU:____
____
____

Lord, bless me that I may be a blessing. Give me Your heart for loving and serving others. Keep Your hand upon me. Keep me from all evil and harm, and let me cause harm to no one. Bind Satan that he have no power over me. All this I pray in subjection to your will and in the strong name of my Lord and Savior, Jesus Christ. Amen.

Rice Krispie Religion

"If you are filled with light, with no dark corners, then your whole life will be radiant, as though a floodlight is shining on you." Luke 11:36

Rice Krispies have been around for three generations or longer, and still going strong. They are even better in cookies. I have always enjoyed the rice krispie "snap, crackle, and pop" when you add milk to the cereal and it begins to explode. Gotta be careful or all those kernels will rise to the top and overflow the bowl. I have noticed they are not nearly as good if you let them sit and get squishee.

> *"I will be filled with joy because of you. I will sing praises to your name, O Most High."*
> *Psalm 9:2 NLT*

There is a lot of wonderful "snap, crackle, and pop" when the pure milk of the gospel is poured into a receptive kernel. We are told that there is great rejoicing in heaven when a sinner repents and receives Jesus as Savior. .

The "snap, crackle, and pop" passion of the new birth in Christ experienced by many believers is not unlike falling in love and getting married. We enjoy a great emotional high and are filled with overflowing joy and passion.

Great as the feelings are, they will not always be enough to sustain a healthy growing relationship with God or with our spouse.

The key to both is in growing into maturity. We should never let either relationship stand still and get mired down in selfishness, self-centered behavior or overcome by the assaults of the flesh, the world, or the devil.

> *"No wonder my heart is filled with joy, and my mouth shouts his praises!"*
> *Acts 2:26 NLT*

As we grow in our love relationship with Christ, the "snap, crackle and pop" of passion can only be sustained by being nourished by His Word daily, and getting to know Him by experience as we grow into the fullness of Christ.

As we grow in our love relationship with our spouses, we need the sustaining power of the fruit of the Spirit and the nourishing power of love if we are to maintain the "snap, crackle and pop" during our life together.

Father, thank you for the sacred delight that is mine through my growing and abiding relationship with you. Amen

Taking it to the Lord...

How can I apply this truth?____

____

Father, I've come to worship and praise you! You are my:_____________________________________

____

I give you all Glory, Honor, and Praise O Lord!

Father, I am sorry that I have sinned by:____

Help me to repent. Cleanse me, strengthen me, restore me.

Father, THANK YOU for all your love, grace, mercy and blessings of life that you continually shower down upon me. Thank you especially for:

1.____________________________________   2.____________________________________

3.____________________________________   4.____________________________________

5.____________________________________   6.____________________________________

THANK YOU for answered prayers:____

Father, I need:____

Father, I ask that YOU:____

____

____

Lord, bless me that I may be a blessing. Give me Your heart for loving and serving others. Keep Your hand upon me. Keep me from all evil and harm, and let me cause harm to no one. Bind Satan that he have no power over me. All this I pray in subjection to your will and in the strong name of my Lord and Savior, Jesus Christ. Amen.

Anchor Deep!

"This confidence is like a strong and trustworthy anchor for our souls. It leads us through the curtain of heaven into God's inner sanctuary. Jesus has already gone in there for us. He has become our eternal High Priest in the line of Melchizedek." Hebrews 6:19

"Through many dangers, toils, and snares I have already come, 'tis grace hath brought me safe thus far, and grace will lead me home". No wonder "Amazing Grace" is perhaps the most beloved and often sung hymn of all time!

> *"I am holding you by your right hand—I, the LORD your God. And I say to you, 'Do not be afraid. I am here to help you."*
>
> *Isaiah 41:13 NLT*

Our lives could be likened to a voyage on the sea. We go through still waters, and some really rough storms. Ships have anchors to help ride out the rough seas and we have God's Word. The deeper we anchor into God's Word, the better able we become to ride out the storms of life.

Here are some samples of the strength and assurances we find in God's Word: *"God is our refuge and strength, always ready to help in times of trouble."*(Psalm 46:1 NLT). *"What do you mean, 'If I can'?"* Jesus asked. *"Anything is possible if a person believes."* (Mark 9:23 NLT) *"For He has not ignored the suffering of the needy. He has not turned and walked away. He has listened to their cries for help."* (Psalm 22:24 NLT)

"But the LORD still waits for you to come to him so he can show you his love and compassion. For the LORD is a faithful God. Blessed are those who wait for him to help them." (Isaiah 20:18 NLT) The more we "anchor deep" into God's Word the more power and strength we receive from it to ride out the storms of life.

> *"For I can do everything with the help of Christ who gives me the strength I need."*
>
> *Philippians 4:13NLT*

Our strength may fail, people will often fail us, and our possessions may all disappear. When we are tossed about with "many a conflict and many a doubt" we need Jesus, "the author and perfector of our faith," the anchor of our souls.

Father, thank you for the grace that you have promised that is sufficient for all our needs. Help me to "anchor deep". Amen

Taking it to the Lord...

How can I apply this truth?____

____

Father, I've come to worship and praise you! You are my:______________________________________

____

I give you all Glory, Honor, and Praise O Lord!

Father, I am sorry that I have sinned by:____

Help me to repent. Cleanse me, strengthen me, restore me.

Father, THANK YOU for all your love, grace, mercy and blessings of life that you continually shower down upon me. Thank you especially for:

1.______________________________________   2.______________________________________

3.______________________________________   4.______________________________________

5.______________________________________   6.______________________________________

THANK YOU for answered prayers:____

Father, I need:____

Father, I ask that YOU:____

____

____

____

Lord, bless me that I may be a blessing. Give me Your heart for loving and serving others. Keep Your hand upon me. Keep me from all evil and harm, and let me cause harm to no one. Bind Satan that he have no power over me. All this I pray in subjection to your will and in the strong name of my Lord and Savior, Jesus Christ. Amen.

Put on the Blinkers!

"Let your eyes look straight ahead, and your eyelids look right before you. Ponder the path of your feet and let all your ways be established. Do not turn to the right or the left; Remove your foot from evil." Proverbs 4:25

Some racehorses get so frightened by crowds that they slow down as they head for home and the big crowds awaiting their arrival. Others get so distracted by horses coming up beside them they tend to slow down or veer to fight or just worry about them.

> *"But my eyes are upon You, O GOD the Lord; In You I take refuge; Do not leave my soul destitute."*
> *Psalm 141:8*

Blinkers are cups worn around the eyes of horses to cut down their line of vision to avoid these fears and distractions that impede their running the race, and they have turned many losers into winners.

Rather than "pluck out the eye" that causes us to sin, perhaps we should just "put on the blinkers" and shut out the distractions and fears that are slowing down our progress in the race of life.

When we turn our eyes upon Jesus, "the author and perfector of our faith" we are focused on what really matters. When our relationship is right with Him, we have the power of the Holy Spirit to overcome the power of sin and temptation to slow us down.

When we major in the major of seeking the kingdom of God first, everything else we need is added. The victor's prize is the crown of righteousness that has already been laid up for us in heaven.

> *"Follow the Lord's rules for doing his work, just as an athlete either follows the rules or is disqualified and wins no prize."*
> *2 Corinthians 2:5 NLT*

In horse racing, there is a big bonus awaiting the horse that wins the Triple Crown. In the kingdom of God, heaven is not a reward but a gift that we receive by faith.

The reward is what we earn by being obedient and being fruitful in the good works for which we were created. When we shut out the distractions we are well on our way to winning the other jewel of God's crown.

Father, by the power of Your Spirit, help me to shut out the distractions and stay focused on running for your "well done." Amen

Taking it to the Lord...

How can I apply this truth?____

____

____

Father, I've come to worship and praise you! You are my:_________________________

____

I give you all Glory, Honor, and Praise O Lord!

Father, I am sorry that I have sinned by:_______________________________________

Help me to repent. Cleanse me, strengthen me, restore me.

Father, THANK YOU for all your love, grace, mercy and blessings of life that you continually shower down upon me. Thank you especially for:

1._____________________________   2._____________________________

3._____________________________   4._____________________________

5._____________________________   6._____________________________

THANK YOU for answered prayers:____

Father, I need:____

Father, I ask that YOU:____

____

____

Lord, bless me that I may be a blessing. Give me Your heart for loving and serving others. Keep Your hand upon me. Keep me from all evil and harm, and let me cause harm to no one. Bind Satan that he have no power over me. All this I pray in subjection to your will and in the strong name of my Lord and Savior, Jesus Christ. Amen.

Wandering Aimlessly Lost

"Household gods give false advice, fortune-tellers predict only lies, and interpreters of dreams pronounce comfortless falsehoods. So my people are wandering like lost sheep, without a shepherd to protect and guide them." Zechariah 10:2 NLT

Although painful, those of us who know what it was like to "wander aimlessly lost" need to sometimes revisit the futility of our lives and the emptiness of our hearts before the Lord found us and called us into saving faith and the abundant life we have in Him.

> *"Some wandered in the desert, lost and homeless. Hungry and thirsty, they nearly died. "LORD, help!" they cried in their trouble, and he rescued them from their distress."*
> *Psalm 107:4-6 NLT*

Thinking about our past should give us even greater passion to seek out and save the lost living among us in our homes, our workplace, and in our everyday lives. It should also trigger a daily wellspring of praise to the Lord of salvation, and the great thing He has done for us.

People today need the Lord as never before. The "household God" called TV has mislead and brainwashed two generations of people with so many lies about what constitutes the good life, and what really matters, no wonder there is so much misery and sin all around us.

> *"My dear brothers and sisters, if anyone among you wanders away from the truth and is brought back again, you can be sure that the one who brings that person back will save that sinner from death and bring about the forgiveness of many sins."*
> *James 5:19,20*

Broken homes, suicide rates, addictions of every kind, have made the age of secular humanism a vast wasteland of broken hearts, shattered dreams, wasted lives and unfilled expectations for millions.

Through it all, we have a God who still loves us all, who would have all men to be saved and who would use us to seek out and proclaim the good news to those who are wandering aimlessly lost, that they might be found before it's too late.

Father, thank you for coming to me when I was lost, and letting me find the "pearl of great price" which is the love, the forgiveness, and the peace and joy I have found in you. Amen

Taking it to the Lord...

How can I apply this truth?____

____

____

Father, I've come to worship and praise you! You are my:_________________________

____

I give you all Glory, Honor, and Praise O Lord!

Father, I am sorry that I have sinned by:____

Help me to repent. Cleanse me, strengthen me, restore me.

Father, THANK YOU for all your love, grace, mercy and blessings of life that you continually shower down upon me. Thank you especially for:

1.________________________________   2.________________________________

3.________________________________   4.________________________________

5.________________________________   6.________________________________

THANK YOU for answered prayers:____

Father, I need:____

Father, I ask that YOU:____

____

____

Lord, bless me that I may be a blessing. Give me Your heart for loving and serving others. Keep Your hand upon me. Keep me from all evil and harm, and let me cause harm to no one. Bind Satan that he have no power over me. All this I pray in subjection to your will and in the strong name of my Lord and Savior, Jesus Christ. Amen.

Wash and Wear Religion

"I will greatly rejoice in the LORD, My soul shall be joyful in my God; For He has clothed me with the garments of salvation, He has covered me with the robe of righteousness," Isaiah 61:10

What joy there is in knowing that, because of our faith in Jesus Christ and His death on the cross for our sins, we have been cleansed and clothed in the righteousness of Christ. This means that when we stand before God, He will not see our sins, but will look at us just as He looks at His Son, in whom He was well pleased! *"Let us go right into the presence of God, with true hearts fully trusting him. For our evil consciences have been sprinkled with Christ's blood to make us clean, and our bodies have been washed with pure water"(Hebrews 10:22)*

> *"Wash me thoroughly from my iniquity, And cleanse me from my sin."*
> *Psalm 51:2*

Who in the world would wants to show up at a wedding with a dirty robe that has not been cleansed by blood of Jesus? Just as sin has no more dominion over our spirit, by the grace of God and by the power of His Spirit, we should not let it have dominion over our flesh. *"No temptation has overtaken you except such as is common to man; but God is faithful, who will not allow you to be tempted beyond what you are able, but with the temptation will also make the way of escape, that you may be able to bear it. (1 Corinthians 10:13)*

> *"Friend, how did you come in here without a wedding garment?' And he was speechless. [13]Then the king said to the servants, 'Bind him hand and foot, take him away, and cast him into outer darkness; there will be weeping and gnashing of teeth."*
> *Matthew 22:12b, 13*

Thank God, He has given us a "wash and wear" robe. Knowing that some of the road dirt of the flesh, the world and the devil is bound to soil our robe, He provides the "living water" which not only takes away our thirst but will keep our robes "white as snow" by daily washing through confession and repentance.

May God forbid that any of us fail to get dressed for the wedding feast!

Father, thank you for cleansing me with the blood of Jesus, and for keeping me clean by the power of Your Spirit. Amen.

Taking it to the Lord...

How can I apply this truth?____

____

Father, I've come to worship and praise you! You are my:______________________

____

I give you all Glory, Honor, and Praise O Lord!

Father, I am sorry that I have sinned by:___________________________________

Help me to repent. Cleanse me, strengthen me, restore me.

Father, THANK YOU for all your love, grace, mercy and blessings of life that you continually shower down upon me. Thank you especially for:

1.______________________________   2.______________________________

3.______________________________   4.______________________________

5.______________________________   6.______________________________

THANK YOU for answered prayers:___________________________________

Father, I need:____

Father, I ask that YOU:____

____

____

Lord, bless me that I may be a blessing. Give me Your heart for loving and serving others. Keep Your hand upon me. Keep me from all evil and harm, and let me cause harm to no one. Bind Satan that he have no power over me. All this I pray in subjection to your will and in the strong name of my Lord and Savior, Jesus Christ. Amen..

Till Misery Do Us Part?

"Therefore shall a man leave his father and his mother, and shall cleave unto his wife: and they shall be one flesh." Genesis 2:24

Do you know of anyone who has gone into a marriage hoping to become miserable or to make life miserable for their spouse? What is it that turns the highest of expectations into depths of misery?

> *"Blessed is everyone who fears the LORD, who walks in His ways"*
> *Psalm 128:1*

A Christian counselor friend of mine says that people who have found misery in marriage will find the root cause in Genesis 2:24. It is either problems with leaving, cleaving, or becoming one flesh.

Leaving family, life style, and all sorts of other accumulated baggage is often not easy. Different backgrounds are especially difficult. Like oil and water believers and nonbelievers don't mix, and sooner or later this will lead to real misery in most cases.

Lack of real cleaving or commitment has made the idea of going into marriage in a disposable, no deposit no return bottle very popular. When we go in thinking we can go out any time we don't get our way, choose not to forgive and forget, and not to honor the commitment made, we are already planting the seeds of disaster. Children, not childishness are supposed to be the fruit of a marriage. When God is not taken into a marriage, the "tie that binds" has no knot.

> *"Nevertheless let each one of you in particular so love his own wife as himself, and let the wife see that she respects her husband."*
> *Ephesians 5:33*

Perceived lack of sexual satisfaction is often a problem. It is interesting to note that surveys find that couples who went into marriage as virgins report much more sexual satisfaction in their marriage. This is another indication that God's way to sexual satisfaction is the best way.

Any good marriage requires a lot of unconditional love. We must learn to love unconditionally, just as God loves us, not because of our shortcomings and sins, but in spite of them.

Father help me understand and practice the essentials of a happy marriage. Amen

Taking it to the Lord...

How can I apply this truth?____

____

Father, I've come to worship and praise you! You are my:_________________________

____

I give you all Glory, Honor, and Praise O Lord!

Father, I am sorry that I have sinned by:_____________________________________

Help me to repent. Cleanse me, strengthen me, restore me.

Father, THANK YOU for all your love, grace, mercy and blessings of life that you continually shower down upon me. Thank you especially for:

1.__________________________________   2.__________________________________
3.__________________________________   4.__________________________________
5.__________________________________   6.__________________________________

THANK YOU for answered prayers:____

Father, I need:____

Father, I ask that YOU:____

____

____

Lord, bless me that I may be a blessing. Give me Your heart for loving and serving others. Keep Your hand upon me. Keep me from all evil and harm, and let me cause harm to no one. Bind Satan that he have no power over me. All this I pray in subjection to your will and in the strong name of my Lord and Savior, Jesus Christ. Amen.

Ride the White Horse

"O foolish Galatians! Who has bewitched you that you should not obey the truth?" Galatians 3.1

Notwithstanding that Horses are not very smart, for many years "horse sense" was widely used as a synonym for "common sense". Tragedy after tragedy of horses running back into a burning barn after they had been turned loose, doesn't make too strong a case for the intelligence of horses.

> *"Do not be like the horse or mule, which have no understanding."*
> *Psalm 32:9*

Before we get too critical and judgmental of the poor horse seeking the security of his stall, we need to consider how we continually run back into the burning barn of our sins after we have been freed by the grace of God through faith in Jesus Christ, and sin has no more dominion over us?

People who have been freed from addictions give up everything to go back to the false security and temporary relief of alcohol, drugs, sex or even food. Abused spouses go back to abusive relationships. We give in to old habits and old lusts as "the roaring lion seeking who he may devour" takes control.

> *"He was clothed in a robe dipped in blood, and His name is called The Word of God. And the armies in heaven, clothed in fine linen, white and clean, followed Him on white horses."*
> *Revelation 19:13*

How we need to know God's wonderful provision to help us through these failures in 1 Corinthians 10:13."*No temptation has overtaken you except such as is common to man; but God is faithful, who will not allow you to be tempted beyond what you are able, but with the temptation will also make the way of escape, that you may be able to bear it."*

Father, thank you for loving and setting me free from bondage to sin and for providing a means of escape through the power of the Holy Spirit. Amen

Taking it to the Lord...

How can I apply this truth?____

____

Father, I've come to worship and praise you! You are my:_______________________

____

I give you all Glory, Honor, and Praise O Lord!

Father, I am sorry that I have sinned by:___________________________________

Help me to repent. Cleanse me, strengthen me, restore me.

Father, THANK YOU for all your love, grace, mercy and blessings of life that you continually shower down upon me. Thank you especially for:

1.___________________________ 2.___________________________

3.___________________________ 4.___________________________

5.___________________________ 6.___________________________

THANK YOU for answered prayers:____

Father, I need:____

Father, I ask that YOU:____

____

____

Lord, bless me that I may be a blessing. Give me Your heart for loving and serving others. Keep Your hand upon me. Keep me from all evil and harm, and let me cause harm to no one. Bind Satan that he have no power over me. All this I pray in subjection to your will and in the strong name of my Lord and Savior, Jesus Christ. Amen.

Understanding That Surpasses All Our Peace

"Now we have received, not the spirit of the world, but the Spirit who is from God, that we might know the things that have been freely given to us by God." 1 Corinthians 2:12

Do you sometimes find yourself wondering what life is all about? Do you often feel that you have more questions than you have answers? Welcome to the Club! This club has a great tradition, is as old as the beginning of time, and has millions of members in every country throughout the world.

> *"The LORD has made known His salvation; his righteousness He has revealed in the sight of the nations."*
> *Psalm 98:2*

One of the great joys of heaven is going to be in having all of our questions answered, and receiving the "understanding that surpasses all our peace".   In the meantime, there is a way that we can get most all of our questions answered. It is called "abiding".

When we abide in and trust God's Word, we abide in Christ, because He is the Word. We don't have to wonder about the mysteries of life, we can know them.

We can know that God created us in His image and placed a longing in our hearts that only a right relationship with Him can satisfy. We can know that free will led to disobedience and we are all born with this inherited weakness that puts us at enmity with God.

We can know that God, in his infinite wisdom and love came up with a cure for this problem. He Himself came in the flesh and blood of a man and after living a perfect sin free life, in perfect obedience allowed Himself to be mocked, humiliated, almost beaten to death, and finally nailed to the cross as the perfect, unblemished Sacrifice to earn us forgiveness for our every sin and act of disobedience and to give us a new, everlasting life through faith in this truth and the one who made it happen.

> *"These things I have written to you who believe in the name of the Son of God, that you may know that you have eternal life, and that you may continue to believe in the name of the Son of God."*
> *1 John 5:13 NLT*

When we abide in God's Word, we receive that quiet understanding and that perfect love that casts out all fear, and we wonder no more.

Father, help me to wonder less, trust and believe more as I abide in Your Word. Amen

Taking it to the Lord...

How can I apply this truth?____

____

____

Father, I've come to worship and praise you! You are my:__________________

____

I give you all Glory, Honor, and Praise O Lord!

Father, I am sorry that I have sinned by:________________________________

Help me to repent. Cleanse me, strengthen me, restore me.

Father, THANK YOU for all your love, grace, mercy and blessings of life that you continually shower down upon me. Thank you especially for:

1.______________________________   2.______________________________

3.______________________________   4.______________________________

5.______________________________   6.______________________________

THANK YOU for answered prayers:_____________________________________

Father, I need:____

Father, I ask that YOU:____

____

____

Lord, bless me that I may be a blessing. Give me Your heart for loving and serving others. Keep Your hand upon me. Keep me from all evil and harm, and let me cause harm to no one. Bind Satan that he have no power over me. All this I pray in subjection to your will and in the strong name of my Lord and Savior, Jesus Christ. Amen.

The Emancipation Proclamation

"Therefore if the Son makes you free, you shall be free indeed." John 8:36

"And by virtue of the power and for the purpose aforesaid, I do order and declare that all persons held as slaves within said designated States and parts of States are, and henceforward shall be, free;" (Abraham Lincoln, September 22, 1862)

Actual and spiritual slaves sometimes both have the same trouble. They cannot handle freedom. When Lincoln abolished slavery and declared all slaves free, many just stayed where they were and as they were. Often prisoners commit crimes to get back into prison because they cannot handle their freedom on the outside.

> *"I will walk in freedom for I have devoted myself to your commandments."*
> *Psalm 119:45 NLT*

Before we get all puffed up with condemnation and wondering how anyone could be so dumb, we need to take a look at our own lives.

Why do we live lives so often in bondage to the will of our flesh instead of lives of freedom controlled by the Spirit of God that is in us?

St. Paul struggled mightily with this same problem. *"But I see another law in my members, warring against the law of my mind, and bringing me into captivity to the law of sin which is in my members. O wretched man that I am! Who will deliver me from this body of death?" (Romans 7:23)*

Thank God for Romans 8 which teaches us that the resurrection power of God is ours to claim by faith. We no longer have to live in bondage to sin of any kind.

> *"For the power of the life-giving Spirit has freed you through Christ Jesus from the power of sin that leads to death."*
> *Romans 8:2 NLT*

The war has been won by Christ's death on the cross. The battle for the control of our will goes on. No matter how many skirmishes we might lose, how many satanic darts hit us, we can stand firm and live victoriously not in our own strength, but in the supernatural strength of the resurrection power of Christ living in us, which is our hope of Glory.

When we appropriate this truth by faith, we fill find that we are free, indeed!

Father, give me your power of the Holy Spirit to live in the freedom Your Son died to give me. Amen

Taking it to the Lord...

How can I apply this truth?____

____

____

Father, I've come to worship and praise you! You are my:_____________________

____

I give you all Glory, Honor, and Praise O Lord!

Father, I am sorry that I have sinned by:__________________________________

Help me to repent. Cleanse me, strengthen me, restore me.

Father, THANK YOU for all your love, grace, mercy and blessings of life that you continually shower down upon me. Thank you especially for:

1.__________________________________   2.__________________________________

3.__________________________________   4.__________________________________

5.__________________________________   6.__________________________________

THANK YOU for answered prayers:_______________________________________

Father, I need:____

Father, I ask that YOU:____

____

____

____

Lord, bless me that I may be a blessing. Give me Your heart for loving and serving others. Keep Your hand upon me. Keep me from all evil and harm, and let me cause harm to no one. Bind Satan that he have no power over me. All this I pray in subjection to your will and in the strong name of my Lord and Savior, Jesus Christ. Amen.

God is Able!

"Daniel, servant of the living God, has your God, whom you serve continually, been able to deliver you from the lions?" Daniel 6:20b

Why, oh why do we doubt God's promises and His ability? Why is it so hard to accept that God, who created the world and everything in it, is not limited in any way? If He has His eyes upon the sparrow, is He not also able to keep His eyes on us?

> *"Be exalted, O LORD, in Your own strength! We will sing and praise Your power."*
> *Psalm 21:13*

The ability of God to work His perfect will in our lives is not limited by His ability, but only by our unbelief. When Jesus asked: *"Do you believe that I am able to do this?" (Matthew 9:28)* only belief was required for the healing to take place.

What confidence we can have when we believe when Paul says: *"So now, brethren, I commend you to God and to the word of His grace, which is able to build you up and give you an inheritance among all those who are sanctified." (Acts 20:32)*

What comfort there is in knowing: *"For in that He Himself has suffered, being tempted, He is able to aid those who are tempted."' (Hebrews 2:18)*

> *"And do not fear those who kill the body but cannot kill the soul. But rather fear Him who is able to destroy both soul and body in hell."*
> *Matthew 10:28*

What hope there is in hearing: *"Now to Him who is able to do exceedingly abundantly above all that we ask or think, according to the power that works in us." (Ephesians 3:20)*

What joy we can have in knowing *"Him who is able to keep you from stumbling, and to present you faultless before the presence of His glory with exceeding joy!"(Jude 1:24)*

Father, I believe that You are able to do all that You have promised. Thank you for the strength I receive in believing this. Amen

Taking it to the Lord...

How can I apply this truth?____

____

____

Father, I've come to worship and praise you! You are my:________________________________

____

I give you all Glory, Honor, and Praise O Lord!

Father, I am sorry that I have sinned by:____

Help me to repent. Cleanse me, strengthen me, restore me.

Father, THANK YOU for all your love, grace, mercy and blessings of life that you continually shower down upon me. Thank you especially for:

1.__________________________________   2.__________________________________

3.__________________________________   4.__________________________________

5.__________________________________   6.__________________________________

THANK YOU for answered prayers:____

Father, I need:____

Father, I ask that YOU:____

____

____

____

Lord, bless me that I may be a blessing. Give me Your heart for loving and serving others. Keep Your hand upon me. Keep me from all evil and harm, and let me cause harm to no one. Bind Satan that he have no power over me. All this I pray in subjection to your will and in the strong name of my Lord and Savior, Jesus Christ. Amen.

Calvary Love

Christ is the end of the law so that there may be righteousness for everyone who believes. Romans 10:4

"It is finished" should be the victory cry of everyone who has received eternal life through faith in Jesus Christ

> *"But I am poor
> and sorrowful;
> Let Your salvation
> O God, set me up
> on high."
> Psalm 69:29*

and what He did on the cross for each and everyone of us. At long last, after hundreds of years of separation from God because of sin, God in His great Love came down as the perfect man to live the perfect life, and serve as the one time perfect sacrifice to fulfill the demands of the Law that He knew that we could never fulfill.

Calvary Love is perfect love. We should never think that there is anything we have to do to add to what God has done for us through Jesus Christ on the cross of Calvary. The only thing that we need do is believe, by the power of the Holy Spirit, that our salvation is assured by the death and resurrection of Jesus Christ.

In thanksgiving and praise for what He did on the Cross for us, we joyfully and thankfully put on the yoke of submission to His will that will allow us to be transformed and renewed and to bear the fruit of His Spirit and enjoy eternal life here and forever by getting to know the Father through the Son that He has sent.

> *"Greater love has no
> one than this, than to lay
> down one's life for his
> friends"
> John 15:13*

Father, I cling to the rugged cross of cavalry. Thank you for the joy of my salvation that cost you so much pain and suffering and shame. Help me to show my appreciation for what you have done. Amen

Taking it to the Lord...

How can I apply this truth?____

____

Father, I've come to worship and praise you! You are my:_____________________

____

I give you all Glory, Honor, and Praise O Lord!

Father, I am sorry that I have sinned by:__________________________________

Help me to repent. Cleanse me, strengthen me, restore me.

Father, THANK YOU for all your love, grace, mercy and blessings of life that you continually shower down upon me. Thank you especially for:

1._________________________________   2._________________________________
3._________________________________   4._________________________________
5._________________________________   6._________________________________

THANK YOU for answered prayers:____

Father, I need:____

Father, I ask that YOU:____

____

____

Lord, bless me that I may be a blessing. Give me Your heart for loving and serving others. Keep Your hand upon me. Keep me from all evil and harm, and let me cause harm to no one. Bind Satan that he have no power over me. All this I pray in subjection to your will and in the strong name of my Lord and Savior, Jesus Christ. Amen.

God Wants to Give You The Desires of Your Heart!

"And I will give you a new heart with new and right desires, and will put a new spirit in you. I will take out your stony heart of sin and give you a new, obedient heart." Ezekial 36:26

One of the key principles of debt counseling is the necessity to know the difference between needs and wants. Bankruptcy courts are full of people who failed to make this distinction, and millions of others are in bondage to credit card and other debts that are suffocating and threatening to overwhelm them.

> *"Delight yourself also in the LORD, And He shall give you the desires of your heart."*
> **Psalm 37:4**

Many believers know by heart and believe: *"And my God shall supply all your need according to His riches in glory by Christ Jesus"* (Philippians 4:19), but miss out on the exceeding joy of understanding that God actually delights in giving us the desires of our new heart.

When we receive Jesus Christ as our Lord and Savior, we receive a heart transplant by the power of the Holy Spirit. This new heart is pure, clean, and debt free, and we no longer have to worry about our sin debt that was suffocating and threatening to overwhelm us. Our debt has been paid in full!

> *"Beloved, if our heart does not condemn us, we have confidence toward God. And whatever we ask we Receive from Him, because we keep His commandments and do those things that are pleasing in His sight."*
> **1 John 3:20**

This new heart we receive is the one Ezekial was talking about…one filled with new and right desires. The love of God gives us no choice but to respond in love and obedience and to want to do the things that please Him and give us the joy, the peace, the love of others, and the security that is the true desire of our new hearts.

Only unbelief, disobedience, and self-centeredness can thwart God's delight in giving us the desires of our heart!

Father, by the power of Your Spirit, help me to understand that you not only want to supply my needs, but that you delight in granting the desires of our new hearts when we are abiding in You. Amen

Taking it to the Lord...

How can I apply this truth?____

____

Father, I've come to worship and praise you! You are my:_______________________________

I give you all Glory, Honor, and Praise O Lord!

Father, I am sorry that I have sinned by:____

Help me to repent. Cleanse me, strengthen me, restore me.

Father, THANK YOU for all your love, grace, mercy and blessings of life that you continually shower down upon me. Thank you especially for:

1._________________________________   2._________________________________

3._________________________________   4._________________________________

5._________________________________   6._________________________________

THANK YOU for answered prayers:____

Father, I need:____

Father, I ask that YOU:____

____

____

____

Lord, bless me that I may be a blessing. Give me Your heart for loving and serving others. Keep Your hand upon me. Keep me from all evil and harm, and let me cause harm to no one. Bind Satan that he have no power over me. All this I pray in subjection to your will and in the strong name of my Lord and Savior, Jesus Christ. Amen.

Now You're "Meddlin"

"Watch and pray, lest you enter into temptation. The spirit indeed is willing, but the flesh is weak."
Matthew 26:41

As a good friend once pointed out: "It's not temptation if you're not tempted!" Think about it! The leprosy of sin that continues to spread throughout the world seems to infect different people with different weaknesses.

> *"How many are my iniquities an sins? Make me know my transgression and my sin."*
> *Job 13:23*

We can listen to sermons condemning weaknesses that we don't have and become infected with a big dose of hypocritical glory if we are not careful. We often have a hard time being sympathetic towards those who succumb to sins that don't tempt us.

It's hard for someone who has not become addicted to alcohol, tobacco, or drugs to understand how someone could be so weak or so dumb as to succumb to such things.

We have a tendency to be judgmental and critical of those who are grossly overweight, who allow themselves to be caught up in an illicit sexual relationship, or any other temptation with which we don't struggle. There is a little bit of the Pharisee in all of us that makes us feel just a little better than those infected with weaknesses we don't have.

When the subject turns to pride, envy, gossip, unforgiveness, or the many forms of idolatry that abound among us, we can get very defensive and start wishing that the preacher would "quit meddling", and sometimes even go into denial that we have a problem. The truth is that we all have sinned and fall

> *"But remember that the temptations that come into your life are no different from what others experience. And God is faithful. He will keep the temptation from becoming so strong that you can't stand up against it. When you are tempted, he will show you a way out so that you will not give in to it."*
> *1 Corinthians 10:13 NLT*

short of the Glory of God. The Good News is that: we have forgiveness in Christ, and that He said: "My grace is sufficient for you, for My strength is made perfect in weakness" (2 Corinthians 12:9)

Father, lead me not into temptation, and deliver me from evil. Amen

Taking it to the Lord...

How can I apply this truth?____
____
____

Father, I've come to worship and praise you! You are my:_____________________
____

I give you all Glory, Honor, and Praise O Lord!

Father, I am sorry that I have sinned by:___________________________________

Help me to repent. Cleanse me, strengthen me, restore me.

Father, THANK YOU for all your love, grace, mercy and blessings of life that you continually shower down upon me. Thank you especially for:

1.______________________________   2.______________________________
3.______________________________   4.______________________________
5.______________________________   6.______________________________

THANK YOU for answered prayers:____
Father, I need:____
Father, I ask that YOU:____
____
____

Lord, bless me that I may be a blessing. Give me Your heart for loving and serving others. Keep Your hand upon me. Keep me from all evil and harm, and let me cause harm to no one. Bind Satan that he have no power over me. All this I pray in subjection to your will and in the strong name of my Lord and Savior, Jesus Christ. Amen.

Things God Hates

"These six things the LORD hates, yes, seven are an abomination to Him: a proud look, a lying tongue, hands that shed innocent blood, a heart that devises wicked plans, feet that are swift in running to evil, a false witness who speaks lies, and one who sows discord among brethren." Proverbs 6:16-19

We know that God being the God of love, hates only one thing, and that is sin. He especially hates the sins against His commandment to love our neighbor, along with the sins against His commandment to love Him.

> *"For whoever finds Me finds life, and obtains favor from the LORD; but he who sins against Me wrongs his own soul; all those who hate Me love death."*
> *Proverbs 8:35, 36*

The good news is that God hates sin but He loves sinners. "As I live," says the Lord GOD, 'I have no pleasure in the death of the wicked, but that the wicked turn from his way and live." (Ezekial 33:11)

God is still standing at the door knocking calling sinners to repentance and salvation through faith in Jesus Christ. There is no sin that God is not longing to forgive.

He forgave Joseph's brothers. He forgave David, Abraham, Peter and the other Apostles, and the prodigal son. He stands ready, willing, able, and even longing to forgive all who call upon His name with Godly sorrow and true repentance.

God's well of forgiveness will never run dry. His love is wider than the ocean, and deeper than the sea. He says: "All that the Father gives Me will come to Me, and the one who comes to Me I will by no means cast out." John 6:37

> *"Therefore, I say to you, her sins, which are many, are forgiven, for she loved much. But to whom little is forgiven, the same loves little."*
> *Luke 7:47*

Know that as much as God hates sin, He loves you even more. He loved you enough to have His own Son die on the cross so that you won't have to die. When we think of how much we have been forgiven, how can we help but love our forgiver even more?

Father, thank you for your forever forgiveness and the power of Your Spirit with which I can win the battles over sin. Amen

Taking it to the Lord...

How can I apply this truth?____

____

Father, I've come to worship and praise you! You are my:______________________

____

I give you all Glory, Honor, and Praise O Lord!

Father, I am sorry that I have sinned by:____________________________________

Help me to repent. Cleanse me, strengthen me, restore me.

Father, THANK YOU for all your love, grace, mercy and blessings of life that you continually shower down upon me. Thank you especially for:

1.__________________________________   2.__________________________________
3.__________________________________   4.__________________________________
5.__________________________________   6.__________________________________

THANK YOU for answered prayers:____

Father, I need:____

Father, I ask that YOU:____

____

____

Lord, bless me that I may be a blessing. Give me Your heart for loving and serving others. Keep Your hand upon me. Keep me from all evil and harm, and let me cause harm to no one. Bind Satan that he have no power over me. All this I pray in subjection to your will and in the strong name of my Lord and Savior, Jesus Christ. Amen.

Be A Pleasure Seeker!

"Do not fear, little flock, for it is your Father's good pleasure to give you the kingdom." Luke 12:32

What a difference perspective makes when it comes to pleasure. From a self-centered perspective, it most always has to do with the gratification of our flesh and what makes us happy.

> *"Let them shout for joy and be glad, who favor my righteous cause; and let them say continually, Let the LORD be magnified, Who has pleasure in the prosperity of His servant."*
> *Psalm 35:27*

From a Christ-centered perspective, it has to do with seeking the pleasure of God. Jesus said: "And He who sent Me is with Me. The Father has not left Me alone, for I always do those things that please Him."(John 8:29)

And what are those things that please God? Loving God and others are certainly at the top of the list. Scripture tells us that "God tests the heart and has pleasure in righteousness." (1 Chronicles 29:17), that "He delights in exercising loving-kindness, judgment, and righteousness." (Jeremiah 9:24), and that "He delights in the way of a good man." (Psalm 37:23)

We are told in Hebrews 13:16: "But do not forget to do good and to share, for with such sacrifices God is well pleased" In Psalm 149:4 we learn: "For the LORD takes pleasure in His people; He will beautify the humble with salvation." Psalm 147:11 tells us that: "The LORD takes pleasure in those who fear Him, In those who hope in His mercy."

> *"But without faith it is impossible to please Him, for he who comes to God must believe that He is, and that He is a rewarder of those who diligently seek Him."*
> *Hebrews 11:6*

Just as Jesus knew the joy of hearing His Father say that He was well pleased with Him, we too can look forward to hearing our Father say "well done thou good and faithful servant" when we seek the pleasure of God by being obedient to His will and doing those things that give Him pleasure. Whose pleasure are you seeking?

Father, help me to seek the real pleasure that comes from living a life fully pleasing to You and fruitful in every good work. Amen.

Taking it to the Lord...

How can I apply this truth?____

____

____

Father, I've come to worship and praise you! You are my:_____________________

____

I give you all Glory, Honor, and Praise O Lord!

Father, I am sorry that I have sinned by:_________________________________

Help me to repent. Cleanse me, strengthen me, restore me.

Father, THANK YOU for all your love, grace, mercy and blessings of life that you continually shower down upon me. Thank you especially for:

1.____________________________   2.____________________________
3.____________________________   4.____________________________
5.____________________________   6.____________________________

THANK YOU for answered prayers:_______________________________________

Father, I need:____

Father, I ask that YOU:____

____

____

Lord, bless me that I may be a blessing. Give me Your heart for loving and serving others. Keep Your hand upon me. Keep me from all evil and harm, and let me cause harm to no one. Bind Satan that he have no power over me. All this I pray in subjection to your will and in the strong name of my Lord and Savior, Jesus Christ. Amen.

Abundant Love

"I have come that they may have life, and have it to the full" John 10:10b

There is a "prosperity gospel" being preached that God wants us all to be rich materially. Scriptures tell us that "a man's life does not consist in the abundance of his possessions." While it is true that we have a heavenly father who loves to give good gifts to his children, we dare not let the world's worship of materialism let us lose sight of the real riches of the abundant life that is ours in Christ.

> *"The Lord is good to all, And His tender mercies are over all His works."*
> *Psalm 145:8*

In the riches of Gods grace that are ours through faith in Christ Jesus, we have the abundance of God's love poured into us with not only the provision for all our physical needs, but for salvation, sanctification, and the capacity to love and be loved by others.

The gift of that "peace that surpasses all understanding" that is ours when we worry about nothing, rejoice about everything, and make our requests and supplications in prayer at the throne of grace should always be a reminder of the abundant love of God that is ours in Christ Jesus.

> *"And all these blessings shall come upon you and overtake you, because you obey the voice of the Lord your God."*
> *Deuteronomy 28:1*

Father, keep me mindful of my overflowing cup of blessings which you in your grace and mercy continually shower down upon me in abundance, and let me be forever thankful. Amen

Taking it to the Lord...

How can I apply this truth?____

____

Father, I've come to worship and praise you! You are my:_____________________

____

I give you all Glory, Honor, and Praise O Lord!

Father, I am sorry that I have sinned by:__________________________________

Help me to repent. Cleanse me, strengthen me, restore me.

Father, THANK YOU for all your love, grace, mercy and blessings of life that you continually shower down upon me. Thank you especially for:

1.________________________________   2.________________________________
3.________________________________   4.________________________________
5.________________________________   6.________________________________

THANK YOU for answered prayers:_______________________________________

Father, I need:____

Father, I ask that YOU:____

____

____

Lord, bless me that I may be a blessing. Give me Your heart for loving and serving others. Keep Your hand upon me. Keep me from all evil and harm, and let me cause harm to no one. Bind Satan that he have no power over me. All this I pray in subjection to your will and in the strong name of my Lord and Savior, Jesus Christ. Amen.

Confident Love

"And my God shall supply all your need according to His riches in glory by Christ Jesus." Philippians 4:19

Self-confidence often leads to pride and arrogance, which are an abomination to the Lord. When we depend on our own strength, sooner or later it is going to fail us. How much better to have our confidence in God's love, and His power to do what He says He will do?

> *"I will go in the strength of the Lord GOD;"*
> *Psalm 71:16a*

God's confident love is assuring love. He makes us confident in all His blessed assurances regarding salvation, blessings and prayer. His promises become our "foretaste of glory divine"!   The power of the Holy Spirit living within us manifests itself in every area of our lives.

When we reach that level of sanctification and spiritual maturity that we truly believe by faith that "God works all things to the good for those who love him and who are called according to his purposes", we experience the confidence of God's unconditional love that leads to Godly contentment and peace.

> *"Now this is the confidence that we have in Him, that if we ask anything according to His will, He hears us."*
> *1 John 5:14*

We should always remember that this Confident love that we receive from him, is the strength to accomplish His purposes and not the self-serving, self-glorifying motivations of our flesh.

May we always live in the confidence of having Christ living in us as our strength and our hope of glory, and may that always be the Glory of God that we seek.

Father, thank you for the confidence of your love and your strength not only for my salvation, but also for my every need as you accomplish your purposes through me. Amen

Taking it to the Lord...

How can I apply this truth?____
____
____

Father, I've come to worship and praise you! You are my:_________________________________
____

I give you all Glory, Honor, and Praise O Lord!

Father, I am sorry that I have sinned by:____

Help me to repent. Cleanse me, strengthen me, restore me.

Father, THANK YOU for all your love, grace, mercy and blessings of life that you continually shower down upon me.
Thank you especially for:

1._________________________________   2._________________________________
3._________________________________   4._________________________________
5._________________________________   6._________________________________
THANK YOU for answered prayers:____
Father, I need:____
Father, I ask that YOU:____
____
____
____

Lord, bless me that I may be a blessing. Give me Your heart for loving and serving others. Keep Your hand upon me. Keep me from all evil and harm, and let me cause harm to no one. Bind Satan that he have no power over me. All this I pray in subjection to your will and in the strong name of my Lord and Savior, Jesus Christ. Amen.

Your Credit Has Been Pre-Approved!

"Finally, there is laid up for me the crown of righteousness, which the Lord, the righteous Judge, will give to me on that Day, and not to me only but also to all who have loved His appearing." 2 Timothy 4:8

Our good credit would not last very long if we took advantage of all the pre-approved credit offers we receive on an ongoing basis. From credit cards to automobiles to home loans, there seems to be a concerted effort to get us into debt. Millions of Americans can give living witness to the pitfalls of easy credit.

> *"I will greatly rejoice in the LORD, my soul shall be joyful in my God; for He has clothed me with the garments of salvation, He has covered me with the robe of righteousness."*
> *Isaiah 61:10*

There is one pre-approved credit that we can be very happy about and excited to have. It's that our faith in Jesus Christ has been credited to us for righteousness in God's bank account! No matter when we go home to be with the Lord, we can be sure that we are going to go clothed in the white robe of righteousness earned for us on the cross and that we will stand before God cleansed and in perfect holiness thanks to the blood of the Lamb.

Our line of credit was established over 2,000 years ago. There is no annual fee or interest charge. There are no credit turndowns, and there is overdraft insurance.

> *"Just as David also describes the blessedness of the man to whom God imputes righteousness apart from works."*
> *Romans 4:6*

There is nothing we can do to earn this priceless gift of righteousness. Jesus Christ did it all! When He said: "it is finished" He meant that He had done all that God required to redeem us and reconcile us to God.

Father, thank You for crediting my account with the righteousness of Your Son so that I might have eternal life. Amen

Taking it to the Lord...

How can I apply this truth?____

____

____

Father, I've come to worship and praise you! You are my:_______________________

____

I give you all Glory, Honor, and Praise O Lord!

Father, I am sorry that I have sinned by:__________________________________

Help me to repent. Cleanse me, strengthen me, restore me.

Father, THANK YOU for all your love, grace, mercy and blessings of life that you continually shower down upon me. Thank you especially for:

1.____________________________   2.____________________________

3.____________________________   4.____________________________

5.____________________________   6.____________________________

THANK YOU for answered prayers:____

Father, I need:____

Father, I ask that YOU:____

____

____

____

Lord, bless me that I may be a blessing. Give me Your heart for loving and serving others. Keep Your hand upon me. Keep me from all evil and harm, and let me cause harm to no one. Bind Satan that he have no power over me. All this I pray in subjection to your will and in the strong name of my Lord and Savior, Jesus Christ. Amen.

God Is Willing!

"Then Jesus, moved with compassion, stretched out His hand and touched him, and said to him, 'I am willing; be cleansed." Mark 1:41

We have a God who was willing to heal the sick, restore sight to the blind, and reward the faithfulness of all who came to Him in faith. If he was willing to sacrifice His own Son that we might live forever, how can anyone question His love, His grace, and His mercy?

> *"To them God willed to make known what are the riches of the glory of this mystery among the Gentiles: which is Christ in you, the hope of glory."*
> *Colossians 1:27*

How can we help but believe that He wills the very best for us, and is willing to do whatever it takes to accomplish His good will? About the only thing God is unwilling about is that any of us should perish. He wants us all to come to repentance and enter into that love relationship with Him through faith in His Son.

The willingness of God is not the problem. The problem is in the unwillingness of man to receive the wonderful gift of salvation, and the unwillingness of all of us to let the yoke of submission to the will of God be placed upon us. *"The Spirit is indeed willing, but the flesh is weak" (Mark 14:38)*

> *"that it might be fulfilled which was spoken by Isaiah the prophet, saying:*
> *"He Himself took our infirmities And bore our sicknesses."*
> *Matthew 8:17b*

We stumble and fall, we "waffle" and we make excuses, and our longsuffering and patient God continues to forgive and forget, and to lovingly chasten and discipline that we might be sanctified and conformed more into the image of Christ as he renews His grace and mercy to us each and every day.

God's willingness to love us and to guide us along the paths of righteousness is exceeded only by His faithfulness in seeing that we do not perish, but have the everlasting life that is ours in Christ.

Father, through the power of Your Spirit living within, me help me to be as willing to receive as You are to give. Amen

Taking it to the Lord...

How can I apply this truth?____
____
____
Father, I've come to worship and praise you! You are my:_____________________________
____
I give you all Glory, Honor, and Praise O Lord!

Father, I am sorry that I have sinned by:____
Help me to repent. Cleanse me, strengthen me, restore me.

Father, THANK YOU for all your love, grace, mercy and blessings of life that you continually shower down upon me. Thank you especially for:

1.___________________________________   2.___________________________________
3.___________________________________   4.___________________________________
5.___________________________________   6.___________________________________

THANK YOU for answered prayers:____
Father, I need:____
Father, I ask that YOU:____
____
____
____

Lord, bless me that I may be a blessing. Give me Your heart for loving and serving others. Keep Your hand upon me. Keep me from all evil and harm, and let me cause harm to no one. Bind Satan that he have no power over me. All this I pray in subjection to your will and in the strong name of my Lord and Savior, Jesus Christ. Amen.

Unholy Passion

"Jesus said, '"Love the Lord your God with all your passion and prayer and intelligence.' This is the most important, the first on any list." Matthew 22:37 MSG

While we usually think of passion in terms of sex, the Bible and history are full of many more passions that have nothing to do with sex. Passion can also mean zeal or burning desire.

> *"They made God angry by building altars to other gods; they made him jealous with their idols."*
> *Psalm 78:58 NLT*

Before being converted on the way to Damascus, Paul had a real passion for persecuting Christians. The crusaders had a passion to take Jerusalem back. Constantine had a passion to Christianize the world and make everyone confess Jesus Christ whether they really believed it or not.

The Spanish inquisition and other stake burnings and persecution of Christians by Christians are sobering examples of unholy passion by those who proclaimed the name of Christ.

Today we have Christians with a passion to uphold traditions and the inerrancy of their interpretations of scripture and doctrine committing all sorts of slander and sins against fellow believers in Jesus Christ who do not agree with them.

We have the "wolves in sheep's clothing" perverting the Word of God to condone what God clearly and repeatedly calls abominations.

We sometimes have a tendency to get so obsessed and caught up in a passion for sports, careers, approval, or possessions that even these good pursuits can become unholy.

> *"Wherever your treasure is, there your heart and thoughts will also be."*
> *Matthew 6:21 NLT*

Anything that takes precedence over God in our lives is unholy. God is not satisfied with minimal devotion. He is worthy of and demands being number one and when we put anything or anyone except Him in that position in our hearts and our lives, we are headed for trouble.

Father, let nothing take your place as number one in my heart. Let my use of time, talents, and treasure reflect my devotion to you.

Taking it to the Lord...

How can I apply this truth?____

____

Father, I've come to worship and praise you! You are my:__________________________________

____

I give you all Glory, Honor, and Praise O Lord!

Father, I am sorry that I have sinned by:____

Help me to repent. Cleanse me, strengthen me, restore me.

Father, THANK YOU for all your love, grace, mercy and blessings of life that you continually shower down upon me. Thank you especially for:

1.____________________________________   2.____________________________________

3.____________________________________   4.____________________________________

5.____________________________________   6.____________________________________

THANK YOU for answered prayers:____

Father, I need:____

Father, I ask that YOU:____

____

____

Lord, bless me that I may be a blessing. Give me Your heart for loving and serving others. Keep Your hand upon me. Keep me from all evil and harm, and let me cause harm to no one. Bind Satan that he have no power over me. All this I pray in subjection to your will and in the strong name of my Lord and Savior, Jesus Christ. Amen.

Wandering Aimlessly Lost

"Household gods give false advice, fortune-tellers predict only lies, and interpreters of dreams pronounce comfortless falsehoods. So my people are wandering like lost sheep, without a shepherd to protect and guide them." Zechariah 10:2 NLT

Although painful, those of us who know what it was like to "wander aimlessly lost" need to sometimes revisit the futility of our lives and the emptiness of our hearts before the Lord found us and called us into saving faith and the abundant life we have in Him.

> *"Some wandered in the desert, lost and homeless. Hungry and thirsty, they nearly died. "LORD, help!" they cried in their trouble and he rescued them from their distress." Psalm 107:4-6 NLT*

Thinking about our past should give us even greater passion to seek out and save the lost living among us in our homes, our workplace, and in our everyday lives. It should also trigger a daily wellspring of praise to the Lord of salvation, and the great thing He has done for us.

People today need the Lord as never before. The "household God" called TV

> *"My dear brothers and sisters, if anyone among you wanders away from the truth and is brought back again, you can be sure that the one who brings that person back will save that sinner from death and bring about the forgiveness of many sins." James 5:19,20*

has mislead and brainwashed two generations of people with so many lies about what constitutes the good life, and what really matters, no wonder there is so much misery and sin all around us.

Broken homes, suicide rates, addictions of every kind, have made the age of secular humanism a vast wasteland of broken hearts, shattered dreams, wasted lives and unfilled expectations for millions.

Through it all, we have a God who still loves us all, who would have all men to be saved and who would use us to seek out and proclaim the good news to those who are wandering aimlessly lost, that they might be found before it's too late.

Father, thank you for coming to me when I was lost, and letting me find the "pearl of great price" which is the love, the forgiveness, and the peace and joy I have found in you. Amen

Taking it to the Lord...

How can I apply this truth?____

____

____

Father, I've come to worship and praise you! You are my:_________________________

____

I give you all Glory, Honor, and Praise O Lord!

Father, I am sorry that I have sinned by:_____________________________________

Help me to repent. Cleanse me, strengthen me, restore me.

Father, THANK YOU for all your love, grace, mercy and blessings of life that you continually shower down upon me. Thank you especially for:

1.________________________________   2.________________________________

3.________________________________   4.________________________________

5.________________________________   6.________________________________

THANK YOU for answered prayers:____

Father, I need:____

Father, I ask that YOU:____

____

____

____

Lord, bless me that I may be a blessing. Give me Your heart for loving and serving others. Keep Your hand upon me. Keep me from all evil and harm, and let me cause harm to no one. Bind Satan that he have no power over me. All this I pray in subjection to your will and in the strong name of my Lord and Savior, Jesus Christ. Amen.

Do You Have God in Your Religion?

"But He will say, 'I tell you I do not know you, where you are from. Depart from Me all you workers of iniquity." Luke 13:27

Someone once said, "Whoever makes religion his god will not have God in his religion." I believe this statement to be true. Sometimes we see people so engrossed in the traditions and doctrines in their church that they squeeze God, His love and the Great Commission right out of the picture.

> *"I will praise You, O LORD, with my whole heart;"*
> *Psalm 9:1*

We have "Don Quixotes" attacking the windmills of the mind, looking for error in every area in the beliefs in their own church and especially in the life and beliefs of other churches. The idea that God is not strong enough to defend the faith without their help is foreign to their thinking. Down through the centuries, we have had zealots dying by the thousands in the crusades, killing by the thousands as in the Spanish Inquisition, and burning so called heretics at the stake.

Somehow, the zealots get the idea that understandings contrary to their own, no matter how scripturally valid they might be, and having nothing to do with salvation and the centrality of the gospel, cannot be tolerated without compromising the truth of their own confessions and beliefs. So-called Christians quarrelling and fighting with each other in the name of religion makes the fury of a woman scorned seem like child's play.

> *"Do not speak evil of one another, brethren. He who speaks evil of a brother and judges his brother, speaks evil of the law and judges the law."*
> *James 4:11*

Christianity is not a religiosity; it is a close personal relationship with Jesus Christ and the belief that He died for our sins so that we would not have to. It's not the label we wear on our backs, it's all about who we have in our hearts.

Father, never let my religiosity be a stumbling block to others. Let me give praise and honor and respect to all who confess Your Son as their hope of glory. Amen

Taking it to the Lord...

How can I apply this truth?____

____

Father, I've come to worship and praise you! You are my:______________________

____

I give you all Glory, Honor, and Praise O Lord!

Father, I am sorry that I have sinned by:__________________________________

Help me to repent. Cleanse me, strengthen me, restore me.

Father, THANK YOU for all your love, grace, mercy and blessings of life that you continually shower down upon me. Thank you especially for:

1.________________________________   2.________________________________
3.________________________________   4.________________________________
5.________________________________   6.________________________________

THANK YOU for answered prayers:____

Father, I need:____

Father, I ask that YOU:____

____

____

Lord, bless me that I may be a blessing. Give me Your heart for loving and serving others. Keep Your hand upon me. Keep me from all evil and harm, and let me cause harm to no one. Bind Satan that he have no power over me. All this I pray in subjection to your will and in the strong name of my Lord and Savior, Jesus Christ. Amen.

All Knowing Love

" Now we can see that you know all things, and that you do not need to have anyone ask you questions. This makes us believe that you came from God." John 16:30

God is omniscient. This is a big word meaning that God knows everything. Nothing is hid from Him. He knows the past, present, and future.

> *"The LORD knows the thoughts of man, That they are futile." Psalm 94:11*

We often deceive ourselves through rationalization and denial. We can even hide the truth from ourselves about ourselves. We have sins that would cause great embarrassment and hurt if they were found out. We can hide the truth from others, and even from ourselves, but we cannot hide any thought, word, or deed from God.

Aren't you glad that an all knowing God who knows everything you have ever done and everything we will ever do still loves you? Isn't it great to have someone you can stand before honestly and confess to freely without condemnation because of our faith in Jesus Christ? It should fill us with Godly sorrow to acknowledge that the God who knows everything about us had to die for our sins.

> *"For it is the God who commanded light to shine out of darkness, who has shone in our hearts to give the light of the knowledge of the glory of God in the face of Jesus Christ." 2 Corinthians 4:6*

May the all knowing love of God through the power of His Spirit within us help us to know that he is truly worth living for.

Father, I realize that I cannot hide anything from you. Help me to come to you to confess openly and with sincere repentance that I am totally dependent upon your grace and mercy which you freely give for the sake of your Son, Jesus Christ. Amen.

Taking it to the Lord...

How can I apply this truth?____
____
____

Father, I've come to worship and praise you! You are my:___________________
____

I give you all Glory, Honor, and Praise O Lord!

Father, I am sorry that I have sinned by:________________________________

Help me to repent. Cleanse me, strengthen me, restore me.

Father, THANK YOU for all your love, grace, mercy and blessings of life that you continually shower down upon me. Thank you especially for:

1.____________________________   2.____________________________
3.____________________________   4.____________________________
5.____________________________   6.____________________________

THANK YOU for answered prayers:____

Father, I need:____

Father, I ask that YOU:____
____
____

Lord, bless me that I may be a blessing. Give me Your heart for loving and serving others. Keep Your hand upon me. Keep me from all evil and harm, and let me cause harm to no one. Bind Satan that he have no power over me. All this I pray in subjection to your will and in the strong name of my Lord and Savior, Jesus Christ. Amen.

Are You Blessable?

"I will bless those who have humble and contrite hearts, who tremble at my word. But those who choose their own ways, delighting in their sins, are cursed. Their offerings will not be accepted." Isaiah 66:2

You would think that we would learn from the history of the children of Israel. Time and time again God rescued, delivered, restored and blessed them, and every time they fell back into idol worship and ignoring God to their peril.

> *"Blessed is every one who fears the LORD, Who walks in His ways."*
> *Psalm 128:1*

Today, we expect God to bless us in spite of our indifference and disobedience….in spite of our putting other gods before him, and willfully ignoring Him.

Thankfully, God is longsuffering, patient, and kind. He longs to bring us into that abiding relationship where He can be our friend, answer our prayers, make us fruitful, give us joy, and let us know His love and be aware of the love of others. God really does long to bless us!

We don't have to be rocket scientists to figure out some simple keys to being blessable.

First of all, obedience brings blessings. All of the old covenants were based on this principle, and this principle holds true today.

Think of the consequences of some of the disobedience in your life and the lives of those around you. We will never know the blessings of God to their fullest if we insist on willfully disobeying God and ignoring the calls of the Holy Spirit to contrition and repentance.

> *"Live in such a way that God's love can bless you as you wait for the eternal life that our Lord Jesus Christ in his mercy is going to give you."*
> *Jude 1:21 NLT*

We learn from Scripture that we are blessable when we are meek, when we mourn, when we hunger and thirst for righteousness, when we are persecuted for the cause of Christ, when we are merciful, when we seek to promote peace, and when we have a clean heart.

We are blessable when we endure temptation and persevere through times of testing, when we are generous, compassionate and kind.

Father, by the power of Your Spirit, help me be blessable. Amen

Taking it to the Lord...

How can I apply this truth?____

____

____

Father, I've come to worship and praise you! You are my:_______________________

____

I give you all Glory, Honor, and Praise O Lord!

Father, I am sorry that I have sinned by:___________________________________

Help me to repent. Cleanse me, strengthen me, restore me.

Father, THANK YOU for all your love, grace, mercy and blessings of life that you continually shower down upon me. Thank you especially for:

1.___________________________________   2.___________________________________
3.___________________________________   4.___________________________________
5.___________________________________   6.___________________________________

THANK YOU for answered prayers:____

Father, I need:____

Father, I ask that YOU:____

____

____

Lord, bless me that I may be a blessing. Give me Your heart for loving and serving others. Keep Your hand upon me. Keep me from all evil and harm, and let me cause harm to no one. Bind Satan that he have no power over me. All this I pray in subjection to your will and in the strong name of my Lord and Savior, Jesus Christ. Amen.

Unconditional Love

"And I pray that you, being rooted and established in love, may have power, together with all the saints, to grasp how wide and long and high and deep is the love of Christ." Ephesians 3:17b, 18 (NIV)

There are times in the lives of the best of Christians when we either sin and fall short of the glory of God, or we fail to meet our expectations or the expectations of others.   Satan will seize upon these times to try to discourage, destroy, and defeat us by raising doubts within our hearts and minds as to whether we are saved or whether God really loves us.

> *"Remember me, O LORD, with the favor You have toward Your people."*
> *Psalm 106:4*

> *"For I am persuaded that neither death nor life, nor angels nor principalities nor powers, nor things present nor things to come, nor height nor depth, nor any other created thing, shall be able to separate us from the love of God which is in Christ Jesus our Lord."*
> *Romans 8:38,39*

We need to pray for spiritual wisdom and discernment to recognize the difference between the Spirit's showing us our sins and giving us Godly sorrow that leads us to confession and repentance; and the Prince of Darkness's tempting us through discouragement and depression to question our salvation.

Christian, stand firm in the realization that your salvation is based not on your performance, but on Christ's performance in living the perfect life and becoming the perfect sacrifice through His death on the Cross for every sin that you have ever committed or will ever commit.   There is nothing that you can do to add to or take away from this truth. God's love is unconditional!

Father, like the apostle Paul, I often do the things that I would not, and do not do the things that I should. I often lose the battles, but thanks be to God, You have won the war for me through the perfect sacrifice of Your son on the cross. Empower me to press on in true repentance and faith. Amen.

Taking it to the Lord...

How can I apply this truth?____

____

Father, I've come to worship and praise you! You are my:_______________________

____

I give you all Glory, Honor, and Praise O Lord!

Father, I am sorry that I have sinned by:_____________________________________

Help me to repent. Cleanse me, strengthen me, restore me.

Father, THANK YOU for all your love, grace, mercy and blessings of life that you continually shower down upon me. Thank you especially for:

1._________________________________   2._________________________________
3._________________________________   4._________________________________
5._________________________________   6._________________________________

THANK YOU for answered prayers:____

Father, I need:____

Father, I ask that YOU:____

____

____

Lord, bless me that I may be a blessing. Give me Your heart for loving and serving others. Keep Your hand upon me. Keep me from all evil and harm, and let me cause harm to no one. Bind Satan that he have no power over me. All this I pray in subjection to your will and in the strong name of my Lord and Savior, Jesus Christ. Amen.

Designer Labels

"For whoever finds Me finds life and wins approval from the LORD. But those who miss Me have injured themselves. All who hate Me love death." Proverbs 8:35 (NLT)

Teenagers seem to place great importance on wearing the right brands as a means of acquiring self-esteem.

> *"And may the Lord our God show us his approval and make our efforts successful. Yes, make our efforts successful!"*
> *Psalm 90:17 NLT*

We seem to have a tendency to want to validate our worth and the approval of our peers by the clothes we wear, the cars we drive, the houses we live in and sometimes even the church we attend.

Many churches sometimes seem to be establishing their own "designer label" by their traditions of worship, interpretations of Scripture, and ideas about how the grace of God is dispensed.

Frankly, God couldn't care less about your outward appearance and your denominational or socio economic labels. He cares only about your heart, and your relationship with Him!

God is the great designer of us all. He created us in His image, for His pleasure, and for His purposes, and for eternity. In His love, He created us with a free will so that we could be free to love Him and fellowship with Him. Unfortunately, this free will led to disobedience by Adam and Eve, and sin entered the world, destroying the earthly paradise that God had created for us.

In His mercy, God ordained that paradise and fellowship with Him would be restored for now and forever by the life, death, and resurrection of His Son, and our Savior, Jesus Christ, for all who believe this, and come into a personal faith relationship with Jesus Christ.

> *"Your approval or disapproval means nothing to me, because I know you don't have God's love within you."*
> *John 5:41 NLT*

The designer label "righteous" which we will wear by faith when we stand before God, is the only label that really matters. Are you wearing this label?

Father, keep me ever mindful that it's not the label on my back, but my relationship with You that counts. Amen

Taking it to the Lord...

How can I apply this truth?____

____

Father, I've come to worship and praise you! You are my:_______________________________

I give you all Glory, Honor, and Praise O Lord!

Father, I am sorry that I have sinned by:____

Help me to repent. Cleanse me, strengthen me, restore me.

Father, THANK YOU for all your love, grace, mercy and blessings of life that you continually shower down upon me. Thank you especially for:

1.______________________________   2.______________________________

3.______________________________   4.______________________________

5.______________________________   6.______________________________

THANK YOU for answered prayers:____

Father, I need:____

Father, I ask that YOU:____

____

____

Lord, bless me that I may be a blessing. Give me Your heart for loving and serving others. Keep Your hand upon me. Keep me from all evil and harm, and let me cause harm to no one. Bind Satan that he have no power over me. All this I pray in subjection to your will and in the strong name of my Lord and Savior, Jesus Christ. Amen.

The Highway of Life

"And this is the way to have eternal life—to know You, the only true God, and Jesus Christ, the one You sent to earth." John 17:3 NLT

There is a "high" way of life and a "low" way of life. The "low" way of foolishness, self centeredness, stubbornness and disobedience, leads to destruction." There is a way that seems right to a man, But its end is the way of death. (Proverbs 16:25)

> *"As for God, His way is perfect. All the LORD'S promises prove true. He is a shield for all who look to Him for protection."*
> *2 Sam 22:31*

The "high" way is the only way to travel if we want to live forever. It begins the minute we receive Jesus Christ as our Savior and continues as we get to know God through getting to know Jesus Christ through His Word.

The "high" way is the road less traveled. As Jesus said: "Enter by the narrow gate; for wide is the gate and broad is the way that leads to destruction, and there are many who go in by it.   Because narrow is the gate and difficult is the way which leads to life, and there are few who find it." (Matthew 7:12)

Sometimes the "High" way of life can be very hard to travel. We often have detours of dalliance and doubt, and continually have to dodge the potholes of pride, selfishness, anger, lust, unforgiveness and idolatry.

> *"Jesus said to him, "I am the way, the truth, and the life. No one comes to the Father except through Me."*
> *John 14:6*

Thank God that as he provided a cloud by day and a pillar of fire by night to guide the Israelites, He provides us with the Holy Spirit to guide us and to give us power to overcome the onslaughts of the world, the flesh, and the devil that would get us off course.

Father, guide me through the potholes of life that I might stay anchored deep in You and following Your "high" way. Amen

Taking it to the Lord...

How can I apply this truth?____

____

Father, I've come to worship and praise you! You are my:__________________________________

I give you all Glory, Honor, and Praise O Lord!

Father, I am sorry that I have sinned by:____

Help me to repent. Cleanse me, strengthen me, restore me.

Father, THANK YOU for all your love, grace, mercy and blessings of life that you continually shower down upon me. Thank you especially for:

1.___________________________________   2.___________________________________

3.___________________________________   4.___________________________________

5.___________________________________   6.___________________________________

THANK YOU for answered prayers:____

Father, I need:____

Father, I ask that YOU:____

____

____

Lord, bless me that I may be a blessing. Give me Your heart for loving and serving others. Keep Your hand upon me. Keep me from all evil and harm, and let me cause harm to no one. Bind Satan that he have no power over me. All this I pray in subjection to your will and in the strong name of my Lord and Savior, Jesus Christ. Amen.

Compassionate Love

"Filled with compassion, Jesus reached out His hand and touched the man." Luke 1:41

If there could only be one word to sum up God's love for us in Christ Jesus, it would have to be compassion.

"And in your compassion you delivered them time after time." Nehemiah 9:28b (NIV)

Jesus had compassion for the lame, the sick, and the blind, and He healed them. He had compassion for the 5000 and He fed them.   He had compassion for Lazarus's sisters and raised him from the dead.

Jesus had the compassion for us that took Him to the Cross to die for our sins. He has the compassion for us that follows us with grace and mercy all the days of our lives.

Although we may harden our hearts toward Him and His commands, although we may try His longsuffering and patience to the limit as we stray from the sheepfold looking for love and pleasure in all the wrong places, we have the confidence that His compassion never fails and that His mercy is renewed every day.

Without God's compassionate love, we would all be without hope. With God's compassionate love, we are without excuse for not showing compassionate love to the hungry, the needy, and the sick that God may place in our path.

"Through the LORD'S mercies we are not consumed, Because His compassions fail not." Lamentations 3:22

Commit your dear Savior's words: "whatever you did for one of the least of these brothers of mine, you did it for me" to your heart, and let it become a law of your life, so that when the time comes to give an account; you will have the compassion you yourself are going to need.

Father, thank you for your compassionate grace and mercy that saved a wretch like me. Keep me ever mindful of where I would be except for your grace and mercy in Christ. Amen

Taking it to the Lord...

How can I apply this truth?____

____

____

Father, I've come to worship and praise you! You are my:_________________________________

____

I give you all Glory, Honor, and Praise O Lord!

Father, I am sorry that I have sinned by:____

Help me to repent. Cleanse me, strengthen me, restore me.

Father, THANK YOU for all your love, grace, mercy and blessings of life that you continually shower down upon me. Thank you especially for:

1.______________________________   2.______________________________

3.______________________________   4.______________________________

5.______________________________   6.______________________________

THANK YOU for answered prayers:____

Father, I need:____

Father, I ask that YOU:____

____

____

____

Lord, bless me that I may be a blessing. Give me Your heart for loving and serving others. Keep Your hand upon me. Keep me from all evil and harm, and let me cause harm to no one. Bind Satan that he have no power over me. All this I pray in subjection to your will and in the strong name of my Lord and Savior, Jesus Christ. Amen.

The Stewardship of Resources

"And God is able to make all grace abound toward you, that you, always having all sufficiency in all things, may have an abundance for every good work." 2 Corinthians 9:8

> *"What shall I give*
> *to the LORD*
> *For all His benefits*
> *toward me?"*
> *Psalm 116:12*

Of all the graces of God, and there are many, the grace of giving is perhaps one of the most neglected and misunderstood. We can readily understand and accept the grace of our salvation, and all of the other undeserved kindnesses of God, but what does grace have to do with giving?

The answer is everything! Apart from God, we can do nothing. We are selfish and self-willed. We are obsessed with accumulating wealth and physical possessions as a validation for our self worth according to the world's standards.

We hear over and over again that "you can't take it with you", and that "you never see a hearse pulling a u haul trailer"; but the clear teaching of scripture that you can send it ahead is conveniently ignored over fear that we might confuse good works with earning our salvation, which is the gift of God and not of works.

Does our Lord Himself not command us to *"lay up for yourselves treasures in heaven, where neither moth nor rust destroys and where thieves do not break in and steal. For where your treasure is, there your heart will be also." (Matthew 6:20)* God is not really after your money, He is after your heart, and He can't get your heart as long as you hold on to your money.

> *"But as you abound in*
> *everything—in faith, in*
> *speech, in knowledge, in*
> *all diligence, and in your*
> *love for us—see that*
> *you abound in this*
> *grace also."*
> *2 Corinthians 8:6*

Just as we cannot out love God, we can never out give Him. Understanding that God provides our abundance so that we can be generous on every occasion is evidence that we do have the grace of giving.

Lord, give me the grace of giving that I might be generous on every occasion just as you have been so generous and gracious to me. Amen

Taking it to the Lord...

How can I apply this truth?____
____
____

Father, I've come to worship and praise you! You are my:_________________________________
____

I give you all Glory, Honor, and Praise O Lord!

Father, I am sorry that I have sinned by:____

Help me to repent. Cleanse me, strengthen me, restore me.

Father, THANK YOU for all your love, grace, mercy and blessings of life that you continually shower down upon me. Thank you especially for:

1._____________________________________   2._____________________________________
3._____________________________________   4._____________________________________
5._____________________________________   6._____________________________________

THANK YOU for answered prayers:____

Father, I need:____

Father, I ask that YOU:____
____
____
____

Lord, bless me that I may be a blessing. Give me Your heart for loving and serving others. Keep Your hand upon me. Keep me from all evil and harm, and let me cause harm to no one. Bind Satan that he have no power over me. All this I pray in subjection to your will and in the strong name of my Lord and Savior, Jesus Christ. Amen.

Wash and Wear Religion

"I will greatly rejoice in the LORD, My soul shall be joyful in my God; For He has clothed me with the garments of salvation, He has covered me with the robe of righteousness," Isaiah 61:10

What joy there is in knowing that, because of our faith in Jesus Christ and His death on the cross for our sins, we have been cleansed and clothed in the righteousness of Christ. This means that when we stand before God, He will not see our sins, but will look at us just as He looks at His Son, in whom He was well pleased! "let us go right into the presence of God, with true hearts fully trusting him. For our evil consciences have been sprinkled with Christ's blood to make us clean, and our bodies have been washed with pure water."(Hebrews 10:22)

> *"Wash me thoroughly from my iniquity, And cleanse me from my sin."*
> *Psalm 51:2*

Who in the world would wants to show up at a wedding with a dirty robe that has not been cleansed by blood of Jesus? Just as sin has no more dominion over our spirit, by the grace of God and by the power of His Spirit, we should not let it have dominion over our flesh. "No temptation has overtaken you except such as is common to man; but God is faithful, who will not allow you to be tempted beyond what you are able, but with the temptation will also make the way of escape, that you may be able to bear it. (1 Corinthians 10:13)

> *"Friend, how did you come in here without a wedding garment?' And he was speechless. 13Then the king said to the servants, 'Bind him hand and foot, take him away, and cast him into outer darkness; there will be weeping and gnashing of teeth."*
> *Matthew 22:12b, 13*

Thank God, He has given us a "wash and wear" robe. Knowing that some of the road dirt of the flesh, the world and the devil is bound to soil our robe, He provides the "living water" which not only takes away our thirst but will keep our robes "white as snow" by daily washing through confession and repentance.

May God forbid that any of us fail to get dressed for the wedding feast!

Father, thank you for cleansing me with the blood of Jesus, and for keeping me clean by the power of Your Spirit. Amen.

Taking it to the Lord...

How can I apply this truth?____

____

____

Father, I've come to worship and praise you! You are my:_______________________

____

I give you all Glory, Honor, and Praise O Lord!

Father, I am sorry that I have sinned by:_____________________________________

Help me to repent. Cleanse me, strengthen me, restore me.

Father, THANK YOU for all your love, grace, mercy and blessings of life that you continually shower down upon me. Thank you especially for:

1.___________________________   2.___________________________

3.___________________________   4.___________________________

5.___________________________   6.___________________________

THANK YOU for answered prayers:___________________________________

Father, I need:____

Father, I ask that YOU:____

____

____

____

Lord, bless me that I may be a blessing. Give me Your heart for loving and serving others. Keep Your hand upon me. Keep me from all evil and harm, and let me cause harm to no one. Bind Satan that he have no power over me. All this I pray in subjection to your will and in the strong name of my Lord and Savior, Jesus Christ. Amen.

Are You the Missing Link?

"So if you break the smallest commandment and teach others to do the same, you will be the least in the Kingdom of Heaven." Matthew 5:19 NLT

Those who teach and believe the false teaching that we are descended from apes are continually searching for the missing link, while thousands are themselves becoming the real "missing links" by failing to obey God's command to teach their children the commandments of God.

> *"He commanded our ancestors to teach them to their children, so the next generation might know them—even the children not yet born—that they in turn might teach their children."*
> *Psalm 78:5,6 NLT*

One of the most Satanic lies ever foisted is the notion that we should not try to influence our children in religious matters, but let them find their own way. This is like thinking we should turn our children loose in a dung heap and they will somehow come out smelling like a rose!

When we break our covenant relationship with God by not passing our faith along to our children, We set in motion a downward spiral with consequences on not only our children, but upon generations to come.

Oftentimes, what we teach by example is worse than what we don't teach because of disobedience. "You tell others not to steal, but do you steal? You say it is wrong to commit adultery, but do you do it? You condemn idolatry, but do you steal from pagan temples? You are so proud of knowing the law, but you dishonor God by breaking it. No wonder the Scriptures say, "The world blasphemes the name of God because of you." (Romans 2:21b NLT)

> *"Teach them to your children. Talk about them when you are at home and when you are away on a journey, when you are lying down and when you are getting up again."*
> *Deut 11:9 NLT*

The consequences of missing links are all around us. The very institution of family itself is being threatened as never before. Let the restoration begin by every believer resolving as did Joshua: *"But as for me and my house, we will serve the LORD." (Joshua 24:15b)*

Father forgive me for not bringing my children up in the nurture and admonition of you as well as I could have or should have. From this day forward, by the power of Your Spirit, help me to do better. Amen

Taking it to the Lord...

How can I apply this truth?____

____

____

Father, I've come to worship and praise you! You are my:_________________________

____

I give you all Glory, Honor, and Praise O Lord!

Father, I am sorry that I have sinned by:____

Help me to repent. Cleanse me, strengthen me, restore me.

Father, THANK YOU for all your love, grace, mercy and blessings of life that you continually shower down upon me. Thank you especially for:

1.____________________________   2.____________________________

3.____________________________   4.____________________________

5.____________________________   6.____________________________

THANK YOU for answered prayers:____

Father, I need:____

Father, I ask that YOU:____

____

____

____

Lord, bless me that I may be a blessing. Give me Your heart for loving and serving others. Keep Your hand upon me. Keep me from all evil and harm, and let me cause harm to no one. Bind Satan that he have no power over me. All this I pray in subjection to your will and in the strong name of my Lord and Savior, Jesus Christ. Amen.

Spiritual Understanding

"For this reason we also, since the day we heard it, do not cease to pray for you, and to ask that you may be filled with the knowledge of His will in all wisdom and spiritual understanding;" Colossians 1:9a

Next to the Gift of Eternal life, God's gift of the Holy Spirit to indwell every believer is perhaps the greatest gift of all others. It is this indwelling presence that gives us the wisdom and spiritual understanding that turns our head knowledge into heart knowledge and empowers us to see God's perspective, and to become Christ centered instead of self centered.

> *"The fear of the LORD is the beginning of wisdom; A good understanding have all those who do His commandments."*
> *Psalm 111:10*

Self-centeredness is all about us and about taking. Christ centeredness is all about Christ and giving. When watching out for Number one, means watching out for ourselves and putting our priorities first, we are never going to be filled with the knowledge of His will in all wisdom and spiritual understanding.

When watching out for Number One means seeking the kingdom of God and His righteousness and putting Him first in our lives, we begin to receive the knowledge of His will in all spiritual wisdom and understanding, along with the power to do it.

The flesh and the spirit are continually warring within us to see which is going to have control of our mind, our will, and our intellect. Even though we have been set free from the dominion and power of sin by Jesus death on the cross, the will of the flesh will continue to creep into our being and stands ready to take control the very minute we let our guard down.

> *"That the righteous requirement of the law might be fulfilled in us who do not walk according to the flesh but according to the Spirit."*
> *Romans 8:4*

"For to be carnally minded is death, but to be spiritually minded is life and peace. Because the carnal mind is enmity against God; for it is not subject to the law of God, nor indeed can be. So then, those who are in the flesh cannot please God."

Father, help me to stay spiritually minded by the power of Your Spirit living with me. Let me put on the full armor of God daily that I might walk in the Spirit and stay free from the control of my flesh. Amen

Taking it to the Lord...

How can I apply this truth?____

____

____

Father, I've come to worship and praise you! You are my:_________________________

____

I give you all Glory, Honor, and Praise O Lord!

Father, I am sorry that I have sinned by:____

Help me to repent. Cleanse me, strengthen me, restore me.

Father, THANK YOU for all your love, grace, mercy and blessings of life that you continually shower down upon me. Thank you especially for:

1._____________________________   2._____________________________

3._____________________________   4._____________________________

5._____________________________   6._____________________________

THANK YOU for answered prayers:______________________________________

Father, I need:____

Father, I ask that YOU:____

____

____

____

Lord, bless me that I may be a blessing. Give me Your heart for loving and serving others. Keep Your hand upon me. Keep me from all evil and harm, and let me cause harm to no one. Bind Satan that he have no power over me. All this I pray in subjection to your will and in the strong name of my Lord and Savior, Jesus Christ. Amen.

Wise Understanding

"The way of life winds upward for the wise, that he may turn away from hell below." Proverbs 15:24

On what do we base our understanding? We get understanding of reading, writing and arithmetic in school.

> *"He has ceased to be wise and to do good." Psalm 36:3b*

Unfortunately, we get a lot of false understanding from the world of TV, Movies, and prevailing standards of morality lived out all around us.

We also acquire understanding by our experiences and relationships with others at work, play, and at school. Someone has written a very winsome and widely read essay on "I learned everything I needed to know in kindergarten".

Many live by the understanding that they should "eat, drink, and be merry" because this is all there is. Others spend their lives "looking out for number one" and find out too late that this is an understanding that reaps no lasting peace.

What is your understanding regarding true happiness? Is based on false assumptions that power, applause, possessions, or people hold the key to your happiness and well being?

> *"But I want you to be wise in what is good, and simple concerning evil." Romans 15:19b*

To be "wise in what is good" (Romans 16a) is to know that there is no true happiness apart from a right relationship with God the Father through Faith in His Son, Jesus Christ.

When we realize that God loves us unconditionally, forgives us for everything we have ever done or will ever do, that He accepts us just the way we are, we are on our way to the wise understanding.

Lord, give me that "wise understanding" that only comes by the power of Your Spirit, revealing Your truths, through Your word. Amen

Taking it to the Lord...

How can I apply this truth?____

____

Father, I've come to worship and praise you! You are my:____

____

I give you all Glory, Honor, and Praise O Lord!

Father, I am sorry that I have sinned by:____

Help me to repent. Cleanse me, strengthen me, restore me.

Father, THANK YOU for all your love, grace, mercy and blessings of life that you continually shower down upon me. Thank you especially for:

1.___________________________________   2.___________________________________

3.___________________________________   4.___________________________________

5.___________________________________   6.___________________________________

THANK YOU for answered prayers:____

Father, I need:____

Father, I ask that YOU:____

____

____

Lord, bless me that I may be a blessing. Give me Your heart for loving and serving others. Keep Your hand upon me. Keep me from all evil and harm, and let me cause harm to no one. Bind Satan that he have no power over me. All this I pray in subjection to your will and in the strong name of my Lord and Savior, Jesus Christ. Amen.

The Timex Award

"To the present hour we both hunger and thirst, and we are poorly clothed, and beaten, and homeless." 2 Corinthians 4:11

Scripture tells of many heroes of the faith who have "takin' a lickin' but keep on tickin'." Joseph certainly had a full plate of betrayal. David spent years hiding out from the murderous obsessions of Saul. The Apostle Paul also endured it all for the sake of the gospel of Jesus Christ.

> *"The Lord also will be a refuge for the oppressed."*
> *Psalm 9:9*

Our Lord himself endured rejection, ridicule, persecution, scourging, desertion by friends, false witnesses, and the humiliation of being crucified naked between two common criminals at the town dump. All this and more by one who never committed a sin in His life. Through it all, He never gave up and prayed for forgiveness for those who had crucified Him with some of His very last words.

Oh what a Savior we have! A man acquainted with sorrows, who can identify with every emotion and physical pain we will ever suffer and who bore the consequences of every sin we have ever committed or will ever commit.

> *"Three times I was beaten with rods; once I was stoned; three times I was shipwrecked; a night and a day I have been in the deep."*
> *2 Corinthians 11:25*

Surely the one who loved us enough to die for us is worth our loving enough to live for! Let us "count it all joy" to suffer the lickings that life hands us, confident that they are for our good and that the patience with which we endure them will have its perfect work in us, that we may be fully conformed to the image of Christ.

Father, thank you for your assurance that we will suffer nothing without your all-sufficient grace to endure and "keep on ticking". Amen

Taking it to the Lord...

How can I apply this truth?____
____
____
Father, I've come to worship and praise you! You are my:______________________________
____
I give you all Glory, Honor, and Praise O Lord!
Father, I am sorry that I have sinned by:____
Help me to repent. Cleanse me, strengthen me, restore me.
Father, THANK YOU for all your love, grace, mercy and blessings of life that you continually shower down upon me. Thank you especially for:

1.__________________________________   2.__________________________________
3.__________________________________   4.__________________________________
5.__________________________________   6.__________________________________
THANK YOU for answered prayers:____
Father, I need:____
Father, I ask that YOU:____
____
____

Lord, bless me that I may be a blessing. Give me Your heart for loving and serving others. Keep Your hand upon me. Keep me from all evil and harm, and let me cause harm to no one. Bind Satan that he have no power over me. All this I pray in subjection to your will and in the strong name of my Lord and Savior, Jesus Christ. Amen.

Revealing Love

"All things have been committed to me by my Father. No one knows the Son except the Father, and no one knows the Father except the Son and those to whom the Son chooses to reveal him." Mt 11:27 (NIV)

Before coming in the Flesh as Jesus Christ, no one had ever seen God. God spoke through the prophets and revealed His presence in many ways, including a burning bush, a cloud by day, a pillar of fire by night, His Shekinah Glory, and behind the veil in the "holy of holies" in the temple.

> *"The LORD has made known His salvation; His righteousness He has revealed in the sight of the nations."*
> *Psalm 98:2*

Now, in His Love, He has revealed Himself through Jesus Christ, God Incarnate, the Living Word! Through the Word, God has given us divine revelation of His Character, His way, His truth, and His gift of eternal life. He has made known to us His will, His promises, and His commands.

When Jesus died on the cross, the veil separating the presence of God was torn from top to bottom, signifying that God has ended His separation from us because of sin, and moved his presence into the hearts of all believers through the indwelling power of the Holy Spirit.

We, like Peter, receive the revelation that "You are the Christ, the Son of the Living God."

Since eternal life is knowing God through knowing Jesus Christ whom He has sent and since we not only have the revelation of Jesus Christ through His Word, but the enlightening power of His Spirit living within us, we are without excuse in not knowing the full love of God that is revealed throughout scripture.

> *"But rise and stand on your feet; for I have appeared to you for this purpose, to make you a minister and a witness both of the things which you have seen and of the things which I will yet reveal to you."*
> *Acts 26:16*

Father, by the power of your Spirit, reveal more of yourself to me as I grown in my knowledge of you through your Word.   Amen

Taking it to the Lord...

How can I apply this truth?____

____

____

Father, I've come to worship and praise you! You are my:_________________________________

____

I give you all Glory, Honor, and Praise O Lord!

Father, I am sorry that I have sinned by:____

Help me to repent. Cleanse me, strengthen me, restore me.

Father, THANK YOU for all your love, grace, mercy and blessings of life that you continually shower down upon me. Thank you especially for:

1.____________________________   2.____________________________

3.____________________________   4.____________________________

5.____________________________   6.____________________________

THANK YOU for answered prayers:____

Father, I need:____

Father, I ask that YOU:____

____

____

Lord, bless me that I may be a blessing. Give me Your heart for loving and serving others. Keep Your hand upon me. Keep me from all evil and harm, and let me cause harm to no one. Bind Satan that he have no power over me. All this I pray in subjection to your will and in the strong name of my Lord and Savior, Jesus Christ. Amen.

Breakfast of Champions

"Imitate those who through faith and patience inherit the promises." Hebrews 6:12b

The advertising of Wheaties as the "breakfast of champions" for over 50 years has been one of the most successful marketing campaigns ever conducted. It is hard to think of or hear the name Wheaties, without immediately thinking of "the breakfast of champions."

"Now in my prosperity I said, "I shall never be moved." Psalm 30:6

Year after year, new sports and Olympic heroes have graced the cereal boxes and held up as examples of the suggestion that you can be a champion if you eat the breakfast of champions.

In the eleventh chapter of Hebrews, God lists His own champions of the faith, and the great things they did because of their faith – which in a manner of speaking, could be called the "breakfast of champions."

When we daily put on the shield of faith, great things begin to happen. We not only are armored to withstand Satan and his attempts to devour us, but we are empowered to please God by trusting Him and "believing that He is, and that He is a rewarder of those who diligently seek Him."(Hebrews 11:6b).

"Who through faith subdued kingdoms, worked righteousness, obtained promises, stopped the mouths of lions, quenched the violence of fire, escaped the edge of the sword, out of weakness were made strong." Hebrews 11:33,34a

When we know by faith that God is on our side and we earnestly seek the knowledge of His will "with all wisdom and spiritual understanding" (Colossians 1:9b), there is no limit to what God can accomplish through us.

Father, let me be a champion for you as I lay hold of the hope that is within me through faith in Jesus Christ. Amen

Taking it to the Lord...

How can I apply this truth?____

____

____

Father, I've come to worship and praise you! You are my:_______________________

____

I give you all Glory, Honor, and Praise O Lord!

Father, I am sorry that I have sinned by:___________________________________

Help me to repent. Cleanse me, strengthen me, restore me.

Father, THANK YOU for all your love, grace, mercy and blessings of life that you continually shower down upon me. Thank you especially for:

1._______________________________   2._______________________________
3._______________________________   4._______________________________
5._______________________________   6._______________________________

THANK YOU for answered prayers:____

Father, I need:____

Father, I ask that YOU:____

____

____

Lord, bless me that I may be a blessing. Give me Your heart for loving and serving others. Keep Your hand upon me. Keep me from all evil and harm, and let me cause harm to no one. Bind Satan that he have no power over me. All this I pray in subjection to your will and in the strong name of my Lord and Savior, Jesus Christ. Amen.

Unwitting Accomplice

"Therefore let us not judge one another anymore, but rather resolve this, not to put a stumbling block or a cause to fall in our brother's way." Romans 14:13

In our self centered, self seeking mode we can easily become oblivious to a very real and present danger with eternal consequences. We often fail to heed the warnings of Scripture with regard to being a stumbling block to others.

> *"Great peace have those who love Your law, and nothing causes them to stumble."*
> *Psalm 119:165*

The great commission to make disciples is not to make others followers or imitators of us, but followers and imitators of Christ.

We have the greatest influence of anyone over our children. They grow up mirroring what they have learned from their parents. If faith is not alive and important to parents, it is almost a certainty that it will not become alive and important to their children.

Even worse, the hypocrisy of parents who "talk the talk" without "walking the walk" will cause untold damage to their children.

The devil has been using people as stumbling blocks since Eve gave Adam the forbidden fruit to eat in the Garden of Eden. Literally millions of souls have been turned away from God by the conduct of legalistic, self righteous and judgmental people professing to be "Christians".

> *"But whoever causes one of these little ones who believe in Me to stumble, it would be better for him if a millstone were hung around his neck, and he were thrown into the sea."*
> *Mark 9:42*

The potential for being a stumbling block or causing harm to others is something that should concern us all. It is bad enough to sin, but when our sin causes harm or hurt to others, it's even worse.

May God keep us from being stumbling blocks to anyone, and may we never be a hindrance to the cause of Christ or anyone coming into or staying in a close personal relationship with Him.

Father, keep your hand upon me and keep me from giving offense or causing harm to others. Amen

Taking it to the Lord...

How can I apply this truth?____
____
____

Father, I've come to worship and praise you! You are my:_________________________
____
I give you all Glory, Honor, and Praise O Lord!

Father, I am sorry that I have sinned by:____
Help me to repent. Cleanse me, strengthen me, restore me.

Father, THANK YOU for all your love, grace, mercy and blessings of life that you continually shower down upon me. Thank you especially for:

1.____________________________________   2.____________________________________
3.____________________________________   4.____________________________________
5.____________________________________   6.____________________________________

THANK YOU for answered prayers:____
Father, I need:____
Father, I ask that YOU:____
____
____

Lord, bless me that I may be a blessing. Give me Your heart for loving and serving others. Keep Your hand upon me. Keep me from all evil and harm, and let me cause harm to no one. Bind Satan that he have no power over me. All this I pray in subjection to your will and in the strong name of my Lord and Savior, Jesus Christ. Amen.

Blessing or Curse?

"For the love of money is a root of all kinds of evil, for which some have strayed from the faith in their greediness, and pierced themselves through with many sorrows." 1 Timothy 6:10

The Old Testament is full of examples of wealth being a blessing from God. Abraham and Isaac were blessed with material wealth. Solomon's great wealth was looked upon as evidence of God's Favor. Job was blessed with great wealth.

> *"So don't be impressed with those who get rich and pile up fame and fortune. They can't take it with them; fame and fortune all get left behind."*
> *Psalm 49:13 MSG*

Wealth becomes a problem when it becomes the spiritual power or object of worship that Jesus mentions in Matthew 6:34: "No one can serve two masters. For you will hate one and love the other, or be devoted to one and despise the other. You cannot serve both God and money."

Whether money and possessions are a blessing or curse depends on how we get them and what we do with them. It has a lot to do with who is the possessor and who the possessee.

God tells us that it is more blessed to give than to receive, so we can be sure that our wealth will be a blessing if we are generous with it. . This is probably also the best antidote for defeating mammon.

The parable of the rich farmer serves a stern warning against hoarding wealth.

When we view whatever wealth we are given as a trust from the Lord, and that we are going to be held accountable for how we use it, we can't help but realize that wealth is a blessing that we are to use to bless others.

> *"but all too quickly the message is crowded out by the cares of this life, the lure of wealth, and the desire for nice things, so no crop is produced."*
> *Mark 4:9 NLT*

The tests that God sends our way in the opportunities he provides for responding to the financial needs of others may very well be the standard which will determine whether our wealth will be a blessing or a curse.

Father, impart to me the grace of giving so that I might be found faithful and a good steward of all that You have given *me*. Amen

Taking it to the Lord...

How can I apply this truth?____

____

____

Father, I've come to worship and praise you! You are my:_______________________

____

I give you all Glory, Honor, and Praise O Lord!

Father, I am sorry that I have sinned by:___________________________________

Help me to repent. Cleanse me, strengthen me, restore me.

Father, THANK YOU for all your love, grace, mercy and blessings of life that you continually shower down upon me. Thank you especially for:

1.____________________________   2.____________________________

3.____________________________   4.____________________________

5.____________________________   6.____________________________

THANK YOU for answered prayers:____

Father, I need:____

Father, I ask that YOU:____

____

____

Lord, bless me that I may be a blessing. Give me Your heart for loving and serving others. Keep Your hand upon me. Keep me from all evil and harm, and let me cause harm to no one. Bind Satan that he have no power over me. All this I pray in subjection to your will and in the strong name of my Lord and Savior, Jesus Christ. Amen.

Time to Clean House

"So clean house! Make a clean sweep of malice and pretense, envy and hurtful talk. You've had a taste of God. Now, like infants at the breast, drink deep of God's pure kindness. Then you'll grow up mature and whole in God." 1 Peter 2:1, 2 MSG

Although "cleanliness is next to godliness" is one of those oft quoted Scriptures that are not in Scripture, Spiritual cleanliness is what faith in God is all about.

> *"He who has clean hands and a pure heart, who has not lifted up his soul to an idol, nor sworn deceitfully."*
> *Psalm 24:4*

When we come to saving faith, we are cleansed by the washing of renewal in baptism. When we become the temple of the Holy Spirit, we need to be aware that we can't expect Him to live in a cesspool of sin. Thank God that He comes with His own janitor service to help us keep His dwelling place clean.

As babes in Christ, we haven't been potty trained. We must rely totally on the sanctifying power of God's Spirit to cleanse us, but we can't expect the Holy Spirit to change our diapers forever. Somewhere along the road to spiritual maturity, we have to get off the breast and on to solid food.

We need to know that we have been made dead to sin and alive in Christ. This new life comes with a new nature, and the cleanliness of Christ becomes the model for growing into His fullness.

> *"Now you Pharisees make the outside of the cup and dish clean, but your inward part is full of greed and wickedness."*
> *Luke 11:39*

When we clean house, we need to check every nook and cranny in every room of our hearts to make sure that all trash, dust and dirt is removed. We need to give ourselves a frequent white glove inspection to make sure that we are providing a clean dwelling place for the honored guest Who has come to live with us.

Father, help me to keep my child like faith and trust, but to grow inwardly and outwardly into the fullness of Christ. Amen.

Taking it to the Lord...

How can I apply this truth?____

Father, I've come to worship and praise you! You are my:____

I give you all Glory, Honor, and Praise O Lord!

Father, I am sorry that I have sinned by:____

Help me to repent. Cleanse me, strengthen me, restore me.

Father, THANK YOU for all your love, grace, mercy and blessings of life that you continually shower down upon me. Thank you especially for:

1.____________________________________ 2.____________________________________

3.____________________________________ 4.____________________________________

5.____________________________________ 6.____________________________________

THANK YOU for answered prayers:____

Father, I need:____

Father, I ask that YOU:____

____

Lord, bless me that I may be a blessing. Give me Your heart for loving and serving others. Keep Your hand upon me. Keep me from all evil and harm, and let me cause harm to no one. Bind Satan that he have no power over me. All this I pray in subjection to your will and in the strong name of my Lord and Savior, Jesus Christ. Amen.

Irreconcilable Differences

"For there is only one God and one Mediator who can reconcile God and people. He is the man Christ Jesus." 1 Timothy 2:5 NLT

The ongoing, apparently never to be resolved, conflicts in the Middle East are just the tip of the iceberg when it comes to irreconcilable differences.

> *"As for our transgressions, You will provide atonement for them."*
> *Psalm 65:3*

We have apparently Irreconcilable differences within and between denominations. We have irreconcilable differences between religions, political parties, and relationships.

"Irreconcilable differences" has become the key reason given in divorce after divorce. It is amazing that none of the differences seemed to matter before marriage, but begin to loom big in the every day process of living life together.

Irreconcilable differences stem from the root cause of the disobedience of man to God in the garden of Eden and the consequences that this caused then and in every succeeding generation.

This disobedience set up irreconcilable differences between the perfect righteousness with which God created us in His perfect image, and the consequences of unrighteousness, rebellion, pride and evil that came into the world as a result of this disobedience.

Righteousness and innocence were lost and sin was found.

We need to thank God without ceasing that, in His love and compassion, He had mercy upon us and provided the means of reconciliation with Him through the perfect obedience of His Son, Jesus Christ!

> *"And what God wants is for us to be made holy by the sacrifice of the body of Jesus Christ once for all time."*
> *Hebrews 10:10 NLT*

Paradise lost has become paradise found! The lion is going to lay down with the lamb. All who call upon the name of the Lord will be saved. Nothing is impossible or irreconcilable for God.

Father, thank you for reconciling me to you and making it possible to be a reconciler to others. Amen

Taking it to the Lord...

How can I apply this truth?____

____

Father, I've come to worship and praise you! You are my:___________________________

I give you all Glory, Honor, and Praise O Lord!

Father, I am sorry that I have sinned by:_____________________________________

Help me to repent. Cleanse me, strengthen me, restore me.

Father, THANK YOU for all your love, grace, mercy and blessings of life that you continually shower down upon me. Thank you especially for:

1._____________________________   2._____________________________

3._____________________________   4._____________________________

5._____________________________   6._____________________________

THANK YOU for answered prayers:____

Father, I need:____

Father, I ask that YOU:____

____

____

Lord, bless me that I may be a blessing. Give me Your heart for loving and serving others. Keep Your hand upon me. Keep me from all evil and harm, and let me cause harm to no one. Bind Satan that he have no power over me. All this I pray in subjection to your will and in the strong name of my Lord and Savior, Jesus Christ. Amen.

God Never Gives Up on Us

"That the saying might be fulfilled which He spoke, "Of those whom You gave Me I have lost none." John 18:9

There is nothing like the faithfulness of God. The fact that He has been faithful in keeping every promise He has ever made gives us every reason to believe that the promise of eternal life in heaven is also something we can count on.

> *"Oh, give thanks to the God of heaven! For His mercy endures forever."*
> *Psalm 136:26*

People will often give up on us. The world will often belittle and minimize us as not being important according to its standards. We often give up on ourselves and fall short of receiving all of the blessings that God prepared for us because we have let the evil one distract us with the darts of doubt, defeat, and depression.

The faithfulness of God is seen time and time again in answered prayers that are God centered and in keeping with His good and perfect will.

Heaven is full of sinners saved by grace as a result of God's faithfulness in answering prayers, and Saints who have been restored and renewed by the regeneration of the Holy Spirit as a result of prayer.

The one thing that we dare not do is to ever give up on God. When the trials of life seem too overwhelming, when God seems to be AWOL, and when we are tempted to follow Job's wife's advice to "curse God and die," we need to call a "time out" and stand on the promises of God.

> *"But if we confess our sins to him, he is faithful and just to forgive us and to cleanse us from every wrong."*
> *1 John 1:9*

God has promised to supply His all sustaining grace to meet our every need, to provide a means of escape from every temptation, to work all things for our good as He conforms us into the image of Christ. Best of all, we can be *"confident of this very thing, that He who has begun a good work in you will complete it until the day of Jesus Christ,"* (Philippians 1:6)

Father, thank you for never giving up on me. For loving me, forgiving me, and sustaining me, no matter what. Amen

Taking it to the Lord...

How can I apply this truth?____

____

Father, I've come to worship and praise you! You are my:___________________

____

I give you all Glory, Honor, and Praise O Lord!

Father, I am sorry that I have sinned by:_________________________________

Help me to repent. Cleanse me, strengthen me, restore me.

Father, THANK YOU for all your love, grace, mercy and blessings of life that you continually shower down upon me. Thank you especially for:

1.______________________________   2.______________________________
3.______________________________   4.______________________________
5.______________________________   6.______________________________

THANK YOU for answered prayers:____

Father, I need:____

Father, I ask that YOU:____

____

____

Lord, bless me that I may be a blessing. Give me Your heart for loving and serving others. Keep Your hand upon me. Keep me from all evil and harm, and let me cause harm to no one. Bind Satan that he have no power over me. All this I pray in subjection to your will and in the strong name of my Lord and Savior, Jesus Christ. Amen.

The Morning After

"I am leaving you with a gift—peace of mind and heart. And the peace I give isn't like the peace the world gives. So don't be troubled or afraid." John 14:27 NLT

It is too easy to think of Christmas as a one day a year thing. We look forward to it with relish, celebrate it with a lot of joy, and then turn our minds to other things as we get up the next morning.

> *"The LORD will give strength to His people; the LORD will bless His people with peace. Psalm 29:11*

We need to remember that Christmas was just the beginning of everything good that we have as believers. The only thing that ended on Christmas was lack of hope for a bright future. The promise of the birth of a Savior was fulfilled.

In living the perfect life that we could never live and becoming the unblemished perfect sacrifice that God's justice required, Jesus fulfilled the promise of His coming, with the promise of the gift He was leaving – "peace of mind and heart."

This, the greatest of all gifts, is not something we throw out with the dead Christmas tree. It is something to be treasured, savored, and claimed every day of our lives.

This peace of mind and heart is the peace that surpasses all understanding. It is the peace that comes from believing that God really does work all things for our good. It is the assurance that God loves us with an everlasting love.

Just as Jesus came into the world to cover our sins with His righteousness, His Spirit remains to cover our weaknesses with God's strength. This peace of mind and heart brings a security and significance that nothing or no one else can give and that nothing or no one else can take away unless we choose to let it.

> *"So Jesus said to them again, "Peace to you! As the Father has sent Me, I also send you." John 20:21*

The morning after Christmas, and every morning after is, as Norman Vincent Peale once said: "the first day of the rest of our lives." Let's rejoice and be glad in them!

Father, let the joy that you brought to me yesterday abide in me everyday. Amen

Taking it to the Lord...

How can I apply this truth?____

____

____

Father, I've come to worship and praise you! You are my:____________________

____

I give you all Glory, Honor, and Praise O Lord!

Father, I am sorry that I have sinned by:_________________________________

Help me to repent. Cleanse me, strengthen me, restore me.

Father, THANK YOU for all your love, grace, mercy and blessings of life that you continually shower down upon me. Thank you especially for:

1.____________________________   2.____________________________
3.____________________________   4.____________________________
5.____________________________   6.____________________________

THANK YOU for answered prayers:_______________________________________

Father, I need:____

Father, I ask that YOU:____

____

____

____

Lord, bless me that I may be a blessing. Give me Your heart for loving and serving others. Keep Your hand upon me. Keep me from all evil and harm, and let me cause harm to no one. Bind Satan that he have no power over me. All this I pray in subjection to your will and in the strong name of my Lord and Savior, Jesus Christ. Amen.

Looking Down on the Looking Downers

"Don't pick on people, jump on their failures, criticize their faults—unless, of course, you want the same treatment. That critical spirit has a way of boomeranging." Matthew 7:1 MSG

A critical, judgmental spirit is one of the thorns of the flesh of far too many Christians--myself included. Why oh why do we fall into the trap of trying to make ourselves think we are better than we are by thinking that others are worse than we are.

> *"The LORD shall judge the peoples; Judge me, O LORD, according to my righteousness, and according to my integrity within me."*
> *Psalm 7:8*

There is only one standard of conduct, and not one of us measures up to it. Jesus Christ came to model this. When we reserve our critical and judgmental spirit for our own sins and shortcomings, we won't have time to worry about the moat in our brother's eye.

It is a scary thought to think about the anger and judgment Jesus reserved for the self-righteousness and hypocrisy of the Scribes and Pharisees of the day.

> *"Every time you criticize someone, you condemn yourself. It takes one to know one. Judgmental criticism of others is a well-known way of escaping detection in your own crimes and misdemeanors."*
> *Romans 2:2 MSG*

Jesus said that He didn't come into the World to judge, but to save. While spiritual discernment includes sometime being fruit inspectors of others in our household or household of faith, we should never let criticism or calling attention to the sins of others be motivated by anything other than love, and sincere concern for that person.

Most importantly, we should discuss the problem with that person instead of about them.

Instead of looking down on the sinful actions of others, we should be looking up to the only one who can change hearts and conduct, and holding ourselves and others who offend us, up in prayer.

Father, help me to look up to you instead of down on others. Amen

Taking it to the Lord...

How can I apply this truth?____

____

Father, I've come to worship and praise you! You are my:_____________________

____

I give you all Glory, Honor, and Praise O Lord!

Father, I am sorry that I have sinned by:_____________________________________

Help me to repent. Cleanse me, strengthen me, restore me.

Father, THANK YOU for all your love, grace, mercy and blessings of life that you continually shower down upon me. Thank you especially for:

1.____________________________   2.____________________________

3.____________________________   4.____________________________

5.____________________________   6.____________________________

THANK YOU for answered prayers:____

Father, I need:____

Father, I ask that YOU:____

____

____

Lord, bless me that I may be a blessing. Give me Your heart for loving and serving others. Keep Your hand upon me. Keep me from all evil and harm, and let me cause harm to no one. Bind Satan that he have no power over me. All this I pray in subjection to your will and in the strong name of my Lord and Savior, Jesus Christ. Amen.

Minimum Daily Requirements

"God is love. When we take up permanent residence in a life of love, we live in God and God lives in us. This way, love has the run of the house, becomes at home and mature in us, so that we're free of worry on Judgment Day—our standing in the world is identical with Christ's. 1 John 4:17 MSG

Vitamins are defined as: "a group of organic substances essential in small quantities to normal metabolism" and "deficiencies of which produce specified disorders".

> *"The people asked, and He brought quail, and satisfied them with the bread of heaven."*
> *Psalm 105:40*

Even though we are probably going to get all of the daily requirements we need just by normal eating; our concern for the health of our physical bodies has made vitamins a "cash cow" for all of the cereals, etc. that are vitamin enriched, and for the billions of dollars spent throughout the world on vitamin supplements.

A lot of us, from time to time, fall far short of the minimum daily requirements for spiritual growth. We never seem to get around to enough prayer, enough reading or hearing God's Word, or enough sharing of our faith, time, talents, or treasures.

God provided just enough manna to meet the minimum daily physical requirements for the children of Israel in the desert. They couldn't store it up or use it except one day at a time.

> *"I am the true bread from heaven. Anyone who eats this bread will live forever and not die as your ancestors did, even though they ate the manna."*
> *John 6:58 NLT*

God provides us with Jesus Christ as the bread of life and the living water that satisfies hunger and thirst daily.

Even though He also gives us the Holy Spirit to call all things to our remembrance and guide us along the pathways of righteousness, we still need to be ever mindful that the greatest vitamin for growing in spiritual maturity and into the fullness of Christ is B1!

Father, let me live out my life as a living celebration of being one with You! Amen

Taking it to the Lord...

How can I apply this truth?____

____

____

Father, I've come to worship and praise you! You are my:______________________

____

I give you all Glory, Honor, and Praise O Lord!

Father, I am sorry that I have sinned by:___________________________________

Help me to repent. Cleanse me, strengthen me, restore me.

Father, THANK YOU for all your love, grace, mercy and blessings of life that you continually shower down upon me. Thank you especially for:

1.___________________________   2.___________________________

3.___________________________   4.___________________________

5.___________________________   6.___________________________

THANK YOU for answered prayers:_______________________________________

Father, I need:____

Father, I ask that YOU:____

____

____

____

Lord, bless me that I may be a blessing. Give me Your heart for loving and serving others. Keep Your hand upon me. Keep me from all evil and harm, and let me cause harm to no one. Bind Satan that he have no power over me. All this I pray in subjection to your will and in the strong name of my Lord and Savior, Jesus Christ. Amen.

Lets Get Personal!

"Yes, a person is a fool to store up earthly wealth, but not have a rich relationship with God." Luke 12:21 NLT

> *"Yes, a person is a fool to store up earthly wealth but not have a rich relationship with God." Luke 12:21 NLT*

Of all the joys of Christmas, what could be better than the reminder God sent Christ to settle His relationship with us so that we could enter into His joy through a close and personal friendship with Him through a personal relationship with His Son and our brother.

When Jesus is our best friend, we have someone who will listen to us, multiply our joy and share our sorrow.

Worldly friends, being sinners just like us, will often disappear and disappoint. Jesus is a friend who will love us and stand beside us no matter what. Even in spite of our sins, He pours out His unconditional love upon us. He is the friend who "sticks closer than a brother".

The key to this rich personal relationship is making room for the Christ Child in the Inn of our heart. When we get our hearts cleansed by the washing of regeneration and we become temples of the Holy Spirit, great things happen.

> *"Now that we have actually received this amazing friendship with God, we are no longer content to simply say it in plodding prose. We sing and shout our praises to God through Jesus, the Messiah!" Romans 5:6-8 MSG*

Although its only an 18 inch journey from head to heart, it is a road less traveled for many of us too much of the time. The old selfish self-centeredness kicks in and our Christ centeredness gets kicked out. The relationship that Christ wants to have with us takes a back seat to the relationship we want to have with the world.

How close and personal is our relationship with God through Jesus Christ? It is not close enough if we are holding back our talents and treasures from Him. It is not close enough if we put anything or any person above Him.

Father, by the power of Your Spirit, draw me into a closer personal relationship with You through a closer friendship with Your Son. Amen

Taking it to the Lord...

How can I apply this truth?____

____

Father, I've come to worship and praise you! You are my:___________________________

____

I give you all Glory, Honor, and Praise O Lord!

Father, I am sorry that I have sinned by:____

Help me to repent. Cleanse me, strengthen me, restore me.

Father, THANK YOU for all your love, grace, mercy and blessings of life that you continually shower down upon me. Thank you especially for:

1.______________________________   2.______________________________
3.______________________________   4.______________________________
5.______________________________   6.______________________________

THANK YOU for answered prayers:____

Father, I need:____

Father, I ask that YOU:____

____

____

Lord, bless me that I may be a blessing. Give me Your heart for loving and serving others. Keep Your hand upon me. Keep me from all evil and harm, and let me cause harm to no one. Bind Satan that he have no power over me. All this I pray in subjection to your will and in the strong name of my Lord and Savior, Jesus Christ. Amen.

Grace Deserves Graciousness

"Now God has us where he wants us, with all the time in this world and the next to shower grace and kindness upon us in Christ Jesus." Ephesians 2

We sometimes fail to appreciate many of the wonderful graces of God. While we accept and sing about the amazing grace of salvation, we often overlook the other graces at the hands of our all-wise, all-powerful, ever present, and ever loving God.

> *"Have compassion on me, LORD, for I am weak. Heal me, LORD, for my body is in agony. I am sick at heart. How long, O LORD, until you restore me?"*
> *Psalm 6:2,3 NLT*

Grace in the Old Testament speaks to the favor, kindness and mercy of God apart from salvation. The psalms are full of pleas for the mercy and compassion of God in time of Need. Other times it is used in conjunction with God making someone favorable in the eyes of another.

St. Paul not only emphasized that salvation is by the undeserved favor of God, but he used grace in terms of attractive speech, giving thanks, gifts for ministry, service, and divine power.

When we come to the realization that we are totally dependent upon the grace of God for every good and perfect gift; we are humbled even more and are lead to trust and obey Him more and seek more grace in every area of our lives.

The idea that we should be gracious as a condition for receiving grace is one of the great principles of Scripture. We see this principle in the Sermon on the Mount, the golden rule, the commandment to forgiveness and loving others.

> *"I am not one of those who treats the grace of God as meaningless."*
> *Galatians 2:21 NIT*

Every kind of grace should abound in every area of our life. If God can be so gracious to the likes of us as unlovable and undeserving as we are at times; how can we refuse to be gracious and loving to the ones we perceive to be unlovable around us?

Father, let your graciousness abound and be reflected in every area of my life. Amen

Taking it to the Lord...

How can I apply this truth?____

____

____

Father, I've come to worship and praise you! You are my:_____________________

____

I give you all Glory, Honor, and Praise O Lord!

Father, I am sorry that I have sinned by:__________________________________

Help me to repent. Cleanse me, strengthen me, restore me.

Father, THANK YOU for all your love, grace, mercy and blessings of life that you continually shower down upon me. Thank you especially for:

1._______________________________ 2._______________________________

3._______________________________ 4._______________________________

5._______________________________ 6._______________________________

THANK YOU for answered prayers:_______________________________________

Father, I need:____

Father, I ask that YOU:____

____

____

Lord, bless me that I may be a blessing. Give me Your heart for loving and serving others. Keep Your hand upon me. Keep me from all evil and harm, and let me cause harm to no one. Bind Satan that he have no power over me. All this I pray in subjection to your will and in the strong name of my Lord and Savior, Jesus Christ. Amen.

Giving In, Up, and Out

"Simon, I've prayed for you in particular that you not give in or give out. When you have come through the time of testing, turn to your companions and give them a fresh start." Luke 22:31 MSG

Why is it so easy to give in to temptation and so hard to give in to God?

"Give in to God, come to terms with him and everything will turn out just fine." Job 22:21 MSG

How come we take in God's blessings so willingly and have a hard time giving them out? The answers are all found in the understanding of our inherited sin nature that is rooted deep within the self-centeredness of our flesh.

Today, as the world's relaxed and casual attitude about sin seems to abound more and more, giving in to sin becomes easier. After all, everybody's doing it, so it must be all right.

Jesus Christ died on the cross to set us free from bondage to our sin nature. He has even promised to provide a means of escape when Satan comes calling with temptations seemingly too good to pass up.

God has provided us with a full set of armor so that we can stand firm against the ongoing attacks from within our flesh and from the world without. The problem is that it can't protect us if we don't put it on daily. Once a week is not enough. Temptations attack on a daily basis.

We need to know that Satan is going to bring disappointments, depression, and all sorts of temptations to try to undermine our faith and get us to give up on God. The good news is that "He who is in you is greater than he who is in the world." (John 4:4b), that God will never give up on you.

"With all these things in mind, dear brothers and sisters, stand firm and keep a strong grip on everything we taught you both in person and by letter." 2 Thessalonians 2:15 NLT

We also need to know that God, in working all things for our good, is going to do whatever it takes to conform us to the image of His Son. Instead of giving up, we should give out praise and thanksgiving that we have a God who loves us enough make us over into the image of His Son.

Father, in the power of Your Spirit, enable me to not give in to sin, but to give out the love you have given to me to others. Amen

Taking it to the Lord...

How can I apply this truth?____

____

____

Father, I've come to worship and praise you! You are my:_____________________

____

I give you all Glory, Honor, and Praise O Lord!

Father, I am sorry that I have sinned by:___________________________________

Help me to repent. Cleanse me, strengthen me, restore me.

Father, THANK YOU for all your love, grace, mercy and blessings of life that you continually shower down upon me. Thank you especially for:

1.________________________________   2.________________________________
3.________________________________   4.________________________________
5.________________________________   6.________________________________

THANK YOU for answered prayers:____

Father, I need:____

Father, I ask that YOU:____

____

____

Lord, bless me that I may be a blessing. Give me Your heart for loving and serving others. Keep Your hand upon me. Keep me from all evil and harm, and let me cause harm to no one. Bind Satan that he have no power over me. All this I pray in subjection to your will and in the strong name of my Lord and Savior, Jesus Christ. Amen.

Is Your Credit Card Maxed?

"In that day the LORD will end the bondage of his people. He will break the yoke of slavery and lift it from their shoulders." Isaiah 10:27

Ever wonder how come getting in debt is so easy, and getting out is so hard? The old song about coal miners "owing their soul to the company store" is not something someone just thought up.

> *"Let us break their chains," they cry, "and free ourselves from this slavery."*
> *Psalm 2:3 NLT*

Bonded servitude and debtors prisons were a part of life for many centuries.

"No payments for 3 years"... "Drive it now and pay later".... "Your Credit has been approved".... "Buy now and save!" are just a few of the enticements paving the way to bondage today.

For those who have lost their credit reputation, "Bad credit no problem" and "Rent to own" are often the cruelest of enticements. (You can be sure that these offers are not generated by charity, but by the opportunity to get an extra high reward for taking a higher risk).

Credit card income has become the "cash cow" for many banks and credit companies. Rented money earns money 24 hours a day, 7 days a week, 365 days a year. When we take the trouble to see how little of what we pay goes to reducing what we owe and how much goes to paying the rent on the money we borrowed or amount we financed often need to ask who owns us.

Debtor's prisons have been done away with by bankruptcy laws. Debtor's have the slate wiped clean, and all debts taken away along with reputation and credit worthiness.

In a sense, Jesus is our referee in bankruptcy for our sin debt. For we who were or are morally bankrupt, He wiped our slate clean with His blood on the cross of Calvary. He has given us a debt counselor called the Holy Spirit, who guides us into all truth, and who will give us the strength and the power to never get this debt maxed out again.

> *"Yes, what joy for those whose sin is no longer counted against them by the Lord."*
> *Romans 4:8 NLT*

Father, thank you for crediting my righteousness account "paid in full" by giving your Son to die for me. Amen

Taking it to the Lord...

How can I apply this truth?____

____

____

Father, I've come to worship and praise you! You are my:_________________________

____

I give you all Glory, Honor, and Praise O Lord!

Father, I am sorry that I have sinned by:____

Help me to repent. Cleanse me, strengthen me, restore me.

Father, THANK YOU for all your love, grace, mercy and blessings of life that you continually shower down upon me. Thank you especially for:

1.___________________________________   2.___________________________________
3.___________________________________   4.___________________________________
5.___________________________________   6.___________________________________

THANK YOU for answered prayers:____

Father, I need:____

Father, I ask that YOU:____

____

Lord, bless me that I may be a blessing. Give me Your heart for loving and serving others. Keep Your hand upon me. Keep me from all evil and harm, and let me cause harm to no one. Bind Satan that he have no power over me. All this I pray in subjection to your will and in the strong name of my Lord and Savior, Jesus Christ. Amen.

Happy Are the Pure in Heart

"Blessed are the pure in heart, for they shall see God." Matthew 5:8

> *"Or who may stand in His holy place? He who has clean hands and a pure heart."*
> *Psalm 24:3b , 4*

The Scribes and Pharisees were long on show and tell, but their hearts were corrupt. They were pleasers of themselves and others, instead of pleasers of God. How could they or anyone think that God, who knows everything, does not know the condition of our hearts?

We can rationalize and deny, fool everyone, even ourselves; but we can't fool God. He knows when our hearts are far from Him. He knows when we are "talking the talk", but not "walking the walk."

Purity of heart can only be gained and maintained by the daily cleansing of our hearts that comes through godly sorrow and true repentance for our sins.

The Good News is that God has sent His Holy Spirit to mend our broken hearts, cleanse our dirty hearts, and do a major heart transplant where necessary. As He chips away at our rough edges, He does what only He can do – change our hearts.

> *"Finally, brethren, whatever things are true, whatever things are noble, whatever things are just, whatever things are pure, whatever things are lovely, whatever things are of good report, if there is any virtue and if there is anything praiseworthy—meditate on these things."*
> *Philippians 4:8*

By His grace, he can turn our anger into self-control, our pride into humility, our self-centeredness into Christ centeredness, and our hate into love. He can change our deceitful and wicked hearts into pure hearts, and then, we will begin to see and experience His love all around us in this life, and meet Him face to face in the next.

Father, create in me a pure heart, and renew a right spirit in me daily. Amen.

Taking it to the Lord...

How can I apply this truth?____

____

Father, I've come to worship and praise you! You are my:______________________

____

I give you all Glory, Honor, and Praise O Lord!

Father, I am sorry that I have sinned by:__________________________________

Help me to repent. Cleanse me, strengthen me, restore me.

Father, THANK YOU for all your love, grace, mercy and blessings of life that you continually shower down upon me. Thank you especially for:

1.____________________________   2.____________________________

3.____________________________   4.____________________________

5.____________________________   6.____________________________

THANK YOU for answered prayers:____

Father, I need:____

Father, I ask that YOU:____

____

____

Lord, bless me that I may be a blessing. Give me Your heart for loving and serving others. Keep Your hand upon me. Keep me from all evil and harm, and let me cause harm to no one. Bind Satan that he have no power over me. All this I pray in subjection to your will and in the strong name of my Lord and Savior, Jesus Christ. Amen.

Spiritual Halitosis

"Finally, brethren, whatever things are true, whatever things are noble, whatever things are just, whatever things are pure, whatever things are lovely, whatever things are of good report, if there is any virtue and if there is anything praiseworthy—meditate on these things." Philippians 4:8 NLT

Halitosis is a multi-million dollar business. We have mouthwashes, mints, breath fresheners of every kind to get rid of bad breath.

> *"My enemies cannot speak one truthful word. Their deepest desire is to destroy others. Their talk is foul, like the stench from an open grave."*
> *Psalm 5:9*

Spiritual halitosis is a major problem for believers and unbelievers alike. The stench of hypocrisy, smut, gossip, slander, character assassination, false witness and vile language fills the air all too often in too many lives.

It has killed marriages, careers, and friendships. It can make us stumbling blocks instead of building blocks. It can grieve the Spirit of God and set back the cause of Christ.

Only when the waters of baptism give us a new tongue to go with our new identify in Christ can we sweeten our spiritual breaths in the power of the Holy Spirit. Our freedom from sin gives us the freedom let our mouth's show forth our praise and give glory to the One who set us free.

We need to be like Job, who vowed: "As long as I live, while I have breath from God, my lips will speak no evil, and my tongue will speak no lies."(Job 27:3).

> *"If you want a happy life and good days, keep your tongue from speaking evil, and keep your lips from telling lies."*
> *1 Peter 3:10 NLT*

Old habits die hard, and it's going to take more than Listerine to sweeten up our spiritual breath. When we cleanse our hearts through confession and repentance and make it a fit dwelling place for the Holy Spirit to dwell and do His will we can get rid of this bad breath.

Father, by the power of Your Spirit clean up my heart so you can help me control of what comes out of my mouth. Amen.

Taking it to the Lord...

How can I apply this truth?____

____

____

Father, I've come to worship and praise you! You are my:________________________

____

I give you all Glory, Honor, and Praise O Lord!

Father, I am sorry that I have sinned by:____________________________________

Help me to repent. Cleanse me, strengthen me, restore me.

Father, THANK YOU for all your love, grace, mercy and blessings of life that you continually shower down upon me. Thank you especially for:

1.__________________________   2.__________________________

3.__________________________   4.__________________________

5.__________________________   6.__________________________

THANK YOU for answered prayers:__________________________________

Father, I need:____

Father, I ask that YOU:____

____

____

Lord, bless me that I may be a blessing. Give me Your heart for loving and serving others. Keep Your hand upon me. Keep me from all evil and harm, and let me cause harm to no one. Bind Satan that he have no power over me. All this I pray in subjection to your will and in the strong name of my Lord and Savior, Jesus Christ. Amen.

Our Greatest Freedom

"You are not slaves; you are free. But your freedom is not an excuse to do evil. You are free to live as God's slaves. Show respect for everyone. Love your Christian brothers and sisters. Fear God. Show respect for the king." 1 Peter 2:16 NLT

When you think of freedom, what do you think of?   The convict thinks of getting out of jail. The ACLU thinks of rights guaranteed by the US Constitution. Children think of getting away from home and on their own.

> *"I will walk in freedom for I have devoted myself to your commandments."*
> *Psalm 119:45*

Every child born of man is born in bondage to sin. Our inherited sin nature makes us slaves to sin and makes it impossible for us to fulfill the righteous demands of the law. We are "dead in trespasses and sin".

By the grace of God, we have been reconciled to Him through faith in Jesus Christ and we have received freedom from this bondage to sin. We have received the freedom to obey! "For you have been called to live in freedom—not freedom to satisfy your sinful nature, but freedom to serve one another in love." (Galations 5:13)

For the first time we are free to hear, obey, and trust God. We are free to worship in spirit and in truth. We are free to produce the fruit of righteousness for which we were created

> *"You are not slaves; you are free. But your freedom is not an excuse to do evil. You are free to live as God's slaves."*
> *1 Peter 2:16 NLT*

We have freedom from condemnation in the eyes of God. Even though we may stumble and fall and sin in the flesh, sin has no more dominion over us spiritually.

Best of all, we are free to obey in love, holiness, and humility with gratitude to the one who first loved us and who set us free.

Father, let me treasure the freedom to obey that you bought for me on the cross with the precious blood of Your beloved Son. In the power of Your Spirit, let me live free. Amen.

Taking it to the Lord...

How can I apply this truth?____

____

____

Father, I've come to worship and praise you! You are my:_________________________

____

I give you all Glory, Honor, and Praise O Lord!

Father, I am sorry that I have sinned by:_______________________________________

Help me to repent. Cleanse me, strengthen me, restore me.

Father, THANK YOU for all your love, grace, mercy and blessings of life that you continually shower down upon me. Thank you especially for:

1.___________________________________   2.___________________________________

3.___________________________________   4.___________________________________

5.___________________________________   6.___________________________________

THANK YOU for answered prayers:____

Father, I need:____

Father, I ask that YOU:____

____

____

Lord, bless me that I may be a blessing. Give me Your heart for loving and serving others. Keep Your hand upon me. Keep me from all evil and harm, and let me cause harm to no one. Bind Satan that he have no power over me. All this I pray in subjection to your will and in the strong name of my Lord and Savior, Jesus Christ. Amen.

You Are One!

"And the Lord said, "Who then is that faithful and wise steward, whom his master will make ruler over his household, to give them their portion of food in due season?" Luke 12:42

Trust funds own a large portion of America's great companies. Some people live well all of their lives as beneficiaries of trusts set up for them years ago.

> *"They put their trust in you and were never disappointed."*
> *Psalm 22:5b NLT*

Have you ever considered that you are a trust fund? Scripture after Scripture affirms that our lives, our talents, and our treasures are trusts on loan from God.

We can learn a very significant lesson from the dishonest but shrewd steward. Although he stored up treasures in the wrong accounts, he was commended for making provisions for his future. Jesus tells us in Matthew 6:19: "Don't store up treasures here on earth, where they can be eaten by moths and get rusty, and where thieves break in and steal. Store your treasures in heaven, where they will never become moth-eaten or rusty and where they will be safe from thieves."

When we realize that we are God's trustees responsible for all that he has given us, we are ready to enter into a fuller joy of the Lord.

Generosity is one of God's greatest lessons. The more faithful we are in being generous with our time, talents, and treasures, the more God will put in our trust account to be generous with. This is a win-win situation for us as the generous ones, and for those God wants to bless through our generosity.

> *"'Well done, my good and faithful servant. You have been faithful in handling this small amount, so now I will give you many more responsibilities. Let's celebrate together!"*
> *Matthew 25:21*

God has given us abundance, so that we can be generous on all occasions. Try as hard as we might, we can never give as abundantly of our time, talent, or treasures as abundantly as God has given them in trust to us.

Father, let the awareness that I am your trust fund keep me focused on being a good trustee. Amen

Taking it to the Lord...

How can I apply this truth?____

____

____

Father, I've come to worship and praise you! You are my:_________________________________

____

I give you all Glory, Honor, and Praise O Lord!

Father, I am sorry that I have sinned by:____

Help me to repent. Cleanse me, strengthen me, restore me.

Father, THANK YOU for all your love, grace, mercy and blessings of life that you continually shower down upon me. Thank you especially for:

1._____________________________________   2._____________________________________

3._____________________________________   4._____________________________________

5._____________________________________   6._____________________________________

THANK YOU for answered prayers:____

Father, I need:____

Father, I ask that YOU:____

____

____

Lord, bless me that I may be a blessing. Give me Your heart for loving and serving others. Keep Your hand upon me. Keep me from all evil and harm, and let me cause harm to no one. Bind Satan that he have no power over me. All this I pray in subjection to your will and in the strong name of my Lord and Savior, Jesus Christ. Amen.

What Will You Leave your Children?

"A good man leaves an inheritance to his children's children," Proverbs 13:22

It is a natural desire of all to leave an inheritance for our children and children's children. When we consider what we will leave, usually the first things we think about are the material things, and how they will be divided among those we leave behind.

> *"Posterity shall serve Him. It will be recounted of the Lord to the next generation."*
> *Psalm 22:30*

We have probably all benefited to some degree by a material bequest willed to us by a family member or close relative, and these have many times turned out to be great blessings to us.

How unfortunate it is when these legacies meant to be blessings turn out to be defiled by sin into curses of jealousy, envy and strife that tear families apart. How sad that substantial inheritances enable the pursuit of an indulgent, fruitless life style by so many.

I hope to bless all my children and children's children with a material inheritance and pray that they will use it wisely and well.

I hope and pray even more that all of my children and children's children will be blessed with a legacy of love and the abundant life in Christ that has been promised to the children and children's children of all who keep God's covenant of grace.

It will bring me no joy to be remembered by how much money I left them. My joy comes in the hope and belief that I will continue to live in their hearts through the love that I have shown them and how much I have cared about their spiritual welfare.

> *"We were also given absolutely terrific promises to pass on to you—your tickets to participation in the life of God after you turned your back on a world corrupted by lust."*
> *2 Peter 1:4 MSG*

I wish for them the joy that I have found in a close personal relationship with God through faith in Jesus Christ. As children of the covenant, this is their birthright, and may God forbid that none of them ever sell it for the pottage of this world.

Father, thank you for the assurances of Your Word that gives me hope for my children and children's children. Amen.

Taking it to the Lord...

How can I apply this truth?____

____

Father, I've come to worship and praise you! You are my:___________________________

____

I give you all Glory, Honor, and Praise O Lord!

Father, I am sorry that I have sinned by:____

Help me to repent. Cleanse me, strengthen me, restore me.

Father, THANK YOU for all your love, grace, mercy and blessings of life that you continually shower down upon me. Thank you especially for:

1._________________________________   2._________________________________
3._________________________________   4._________________________________
5._________________________________   6._________________________________

THANK YOU for answered prayers:____

Father, I need:____

Father, I ask that YOU:____

____

____

____

Lord, bless me that I may be a blessing. Give me Your heart for loving and serving others. Keep Your hand upon me. Keep me from all evil and harm, and let me cause harm to no one. Bind Satan that he have no power over me. All this I pray in subjection to your will and in the strong name of my Lord and Savior, Jesus Christ. Amen.

Dance With the One Who Brought You

"For we are God's masterpiece. He has created us anew in Christ Jesus, so that we can do the good things he planned for us long ago." Ephesians 2:10 NLT

There seem to be a lot of "singles" trying to cut in on our dance with the Lord in the ballroom of life.   They are like a bunch of ticks trying to sink their teeth in us and suck the true joy of life out of us.

> *"I am the LORD, that is My name; and My glory I will not give to another."*
> *Isaiah 42.8*

They often seem to be more exciting than the one who brought us to the dance.

These pride-based, demon inspired princes of the world come gift wrapped up in tinsels of gold, and promise the pleasure, approval, satisfaction, and validation we all seek. It is only by the grace of God that any of us can reject their flirtations.

Not only does God supply us His grace, He even provides a chaperone! He indwells us with the Holy Spirit to guide us into all truth, and the power to resist and escape all of the temptations that surround us.

Jesus was the only one ever born of woman who refused to dance with them. "For we do not have a High Priest who cannot sympathize with our weaknesses, but was in all points tempted as we are, yet without sin." (Hebrews 4:15)

> *"But you must remain faithful to the things you have been taught."*
> *2 Timothy 3:14*

Our God is a jealous God. He created us for His pleasure and His Glory, and for fellowship with Him. We need to join the Psalmist in 119:73 who said: "You made me; you created me. Now give me the sense to follow your commands."

Scripture makes it abundantly clear that we can worship and praise through, and should even enjoy dancing. When dancing to the joy of life, we should never forget the one who brought us into this life and the life eternal.

Father, don't let anyone or anything cut into the dance of life to which you have brought me. Amen

Taking it to the Lord...

How can I apply this truth?____

____

Father, I've come to worship and praise you! You are my:___________________________

____

I give you all Glory, Honor, and Praise O Lord!

Father, I am sorry that I have sinned by:_______________________________________

Help me to repent. Cleanse me, strengthen me, restore me.

Father, THANK YOU for all your love, grace, mercy and blessings of life that you continually shower down upon me. Thank you especially for:

1._______________________________   2._______________________________

3._______________________________   4._______________________________

5._______________________________   6._______________________________

THANK YOU for answered prayers:____

Father, I need:____

Father, I ask that YOU:____

____

____

Lord, bless me that I may be a blessing. Give me Your heart for loving and serving others. Keep Your hand upon me. Keep me from all evil and harm, and let me cause harm to no one. Bind Satan that he have no power over me. All this I pray in subjection to your will and in the strong name of my Lord and Savior, Jesus Christ. Amen.

Authentic Christianity

"Examine yourselves to see if your faith is really genuine. Test yourselves. If you cannot tell that Jesus Christ is in you, it means you have failed the test." 2 Corinthians 13:5 NLT

Phony, carnal Christians have probably done more harm to the cause of Christ than any other group. Our Lord reserved His severest judgment and anger for the Scribes and Pharisees who praised God with their lips, but whose hearts were far from him, and whose worship was a farce. (See Matthew 15.)

Children are often the best judges and worst victims of phony religion. All of the "talking the talk" in the world will not cover failures to "walk the walk" by parents. Parental influence (or lack of) is the most powerful influence, for bad or good in the lives of children.

> *"My heart is steadfast, O God, my heart is steadfast; I will sing and give praise."*
> *Psalm 57:6*

Do we model the love of Christ in the way we treat others? Do we know what Jesus did, so that we know what He would do in any given situation? Are we known as a contagious Christian?

Have we bought into the prosperity gospel that can be so cruel and devastating? Does our observance of traditions and a strict set of rules define our faith? Have we made religion our God instead of God?

Authentic Christianity embraces genuine love that is unconditional, forgiving, and accepting. We must hate the sin, but love the sinner.

When we consider that God knows our hearts, that we are going to need all of the grace and mercy that we can find to cover our own shortcomings, dare we presume upon the grace of God?

> *"And though I have the gift of prophecy, and understand all mysteries and all knowledge, and though I have all faith, so that I could remove mountains, but have not love, I am nothing."*
> *1 Corinthians 13:2 NLT*

We authenticate our Christianity by worshipping God in Spirit and in truth. Is there anything in our lives other than lip service or church attendance that validates our faith to others?

Father, may my heart, my mouth, and my deeds be genuine expressions of my love in Your sight, Oh Lord. Amen

Taking it to the Lord...

How can I apply this truth?____

____

Father, I've come to worship and praise you! You are my:_______________________

____

I give you all Glory, Honor, and Praise O Lord!

Father, I am sorry that I have sinned by:___________________________________

Help me to repent. Cleanse me, strengthen me, restore me.

Father, THANK YOU for all your love, grace, mercy and blessings of life that you continually shower down upon me. Thank you especially for:

1.____________________________　　2.____________________________
3.____________________________　　4.____________________________
5.____________________________　　6.____________________________

THANK YOU for answered prayers:__________________________________

Father, I need:____

Father, I ask that YOU:____

____

____

Lord, bless me that I may be a blessing. Give me Your heart for loving and serving others. Keep Your hand upon me. Keep me from all evil and harm, and let me cause harm to no one. Bind Satan that he have no power over me. All this I pray in subjection to your will and in the strong name of my Lord and Savior, Jesus Christ. Amen.

Mysteries of Life

"Indeed we count them blessed who endure. You have heard of the perseverance of Job and seen the end intended by the Lord—that the Lord is very compassionate and merciful." James 5:11

Those who preach the prosperity gospel must not believe that one of the oldest and significant books in the Bible is the Word of God. Those who can't understand why bad things happen to good people need to read and think about this book also.

"You talk like a godless woman. Should we accept only good things from the hand of God and never anything bad?"
Job 2:10 NLT

When we get over simplistic and think that we have the answers to all of the perplexing problems of life, instead of trying to tell others why they are going through such suffering we need to read the book of Job.

We all can usually understand and accept the justice of deserved suffering as a consequence of sin and one getting what he or she deserves. It's the undeserved suffering that troubles us.   As we get older and realize more and more the futility of trying to understand why bad things happen to good people and good things happen to bad people, we realize more and more that this is one of the mysteries of life that we are never going to fully understand.

"To me, who am less than the least of all the saints, this grace was given, that I should preach among the Gentiles the unsearchable riches of Christ."
Ephesians 3:8

When we are knocking ourselves out trying to do good and find our selves getting knocked down, we can find solace and comfort through reading the book of Job, by and believing that God is always working in our lives for our good, and to conform us into the image of Christ.

In James, we find perhaps the best explanation of the lesson to be learned through Job – perseverance in faith, no matter what.

When we echo the questions of Job, we come closer to understanding the meaning of the mystery of God. We can take comfort in knowing that one of these days, all things shall be revealed.

Father, thank you for comfort and encouragement we find in the book of Job. Amen

Taking it to the Lord...

How can I apply this truth?____

____

Father, I've come to worship and praise you! You are my:___________________________

____

I give you all Glory, Honor, and Praise O Lord!

Father, I am sorry that I have sinned by:_______________________________________

Help me to repent. Cleanse me, strengthen me, restore me.

Father, THANK YOU for all your love, grace, mercy and blessings of life that you continually shower down upon me. Thank you especially for:

1.____________________________   2.____________________________
3.____________________________   4.____________________________
5.____________________________   6.____________________________

THANK YOU for answered prayers:_____________________________________

Father, I need:____

Father, I ask that YOU:____

____

____

Lord, bless me that I may be a blessing. Give me Your heart for loving and serving others. Keep Your hand upon me. Keep me from all evil and harm, and let me cause harm to no one. Bind Satan that he have no power over me. All this I pray in subjection to your will and in the strong name of my Lord and Savior, Jesus Christ. Amen

Who Can You Depend On?

"Depend on it: God keeps his word even when the whole world is lying through its teeth." Romans 3:3 MSG

Dependability is one of the greatest virtues of character anyone can have. Whether as an individual, employer, team member, or soldier, having people you can depend on is one of the greatest blessings of life.

> *"Those who trust in GOD are like Zion Mountain: Nothing can move it, a rock-solid mountain you can always depend on."*
> *Psalm 125:1 MSG*

The bigger the business, the greater the need for dependable people. Even self-employed and self-sufficient people at times find they need someone on whom they can depend.

If an emergency or misfortune should strike today, who could you depend on to drop everything and help. Among my greatest treasures, is the handful of people I know that I can depend on no matter what!

A reputation for being on time for an appointment, meeting, or work; for doing what you promise when you promise to do it, for fulfilling your commitments to spouses, family and friends are all linked to dependability.

Jesus knew a lot about dependability. His disciples carried to their grave the sadness that they didn't stay awake while He prayed, that they disappeared when the going got rough.

It is an all too unfortunate fact of this life that many people you depend on are going to disappoint you. Perhaps the greatest fact of eternal life in Christ is that when we enter into a relationship with someone in whom we can depend totally and without reservation.

> *"I work very hard at this, as I depend on Christ's mighty power that works within me."*
> *Colossians 1:29*

You can trust in other people, in possessions, looks, and your own abilities all you want, but without trust in the Lord and His promises that are ours in Christ, there is coming a time when He is all we have to depend on.

Father, thank you for the realization that I am totally dependent upon You for every breath I take, every day I live. Keep me ever mindful that You are faithful and dependable. Amen

Taking it to the Lord...

How can I apply this truth?____
____
____

Father, I've come to worship and praise you! You are my:___________________________
____
I give you all Glory, Honor, and Praise O Lord!

Father, I am sorry that I have sinned by:____
Help me to repent. Cleanse me, strengthen me, restore me.

Father, THANK YOU for all your love, grace, mercy and blessings of life that you continually shower down upon me. Thank you especially for:

1.___________________________________   2.___________________________________
3.___________________________________   4.___________________________________
5.___________________________________   6.___________________________________

THANK YOU for answered prayers:____
Father, I need:____
Father, I ask that YOU:____
____
____
____

Lord, bless me that I may be a blessing. Give me Your heart for loving and serving others. Keep Your hand upon me. Keep me from all evil and harm, and let me cause harm to no one. Bind Satan that he have no power over me. All this I pray in subjection to your will and in the strong name of my Lord and Savior, Jesus Christ. Amen.

Unfailing Love

"In your unfailing love, you will lead the people you have redeemed. In your strength you will guide them to your holy dwelling." Ex 15:13 (NIV)

Failure is one of the most feared and yet one of the most common experiences in our human experience. From grades in school to grades in life, no one consciously seeks to fail. We struggle through failed relationships, failed marriages, financial failures, failing health, and failed parenting. One of the biggest roadblocks to success in these areas is the fear of failure.

> *"Turn, O LORD, and deliver me;*
> *save me because of your unfailing love."*
> *Psalm 6:4 (NIV)*

Like the unfaithful steward who buried his talent in the ground for fear of failure, or the unfaithful children of Israel who wandered in the desert for 40 years because of their fear of failure in occupying the land that God had promised them, we often pass up so many opportunities to give and receive blessings to others because of our fear of failure.

When people, plans, and our own efforts fail us, we can find great comfort in knowing that God's love for us is unfailing.

> *"Through the LORD's mercies we are not consumed, Because His compassions fail not.*
> *They are new every morning; Great is Your faithfulness."*
> *Lamentations 3:22,23*

He is there in the midst of our failures to comfort us, to strengthen us, and to reassure us that He is with us always, that He will never fail, leave or forsake us!

Father, I fail you so often, and I am so sorry for these failures that happen in spite of my best intentions. Thank you for your forgiveness and your unfailing love that anchors my faith in you. Amen

Taking it to the Lord...

How can I apply this truth?____

____

Father, I've come to worship and praise you! You are my:____________________________________

____

I give you all Glory, Honor, and Praise O Lord!

Father, I am sorry that I have sinned by:____

Help me to repent. Cleanse me, strengthen me, restore me.

Father, THANK YOU for all your love, grace, mercy and blessings of life that you continually shower down upon me. Thank you especially for:

1.______________________________________   2.______________________________________
3.______________________________________   4.______________________________________
5.______________________________________   6.______________________________________

THANK YOU for answered prayers:____

Father, I need:____

Father, I ask that YOU:____

____

____

Lord, bless me that I may be a blessing. Give me Your heart for loving and serving others. Keep Your hand upon me. Keep me from all evil and harm, and let me cause harm to no one. Bind Satan that he have no power over me. All this I pray in subjection to your will and in the strong name of my Lord and Savior, Jesus Christ. Amen.

Taking Care of Business

"Why did you seek Me? Did you not know that I must be about My Father's business? Luke 2:49

Distraction is one of the favorite darts of the evil one. If he can get us as individuals or as a body of believers distracted, he can win another battle in the war that he has already lost.

> *"All goes well for those who are generous, who lend freely and conduct their business fairly."*
> *Psalm 112:5 NLT*

When any business loses focus on its market and purpose, it is going to have major problems.

All of the energy spent by a church in pursuing agendas other than that for which they were created is energy that drains the church of its ability to be true to its calling.

All of the energy spent by a pastor in draining the swamps of division and pursuing agendas of men instead of the purposes of God distracts and sometimes even destroys his ability to be true to his calling.

Our lives abound with distractions as we go about trying to make a living, raise a family, and survive in a sin sick world. We can become so filled with the cares of this world and in seeking the treasures and pleasures of the world that we can easily get our priorities mixed up.

What did Jesus mean when He said "do business until I come'?

> *"He said, 'That's what I mean: Risk your life and get more than you ever dreamed of. Play it safe and end up holding the bag."*
> *Luke 19:26 MSG*

Only when we realize that God created good works for us to do even before we were born can we begin to understand the fact that we were given our lives for God's pleasure and glory – not ours – and that we need to get serious about "taking care of God's business".

After the wood, hay, and straw is burned away, will there be anything left as evidence that we have been about our Father's business?

Father, by the power of Your Holy Spirit, enable me to do those things in life that are pleasing to you and that I will hear your "well done!" when I see you face to face in heaven. Amen

Taking it to the Lord...

How can I apply this truth?____

____

____

Father, I've come to worship and praise you! You are my:____________________

____

I give you all Glory, Honor, and Praise O Lord!

Father, I am sorry that I have sinned by:_________________________________

Help me to repent. Cleanse me, strengthen me, restore me.

Father, THANK YOU for all your love, grace, mercy and blessings of life that you continually shower down upon me. Thank you especially for:

1.____________________________   2.____________________________

3.____________________________   4.____________________________

5.____________________________   6.____________________________

THANK YOU for answered prayers:_____________________________________

Father, I need:____

Father, I ask that YOU:____

____

____

____

Lord, bless me that I may be a blessing. Give me Your heart for loving and serving others. Keep Your hand upon me. Keep me from all evil and harm, and let me cause harm to no one. Bind Satan that he have no power over me. All this I pray in subjection to your will and in the strong name of my Lord and Savior, Jesus Christ. Amen.

Priming the Pump

"He who believes in Me, as the Scripture has said, out of his heart will flow rivers of living water." John 7:38

Only one who has ever experienced the frustration of a pump losing its prime can really appreciate this illustration. Simply put, pumps work on a vacuum principle and if air gets in the line they lose their prime and do not work. When a pump is first installed, it is primed by filling with the liquid being pumped and "bleeding" any air pockets so that there is an uninterrupted flow.

> *"Therefore with joy you will draw water from the wells of salvation."*
> *Isaiah 12:3*

When it comes to receiving God's wonderful gift of salvation, the Holy Spirit primes the pump of Living Water by convicting us of our sinfulness and our need for a Savior. We get our lifeline purged by the blood of Jesus and become alive in Him.

Just as it only takes a spark to get a fire going, when we experience God's love, we want to pass it on by being instruments for "priming the pump for others" through sharing the Good News.

God's pump is self-sealing with a double lifetime warranty guaranteeing our inheritance of eternal life. When the air pockets of sin and disobedience try to shut down our system, our guarantor convicts us and works forgiveness and repentance in our hearts when we confess.

> *"But whoever drinks of the water that I shall give him will never thirst. But the water that I shall give him will become in him a fountain of water springing up into everlasting life."*
> *John 4:14*

The priming principal has many other applications for growing into the fullness of Christ. We "prime the pump" of God's relational and financial blessings by initiating love to others and love to God through our giving.

God will often use us to "prime the pump" or "fan the fire" of faith by being sermons in shoes and letting the light of God's love flow through us.

May we all be "pump primers" for Christ by the examples we set and the lives we lead!

Father, by the power of Your Spirit, let your streams of living water flow through me and into the lives of others. Amen

Taking it to the Lord...

How can I apply this truth?____

____

____

Father, I've come to worship and praise you! You are my:_______________________

____

I give you all Glory, Honor, and Praise O Lord!

Father, I am sorry that I have sinned by:_________________________________

Help me to repent. Cleanse me, strengthen me, restore me.

Father, THANK YOU for all your love, grace, mercy and blessings of life that you continually shower down upon me. Thank you especially for:

1.______________________________   2.______________________________

3.______________________________   4.______________________________

5.______________________________   6.______________________________

THANK YOU for answered prayers:_________________________________

Father, I need:____

Father, I ask that YOU:____

____

____

Lord, bless me that I may be a blessing. Give me Your heart for loving and serving others. Keep Your hand upon me. Keep me from all evil and harm, and let me cause harm to no one. Bind Satan that he have no power over me. All this I pray in subjection to your will and in the strong name of my Lord and Savior, Jesus Christ. Amen.

Beware of the Undertow!

"You therefore, beloved, since you know this beforehand, beware lest you also fall from your own steadfastness, being led away with the error of the wicked;" 2 Peter 3:17

From the beginning, there has been a red tide of disobedience and rebellion. Satan, who is out to destroy us, began his temptation to disobedience by asking Eve if God really said what He said about eating the fruit of the tree of life.

> *"Keep me from lying to myself; give me the privilege of knowing your law."*
> *Psalm 119:29 NLT*

All of mankind got caught up in the undertow of this disobedience and washed away in the tide of sin that was brought into the world.

Today, as God pours out wave after wave of His love, grace, and mercy, Satan is surfing right along creating an undertow of disobedience and destruction through His agents that He has planted within Christ's Church to create doubt, division, and disobedience.

Scripture is being reinterpreted and even ignored as a means of trying to undermine God's authority as clearly expressed in Scripture, and casting doubt on whether God's abominations and clear definition of sins are really sins. What a tragedy that the greatest enemies of Christ have infiltrated His Church and are wreaking such havoc in His name.

We should not be surprised by this. Scripture after scripture warns about the false prophets and wolves in sheep's clothing. They are alive and well and apparently growing stronger day by day, denomination by denomination.

> *"They will cleverly teach their destructive heresies about God and even turn against their Master who bought them."*
> *2 Peter 2:1b NLT*

Matthew says that we will know them by their fruits. Today, more than ever, we need to be fruit inspectors and be filled with wisdom and spiritual discernment in order to avoid being pulled down by the undertow. We need to heed God's admonishment that we who think we stand "take heed lest we fall."

Father, let me not be deceived by relative truth, or that you don't really mean what you say. Amen

Taking it to the Lord...

How can I apply this truth?____

____

____

Father, I've come to worship and praise you! You are my:_______________________

____

I give you all Glory, Honor, and Praise O Lord!

Father, I am sorry that I have sinned by:_______________________________________

Help me to repent. Cleanse me, strengthen me, restore me.

Father, THANK YOU for all your love, grace, mercy and blessings of life that you continually shower down upon me. Thank you especially for:

1.___________________________   2.___________________________

3.___________________________   4.___________________________

5.___________________________   6.___________________________

THANK YOU for answered prayers:____

Father, I need:____

Father, I ask that YOU:____

____

____

____

Lord, bless me that I may be a blessing. Give me Your heart for loving and serving others. Keep Your hand upon me. Keep me from all evil and harm, and let me cause harm to no one. Bind Satan that he have no power over me. All this I pray in subjection to your will and in the strong name of my Lord and Savior, Jesus Christ. Amen.

Unchanging Love

"Remember your leaders, who spoke the word of God to you. Consider the outcome of their way of life and imitate their faith. Jesus Christ is the same yesterday, today, and forever". Hebrews 13:7, 8

Change is constant. Day by day, year-by-year, generation-by-generation, we see changes all about us. Credit cards and the Internet have changed the way we live and do business.

Advances in medical knowledge and technologies have made miracles commonplace. Declines in moral values and standards of conduct give cause for weeping and sorrow.

Many long for the "good old days" because we all have a tendency to remember the

> **"Forever, O LORD, Your word is settled in heaven."**
> **Psalm 119:89**

good and forget the bad. The truth is that sin has infected every generation and has always been and will always be a condition of the world until the kingdom of God is reestablished or until we go to our heavenly home of sinless perfection.

> **"That by two immutable things, in which it is impossible for God to lie, we might have strong consolation, who have fled for refuge to lay hold of the hope set before us."**
> **Hebrews 6:18**

What a joy to know that we have the unchanging love of God through faith in Jesus Christ. With disappointments, sorrow, and sin all around us, with the "unholy trinity" of the flesh, the world, and the devil constantly seeking to devour us, how good it is to "anchor deep" in the blessed assurances of an unchanging God, who cannot lie.

Father, daily we see signs of man's inhumanity to man and the depravity of a sin sick world. Thank you for the security of your unchanging love and the faith to know that you are in control, and that your promises stand forever. Amen

Taking it to the Lord...

How can I apply this truth?____

____

____

Father, I've come to worship and praise you! You are my:___________________________

____

I give you all Glory, Honor, and Praise O Lord!

Father, I am sorry that I have sinned by:____

Help me to repent. Cleanse me, strengthen me, restore me.

Father, THANK YOU for all your love, grace, mercy and blessings of life that you continually shower down upon me. Thank you especially for:

1.___________________________________   2.___________________________________

3.___________________________________   4.___________________________________

5.___________________________________   6.___________________________________

THANK YOU for answered prayers:____

Father, I need:____

Father, I ask that YOU:____

____

____

Lord, bless me that I may be a blessing. Give me Your heart for loving and serving others. Keep Your hand upon me. Keep me from all evil and harm, and let me cause harm to no one. Bind Satan that he have no power over me. All this I pray in subjection to your will and in the strong name of my Lord and Savior, Jesus Christ. Amen.

Are You Fit?

"Prove by the way you live that you have really turned from your sins and turned to God." Matthew 3:8 NLT

"Happy are those who are strong in the LORD, who set their minds on a pilgrimage to Jerusalem." Psalm 84:5 NLT

After the call to salvation comes is the call to sanctification. Simply put, this is the call to "walking the walk" after "talking the talk". We confess Jesus Christ as Lord to get there, and we exercise the discipline of believers to grow there.

Our life long pilgrimage is a day by day, year by year walk with Jesus, not only the Author, but also the Perfecter of our faith.

As we come to faith through the milk of the Word, we grow and are sustained by the meat of the Word and spiritual exercise.

Spiritual exercise is the discipline of growing in the knowledge of God through growing in our knowledge of Christ......Who He Was and Is...Why He came and comes......what He did and does....and How He calls and reveals Himself to us.

He speaks to us through His written and preached Word, through prayer, circumstances, and the wise counsel of fellow believers. He continually inspects, corrects, and perfects us through the power of the Holy Spirit living within us.

"Physical exercise has some value, but spiritual exercise is much more important, for it promises a reward in both this life and the next." 1 Timothy 4:8 NLT

Our transformation begins our life long conformation into the likeness of Christ. The more we cooperate with this process through spiritual exercise and discipline, the less chastening and disciplining God will have to do to accomplish this.

At the bare minimum, we should devote more time to Spiritual exercise than we do to physical. As St. Paul says, the rewards are great in this life and in the next.

Father, by the power of Your Spirit, help me to make Spiritual Fitness a top priority in my life. Amen

Taking it to the Lord...

How can I apply this truth?____

____

____

Father, I've come to worship and praise you! You are my:_____________________

____

I give you all Glory, Honor, and Praise O Lord!

Father, I am sorry that I have sinned by:__________________________________

Help me to repent. Cleanse me, strengthen me, restore me.

Father, THANK YOU for all your love, grace, mercy and blessings of life that you continually shower down upon me. Thank you especially for:

1.___________________________   2.___________________________
3.___________________________   4.___________________________
5.___________________________   6.___________________________

THANK YOU for answered prayers:_______________________________________

Father, I need:____

Father, I ask that YOU:____

____

____

Lord, bless me that I may be a blessing. Give me Your heart for loving and serving others. Keep Your hand upon me. Keep me from all evil and harm, and let me cause harm to no one. Bind Satan that he have no power over me. All this I pray in subjection to your will and in the strong name of my Lord and Savior, Jesus Christ. Amen.

Happy Are Those Who Hunger and Thirst

"Blessed are those who hunger and thirst for righteousness, for they shall be filled." Matthew 5:6

We have been given an appetite for food and water so that our bodies might be sustained and nourished. Without food and water, we perish.

> *"O God, You are my God;*
> *early will I seek You;*
> *my soul thirsts for You;*
> *my flesh longs for You."*
> *Psalm 63:1*

When we experience a new birth in Christ, we are given an appetite for the true Bread of Life and living water for our souls. To hunger and thirst for more and more of Christ is the work of sanctification (or making us more holy and Christ-like) that the Holy Spirit works in us.

Our hunger and thirst for righteousness fills us with the joy of our salvation, when we receive Jesus Christ as our Savior. Once we have received salvation, the Holy Spirit who has come to live within us fills us with the hunger and thirst to be more like Christ and to lead a life pleasing to God. We need the sustenance of the Word and the power of the Holy Spirit to accomplish this.

In the flesh, we hunger and thirst after many other things, which we think important and necessary. We hunger for material treasures, for the applause of others, for anything that we think will fill us with happiness. The trouble is, that when we seek happiness and fulfillment in these things at the expense of seeking the righteousness of Christ, we are going to be disappointed.

> *"Whoever drinks of this water will thirst again, but whoever drinks of the water that I shall give him will never thirst. But the water that I shall give him will become in him a fountain of water springing up into everlasting life."*
> *John 4:13*

Love is the only thing that never fails. When we are filled with the Love of God in Christ Jesus we are truly filled.

Father, by the power of Your Spirit, instill the fervent desire to know You through the Son that You have sent, so that I may be continually filled. Amen

Taking it to the Lord...

How can I apply this truth?____

____

____

Father, I've come to worship and praise you! You are my:_________________________________

____

I give you all Glory, Honor, and Praise O Lord!

Father, I am sorry that I have sinned by:____

Help me to repent. Cleanse me, strengthen me, restore me.

Father, THANK YOU for all your love, grace, mercy and blessings of life that you continually shower down upon me. Thank you especially for:

1.__________________________________ 2.__________________________________

3.__________________________________ 4.__________________________________

5.__________________________________ 6.__________________________________

THANK YOU for answered prayers:____

Father, I need:____

Father, I ask that YOU:____

____

____

Lord, bless me that I may be a blessing. Give me Your heart for loving and serving others. Keep Your hand upon me. Keep me from all evil and harm, and let me cause harm to no one. Bind Satan that he have no power over me. All this I pray in subjection to your will and in the strong name of my Lord and Savior, Jesus Christ. Amen.

Sacrificial Love

"Through Jesus, therefore, let us continually offer to God a sacrifice of praise—the fruit of lips that confess his name. And do not forget to do good and share with others, for with such sacrifices God is pleased." Hebrews 13:15,16

No love surpasses the love of God in sacrificing His beloved son on the Cross of Calvary as payment for every sin that we have ever committed or will ever commit. While this salvation is God's free gift of love to us we must never forget that it cost God His very own son. We were bought at a tremendous price and, when we are honest with ourselves, we must admit that we can never be worthy of the price God paid; but we should at least be thankful.

> *"For You have delivered*
> *my soul from death,*
> *My eyes from tears,*
> *And my feet from falling."*
> *Psalm 116:8*

To think that we can do anything to earn what has already been earned diminishes the magnitude of the supreme sacrifice that God made for us in Christ. Rather we should accept this Amazing Grace of God that saves us with "thanksliving" expressed in lives of submission to the will of God, lives controlled by the Spirit of God, and lives worthy of our calling as sons and daughters of the Living God.

> *"But this Man, after He*
> *had offered one*
> *sacrifice for sins*
> *forever, sat down at the*
> *right hand of God."*
> *Hebrews 10:12*

In short, we don't have to do or not do anything to earn our salvation; but our Love for God because of what he has done for us should give us no choice but to offer sacrifices of thanksgiving, praise, and love to Him and others in joyful response to His perfect sacrifice.

Father, the magnitude of your sacrificial love is so great it defies my understanding. Thank you giving me enough *understanding to* want to thank you by glorifying you in the way I live my life. Amen

Taking it to the Lord...

How can I apply this truth?____

____

Father, I've come to worship and praise you! You are my:___________________

____

I give you all Glory, Honor, and Praise O Lord!

Father, I am sorry that I have sinned by:_________________________________

Help me to repent. Cleanse me, strengthen me, restore me.

Father, THANK YOU for all your love, grace, mercy and blessings of life that you continually shower down upon me. Thank you especially for:

1._____________________________________   2._____________________________________

3._____________________________________   4._____________________________________

5._____________________________________   6._____________________________________

THANK YOU for answered prayers:____

Father, I need:____

Father, I ask that YOU:____

____

____

Lord, bless me that I may be a blessing. Give me Your heart for loving and serving others. Keep Your hand upon me. Keep me from all evil and harm, and let me cause harm to no one. Bind Satan that he have no power over me. All this I pray in subjection to your will and in the strong name of my Lord and Savior, Jesus Christ. Amen.

Having and Being

"And even we Christians, although we have the Holy Spirit within us as a foretaste of future glory, also groan to be released from pain and suffering." Romans 8:23

Another legacy left us by the fall of Adam and Eve is pain and suffering. It starts with childbirth and continues throughout our lives on this earth.

"But even the best of these years are filled with pain and trouble; soon they disappear, and we are gone." Psalm 90:10b NLT

We will have physical pains through illness, disease, and injury; and emotional pain from relational conflicts and problems within families, churches, and neighborhoods.

It's not a question of if, but only when, and we need to constantly give God thanks that he has spared us so much pain and suffering, and has promised his power and his presence to see us through the pain and suffering He allows.

If no one really chooses or wants to have pain, why do so many choose to be a pain?

Why do so many choose anger, selfishness, jealousy, critical and judgmental spirits, along with self-pity and self-centeredness and become a pain to everyone around them?

Paul had his thorn in the flesh, and we have our "bees in our bonnets" that make us a pain to live with or even be around.

We can seldom control the circumstances that cause us pain, but we can always control our actions and disposition.

"For God can use sorrow in our lives to help us turn away from sin and seek salvation." 2 Corinthians 7:9 NLT

By the power of the Holy Spirit living within us, we can bear the fruit of the Spirit, and live with love, joy, peace, longsuffering, kindness, goodness, faithfulness, gentleness, and self-control.

When our hearts are filled with this fruit, we don't have room to be the "bad apples" that rob others of their joy and us of our witness.

Father, keep me ever mindful that although I may have to suffer pain, I certainly don't have to be one. Amen

Taking it to the Lord...

How can I apply this truth?____

____

____

Father, I've come to worship and praise you! You are my:_____________________

____

I give you all Glory, Honor, and Praise O Lord!

Father, I am sorry that I have sinned by:__________________________________

Help me to repent. Cleanse me, strengthen me, restore me.

Father, THANK YOU for all your love, grace, mercy and blessings of life that you continually shower down upon me. Thank you especially for:

1.______________________________ 2.______________________________

3.______________________________ 4.______________________________

5.______________________________ 6.______________________________

THANK YOU for answered prayers:____

Father, I need:____

Father, I ask that YOU:____

____

____

Lord, bless me that I may be a blessing. Give me Your heart for loving and serving others. Keep Your hand upon me. Keep me from all evil and harm, and let me cause harm to no one. Bind Satan that he have no power over me. All this I pray in subjection to your will and in the strong name of my Lord and Savior, Jesus Christ. Amen.

Like Father Like Son

"Imitate me, just as I also imitate Christ." 1 Corinthians 11:1

The influence of parents affects every area of a child's life long after they are grown and even after parents are

> *"The LORD is my strength and my shield; My heart trusted in Him, and I am helped."*
> *Psalm 28:7*

dead and buried. In addition to inherited physical traits, we seem to inherit emotional and personality traits as well. Musical talents seem to be passed on a regular basis.

For better or for worse, we all too often find ourselves growing into and becoming the kind of people our parents are or were.

Jesus made no excuses for doing only what His Father told Him to do.

Above all, He was obedient, even to willingly suffering and dying for us.

He was the perfect example of loving and honoring God, and His parents.

He had the perfect example to emulate, and He set the standard for us parents to imitate.

If children do not receive love and affirmation at home they are going to have a hard time giving love and affirmation to others. If they see parents "talking the talk" but not "walking the walk", they are going to be turned off and have a hard time knowing the joy of the Lord..

> *"Most assuredly, I say to you, the Son can do nothing of Himself, but what He sees the Father do; for whatever He does, the Son also does in like manner."*
> *John 5:19*

If they see parents divorcing and breaking commitments, they are learning that commitment doesn't mean anything. If they see parents breaking commandments, they are learning that God's commandments don't mean anything.

In considering a mate, see how they treat their parents, and what kind of parents they have. The apple doesn't fall far from the tree, so be forewarned that you will most likely be treated the way your spouse treats his or her mother or father.

When God commands us to be "imitators of Christ", He is giving good advice. He not only sent Christ to die for us, but to live for us and show us how to live, love, and forgive.

Father, thank you for giving me the perfect role model in Your Son and my Lord and Savior, Jesus Christ. Amen.

Taking it to the Lord...

How can I apply this truth?____

____

____

Father, I've come to worship and praise you! You are my:_________________________________

____

I give you all Glory, Honor, and Praise O Lord!

Father, I am sorry that I have sinned by:____

Help me to repent. Cleanse me, strengthen me, restore me.

Father, THANK YOU for all your love, grace, mercy and blessings of life that you continually shower down upon me. Thank you especially for:

1.______________________________   2.______________________________

3.______________________________   4.______________________________

5.______________________________   6.______________________________

THANK YOU for answered prayers:____

Father, I need:____

Father, I ask that YOU:____

____

____

____

Lord, bless me that I may be a blessing. Give me Your heart for loving and serving others. Keep Your hand upon me. Keep me from all evil and harm, and let me cause harm to no one. Bind Satan that he have no power over me. All this I pray in subjection to your will and in the strong name of my Lord and Savior, Jesus Christ. Amen.

24-7-365!

"In everything give thanks; for this is the will of God in Christ Jesus for you." Ephesians 5:18

When we stop and consider how totally dependent we are upon God, we should be filled with thanksgiving throughout our being 24 hours a day, seven days a week, and three hundred and sixty five days of every year.

> *"Give thanks to the God of heaven. His faithful love endures forever."*
> *Psalm 136:26 NLT*

. Every breath we take, every day we live is a gift from God. His blanket of love covers us and protects us from those things that kill not only the body, but also the soul.

God's love is like an iceberg. What we don't often see is much deeper and more meaningful than what we do see. We take so much for granted and have to lose it before we can fully appreciate it.

Giving thanks is not an option. It is a command. Giving thanks for all things means being thankful for the things that we perceive to be bad that God means for our good.

If, by the power of the Holy Spirit, we truly believe that God works all things for our good, how can we not give thanks for all things? In our own strength it is impossible to give thanks for the heartaches and disappointments that often come into our lives.

When, in obedience to God's commands we learn to give thanks regardless of the physical, emotional, or relational pain we are experiencing we are going to experience Spirit powered peace, all sustaining grace, and confident hope that is ours in Christ.

> *"And you will always give thanks for everything to God the Father in the name of our Lord Jesus Christ."*
> *Ephesians 5:20 NLT*

God has allowed us to learn from Joseph, David, the Apostle Paul, and Our Lord Jesus Christ Himself the truth about being thankful in everything.

Father, let my thanksgiving turn into my thanksliving every day of my life. Amen.

Taking it to the Lord...

How can I apply this truth?____

____

____

Father, I've come to worship and praise you! You are my:___________________

____

I give you all Glory, Honor, and Praise O Lord!

Father, I am sorry that I have sinned by:_________________________________

Help me to repent. Cleanse me, strengthen me, restore me.

Father, THANK YOU for all your love, grace, mercy and blessings of life that you continually shower down upon me. Thank you especially for:

1.______________________________   2.______________________________

3.______________________________   4.______________________________

5.______________________________   6.______________________________

THANK YOU for answered prayers:_______________________________________

Father, I need:____

Father, I ask that YOU:____

____

____

____

Lord, bless me that I may be a blessing. Give me Your heart for loving and serving others. Keep Your hand upon me. Keep me from all evil and harm, and let me cause harm to no one. Bind Satan that he have no power over me. All this I pray in subjection to your will and in the strong name of my Lord and Savior, Jesus Christ. Amen.

No Democrats in Heaven!

"All that I know now is partial and incomplete, but then I will know everything completely, just as God knows me now." 1 Corinthians 13:12b NLT

Before any republicans start dancing for joy, we should remind them that there will not be any republicans there either. There will be no politics in heaven! Doesn't that just make you long to go there?

"I—yes, I alone—am the one who blots out your sins for my own sake and will never think of them again." Isaiah 43:25 NLT

While it is true that God says that all authorities are given by Him, it seems that the forces of evil are also given authority through the permissive will of God and we see this evil in the world all around us.

Satan promised all of the authority over the world kingdoms that were his if Jesus would bow down and worship him. He continues to offer fame, fortune, and the pleasures of this world to those who will sell their souls to him.

The politics of the world today are too often sad reminders of the forces of the world and the flesh that are undermining society and trying to wipe out the worship of God.

The politics of personal character assassination, misleading and downright untrue rhetoric, hidden agendas, and ulterior motives are all around.

Politics in the Church surely bring tears to the eyes of the One Who died to establish it. When the agenda's are self-centered instead of Christ centered, and self-glorifying rather than God glorifying, they bring dissension, evil, shame and disgrace to the name of Christ.

"Nothing evil will be allowed to enter—no one who practices shameful idolatry and dishonesty— but only those whose names are written in the Lamb's Book of Life." Revelation 21:27 NLT

In view of all this, it's so good to know that we have a God who is sovereign, who is still in control, who has already won our war for us on the cross. No politics in the world today can separate us from the love of God that is ours through faith in Jesus Christ.

Father, thank you for your assurance that the Lion is going to lay down with the lamb, and that all who call upon your name will be elected regardless of our political affiliation. Amen

Taking it to the Lord...

How can I apply this truth?____

____

____

Father, I've come to worship and praise you! You are my:______________________

____

I give you all Glory, Honor, and Praise O Lord!

Father, I am sorry that I have sinned by:___________________________________

Help me to repent. Cleanse me, strengthen me, restore me.

Father, THANK YOU for all your love, grace, mercy and blessings of life that you continually shower down upon me. Thank you especially for:

1.______________________________   2.______________________________

3.______________________________   4.______________________________

5.______________________________   6.______________________________

THANK YOU for answered prayers:____

Father, I need:____

Father, I ask that YOU:____

____

____

Lord, bless me that I may be a blessing. Give me Your heart for loving and serving others. Keep Your hand upon me. Keep me from all evil and harm, and let me cause harm to no one. Bind Satan that he have no power over me. All this I pray in subjection to your will and in the strong name of my Lord and Savior, Jesus Christ. Amen.

"Wise as Serpents and Harmless as Doves"

"For I know this, that after my departure savage wolves will come in among you, not sparing the flock."
Acts 20:29

This probably won't come as a shock to you, but all people who belong to a church, and who profess faith in Jesus Christ are not Christians. The world came into the Church big time when zealous leaders like Constantine and some early popes and kings in their well meaning passion to evangelize decreed that all would become Christians under penalty of death whether they really believed or not.

> *"Search me, O God, and know my heart; Try me, and know my anxieties;*
> *And see if there is any wicked way in me, and lead me in the way everlasting."*
> **Psalm 139:23,24**

Latter day scribes and Pharisees are alive and well in many churches, and we know what our Lord thinks about them. Time and time again, Our Lord warns *"Beware of false prophets, who come to you in sheep's clothing, but inwardly they are ravenous wolves."(Matthew 7:15)*

We are not to be judgmental and certainly not hypocritical, but realizing that since Satan is working in the Church and in fellow believers, we need to "be wise as serpents and harmless as doves" (Matthew 10:16b). We need to daily pray for wisdom and spiritual discernment, and to always be aware that there is sin lurking from within as well as from without.

> *"For false Christs and false prophets will rise and show signs and wonders to deceive, if possible, even the elect."* **Mark 13:22**

It is especially important to know Scripture and what God says so that we can "test the spirits". If we don't anchor deep into God's Word and know where we stand, we can easily fall for any good sounding philosophy or idea that is a perversion of God's truth.

Father, let me grow in your Word so that I might grow in spiritual discernment to separate the genuine from the counterfeit. Amen

Taking it to the Lord...

How can I apply this truth?____

____

____

Father, I've come to worship and praise you! You are my:_______________________

____

I give you all Glory, Honor, and Praise O Lord!

Father, I am sorry that I have sinned by:___________________________________

Help me to repent. Cleanse me, strengthen me, restore me.

Father, THANK YOU for all your love, grace, mercy and blessings of life that you continually shower down upon me. Thank you especially for:

1.________________________________   2.________________________________
3.________________________________   4.________________________________
5.________________________________   6.________________________________

THANK YOU for answered prayers:____

Father, I need:____

Father, I ask that YOU:____

____

____

Lord, bless me that I may be a blessing. Give me Your heart for loving and serving others. Keep Your hand upon me. Keep me from all evil and harm, and let me cause harm to no one. Bind Satan that he have no power over me. All this I pray in subjection to your will and in the strong name of my Lord and Savior, Jesus Christ. Amen.

Burger King Religion

"There is a way that seems right to a man, but its end is the way of death." Proverbs 16:25

We are into our 2nd fast food generation. Instant gratification is at practically every interstate exit, and certainly in any town or city of any size at all. We have McDonalds, Wendy's, Taco Bell, etc. satisfying the cravings of our tummies almost instantly. One of Burger King's most successful advertising campaigns has been "Have it your way"!

> *"Every way of a man is right in his own eyes, But the LORD weighs the hearts."*
> *Proverbs 21:2*

Unfortunately, this has become the biggest appeal of the only religion still taught in our schools and secular circles. It's called secular humanism, which teaches there is no such thing as sin, that we are in control of our lives and destiny, that man is basically good, that all truth is relative, that this life is all there is, and that "if it feels good, do it!"

We can't "have it our way" without getting God out of the way, so He is mocked, ridiculed, dismissed, and banned.

Even among many Christians, we have a tendency to "pick and choose" which parts of God's Word we will believe and which "suggestions" we will obey. As Satan tempted Eve by saying God didn't really say that, he tempts us today by saying that God didn't really mean that.

God's Word says: "For we do not wrestle against flesh and blood, but against principalities, against powers, against the rulers of the darkness of this age, against spiritual hosts of wickedness in the heavenly places" (Ephesians 6:12). The battle going on for the souls of men many times seems to be going against God and in favor of these forces of evil. Fortunately, we have the death and resurrection of Jesus Christ from the dead as proof that the war has been won for those who believe and choose to "have it God's way"!

> *"And yet I show you a more excellent way."*
> *1 Corinthians 12:31b*

Father, by the power of your Spirit living within me, help me to get over my self centered desire to have everything my way, and to concentrate on living and loving your way. Amen

Taking it to the Lord...

How can I apply this truth?____

____

Father, I've come to worship and praise you! You are my:___________________________

____

I give you all Glory, Honor, and Praise O Lord!

Father, I am sorry that I have sinned by:____

Help me to repent. Cleanse me, strengthen me, restore me.

Father, THANK YOU for all your love, grace, mercy and blessings of life that you continually shower down upon me. Thank you especially for:

1.__________________________________   2.__________________________________

3.__________________________________   4.__________________________________

5.__________________________________   6.__________________________________

THANK YOU for answered prayers:____

Father, I need:____

Father, I ask that YOU:____

____

____

Lord, bless me that I may be a blessing. Give me Your heart for loving and serving others. Keep Your hand upon me. Keep me from all evil and harm, and let me cause harm to no one. Bind Satan that he have no power over me. All this I pray in subjection to your will and in the strong name of my Lord and Savior, Jesus Christ. Amen.

Don't Leave Home Without It!

"Put on the whole armor of God, that you may be able to stand against the wiles of the devil." Ephesians 6:11

The minefields of sin are all around us. They explode into our lives from every direction. Whether tripped by anger, pride, rebellion, envy, jealousy, gossip, unforgiveness, sexual immorality, or some other evil, they happen. The question is not if they come, but when they come, how do we respond.

> *"For You have been my defense And refuge in the day of my trouble."*
> *Psalm 59:16b*

God, in His mercy, has provided us with a defense from such explosions. He has given us a belt of truth, a breastplate of righteousness, sandals of gospel power, a helmet of salvation, shield of faith, and the sword of the Spirit.

He has promised that no temptation will be given without a means of an escape route. He has determined that sin will no longer have dominion over us. When we walk in the Christ centered power of the Spirit there is nothing that Satan or any of his agents can do to penetrate the armor God has provided.

> *"For your obedience has become known to all. Therefore I am glad on your behalf; but I want you to be wise in what is good, and simple concerning evil. And the God of peace will crush Satan under your feet shortly."*
> *Romans 16:19,20*

This armor doesn't do a bit of good stored in the closet, or just worn on Sundays. We need to put it on every day just as we need to die daily to sin and become alive in Christ through confession and repentance.

God has also cleared a path through the minefields of life. It's called the pathway of obedience. With the Holy Spirit as our personal guide, we are guaranteed a safe passage!

Father, keep me safe from the minefields of sin by the power of the Holy Spirit. Amen

Taking it to the Lord...

How can I apply this truth?____

____

Father, I've come to worship and praise you! You are my:_________________________

____

I give you all Glory, Honor, and Praise O Lord!

Father, I am sorry that I have sinned by:______________________________________

Help me to repent. Cleanse me, strengthen me, restore me.

Father, THANK YOU for all your love, grace, mercy and blessings of life that you continually shower down upon me. Thank you especially for:

1.__________________________________   2.__________________________________

3.__________________________________   4.__________________________________

5.__________________________________   6.__________________________________

THANK YOU for answered prayers:____

Father, I need:____

Father, I ask that YOU:____

____

____

Lord, bless me that I may be a blessing. Give me Your heart for loving and serving others. Keep Your hand upon me. Keep me from all evil and harm, and let me cause harm to no one. Bind Satan that he have no power over me. All this I pray in subjection to your will and in the strong name of my Lord and Savior, Jesus Christ. Amen.

The Stewardship of Life

"We must all appear before the judgment seat of Christ ..." (2 Corinthians 5:10)

The parable of the mina is a sobering reminder that we are going to be held accountable for our use of the life God has given us for the good works for which "God created beforehand that we should walk in them" Ephesians 2:2b.

> *"My eyes shall be on the faithful of the land, That they may dwell with me."*
> *Psalm 101:3*

When Christ returns and we stand before Him at the "resurrection of the just", what is going to remain after the "wood hay and stubble" of our lives has been burned away? Will God be able to say "well done, good and faithful servant"?

We must never confuse our salvation, which is the gift of God and "not of works lest any man should boast" with the account we are going to give of our lives in heaven at the judgment seat of Christ.

For those who love God and respond to His love by loving Him and wanting to live for Him, what greater joy could there be than receiving our Lord's "well done"?

> *"So he called ten of his servants, delivered to them ten minas, and said to them, 'Do business till I come."*
> *Luke 19:13*

Whether the good works for which we were created is in obeying the great commandment or great commission, or in bringing up our children in the fear and admonition of the Lord, we should always be mindful that every thing we have, every breath we take comes from God and we will be held accountable for the stewardship of the lives we have been given.

Father, by the Power of the Holy Spirit, help me to be about Fulfilling the purposes for which you created me. Amen

Taking it to the Lord...

How can I apply this truth?____

____

____

Father, I've come to worship and praise you! You are my:____________________

____

I give you all Glory, Honor, and Praise O Lord!

Father, I am sorry that I have sinned by:___________________________________

Help me to repent. Cleanse me, strengthen me, restore me.

Father, THANK YOU for all your love, grace, mercy and blessings of life that you continually shower down upon me. Thank you especially for:

1.___________________________   2.___________________________

3.___________________________   4.___________________________

5.___________________________   6.___________________________

THANK YOU for answered prayers:___________________________________

Father, I need:____

Father, I ask that YOU:____

____

____

Lord, bless me that I may be a blessing. Give me Your heart for loving and serving others. Keep Your hand upon me. Keep me from all evil and harm, and let me cause harm to no one. Bind Satan that he have no power over me. All this I pray in subjection to your will and in the strong name of my Lord and Savior, Jesus Christ. Amen.

Batten Down the Hatches

"Since he himself has gone through suffering and temptation, he is able to help us when we are being tempted." Hebrews 2:18 NLT

When the seas got rough, closing the cargo hatches to keep waters from roaring in and flooding, and making sure all the cargo is tied down was a must for survival.

> *"Let them continually say, "Great is the LORD, who enjoys helping his servant." Psalm 35:27 NLT*

It's now a matter of if, but only a matter of when the storms of life come, how do we "batten down the hatches"?

Just as the permissive will of God allows the free will to reject His offer of salvation, it also allows the sin of the world to manifest itself in our lives, our families, and our churches.

God will also use the storms of life to test, inspect, correct, and perfect us. God's course in character development is taught in the Bible and in the life of Jesus Christ. The laboratory is our homes, schools, work places, and churches.

We prepare for the tests by doing our homework and anchoring our faith deep in God's Word. We learn to know what we stand for so that we will know what not to fall for.

It's only when we know what Jesus did that we can know what He would do in our situation. He knew and quoted scripture, He prayed, He fasted, He submitted to the will of His father and was obedient even to death.

> *"So be truly glad! There is wonderful joy ahead, even though it is necessary for you to endure many trials for a while." 1 Peter 1:6 NLT*

We should never be surprised or disgruntled when we are called to walk through a storm. We have the Good Shepherd leading us, the Holy Spirit giving us power from on high, and the promises of the God Who cannot lie to sustain and strengthen us.

Because of the grace of God, we should never be tossed about by conflict and doubt. God has provided us with His armor. We best learn how to use it before the next emergency.

Father, keep me prepared and empowered to sail through the storms of life. Amen

Taking it to the Lord...

How can I apply this truth?____

____

Father, I've come to worship and praise you! You are my:_________________________

____

I give you all Glory, Honor, and Praise O Lord!

Father, I am sorry that I have sinned by:____

Help me to repent. Cleanse me, strengthen me, restore me.

Father, THANK YOU for all your love, grace, mercy and blessings of life that you continually shower down upon me. Thank you especially for:

1.__________________________________   2.__________________________________
3.__________________________________   4.__________________________________
5.__________________________________   6.__________________________________

THANK YOU for answered prayers:____

Father, I need:____

Father, I ask that YOU:____

____

____

Lord, bless me that I may be a blessing. Give me Your heart for loving and serving others. Keep Your hand upon me. Keep me from all evil and harm, and let me cause harm to no one. Bind Satan that he have no power over me. All this I pray in subjection to your will and in the strong name of my Lord and Savior, Jesus Christ. Amen.

Abiding Gives Us Jesus' Joy

"These things I have spoken to you, that My joy may remain in you, and that your joy may be full." John 15:9

Is the joy of the Lord your peace? Are you filled to overflowing with the joy of your salvation, which was won for you on the cross of Calvary? Have you surveyed the wondrous cross?

"But let all those rejoice who put their trust in You; Let them ever shout for joy." Psalm 5:11

One of the greatest gifts to all believers is the gift of joy. As we abide in Christ more, our joy becomes overwhelming. We can rejoice in our trials knowing that God works all things for our good.

When we come into the fullness of Christ's joy, we become contagious Christians, through whom the joy of the Lord shines through to others.

Best of all, with the joy comes that priceless peace that surpasses all understanding. We know that we are unconditionally loved forever forgiven and covered with the righteousness of Christ.

"But none of these things move me; nor do I count my life dear to myself, so that I may finish my race with joy," Acts 20:24

We become "strengthened with all might, according to His glorious power, for all patience and longsuffering with joy;" Colossians 1:11

This peace is the treasure of our being. When we abide to the extent that the mystery that "Christ in us is our hope of glory" (Colossians 1:27) is not longer a mystery but a reality in our hearts. The fullness of Christ's joy becomes our joy and we will never be the same.

Lord, thank you for my joy. May it ever increase as I grow into your fullness. Amen

Taking it to the Lord...

How can I apply this truth?____

____

____

Father, I've come to worship and praise you! You are my:_______________________

____

I give you all Glory, Honor, and Praise O Lord!

Father, I am sorry that I have sinned by:_____________________________________

Help me to repent. Cleanse me, strengthen me, restore me.

Father, THANK YOU for all your love, grace, mercy and blessings of life that you continually shower down upon me. Thank you especially for:

1._________________________________   2._________________________________

3._________________________________   4._________________________________

5._________________________________   6._________________________________

THANK YOU for answered prayers:____

Father, I need:____

Father, I ask that YOU:____

____

____

Lord, bless me that I may be a blessing. Give me Your heart for loving and serving others. Keep Your hand upon me. Keep me from all evil and harm, and let me cause harm to no one. Bind Satan that he have no power over me. All this I pray in subjection to your will and in the strong name of my Lord and Savior, Jesus Christ. Amen.

Don't Give Till it Hurts!

"Will a man rob God? Yet you have robbed Me! But you say, 'In what way have we robbed You?' In tithes and offerings." Malachi 3:8

God's economy is beyond human understanding. The truth that the more we give, the more we will have runs contrary to human reasoning. God's word makes it clear that we are not to give under compulsion or grudgingly, like someone is holding a gun to our head. Instead of giving till it hurts, we need to give until it <u>feels good</u>!

"May He remember all your offerings," Psalm 20:3

If we have never experienced the joy of giving whether it be of our treasure, our time, our talents or our love we have missed one of the great joys of life. God is love, and love is a giving relationship. (God so loved the world that he <u>gave</u> His only begotten Son so that whoever believes in Him would not perish, but have eternal life") The world seems to be made up of "givers" or "takers". Takers seem never satisfied, and always wanting more and more. Givers seem to enjoy godly contentment in always having enough.

When we respond to God's love and all that He has given us, we feel good about giving Him from the abundance of our love. Whether it's money, praise, or service the grace of giving springs up from the heart in an attitude of gratitude. We can never out give God and we can never out love Him! When we realize that any abundance we have has been given so that we might be generous on every occasion we can find great joy and really feel good about giving to the Lord.

"And God is able to make all grace abound toward you, that you, always having all sufficiency in all things, may have an abundance for every good work." 2 Corinthians 9:8

We seem to hear a lot of complaints about the church always asking for money. Ever wonder about how God might feel about us always asking for blessings of every description and then having the gall to complain when He asks us for our treasure, time, or talents for the up building of His kingdom?

Father, help me to discover the joy of giving that comes only from being filled with the grace of giving. Amen

Taking it to the Lord...

How can I apply this truth?____

____

____

Father, I've come to worship and praise you! You are my:_______________________

____

I give you all Glory, Honor, and Praise O Lord!

Father, I am sorry that I have sinned by:____________________________________

Help me to repent. Cleanse me, strengthen me, restore me.

Father, THANK YOU for all your love, grace, mercy and blessings of life that you continually shower down upon me. Thank you especially for:

1.__________________________________   2.__________________________________

3.__________________________________   4.__________________________________

5.__________________________________   6.__________________________________

THANK YOU for answered prayers:____

Father, I need:____

Father, I ask that YOU:____

____

____

____

Lord, bless me that I may be a blessing. Give me Your heart for loving and serving others. Keep Your hand upon me. Keep me from all evil and harm, and let me cause harm to no one. Bind Satan that he have no power over me. All this I pray in subjection to your will and in the strong name of my Lord and Savior, Jesus Christ. Amen.

Trickle Down Love

"Tell them to go after God, who piles on all the riches we could ever manage—to do good, to be rich in helping others, to be extravagantly generous. If they do that, they'll build a treasury that will last, gaining life that is truly life." 1 Timothy 6:17 MSG

Republicans preach "trickle down economics" wherein people make money and then reinvest it to create jobs and prosperity for other people.

> *"All goes well for those who are generous, who lend freely and conduct their business fairly."*
> *Psalm 112:5 NLT*

God teaches "trickle down love" where He fills us with His love to overflowing, so that it spills out into the lives of those around us.

Just as you can't give money you don't have, you can't give away love you don't have. When we seek love in all the wrong places, we will never be happy or satisfied, and will never fill that longing for Him that God has placed in the heart of all people.

When we realize that God loves us unconditionally, forgives us for everything we have ever done or will ever do, accepts us just the way we are, and has a perfect plan for our lives, we cannot help but respond with love and thanksgiving.

God replaces "I would be happy if…into "I am happy because…" when we find the joy of the Lord by faith. When God fills our hearts to overflowing with His love, we cannot help but pass it on. When we "reinvest" this love by loving others, we impact lives and become faithful to the great commission to make disciples.

> *"And God is able to make all grace abound toward you, that you, always having all sufficiency in all things, may have an abundance for every good work."*
> *2 Corinthians 9:8*

Best of all, the fact that we cannot out give God also means that we cannot "out love" God! When we are in a right love relationship with God through abiding in His Word and seeking to imitate Christ, His stream of living water becomes an ocean in our life, and we become better witnesses and the world becomes a better place.

Father, keep me filled with your overflowing cup of blessings so that I can pass them on to others. Amen

Taking it to the Lord...

How can I apply this truth?____

____

____

Father, I've come to worship and praise you! You are my:_______________________

____

I give you all Glory, Honor, and Praise O Lord!

Father, I am sorry that I have sinned by:___________________________________

Help me to repent. Cleanse me, strengthen me, restore me.

Father, THANK YOU for all your love, grace, mercy and blessings of life that you continually shower down upon me. Thank you especially for:

1.____________________________   2.____________________________

3.____________________________   4.____________________________

5.____________________________   6.____________________________

THANK YOU for answered prayers:____

Father, I need:____

Father, I ask that YOU:____

____

____

Lord, bless me that I may be a blessing. Give me Your heart for loving and serving others. Keep Your hand upon me. Keep me from all evil and harm, and let me cause harm to no one. Bind Satan that he have no power over me. All this I pray in subjection to your will and in the strong name of my Lord and Savior, Jesus Christ. Amen.

The Place of Understanding

"But where shall wisdom be found? And where is the place of understanding?" Job 28:12

Self help books and videos have become a multi-billion dollar industry. We can learn how to win friends and influence people, how to lose weight, how to do about anything, and what to believe about everything by simply reading the books or watching the videos.

> *"Trust in the Lord with all your heart, And lean not on your own understanding." Proverbs 3:5*

The truth is that our information highway has become a super highway as the wealth of knowledge and access has never been greater in the history of the world.

This being the case, why is the world in such a mess? As secular humanism takes over in our schools, our homes, our work place, and "relative truth" becomes the prevailing standard of morality, our problems with morality, mental illness, substance abuse, and any number of other maladies seem to go from bad to worse.

Can it possibly be that we are losing the source of all true wisdom and understanding? Can it possibly be that we are losing our "fear of the Lord?' which is "the beginning of wisdom?" (Proverbs 9:10)

> *¹So let us stop going over the basics of Christianity again and again. Let us go on instead and become mature in our understanding." Hebrews 6:1*

Much like animals who lose their inbred fear of humans, we humans who lose or never acquire "the fear of the Lord" are like runaway trains going full steam ahead with no brakes headed for eternal damnation and separation from God

Father, never let unconfessed and unrepented sins overpower me and let me lose my fear and reverence of you and your will on how I should live. Let my understanding increase as my knowledge of you increases as I grow in your Word and ways. Amen

Taking it to the Lord...

How can I apply this truth?____

____

Father, I've come to worship and praise you! You are my:____________________

____

I give you all Glory, Honor, and Praise O Lord!

Father, I am sorry that I have sinned by:_________________________________

Help me to repent. Cleanse me, strengthen me, restore me.

Father, THANK YOU for all your love, grace, mercy and blessings of life that you continually shower down upon me. Thank you especially for:

1.______________________________   2.______________________________
3.______________________________   4.______________________________
5.______________________________   6.______________________________

THANK YOU for answered prayers:____

Father, I need:____

Father, I ask that YOU:____

____

____

____

Lord, bless me that I may be a blessing. Give me Your heart for loving and serving others. Keep Your hand upon me. Keep me from all evil and harm, and let me cause harm to no one. Bind Satan that he have no power over me. All this I pray in subjection to your will and in the strong name of my Lord and Savior, Jesus Christ. Amen.

Abiding Brings Friendship with God

"Your are my friends if you do what I command you. No longer do I call you servants, for a servant does not know what his master is doing; but I have called you friends, for all things that I heard from My Father I have made known to you." John 15:14,15

Do you have friendship with God? Does He diminish your sorrow and multiply your joy? Does He walk with you and talk with you through His Word and Spirit?

> *"A man who has friends must himself be friendly, but there is a friend who sticks closer than a brother."*
> *Proverbs 18:24*

Abraham was called a Friend of God because He did what God commanded. Jesus says that you are His friend if you do what He commands. To love God with all our hearts and to love others as He has loved us makes this friendship a reality in our lives.

We were created for fellowship or friendship with God. We were created in His image and given this capacity. God calls us into a close and personal relationship with Him through His Son, Who makes known to us all that He has heard from the Father.

In His grace and mercy God has restored us to righteousness in His sight, and made us joint heirs with Christ in enjoying all of the blessings of friendship and fellowship with Him.

> *"You are My friends if you do whatever I command you."*
> *John 15:14*

As we abide in Him and His Word more and more, we enjoy the incredible blessing of friendship with God more and more. The better we get to know Him, the more we love Him and appreciate the wonders of His love.

Is there any higher calling than that of being called "Friend" by our Lord and Savior? May God grant us all the incredible blessings of His friendship.

Lord, I want to be called your friend. By the power of your Spirit, help me to get to know you better and obey you fully. Amen

Taking it to the Lord...

How can I apply this truth?____
____
____

Father, I've come to worship and praise you! You are my:____________________________________
____
I give you all Glory, Honor, and Praise O Lord!

Father, I am sorry that I have sinned by:____
Help me to repent. Cleanse me, strengthen me, restore me.

Father, THANK YOU for all your love, grace, mercy and blessings of life that you continually shower down upon me. Thank you especially for:

1.___________________________________   2.___________________________________
3.___________________________________   4.___________________________________
5.___________________________________   6.___________________________________

THANK YOU for answered prayers:____
Father, I need:____
Father, I ask that YOU:____
____
____

Lord, bless me that I may be a blessing. Give me Your heart for loving and serving others. Keep Your hand upon me. Keep me from all evil and harm, and let me cause harm to no one. Bind Satan that he have no power over me. All this I pray in subjection to your will and in the strong name of my Lord and Savior, Jesus Christ. Amen.

Is God On Your Leftover List?

"But seek first the kingdom of God and His righteousness, and all these things shall be added to you. Matthew 6:33 NLT

One of my favorite things about Thanksgiving feasts is the leftover turkey for sandwiches that make dill pickles taste so good, and my wife's spectacular Turkey casseroles. Leftovers may be ok for eating, but they are not OK for God.

> *"The one thing I ask of the LORD-- the thing I seek most- - is to live in the house of the LORD all the days of my life, delighting in the LORD'S perfections."*
> *Psalm 27:4 NLT*

We seem to have a hard time remembering our Lord's command to seek first the Kingdom of God and His righteousness. In our own self centered, self-absorbed world, we have a problem with priorities, and God often ends up on the leftover list.

We will give God money, if we have any leftover. We will give Him time or talents if we have any left over after we have supplied all of our needs and wants and those of our family.

As long suffering and patient, as kind and loving as God is we dare not forget that God is a jealous God who will not tolerate playing second fiddle to anyone or anything in our affection or priorities. Even returning home to bury one's father (Luke 9:59) was not more important to God than becoming His disciple.

> *"Should people cheat God? Yet you have cheated me! "But you ask, 'What do you mean? When did we ever cheat you?'"*
> *Malachi 3:3*

God certainly didn't give us a leftover when He gave us His only begotten Son as the perfect, unblemished sin offering for us. He has never been known to tell anyone that He will bless them if He has any blessings left over.

Our God is not a stingy God for stingy people. He is more generous in love and temporal blessings of every kind than we can ever comprehend, especially to those who are generous to Him.

He belongs at the top in our hearts and in our thoughts. .

Father, forgive me for the times I have put you on my leftover list. Through the power of the Holy Spirit, help me to keep you where you belong at the top of my list. Amen

Taking it to the Lord...

How can I apply this truth?____

____

____

Father, I've come to worship and praise you! You are my:_______________________

____

I give you all Glory, Honor, and Praise O Lord!

Father, I am sorry that I have sinned by:_______________________________

Help me to repent. Cleanse me, strengthen me, restore me.

Father, THANK YOU for all your love, grace, mercy and blessings of life that you continually shower down upon me. Thank you especially for:

1.______________________________   2.______________________________

3.______________________________   4.______________________________

5.______________________________   6.______________________________

THANK YOU for answered prayers:_______________________________

Father, I need:____

Father, I ask that YOU:____

____

Lord, bless me that I may be a blessing. Give me Your heart for loving and serving others. Keep Your hand upon me. Keep me from all evil and harm, and let me cause harm to no one. Bind Satan that he have no power over me. All this I pray in subjection to your will and in the strong name of my Lord and Savior, Jesus Christ. Amen.

Allied or Mayflower?

"I assure you, even if you had faith as small as a mustard seed you could say to this mountain, 'Move from here to there,' and it would move. Nothing would be impossible." Matthew 17:20

There are movers for everything from earth to buildings, but nobody can move like God. He moved the children of Israel through the Red Sea without a scratch. He moved His presence from within the holy of holy of the temple into the hearts of all believers. He moved the Good News of the Gospel to the four corners of the World.

> *"You cried to me in trouble, and I saved you; I answered out of the thundercloud."*
> *Psalm 81:7*

God's prayer fueled moving was awesome to behold when Elisha used it to destroy the 500 prophets of Baal. Christ used it to heal the sick, give sight to the blind, to make the lame walk, and to raise the dead.

When it comes to moving mountains, Jesus reminds us that nothing is impossible for God.

Whether it is a mountain of fear or a mountain of doubt; a mountain of illness or a mountain of suffering - God specializes in moving mountains.

> *"I tell you the truth, if anyone says to this mountain, 'Go, throw yourself into the sea,' and does not doubt in his heart but believes that what he says will happen, it will be done for him."*
> *Mark 11:23 NIV*

We see the results of God's moving the hearts of men from unbelief to faith in the lives of the disciples, who went from fear to courageous witnessing and martyrdom without a whimper. We see God's moving the heart of Saul, the persecutor, into Paul the sinner saved by grace.

The only things limiting God's power are unrepented sins, unbelief and self-will seeking instead of God's-will-seeking. He promises that whatsoever we ask in accordance with His will, will be done.

Father, give me that mountain moving faith that I might live a life fully pleasing to you and fruitful in every good work. Amen

Taking it to the Lord...

How can I apply this truth?____

____

Father, I've come to worship and praise you! You are my:_________________________________

____

I give you all Glory, Honor, and Praise O Lord!

Father, I am sorry that I have sinned by:____

Help me to repent. Cleanse me, strengthen me, restore me.

Father, THANK YOU for all your love, grace, mercy and blessings of life that you continually shower down upon me. Thank you especially for:

1.___________________________________   2.___________________________________
3.___________________________________   4.___________________________________
5.___________________________________   6.___________________________________

THANK YOU for answered prayers:____

Father, I need:____

Father, I ask that YOU:____

____

____

____

Lord, bless me that I may be a blessing. Give me Your heart for loving and serving others. Keep Your hand upon me. Keep me from all evil and harm, and let me cause harm to no one. Bind Satan that he have no power over me. All this I pray in subjection to your will and in the strong name of my Lord and Savior, Jesus Christ. Amen.

Understanding of Abundance

I have come that they may have life, and that they may have it more abundantly. John 10:10b

What constitutes the "abundant life"? For those who teach and preach the "prosperity gospel" it means material prosperity, or "health, wealth, and happiness", and that we should "give to get"!

> *"He himself shall dwell in prosperity, And his descendants shall inherit the earth."*
> *Psalm 25:13*

While there is nothing inherently wrong with any of these blessings which all come from God, "who is able to do exceedingly abundantly above all that we ask or think" (Ephesians 3:20b), these should never be misunderstood as the defining criteria of the abundant life.

The real understanding of the abundant life comes with the realization of who possesses you! When we, by faith, and in the power of the Holy Spirit, come to the realization that we are the blood bought children of the God who loved us so much that *"He gave his only begotten Son to die for us," (John 3:16b),* we give up possession and bondage by our sinful nature, and are set free to live the abundant life to which God has called us.

> *"Command those who are rich in this present age not to be haughty, nor to trust in uncertain riches but in the living God, who gives us richly all things to enjoy."*
> *1 Timothy 6:17*

We discover the true riches of God's love in Christ, the fullness of joy that comes only through a deep and abiding relationship with Him, and the realization that *"we are His workmanship, created in Christ Jesus for good works, which God prepared beforehand that we should walk in them." (Ephesians 2:10)* The abundant life consists of giving God's love to others, and in giving, receiving the peace and joy. This is the true treasure of the abundant life.

Father, let me live and enjoy the abundant life by glorifying you and being a conduit of your love to others in every area of my life. Amen

Taking it to the Lord...

How can I apply this truth?____

____

Father, I've come to worship and praise you! You are my:_________________________________

____

I give you all Glory, Honor, and Praise O Lord!

Father, I am sorry that I have sinned by:____

Help me to repent. Cleanse me, strengthen me, restore me.

Father, THANK YOU for all your love, grace, mercy and blessings of life that you continually shower down upon me. Thank you especially for:

1._______________________________   2._______________________________
3._______________________________   4._______________________________
5._______________________________   6._______________________________

THANK YOU for answered prayers:____

Father, I need:____

Father, I ask that YOU:____

____

____

Lord, bless me that I may be a blessing. Give me Your heart for loving and serving others. Keep Your hand upon me. Keep me from all evil and harm, and let me cause harm to no one. Bind Satan that he have no power over me. All this I pray in subjection to your will and in the strong name of my Lord and Savior, Jesus Christ. Amen.

Road Dirt

"How much more shall the blood of Christ, who through the eternal Spirit offered Himself without spot to God, cleanse your conscience from dead works to serve the living God?" Hebrews 9:14

In Jesus' day, walking in sandals on dirt roads was the main means of getting around. The practice of washing off the road dirt even after going to the community bath was the custom of the day. In houses with servants, the job of washing feet was given to the lowliest of servants.

> **"How can a young man cleanse his way? By taking heed according to Your word."**
> **Psalm 119:11**

We have the filth of our original sin washed away by the blood of Jesus on the Cross and through the one time washing of baptism.

Because we live in the flesh in a sinful world, we continually pick up the road dirt of sin as we walk through life. We need the daily cleansing of confession and repentance so that the Holy Spirit can continue the good work that was begun when we received Jesus Christ as our Savior and the forgiveness of our sins.

In washing the disciples feet, Jesus was showing how much He loved them. He was also teaching that there is nothing below doing for the sake of glorifying God. Most importantly he was teaching the importance of spiritual cleansing from the pollution of sin.

> **"And since I, the Lord and Teacher, have washed your feet, you ought to wash each other's feet."**
> **John 13:14 NLT**

Pride should never allow us to reject the forgiveness of God that is ours through confession and repentance. Pride should never allow us to reject the help of a brother or sister in Christ, or fail to help them.

When we see our Master serving, we learn the truth that greatness is not to be found in domineering but in serving.

Father, give me that daily washing cleanses me from the road dirt of life. Amen.

Taking it to the Lord...

How can I apply this truth?____
____
____

Father, I've come to worship and praise you! You are my:_______________
____

I give you all Glory, Honor, and Praise O Lord!

Father, I am sorry that I have sinned by:______________________________

Help me to repent. Cleanse me, strengthen me, restore me.

Father, THANK YOU for all your love, grace, mercy and blessings of life that you continually shower down upon me. Thank you especially for:

1.____________________________   2.____________________________
3.____________________________   4.____________________________
5.____________________________   6.____________________________

THANK YOU for answered prayers:_______________________________________

Father, I need:____

Father, I ask that YOU:____
____
____

Lord, bless me that I may be a blessing. Give me Your heart for loving and serving others. Keep Your hand upon me. Keep me from all evil and harm, and let me cause harm to no one. Bind Satan that he have no power over me. All this I pray in subjection to your will and in the strong name of my Lord and Savior, Jesus Christ. Amen.

Sinning Practice at 7?

"Everyone who makes a practice of doing evil, addicted to denial and illusion, hates God-light and won't come near it, fearing a painful exposure." John 3:19" MSG

A typographical error in the church bulletin that changed singing into sinning could really raise some eyebrows. If children are not taught to obey, to share, play fair, and the difference between right and wrong, they are going to grow up in the practice of sinning.   David's sons should be a warning to all that sin practice by our children should not be tolerated or encouraged.

> *"Do not incline my heart to any evil thing, to practice wicked works with men who work iniquity; and do not let me eat of their delicacies."*
> *Psalm 141:4*

Adolph Hitler did not become the evil one he became overnight. He had a lot of practice.

We all have probably gotten good at some sin by repeated practice. Whether the sin of worry, gossip, pride, jealousy, lust or forsaking the assembling of ourselves together, it can become a habit and we can become very good at it with practice.

Even when we become dead to sin and alive in Christ, old habits die hard.

Without Spirit Control over our self-control, we can easily find ourselves reverting back to the sins of the flesh, the world, or the devil.

> *"We know that those who have become part of God's family do not make a practice of sinning, for God's Son holds them securely, and the evil one cannot get his hands on them."*
> *1 John 5:18 NLT*

Thank God that in His love, He made provision for us not only for the grace to save us, but with His sustaining grace to sanctify us and make us more like Christ as we practice prayer, studying and hearing God's Word, and receiving the encouragement of fellowship with other believers.

We need to practice and become really good at showing our love for God and others. Maybe we should start having love practice with hospital and nursing home visits, in jails and prisons, at schools and workplaces. It might even be a good idea to start love practice at home with our spouses and family.

Father, help me to practice obeying more and sinning less. Amen

Taking it to the Lord...

How can I apply this truth?____
____
____

Father, I've come to worship and praise you! You are my:_________________________________
____
I give you all Glory, Honor, and Praise O Lord!

Father, I am sorry that I have sinned by:____
Help me to repent. Cleanse me, strengthen me, restore me.

Father, THANK YOU for all your love, grace, mercy and blessings of life that you continually shower down upon me. Thank you especially for:

1.____________________________________   2.____________________________________
3.____________________________________   4.____________________________________
5.____________________________________   6.____________________________________

THANK YOU for answered prayers:____
Father, I need:____
Father, I ask that YOU:____
____
____

Lord, bless me that I may be a blessing. Give me Your heart for loving and serving others. Keep Your hand upon me. Keep me from all evil and harm, and let me cause harm to no one. Bind Satan that he have no power over me. All this I pray in subjection to your will and in the strong name of my Lord and Savior, Jesus Christ. Amen.

Our Equal Opportunity God

"The Lord is not slack concerning His promise, as some count slackness, but is longsuffering toward us, not willing that any should perish but that all should come to repentance." 2 Peter 3:9

God is no respecter of persons. He pours out His love to all. He makes the sun to shine on the just and the unjust. He wants all to enter His joy and to share in the treasures of His grace.

> *"The LORD is good to everyone. He showers compassion on all his creation."*
> *Psalm 145:9 NLT*

We are all given a life and accountable for it. We will be held accountable for our stewardship of the talents and abilities that we have been given. To whom much is given, much is expected.

Some have been gifted to be chiefs. Some have been gifted to be foot soldiers. It's not a matter of what gifts we have been given, but it's all about what we have done with what we have been given. God is not nearly as pleased with sacrifices that really cost us nothing. In money, time, talents, and love, it's all about proportionality – not the amount but the proportion of what we have been given. "Praise our God, all you His servants and those who fear Him, both small and great!" (Rev 19:5)

God called all to the wedding feast. Those who were too busy, too self-absorbed, too rich, and too prideful to attend, were replaced by those who gratefully accepted the invitation.

> *"After this I saw a vast crowd, too great to count, from every nation and tribe and people and language, standing in front of the throne and before the Lamb."*
> *Revelation 7:9 NLT*

God wants us all to take advantage of the opportunities He gives us, not only in our opportunity for salvation, but also for ministry or servanthood. Here even the least gifted have the opportunity to be the greatest, and the greatest are commanded to become the least.

Are you an equal opportunity witness? Do you give everyone God sends across your path the opportunity to want to know Him through you?

Father, help me to make the most of all the opportunities you continue to provide for worship, witness, and service. Amen

Taking it to the Lord...

How can I apply this truth?____
____
____

Father, I've come to worship and praise you! You are my:_______________________________
____

I give you all Glory, Honor, and Praise O Lord!

Father, I am sorry that I have sinned by:____

Help me to repent. Cleanse me, strengthen me, restore me.

Father, THANK YOU for all your love, grace, mercy and blessings of life that you continually shower down upon me. Thank you especially for:

1._________________________________   2._________________________________
3._________________________________   4._________________________________
5._________________________________   6._________________________________

THANK YOU for answered prayers:____

Father, I need:____

Father, I ask that YOU:____
____
____
____

Lord, bless me that I may be a blessing. Give me Your heart for loving and serving others. Keep Your hand upon me. Keep me from all evil and harm, and let me cause harm to no one. Bind Satan that he have no power over me. All this I pray in subjection to your will and in the strong name of my Lord and Savior, Jesus Christ. Amen.

Amazing Love

"Although I am the least of all God's people, this grace was given to me to preach to the Gentiles the unsearchable riches of Christ." Eph 3:8

Who can fathom the Amazing love of God manifested in the life, death, and resurrection of Jesus Christ? It is beyond human understanding as to how a righteous and holy God would give up His majesty and glory to take on the nature of a servant and humble himself and become obedient even unto death so that we who believe might live forever. The grace of God that gives us what we don't deserve, the mercy of God that does not give us what we do deserve, defies reason and leaves all who claim the title of Christian pondering the depth of the riches that are ours in Christ Jesus.

> *"As for me, I will seek your face and I shall be satisfied when I awake in your likeness."*
> *Psalm 17:15*

> *"Oh, the depth of the riches both of the wisdom and knowledge of God."*
> *Romans 11:33*

This Amazing love has freed us from the bondage of sin and death and given us a new life that allows us to walk by faith and not by sight into the eternal bliss of peace with God for now and forever. That we will stand before God clothed in the righteousness of Christ and welcomed into the heavenly kingdom as joint heirs with Christ should never cease to amaze us or to make us forever thankful.

Father, the wonder of your love is too awesome for me to ever fully understand. Thank you for indwelling me with the Holy Spirit to give me all the faith I need to be secure in my love relationship with you. Amen.

Taking it to the Lord...

How can I apply this truth?____

____

Father, I've come to worship and praise you! You are my:_________________________________

____

I give you all Glory, Honor, and Praise O Lord!

Father, I am sorry that I have sinned by:____

Help me to repent. Cleanse me, strengthen me, restore me.

Father, THANK YOU for all your love, grace, mercy and blessings of life that you continually shower down upon me. Thank you especially for:

1.______________________________   2.______________________________
3.______________________________   4.______________________________
5.______________________________   6.______________________________

THANK YOU for answered prayers:____

Father, I need:____

Father, I ask that YOU:____

____

____

____

Lord, bless me that I may be a blessing. Give me Your heart for loving and serving others. Keep Your hand upon me. Keep me from all evil and harm, and let me cause harm to no one. Bind Satan that he have no power over me. All this I pray in subjection to your will and in the strong name of my Lord and Savior, Jesus Christ. Amen.

Supernatural Understanding

"And the peace of God, which surpasses all understanding, will guard your hearts and minds through Christ Jesus." Philippians 4:7

"And no one can say that Jesus is Lord except by the Holy Spirit" (1 Cor.12:3b), "For the message of the cross is foolishness to those who are perishing, but to us who are being saved it is the power of God. " (1 Cor.1:18)

> **"Such knowledge is too wonderful for me; It is high, I cannot attain it."**
> **Psalm 139:6**

Verse after verse of scripture make it abundantly clear that only the supernatural power of the Holy Spirit can affect faith in the heart of anyone. We can and should testify and be ready to "give a defense to everyone who asks you for a reason for the hope that is within you."(1 Pet. 3:15), but we need to understand that only the intervention of the Holy Spirit will work understanding in the heart of anyone who hears the good news.

It is so hard and frustrating at times, especially with those that we love, when we cannot get through to them concerning salvation and their relationship with God. Our God given free will includes the will to reject. God will not force faith on anyone.

Our prayer should be that God would get through to them and give them that supernatural understanding that they are sinners and need a Savior, and call them into a saving relationship through Jesus Christ by the power of the Holy Spirit.

> **"And my speech and my preaching were not with persuasive words of human wisdom, but in demonstration of the Spirit and of power, ⁵that your faith should not be in the wisdom of men but in the power of God."**
> **1 Corinthians 2:3,4**

The power is in God's Word, not ours. We need to intercede for those lost friends and loved ones at the throne of Grace by continually praying that God would prepare their hearts to receive the supernatural understanding that they are separated from God by their sinfulness, that there is forgiveness, and that by acknowledging this and believing that Jesus Christ died on the Cross to pay their sin debt in full; that they do receive eternal life.

Father, by your grace and in your mercy give _____________ that supernatural understanding needed that they might receive that saving faith of the gospel which you wish for all. Amen

Taking it to the Lord...

How can I apply this truth?____

____

____

Father, I've come to worship and praise you! You are my:________________________

____

I give you all Glory, Honor, and Praise O Lord!

Father, I am sorry that I have sinned by:_____________________________________

Help me to repent. Cleanse me, strengthen me, restore me.

Father, THANK YOU for all your love, grace, mercy and blessings of life that you continually shower down upon me. Thank you especially for:

1.____________________________   2.____________________________

3.____________________________   4.____________________________

5.____________________________   6.____________________________

THANK YOU for answered prayers:____

Father, I need:____

Father, I ask that YOU:____

____

____

Lord, bless me that I may be a blessing. Give me Your heart for loving and serving others. Keep Your hand upon me. Keep me from all evil and harm, and let me cause harm to no one. Bind Satan that he have no power over me. All this I pray in subjection to your will and in the strong name of my Lord and Savior, Jesus Christ. Amen.

The Rose Among Thorns

"For we do not have a High Priest who cannot sympathize with our weaknesses, but was in all points tempted as we are, yet without sin. Let us therefore come boldly to the throne of grace that we may obtain mercy and find grace to help in time of need." Hebrews 4:15

What a mess Adam and Eve got us into!   They turned the Garden of Eden into a garden of evil often filled with more thorns than roses.

> *"Give your burdens to the LORD, and he will take care of you. He will not permit the godly to slip and fall."*
> *Psalm 55:22 NLT*

There are going to be all kinds of problems in the life of every person ever born of woman as long as we live on this earth. The illness free, sin free, problem free life of bliss is reserved for heaven.

While we can minimize the consequences of sin by living Spirit filled lives free from bondage to it, we are still going to need the strength of God to cover our weaknesses in this life until the next.

> *"Three different times I begged the Lord to take it away. Each time he said, "My gracious favor is all you need. My power works best in your weakness." So now I am glad to boast about my weaknesses, so that the power of Christ may work through me."*
> *2 Corinthians 12:8,9 NLT*

Our Lord Jesus Christ was the only perfect man who ever lived, and we know what pain and suffering He had to endure. The Apostle Paul became one of the most Godly men who ever lived. Even after earnestly praying for relief, he still had to carry his thorn in the flesh all the days of his life.

As we endure the prickliness of life, we look to the Problem Solver instead of the problem. We need to claim that "all sufficient grace" that He promises. His purpose is to shape us in the image of Christ and mature us in the faith so that by and through His grace that everything will "come up roses!"

Father, thank You for Your all-sufficient grace that will sustain me through every trial. Amen

Taking it to the Lord...

How can I apply this truth?____

____

Father, I've come to worship and praise you! You are my:___________________________

____

I give you all Glory, Honor, and Praise O Lord!

Father, I am sorry that I have sinned by:____

Help me to repent. Cleanse me, strengthen me, restore me.

Father, THANK YOU for all your love, grace, mercy and blessings of life that you continually shower down upon me. Thank you especially for:

1.___________________________   2.___________________________
3.___________________________   4.___________________________
5.___________________________   6.___________________________

THANK YOU for answered prayers:____

Father, I need:____

Father, I ask that YOU:____

____

____

Lord, bless me that I may be a blessing. Give me Your heart for loving and serving others. Keep Your hand upon me. Keep me from all evil and harm, and let me cause harm to no one. Bind Satan that he have no power over me. All this I pray in subjection to your will and in the strong name of my Lord and Savior, Jesus Christ. Amen.

Confident Living and Loving

"For God has not given us a spirit of fear, but of power and of love and of a sound mind." 2 Timothy 1:7

> *"Yet I am confident that I will see the LORD'S goodness while I am here in the land of the living." Psalm 27:13 NLT*

If perfect love casts away all fear, and we love the Lord with all our heart, why is it sometimes so hard for some of us to live and love confidently?

Sometimes even we Christians fall into the trap of depression forgetful of the hope that is in us through Christ. We worry too much and trust too little. We bear needless grief and pain because we do not take it to the Lord in confident prayer.

We can all live confidently and joyfully when everything is going our way. The test of our faith is in living confidently and joyfully when our comfort zone is getting squeezed.

Loving confidently is probably even more difficult for some than living confidently. We are afraid to risk rejection, disappointment, and the vulnerability of reaching out in love to others in the confidence of God's love.

> *"We can rejoice, too, when we run into problems and trials, for we know that they are good for us— they help us learn to endure. And endurance develops strength of character in us, and character strengthens our confident expectation of salvation." Romans 5:3, 4 NLT*

We get burned and sometimes taken to the cleaners in trying to love and help others, and use this as an excuse for ignoring the needs and pleas of others around us.

When I think of the many times God has gotten burned and taken to the cleaners in loving me, I am ashamed of not being able to love others as He loves me.

This is what being conformed into the image of Christ is all about. As we struggle through the trials and temptations of life, we see the love of God manifested, and as we grow in confidence in His love, we are able to live and to love more confidently.

Father, help me to live and love more confidently. Amen

Taking it to the Lord...

How can I apply this truth?____

____

____

Father, I've come to worship and praise you! You are my:_________________________

____

I give you all Glory, Honor, and Praise O Lord!

Father, I am sorry that I have sinned by:____

Help me to repent. Cleanse me, strengthen me, restore me.

Father, THANK YOU for all your love, grace, mercy and blessings of life that you continually shower down upon me. Thank you especially for:

1._________________________________   2._________________________________

3._________________________________   4._________________________________

5._________________________________   6._________________________________

THANK YOU for answered prayers:____

Father, I need:____

Father, I ask that YOU:____

____

____

____

Lord, bless me that I may be a blessing. Give me Your heart for loving and serving others. Keep Your hand upon me. Keep me from all evil and harm, and let me cause harm to no one. Bind Satan that he have no power over me. All this I pray in subjection to your will and in the strong name of my Lord and Savior, Jesus Christ. Amen.

The Art of the Deal

"Jesus told him, "If you want to be perfect, go and sell all you have and give the money to the poor, and you will have treasure in heaven. Then come, follow me." But when the young man heard this, he went sadly away because he had many possessions." Matthew 19:21

Real Estate tycoon Donald Trump wrote a book called "The Art of the Deal." There are courses in salesmanship that could well be called "the art of the deal."

One of the biggest concerns of any salesman or dealmaker is closing the deal. Transactions often go right up to closing and signing all the paper work when the "deal breaker" shows up. Auto dealers and other merchants use their top salesmen or sales managers as take over artists to close the deal. Many salesmen are threatened with firing if they let a customer leave without being turned over to the closer.

Jesus was undoubtedly the greatest "salesman" who ever lived, selling the greatest "product" ever offered and He has always had to deal with "deal killers". The Scribes and Pharisees rejected Him and turned others against Him. The often experienced and taught His disciples that unbelief killed the deal for healing and salvation for so many.

Humanistic pride in our ability to be self sufficient in our own abilities and to have no need for a Savior probably heads the list of deal breakers today. The love of money, and possessions can be a real stumbling block. The love of the world and all its so-called pleasures discourage others.

> *"And it is true that the citizens of this world are more shrewd than the godly are."*
> *Luke 16:b*

Once we have, by the power of the Holy Spirit, overcome the deal breakers of salvation; we need to concentrate on perfecting the art of the deal in leading others into a saving, sanctifying, and fulfilling relationship with God through faith in Jesus Christ. We need to always be dealmakers and never deal breakers in his regard.

Father, teach me "the art of the deal" in winning souls for you. Amen

Taking it to the Lord...

How can I apply this truth?____

____

____

Father, I've come to worship and praise you! You are my:_________________________

____

I give you all Glory, Honor, and Praise O Lord!

Father, I am sorry that I have sinned by:____

Help me to repent. Cleanse me, strengthen me, restore me.

Father, THANK YOU for all your love, grace, mercy and blessings of life that you continually shower down upon me. Thank you especially for:

1.____________________________   2.____________________________

3.____________________________   4.____________________________

5.____________________________   6.____________________________

THANK YOU for answered prayers:____

Father, I need:____

Father, I ask that YOU:____

____

____

____

Lord, bless me that I may be a blessing. Give me Your heart for loving and serving others. Keep Your hand upon me. Keep me from all evil and harm, and let me cause harm to no one. Bind Satan that he have no power over me. All this I pray in subjection to your will and in the strong name of my Lord and Savior, Jesus Christ. Amen.

What's Your Major?

"Blind guides! You strain your water so you won't accidentally swallow a gnat; then you swallow a camel!" Matthew 23:24 NLT

Anyone attending, about to attend, or having attended college have been asked about their major many times.

Churches and believers need to ask themselves this question frequently, and be honest in their answers.

> *"With all my heart I will praise you, O Lord my God. I will give glory to your name forever."*
> *Psalm 86:12 NLT*

Satan sends many distractions into a body of believers to draw their attention and energies off of the major and onto the minor. Hurt feelings and divisions over the color of choir robes, how and how often communion should be celebrated, and other agendas often take precedence and impede progress in accomplishing the purpose for which we became a church, and for which we became saved – To Glorify God and make disciples!

How many you running? Is often the first question asked among pastors at conventions and convocations. The big building program is often a hot topic. A lot of times, the better question might be "How many you ruining?

Satan has used a lot o minors within church bodies and denominations to give offense and cause a falling away and division within a body. He uses the same tactic with believers on a personal level to keep us from focusing on the purpose for which we were created.

Is anything other than glorifying God and making disciples taking precedence in your church? Is anything other than the "good works for which we were created beforehand" taking precedence in your personal life.

> *"God's purpose was that we who were the first to trust in Christ should praise our glorious God."*
> *Ephesians 1:12 NLT*

There are a lot of good minors, both corporately and personally, as long as we don't forget the major of seeking first the kingdom of God and His righteousness for ourselves and for those who haven't received the righteousness of Christ.

Father, don't let me fall into the trap of majoring in minors. Keep me ever mindful of your great commission and great commandment. Amen.

Taking it to the Lord...

How can I apply this truth?____

____

____

Father, I've come to worship and praise you! You are my:_____________________

____

I give you all Glory, Honor, and Praise O Lord!

Father, I am sorry that I have sinned by:__________________________________

Help me to repent. Cleanse me, strengthen me, restore me.

Father, THANK YOU for all your love, grace, mercy and blessings of life that you continually shower down upon me. Thank you especially for:

1.___________________________   2.___________________________

3.___________________________   4.___________________________

5.___________________________   6.___________________________

THANK YOU for answered prayers:_______________________________________

Father, I need:____

Father, I ask that YOU:____

____

____

____

Lord, bless me that I may be a blessing. Give me Your heart for loving and serving others. Keep Your hand upon me. Keep me from all evil and harm, and let me cause harm to no one. Bind Satan that he have no power over me. All this I pray in subjection to your will and in the strong name of my Lord and Savior, Jesus Christ. Amen.

Don't Just do Something, Stand There!

"Finally, all of you should be of one mind, full of sympathy toward each other, loving one another with tender hearts and humble minds." 1 Peter 3:8 NLT

For many, going to visit someone who is dying, or going to a funeral visitation is a very hard thing to do, mainly because we don't know what to say. Often, out of our insecurity in not knowing what to say, we end up engaging in mindless chatter that comforts no one.

> *"A time to tear,*
> *a time to sew; time to keep*
> *silence And a time to speak;"*
> *Ecclesiastes 3:7*

One of the hardest things for any believer to acquire is the wisdom and spiritual discernment in knowing when and what to say, and when not to say anything.

The pleasure of our presence and company that lets someone know that we care enough to come and be with them is a blessing that needs no verbal amplification. Often as we pray in silence while offering the comfort of our presence, the Holy Spirit will tell us what, if anything, we should say in this particular situation.

> *"He comes alongside us*
> *when we go through hard*
> *times, and before you know*
> *it, he brings us alongside*
> *someone else who is going*
> *through hard times so that we*
> *can be there for that person*
> *just as God was there for us."*
> *2 Corinthians 1:3 MSG*

Rather than come on too strong and with a false bravado or trite Polly Anna chatter, it might be well to be still, and let the Holy Spirit lead us. We need to be sensitive and caring and sometimes the best way to do this is just to stand there.

One of God's greatest gifts to the believer is the awareness of the love of others that He gives. We can sense the prayers that are going out for us in our times of need.

Just as a picture is sometimes worth a thousand words, so the sight of our presence alone is the best balm for the soul in many situations.

Father, just as you comfort me with Your presence, let me be a comforter through my presence with others. Amen

Taking it to the Lord...

How can I apply this truth?____

____

____

Father, I've come to worship and praise you! You are my:_________________________

____

I give you all Glory, Honor, and Praise O Lord!

Father, I am sorry that I have sinned by:____

Help me to repent. Cleanse me, strengthen me, restore me.

Father, THANK YOU for all your love, grace, mercy and blessings of life that you continually shower down upon me. Thank you especially for:

1._________________________________   2._________________________________
3._________________________________   4._________________________________
5._________________________________   6._________________________________

THANK YOU for answered prayers:____

Father, I need:____

Father, I ask that YOU:____

____

____

____

Lord, bless me that I may be a blessing. Give me Your heart for loving and serving others. Keep Your hand upon me. Keep me from all evil and harm, and let me cause harm to no one. Bind Satan that he have no power over me. All this I pray in subjection to your will and in the strong name of my Lord and Savior, Jesus Christ. Amen.

Location, Location, Location!

"Yes, a person is a fool to store up earthly wealth but not have a rich relationship with God." Luke 12:21 NLT

The difference between a $100 acre of land and $1,000,000 acre of land is location! In real estate, retail trade, and about every other area of commerce location is the key factor.

> *"GOD rewrote the text of my life when I opened the book of my heart to his eyes."*
> *Psalm 18:1 MSG*

Location is also a key factor in the life of every professing believer in Jesus Christ. It's the location of Jesus in our lives. Is he in our head or in our hearts?

As great as head knowledge is, it's not where the love of Christ dwells. We can have all the proper knowledge and theology, we can dance through all the hoops of tradition and playing church, but Jesus in the head is not the Christian religion.. Jesus came to dwell in the heart of all believers.

Christianity is not about religion, it's all about a close and personal love relationship with God through faith in Jesus Christ. When Jesus is in your heart, commandment to Love God and to Love others has been fulfilled.

Jesus said: *"A good man out of the good treasure of his heart brings forth good; and an evil man out of the evil treasure of his heart brings forth evil. For out of the abundance of the heart his mouth speaks." (Luke 6:45)*

> *"So now we can rejoice in our wonderful new relationship with God—all because of what our Lord Jesus Christ has done for us in making us friends of God."*
> *Romans 5:11 NLT*

When we receive Jesus into our hearts, we begin a deep and abiding relationship with a "friend who sticks closer than a brother". As we grow in our knowledge of Him through abiding in the Word, we grow more like Him as we experience the supernatural transformation by the renewing of our minds. We begin a lifelong process of being perfected in His image.

Oh what a friend! Oh what a Savior! Oh what blessings when Jesus finds that location in our hearts!

Father, Thank you for making it possible to have friendship with you through a love relationship with your Son and my Savior and best friend, Jesus Christ. Amen

Taking it to the Lord...

How can I apply this truth?____
____
____

Father, I've come to worship and praise you! You are my:_________________________________
____

I give you all Glory, Honor, and Praise O Lord!

Father, I am sorry that I have sinned by:____

Help me to repent. Cleanse me, strengthen me, restore me.

Father, THANK YOU for all your love, grace, mercy and blessings of life that you continually shower down upon me. Thank you especially for:

1._____________________________________   2._____________________________________
3._____________________________________   4._____________________________________
5._____________________________________   6._____________________________________

THANK YOU for answered prayers:____

Father, I need:____

Father, I ask that YOU:____
____
____
____

Lord, bless me that I may be a blessing. Give me Your heart for loving and serving others. Keep Your hand upon me. Keep me from all evil and harm, and let me cause harm to no one. Bind Satan that he have no power over me. All this I pray in subjection to your will and in the strong name of my Lord and Savior, Jesus Christ. Amen.

Worms Anyone?

"Depression haunts my days. My weary nights are filled with pain as though something were relentlessly gnawing at my bones." Job 30:16 NLT

Ever been there? Has it ever been hard to get up and face the world some mornings? Ever wanted to go "eat that worm and die?" Welcome to the club!

> *"In your righteousness, bring me out of this distress."*
> *Psalm 143:11b NLT*

Depression to some degree is a reality of life for everyone. If it is physical, treatment is fairly simple. This is why God gives us Doctors.

Depression does not come from God, but He may allow it to discipline, test or strengthen us. Depression is one of the favorite tools of the tyrant to try to get us to doubt our salvation and God's love and promises.

Satan often uses depression to trigger a crisis of confidence whenever God is about to accomplish something through us. He often uses it when we face changes in jobs or other circumstances.

> *"Don't worry about anything; instead, pray about everything. Tell God what you need, and thank him for all he has done. If you do this, you will experience God's peace, which is far more wonderful than the human mind can understand."*
> *Philippians 4:6,7 NLT*

David wrote the book on depression throughout Psalms. Relentlessly pursued by Saul and utterly exhausted and forlorn, he gives us one of the best cures for depression in Psalm 42:6 "Now I am deeply discouraged, but I will remember your kindness—" When we focus on God and all of the love and tender mercies He has showered upon us in the past and all of the promises we can bank on for the present and future, we receive strength and comfort to overcome depression.

When we quit focusing on our problems and onto the problem solver, when we move from self-pity to God praise, we are going to find our depression left behind.

Father, don't let the sin of depression have dominion over me. Restore unto me the joy of my salvation and that wonderful peace that surpasses all understanding. Amen

Taking it to the Lord...

How can I apply this truth?____

____

____

Father, I've come to worship and praise you! You are my:___________________________________

____

I give you all Glory, Honor, and Praise O Lord!

Father, I am sorry that I have sinned by:____

Help me to repent. Cleanse me, strengthen me, restore me.

Father, THANK YOU for all your love, grace, mercy and blessings of life that you continually shower down upon me. Thank you especially for:

1.______________________________　　2.______________________________

3.______________________________　　4.______________________________

5.______________________________　　6.______________________________

THANK YOU for answered prayers:____

Father, I need:____

Father, I ask that YOU:____

____

____

____

Lord, bless me that I may be a blessing. Give me Your heart for loving and serving others. Keep Your hand upon me. Keep me from all evil and harm, and let me cause harm to no one. Bind Satan that he have no power over me. All this I pray in subjection to your will and in the strong name of my Lord and Savior, Jesus Christ. Amen.

Giver or Taker?

"Help and give without expecting a return. You'll never—I promise—regret it. Live out this God-created identity the way our Father lives toward us, generously and graciously, even when we're at our worst. Our Father is kind; you be kind." Luke 6:35 MSG

> *"What can I offer the LORD for all he has done for me?"*
> *Psalm 116:12 NLT*

It seems that our world is made up of givers and takers. Those who look out for Number 1 to the exclusion of everyone and everything are never satisfied and will go to their graves "on the take"!

Takers are selfish, demanding, pushy and seldom satisfied. They always want more. It's all about them and their needs and wants. They use others to fulfill their purposes, and achieve them at the expense of others.

Their river of life becomes stagnant as they soak up everything they think they need or want and give nothing out in return. It is interesting to note how often Scripture mentions the sin of greed right up there with sexual immorality and idolatry.

Givers are those who receive the love of God gladly, and the stream of living water He provides, and pour out this living water of love in ministry or blessing to others.

Love is all about giving. God initiated love by giving His only begotten Son so that whoever believed in Him would not perish but have everlasting life. Jesus Christ modeled giving out of a heart overflowing with love and compassion.

> *"Don't think only about your own affairs, but be interested in others, too, and what they are doing."*
> *Philippians 2:4 NLT*

He healed the sick, fed the hungry, loved the unlovable, and washed the feet of His disciples as examples of giving love. He forgave those who persecuted and betrayed Him with forgiving love.

We are like beggars begging for bread when we receive the grace of God and eternal life through the gift of His son. We cannot take this love and hoard it. We have to be givers by "passing it on."

Father help me to be a generous giver and not a selfish taker in every area of my life. Amen

Taking it to the Lord...

How can I apply this truth?____

Father, I've come to worship and praise you! You are my:____

I give you all Glory, Honor, and Praise O Lord!

Father, I am sorry that I have sinned by:____

Help me to repent. Cleanse me, strengthen me, restore me.

Father, THANK YOU for all your love, grace, mercy and blessings of life that you continually shower down upon me. Thank you especially for:

1._____________________________________   2._____________________________________

3._____________________________________   4._____________________________________

5._____________________________________   6._____________________________________

THANK YOU for answered prayers:____

Father, I need:____

Father, I ask that YOU:____

Lord, bless me that I may be a blessing. Give me Your heart for loving and serving others. Keep Your hand upon me. Keep me from all evil and harm, and let me cause harm to no one. Bind Satan that he have no power over me. All this I pray in subjection to your will and in the strong name of my Lord and Savior, Jesus Christ. Amen.

Are You a Door Knocker Downer?

"We use God's mighty weapons, not mere worldly weapons, to knock down the Devil's strongholds." 2 Corinthians 10:4 NLT

The disciples had a lot to learn about knocking down obstacles. Peter cut off the ear of one who was going to arrest Jesus. Luke 9:53 tells of James and John wanting to bring down fire from heaven and burn up a Samaritan village because they would not receive Jesus.

> *"Turn away from evil and do good. Work hard at living in peace with others." Psalm 34:10 NLT*

David had ample opportunities to end Saul's pursuit and persecution of him, but would not lay a hand on God's anointed one, but put to death the one that did. We are all greatly blessed by the Psalms David wrote while hiding out and fleeing the unjust persecution and attempts to kill him.

Before we respond to anything by over reacting or reacting to anything without our brains fully loaded, we can learn a lot from David about the rewards of long suffering and patience. He was "the man after God's own heart".

A lot of problems need to be left alone and given a chance to work themselves out. Premature rushes to judgment or over reaction often provide fuel for a fire that would otherwise soon burn out. A short fuse is dangerous in fireworks and in life.

God's "mighty weapons" of truth, righteousness, the Good News, faith, salvation, the Word of God, and prayer somehow don't seem all that powerful to our finite minds, but we live in a kingdom that has been built and is being built with them.

> *"A final word: Be strong with the Lord's mighty power. Put on all of God's armor so that you will be able to stand firm against all strategies and tricks of the Devil." Ephesians 6:10, 11 NLT*

Oh that God would give us wisdom and spiritual discernment to know when to speak and when to remain silent, how to react without over reacting, and how to be proactive in fulfilling the Great Commission and tearing down the walls of hate and prejudice.

Father, keep me from rash responses and actions. Amen

Taking it to the Lord...

How can I apply this truth?____

____

____

Father, I've come to worship and praise you! You are my:_________________________________

____

I give you all Glory, Honor, and Praise O Lord!

Father, I am sorry that I have sinned by:____

Help me to repent. Cleanse me, strengthen me, restore me.

Father, THANK YOU for all your love, grace, mercy and blessings of life that you continually shower down upon me. Thank you especially for:

1.___________________________________   2.___________________________________

3.___________________________________   4.___________________________________

5.___________________________________   6.___________________________________

THANK YOU for answered prayers:____

Father, I need:____

Father, I ask that YOU:____

____

____

____

Lord, bless me that I may be a blessing. Give me Your heart for loving and serving others. Keep Your hand upon me. Keep me from all evil and harm, and let me cause harm to no one. Bind Satan that he have no power over me. All this I pray in subjection to your will and in the strong name of my Lord and Savior, Jesus Christ. Amen.

Under a Sea of Grief

"And God will wipe away every tear from their eyes; there shall be no more death, nor sorrow, nor crying. There shall be no more pain, for the former things have passed away." Revelation 21:4

Each of us has been or will be under a sea of grief many times. We grieve for loved ones who become afflicted or die. We suffer setbacks and failures, heartbreak, disappointment, and sorrow.

> *"But the LORD is in His holy temple.*
> *Let all the earth keep silence before Him."*
> *Habakkuk 2:20*

It is hard not to question God when bad things happen to good people, and when the ungodly seem to prosper and prevail. God welcomes the questions and has given most of the answers and will ultimately give them all.

As believers, we find great comfort through knowing that God is all loving and generous in grace and mercy to all who ask. We know that He works all things for our good and His glory, even though His ways are higher, his time table different. Just because God remains silent and doesn't seem to be anywhere to be found in a given situation does not mean that He is not at work and in control.

What comfort there is in understanding that the all-sufficient grace of God abounds and is made manifest in suffering and sorrow. We cannot appreciate it in times of prosperity and great joy unless we have experienced it when He is all we have, and find that He is all we need.

The Good News is that, <u>no matter what</u>, as children of God, we are joint heirs with Christ and are free spiritually and will be freed from physical, emotional, and relational pain and suffering many times in this life. Even better, we can be sure that we will have total freedom from all pain, sorrow, and sadness when we receive the ultimate healing that Jesus Christ died to give us.

> *"Yet what we suffer now is nothing compared to the glory he will give us later."*
> *Romans 8:18 NLT*

Father, when the storms threaten to drown me let me take refuge in your all-sufficient grace that covers my weakness with Your strength. Amen

Taking it to the Lord...

How can I apply this truth?____

____

Father, I've come to worship and praise you! You are my:___________________

____

I give you all Glory, Honor, and Praise O Lord!

Father, I am sorry that I have sinned by:________________________________

Help me to repent. Cleanse me, strengthen me, restore me.

Father, THANK YOU for all your love, grace, mercy and blessings of life that you continually shower down upon me. Thank you especially for:

1.______________________________   2.______________________________
3.______________________________   4.______________________________
5.______________________________   6.______________________________

THANK YOU for answered prayers:____

Father, I need:____

Father, I ask that YOU:____

____

____

Lord, bless me that I may be a blessing. Give me Your heart for loving and serving others. Keep Your hand upon me. Keep me from all evil and harm, and let me cause harm to no one. Bind Satan that he have no power over me. All this I pray in subjection to your will and in the strong name of my Lord and Savior, Jesus Christ. Amen.

Taking Inventory

"Not that I seek the gift, but I seek the fruit that abounds to your account." Philippians 4:17

An accurate inventory of cash, receivables, merchandise, supplies and equipment is the only way any business can determine whether it made a profit or loss, detect theft or pilferage, and come up with a net worth.

> *"Moreover by them your servant is warned, and in keeping them is great reward."*
> *Psalm 19:11*

On the personal level, when we add our cash, savings, investments, and possessions, and subtract what we owe, we determine our personal net worth.

On the spiritual level, we all need to be constantly taking inventory of the debit and credit balances in God's book of life. Scripture tells us that, our faith in Jesus Christ has been credited as righteousness by God--with overdraft protection. Because of this imputed righteousness our destination is assured. Heaven is a gift and we do not earn it!

Scripture also tells us that when arrive at our heavenly destination there is going to be an inventory taken of all the treasures we have stored up in heaven consisting of the good works we did and fruit we produced that glorified God during our sojourn on earth. These are what will remain after the fire has burned away the "wood, hay and straw" of wasted lives and missed opportunities.

We will find our account credited for loving God and others, for bringing others to Christ, and those things through which we have t glorified God on a personal, private, public, and church level.

> *"Store up your treasures in heaven, where they will never become moth-eaten or rusty and where they will be safe from thieves."*
> *Matthew 6:20 NLT*

To be called "good and faithful servant" by God and to be given even more ministry privileges in heaven are opportunities we surely don't want to miss.

Father, thank you for taking the cup of death for the wages of sin away from me by sending Jesus to die for my sins on the Cross at Calvary. Amen

Taking it to the Lord...

How can I apply this truth?____

____

Father, I've come to worship and praise you! You are my:_________________________________

____

I give you all Glory, Honor, and Praise O Lord!

Father, I am sorry that I have sinned by:____

Help me to repent. Cleanse me, strengthen me, restore me.

Father, THANK YOU for all your love, grace, mercy and blessings of life that you continually shower down upon me. Thank you especially for:

1.____________________________________   2.____________________________________

3.____________________________________   4.____________________________________

5.____________________________________   6.____________________________________

THANK YOU for answered prayers:____

Father, I need:____

Father, I ask that YOU:____

____

____

Lord, bless me that I may be a blessing. Give me Your heart for loving and serving others. Keep Your hand upon me. Keep me from all evil and harm, and let me cause harm to no one. Bind Satan that he have no power over me. All this I pray in subjection to your will and in the strong name of my Lord and Savior, Jesus Christ. Amen.

The Gold Standard

"How much better to get wisdom than gold! And to get understanding is to be chosen rather than silver."
Proverbs 16:16

Prior to 1971, the United States of America was on the Gold Standard, and our paper money was backed by and

> *"The idols of the nations are silver and gold. The work of of men's hands."*
> *Psalm 135:15*

redeemable for gold. Today, our paper money is backed by nothing more than the credit of the United States government and has continued to become worth less and less as government debt has increased more and more.

Up until around 1950, God's Word was the standard for morality and civil and criminal law in this country. Today, our standard for morality and civil and criminal law in this country has seemingly forgotten God and been replaced by the wisdom of man with disastrous results.

Our new age of enlightenment has given us abortion on demand, respectable homosexuality, a 66% divorce rate, relative truth, AIDS, drug addiction and substance abuse, pornography addiction, etc. We have seen the Word of God banned and condoms distributed in our public schools. Out of wedlock births have skyrocketed. Our "liberation" from God's moral restraints has brought more bondage and misery instead.

> *"That the genuineness of your faith, being much more precious than gold that perishes, though it is tested by fire, may be found to praise, honor, and glory at the revelation of Jesus Christ."*
> *1 Peter 1:7*

Through it all, those who persevere in the faith have the ultimate gold standard, backed by the death of and validated by the resurrection of Jesus Christ. Whether the streets of heaven are paved with gold doesn't matter. What counts is that we have a future and a hope that is incorruptible and will never fail.

Father, let my sadness and concern over the abandonment of Your standards by so much of this world be comforted by the assurance I have through faith that You are still in Control. Amen

Taking it to the Lord...

How can I apply this truth?____

____

Father, I've come to worship and praise you! You are my:_____________________

____

I give you all Glory, Honor, and Praise O Lord!

Father, I am sorry that I have sinned by:_________________________________

Help me to repent. Cleanse me, strengthen me, restore me.

Father, THANK YOU for all your love, grace, mercy and blessings of life that you continually shower down upon me. Thank you especially for:

1.__________________________   2.__________________________

3.__________________________   4.__________________________

5.__________________________   6.__________________________

THANK YOU for answered prayers:________________________________

Father, I need:____

Father, I ask that YOU:____

____

____

Lord, bless me that I may be a blessing. Give me Your heart for loving and serving others. Keep Your hand upon me. Keep me from all evil and harm, and let me cause harm to no one. Bind Satan that he have no power over me. All this I pray in subjection to your will and in the strong name of my Lord and Savior, Jesus Christ. Amen.

Let Freedom Ring!

"Stand fast therefore in the liberty by which Christ has made us free, and do not be entangled again with a yoke of bondage." Galatians 5:1

The idea that we are born with an inherited birth defect called sin is not a very popular concept these days.

> *"And you shall know the truth, and the truth shall make you free."*
> *John 8:32*

Enlightened humanists and liberal politicians have ignored the reality of original sin to our peril. Liberals and humanists say that all crime stems from a bad environment, and that if we improve the environment we will eliminate crime and have utopia. The razed housing projects in many major cities belie that myth.

The disobedience of Adam and Eve caused all mankind to be kicked out of paradise and to be separated from God. *"Therefore, just as through one man sin entered the world, and death through sin, and thus death spread to all men, because all sinned." (Romans 5:12)*

The "good news" is that by His death on the cross, Jesus Christ has ended the separation from God and freed all who believe from eternal death! *"But now having been set free from sin, and having become slaves of God, you have your fruit to holiness, and the end, everlasting life. (Romans 6:18)*

Think about it! For the very first time, we are free from bondage and domination by sin. We can actually, with the power of the Holy Spirit living within us live a life fully pleasing to God and bearing the fruit of the Spirit.

> *"But he who looks into the perfect law of liberty and continues in it, and is not a forgetful hearer but a doer of the work, this one will be blessed in what he does."*
> *James 1:25*

Although we may momentarily stumble and fall into sins of the flesh, we are no longer sinners, but saints No longer can we use the excuse "I'm only human" to justify our continual sinful behavior. We are no longer slaves to sin, but slaves of righteousness and our love of God leaves us no choice but to want to do the things that please Him. Shouldn't we start rejoicing and living in our freedom?

Father, thank You for setting me free from sin so that I can become a slave to Your righteousness. Amen

Taking it to the Lord...

How can I apply this truth?____

____

____

Father, I've come to worship and praise you! You are my:_____________________

____

I give you all Glory, Honor, and Praise O Lord!

Father, I am sorry that I have sinned by:_________________________________

Help me to repent. Cleanse me, strengthen me, restore me.

Father, THANK YOU for all your love, grace, mercy and blessings of life that you continually shower down upon me. Thank you especially for:

1.__________________________   2.__________________________

3.__________________________   4.__________________________

5.__________________________   6.__________________________

THANK YOU for answered prayers:_______________________________________

Father, I need:____

Father, I ask that YOU:____

____

____

Lord, bless me that I may be a blessing. Give me Your heart for loving and serving others. Keep Your hand upon me. Keep me from all evil and harm, and let me cause harm to no one. Bind Satan that he have no power over me. All this I pray in subjection to your will and in the strong name of my Lord and Savior, Jesus Christ. Amen.

Are You an Identity Theft Victim?

"The thief does not come except to steal, and to kill, and to destroy. I have come that they may have life, and that they may have *it* more abundantly." John 10:10

Credit card identity theft has reached mega million dollar proportions. By hook or crook, by means only an evil genius could devise, credit card fraud has stolen the identity of hundreds of thousands of innocent people, often with disastrous results.

> *"Then he said, "Are you really my son Esau?" He said, "I am." Genesis 27:24*

Today's identity theft is nothing compared to what Jacob did to Esau. He stole the irrevocable blessing of Isaac by falsifying his identity.

The real tragedy of identity theft comes when Satan comes like a thief in the night, seeking whom he may devour. He will lie, cheat and offer every temptation imaginable to try to steal the believer's birth right of their new life in Christ.

He will come in sheep's clothing, promising riches, pleasure, fame, and any other inducement that might work to destroy the believer   Once he has a believer hooked real good; fear, doubt, and despair take over and even the strongest of faiths are shaken.

> *"For those who are such do not serve our Lord Jesus Christ, but their own belly, and by smooth words and flattering speech deceive the hearts of the simple." Romans 16:18*

The good news is that our new identity in Christ is an identity may be stolen or severely bruised from time to time, but never stolen completely.

God assures us through Paul: *"And I am convinced that nothing can ever separate us from his love. Death can't, and life can't. The angels can't, and the demons can't. "Our fears for today, our worries about tomorrow, and even the powers of hell can't keep God's love away." (Romans 8:38 NLT)*

Father, keep me ever mindful of who I am in you and never let sin destroy this identity. Amen

Taking it to the Lord...

How can I apply this truth?____

____

____

Father, I've come to worship and praise you! You are my:_______________________

____

I give you all Glory, Honor, and Praise O Lord!

Father, I am sorry that I have sinned by:___________________________________

Help me to repent. Cleanse me, strengthen me, restore me.

Father, THANK YOU for all your love, grace, mercy and blessings of life that you continually shower down upon me. Thank you especially for:

1.___________________________   2.___________________________

3.___________________________   4.___________________________

5.___________________________   6.___________________________

THANK YOU for answered prayers:___________________________________

Father, I need:____

Father, I ask that YOU:____

____

____

____

Lord, bless me that I may be a blessing. Give me Your heart for loving and serving others. Keep Your hand upon me. Keep me from all evil and harm, and let me cause harm to no one. Bind Satan that he have no power over me. All this I pray in subjection to your will and in the strong name of my Lord and Savior, Jesus Christ. Amen.

You Are Wondrously Made!

"I praise you because I am fearfully and wonderfully made; your works are wonderful, I know that full well" Psalm 139:14 NIV

If we have a poor self-image, it's probably our own fault. We look at others and don't like the comparison

> *"Let every created thing give praise to the LORD, for he issued his command, and they came into being."*
> *Psalm 148:5*

Scripture says that we are *"God's masterpiece" (Ephesians 2:10).* We are not only wondrously made, but we are uniquely made. DNA, fingerprints, and many other means of measurement point out the fact that there are no two people exactly alike.

Perhaps even worse than a poor self image is the delusion that we are better than others. This puffs up pride, which God hates, and tends to make us more self-centered about how great we are rather than Christ centered about how great He is.

The truth is that God gave us a heart and a soul that sets us apart from all creation. Abraham, Noah, and Enoch are known as ones who walked with God. Solomon's prayer includes: *"You have shown great mercy to Your servant David my father, because he walked before You in truth, in righteousness, and in uprightness of heart with You" (1 Kings 3:6)*

We have all been created with this capacity to walk before God in truth, righteousness and uprightness of heart. It has nothing to do with our appearance, our possessions, or our talents.

God is no respecter of persons. He is an equal opportunity God with mercy, longsuffering, patience, kindness and love for all. God has made you inferior to no one, and so you should not make yourself to feel inferior to anyone. God has made you superior to no one, so don't get the "big head'.

> *"That the man of God may be complete, thoroughly equipped for every good work."*
> *2 Timothy 3:17*

You are "fearfully and wondrously made." You are equipped with an instruction manual.   Rejoice and be glad in it! Seek to discover and do those things for which you were created.

Father, let me never get down on myself because of what I don't have, but rather let me rejoice in what I do have in you. Amen

Taking it to the Lord...

How can I apply this truth?____

____

____

Father, I've come to worship and praise you! You are my:_______________________________

____

I give you all Glory, Honor, and Praise O Lord!

Father, I am sorry that I have sinned by:____

Help me to repent. Cleanse me, strengthen me, restore me.

Father, THANK YOU for all your love, grace, mercy and blessings of life that you continually shower down upon me. Thank you especially for:

1.___________________________________   2.___________________________________

3.___________________________________   4.___________________________________

5.___________________________________   6.___________________________________

THANK YOU for answered prayers:____

Father, I need:____

Father, I ask that YOU:____

____

____

Lord, bless me that I may be a blessing. Give me Your heart for loving and serving others. Keep Your hand upon me. Keep me from all evil and harm, and let me cause harm to no one. Bind Satan that he have no power over me. All this I pray in subjection to your will and in the strong name of my Lord and Savior, Jesus Christ. Amen.

Things are Looking Up!

"And let us run with endurance the race that God has set before us. We do this by keeping our eyes on Jesus, on whom our faith depends from start to finish." Hebrews 12:1b, 2a NLT

> *"Then you will delight yourself in the Almighty and look up to God. You will pray to him, and he will hear you, and you will fulfill your vows to him."*
> *Job 22:26,27 NLT*

I had an acquaintance who had been suffering through an assortment of illnesses fairly common for those in their 80s. I hadn't seen her much lately. When I did and inquired about how she was doing, her response was "things are looking up!" It took a while for it to dawn on me that this was her way of saying that she was dying.

Alcoholics Anonymous and many other substance abuse programs are based on the understanding that the only way to help any addict is to pin them down to where they admit they have a problem, and then help them to look up to that higher power Who can cover their weaknesses with His strength to overcome their problem one day at a time.

Sometimes God has to lay us low in order to make us look up. He does have a way of getting our attention when we stray and quit looking up to Him.

The bottom line is where are you looking when problems come. Are you looking down in defeat and despair like one who has no hope? Are you looking down at the problem instead of up to the problem solver?

The closer we get to our last day on this earth, the less we look up to the things we used to look up to. Somehow, the status symbols and the toys don't seem that important.

> *"Because of Christ and our faith in him, we can now come fearlessly into God's presence, assured of his glad welcome."*
> *Ephesians 3:12 NLT*

When we look up, faith kicks in and kicks fear out. We will see the Glory of the Lord and the wonderful future we have with Him. It is a future worth living for, and a future worth dying for.

Things are always "looking up" for those whose trust is in the Lord.

Father, give me the faith and the courage to look up and beyond the temporary trials and troubles of this life. Amen

Taking it to the Lord...

How can I apply this truth?____

____

____

Father, I've come to worship and praise you! You are my:___________________

____

I give you all Glory, Honor, and Praise O Lord!

Father, I am sorry that I have sinned by:_________________________________

Help me to repent. Cleanse me, strengthen me, restore me.

Father, THANK YOU for all your love, grace, mercy and blessings of life that you continually shower down upon me. Thank you especially for:

1.____________________________   2.____________________________

3.____________________________   4.____________________________

5.____________________________   6.____________________________

THANK YOU for answered prayers:___________________________________

Father, I need:____

Father, I ask that YOU:____

____

____

Lord, bless me that I may be a blessing. Give me Your heart for loving and serving others. Keep Your hand upon me. Keep me from all evil and harm, and let me cause harm to no one. Bind Satan that he have no power over me. All this I pray in subjection to your will and in the strong name of my Lord and Savior, Jesus Christ. Amen.

Still Rowing Your Own Boat?

"And He said to me, "My grace is sufficient for you, for My strength is made perfect in weakness." 2 Corinthians 12:9

There is something about pride that blinds. When we insist on doing it our way, we disable the grace of God and set ourselves up for a big fall.

> *"I love you, LORD; you are my strength." Psalm 18.1 NLT*

It doesn't matter how big and strong we are physically, how smart we are mentally, and how secure we are in our own strength and goodness emotionally, or how successful we are from the world's perspective.

There is going to come a point in time when all of these attributes fail. Paul understood that his thorn in the flesh was given to keep him humble and totally dependent upon the grace of God.

When we get so self sufficient and filled with pride in our own abilities that we rob God of His glory and appropriate it for ourselves, we set ourselves up to go down big time. *"God opposes the proud, but gives grace to the humble". (1 Peter 5:5 NIV)*

How could anyone prefer their own strength to strength of the Almighty One, who created and controls the world and everything in it? This is beyond my comprehension.

That *"way that seems right to man" is the "way of death" (Proverbs 14:12)*. The way that God chose to come in the lowliness of a stable, to a bunch of publicans and sinners, and call a rag tag bunch of disciples to show how His power perfects any weakness should be more than enough to convince anyone that He is the way.

> *"And God's weakness is far stronger than the greatest of human strength." 1 Corinthians 1:27 NLT*

Which way are you going?

Father, help me to avoid the shipwrecks of life that come from insisting on living it my way instead of your way. Amen

Taking it to the Lord...

How can I apply this truth?____

____

Father, I've come to worship and praise you! You are my:_________________________

____

I give you all Glory, Honor, and Praise O Lord!

Father, I am sorry that I have sinned by:_________________________________

Help me to repent. Cleanse me, strengthen me, restore me.

Father, THANK YOU for all your love, grace, mercy and blessings of life that you continually shower down upon me. Thank you especially for:

1._________________________________   2._________________________________
3._________________________________   4._________________________________
5._________________________________   6._________________________________

THANK YOU for answered prayers:____

Father, I need:____

Father, I ask that YOU:____

____

____

Lord, bless me that I may be a blessing. Give me Your heart for loving and serving others. Keep Your hand upon me. Keep me from all evil and harm, and let me cause harm to no one. Bind Satan that he have no power over me. All this I pray in subjection to your will and in the strong name of my Lord and Savior, Jesus Christ. Amen.

Silence of the Lambs

"And how can they believe in him if they have never heard about him? And how can they hear about him unless someone tells them?" Romans 10:14b

When thinking of lambs, we think mostly of sacrifice. We think of Jesus as the Lamb of God, most holy, given as the perfect sacrifice for our sins. The truth is that all believers are lambs of God, the sheep of His pasture who dwell in the security and love of the Good Shepherd.

> *"Save me, so I can praise you publicly at Jerusalem's gates, so I can rejoice that you have rescued me."*
> *Psalm 9:14 NLT*

When we have been redeemed by the blood of the lamb, through faith in Him, we become followers of Him. As followers we are called to the great commandment to love one another, and the great commission to go out into the world and make disciples. We cannot be silent lambs. We can and should be humble and obedient, but never silent unless our conduct is so bad it ruins our witness.

Just as Jesus told the demon possessed man to *"go back to your family and tell them all the wonderful things God has done for you" (Luke 8:39)*, He tells us to go out and make disciples of all nations.

We dare not remain silent and let our friends and loved ones wander aimlessly lost without telling them about the Love of God that is in Christ Jesus. Jesus is the only hope for a sin sick world, and we dare not fail to tell about Him or help to send others to tell about Him throughout the world.

> *"Look, I am sending you out as sheep among wolves. Be as wary as snakes and harmless as doves."*
> *Matthew 10:16 NLT*

"Talking the talk" without "walking the walk" makes us stumbling blocks that can do more harm than good to the building up of God's kingdom on earth. If we are bearing the name with shame, maybe our silence is golden. We might even need to ask ourselves how to get back from the pigpen to our Father's house.

Father, give me the power to witness by words backed up by the fruits I am known by. Amen

Taking it to the Lord...

How can I apply this truth?____
____
____

Father, I've come to worship and praise you! You are my:_____________________
____

I give you all Glory, Honor, and Praise O Lord!

Father, I am sorry that I have sinned by:___________________________________

Help me to repent. Cleanse me, strengthen me, restore me.

Father, THANK YOU for all your love, grace, mercy and blessings of life that you continually shower down upon me. Thank you especially for:

1.__________________________________   2.__________________________________
3.__________________________________   4.__________________________________
5.__________________________________   6.__________________________________

THANK YOU for answered prayers:____
Father, I need:____
Father, I ask that YOU:____
____
____
____

Lord, bless me that I may be a blessing. Give me Your heart for loving and serving others. Keep Your hand upon me. Keep me from all evil and harm, and let me cause harm to no one. Bind Satan that he have no power over me. All this I pray in subjection to your will and in the strong name of my Lord and Savior, Jesus Christ. Amen.

When Nature Calls

"But Jesus didn't trust them, because he knew what people were really like. No one needed to tell him about human nature." John 2:23, 24 NLT

We are talking about that old dead man that keeps calling us from the grave back into the depths of despair and the fleeting pleasure of sin.

> *"Keep back Your servant also from presumptuous sins; let them not have dominion over me." Psalm 19:12 NLT*

Once we were dead in trespasses and sin, and now we are dead to trespasses and sin, thanks to our saving faith that Jesus Christ died on the cross for our sins. Sin no longer has dominion over us, nor does it have the power to separate us from the love of God that is in Christ Jesus.

With all this being said in Scripture and believed in faith, why oh why do we hear the call of our sin nature daily?

We hear the call of anger and depression, the call of lust and unholy passion, the call of selfish ambition, the call of pride and rebellion.

"For the Devil has come down to you in great anger, and he knows that he has little time." (Revelation 12:12b NLT) We see the power of evil all around us and throughout the world.

> *"So, dear brothers and sisters you have no obligation whatsoever to do what your sinful nature urges you to do." Romans 8:12 NLT*

While God does not tempt us to sin, His permissive will allows us to be tempted and tried as part of the purification process He uses to conform us into the image of His Son.

If we try to fight these battles in our own strength, we are going to lose. When we ask God to cover our weaknesses with His strength, we are reassured and believe God when He says that He will not allow any temptation without providing a means of escape, that He who is in us is greater than he who is in the world.

As believers we have no obligation to answer the call of nature.

Father, as you have overcome death for me, give me the strength to overcome the calls of the old Adam within me. Amen.

Taking it to the Lord...

How can I apply this truth?____

____

Father, I've come to worship and praise you! You are my:__________________

____

I give you all Glory, Honor, and Praise O Lord!

Father, I am sorry that I have sinned by:_______________________________

Help me to repent. Cleanse me, strengthen me, restore me.

Father, THANK YOU for all your love, grace, mercy and blessings of life that you continually shower down upon me. Thank you especially for:

1.__________________________   2.__________________________

3.__________________________   4.__________________________

5.__________________________   6.__________________________

THANK YOU for answered prayers:______________________________________

Father, I need:____

Father, I ask that YOU:____

____

____

Lord, bless me that I may be a blessing. Give me Your heart for loving and serving others. Keep Your hand upon me. Keep me from all evil and harm, and let me cause harm to no one. Bind Satan that he have no power over me. All this I pray in subjection to your will and in the strong name of my Lord and Savior, Jesus Christ. Amen.

The Fellowship of Growing

"So let's keep focused on that goal, those of us who want everything God has for us. If any of you have something else in mind, something less than total commitment, God will clear your blurred vision—you'll see it yet! Now that we're on the right track, let's stay on it." Philippians 3:15 MSG

There are few things sweeter or more rewarding than growing in our relationship with Christ as we grow in our relationship with brothers and sisters in the Lord. The body of Christ is a living organism and it will grow according to how well members of a particular body are growing in their relationship with God through His Word and in their relationships with each other.

"But the godly will flourish like palm trees and grow strong like the cedars of Lebanon."
Psalm 92:12 NLT

The shared joy of being part of something bigger than any individual, is a joy reserved for those who join together in unity of purpose and spirit to glorify God and to build up His kingdom. Whether it's in growing a ministry or growing into the fullness of Christ; the fellowship of growing is an awesome experience.

Growing Christians are those growing in fellowship with other believers. It is through this fellowship that we receive the encouragement, the love and support, and the accountability that we need to keep growing in the Word and into the image of Christ.

"Godliness leads to love for other Christians, and finally you will grow to have genuine love for everyone."
2 Peter 1:7 NLT

When we "church hop" we miss out on this joy. When we remain aloof from the fellowship of believers through not getting involved, we miss out on this joy. God calls us not only to salvation, but also to holiness, ministry, and mission. We cannot even recognize, much less answer these calls without the fellowship of growing.

Father, help me to know the blessings of the fellowship of growing. Amen

Taking it to the Lord...

How can I apply this truth?____

____

____

Father, I've come to worship and praise you! You are my:_______________________

____

I give you all Glory, Honor, and Praise O Lord!

Father, I am sorry that I have sinned by:_____________________________________

Help me to repent. Cleanse me, strengthen me, restore me.

Father, THANK YOU for all your love, grace, mercy and blessings of life that you continually shower down upon me. Thank you especially for:

1._________________________________   2._________________________________
3._________________________________   4._________________________________
5._________________________________   6._________________________________

THANK YOU for answered prayers: _______________________________________

Father, I need:____

Father, I ask that YOU: ____

____

____

Lord, bless me that I may be a blessing. Give me Your heart for loving and serving others. Keep Your hand upon me. Keep me from all evil and harm, and let me cause harm to no one. Bind Satan that he have no power over me. All this I pray in subjection to your will and in the strong name of my Lord and Savior, Jesus Christ. Amen.

Our Just Desserts

"Let us therefore come boldly to the throne of grace, that we may obtain mercy and find grace to help in time of need. Hebrews 4:16

If God gave us what we deserved, we would all be in big trouble. *"There is none righteous, no not one."* (Romans 3:10)

> *"Do not remember the sins of my youth, nor my transgressions; according to Your mercy remember me, for Your goodness' sake, O Lord"*
> *Psalm 25:7*

If God had given Abraham what he deserved when he passed Sarah off as his sister where would we be? If God had dealt with Paul as he deserved for killing and persecuting Christians how would we gentiles known have known that God's salvation was for us also? What if God had given Peter what he deserved for denying Christ?

As much in denial as I am, as much as I gloss over and make light of my sins when the self righteousness of my flesh takes over, the reality of my own sins still send me running to the throne of grace for the undeserved grace and mercy of God.

We often rise up in righteous indignation demanding justice for others when if we received the justice we demanded for others we would be doomed.

The thief on the cross knew what he deserved and was overcome with awe and joy with what he got.

The unforgiving steward is a stark reminder that it's best not to test God's patience when it comes to not being merciful. We had best remember *that "blessed are the merciful, for they shall receive mercy."(Matthew 5:7)*

> *"Through the heartfelt mercies of our God, God's Sunrise will break in upon us, Shining on those in the darkness, those sitting in the shadow of death."*
> *Luke 1:78 MSG*

When we know what we were, what we sometimes revert to being, we know that our only hope is that God will not deal with us as we deserve, but as His exceedingly abundant grace and mercy allows.

Father, thank you for all the times you have not given me what I deserved. May your face continue to shine upon me and may you continue to be gracious to me. Amen

Taking it to the Lord...

How can I apply this truth?____
____
____

Father, I've come to worship and praise you! You are my:_____________________________________
____

I give you all Glory, Honor, and Praise O Lord!

Father, I am sorry that I have sinned by:____

Help me to repent. Cleanse me, strengthen me, restore me.

Father, THANK YOU for all your love, grace, mercy and blessings of life that you continually shower down upon me. Thank you especially for:

1._______________________________   2._______________________________
3._______________________________   4._______________________________
5._______________________________   6._______________________________

THANK YOU for answered prayers: ____

Father, I need:____

Father, I ask that YOU: ____
____
____

Lord, bless me that I may be a blessing. Give me Your heart for loving and serving others. Keep Your hand upon me. Keep me from all evil and harm, and let me cause harm to no one. Bind Satan that he have no power over me. All this I pray in subjection to your will and in the strong name of my Lord and Savior, Jesus Christ. Amen.

God Loves Telemarketers

"Don't forget to show hospitality to strangers, for some who have done this have entertained angels without realizing it!" Hebrews 13:2 NLT

Ouch! You mean we need to be kind to telemarketers? Talk about loving the unlovable! Telemarketers trespass upon our privacy, often in the middle of dinner, and if God has sent them as a test of my love, patience, and forbearance, I have failed the test!

> *"There are many who say, "Who will show us any good?"*
> *Psalm 4:2*

Every time we get a telemarketer call, we should at first thank God that we don't have to make a living that way. Can you just imagine the rejection, ridicule and abuse they have to endure every day?

Could one of these telemarketer calls possibly be a divine appointment set up by God for you to win someone for Christ? I intend to find out. From this day until something tells me to stop, I am going to be a telemarketer for the Gospel to them.

When they say "Hello, my name is Tom how are you doing?" I am going to try something like. "Hi Tom! I'm Bob. How nice of you to call. Can I ask you a couple of questions? Tom, if you were to die tonight, are you sure you would go to heaven?" followed by "Tom, if you were to die tonight and God should ask 'why should I let you in my heaven?' what would your answer be?"

> *"And whatever you do or say, let it be as a representative of the Lord Jesus, all the while giving thanks through him to God the Father."*
> *Colossians 3:17*

Only God knows, but think how great it would be to have Tom come up to you in heaven and thank you for leading him into a saving relationship through faith in Jesus Christ.

God can do anything. He can even make the caller the callee. Would you care to join me in this effort to spread the Gospel to telemarketers?

Father, when I think about how unlovable I am sometimes, use this to help me to love the unlovable. Amen.

Taking it to the Lord...

How can I apply this truth?____
____
____

Father, I've come to worship and praise you! You are my:___________________________
____

I give you all Glory, Honor, and Praise O Lord!

Father, I am sorry that I have sinned by:____

Help me to repent. Cleanse me, strengthen me, restore me.

Father, THANK YOU for all your love, grace, mercy and blessings of life that you continually shower down upon me. Thank you especially for:

1.________________________________   2.________________________________
3.________________________________   4.________________________________
5.________________________________   6.________________________________

THANK YOU for answered prayers: ____

Father, I need:____

Father, I ask that YOU: ____
____
____
____

Lord, bless me that I may be a blessing. Give me Your heart for loving and serving others. Keep Your hand upon me. Keep me from all evil and harm, and let me cause harm to no one. Bind Satan that he have no power over me. All this I pray in subjection to your will and in the strong name of my Lord and Savior, Jesus Christ. Amen.

Do You Shortchange God?

"Jesus said to him, "You shall love the Lord your God with all your heart, with all your soul, and with all your mind. This is the first and great commandment. And the second is like it: 'You shall love your neighbor as yourself.'" Matthew 22:37-39

"All" is a big little word. We can rationalize and deceive ourselves, but we can't deceive God. He knows what our "all" is and what it should be.

> *Your precepts concerning all things I consider to be right; I hate every false way."*
> *Psalm 119:128*

God knew that the widow gave all the worldly treasure that she had and was very pleased. God knew that Ananias and Sapphira had shortchanged Him and He destroyed them on the spot

When God calls us robbers, (Malachi 3:8) He is not just talking about money.

He is also talking about our time, our talents and other resources which we lavish upon ourselves and our own agendas, and shortchange Him..

Whether considering our time, talents, or treasure, God knows the heart. He knows when we are offering our sacrifices of praise grudgingly and under compulsion or in joyful, cheerful response to His great love and great gifts to us. *" If you give, you will receive. Your gift will return to you in full measure, pressed down, shaken together to make room for more, and running over. Whatever measure you use in giving—large or small—it will be used to measure what is given back to you." (Luke 6:38 NLT)*

We don't have to be rocket scientists to figure out that when we shortchange God, we are actually only shortchanging ourselves from receiving all of the blessings God wants to shower upon us.

> *"Do all things without complaining and disputing, that you may become blameless and harmless, children of God without fault in the midst of a crooked and perverse generation, among whom you shine as lights in the world."*
> *Philippians 2:14 NLT*

Father, by the power of your Spirit, help me to excel in the grace of giving in every area of my life. Amen.

Taking it to the Lord...

How can I apply this truth?____

____

____

Father, I've come to worship and praise you! You are my:__________________

____

I give you all Glory, Honor, and Praise O Lord!

Father, I am sorry that I have sinned by:_______________________________

Help me to repent. Cleanse me, strengthen me, restore me.

Father, THANK YOU for all your love, grace, mercy and blessings of life that you continually shower down upon me.

Thank you especially for:

1.______________________________   2.______________________________
3.______________________________   4.______________________________
5.______________________________   6.______________________________

THANK YOU for answered prayers:_______________________________________

Father, I need:____

Father, I ask that YOU:____

____

____

Lord, bless me that I may be a blessing. Give me Your heart for loving and serving others. Keep Your hand upon me. Keep me from all evil and harm, and let me cause harm to no one. Bind Satan that he have no power over me. All this I pray in subjection to your will and in the strong name of my Lord and Savior, Jesus Christ. Amen.

Friends in High Places

"God will surely do this for you, for he always does just what he says, and he is the one who invited you into this wonderful friendship with his Son, Jesus Christ our Lord."1 Corinthians 1:9 NLT

The politics of having friends in high places has gone on for a long time, and will continue regardless of all the campaign reform laws and other measures.

> *"You didn't choose me. I chose you. I appointed you to go and produce fruit that will last, so that the Father will give you whatever you ask for, using my name."*
> *John 15:16 NLT*

Special interest groups representing minorities and other bloc voters seem to wield a very disproportionate influence because they elect people who cater to their interests..

Professional lobbying is a zillion dollar industry with millions in contributions spent to elect or gain access to friends in high places.

One of the great shames of our political system is the selling out of common interest to the special interest groups who control enough votes to intimidate and control certain agendas in this country.

As believers, it is very encouraging to know that we have two of the best friends in the very highest of places. They can't be bought, intimidated and they will never sell out to the opposition.

The Holy Spirit is continually making intercession for us even when we don't know for what to pray.

> *"And the Father who knows all hearts knows what the Spirit is saying, for the Spirit pleads for us believers in harmony with God's own will."*
> *Romans 8:26 NLT*

Best of all, Jesus Himself is our great high priest who is sitting at the right hand of God making intercession on our behalf so that God will not see us as the sinners we are, but as brothers and sisters of Christ.

His one time sacrifice of dying on the cross for us fulfilled all the righteous demands of the law and has restored our relationship with God.

Aren't you glad you've got such good friends in high places?

Father, what joy there is to knowing that my friendship with Your gives me access to your throne of grace. Amen

Taking it to the Lord...

How can I apply this truth?____

____

Father, I've come to worship and praise you! You are my:_______________________

____

I give you all Glory, Honor, and Praise O Lord!

Father, I am sorry that I have sinned by:_____________________________________

Help me to repent. Cleanse me, strengthen me, restore me.

Father, THANK YOU for all your love, grace, mercy and blessings of life that you continually shower down upon me. Thank you especially for:

1.____________________________________   2.____________________________________

3.____________________________________   4.____________________________________

5.____________________________________   6.____________________________________

THANK YOU for answered prayers: ____

Father, I need:____

Father, I ask that YOU: ____

____

____

Lord, bless me that I may be a blessing. Give me Your heart for loving and serving others. Keep Your hand upon me. Keep me from all evil and harm, and let me cause harm to no one. Bind Satan that he have no power over me. All this I pray in subjection to your will and in the strong name of my Lord and Savior, Jesus Christ. Amen.

Coming Up Short

"For all have sinned; all fall short of God's glorious standard. Yet now God in his gracious kindness declares us not guilty." Romans 3:23 NLT

We all probably come up short or have come up short in some areas of our lives. We sometimes come up short

> *"The LORD upholds all who fall, and raises up all who are bowed down."*
> *Psalm 145:14*

financially, where there doesn't seem to be enough to pay the bills or maintain the life style that we have chosen. Many come up short of the expectations of their bosses and get fired or demoted.

Others come up short in meeting the expectations of their spouses and break their marriage covenant with not only their spouses, but with God.

In my horse racing days, I had an awful lot of horses that came up way short.

As believers, we have sometimes become so indoctrinated against good works that we stand in danger of coming up short when God passes out His rewards to believers on judgment day.

We can be assured and look forward to eternal life in heaven because Jesus was good enough and imputed His goodness to us through His death on the cross. There is no good work that can earn this.

> *"If you try to keep your life for yourself, you will lose it. But if you give up your life for me, you will find true life."*
> *Luke 9:24 NLT*

It is so refreshing to note that seemingly just over the past few years many outstanding preachers and bible scholars have been gifted with spiritual insight to articulate a better understanding of the rewards in heaven.

What we do here with the time, talents, and treasures we have been given does matter, and may well determine what we will be doing for eternity.

Father, help me to be about doing those things that you created me for before I was ever born, so that I don't come up short at the resurrection of the just. Amen

Taking it to the Lord...

How can I apply this truth?____

____

____

Father, I've come to worship and praise you! You are my:_____________________

____

I give you all Glory, Honor, and Praise O Lord!

Father, I am sorry that I have sinned by:__________________________________

Help me to repent. Cleanse me, strengthen me, restore me.

Father, THANK YOU for all your love, grace, mercy and blessings of life that you continually shower down upon me. Thank you especially for:

1._________________________________   2._________________________________

3._________________________________   4._________________________________

5._________________________________   6._________________________________

THANK YOU for answered prayers:____

Father, I need:____

Father, I ask that YOU:____

____

____

____

Lord, bless me that I may be a blessing. Give me Your heart for loving and serving others. Keep Your hand upon me. Keep me from all evil and harm, and let me cause harm to no one. Bind Satan that he have no power over me. All this I pray in subjection to your will and in the strong name of my Lord and Savior, Jesus Christ. Amen.

Thank You, Dr. Heimlich!

"Looking carefully lest anyone fall short of the grace of God; lest any root of bitterness springing up cause trouble, and by this many become defiled;" Hebrews 12:15

It is a terrifying thing to get a food particle stuck in your esophagus. You can't breathe, you can't get it to go down, and panic sets in. I have had a lot of near misses, and once had to have this life saving maneuver performed on me by my son at a restaurant. I don't know whether Heimlich is a person or the maneuver, but either way I am thankful for it.

> *"Then I realized how bitter I had become, how pained I had been by all I had seen."*
> *Psalm 73:21 NLT*

Just as food getting stuck in our esophagus poses a real and present danger to our body, resentment and bitterness can cause the same danger to our souls if we don't get rid of them.

When we harbor unforgiveness and resentment against God or someone who has harmed or offended us, we are going to end up choking on it and the damage we inflict on ourselves is going to far worse than the damages the offense we refuse to forgive caused. Many studies link illnesses of every kind to the poison of resentment or bitterness that we let "stick in our craw."

Instead of trying to be reconciled with one who has offended us by talking to them about it in a kind and loving way, we want to talk about it to others and let the root take hold.

> *"But if you have bitter envy and self-seeking in your hearts, do not boast and lie against the truth."*
> *James 3:14*

God has provided an excellent maneuver to help us avoid the inevitable consequences of allowing resentment or bitterness to take root within us. It is called forgive and forget. If God can do this for us, we can certainly do it for others.

Father, don't let any seed of bitterness take root in me. By the power of Your Spirit living within me, help me to forgive and forget. Amen

Taking it to the Lord...

How can I apply this truth?____
____
____

Father, I've come to worship and praise you! You are my:_________________________________
____

I give you all Glory, Honor, and Praise O Lord!

Father, I am sorry that I have sinned by:____

Help me to repent. Cleanse me, strengthen me, restore me.

Father, THANK YOU for all your love, grace, mercy and blessings of life that you continually shower down upon me. Thank you especially for:

1._________________________________   2._________________________________
3._________________________________   4._________________________________
5._________________________________   6._________________________________

THANK YOU for answered prayers: ____

Father, I need:____

Father, I ask that YOU: ____
____
____

Lord, bless me that I may be a blessing. Give me Your heart for loving and serving others. Keep Your hand upon me. Keep me from all evil and harm, and let me cause harm to no one. Bind Satan that he have no power over me. All this I pray in subjection to your will and in the strong name of my Lord and Savior, Jesus Christ. Amen.

Mutiny

"So then, my beloved brethren, let every man be swift to hear, slow to speak, slow to wrath; for the wrath of man does not produce the righteousness of God." James 1:19

There is a major battle for control going on in a lot of households. It's the battle for control of the remote control of the "boob tube." Some of my grown kids and grand kids channel surfing drives me nuts. I have a friend who seems to have a built in sensor and can mute a commercial before it even starts.

> *'But I, like a deaf man, do not hear; and I am like a mute who does not open his mouth."*
> *Psalm 38:14*

The mute button is a wonderful invention when it comes to TV, but it can be either a deadly weapon of destruction or a great piece of armor in the battle of life.

When we mute out God's call to salvation we are lost forever. When we miss His calls to righteousness and to doing the good works for which He created us, we are in danger of losing our heavenly rewards.

We need to deal with temptation by hitting the mute button when the responses of the flesh or the deceits of the devil start to trigger sinful thoughts and responses. When our spiritual batteries are fully charged and we are walking in power of the Spirit, we can hit the mute button and break the bondage to sin.

> *"But He answered and said to them, 'My mother and My brothers are these who hear the word of God and do it."*
> *Luke 7:21*

I don't know about you, but I am very thankful and grateful to God that he hasn't hit his mute button on me. He still hears my calls for forgiveness, strength, relational, physical, spiritual, and material blessings.

He hears the prayers of the Holy Spirit who is constantly interceding for me, and he hears and answers my prayers for others in accordance with His good and gracious will.

Father, give me the spiritual discernment to know how and when to use the mute button of my mind. Amen.

Taking it to the Lord...

How can I apply this truth?____

____

Father, I've come to worship and praise you! You are my:___________________________

____

I give you all Glory, Honor, and Praise O Lord!

Father, I am sorry that I have sinned by:____

Help me to repent. Cleanse me, strengthen me, restore me.

Father, THANK YOU for all your love, grace, mercy and blessings of life that you continually shower down upon me. Thank you especially for:

1.____________________________   2.____________________________
3.____________________________   4.____________________________
5.____________________________   6.____________________________

THANK YOU for answered prayers:____

Father, I need:____

Father, I ask that YOU:____

____

____

Lord, bless me that I may be a blessing. Give me Your heart for loving and serving others. Keep Your hand upon me. Keep me from all evil and harm, and let me cause harm to no one. Bind Satan that he have no power over me. All this I pray in subjection to your will and in the strong name of my Lord and Savior, Jesus Christ. Amen.

Ruffled Feathers

"Stop your anger! Turn from your rage! Do not envy others—it only leads to harm." Psalm 37:8 NLT

It seems that we are constantly getting our comfort zone squeezed. We take offense when none is intended, we get our feelings hurt when others reject our ideas or suggestions. Our response to any kind of conflict seems to bring out the worst in us instead of God's best.

> *"Don't sin by letting anger gain control over you. Think about it overnight and remain silent."*
> *Psalm 4:4 NLT*

Road rage is an ever increasing and dangerous anger problem. We Christians sometimes lash out in a manner that brings shame to the name we claim. Satan seems to know where our fuse is the shortest and how to light it.

Solomon, recognized as the wisest man who ever lived has some comments on anger worth repeating from Proverbs: *"Those who control their anger have great understanding; those with a hasty temper will make mistakes."* (14:29) – *"A gentle answer turns away wrath, but harsh words stir up anger."* (15:1) – *"People with good sense restrain their anger; they earn esteem by overlooking wrongs."* (19:11) *"As surely as a wind from the north brings rain, so a gossiping tongue causes anger!"* (25:23)- *"Anger is cruel, and wrath is like a flood, but who can survive the destructiveness of jealousy?"* (27:4) *"Mockers can get a whole town agitated, but those who are wise will calm anger."*(29:8 T) *"A fool gives full vent to anger, but a wise person quietly holds it back".* (29:11) (All references from NLT) Perhaps worse than anger itself, is the devastating consequence of resentment and unforgiveness. We all need to be more like God who is " *Slow to anger and rich in unfailing love, forgiving every kind of sin and rebellion". (Numbers 14:18 NLT)*

> *"Don't sin by letting anger gain control over you."* *Don't let the sun go down while you are still angry, 27for anger gives a mighty foothold to the Devil."*
> *Ephesians 4:26 NLT*

Father it is only the power of Your Spirit in producing the fruit of self-control, long suffering, patience, kindness, and love that will keep me from the destructiveness of anger. Fill me with Your Spirit! Amen

Taking it to the Lord...

How can I apply this truth?____

____

Father, I've come to worship and praise you! You are my:_____________________

____

I give you all Glory, Honor, and Praise O Lord!

Father, I am sorry that I have sinned by:___________________________________

Help me to repent. Cleanse me, strengthen me, restore me.

Father, THANK YOU for all your love, grace, mercy and blessings of life that you continually shower down upon me. Thank you especially for:

1.________________________________   2.________________________________
3.________________________________   4.________________________________
5.________________________________   6.________________________________

THANK YOU for answered prayers:____

Father, I need:____

Father, I ask that YOU:____

____

____

Lord, bless me that I may be a blessing. Give me Your heart for loving and serving others. Keep Your hand upon me. Keep me from all evil and harm, and let me cause harm to no one. Bind Satan that he have no power over me. All this I pray in subjection to your will and in the strong name of my Lord and Savior, Jesus Christ. Amen.

Lightning Rod

"For as the lightning lights up the entire sky, so it will be when the Son of Man comes." Matthew 24:27 NLT

Lightning is one of the most explosive and terrifying forces in God's creation. Living in one of the highest and most severe lightning belts in the world makes me acutely aware of this danger.

> *"His lightning flashes out across the world. The earth sees and trembles."*
> *Psalm 97:4*

A hi-tech multi-million dollar truck weight station had to be shutdown and dismantled because of lightning. Over the years, several thousand horses have been struck down by lightning as they sought the shelter beneath trees that draw lightning like honey draws a fly.

Lightning rods are still a big business in this area. I have spent several thousand dollars on them myself not knowing if they would really do any good, but just for the comfort of thinking they would. What a comfort there is in knowing that we have the only reliable and proven lightning rod ever created!

> *"Then, in heaven, the Temple of God was opened and the Ark of his covenant could be seen inside the Temple. Lightning flashed, thunder crashed and roared; there was a great hailstorm, and the world was shaken by a mighty earthquake."*
> *Revelation 11:17 NLT*

Jesus Christ came into the world to be our lightning rod. He draws all of the anger and wrath of God because of our sins upon Himself, and grounds them into the dirt where they belong.

Because He was good enough, we don't have to be, but we sure ought to want to be.

He is our high tower who insulates us from the ravages of sin and turns its negative force into a Spirit filled, positive life giving force for the present and for all of eternity.

Doesn't this realization make you want to praise Him by pleasing Him in every area of your life?

Father, thank you for taking the power of sin and burying it with Your Son and my Savior, Jesus Christ. Amen

Taking it to the Lord...

How can I apply this truth?____

____

Father, I've come to worship and praise you! You are my:_____________________________

I give you all Glory, Honor, and Praise O Lord!

Father, I am sorry that I have sinned by:______________________________________

Help me to repent. Cleanse me, strengthen me, restore me.

Father, THANK YOU for all your love, grace, mercy and blessings of life that you continually shower down upon me. Thank you especially for:

1.__________________________________ 2.__________________________________

3.__________________________________ 4.__________________________________

5.__________________________________ 6.__________________________________

THANK YOU for answered prayers:____

Father, I need:____

Father, I ask that YOU:____

____

____

Lord, bless me that I may be a blessing. Give me Your heart for loving and serving others. Keep Your hand upon me. Keep me from all evil and harm, and let me cause harm to no one. Bind Satan that he have no power over me. All this I pray in subjection to your will and in the strong name of my Lord and Savior, Jesus Christ. Amen.

Selling Out Fast

"Seek the LORD while He may be found, call upon Him while He is near." Isaiah 55:6 NLT

> *"And the Good News about the Kingdom will be preached throughout the whole world, so that all nations will hear it; and then, finally, the end will come."*
> *Matthew 24:14 NLT*

It may be later than you think! The Gospel has been preached and heard throughout the whole world, thanks to satellite TV and the dedicated efforts of so many ministries.

There are signs of a great awakening among Jews to the reality of Jesus Christ being the Messiah.

The generally accepted understanding of Scripture is that when the Gospel has been preached to all nations, and when the complete number of Jews receive Jesus Christ as Savior and Lord, the end will come. Scripture time and time again warns us all to be ready.

To those who look to the thief on the cross as assurance that they can take their time opening the door when Jesus comes knocking with the power of the Holy Spirit had better look at the admonition in today's message from Isaiah.

> *"Then I saw the Lamb standing on Mount Zion, and with him were 144,000 who had his name and his Father's name written on their foreheads."*
> *Revelation 14:1 NLT*

The disappointment we have experienced when we have responded too late to great savings opportunities and found them "sold out" when we finally make up our minds is trivial. Even the remote possibility that we may delay too long in receiving Jesus Christ should be cause for real concern.

May God forbid that we not find ourselves sold out and shut out from the joys of eternal life here and forever either through our death, or His return before we answer His call to salvation.

Father, I pray that those I love who do not yet know You will respond to Your call before it's too late. Amen

Taking it to the Lord...

How can I apply this truth?____

____

____

Father, I've come to worship and praise you! You are my:____________________

____

I give you all Glory, Honor, and Praise O Lord!

Father, I am sorry that I have sinned by:__________________________________

Help me to repent. Cleanse me, strengthen me, restore me.

Father, THANK YOU for all your love, grace, mercy and blessings of life that you continually shower down upon me. Thank you especially for:

1.________________________________   2.________________________________

3.________________________________   4.________________________________

5.________________________________   6.________________________________

THANK YOU for answered prayers:____

Father, I need:____

Father, I ask that YOU:____

____

____

Lord, bless me that I may be a blessing. Give me Your heart for loving and serving others. Keep Your hand upon me. Keep me from all evil and harm, and let me cause harm to no one. Bind Satan that he have no power over me. All this I pray in subjection to your will and in the strong name of my Lord and Savior, Jesus Christ. Amen.

A 2-4-1 Special You Can't Afford to Miss

"May you experience the love of Christ, though it is so great you will never fully understand it. Then you will be filled with the fullness of life and power that comes from God." Ephesians 3:19 NLT

As great as heaven is going to be, and as great as our assurance of going to be with the Lord in heaven is; we should always be mindful of the fact that eternal life also means an abundant, fruitful life on this earth, and begins with our new birth in Christ.

> *"Everyone will share the story of your wonderful goodness; they will sing with joy of your righteousness."*
> *Psalm 145:7 NLT*

God has promised to heal us and let us *"enjoy abundant peace and security",* (Jeremiah 33:6). In John 10:10b, Jesus says: "My purpose is to give life in all its fullness." (NLT)

Although we will experience pain and suffering in this life because of the sin that is in this world, we are also promised *"peace that surpasses all understanding", "the joy of the Lord", "Friendship with God", "means of escape"* from every temptation, *"very present help in time of trouble, all sufficient grace",* and even *"the desires of our heart".*

God makes us a "2 for 1" offer that many seem to think is too good to be true judging by the way they turn it down time and time again.

We often become discouraged and cling to the rock of our salvation knowing that God is going to wipe away every tear and that there will be no more sorrow or sadness in heaven.

> *"But if you stay joined to me and my words remain in you, you may ask any request you like, and it will be granted!"*
> *John 15:7 NLT*

We should be even more encouraged to know that there is inexpressible joy for us in this life as we become filled with the Love of God that is ours through faith in Christ Jesus and can live in the freedom and joy of our salvation through the power of the Holy Spirit living within us. It's to be found in abiding.

Father, keep me ever mindful and thankful for the double blessing I have of the abundant life here, and the future joys of heaven to come. Amen

Taking it to the Lord...

How can I apply this truth?____

____

____

Father, I've come to worship and praise you! You are my:___________________

____

I give you all Glory, Honor, and Praise O Lord!

Father, I am sorry that I have sinned by:________________________________

Help me to repent. Cleanse me, strengthen me, restore me.

Father, THANK YOU for all your love, grace, mercy and blessings of life that you continually shower down upon me. Thank you especially for:

1._________________________________   2._________________________________

3._________________________________   4._________________________________

5._________________________________   6._________________________________

THANK YOU for answered prayers:____

Father, I need:____

Father, I ask that YOU:____

____

____

Lord, bless me that I may be a blessing. Give me Your heart for loving and serving others. Keep Your hand upon me. Keep me from all evil and harm, and let me cause harm to no one. Bind Satan that he have no power over me. All this I pray in subjection to your will and in the strong name of my Lord and Savior, Jesus Christ. Amen.

Get Out of the Boat!

"Then Jesus told them, "I assure you, if you have faith and don't doubt, you can do things like this and much more. You can even say to this mountain, 'May God lift you up and throw you into the sea,' and it will happen. If you believe, you will receive whatever you ask for in prayer." Matthew 21:21, 22 NLT

Faith is the living, growing certainty of the reality of God and His promises for now and forever. Faith is what gives ordinary people the power to accomplish extraordinary things. Lack of faith or unbelief is the means through which Satan keeps even believers from growing into the fullness of Christ and from enjoying all of the abundance of life that this affords.

> *"When I pray,*
> *You answer me;*
> *You encourage me*
> *by giving me the*
> *strength I need."*
> *Psalm 138:3 NLT*

We are never going to know the joy of walking on water until we get out of the boat. When we let doubt and despair, fear of failure, and love of our "comfort zone" keep us glued to our seats, we are going to miss out on the opportunities for blessings and fruitfulness that God has purposed for us.

As someone very wise once said: "if you believe you can, or believe you can't - you're right!"

> *"What is faith? It is the confident assurance that what we hope for is going to happen. It is the evidence of things we cannot yet see. God gave his approval to people in days of old because of their faith."*
> *Hebrews 11:1 NLT*

The children of Israel wandered in the wilderness for 40 years because they would not get out of the boat. The rich young ruler is spending eternity in hell because he trusted his riches instead of the one who provided them.

What is the sea of doubt keeping you from doing right now? If it is something that would glorify God and be fully pleasing to Him, better get your feet wet!

Father, your perfect love casts out all fear. Give me the courage and the power to walk on the water of faith that I might know the fullness of your love. Amen

Taking it to the Lord...

How can I apply this truth?____

____

Father, I've come to worship and praise you! You are my:_____________________

____

I give you all Glory, Honor, and Praise O Lord!

Father, I am sorry that I have sinned by:_________________________________

Help me to repent. Cleanse me, strengthen me, restore me.

Father, THANK YOU for all your love, grace, mercy and blessings of life that you continually shower down upon me. Thank you especially for:

1._________________________________   2._________________________________
3._________________________________   4._________________________________
5._________________________________   6._________________________________

THANK YOU for answered prayers:____

Father, I need:____

Father, I ask that YOU:____

____

____

Lord, bless me that I may be a blessing. Give me Your heart for loving and serving others. Keep Your hand upon me. Keep me from all evil and harm, and let me cause harm to no one. Bind Satan that he have no power over me. All this I pray in subjection to your will and in the strong name of my Lord and Savior, Jesus Christ. Amen.

Fellowship for the Suffering

"Since he himself has gone through suffering and temptation, he is able to help us when we are being tempted." Hebrews 2:18 NLT

Alcoholics Anonymous has for over half a century been the most effective treatment yet devised for alcoholism. The same 12 basic steps have also had much success treating other addictions including drugs and gambling.

> *"The LORD helps the fallen and lifts up those bent beneath their loads."*
> **Psalm 145:14**

All of these programs provide a fellowship for the suffering to share their experiences, strength, and hope with each other for the purpose of overcoming.

Support groups provide a fellowship for the suffering of not only many problems, but also for the families of those afflicted.

Providing fellowship for the suffering is what Christ's Church is all about. Whether it's through sharing your testimony as to how you received Jesus Christ as your savior and helping others to get to know the peace and joy of salvation; or through sharing experiences that help strengthen and comfort others facing or going through problems and illnesses that you have been through, you are part of the fellowship for the suffering.

Even when we cannot speak from experience about a problem we have never encountered, we can always talk about the one who knows exactly what anyone is going through.

> *"He comforts us in all our troubles so that we can comfort others."*
> **2 Corinthians 1:4 NLT**

You never have to look very far to find someone who is suffering. As believers commanded to love others, we can find great joy in bringing comfort and strength to others through not only shared experience, but also through fervent prayer.

We are all going to need the fellowship for sufferers at some point in time.

Father, thank you for calling me into the fellowship of believers through faith in Jesus Christ   Help me to strengthen and encourage the suffering with you love. Amen

Taking it to the Lord...

How can I apply this truth?____

____

Father, I've come to worship and praise you! You are my:_________________________________

____

I give you all Glory, Honor, and Praise O Lord!

Father, I am sorry that I have sinned by:____

Help me to repent. Cleanse me, strengthen me, restore me.

Father, THANK YOU for all your love, grace, mercy and blessings of life that you continually shower down upon me. Thank you especially for:

1._________________________________   2._________________________________

3._________________________________   4._________________________________

5._________________________________   6._________________________________

THANK YOU for answered prayers:____

Father, I need:____

Father, I ask that YOU:____

____

____

Lord, bless me that I may be a blessing. Give me Your heart for loving and serving others. Keep Your hand upon me. Keep me from all evil and harm, and let me cause harm to no one. Bind Satan that he have no power over me. All this I pray in subjection to your will and in the strong name of my Lord and Savior, Jesus Christ. Amen.

"But For...."

"And He said to me, "My grace is sufficient for you, for My strength is made perfect in weakness." 2 Corinthians 12:9

It is so easy to take God for granted. We often seem to go through life whining and complaining about "minors" without even giving a thought to all of the unseen and unknown "majors" from which God has spared and shielded us

> *'He orders his angels to protect you. And they will hold you with their hands to keep you from striking your foot on a stone."*
> *Psalm 91:11*

It is only when we come upon someone experiencing a really terrible illness, circumstance, or experience that the Holy Spirit reminds us that there "But For" the grace of God go I." Like the man who cried because he had no shoes until he saw a man who had no feet, we need to view the misfortunes of others with not only sympathy and compassion, but also with thanksgiving and praise to God that we have been spared such a fate.

> *"For the Lord God is a sun and shield; the Lord will give grace and glory; no good thing will He withhold from those who walk uprightly."*
> *Psalm 84:11 NLT*

I thank God continually that by His grace, I have been shielded and spared so many of the heartaches and tragedies I see all around me. I think that maybe God knows how weak I really am, and in His mercy and love shields me from things He knows I am not strong enough to handle.

When we think of all the things we have been spared by the grace of God, we should be humbled and ashamed that we would ever dare complain about anything.

Father, keep me ever mindful of your tender mercy and loving kindness shielding me from so many of the tragedies and suffering I see all around me, and forgive me for taking all of my blessings for granted. Amen

Taking it to the Lord...

How can I apply this truth?____

____

____

Father, I've come to worship and praise you! You are my:_______________________

____

I give you all Glory, Honor, and Praise O Lord!

Father, I am sorry that I have sinned by:_______________________________________

Help me to repent. Cleanse me, strengthen me, restore me.

Father, THANK YOU for all your love, grace, mercy and blessings of life that you continually shower down upon me. Thank you especially for:

1.______________________________   2.______________________________

3.______________________________   4.______________________________

5.______________________________   6.______________________________

THANK YOU for answered prayers:______________________________________

Father, I need:____

Father, I ask that YOU:____

____

____

Lord, bless me that I may be a blessing. Give me Your heart for loving and serving others. Keep Your hand upon me. Keep me from all evil and harm, and let me cause harm to no one. Bind Satan that he have no power over me. All this I pray in subjection to your will and in the strong name of my Lord and Savior, Jesus Christ. Amen.

Dead Men Walking

"You were dead because of your sins and because your sinful nature was not yet cut away. Then God made you alive with Christ. He forgave all our sins." Colossians 2:13 NLT

Everywhere we go they are all around us. Our world, our lives, our daily activities are filled with people who need the Lord.

> *"When you send Your Spirit, new life is born to replenish all the living of the earth."*
> *Psalm 104:30 NLT*

The ranks of the eternally doomed are growing throughout the world. The age of enlightenment has cast darkness into the real understanding of life. Without knowledge of and faith in God, there is no enlightenment.

Many of us who have been "dead men walking" before we came to Christ are uniquely equipped to recognize, identify with, and minister to people who need the Lord.

All of us have been brought from death in trespasses and sin to life in Jesus Christ through the influence of someone. We have a privilege and obligation to "pass it on!" by being the messenger of God's love and grace to someone else. There is no higher calling in this life!

There is a special recognition in heaven for those who do "pass it on!" *"Those who are wise shall shine like the brightness of the firmament, and those who turn many to righteousness like the stars forever and ever" (Daniel 12:3 NLT).*

> *"Once you were dead, doomed forever because of your many sins. ²You used to live just like the rest of the world, full of sin, obeying Satan, the mighty prince of the power of the air."*
> *Ephesians 2:1 NLT*

As much as we need to have compassion and sorrow for the "dead men walking" around us, we need even more to use the power of prayer and supplication, and a Spirit powered witness as God's agents called to proclaim the Good News of new life in Christ.

Father, make me sensitive to the "dead men walking" around me, and use me as a conduit of your saving grace to them. Amen

Taking it to the Lord...

How can I apply this truth?____

____

____

Father, I've come to worship and praise you! You are my:_______________________

____

I give you all Glory, Honor, and Praise O Lord!

Father, I am sorry that I have sinned by:_____________________________________

Help me to repent. Cleanse me, strengthen me, restore me.

Father, THANK YOU for all your love, grace, mercy and blessings of life that you continually shower down upon me. Thank you especially for:

1.____________________________   2.____________________________

3.____________________________   4.____________________________

5.____________________________   6.____________________________

THANK YOU for answered prayers:_______________________________________

Father, I need:____

Father, I ask that YOU:____

____

____

Lord, bless me that I may be a blessing. Give me Your heart for loving and serving others. Keep Your hand upon me. Keep me from all evil and harm, and let me cause harm to no one. Bind Satan that he have no power over me. All this I pray in subjection to your will and in the strong name of my Lord and Savior, Jesus Christ. Amen.

Stand Tall!

"May our Lord Jesus Christ and God our Father, who loved us and in his special favor gave us everlasting comfort and good hope, comfort your hearts and give you strength in every good thing you do and say." 2 Thessalonians 2:16 NLT

Standing tall requires a special measure of grace that God will always provide when we are abiding in Him and doing those good things that glorify Him and bring a smile to His face.

> **"You are good and do only good; teach me your principles."**
> **Psalm 119:68**

Someone once said that we "never stand so tall as when we stoop to help someone else." The life of every believer should be a life of ministry. We are all called to not only love God, but to be conduits of His love to others.

We can stand tall in the eyes of others by accumulating power, wealth, or popularity. Many "stand tall" in the eyes of others by their athletic prowess, or outstanding accomplishments.

There is really nothing wrong with any of these worldly denominators of success, but they are really not what "standing tall" is all about from God's perspective. The fleeting approval of self and others is the only reward we are going to get out of these things.

The widow who gave her mite is one of the best examples of "standing tall" in God's eyes. When we take the time to comfort the hurting, encourage the failing, help someone financially, or showing kindness in any other way, we are going to "stand tall" in God's eyes.

Jesus said: "*Assuredly, I say to you, inasmuch as you did it to one of the least of these My brethren, you did it to Me.*"

> **"It is God who gives us, along with you, the ability to stand firm for Christ."**
> **2 Corinthians 1:21 NLT**

Jesus "stood tall" when he stooped to wash the feet of the disciples. He "stood tall" when he gladly allowed Himself to be crushed by the load of our sins. May we "stand tall" in the joy and delight of the Lord when we have the opportunities to reflect His love by stooping to help others.

Father, thank You for empowering me to stand tall in your sight by being about your business of loving others. Amen

Taking it to the Lord...

How can I apply this truth?____
____
____

Father, I've come to worship and praise you! You are my:_________________________________
____

I give you all Glory, Honor, and Praise O Lord!

Father, I am sorry that I have sinned by:____

Help me to repent. Cleanse me, strengthen me, restore me.

Father, THANK YOU for all your love, grace, mercy and blessings of life that you continually shower down upon me. Thank you especially for:

1.___________________________________   2.___________________________________
3.___________________________________   4.___________________________________
5.___________________________________   6.___________________________________

THANK YOU for answered prayers:____

Father, I need:____

Father, I ask that YOU:____
____
____

Lord, bless me that I may be a blessing. Give me Your heart for loving and serving others. Keep Your hand upon me. Keep me from all evil and harm, and let me cause harm to no one. Bind Satan that he have no power over me. All this I pray in subjection to your will and in the strong name of my Lord and Savior, Jesus Christ. Amen.

Let the Walls Come Down!

"So that there should be no division in the body, but that its parts should have equal concern for each other. 1 Corinthians 12:25 NIV

The Great Wall of China is truly one of the great wonders of the world. As impressive as it is from pictures, they do not begin to match the experience of actually climbing and walking on it.

> *"The name of the LORD is a strong tower; the righteous run to it and are safe."*
> *Proverbs 18:10*

Since the beginning of man, walls seem to have been the means of protection from hostile attacks.

On the spiritual level, walls of denominationalism and race, division and disagreement, jealousy and pride, fear and resentment, are often walls of sin that separate us from being obedient to both the great commandment to love others and the Great Commission to make disciples of all nations.

Contrary too many beliefs, all believers in Jesus Christ are members of the body of Christ first and members of a denomination second. There are not going to be any Lutherans, Baptists, Catholics or any other denominations in heaven. There will be only blood bought children of God who have received the righteousness of Christ by faith in His death on the cross for their sins.

> *"So whenever you speak, or whatever you do, remember that you will be judged by the law of love, the law that set you free."*
> *James 5:12 NLT*

Christian liberty allows for a lot of freedom in how we should worship. The only non negotiable is Who we should worship.

We had better get used to the idea of co existing in heaven with people of other color and other denominations. The walls that we have built up here are all going to come tumbling down there!

Father, forgive me for the walls of prejudice that I have built up against others. Help me to believe and celebrate the unity of all believers who are in Christ. Amen

Taking it to the Lord...

How can I apply this truth?____

____

Father, I've come to worship and praise you! You are my:_________________________________

____

I give you all Glory, Honor, and Praise O Lord!

Father, I am sorry that I have sinned by:____

Help me to repent. Cleanse me, strengthen me, restore me.

Father, THANK YOU for all your love, grace, mercy and blessings of life that you continually shower down upon me. Thank you especially for:

1.______________________________   2.______________________________
3.______________________________   4.______________________________
5.______________________________   6.______________________________

THANK YOU for answered prayers:____

Father, I need:____

Father, I ask that YOU:____

____

____

Lord, bless me that I may be a blessing. Give me Your heart for loving and serving others. Keep Your hand upon me. Keep me from all evil and harm, and let me cause harm to no one. Bind Satan that he have no power over me. All this I pray in subjection to your will and in the strong name of my Lord and Savior, Jesus Christ. Amen.

Fellowship of Winners

"God blesses the people who patiently endure testing. Afterward they will receive the crown of life that God has promised to those who love him." James 1:12 NLT

Some of the greatest joys of life are found in being a part of something bigger than your self. In sports, it's the joy of the shared experience of being on a team, hopefully to win.

> *"Blessed is the man who fears the LORD, who delights greatly in His commandments. His descendants will be mighty on earth; The generation of the upright will be blessed."*
> *Psalm 112:1,2 NLT*

Winners of World War II are still holding reunions to relive the joy of their victory.

The disciples are an exciting example of how God can use ordinary people to accomplish extraordinary things when they bond together in unity of purpose and common vision. When they saw Jesus resurrected and alive among them, they saw the greatest victory ever won and proceeded to change the world.

Today, as a believer that Jesus Christ died on the cross for your salvation and gives you the victory over death by faith, you are a member of the winning team!

As a winner, you have "Victory in Jesus" and the privilege of becoming a member of the fellowship of winners. "Oh what fellowship, oh what joy divine, leaning on the everlasting arms, what a blessedness, what peace is mine, leaning on the everlasting arms."

> *"For every child of God defeats this evil world by trusting Christ to give the victory."*
> *1 John 5:4*

As a member of this fellowship, you have the responsibility and the privilege of living out the great commandment and great commission in many different ways. Whether we are building the kingdom through evangelism, missions, or just being a godly parent or faithful witness by the life we live, we need to be in fellowship with other winners in order to be strengthened and encouraged for fulfilling God's purposes for our lives.

Father, keep me ever mindful of my need for the fellowship of winners in You, so that my joy may be full. Amen

Taking it to the Lord...

How can I apply this truth?____

____

____

Father, I've come to worship and praise you! You are my:_____________________

____

I give you all Glory, Honor, and Praise O Lord!

Father, I am sorry that I have sinned by:_________________________________

Help me to repent. Cleanse me, strengthen me, restore me.

Father, THANK YOU for all your love, grace, mercy and blessings of life that you continually shower down upon me. Thank you especially for:

1._________________________________   2._________________________________

3._________________________________   4._________________________________

5._________________________________   6._________________________________

THANK YOU for answered prayers:_______________________________________

Father, I need:____

Father, I ask that YOU:____

____

____

Lord, bless me that I may be a blessing. Give me Your heart for loving and serving others. Keep Your hand upon me. Keep me from all evil and harm, and let me cause harm to no one. Bind Satan that he have no power over me. All this I pray in subjection to your will and in the strong name of my Lord and Savior, Jesus Christ. Amen.

Caller ID

"And now, Israel, what does the LORD your God require of you? He requires you to fear him, to live according to his will, to love and worship him with all your heart and soul, and to obey the LORD'S commands and laws that I am giving you today for your own good." Deuteronomy 10:12 NLT

Many use caller ID on their phones to filter out telemarketing calls and other calls they don't care to take. They look at who's calling and then choose to ignore or answer.

> *"Answer me when I call, O God who declares me innocent. Take away my distress. Have mercy on me and hear my prayer."*
> *Psalm 4:1 NLT*

Aren't you glad that God doesn't filter us out with caller ID? Aren't you glad that He doesn't think about us and treat us the way most of us think about and treat telemarketers?

Unfortunately, we miss too many of God's calls because we haven't taken the time to get to know God through His Word and to recognize His voice. We sometimes don't recognize the circumstances or voices of other believers through which God is calling.

Sometimes we recognize the caller, but choose to ignore because we simply don't want to hear what we know He is going to say about our conduct or willful disobedience.

Often we make the wrong identification of the caller. We answer the call to what we perceive to be pleasure when it is really a call to pain and suffering. We pick up the call of the wolf in sheep's clothing because we have not learned to recognize the voice of the Good Shepherd.

> *"The gatekeeper opens the gate for him, and the sheep hear his voice and come to him. He calls his own sheep by name and leads them out."*
> *John 10:3 NLT*

It is great to be able to spot the unwanted calls from unwelcome callers through Caller ID, but we need to pray for wisdom and spiritual discernment so that we do not ignore the calls of the one who knows and calls us by name into an on going and ever growing relationship with Him.

Father, help me to identify and be sensitive and obedient to all Your calls. Amen

Taking it to the Lord...

How can I apply this truth?____

____

____

Father, I've come to worship and praise you! You are my:_______________________

____

I give you all Glory, Honor, and Praise O Lord!

Father, I am sorry that I have sinned by:____________________________________

Help me to repent. Cleanse me, strengthen me, restore me.

Father, THANK YOU for all your love, grace, mercy and blessings of life that you continually shower down upon me. Thank you especially for:

1.______________________________   2.______________________________

3.______________________________   4.______________________________

5.______________________________   6.______________________________

THANK YOU for answered prayers:____

Father, I need:____

Father, I ask that YOU:____

____

____

Lord, bless me that I may be a blessing. Give me Your heart for loving and serving others. Keep Your hand upon me. Keep me from all evil and harm, and let me cause harm to no one. Bind Satan that he have no power over me. All this I pray in subjection to your will and in the strong name of my Lord and Savior, Jesus Christ. Amen.

Sunny Side Up

"Martha, Martha," the Lord answered, "you are worried and upset about many things," Luke 10:41 NIV

How anyone can stand their eggs "sunny side up" is beyond me. They look pretty, but they are too raw for my tastes. I am sure glad that there are other choices like scrambled, over medium, or omelets.

> *"Sing to God, sing praise to his name,*
> *extol him who rides on the clouds his name is the LORD -*
> *and rejoice before him."*
> *Psalm 68:4*

When it comes to attitude and disposition, "sunny side up" tastes good to you and to everyone around you. When those two big yolks of love and joy pop out they light up lives.

There is probably no more effective witnessing tool than living "sunny side up" in the joy of the Lord and having those around you be drawn like a magnet to you and ask why you are always so upbeat and happy.

> *"And we rejoice in the hope of the glory of God. Not only so, but we also rejoice in our sufferings, because we know that suffering produces perseverance; perseverance, character; and character, hope."*
> *Romans 5:2b-4 NIV*

When Paul and Silas responded to their beating and jailing by praying and singing hymns, God showed up big time, and even the jailer and his household were saved. Jesus commands, "rejoice and be glad" and promises a reward in heaven for those who are persecuted.

The Fact that Scripture mentions "rejoice" and "joy" almost 500 times makes it very clear that they should be and integral part of the life of every believer.

Smile and the world smiles with you or whine and complain and be a wet blanket to all those around you. Do you really wanna go through life as a grump?

Most importantly, how in the world can we expect the Holy Spirit to dwell in a temple of gloom and doom?

Father, give me your joy on the inside so that I can live "sunny side up" on the outside. Amen

Taking it to the Lord...

How can I apply this truth?____

____

Father, I've come to worship and praise you! You are my:_______________________

____

I give you all Glory, Honor, and Praise O Lord!

Father, I am sorry that I have sinned by:_____________________________________

Help me to repent. Cleanse me, strengthen me, restore me.

Father, THANK YOU for all your love, grace, mercy and blessings of life that you continually shower down upon me. Thank you especially for:

1._____________________________   2._____________________________

3._____________________________   4._____________________________

5._____________________________   6._____________________________

THANK YOU for answered prayers:___________________________________

Father, I need:____

Father, I ask that YOU:____

____

____

Lord, bless me that I may be a blessing. Give me Your heart for loving and serving others. Keep Your hand upon me. Keep me from all evil and harm, and let me cause harm to no one. Bind Satan that he have no power over me. All this I pray in subjection to your will and in the strong name of my Lord and Savior, Jesus Christ. Amen.

After God's Own Heart

"But God removed him from the kingship and replaced him with David, a man about whom God said, 'David son of Jesse is a man after my own heart, for he will do everything I want him to." Acts 13:22 NLT

The eighteen inches from the mind to the heart is a river too wide for many. Unless we take this road less traveled, we will never be able to enjoy the fullness of a close personal relationship with God through Jesus, and we will miss out on the sacred delight of God's delight in us.

"I will bless the LORD who guides me; even at night my heart instructs me."
Psalm 16:7 NLT

David was not a man after God's own heart because of His courage or His song writing ability. He was loved by God because *"he will do everything I want him to do".*

David reverenced God. He was a man of prayer.   He sought God's will continually and always obeyed God. David was strong and courageous, kind and compassionate, and he delighted in the Lord.

"For if you confess with your mouth that Jesus is Lord and believe in your heart that God raised him from the dead, you will be saved"
Romans 10:9

When God denied his request to build the temple David accepted the sovereign Will of God graciously and willingly. Through Solomon the physical temple was built. Later, through the lineage of David, the kingdom of eternal life through faith in Jesus Christ was established forever.

We too, can become the man or woman after God's own heart. By growing into the fullness of Christ through abiding in the Word, and by obedience and willingness to do everything God wants, we too can have the sacred delight of God's friendship and delight.

Best of all, we can by faith appropriate the heart of Jesus, so that we can love others as He did, love God as He did, think like Him and live for Him.

Father, by the power of Your Spirit give me a heart filled with reverence and obedience that I might be a man after your own heart. Amen.

Taking it to the Lord...

How can I apply this truth?____

____

____

Father, I've come to worship and praise you! You are my:_________________________________

____

I give you all Glory, Honor, and Praise O Lord!

Father, I am sorry that I have sinned by:____

Help me to repent. Cleanse me, strengthen me, restore me.

Father, THANK YOU for all your love, grace, mercy and blessings of life that you continually shower down upon me. Thank you especially for:

1.______________________________   2.______________________________
3.______________________________   4.______________________________
5.______________________________   6.______________________________

THANK YOU for answered prayers:____

Father, I need:____

Father, I ask that YOU:____

____

____

____

Lord, bless me that I may be a blessing. Give me Your heart for loving and serving others. Keep Your hand upon me. Keep me from all evil and harm, and let me cause harm to no one. Bind Satan that he have no power over me. All this I pray in subjection to your will and in the strong name of my Lord and Savior, Jesus Christ. Amen.

Patience Practice

"Strengthened with all might, according to His glorious power, for all patience and longsuffering with joy;" Colossians 1:11 NLT

Patience is a character virtue that we believers seem to have quite a problem in developing. The oft-quoted phrase: "Give me patience Lord, but please hurry" says a lot about our lack of patience.

> *"Yet though he did all this for them, they continued to test his patience."*
> *Psalm 78:56 NLT*

The Holy Spirit sure knows how to give us patience lessons in every area of everyday life. .

I have had some really memorable patience practice sessions with the Social Security Administration via telephone on behalf of a dear friend of mine. Computer tech support services can sure teach a lot about patience. Even trying to communicate with your local bank via telephone to a records department thousands of miles away can be quite a patience practice session.

Whether in potty training children, house breaking pets, or finding a misplaced article; we can get some real good patience practice. These are just shallow examples. When we get into patience waiting for answers to prayers, delayed gratification, or persevering through illness, rejection, and other problems, we realize the need for the Spirit empowered gift of patience.

> *"May God, who gives this patience and encouragement, help you live in complete harmony with each other—each with the attitude of Christ Jesus toward the other."*
> *Romans 15:5 NLT*

The Holy Spirit is at work in the lives of every believer producing the godly fruits of the character of Christ in us. Through learning patience, we need to know that we are being conformed to the image of Christ and being made more Christ like every day of our lives.

Whether for salvation or developing the godly character of Christ in us, God exercises more longsuffering and patience than we will ever be called upon to practice.

Father, forgive my impatience and help me to respond with patience and love in every circumstance. Amen

Taking it to the Lord...

How can I apply this truth?____

____

____

Father, I've come to worship and praise you! You are my:_______________________

____

I give you all Glory, Honor, and Praise O Lord!

Father, I am sorry that I have sinned by:_______________________________________

Help me to repent. Cleanse me, strengthen me, restore me.

Father, THANK YOU for all your love, grace, mercy and blessings of life that you continually shower down upon me. Thank you especially for:

1.______________________________   2.______________________________

3.______________________________   4.______________________________

5.______________________________   6.______________________________

THANK YOU for answered prayers:____

Father, I need:____

Father, I ask that YOU:____

____

____

Lord, bless me that I may be a blessing. Give me Your heart for loving and serving others. Keep Your hand upon me. Keep me from all evil and harm, and let me cause harm to no one. Bind Satan that he have no power over me. All this I pray in subjection to your will and in the strong name of my Lord and Savior, Jesus Christ. Amen.

Virus Alert!

"But it takes only one wrong person among you to infect all the others—a little yeast spreads quickly through the whole batch of dough!" Galatians 5:9

The ongoing threat and damage of computer viruses is big news throughout the world whenever it happens. Try as hard as these hackers might, they will never be as successful or last as long as the "master hacker" a/k/a Satan.

> **"The LORD nurses them when they are sick and eases their pain and discomfort. 'O LORD,' I prayed, have mercy on me. Heal me, for I have sinned against you."**
> **Psalm 41:2,4 NLT**

Even though mortally wounded and defeated he continues to break down our defenses and infect every area of our personal, congregational, family and vocational life.

He uses the virus of doubt to hack away at the truth of Scripture inerrancy, and sends wolves in among the sheep to espouse that commandments are only suggestions, and that any belief is ok as long as you're sincere.

Gossip, self-focus, and pride are some of the carriers he uses to spread his evil among us. Rationalization and denial will only prolong the problem.

Thank God, we have the master hardware and software inventor on our side. In his love and mercy, He gives us a patch to disable every virus thrown at us before it becomes fatal.

Jesus Christ won the ultimate victory over the condemnation and destruction of any sin virus by his death on the cross for all who would receive Him by faith as Savior and Lord.

> *"Put on all of God's armor so that you will be able to stand firm against all strategies and tricks of the Devil."*
> *Ephesians 6:10*

He provides this "patch" for all through confession and Godly sorrow leading to repentance and saving faith. He then supplies the anti-virus serum through the indwelling of the Holy Spirit.

With the helmet of salvation and sword of the Spirit, which is the Word of God, He provides a means of escape and protection from every virus that comes our way.

Father, thank you for giving me a firewall to protect me from the virus of sin. Help me to use it 24/7. Amen

Taking it to the Lord...

How can I apply this truth?____

____

____

Father, I've come to worship and praise you! You are my:____________________

____

I give you all Glory, Honor, and Praise O Lord!

Father, I am sorry that I have sinned by:________________________________

Help me to repent. Cleanse me, strengthen me, restore me.

Father, THANK YOU for all your love, grace, mercy and blessings of life that you continually shower down upon me. Thank you especially for:

1.___________________________   2.___________________________

3.___________________________   4.___________________________

5.___________________________   6.___________________________

THANK YOU for answered prayers:____

Father, I need:____

Father, I ask that YOU:____

____

____

Lord, bless me that I may be a blessing. Give me Your heart for loving and serving others. Keep Your hand upon me. Keep me from all evil and harm, and let me cause harm to no one. Bind Satan that he have no power over me. All this I pray in subjection to your will and in the strong name of my Lord and Savior, Jesus Christ. Amen.

As Others Do

"He always keeps his word. Let's see how inventive we can be in encouraging love and helping out, not avoiding worshiping together as some do but spurring each other on, especially as we see the big Day approaching. Hebrews 10:24 MSG

The master of deceit and denial is also a master fisherman. He knows more about denial and disobedience than anyone. He wants us to deny that we were created for worship, and that corporate worship with other believers is not a suggestion, but a commandment!

"Lift high your praises when the people assemble, shout Hallelujah when the elders meet!"
Psalm 107:32 MSG

It's not as if he needed any help within the church to reel us in. He has the world to compete for our attention and devotion to God by offering all sorts of sparkling trinkets to make us one of the "some dos" in our text. He uses the golf course, fishing, stock car racing, ball games, and a number of other attractions that seem so much more attractive than going to church and encouraging fellow believers by our presence.

If the attractions of the world are not enough, Satan can always prey on the inherent weaknesses of our flesh to accomplish his purpose of separating us from the love and encouragement we find in corporate worship. He uses sleeping in, a critical spirit in focusing on all of the shortcomings of our church and its members, stubborn self will that tells us we don't need the fellowship of the "communion of saints" or the grace that is imparted through corporate worship to pull us out of the living water.

"We are all parts of his one body, and each of us has different work to do. And since we are all one body in Christ, we belong to each other, and each of us needs all the others."
Romans 12:5 NLT

Worst of all, our relegation of corporate worship to an Easter and Christmas ritual (if even that) sets a terrible example for any children, grand children, or other believers who may be lead astray by our example.

Do you really want to be a "some do"?

Father, don't let the weakness of our flesh or the tricks of the evil one rob us of the joy of corporate worship. Amen

Taking it to the Lord...

How can I apply this truth?____

____

____

Father, I've come to worship and praise you! You are my:_____________________

____

I give you all Glory, Honor, and Praise O Lord!

Father, I am sorry that I have sinned by:__________________________________

Help me to repent. Cleanse me, strengthen me, restore me.

Father, THANK YOU for all your love, grace, mercy and blessings of life that you continually shower down upon me. Thank you especially for:

1._________________________________ 2._________________________________

3._________________________________ 4._________________________________

5._________________________________ 6._________________________________

THANK YOU for answered prayers:____

Father, I need:____

Father, I ask that YOU:____

____

____

Lord, bless me that I may be a blessing. Give me Your heart for loving and serving others. Keep Your hand upon me. Keep me from all evil and harm, and let me cause harm to no one. Bind Satan that he have no power over me. All this I pray in subjection to your will and in the strong name of my Lord and Savior, Jesus Christ. Amen.

Every Day Low Price

"They took the thirty pieces of silver—the price at which he was valued by the people of Israel—and purchased the potter's field, as the Lord directed." Matthew 27:9 NLT

In my business career, I promoted about every kind of sale imaginable. When some cult began getting ready for the end of the world, I even contemplated and "End of the World Sale" promising your purchase free if the world came to an end!

> *"Redemption does not come so easily, for no one can ever pay enough to live forever and never see the grave." Psalm 49:8*

Judas put Jesus on sale for thirty pieces of silver. Before we condemn so quickly, we need to think about the times that we have deliberately sold out to sin for far less than thirty dollars. Whether to satisfy greed, lust, pride, or other fleshly needs, we often choose to forget: *"for God bought you with a high price. So you must honor God with your body.(1 Corinthians 6:20)* Our highest calling is to honor God with our lives.

God has never been on sale! He set the price for all when he declared Abraham righteous by faith. He confirmed His "every day low price" through sending Jesus Christ to give us the priceless treasure of eternal life as a free gift of faith. We can't pay anymore and He won't accept any less. His price is non negotiable, and is limited to one per person.

> *"Pay all your debts, except the debt of love for others. You can never finish paying that! If you love your neighbor, you will fulfill all the requirements of God's law." Romans 13:8*

While the price of eternal life for us is low, it certainly wasn't cheap for God's only Son who bought us the right to be called children of God and heirs to the promises of God. He had to go through terrible suffering and torment and death itself so that we will not have to.

If Jesus thought us worth dying for, can't we show that He is worth living for with an every day life of worship and praise in every area of our lives?

Father, keep me ever mindful that although your price to me was low, it was not cheap. Never let me abuse this gift of Your grace. Amen

Taking it to the Lord...

How can I apply this truth?____

____

Father, I've come to worship and praise you! You are my:_________________________________

____

I give you all Glory, Honor, and Praise O Lord!

Father, I am sorry that I have sinned by:____

Help me to repent. Cleanse me, strengthen me, restore me.

Father, THANK YOU for all your love, grace, mercy and blessings of life that you continually shower down upon me. Thank you especially for:

1._____________________________________   2._____________________________________
3._____________________________________   4._____________________________________
5._____________________________________   6._____________________________________

THANK YOU for answered prayers:____

Father, I need:____

Father, I ask that YOU:____

____

____

Lord, bless me that I may be a blessing. Give me Your heart for loving and serving others. Keep Your hand upon me. Keep me from all evil and harm, and let me cause harm to no one. Bind Satan that he have no power over me. All this I pray in subjection to your will and in the strong name of my Lord and Savior, Jesus Christ. Amen.

Fathoming the Unfathomable

"For My thoughts are not your thoughts, nor are your ways My ways," says the LORD. For as the heavens are higher than the earth, so are My ways higher than your ways, and My thoughts than your thoughts." Isaiah 55:8,9

> *"As far as I am concerned, God turned into good what you meant for evil."*
> *Genesis 50:20 NLT*

How did I get all the way from Florida to Mackinac Island Michigan and meet my wife from Wisconsin? How did I happen to run into some casual acquaintances at breakfast in a transient mess hall, and leave with them as a crewmember on the commanding general's plane? How did I get into the furniture business? Coincidences or God at Work? I am sure you have many similar questions about circumstances in your life. Of all the things that we are never going to fully comprehend this side of heaven are the ways God is continually working in our lives, and the lives of others to accomplish His purposes.

All too often we dismiss evidence of God at work as coincidences and fail to recognize Him at work. Scripture is filled with examples of How God caused things to happen to accomplish His purposes. That He continually uses the evil acts of others to accomplish His purposes is another oft-repeated Biblical truth.

Was it coincidence that Joseph was sold into slavery and ended up as defacto ruler of Egypt? Was it just a coincidence that Esther found favor with King Xerxes and saved her people? Was it just a coincidence that Abraham found a lamb caught in a briar patch?

Of all of the delights in this life, there is nothing to compare with those sacred delights through which we experience God at work in His wonderful and mysterious ways. It may be manifested through answered prayers, or confirmation of a thought or answer to a question. It may be in seeing a transformed life. Sometimes we can't even see the hand of God in a situation until much later.

> *"May you experience the love of Christ, though it is so great you will never fully understand it. Then you will be filled with the fullness of life and power that comes from God."*
> *Ephesians 3:19 NLT*

The secret of enjoying these sacred delights is thru abiding in God's Word and receiving the wisdom and spiritual discernment to recognize them when we see them.

Father, help me discern your work all around me and delight in it. Amen

Taking it to the Lord...

How can I apply this truth?____

____

Father, I've come to worship and praise you! You are my:_______________________

____

I give you all Glory, Honor, and Praise O Lord!

Father, I am sorry that I have sinned by:_____________________________________

Help me to repent. Cleanse me, strengthen me, restore me.

Father, THANK YOU for all your love, grace, mercy and blessings of life that you continually shower down upon me. Thank you especially for:

1._______________________________   2._______________________________
3._______________________________   4._______________________________
5._______________________________   6._______________________________

THANK YOU for answered prayers:____

Father, I need:____

Father, I ask that YOU:____

____

Lord, bless me that I may be a blessing. Give me Your heart for loving and serving others. Keep Your hand upon me. Keep me from all evil and harm, and let me cause harm to no one. Bind Satan that he have no power over me. All this I pray in subjection to your will and in the strong name of my Lord and Savior, Jesus Christ. Amen.

Getting in God's Way

"And this I pray, that your love may abound still more and more in knowledge and all discernment, that you may approve the things that are excellent, that you may be sincere and without offense till the day of Christ, being filled with the fruits of righteousness which are by Jesus Christ, to the glory and praise of God." Philippians 1:10, 11

Getting in God's way should be one of the real concerns of all believers It can cause terrible consequences for us and for others. While it is comforting to know that God can work our mistakes for his good and to accomplish His purposes, the godly sorrow that we sometimes have to bear forever is not a happy sorrow.

> *"O LORD, listen to my cry; give me the discerning mind you promised."*
> *Psalm 119:169 NLT*

We often get in God's way without even realizing it. One of the most common ways is when deceive ourselves into thinking our agenda is God's agenda. This is especially prevalent in many areas of church life.

By over reacting to circumstances we can thwart God's healing or disciplining process in the lives of those we love by not letting God's process run its course and by short-circuiting the consequences that lead to godly repentance and restoration.

How many marriages have failed because well meaning parents made it too attractive and too easy to come home? How many relationships have been irreparably damaged because of our getting involved, or taking sides in other's conflicts?

Worst of all, how many have been kept from coming into a saving relationship with Jesus Christ by the terrible witness of one professing to be a Christian? The devil has a field day when God's saints, spew hatred and malice, and fight and quarrel among themselves.

> *"And do not grieve the Holy Spirit of God, by whom you were sealed for the day of redemption."*
> *Ephesians 4:30*

No wonder the Bible has so many prayers asking for wisdom and spiritual discernment! This is what it takes to stay our of God's way.

Father, Give me the wisdom and spiritual discernment. Let me be a building block and never a stumbling block. Amen

Taking it to the Lord...

How can I apply this truth?____

____

Father, I've come to worship and praise you! You are my:_______________________________

____

I give you all Glory, Honor, and Praise O Lord!

Father, I am sorry that I have sinned by:____

Help me to repent. Cleanse me, strengthen me, restore me.

Father, THANK YOU for all your love, grace, mercy and blessings of life that you continually shower down upon me. Thank you especially for:

1._____________________________________ 2._____________________________________

3._____________________________________ 4._____________________________________

5._____________________________________ 6._____________________________________

THANK YOU for answered prayers:____

Father, I need:____

Father, I ask that YOU:____

____

____

Lord, bless me that I may be a blessing. Give me Your heart for loving and serving others. Keep Your hand upon me. Keep me from all evil and harm, and let me cause harm to no one. Bind Satan that he have no power over me. All this I pray in subjection to your will and in the strong name of my Lord and Savior, Jesus Christ. Amen.

Magnify!

"And Mary said: 'My soul magnifies the Lord, and my spirit has rejoiced in God my Savior. For He has regarded the lowly state of His maidservant; for behold, henceforth all generations will call me blessed. For He who is mighty has done great things for me, and holy is His name. Luke 1:46-49.

Although magnify does mean praise, it also means to enlarge or make bigger. Oh that we would be as good at making God as big as we make our problems!!

> *"Oh, magnify the LORD with me, and let us exalt His name together."*
> *Psalm 34:3*

We can learn a lot from Mary. Se chose to magnify God. She magnified the sovereignty and grace of God and rejoiced and praised Him.

We are usually only be as big as the things that bother us. We too often have the tendency to "major in the minors" like Martha, who chose to react to Christ's presence in her home by complaining and worrying.

The larger we magnify the Lord the less the minor irritations will bother us. When we enlarge our understanding of and faith in God, we enlarge our capacity to love and obey God. As believers, we have a "Spirit powered" microscope that magnifies the all sufficiency of God's grace to cover our every weakness. It magnifies the wonders of God's grace, the power of His love, and the security of His promises above all other powers, wisdom, and ways of man.

> *"Remember to magnify His work, of which men have sung. Everyone has seen it; man looks on it from afar."*
> *Job 36:24*

Before we shrink back into withdrawal or defeat, let's turn up the magnification on our built in microscope and focus on the bigness of the problem solver instead of the problem. As the old hymn says, "Oh what peace we often forfeit, oh what needless pain we bear, all because we do not carry everything to God in prayer."

Father, let my soul magnify You above all and let me be ever mindful of all the great things You have done and are going to do for me. Amen

Taking it to the Lord...

How can I apply this truth?____

Father, I've come to worship and praise you! You are my:____

I give you all Glory, Honor, and Praise O Lord!

Father, I am sorry that I have sinned by:____

Help me to repent. Cleanse me, strengthen me, restore me.

Father, THANK YOU for all your love, grace, mercy and blessings of life that you continually shower down upon me. Thank you especially for:

1.___________________________________   2.___________________________________

3.___________________________________   4.___________________________________

5.___________________________________   6.___________________________________

THANK YOU for answered prayers:____

Father, I need:____

Father, I ask that YOU:____

Lord, bless me that I may be a blessing. Give me Your heart for loving and serving others. Keep Your hand upon me. Keep me from all evil and harm, and let me cause harm to no one. Bind Satan that he have no power over me. All this I pray in subjection to your will and in the strong name of my Lord and Savior, Jesus Christ. Amen.

Whose Fool Are You?

"Stop fooling yourselves. If you think you are wise by this world's standards, you will have to become a fool so you can become wise by God's standards. For the wisdom of this world is foolishness to God." 1 Corinthians 3:18,19 NLT

It's a fact of life that we are all somebody's "fool". We all believe in somebody or something. Some let drugs, booze, sex, possessions, popularity, or pride make a fool of them. Some let customs, traditions, or godless humanism make a fool out of them. Others let dead religions with dead prophets fool them.

> *"The fool has said in his heart, 'there is no God"*
> *Psalm 14:1*

All of this begs the question: "What if you're wrong?" Scripture says, *"There is a way that seems right to man, but its end is the way of death."(Proverbs 14:12)*

Praise God that those of us who become fools so that we can become wise by God's standards have the documented, witnessed, and historical proof of the resurrection of Jesus Christ to validate our faith in the living God who gives us everlasting life by faith.

Anything other than saving faith in Jesus Christ has no margin for error. How sad to be so foolish as to think that this life is all there is, and to die with no future and no hope.

> *"Who but a fool would make his own god-an idol that cannot help him one bit."*
> *Isaiah 44:10*

In this deadly struggle for eternal life, it's hard to imagine anyone not wanting to be on the winning team. The real foolishness is to disregard the clear call to salvation and eternal life that God extends to all.

The streets of heaven are not going to be paved with fool's gold. Those foolish enough to reject heaven and accept what this world has to offer as their reward are going to get cheated big time.

Father, I have done a lot of foolish things in my life, but coming to know you through Jesus Christ was not one of them. Glory be to You, Oh Lord! Amen

Taking it to the Lord...

How can I apply this truth?____

____

____

Father, I've come to worship and praise you! You are my:_____________________

____

I give you all Glory, Honor, and Praise O Lord!

Father, I am sorry that I have sinned by:__________________________________

Help me to repent. Cleanse me, strengthen me, restore me.

Father, THANK YOU for all your love, grace, mercy and blessings of life that you continually shower down upon me. Thank you especially for:

1.____________________________   2.____________________________

3.____________________________   4.____________________________

5.____________________________   6.____________________________

THANK YOU for answered prayers:____

Father, I need:____

Father, I ask that YOU:____

____

____

Lord, bless me that I may be a blessing. Give me Your heart for loving and serving others. Keep Your hand upon me. Keep me from all evil and harm, and let me cause harm to no one. Bind Satan that he have no power over me. All this I pray in subjection to your will and in the strong name of my Lord and Savior, Jesus Christ. Amen.

No! I Won't Go!

"Now I say to you that you are Peter, and upon this rock I will build my church, and all the powers of hell will not conquer it." Matthew 16:18 NLT

It is a terrible mistake to deny the reality of hell. It is too late to deny it, when someone gets there by their own free will, or by being deceived by the devil, humanists and other unbelievers who say there is no such place.

> *"The path of the wise leads to life above; they leave the grave behind."*
> *Proverbs 15:24*

Peter's profession of faith *"You are the Christ, the Son of the Living God." (Matthew 16:15)* is the solid rock of faith on which we can base our assurance of eternal life and freedom from the torment of hell.

The witnessed and recorded resurrection and ascension of Jesus Christ into heaven gives further blessed assurance for the blessed hope of all believers.

Whether the darts of doubt cause us to deny the reality of hell, or to question our salvation, we have the "shield of faith" – God's Word – with which to overcome all concerns and doubts about our destination.

What promise and comfort there are in these words of the Apostle Paul: *"And I am convinced that nothing can ever separate us from His love. Death can't and life can't. The angels can't and the demons can't. Our fears for today, our worries about tomorrow, and even the powers of hell can't keep God's love away." (Romans 8:38 NLT)*

> *"These are the ones coming out of the great tribulation. They washed their robes in the blood of the Lame and made them white."*
> *Revelation 7:14b NLT*

I personally think that it is a grave mistake that many churches and pastors seem to be getting away from declaring the reality of hell and using this reality to move people into a saving, love relationship with Jesus Christ.

Whether through making us to go to heaven or simply not want to go to hell, the important thing is that God calls through the Holy Spirit and would have all receive Him into our hearts.

Father, thank you for teaching me about the reality of hell, and for providing the means of escape from it through faith in Jesus. Amen

Taking it to the Lord...

How can I apply this truth?____

____

Father, I've come to worship and praise you! You are my:_______________________________

____

I give you all Glory, Honor, and Praise O Lord!

Father, I am sorry that I have sinned by:____

Help me to repent. Cleanse me, strengthen me, restore me.

Father, THANK YOU for all your love, grace, mercy and blessings of life that you continually shower down upon me. Thank you especially for:

1.________________________________   2.________________________________

3.________________________________   4.________________________________

5.________________________________   6.________________________________

THANK YOU for answered prayers:____

Father, I need:____

Father, I ask that YOU:____

____

____

Lord, bless me that I may be a blessing. Give me Your heart for loving and serving others. Keep Your hand upon me. Keep me from all evil and harm, and let me cause harm to no one. Bind Satan that he have no power over me. All this I pray in subjection to your will and in the strong name of my Lord and Savior, Jesus Christ. Amen.

Have You Checked with your Parole Officer?

"If you do this, you will experience God's peace, which is far more wonderful than the human mind can understand. His peace will guard your hearts and minds as you live in Christ Jesus." Philippians 4:7 NLT

After being set free from prison, most offenders are required to check in regularly with a Parole Officer who is supposed to monitor their conduct and help them stay free.

> *"Keep me from deliberate sins!*
> *'t let them control me.*
> *Then I will be free of guilt and innocent of great sin."*
> *Psalm 19:13 NLT*

When you think about it, that's not a bad idea for each of us who claim the name of Christ. We have been set free from bondage to sin, from its power and control and walk into a new life of freedom in the Spirit.

The only way this freedom cannot be turned into a license is by regular check ins with our Parole Officer, a/k/a the Holy Spirit!

Rehabilitation of old habits, old reactions, and old lifestyles, is never easy. Even though we are instantly cured of our sin condition in the eyes of God when we receive Jesus Christ as our Savior and Lord, we need a lot of help in being transformed by the renewing of our minds and hearts, and it seldom happens over night.

God knows us better than we know ourselves, and in His love and mercy, He gives us a helper to lead, guide, and conform us into the image of Christ.

God will speak to us through the Spirit as we check in through prayer, bible study, and fellowship with other believers. He will even supply us with armor with which to stand against the roaring lion who is seeking to destroy us.

> *[16]And I will pray the Father, and He will give you another Helper, that He may abide with you forever—*
> *John 14:16 NLT*

Without frequent check ins and close communication with our "Parole Officer", we are fair game to go back into the prison of sin and will never be able to lead "lives filled with wisdom and spiritual discernment, fully pleasing to Him, fruitful in every good work," and most importantly: "strengthened will all might, according to His glorious power." (Colossians 1:9:11) May God forbid that none of us will violate our parole.

Father, I need you every hour! Keep me on the road to holiness by the power of your Spirit. Amen

Taking it to the Lord...

How can I apply this truth?____

____

____

Father, I've come to worship and praise you! You are my:_____________________

____

I give you all Glory, Honor, and Praise O Lord!

Father, I am sorry that I have sinned by:_________________________________

Help me to repent. Cleanse me, strengthen me, restore me.

Father, THANK YOU for all your love, grace, mercy and blessings of life that you continually shower down upon me. Thank you especially for:

1.__________________________________   2.__________________________________
3.__________________________________   4.__________________________________
5.__________________________________   6.__________________________________

THANK YOU for answered prayers:_______________________________________

Father, I need:____

Father, I ask that YOU:____

____

____

Lord, bless me that I may be a blessing. Give me Your heart for loving and serving others. Keep Your hand upon me. Keep me from all evil and harm, and let me cause harm to no one. Bind Satan that he have no power over me. All this I pray in subjection to your will and in the strong name of my Lord and Savior, Jesus Christ. Amen.

Climb Every Mountain

**"Nothing, not even a mighty mountain, will stand in Zerubbabel's way; it will flatten out before him!"
Zechariah 4:7 NLT**

There are good and bad mountains of life. Hopefully, we all have a lot of mountain top experiences that fill us with joy and we remember forever.

"He makes me as surefooted as a deer, leading me safely along the mountain heights." Psalm 18:33 NLT

Marriage, getting our first driver's license, graduating from high school or college, entering into that friendship with God through faith in Jesus Christ are some of the big and small mountain top experiences we remember and cherish. The transfiguration of Jesus was certainly was a mountain top experience for the disciples present. They even wanted to build an altar to commemorate.

There are other mountains that loom ahead of us as unsolvable, terrifying problems, that we feel are as immovable as the literal mountains that Jesus said we could move by faith. As we look at the mountains of fear, illness, rejection, financial problems, addiction, from our valley of despair, we need to respond in at least four ways:

"You didn't have enough faith," Jesus told them. "I assure you, even if you had faith as small as a mustard seed you could say to this mountain, 'Move from here to there,' and it would move. Nothing would be impossible." Matthew 17:20 NLT

1. <u>Examine</u> ourselves to see if we are suffering the consequences of any unconfessed or unrepented sin. Confess and repent and throw yourself on the mercy of God.

2. <u>Magnify</u> the Lord through prayer, worship, getting to know Him better through His Word, and praise to make Him bigger and our mountain smaller.

3. <u>Recount</u> all the other mountains where God has come through big time in Scripture and your own life and be strengthened and encouraged.

4. <u>Reaffirm</u> your belief that God does work all things to the good for those who love him and are called according His purposes, and that He promises that nothing can separate us from His love.

Father, I believe that you can move or remove the mountains of life. Help my unbelief. Amen

Taking it to the Lord...

How can I apply this truth?____

____

____

Father, I've come to worship and praise you! You are my:_______________________

____

I give you all Glory, Honor, and Praise O Lord!

Father, I am sorry that I have sinned by:_____________________________________

Help me to repent. Cleanse me, strengthen me, restore me.

Father, THANK YOU for all your love, grace, mercy and blessings of life that you continually shower down upon me. Thank you especially for:

1.__________________________________   2.__________________________________

3.__________________________________   4.__________________________________

5.__________________________________   6.__________________________________

THANK YOU for answered prayers:____

Father, I need:____

Father, I ask that YOU:____

____

____

____

Lord, bless me that I may be a blessing. Give me Your heart for loving and serving others. Keep Your hand upon me. Keep me from all evil and harm, and let me cause harm to no one. Bind Satan that he have no power over me. All this I pray in subjection to your will and in the strong name of my Lord and Savior, Jesus Christ. Amen.

Wanna Horse Around?

"We can make a large horse turn around and go wherever we want by means of a small bit in its mouth." James 3:3

If you are going to "horse around", you need to know one thing. Whether riding or training, horses move away from pressure. They stop or back up to relieve the pressure of a bit, they move forward when you kick them or hit them with a crop. Most runaways are caused when a rider tenses up and grips too tightly with their legs, unknowingly telling a horse to go. All training is based on a horse's responding to pressure.

> *"Lead me to the towering rock of safety, for you are my safe refuge, a fortress where my enemies cannot reach me."*
> *Psalm 61:2b.3*

When it comes to the pressures of life, we are hopefully a little smarter than the average horse. We can choose how we are going to respond to pressure.

The pressure of temptation to sin is always present. God has promised a means of escape. There are certainly pressures from which we need to move away, and by the grace o God and with the power of His Spirit we can.

The pressures of failure take a lot of wisdom and spiritual discernment. Sometimes we need to move away and move on, secure in God's love, acceptance, and forgiveness no matter what. Other times we need to persevere and see our careers, our marriages, our relationships with others, or our finances through some very trying times and circumstances, confident that God does work all things for our good.

> *"So humble yourselves before God. Resist the devil, and he will flee from you."*
> *James 4:7*

The pressures of our illnesses or the illnesses of those around us are things that we cannot move away from, but only endure with courage, confidence, and trust in God.

The pressures of weariness and fear caused even the disciples to run away from the pressure of fear; but like the runaway horses who eventually come back to the barn, they too found their way back - humbler, wiser, and stronger in the strength of God's Spirit.

Father, help me to bridle my tongue, rein in my pride and self-centeredness, and respond to all pressures with the power of your Spirit. Amen

Taking it to the Lord...

How can I apply this truth?____

____

____

Father, I've come to worship and praise you! You are my:______________________

____

I give you all Glory, Honor, and Praise O Lord!

Father, I am sorry that I have sinned by:____________________________________

Help me to repent. Cleanse me, strengthen me, restore me.

Father, THANK YOU for all your love, grace, mercy and blessings of life that you continually shower down upon me. Thank you especially for:

1._________________________________   2._________________________________

3._________________________________   4._________________________________

5._________________________________   6._________________________________

THANK YOU for answered prayers:____

Father, I need:____

Father, I ask that YOU:____

____

____

Lord, bless me that I may be a blessing. Give me Your heart for loving and serving others. Keep Your hand upon me. Keep me from all evil and harm, and let me cause harm to no one. Bind Satan that he have no power over me. All this I pray in subjection to your will and in the strong name of my Lord and Savior, Jesus Christ. Amen.

Faulty Vision

"Nothing in all creation is hidden from God's sight. Everything is uncovered and laid bare before the eyes of him to whom we must give account" Hebrews 4:13 NIV

Next to spiritual heart disease, faulty eyesight is probably the biggest health problem of believers and nonbelievers alike. God has recently unlocked the keys of knowledge for dealing with physical eye problems, just as He gave the key for dealing with our spiritual vision in the Word centuries ago.

> *"The LORD gives sight to the blind, the LORD lifts up those who are bowed down, the LORD loves the righteous."*
> *Psalm 146:8 NIV*

For the near sighted, who can only see instant gratification as their standard of living and conduct, God cures by giving faith to live by instead of sight.

For the far sighted, God reminds us that our days are in His hands, and that we need to be ready to meet Him face to face at all times. We should never put off the day of our salvation when Jesus stands at the door and knocks.

For the spiritually blind, God will remove the scales from our eyes as He did for Paul, so that we can see as well as know His will and His plan for our life.

He can give us the ability to see trials as opportunities, to see everyone we meet as mission prospects. Best of all, He can give us the desire and the power to see Jesus in all His fullness. He gives us the indwelling presence of the Holy Spirit to help us see our sin and to see truth, to "preserve sound judgment and discernment", and not let them out of our sight

> *"Woe to those who are wise in their own eyes and clever in their own sight."*
> *Isaiah 5:21 NIV*

God doesn't have any vision problem. He not only controls all, and knows all, but He sees all! We are precious in His sight! In life and even at death, *(Precious in the sight of the LORD is the death of his saints. Psalm 116:15),* God sees us as dear and beloved brothers of Christ.

Father, let the light of your love shine brightly that I might see Jesus! Amen

Taking it to the Lord...

How can I apply this truth?____

____

____

Father, I've come to worship and praise you! You are my:_____________________

____

I give you all Glory, Honor, and Praise O Lord!

Father, I am sorry that I have sinned by:_________________________________

Help me to repent. Cleanse me, strengthen me, restore me.

Father, THANK YOU for all your love, grace, mercy and blessings of life that you continually shower down upon me. Thank you especially for:

1.___________________________________   2.___________________________________

3.___________________________________   4.___________________________________

5.___________________________________   6.___________________________________

THANK YOU for answered prayers:_____________________________________

Father, I need:____

Father, I ask that YOU:____

____

____

____

Lord, bless me that I may be a blessing. Give me Your heart for loving and serving others. Keep Your hand upon me. Keep me from all evil and harm, and let me cause harm to no one. Bind Satan that he have no power over me. All this I pray in subjection to your will and in the strong name of my Lord and Savior, Jesus Christ. Amen.

Distractions, Distractions

**"But seek first the kingdom of God and His righteousness, and all these things shall be added to you."
Matthew 6:33**

The devil seems to work overtime, coming up with distractions to take our attention away from the kingdom of God, and into his playground of sin, worry, and preoccupation with other harmful things. This derails our good intentions and leads us down many detours with many potholes on our journey through life. He seems to work the hardest just when we are about to make a spiritual breakthrough and on the verge of doing something to build up the kingdom of God.

> *"Wait patiently for the Lord. Be brace and courageous. Yes, wait patiently on the Lord.*
> *Psalm 27:10*

As we seek wealth, fame and fortune, approval of peers, or whatever else we think will make us happy, we can get so caught up in these distractions that it becomes easy to forget to keep the main thing the main thing – seeking first the kingdom of God and His righteousness!

How much energy must we waste, frustration we suffer, and needless pain we bear before we realize that happiness and real significance in life are added only after we put God first?

Solomon was the wisest man who ever lived. After seeking pleasure and meaning to life in all the wrong places, he concluded: *"But as I looked at everything I had tried so hard to accomplish, it was all so meaningless. It was like chasing the wind. There was nothing really worthwhile anywhere." (Ecclesiastes 2:11)*

Whether individually or as a body of believers, we need to be on the lookout for destructive distractions that obscure our vision of the kingdom of God.

Father, give me the wisdom and spiritual discernment I need to recognize and deal with the distractions that Satan sends my way. Amen

Taking it to the Lord...

How can I apply this truth?____

____

Father, I've come to worship and praise you! You are my:_______________________________________

____

I give you all Glory, Honor, and Praise O Lord!

Father, I am sorry that I have sinned by:____

Help me to repent. Cleanse me, strengthen me, restore me.

Father, THANK YOU for all your love, grace, mercy and blessings of life that you continually shower down upon me. Thank you especially for:

1.____________________________________   2.____________________________________
3.____________________________________   4.____________________________________
5.____________________________________   6.____________________________________

THANK YOU for answered prayers:____

Father, I need:____

Father, I ask that YOU:____

____

____

Lord, bless me that I may be a blessing. Give me Your heart for loving and serving others. Keep Your hand upon me. Keep me from all evil and harm, and let me cause harm to no one. Bind Satan that he have no power over me. All this I pray in subjection to your will and in the strong name of my Lord and Savior, Jesus Christ. Amen.

Thy Will Be Done

"The Lord isn't really being slow about his promise to return, as some people think. No, He is being patient for your sake. He does not want anyone to perish, so He is giving more time for everyone to repent." 2 Peter 3:9 NLT

> *"Rescue me from my rebellion, for even fools mock me when I rebel."*
> *Psalm 39:8 NLT*

We are not the only ones who say "Thy will be done!" Our Lord Himself says the same thing to us. This is why we need to be very careful about exercising the freed of the will that God gives to everyone born of woman. Eve's will was to know as much as God, and she chose to disobey God. We are all still payin' the price for the curse of sin that she brought into the world by exercising her free will.

The prodigal son's will was to go out and live it up and soak up all of the pleasure the world had to offer. His road to the pigpen was not anything we would choose for even our worst enemies.

God doesn't make junk or robots. Although we come into this world with an inherited sin nature, we also come created in the image of God, with a capacity to love and be loved, and to produce the good works for which He created us.

> *"Come to Me with your ears wide open. Listen for the life of your soul is as stake. I am ready to make an everlasting covenant with you. I will give you all the mercies and unfailing love that I promised to David."*
> *Isaiah 55:3*

God gave us a free will to receive His wonderful gift of salvation by faith, and to live free from the condemnation of sin and bondage of the will. He is not going to force His love on anyone, and He allows "thy will be done" and all of its present and eternal consequences if we choose to reject Him when He stands at the door and knocks.

Let our prayer be "let not my will but Thine be done in all things."

Father, take away the bondage of my will to sin and rebellion against You and give me the power of Your Spirit to pray and mean "Thy will be done." Amen

Taking it to the Lord...

How can I apply this truth?____

____

Father, I've come to worship and praise you! You are my:_________________________

____

I give you all Glory, Honor, and Praise O Lord!

Father, I am sorry that I have sinned by:____

Help me to repent. Cleanse me, strengthen me, restore me.

Father, THANK YOU for all your love, grace, mercy and blessings of life that you continually shower down upon me. Thank you especially for:

1.__________________________________   2.__________________________________

3.__________________________________   4.__________________________________

5.__________________________________   6.__________________________________

THANK YOU for answered prayers:____

Father, I need:____

Father, I ask that YOU:____

____

____

Lord, bless me that I may be a blessing. Give me Your heart for loving and serving others. Keep Your hand upon me. Keep me from all evil and harm, and let me cause harm to no one. Bind Satan that he have no power over me. All this I pray in subjection to your will and in the strong name of my Lord and Savior, Jesus Christ. Amen.

Multiply Joy, Divide Sorrow

"Think of ways to encourage one another to outbursts of love and good deeds. And let us neglect our meeting together, as some people do, but encourage and warn each other, especially now that the day of His coming back again is drawing near." Hebrews 10:24,25 NLT

God not only created us for fellowship with Him, but for fellowship with other believers. Outside of saving faith and a loving spouse and family, there is no greater treasure than a friend who is also a brother or sister in Christ. There is no better way to find such a treasure than through fellowship in the Word.

> *"They will talk together about the glory of your kingdom; they will celebrate examples of your power."*
> Psalm 145:11 NLT

As we grow together in the Word, we become more transparent and find accountability and strength in others. *"As iron sharpens iron, a friend sharpens a friend." (Proverbs 27:17).* Just as joy is multiplied when we share it with others, our sorrows are diminished and our strength increased when we share our pain with others.

We can only find real strength and real joy with Christian friends. Just as in any good marriage, if God is not in the relationship, whoever or whatever takes His place I not an acceptable substitute.

Coming together for corporate worship and for fellowship in the Word in small groups where we can get to know God and each other better are great privileges that afford many blessings.

> *"When others are happy, be happy with them. If they are sad, share their sorrow."*
> Romans 12:15 NLT

God speaks to us through His Word, through prayer, through circumstances, and through Christian friends. Satan speaks to us through the world, the flesh, and unbelieving friends. To whom do you think you should be listening?

Father, thank you for my brothers and sisters in Christ with whom I can multiply my joy and divide my sorrows by sharing both with them. Amen

Taking it to the Lord...

How can I apply this truth?____

____

____

Father, I've come to worship and praise you! You are my:________________________________

____

I give you all Glory, Honor, and Praise O Lord!

Father, I am sorry that I have sinned by:____

Help me to repent. Cleanse me, strengthen me, restore me.

Father, THANK YOU for all your love, grace, mercy and blessings of life that you continually shower down upon me. Thank you especially for:

1.___________________________________   2.___________________________________
3.___________________________________   4.___________________________________
5.___________________________________   6.___________________________________

THANK YOU for answered prayers:____

Father, I need:____

Father, I ask that YOU:____

____

____

Lord, bless me that I may be a blessing. Give me Your heart for loving and serving others. Keep Your hand upon me. Keep me from all evil and harm, and let me cause harm to no one. Bind Satan that he have no power over me. All this I pray in subjection to your will and in the strong name of my Lord and Savior, Jesus Christ. Amen.

"Rent to Own" Religion

"What do you have that God hasn't given you? And if all you have is from Gold, why boast as though you have accomplished something on your own?" 1 Corinthians 4:7 NLT

I am not a big Rush Limbaugh fan, but one of the things he says seemingly tongue in check is true whether he really believes it or not. "Talent on loan from God" is probably the best and most irrefutable thing he has ever said.

> *"Trust in the Lord with all your hear; do not lean on your own understanding. Seek His will in all you do, and He will direct your paths."*
> *Proverbs 3:5 NLT*

"Rent to Own" businesses seem to flourish and make goods available to people who have acquired a reputation for paying too weakly for normal creditors. If we are honest about it, this is the way God makes good things available to sinners like us who have all sinned and fallen short of the glory of God.

While we were wandering aimlessly lost wasting our purpose and inheritance on the trivial pursuits of life controlled by our flesh, God came along beside us and called us by name into a relationship with Him that erases our sin debt forever and allows us to start living a debt free life with no more payments and no more repossessions.

When we respond to His love with obedience and faithfulness, we begin to realize that Jesus has paid our rent for our home in heaven. We want to live out our lives in Christ to the glory of God, and for producing the fruit for which he created us and gifted us before we were even born.

> *"For we are not our own masters when we live or when we die."*
> *Romans 14:7 NLT*

We need to know that everything we have including life itself is on loan from God and we are only going to own the treasures that we store up in heaven by using our time, talents, and resources glorifying Him here on this earth.

May we all live daily lives for Him on earth so that we will be able to rejoice in the accounting that is to come in heaven.

Father, thank you for paying my rent so that I can own all of the joys of this life and the life that is to come. Amen

Taking it to the Lord...

How can I apply this truth?____

____ .

____

Father, I've come to worship and praise you! You are my:_________________________________

____

I give you all Glory, Honor, and Praise O Lord!

Father, I am sorry that I have sinned by:____

Help me to repent. Cleanse me, strengthen me, restore me.

Father, THANK YOU for all your love, grace, mercy and blessings of life that you continually shower down upon me. Thank you especially for:

1.______________________________________   2.______________________________________
3.______________________________________   4.______________________________________
5.______________________________________   6.______________________________________

THANK YOU for answered prayers:____

Father, I need:____

Father, I ask that YOU:____

____

____

Lord, bless me that I may be a blessing. Give me Your heart for loving and serving others. Keep Your hand upon me. Keep me from all evil and harm, and let me cause harm to no one. Bind Satan that he have no power over me. All this I pray in subjection to your will and in the strong name of my Lord and Savior, Jesus Christ. Amen.

Trivial Pursuits

"Now we see things imperfectly as in a mirror, but then we will see everything with perfect clarity. All that I know now is partial and incomplete, but then I will know everything completely, just as God knows me now." 1 Corinthians 13:12 NLT

Trivial Pursuits is a fun parlor game that has been around for years and is still going strong. It is also a life style that has been around far too long and keeps getting more popular.

> *"Oh my people, listen to my teaching. Open your ears to what I am saying."*
> *Psalm 78:1 NLT*

In spite of Jesus clearly stating: *"However, no one knows the day or the hour when these things will happen, not even the angels in heaven or the Son himself. Only the Father knows" (Matthew 24:36 NLT)*, many Christians and especially pastors and Bible scholars seem to be preoccupied with trying to figure out the hour and day of Christ's return. Talk about trivial pursuits!

> *"Now anyone who builds on that foundation may use gold, silver, jewel, wood, hay, or straw. ¹³But there is going to come a time of testing at the judgment day to see what kind of work each builder has done."*
> *1 Corinthians 3:12,13 NLT*

The reality for all believers that the fruit our lives are going to be tested by fire, and that all the wood, hay, and straw or trivial pursuits will be burned away should be the real concern for us all.

Our pursuit of what we mistakenly think will make us happy will most often turn out to be wood, hay, and stubble. We will have cause to regret and wonder how we could have spent so much on such a meaningless effort. Wealth, prestige, popularity and power are just a few of the trivial pursuits that cannot provide any lasting happiness or validation for our lives.

Our time, treasure, and talents are on loan from God. We are only stewards. May we all have a lot of credits to our account after the trivial pursuits have been burned away.

Father, give me the wisdom and spiritual discernment to live a life fully pleasing to you and fruitful in every good work. Amen

Taking it to the Lord...

How can I apply this truth?____

____

Father, I've come to worship and praise you! You are my:_____________________________________

____

I give you all Glory, Honor, and Praise O Lord!

Father, I am sorry that I have sinned by:____

Help me to repent. Cleanse me, strengthen me, restore me.

Father, THANK YOU for all your love, grace, mercy and blessings of life that you continually shower down upon me. Thank you especially for:

1.____________________________________   2.____________________________________

3.____________________________________   4.____________________________________

5.____________________________________   6.____________________________________

THANK YOU for answered prayers:____

Father, I need:____

Father, I ask that YOU:____

____

____

Lord, bless me that I may be a blessing. Give me Your heart for loving and serving others. Keep Your hand upon me. Keep me from all evil and harm, and let me cause harm to no one. Bind Satan that he have no power over me. All this I pray in subjection to your will and in the strong name of my Lord and Savior, Jesus Christ. Amen.

U Turns Allowed

"You can enter God's Kingdom only through the narrow gate. The highway to hell is broad, and its gate is wide for the many who choose the easy way. But the gateway to life is small and the road is narrow." Matthew 7:13,14 NLT

About the only good thing about the highway to hell is that U turns are allowed. The thief on the cross gives witness to the fact that you can turn even at the very end.

> *"Turn from evil and do good, and you will live in the land forever."*
> *Psalm 37:27 NLT*

No matter how badly we have messed up, no matter how bad the pigpen of our sins smells, we can take heart in knowing that help is only a prayer of confession and repentance away.

The apostle Paul did a u-turn from persecutor and murderer to God's chosen one for proclaiming salvation to the gentiles. Peter and he other disciples did u-turns from denial and running away to boldly proclaiming the gospel and dying with courage and joy for the cause of Christ.

The prodigal son is probably the one with whom we can most easily relate. In our time of rebellion and running away from God, we can expect to reap a whirlwind of consequences every bit as bad or worse than slopping and eating with pigs. Thanks be to God that He does allow u turns when we stumble and fall short of His glory. He stands ever ready to welcome us back into His kingdom of love, mercy, and grace Many times whether for salvation or restoration, we have to get to the end of our own strength before we accept the life line that God throws out to all who make a u turn back to Him.

> *"I am the one who corrects and disciplines everyone I love. Be diligent and turn from your indifference."*
> *Revelation 3:19 NLT*

It is so much better to enjoy the abundant life lived in the will of the Lord, than choosing to pursue a life of willful sin and rebellion and their consequences.

Thanks be to God that He is always willing for us to turn back in true repentance and godly sorrow when we stumble and fall.

Father, thank you for allowing me to make u turns back into your kingdom. Amen

Taking it to the Lord...

How can I apply this truth?____
____
____

Father, I've come to worship and praise you! You are my:_____________________
____

I give you all Glory, Honor, and Praise O Lord!

Father, I am sorry that I have sinned by:_________________________________

Help me to repent. Cleanse me, strengthen me, restore me.

Father, THANK YOU for all your love, grace, mercy and blessings of life that you continually shower down upon me. Thank you especially for:

1._________________________________   2._________________________________
3._________________________________   4._________________________________
5._________________________________   6._________________________________

THANK YOU for answered prayers:____

Father, I need:____

Father, I ask that YOU:____
____
____

Lord, bless me that I may be a blessing. Give me Your heart for loving and serving others. Keep Your hand upon me. Keep me from all evil and harm, and let me cause harm to no one. Bind Satan that he have no power over me. All this I pray in subjection to your will and in the strong name of my Lord and Savior, Jesus Christ. Amen.

How Deep's the Water?

"Whether we are high above the sky or in the deepest ocean, nothing in all creation will ever be able to separate us from the love of God that is revealed in Christ Jesus our Lord. Romans 8:39 NLT

Perhaps nothing symbolizes both life and death as much as water. It is life giving both spiritually and physically, and it is at the same time life threatening either by drowning, poisoning, or thirst.

> *"Deeper and deeper
> I sink into the mire;
> I can't find a foothold to
> stand on. I am in deep
> water, and the floods
> overwhelm me."
> Psalm 69:2 NLT*

Baptism symbolizes the drowning of the old sinful man and the filling of the new man with the living water of the Holy Spirit from an ocean of love that will never run dry.

"If you believe in me, come and drink! For the Scriptures declare that rivers of living water will flow out from within."⁹(When he said "living water," he was speaking of the Spirit, who would be given to everyone believing in him. But the Spirit had not yet been given, because Jesus had not yet entered into his glory.)"

(John 7:38,39 NLT)

Peter jumped out of the water and began walking in faith until the saw the waves and became terrified. Sometimes we find ourselves in such a flood of troubles that we feel we will surely drown. These are the times when we should remember to do what Peter did - cry out to God!

> *"Jesus replied, "If you only
> knew the gift God has for you
> and who I am, you would ask
> me, and I would give you
> living water."
> John 4:10 NLT*

Whether we find drowning in a sea of debt, disease, or sin, we need to remember that God owns more lifeboats than all of the cruise lines combined. He has been sending them our on rescue missions since the beginning of time and He promises all believers that He will respond to any distress signal.

Father, when through the deep waters you call me to go, let my rivers of sorrow never be overflowed. Amen

When we "anchor deep" in God's Word, we anchor into a spring of living water that will never run dry.

Taking it to the Lord...

How can I apply this truth?____

____

____

Father, I've come to worship and praise you! You are my:____________________

____

I give you all Glory, Honor, and Praise O Lord!

Father, I am sorry that I have sinned by:__________________________________

Help me to repent. Cleanse me, strengthen me, restore me.

Father, THANK YOU for all your love, grace, mercy and blessings of life that you continually shower down upon me. Thank you especially for:

1.___________________________________   2.___________________________________

3.___________________________________   4.___________________________________

5.___________________________________   6.___________________________________

THANK YOU for answered prayers:____

Father, I need:____

Father, I ask that YOU:____

____

____

Lord, bless me that I may be a blessing. Give me Your heart for loving and serving others. Keep Your hand upon me. Keep me from all evil and harm, and let me cause harm to no one. Bind Satan that he have no power over me. All this I pray in subjection to your will and in the strong name of my Lord and Savior, Jesus Christ. Amen.

The Ingrown Church

"You also, like living stones, are being built into a spiritual house to be a holy priesthood, offering spiritual sacrifices acceptable to God through Jesus Christ." Peter 2:5 NIV

The body of Christ is a vital, living organism. If it is not growing, it is not healthy. The fact that thousands of churches are closing every year, and thousands of others are losing members in droves begs the question: "why"?

> *"My soul yearns, even faints, for the courts of the LORD; my heart and my flesh cry out for the living God."*
> *Psalm 84:2 NIV*

One of the big reasons that I have seen is that many churches and seemingly many denominations have become ingrown. Focus is too often on worshipping tradition and defending the faith rather than on obeying the great commandment and great commission.

Many ingrown churches seem to be operating more as sanctuaries for saints rather than hospitals for sinners. They "major in minors" and let visitors come and go unnoticed and unwelcome while they congregate in cliques and are oblivious to the fact that people who need the Lord are coming in and out of their doors without having their need met.

> *"I know your deeds; you have a reputation of being alive, but you are dead. Wake up! Strengthen what remains and is about to die, for I have not found your deeds complete in the sight of my God."*
> *Revelation 3:1,2 NIV*

There are many vital, doctrinally sound, bible-believing churches growing by leaps and bounds throughout the country. These contradict the rationalization of the dying churches that hide behind the excuse that their "purity of doctrine" is weeding out the unbelievers, and that numbers do not mean anything.

We are called to be "contagious Christians" in churches where God is at work through ministry within and without. Church should be a place that we can't wait to get to celebrate the love, peace, and joy of our salvation in Christ through authentic worship that encourages us--other believers and any seekers who might show up on any given Sunday.

We need to be conservative in doctrine, and liberal in love. Growing within doesn't mean being ingrown. We cannot grow within without growing out in ministry.

Father, keep me ever mindful that you are alive and relevant, and let your church be true to its calling.
Amen   ### Taking it to the Lord...

How can I apply this truth?____
____
____

Father, I've come to worship and praise you! You are my:_________________
____
I give you all Glory, Honor, and Praise O Lord!

Father, I am sorry that I have sinned by:________________________________
Help me to repent. Cleanse me, strengthen me, restore me.

Father, THANK YOU for all your love, grace, mercy and blessings of life that you continually shower down upon me. Thank you especially for:

1.________________________________   2.________________________________
3.________________________________   4.________________________________
5.________________________________   6.________________________________

THANK YOU for answered prayers:____
Father, I need:____
Father, I ask that YOU:____
____

Lord, bless me that I may be a blessing. Give me Your heart for loving and serving others. Keep Your hand upon me. Keep me from all evil and harm, and let me cause harm to no one. Bind Satan that he have no power over me. All this I pray in subjection to your will and in the strong name of my Lord and Savior, Jesus Christ. Amen.

When is Enough not Enough?

"You say, 'I am rich; I have acquired wealth and do not need a thing.' But you do not realize that you are wretched, pitiful, poor, blind and naked. " Revelation 3: 17 NIV

Idolatry is one the greatest sources of unhappiness and dissatisfaction in the world today. When we become possessed by possessions, power, prestige, lust or any trivial pursuits, we can never know the joy and Godly contentment of having the peace that surpasses all understanding. When we worship at the throne of any of these idols, enough will never be enough – we will always want more!

> *"Blessed is the man who makes the LORD his trust, who does not look to the proud, to those who turn aside to false gods."*
> *Psalm 40:4 NIV*

Becoming driven by the need to validate our worth and seeking happiness through anything other than a right relationship with God through faith in Jesus Christ is driving down the highway to despair.

These idols will, usually sooner than later, turn out to be the false Gods that they are, and we are left holding the bag of emptiness.

> *"For you have spent enough time in the past doing what pagans choose to do--living in debauchery, lust, drunkenness, orgies, carousing and detestable idolatry."*
> *1 Peter 4:3 NIV*

When we have the blessings of true joy, knowing the love of God and others, learning to be content in knowing that God's power is made perfect in our weaknesses, and that He will supply His all sufficient grace and meet our every need according to His riches in Christ Jesus, we have more than enough.

We will have more than enough love so that we can pass some on to others, we will have more than enough forgiveness so that we can pass some on others, and we will have more than enough joy go around.

Without this, we will never enjoy life to the fullest.

Father, let abiding in You through Your Word be more than enough for me. Amen

Taking it to the Lord...

How can I apply this truth?____
____

Father, I've come to worship and praise you! You are my:________________________
____

I give you all Glory, Honor, and Praise O Lord!

Father, I am sorry that I have sinned by:___________________________________

Help me to repent. Cleanse me, strengthen me, restore me.

Father, THANK YOU for all your love, grace, mercy and blessings of life that you continually shower down upon me. Thank you especially for:

1.________________________________   2.________________________________
3.________________________________   4.________________________________
5.________________________________   6.________________________________

THANK YOU for answered prayers:____

Father, I need:____

Father, I ask that YOU:____
____
____

Lord, bless me that I may be a blessing. Give me Your heart for loving and serving others. Keep Your hand upon me. Keep me from all evil and harm, and let me cause harm to no one. Bind Satan that he have no power over me. All this I pray in subjection to your will and in the strong name of my Lord and Savior, Jesus Christ. Amen.

Tent Dwellers Arise!

"I think it is right to refresh your memory as long as I live in the tent of this body, because I know that I will soon put it aside, as our Lord Jesus Christ has made clear to me." 2 Peter 1:13,14 NIV

God has been a tent dweller for many generations. In Exodus 40:34 we find: *"Then the cloud covered the Tent of Meeting, and the glory of the Lord filled the tabernacle."* God's presence filled the Tent of Meeting, and only left the tent to dwell in the temple. When Jesus Christ died on the cross, God's presence left the temple and took up residence of these earthly tents we live through His Holy Spirit.

> *" If you make the Most High your dwelling-even the LORD, who is my refuge-then no harm will befall you, no disaster will come near your tent."*
> *Psalm 91:9,10 NIV*

There is nothing permanent about tents. They endure the wind and rain, snow and hail, a start wearing out the day they are pitched. This tent we are living in is not permanent either. It starts dying the day we are born, and sooner or later we are going to have to leave it.

The good news for believers is that we are going to receive a brand new, incorruptible, permanent home at the resurrection of the just. Our new one will know no more suffering, no more pain, no more destruction, no more tears.

> *"Now we know that if the earthly tent we live in is destroyed, we have a building from God, an eternal house in heaven, not built by human hands".*
> *2 Corinthians 5:1 NIV*

The master builder with a master plan has even sent His son ahead to prepare a place for us--our new permanent home. It is going to be so wonderful we cannot begin to comprehend. As Paul says: *"No eye has seen, no ear has heard, no mind has conceived what God has prepared for those who love him" [1 Corinthians 2:9)*

Father as I get older and more aware of how temporary my tent is, help me to "keep my eye on the prize" and be comforted by your peace and joy. Amen

Taking it to the Lord...

How can I apply this truth?____

____

____

Father, I've come to worship and praise you! You are my:_______________________

____

I give you all Glory, Honor, and Praise O Lord!

Father, I am sorry that I have sinned by:_____________________________________

Help me to repent. Cleanse me, strengthen me, restore me.

Father, THANK YOU for all your love, grace, mercy and blessings of life that you continually shower down upon me. Thank you especially for:

1.________________________________   2.________________________________

3.________________________________   4.________________________________

5.________________________________   6.________________________________

THANK YOU for answered prayers:____

Father, I need:____

Father, I ask that YOU:____

____

____

____

Lord, bless me that I may be a blessing. Give me Your heart for loving and serving others. Keep Your hand upon me. Keep me from all evil and harm, and let me cause harm to no one. Bind Satan that he have no power over me. All this I pray in subjection to your will and in the strong name of my Lord and Savior, Jesus Christ. Amen.

Subway Religion

"He humbled you, causing you to hunger and then feeding you with manna, which neither you nor your fathers had known, to teach you that man does not live on bread alone but on every word that comes from the mouth of the LORD" Deuteronomy 8:3

Only Christ's church offers more franchise locations than Subway sandwich shops.   While you can find Italian, Wheat, Honey Oat, Monterey Cheddar, Parmesan/Oregano, Roasted Garlic, Hearty Italian, Italian Herbs and Cheese, or Sourdough, at Subway, You can partake of the "bread of life" at hundreds of Christian denominations throughout the world!

> *"They ate the food of angels! God gave them all they could hold."*
> *Psalm 78:15 NLT*

Perhaps our creator, who made us all with many different physical, mental, and emotional make-ups, allowed denominations to come into His church so that we could all find a place to worship in the heart language that He has given us.

Some denominations serve the bread of life with "a little bit country". Others feature "a little bit rock and roll". Whether you like formal or casual, traditional or contemporary, storefronts or cathedrals, you can find a place to worship just right for you. It's not the label, but the heart that counts.

Our freedom and liberty in Christ gives us a lot of latitude as to how and where we can worship. As long as salvation by grace alone through faith in Jesus Christ alone by authority of the inerrant truth of Scripture alone is proclaimed, God will be present and pleased with wherever we choose to worship.

> *"Jesus replied, "I am the bread of life. No one who comes to me will ever be hungry again. Those who believe in me will never thirst."*
> *John 6:35*

Whether you want to dance, clap your hands, lift your hands, or reverently worship quietly doesn't bother God, and it shouldn't bother you.

The world has been in the church for many centuries, and brought a lot of heresy and false teachings. Truth has too often become relative truth, tradition and legalism has overtaken relationship and mission, and hypocritical glory too often robs God of His glory.

Perhaps now, more than ever before, we should "beware of the leaven of the scribes and Pharisees", as we seek to worship God in spirit and in truth.

Father, fill me with all wisdom and spiritual discernment that I might feed on the true bread of life. Amen

Taking it to the Lord...

How can I apply this truth?____

____

____

Father, I've come to worship and praise you! You are my:____

____

I give you all Glory, Honor, and Praise O Lord!

Father, I am sorry that I have sinned by:____

Help me to repent. Cleanse me, strengthen me, restore me.

Father, THANK YOU for all your love, grace, mercy and blessings of life that you continually shower down upon me. Thank you especially for:

1.______________________________________   2.______________________________________

3.______________________________________   4.______________________________________

5.______________________________________   6.______________________________________

THANK YOU for answered prayers:____

Father, I need:____

Father, I ask that YOU:____

____

____

Lord, bless me that I may be a blessing. Give me Your heart for loving and serving others. Keep Your hand upon me. Keep me from all evil and harm, and let me cause harm to no one. Bind Satan that he have no power over me. All this I pray in subjection to your will and in the strong name of my Lord and Savior, Jesus Christ. Amen.

Not What but Who!

"I will give them a heart to know me, that I am the LORD. They will be my people, and I will be their God, for they will return to me with all their heart. Jeremiah 24:7

> *"Continue your love to those who know you, your righteousness to the upright in heart."*
> **Psalm 36:10**

The scribes and the Pharisee's thought that they knew all there was to know about God. They spent a lifetime in study, prayer, and observing the law and yet our Lord called them a *"brood of vipers". (Matthew 3:7)*

Our Lord also said: *"But blessed are your eyes because they see, and your ears because they hear. "For I tell you the truth, many prophets and righteous men longed to see what you see but did not see it, and to hear what you hear but did not hear it."* *(Matthew 13:11)*

The key to the kingdom of God and receiving the righteousness of Christ is found in John 17:3: *"Now this is eternal life: that they may know you, the only true God, and Jesus Christ, whom you have sent."*

Clearly, our eternal life is not based on what we know but on Who we know! God calls us into a <u>close</u> and <u>personal</u> relationship with His Son and our brother, Jesus Christ. Eternal life begins the minute we know Him by faith as our Savior. It continues as we grow into His fullness by getting to know Him as He speaks to us through His Word, through prayer, through circumstances, and through other believers.

> *"We know that we have come to know him if we obey his commands."*
> **1 John 2:3 NIV**

We can and should learn to know as much about God as we can, but we need to always remember it's not <u>what</u> we know, but <u>who</u> we know that counts!

The Pharisees made religion their God, and as a result, did not have God in their religion. Many seem to acquire a lot of head knowledge and doctrinal knowledge without having a clue as to what heart knowledge is all about. Unless we have Jesus in our hearts, all of the sacraments and ordinances of any church are worthless.

Father, keep me ever mindful that knowing you through a real and personal relationship with Your Son is what's really important. Amen

Taking it to the Lord...

How can I apply this truth?____
____
____

Father, I've come to worship and praise you! You are my:_________________________________
____

I give you all Glory, Honor, and Praise O Lord!

Father, I am sorry that I have sinned by:____

Help me to repent. Cleanse me, strengthen me, restore me.

Father, THANK YOU for all your love, grace, mercy and blessings of life that you continually shower down upon me. Thank you especially for:

1._______________________________   2._______________________________
3._______________________________   4._______________________________
5._______________________________   6._______________________________

THANK YOU for answered prayers:____

Father, I need:____

Father, I ask that YOU:____
____
____

Lord, bless me that I may be a blessing. Give me Your heart for loving and serving others. Keep Your hand upon me. Keep me from all evil and harm, and let me cause harm to no one. Bind Satan that he have no power over me. All this I pray in subjection to your will and in the strong name of my Lord and Savior, Jesus Christ. Amen.

Are You Full of It?

"So now we can rejoice in our wonderful new relationship with God--all because of what our Lord Jesus Christ has done for us in making us friends of God." Romans 5:11 NIV

"Delight," "happiness," "satisfaction," "bliss," "exceptionally good:" all of these words are used to define one little word – joy! Scripture after Scripture affirms that joy should be an integral part of the life of every Christian.

> *"But let all who take refuge in you rejoice; let them sing joyful praises forever. Protect them, so all who love your name may be filled with joy."*
> *Psalm 5:11*

Unfortunately we Christians all too often lose sight of the fact that Jesus said: *"I have told you this so that you will be filled with my joy. Yes, your joy will overflow!" (John 15:11)*

It is this joy in the Lord and what He has done for us that turns our "have-tos" into "want-tos." The joy of the Lord makes us want to do the things that please Him.

God, who loves us with an everlasting love, "loves a cheerful giver"- one who gives of treasures, time, and talents out of joy and not out of compulsion.

> *"We can rejoice, too, when we run into problems and trials, for we know that they are good for us--they help us learn to endure."*
> *Romans 5:3*

We sing: "the joy of the Lord is my strength", and many other hymns of joy. 1 John 1:4 says: "We *are writing these things so that your joy will be complete."* St Paul says in Philippians 4:4: *"Always be full of joy in the Lord. I say it again-- rejoice!"*

When people, circumstances, or things try to rob you of your joy, always remember that the joy of the Lord is your strength and your peace.

Let your joy overflow into the lives of all those around you!

Father, let nothing or no one rob me of my joy that I have in You. Amen

Taking it to the Lord...

How can I apply this truth?____

____

Father, I've come to worship and praise you! You are my:______________________

____

I give you all Glory, Honor, and Praise O Lord!

Father, I am sorry that I have sinned by:__________________________________

Help me to repent. Cleanse me, strengthen me, restore me.

Father, THANK YOU for all your love, grace, mercy and blessings of life that you continually shower down upon me. Thank you especially for:

1.________________________________   2.________________________________

3.________________________________   4.________________________________

5.________________________________   6.________________________________

THANK YOU for answered prayers:____

Father, I need:____

Father, I ask that YOU:____

____

____

Lord, bless me that I may be a blessing. Give me Your heart for loving and serving others. Keep Your hand upon me. Keep me from all evil and harm, and let me cause harm to no one. Bind Satan that he have no power over me. All this I pray in subjection to your will and in the strong name of my Lord and Savior, Jesus Christ. Amen.

Are You A Pot?

"Do not judge, and you will not be judged. Do not condemn, and you will not be condemned. Forgive, and you will be forgiven." Luke 6:37 NIV

Too many of us seem enjoy and spend too much time worrying about those "kettles". When our fleshly critical and judgmental spirits take over, grace gets cast aside and we have a ball making ourselves look good by making others look bad.

> *"And the heavens proclaim his righteousness, for God himself is judge."*
> *Psalm 50:6 NIV*

Many seem to have a need to feel that they are better than some one else. Racial and Religious prejudice and discrimination spring from this root cause. The victims of such prejudice often turn right around and practice the same thing against others they deem further down the economic, racial, or social ladder. Sadly, some many pastors and many churches are the worst offenders.

While we need to recognize and hate sin of all kinds, admonish our brothers and sisters in Christ in Christian love when their sinful behavior calls for it; we must be like Christ, who always hated the sin, but always loved the sinners, except the self-righteousness and hypocrisy of the scribes and Pharisees.

> *"You, therefore, have no excuse, you who pass judgment on someone else, for at whatever point you judge the other, you are condemning yourself, because you who pass judgment do the same things."*
> *Romans 2:1 NIV*

Scripture teaches that we would be better off spending our time judging ourselves. *"But if we judged ourselves, we would not come under judgment." (1 Corinthians 11:31 NIV)* Whether in taking communion, or in daily confession and repentance, we can save ourselves the pain and God the sorrow of having to discipline us more severely.

Frankly, I cannot afford the luxury of judging, condemning, and not forgiving others. I need all of the grace and mercy available to atone for my own sins, and I dare not forget our Lord's admonishment: *"But if you do not forgive men their sins, your Father will not forgive your sins." (Matthew 6:15 NIV)*

Father, take away my critical spirit, and replace it with the grace that abounds even more than sin.
Amen   **Taking it to the Lord...**

How can I apply this truth?____

____

Father, I've come to worship and praise you! You are my:______________________

____

I give you all Glory, Honor, and Praise O Lord!

Father, I am sorry that I have sinned by:__________________________________

Help me to repent. Cleanse me, strengthen me, restore me.

Father, THANK YOU for all your love, grace, mercy and blessings of life that you continually shower down upon me. Thank you especially for:

1._________________________________   2._________________________________

3._________________________________   4._________________________________

5._________________________________   6._________________________________

THANK YOU for answered prayers:____

Father, I need:____

Father, I ask that YOU:____

____

____

Lord, bless me that I may be a blessing. Give me Your heart for loving and serving others. Keep Your hand upon me. Keep me from all evil and harm, and let me cause harm to no one. Bind Satan that he have no power over me. All this I pray in subjection to your will and in the strong name of my Lord and Savior, Jesus Christ. Amen.

Have you "Defragged" Lately?

"Create in me a clean heart, O God. Renew a right spirit within me. Do not banish me from your presence, and don't take your Holy Spirit from me. Restore to me again the joy of your salvation, and make me willing to obey you." Psalm 51:10-12 NLT

While only the computer literate have ever heard of "defragging." It's not a bad concept for all believers. Simply put, it's an operation whereby all fragments on your computer's hard disk are consolidated, and disk space is freed up. This, along with disk clean up can make remarkable improvement in the operation of a computer.

> *"How can I know all the sins lurking in my heart? Cleanse me from these hidden faults."*
> *Psalm 19:12 NLT*

If we are ever going to grow into the fullness of Christ we need constant "defragging" and clean up of our minds and souls.

When we take our sins and burdens to the cross, we free up our strength and energy to be filled with the Love of God and the strength of His Spirit.

When we confess and dump any lingering bitterness or resentment, we free up a lot of wasted space for joy. When we dump any jealousy, envy, lust, or idolatry, we are freed to become Christ centered instead of self-centered. When we get rid of anger and impatience, we make room for that "peace that surpasses all understanding." When we get rid of all the fragments of time wasted on trivial pursuits, we free up time to be about our Father's business – doing those things for which He created us.

> *"Therefore, cleanse your sinful hearts and stop being stubborn."*
> *Deuteronomy 10:16 NLT*

Thanks be to God that He has given us the means for continual "defragging" and clean up through daily confession, repentance, and abiding in the power of the Holy Spirit.

Father, equip me to "fight the good fight" and "run the good race" by getting rid of all those things that hold me back. Amen

Taking it to the Lord...

How can I apply this truth?____
____
____

Father, I've come to worship and praise you! You are my:_________________________________
____

I give you all Glory, Honor, and Praise O Lord!

Father, I am sorry that I have sinned by:____

Help me to repent. Cleanse me, strengthen me, restore me.

Father, THANK YOU for all your love, grace, mercy and blessings of life that you continually shower down upon me. Thank you especially for:

1.______________________________________   2.______________________________________
3.______________________________________   4.______________________________________
5.______________________________________   6.______________________________________

THANK YOU for answered prayers:____
Father, I need:____
Father, I ask that YOU:____
____
____

Lord, bless me that I may be a blessing. Give me Your heart for loving and serving others. Keep Your hand upon me. Keep me from all evil and harm, and let me cause harm to no one. Bind Satan that he have no power over me. All this I pray in subjection to your will and in the strong name of my Lord and Savior, Jesus Christ. Amen.

The Heart of the Matter

"And I will give you a new heart with new and right desires, and I will put a new spirit in you. I will take out your stony heart of sin and give you a new, obedient heart. And I will put my Spirit in you so you will obey my laws and do whatever I command. Ezekial 36:26,27 NLT

Heart disease is not only the #1 cause of physical death, it is also the #1 cause of spiritual death.

> *"God is my shield, saving those whose hearts are true and right."*
> *Psalm 7:10 NLT*

Daily miracles are now commonplace throughout the world. God has provided skilled doctors to deal with heart disease as never before. However, sooner or later, hearts are going to stop beating, and all are going to die physically.

As sin and man's inhumanity to man becomes increasingly worse throughout the world we need to understand the "heart of the matter" is that only God can change hearts.

Rather than pray for World Peace, an end to abortions, pain and suffering in the world, it might would be better to ask God to have mercy on this sin-sick, depraved world, and bring heart changing renewal, revival, and rebirth.

When the hearts filled with hatred, jealousy, prejudice, deceit, and all of the other sins that seem to plague this world receive a transplant and become alive in Christ and filled with the love of God, which is ours through faith in Christ Jesus, everything else will fall into place.

God is looking into the heart of believers and unbelievers alike, and can seldom like what He sees. So far, In His forbearing, longsuffering, patient, and merciful love, He has allowed sin, death and destruction to run its course and have its way.

> *"Realizing this man's understanding, Jesus said to him, "You are not far from the Kingdom of God."*
> *Luke 12:34 NLT*

How much longer His grace will abound over the sin of the world is cause for concern especially for the billions of people who have not received a heart transplant. This is the "heart of the matter".

Father, bring renewal and revival into the world, and let it begin within me. Amen

Taking it to the Lord...

How can I apply this truth?____

____

____

Father, I've come to worship and praise you! You are my:_______________________

____

I give you all Glory, Honor, and Praise O Lord!

Father, I am sorry that I have sinned by:_____________________________________

Help me to repent. Cleanse me, strengthen me, restore me.

Father, THANK YOU for all your love, grace, mercy and blessings of life that you continually shower down upon me. Thank you especially for:

1.__________________________________   2.__________________________________

3.__________________________________   4.__________________________________

5.__________________________________   6.__________________________________

THANK YOU for answered prayers:____

Father, I need:____

Father, I ask that YOU:____

____

____

____

Lord, bless me that I may be a blessing. Give me Your heart for loving and serving others. Keep Your hand upon me. Keep me from all evil and harm, and let me cause harm to no one. Bind Satan that he have no power over me. All this I pray in subjection to your will and in the strong name of my Lord and Savior, Jesus Christ. Amen.

Watch out for the Minefields!

"Be self-controlled and alert. Your enemy the devil prowls around like a roaring lion looking for someone to devour." 1 Peter 5:8 NIV

Minefields planted during a war seem to harm and plague the people for years after the war is over. Unsuspecting children and adults have stepped on one--years later--and been killed or severely injured.

> *"Keep me from the snares they have laid for me, from the traps set by evildoers."*
> *Psalm 141.9 NIV*

Although the war is over and Satan has been defeated the battlefield of life is still strewn with minefields through which he seeks to destroy our faith and control our baser instincts.

We too often forget that life is a battleground where we walk daily through the minefields planted by the sins of the world in addition to pride, idolatry, anger, lust, jealousy, and other rebellion against God.

> *"Everything we do wrong is sin, but not all sin is fatal.*
> *We know that none of the God-begotten makes a practice of sin--fatal sin. The God-begotten are also the God-protected. The Evil One can't lay a hand on them."*
> *1 John 5:17,18 MSG*

This is the battleground through which our Savior walked without tripping on any of the mines, and defused them by His death on the cross so that they no longer have the power to destroy us.

We should also remember that although they cannot destroy us, they can cause great harm to us, to those we love, and to the cause of Christ. This is why it is so important that we daily *"put on the full armor of God, so that when the day of evil comes, you may be able to stand your ground, and after you have done everything, to stand." (Ephesians 6:13)*

Father, by the power of Your Spirit, protect me from the minefields that are still hurtful to me and to others. Amen

Taking it to the Lord...

How can I apply this truth?____

____

Father, I've come to worship and praise you! You are my:_____________________________

____

I give you all Glory, Honor, and Praise O Lord!

Father, I am sorry that I have sinned by:____

Help me to repent. Cleanse me, strengthen me, restore me.

Father, THANK YOU for all your love, grace, mercy and blessings of life that you continually shower down upon me. Thank you especially for:

1.________________________________   2.________________________________
3.________________________________   4.________________________________
5.________________________________   6.________________________________

THANK YOU for answered prayers:____

Father, I need:____

Father, I ask that YOU:____

____

____

Lord, bless me that I may be a blessing. Give me Your heart for loving and serving others. Keep Your hand upon me. Keep me from all evil and harm, and let me cause harm to no one. Bind Satan that he have no power over me. All this I pray in subjection to your will and in the strong name of my Lord and Savior, Jesus Christ. Amen.

Hope at the End of the Rope

"Dear brothers and sisters, whenever trouble comes your way, let it be an opportunity for joy. For when your faith is tested, your endurance has a chance to grow. So let it grow, for when your endurance is fully developed, you will be strong in character and ready for anything." James 1:2-4 NLT

Along with the cup of living water, joy, and blessings; everyone at some time or another is going to drink from the cups of sorrow and suffering.

> *"I have been dismissed as one who is dead, like a strong man with no strength left."*
> *Psalm 88:4 NLT*

Whether we grieve over the death of a loved one, a sin, a broken relationship – whether our suffering is physical, emotional, or financial, it is real and it hurts. When these hurts pile up, we sometimes find ourselves at the end of our ropes. We just can't handle anymore! The good news is that we don't have to!

We have a God who is no stranger to sorrow and suffering. *"He was despised and rejected by men, a man of sorrows, and familiar with suffering, whom men hide their faces he was despised, and we esteemed him not." (Isaiah 53:3)*

Our God who cannot lie is the God who works all things for our good. *"And God is faithful; he will not let you be tempted beyond what you can bear. But when you are tempted, he will also provide a way out so that you can stand up under it." (1 Corinthians 10:13)*

> *"For the Lord does not abandon anyone forever. Though he brings grief, he also shows compassion according to the greatness of his unfailing love. For he does not enjoy hurting people or causing them sorrow."*
> *Lamentations 3:31 NLT*

Rather than fall into the pit of depression and despair, we need to lay hold of the hope at the end of the rope. We need to trust in the One who loves us with an everlasting love, the One who says:

"My grace is sufficient for you, for my power is made perfect in weakness." (1 Corinthians 12:9) NIV

Father, thank you for being my "bridge over troubled waters," my "hope at the end of the rope." Amen

Taking it to the Lord...

How can I apply this truth?____

____

____

Father, I've come to worship and praise you! You are my:_______________________

____

I give you all Glory, Honor, and Praise O Lord!

Father, I am sorry that I have sinned by:_____________________________________

Help me to repent. Cleanse me, strengthen me, restore me.

Father, THANK YOU for all your love, grace, mercy and blessings of life that you continually shower down upon me. Thank you especially for:

1.____________________________________   2.____________________________________

3.____________________________________   4.____________________________________

5.____________________________________   6.____________________________________

THANK YOU for answered prayers:____

Father, I need:____

Father, I ask that YOU:____

____

____

____

Lord, bless me that I may be a blessing. Give me Your heart for loving and serving others. Keep Your hand upon me. Keep me from all evil and harm, and let me cause harm to no one. Bind Satan that he have no power over me. All this I pray in subjection to your will and in the strong name of my Lord and Savior, Jesus Christ. Amen.

Hold That Thought

"We demolish arguments and every pretension that sets itself up against the knowledge of God, and we take captive every thought to make it obedient to Christ." 2 Corinthians 10:5 NIV

It starts with our thoughts! A seed of doubt, lust, envy, pride, or bitterness, begins with the thought, and takes root in our heart and then possession of our mind and our will and we allow ourselves to be overcome and dominated by sin.

> *"May he be pleased by all these thoughts about him, for I rejoice in the LORD. Psalm 104:34*

King Saul's jealousy and hatred of David sprang from hearing *"Saul has killed his Thousands and David his ten thousands!" (Samuel 18:7b).* David's sin with Bathsheba all started when he saw her and lusted for her.

Why do we allow ourselves to be overcome and dominated by sin, when our new birth in Christ has set us free? *"For sin shall not have dominion over you, for you are not under law but under grace." (Romans 6:14)*

The answer has something to do with our fleshly thoughts taking over our spiritual. When we allow our free will to choose to let those thoughts take us where we should not go, we have dropped our guard and left home without the "full armor of God."

> *"Fix your thoughts on what is true and honorable and right. Ephesians 4:8 b*

By the power of the Holy Spirit living within the heart of every believer, we can "just say no" to the darts of evil thoughts the evil one is constantly throwing at us.

If Eve had just taken the thought to disobey God captive, we would not be dealing with this problem today. When we realize that God is not going to give us any temptation without the grace to overcome, and without providing a means of escape from it, we can begin to filter every thought through the mind of Christ, and put the ones that don't reflect Him and His glory on permanent hold.

Father, help me to control my thoughts that the sinful ones not have their way within me. Amen

Taking it to the Lord...

How can I apply this truth?____

____

Father, I've come to worship and praise you! You are my:_________________________

____

I give you all Glory, Honor, and Praise O Lord!

Father, I am sorry that I have sinned by:____

Help me to repent. Cleanse me, strengthen me, restore me.

Father, THANK YOU for all your love, grace, mercy and blessings of life that you continually shower down upon me. Thank you especially for:

1.______________________________   2.______________________________
3.______________________________   4.______________________________
5.______________________________   6.______________________________

THANK YOU for answered prayers:_______________________________________

Father, I need:____

Father, I ask that YOU:____

____

____

Lord, bless me that I may be a blessing. Give me Your heart for loving and serving others. Keep Your hand upon me. Keep me from all evil and harm, and let me cause harm to no one. Bind Satan that he have no power over me. All this I pray in subjection to your will and in the strong name of my Lord and Savior, Jesus Christ. Amen.

You Can't Take it With you

"**If the work survives the fire, that builder will receive a reward. But if the work is burned up, the builder will suffer great loss. The builders themselves will be saved, but like someone escaping through a wall of flames." 1 Corinthians 3:14 NLT**

The idea of sending ahead treasures in heaven has unjustly fallen in disrepute for far too long among many Christians. Partly from a reaction to the selling of indulgences and mostly from failure to distinguish between our destination and what we will do when we get there has caused many of us to give little thought that there are rewards in heaven other than heaven itself.

> *"Moreover by them Your servant is warned, And in keeping them there is great reward."*
> *Psalm 19:11*

As St. Paul emphasizes in Ephesians 2:9*: "Salvation is not a reward for the good things we have done, so none of us can boast about it". NLT.* Scripture after Scripture attests to the fact that Heaven is our destination by grace through faith and not of works.

This being the case, why does Scripture after Scripture mention rewards in Heaven*?). "Be happy about it! Be very glad! For a great reward awaits you in heaven." Matthew 5:1. "If the master returns and finds that the servant has done a good job, there will be a reward." Matthew 24:6 "And you will be blessed, because they cannot repay you; for you shall be repaid at the resurrection of the just." Luke 14:14 "See, I am coming soon, and my reward is with me, to repay all according to their deed." Rev. 22:12*

> *"But lay up for yourselves treasures in heaven, where neither moth nor rust destroys and here thieves do not break in and steal."*
> *Matthew 6:20*

And what could be better than heaven? Personally, I can't wait to find out. For those who love the Lord, to hear *"Well done thou good and faithful servant"* would be a great reward in itself. The prospect of getting a "good job in heaven" so that we can love the Lord even more by serving Him more would be even greater. One thing is sure: Although we can't take our time, talents, and treasures with us, <u>we can send them ahead!</u>

Father, thank you for your free gift of heaven. Help me to do those good works here for which you created me before I was born so that I can receive the rewards that you promise. Amen

Taking it to the Lord...

How can I apply this truth?____

____

____

Father, I've come to worship and praise you! You are my:__________________________

____

I give you all Glory, Honor, and Praise O Lord!

Father, I am sorry that I have sinned by:_______________________________________

Help me to repent. Cleanse me, strengthen me, restore me.

Father, THANK YOU for all your love, grace, mercy and blessings of life that you continually shower down upon me. Thank you especially for:

1.____________________________   2.____________________________

3.____________________________   4.____________________________

5.____________________________   6.____________________________

THANK YOU for answered prayers:____

Father, I need:____

Father, I ask that YOU:____

____

____

Lord, bless me that I may be a blessing. Give me Your heart for loving and serving others. Keep Your hand upon me. Keep me from all evil and harm, and let me cause harm to no one. Bind Satan that he have no power over me. All this I pray in subjection to your will and in the strong name of my Lord and Savior, Jesus Christ. Amen.

Does Your Standard of Giving
Match Your Standard of Living?

"Much is required from those to whom much is given, and much more is required from those to whom much more is given." Luke 12:48 NLT

We can say we love God all our lives, but where's the evidence? Perhaps the best answer is found in how freely we give of our time, talents, and treasures as conduits of God's love to others. St Paul says that giving *"is one way to prove your love is real."* (2:Corinthians 8:8b)

> *"Once I was young, and now I am old. Yet I have never seen the godly forsaken, nor seen their children begging for bread."*
> *Psalm 37:25 NLT*

One of the greatest robberies Satan and our flesh can ever commit is to rob us of the joy of giving. It's easy to experience this joy when we give to our spouses or family or friends, but for some reason, Satan or our flesh wants to step in and harden our hearts and pocketbooks to the Lord and others in need.

If God had responded to us the way we all too often respond to giving of any kind – graceless, condemningly, grudgingly and self centered - we would all be doomed to eternal damnation. Praise be to God, that: *"God showed his great love for us by sending Christ to die for us while we were still sinners." Romans 5:8 NLT*

The truth is that God does not need our time, talents, or treasures nearly as much as we need to give them. He owns them all, and just loans them out to us. *" For we are His workmanship, created in Christ Jesus for good works, which God prepared beforehand that we should walk in them."* *Ephesians 2:10*

> *"Since you excel in so many ways—you have so much faith, such gifted speakers, such knowledge, such enthusiasm, and such love for us□—now I want you to excel also in this gracious ministry of giving."*
> *2 Corinthians 8:7 NLT*

We need to be possessed by God instead of the treasures and "trivial pursuits" that all too often seem to possess us.

If God has blessed you with a standard of living that affords leisure time, abundant financial resources, and special talents, does your standard of giving give Him the glory for this?

Father, help my standard of giving to match my standard of living that I might glorify you and be a good and faithful steward. Amen

Taking it to the Lord...

How can I apply this truth?____
____
____

Father, I've come to worship and praise you! You are my:_________________________________
____

I give you all Glory, Honor, and Praise O Lord!

Father, I am sorry that I have sinned by:____

Help me to repent. Cleanse me, strengthen me, restore me.

Father, THANK YOU for all your love, grace, mercy and blessings of life that you continually shower down upon me. Thank you especially for:

1.___________________________________   2.___________________________________
3.___________________________________   4.___________________________________
5.___________________________________   6.___________________________________

THANK YOU for answered prayers:____

Father, I need:____

Father, I ask that YOU:____
____
____

Lord, bless me that I may be a blessing. Give me Your heart for loving and serving others. Keep Your hand upon me. Keep me from all evil and harm, and let me cause harm to no one. Bind Satan that he have no power over me. All this I pray in subjection to your will and in the strong name of my Lord and Savior, Jesus Christ. Amen.

Practice Makes Perfect

"Keep putting into practice all you learned from me and heard from me and saw me doing, and the God of peace will be with you." Philippians 4:9 NLT

Sometimes it seems that all we ever do is practice. We practice singing, dancing, driving, golfing, speaking. I remember having to practice what to do if my plane had to ditch in the ocean. After years of nap practice, I find that I can nap about anywhere, any place, and under any circumstances.

> *"Give me understanding and I will obey your law; I will put it into practice   with all my heart."*
> *Psalm 119:34*

Most of us haven't had to go to sin-practice, it just seems something that we are naturally good at. The willful and deliberate practice of a sin bears consequences for ourselves, and others that we really can't afford.

When you think about it, life is really one big practice for the life that is to come for all believers in Jesus Christ.

Spiritual maturity doesn't come overnight. It takes a lot of grace, a lot of practice, and God discipline. Fortunately God knew this and gave us the Holy Spirit to help us.

Practicing prayer *("The earnest prayer of a righteous person has great power and wonderful results." (James 5:16b NLT);* abiding in the Word (*He replied, "But even more blessed are all who hear the word of God and put it into practice." (Luke 11:28);* daily dying to sin *"So you should consider yourselves dead to sin and able to live for the glory of God through Christ Jesus." (Romans 6:11)*; and persevering through trials and disappointments *("But he who endures to the end shall be saved." (Matthew 24:13)* are the means through which we grow into the fullness of Christ. As we practice these spiritual disciplines, we begin to enjoy the "foretaste of glory" that awaits us in heaven.

> *"Whoever does not practice righteousness is not of God, nor is he who does not love his brother."*
> *1 John 3:10*

Father, Help me to practice "walking the walk" into spiritual maturity by the power of Your Spirit. Amen

Taking it to the Lord...

How can I apply this truth?____

____

Father, I've come to worship and praise you! You are my:_____________________

____

I give you all Glory, Honor, and Praise O Lord!

Father, I am sorry that I have sinned by:__________________________________

Help me to repent. Cleanse me, strengthen me, restore me.

Father, THANK YOU for all your love, grace, mercy and blessings of life that you continually shower down upon me. Thank you especially for:

1.____________________________   2.____________________________

3.____________________________   4.____________________________

5.____________________________   6.____________________________

THANK YOU for answered prayers:____

Father, I need:____

Father, I ask that YOU:____

____

____

Lord, bless me that I may be a blessing. Give me Your heart for loving and serving others. Keep Your hand upon me. Keep me from all evil and harm, and let me cause harm to no one. Bind Satan that he have no power over me. All this I pray in subjection to your will and in the strong name of my Lord and Savior, Jesus Christ. Amen.

Wanna Speak to the Owner?

"Do not let sin control the way you live; do not give in to its lustful desires. Do not let any part of your body become a tool of wickedness," Romans 6:12 NLT

> *The precepts of the LORD are right, giving joy to the heart. The commands of the LORD are radiant, giving sight to my eyes."*
> *Psalm 19:8 NIV*

We don't like to admit that we have an owner. "I did it my way", "Be all that YOU can be", and other songs reaffirm that it is all about us and that we are the "captains of our fate"!   And then we give up control of our lives to a pill, alcohol, lust, pride, power, idolatry or any number of other severe taskmasters.

Thankfully we Christians have an owner who is always ready to take calls, even collect calls. We were bought and paid for by the blood of Jesus Christ on the Cross at Calvary, and He rightfully owns us. We no longer have to be slaves to sin, but can actually be slaves to righteousness, because God has destroyed sin's control over us and set us free from its bondage.

Our new owner has plenty to say to us. *"Don't be conformed to this world, but be transformed by the renewing of your mind," "Put on the full armor of God", "Resist the devil and he will flee", "thou shall have no other Gods before me"* are just a few that come to mind.

When our owner comes, and asks us to give an accounting of the life that He has given us, are we going to have any fruit to show worthy of the price He paid for us?

> *"But God is so rich in mercy, and he loved us so very much, that even while we were dead because of our sins, he gave us life when he raised Christ from the dead."*
> *Ephesians 2:4,5*

We know that we can never be worthy, but we can surely be thankful and let our thanks be known by the fruits of righteousness that we can lay before the King. Are you ready to "speak to the owner?"

Father, thank you for taking ownership of me. By the power of Your Spirit, help me to do the good things you planned for me to do before I was even born. Amen

Taking it to the Lord...

How can I apply this truth?____

____

Father, I've come to worship and praise you! You are my:___________________________

____

I give you all Glory, Honor, and Praise O Lord!

Father, I am sorry that I have sinned by:____

Help me to repent. Cleanse me, strengthen me, restore me.

Father, THANK YOU for all your love, grace, mercy and blessings of life that you continually shower down upon me. Thank you especially for:

1.___________________________________   2.___________________________________
3.___________________________________   4.___________________________________
5.___________________________________   6.___________________________________

THANK YOU for answered prayers:____

Father, I need:____

Father, I ask that YOU:____

____

____

Lord, bless me that I may be a blessing. Give me Your heart for loving and serving others. Keep Your hand upon me. Keep me from all evil and harm, and let me cause harm to no one. Bind Satan that he have no power over me. All this I pray in subjection to your will and in the strong name of my Lord and Savior, Jesus Christ. Amen.

Oral Hygiene

"If you want a happy life and good days, keep your tongue from speaking evil, and keep your lips from telling lies." 1 Peter 3:10

Oral Hygiene is a mega-billion dollar business worldwide. We have electric toothbrushes, teeth whiteners, all sorts of mouth washes, and of course, your favorite flavor toothpaste. Which brings up an interesting question…have you ever tried to put toothpaste back into the tube?

"Who may worship in your sanctuary, LORD?
"Who may enter your presence on your holy hill? Those who lead blameless lives and do what is right, speaking the truth from sincere hearts."
Psalm 15:1, 2

As impossible as that might be, it is still easier than taking back those words spoken in thoughtlessness, anger, pride, or conceit that are better left unspoken. Once out of our mouth they can kill relationships, fuel fires, and destroy our Christian witness.

As funny as some jokes might be to us, the embarrassment that comes from people being offended by their content is not funny at all.

Not only what you say, but the way you say it, can be more abrasive than sandpaper and do a lot of damage. *"For whatever is in your heart determines what you say. A good person produces good words from a good heart, and an evil person produces evil words from an evil heart." Matthew 12:34b, 35 NLT*

"If you claim to be religious but don't control your tongue, you are just fooling yourself, and your religion is worthless."
James 1:26

It is better to let an argument die from lack of fuel than to jump in and fan the flames. It still takes two to argue. There is no breath sweetener made that can match the sweetness of God's Spirit within us. *"Surely it is God's Spirit within people, the breath of the Almighty within them, that makes them intelligent." Job 32:8*

Father, help me to "clean up my act" by letting what comes out of my mouth, reflect your love, your grace, and your kindness. Amen

Taking it to the Lord…

How can I apply this truth?____

____

Father, I've come to worship and praise you! You are my:__________________________________

____

I give you all Glory, Honor, and Praise O Lord!

Father, I am sorry that I have sinned by:____

Help me to repent. Cleanse me, strengthen me, restore me.

Father, THANK YOU for all your love, grace, mercy and blessings of life that you continually shower down upon me. Thank you especially for:

1.___________________________________   2.___________________________________

3.___________________________________   4.___________________________________

5.___________________________________   6.___________________________________

THANK YOU for answered prayers:____

Father, I need:____

Father, I ask that YOU:____

____

____

____

Lord, bless me that I may be a blessing. Give me Your heart for loving and serving others. Keep Your hand upon me. Keep me from all evil and harm, and let me cause harm to no one. Bind Satan that he have no power over me. All this I pray in subjection to your will and in the strong name of my Lord and Savior, Jesus Christ. Amen.

How Do You Like Your Eggs?

"Restore to me again the joy of your salvation, and make me willing to obey you." Psalm 51:12

Nobody likes to get "egg in the face" by committing some big blunder or making a bad choice. Once the yolk is broken, and the egg whites and yolks are mixed, you surely can't have your eggs unscrambled!

> *"You have forgiven the iniquity of Your people; You have covered all their sin"*
> *Psalm 85:2*

The lives of Christians are filled with growth pills disguised as problems. God often arranges circumstances to discipline, test, humble, and confound us in the process of refining us and conforming us into the image of Christ.

Most of the time, we make the beds that we have to lie in through willful disobedience and trading God control for self-control, and we have to suffer the consequences that often will plague us for the rest of our lives.

The question is not if, but when we get egg in our face, undergo God's discipline and chastening, or slip into our flesh mode. How do we respond? We can blame others, rationalize, deny, fall into self-pity and feel sorry for ourselves. The worst mistake we can make is to get angry at God.

That "roaring lion" is just waiting to step up when we step down to self-centered justification instead of Christ centered confession and repentance.

> *"But may the God of all grace, who called us to His eternal glory by Christ Jesus, after you have suffered a while, perfect, establish, strengthen, and settle you."*
> *1 Peter 5:10*

When we "blow it" we join an all-star lineup of Saints who did the same thing. Starting with Adam and Eve, Moses, Jonah, David, Peter and Paul, just to name a few.

When the "Master Chef: seasons our sins with forgiveness and grace, he can turn our "scrambled eggs" fit to serve the King!

Father, help me to know that you are always more ready to forgive than I am to be forgiven. Amen

Taking it to the Lord...

How can I apply this truth?____

____

Father, I've come to worship and praise you! You are my:_______________________________

____

I give you all Glory, Honor, and Praise O Lord!

Father, I am sorry that I have sinned by:____

Help me to repent. Cleanse me, strengthen me, restore me.

Father, THANK YOU for all your love, grace, mercy and blessings of life that you continually shower down upon me. Thank you especially for:

1.__________________________________   2.__________________________________

3.__________________________________   4.__________________________________

5.__________________________________   6.__________________________________

THANK YOU for answered prayers:____

Father, I need:____

Father, I ask that YOU:____

____

____

Lord, bless me that I may be a blessing. Give me Your heart for loving and serving others. Keep Your hand upon me. Keep me from all evil and harm, and let me cause harm to no one. Bind Satan that he have no power over me. All this I pray in subjection to your will and in the strong name of my Lord and Savior, Jesus Christ. Amen.

Are you Illegitimate?

"These trials are only to test your faith, to show that it is strong and pure. It is being tested as fire tests and purifies gold—and your faith is far more precious to God than mere gold" 1 Peter 1:7

I think I first heard this from Max Lucado, and if not him, I thank whoever gave me this thought to ponder: "God loves you just the way you are, but too much to let you stay that way."

> *"I know, O LORD, that your decisions are fair; you disciplined me because I needed it."*
> *Psalm 119:75*

When we think that God promised us a rose garden in this life, we are in for some big surprises. As works in progress, we are going to find that the Lord who loves us with an everlasting love also loves us with a "tough love" and is going to do whatever it takes to conform us into the image of His Son.

The slower we learn that God's ways are really the best ways for living the abundant, fulfilling life on this earth, the more mistakes, heartaches, and needless pain we are going to have to endure before we learn to totally abide in Him.

Although we are no longer bound to the law for salvation, the Holy Spirit still uses the law to convict us of our sins, and as a guide and a curb. Whenever we overstep the boundaries of the law, we can fully expect that God will give us whatever degree of reproof, chastening, or scourging He deems necessary to bring us back onto the path of righteousness.

> *"If God doesn't discipline you as he does all of his children, it means that you are illegitimate and are not really his children after all."*
> *Hebrews 12:8*

Does this mean that we should respond in anger or by doubting God's love when we experience God's chastening? Does it mean that we should go "eat a worm and die" in self-pity? Of course not!

We should respond by 1. Rejoicing in God's love 2. Repenting 3. Moving on!

Father, by the power of your Holy Spirit, give me a faith that will not fail, a hope that will not disappear, and your all sufficient grace to see me through your process of conforming me into the image of Jesus. Amen

Taking it to the Lord...

How can I apply this truth?____

____

Father, I've come to worship and praise you! You are my:___________________

____

I give you all Glory, Honor, and Praise O Lord!

Father, I am sorry that I have sinned by:_________________________________

Help me to repent. Cleanse me, strengthen me, restore me.

Father, THANK YOU for all your love, grace, mercy and blessings of life that you continually shower down upon me. Thank you especially for:

1.____________________________   2.____________________________

3.____________________________   4.____________________________

5.____________________________   6.____________________________

THANK YOU for answered prayers:_______________________________________

Father, I need:____

Father, I ask that YOU:____

____

____

Lord, bless me that I may be a blessing. Give me Your heart for loving and serving others. Keep Your hand upon me. Keep me from all evil and harm, and let me cause harm to no one. Bind Satan that he have no power over me. All this I pray in subjection to your will and in the strong name of my Lord and Savior, Jesus Christ. Amen.

"Itchy" Ears?

"For the time will come when they will not endure sound doctrine, but according to their own desires, *because* they have itching ears, they will heap up for themselves teachers; and they will turn *their* ears away from the truth, and be turned aside to fables" 2 Timothy 4:3,4

There is a great epidemic of "ear itch" going on throughout the world. Many have become completely deaf, and even worse, others have misinterpreted God's Word into fables that make "Alice in Wonderland" more believable.

> *"Listen, for I will speak of excellent things, And from the opening of my lips will come right things; For my mouth will speak truth."*
> *Proverbs 8:6,7a)*

Truth has become relative truth, the 10 commandments have become the ten suggestions, marriage has been redefined to include those of the same sex, and sin has become an irrelevant word. Many hear what they want to hear and choose to ignore or spin what we don't want to hear in the name of tolerance, women's rights, gay rights, or a mistaken concept of love.

> *"For the hearts of these people are hardened, and their ears cannot hear, and they have closed their eyes—so their eyes cannot see, and their ears cannot hear, and their hearts cannot understand, and they cannot turn to me and let me heal them."*
> *Matthew 13:15*

God makes it very clear *"that no prophecy of Scripture is of any private interpretation, for prophecy never came by the will of man, but holy men of God spoke as they were moved by the Holy Spirit." (2 Peter 1:20)* Or how about *"All Scripture is given by inspiration of God, and is profitable for doctrine, for reproof, for correction, for instruction in righteousness," (1 Timothy 3:16)*

If we would know truth, we had better get to know Jesus and what He stands for, or we are apt to fall for anything that our "itchy ears" hear through the world, the flesh, and the devil.

Have you checked your hearing lately?

Father, thank you for giving me the Holy Spirit so that my eyes can see, my ears can hear, my mind can comprehend.

Taking it to the Lord...

How can I apply this truth?____

____

Father, I've come to worship and praise you! You are my:______________________

____

I give you all Glory, Honor, and Praise O Lord!

Father, I am sorry that I have sinned by:___________________________________

Help me to repent. Cleanse me, strengthen me, restore me.

Father, THANK YOU for all your love, grace, mercy and blessings of life that you continually shower down upon me. Thank you especially for:

1._________________________________   2._________________________________
3._________________________________   4._________________________________
5._________________________________   6._________________________________

THANK YOU for answered prayers:____

Father, I need:____

Father, I ask that YOU:____

____

____

Lord, bless me that I may be a blessing. Give me Your heart for loving and serving others. Keep Your hand upon me. Keep me from all evil and harm, and let me cause harm to no one. Bind Satan that he have no power over me. All this I pray in subjection to your will and in the strong name of my Lord and Savior, Jesus Christ. Amen.

Are You "World Class"?

"And do not be conformed to this world, but be transformed by the renewing of your mind, that you may prove what *is* that good and acceptable and perfect will of God." Romans 12:2

We often hear "world class" used to describe outstanding athletes, orchestras, tourist attractions, as being among the best in the world.

> *"In this life they consider themselves fortunate, and the world loudly applauds their success."*
> *Psalm 49*

The problem is that the world's standards of morality and life have deteriorated so badly that it is producing "world class" sinners.

Satan is doing everything possible to get us to "curse God and die" like the rest of the world. As the world comes into our homes through TV, the internet, and newspapers, we are targeted from the age of 3 up to find our needs satisfaction in the latest toy, cartoon, beer, or perfume.

The Christian faith and lifestyle is constantly being challenged and undermined in so many subtle and not so subtle ways it takes all the spiritual discernment and strength from the Holy Spirit we can get to keep from being sucked into the cesspool of the world view.

Family values have been undermined for 2 generations on TV shows showing dads as idiots and God as a butt of jokes. Now TV shows are blatantly flaunting homosexuality, fornication, greed, and idolatry of every kind as the "world class" standard for living, loving, and finding true happiness. Does the one with the most toys really win?

> *"For all that is in the world—the lust of the flesh, the lust of the eyes, and the pride of life—is not of the Father but is of the world."*
> *1 John 2:16*

In a world obsessed with sex and materialism, the call to living Holy, "set apart" lives is falling more and more on deaf ears, but to those who claim Jesus Christ as Lord and Savior, it's a call to becoming saints who are still the salt and the light of the world.

Father, let me not fall in love with my self or the world. Let me be transformed into the image of Christ. Amen

Taking it to the Lord...

How can I apply this truth?____

____

Father, I've come to worship and praise you! You are my:_______________________

____

I give you all Glory, Honor, and Praise O Lord!

Father, I am sorry that I have sinned by:____________________________________

Help me to repent. Cleanse me, strengthen me, restore me.

Father, THANK YOU for all your love, grace, mercy and blessings of life that you continually shower down upon me. Thank you especially for:

1.______________________________   2.______________________________
3.______________________________   4.______________________________
5.______________________________   6.______________________________

THANK YOU for answered prayers:____

Father, I need:____

Father, I ask that YOU:____

____

____

Lord, bless me that I may be a blessing. Give me Your heart for loving and serving others. Keep Your hand upon me. Keep me from all evil and harm, and let me cause harm to no one. Bind Satan that he have no power over me. All this I pray in subjection to your will and in the strong name of my Lord and Savior, Jesus Christ. Amen.

Have You Ordered Yours?

"I tell you the truth, if anyone keeps my word, he will never see death." John 8:51

> *"I will abide in Your tabernacle forever; I will trust in the shelter of Your wings."*
> *Psalm 61:4*

There is a relative new "bon voyage" gift that you can buy for yourself or tell your loved ones you to get it for you. You can get one to express the passion of your life, or your pride in your alma mater. You can attend your going away party in a Commemorative Casket!

Commemorative Memorials in Macon Georgia have licensing rights from most colleges to use the school colors and seal on caskets, and now die hard fans and alums can express their admiration for their college or university right up to the end. (Nebraska Cornhusker and Tennessee Volunteer fans have so far been the best customers).

Actually, we shouldn't spend too much or worry at all about caskets, because we are not going to be there! I died and was buried when I was baptized. *"We were therefore buried with him through baptism into death in order that, just as Christ was raised from the dead through the glory of the Father, we too may live a new life." (Romans 6:4)* This new life that we have through faith in Jesus Christ is eternal life, which means we are going to live forever! *"I tell you the truth, whoever hears my word and believes him who sent me has eternal life and will not be condemned; he has crossed over from death to life."*

When we have completed God's purposes and we leave this corruptible body behind, our spirits will be instantly transported into the presence of God! *"I tell you the truth, today you will be with me in paradise" (Luke 23:43).* There we will wait for our new bodies at the "resurrection of the just."

> *"How we thank God, who gives us victory over sin and death through Jesus Christ our Lord!"*
> *1 Corinthians 15:57*

Frankly, rather than spending money on a commemorative casket, I would rather have it spent on a great praise band and dinner party. For the believer, death is not the end of anything, but the beginning of everything! And that's cause for real celebration!

Father, thank you for giving me the faith to know that because You live I can face all the tomorrows with your joy in this life and in eternity. Amen

Taking it to the Lord...

How can I apply this truth?____

____

Father, I've come to worship and praise you! You are my:___________________________________

____

I give you all Glory, Honor, and Praise O Lord!

Father, I am sorry that I have sinned by:____

Help me to repent. Cleanse me, strengthen me, restore me.

Father, THANK YOU for all your love, grace, mercy and blessings of life that you continually shower down upon me. Thank you especially for:

1._____________________________________   2._____________________________________

3._____________________________________   4._____________________________________

5._____________________________________   6._____________________________________

THANK YOU for answered prayers:____

Father, I need:____

Father, I ask that YOU:____

____

____

Lord, bless me that I may be a blessing. Give me Your heart for loving and serving others. Keep Your hand upon me. Keep me from all evil and harm, and let me cause harm to no one. Bind Satan that he have no power over me. All this I pray in subjection to your will and in the strong name of my Lord and Savior, Jesus Christ. Amen.

Webster Has Been Bridged!

"For I know the plans I have for you," declares the LORD, "plans to prosper you and not to harm you, plans to give you hope and a future." Jeremiah 29:11

I am happy to report that Webster's New Dictionary is no longer unabridged! The Lord has given me a new word that should be in every one's vocabulary and all dictionaries. This word can change your perspective and give you a whole new way of living. The new word is blessitunity, and it means" the opportunity to give or receive a blessing".

> *"Blessed is the man who fears the LORD, Who delights greatly in His commandments."*
> *Psalm 112:1*

While we are looking for opportunities to advance our careers, our own agendas, and our standing among our peers; we often miss out on the opportunity for a blessing that might be found in not only the best but even in the worst of circumstances.

God's Word abounds on how we might enjoy blessitunities. We find blessed, bless, etc. almost 300 times in the Bible, and Jesus Himself tells how to be blessed over 20 times starting with the beatitudes. *"Blessed are those servants whom the master, when he comes, will find watching." (Luke 12:37), and "But He said, "More than that, blessed are those who hear the word of God and keep it!" (Luke 11:28)* are a couple of my personal favorites.

Is your glass half empty or half full? Do you respond to problems by self-pity or by looking for what possible blessing might be there? Do you know what God's idea of blessings is? His ways are higher than our ways, and His thoughts are beyond our comprehension.

> *"Blessed are the pure in heart, For they shall see God."*
> *Matthew 5:3*

This is where faith comes in. God says that when we rejoice, are thankful, and pray, we will be blessed with that "peace that surpasses all understanding." Blessitunities are all around us! Would someone please call Mr. Webster?

Father, help me to be sensitive to the blessitunities that you provide on a daily basis and bless me so that I can be a blessing to others. Amen

Taking it to the Lord...

How can I apply this truth?____
____
____

Father, I've come to worship and praise you! You are my:_______________________
____

I give you all Glory, Honor, and Praise O Lord!

Father, I am sorry that I have sinned by:____________________________________

Help me to repent. Cleanse me, strengthen me, restore me.

Father, THANK YOU for all your love, grace, mercy and blessings of life that you continually shower down upon me. Thank you especially for:

1._________________________________   2._________________________________
3._________________________________   4._________________________________
5._________________________________   6._________________________________

THANK YOU for answered prayers:____

Father, I need:____

Father, I ask that YOU:____
____
____

Lord, bless me that I may be a blessing. Give me Your heart for loving and serving others. Keep Your hand upon me. Keep me from all evil and harm, and let me cause harm to no one. Bind Satan that he have no power over me. All this I pray in subjection to your will and in the strong name of my Lord and Savior, Jesus Christ. Amen.

Saint or Sinner?

"Taste and see that the LORD is good; blessed is the man who takes refuge in him. Fear the LORD, you his saints, for those who fear him lack nothing. [1]The lions may grow weak and hungry, but those who seek the LORD lack no good thing." Psalm 34:8-10

We have a tendency to undervalue the wonderful inheritance that we have when we by faith in Jesus Christ became joint heirs with Him. We become dead to sin and alive in Christ. We receive all of the rights of sonship, which means that we have been sanctified and made holy in the sight of God and have become Saints in the household of faith.

> *"I will listen to what God the LORD will say; He promises peace to his people, his saints- but let them not return to folly."*
> *Psalm 85.8*

There are times that we don't feel like saints. There are certainly times that we don't act like saints. Thank God, our sainthood is not based on our feelings or performance, but on the performance of Jesus Christ in dying on the cross for us, so that we could be reconciled to God and become saints in His eyes.

We need to understand that there are two types of sin. One has to do with our inherited curse of sin, the other with our sinful actions..

When we accept or accepted Jesus Christ as our Savior, our inheritance changed from sinner to saint. We are set free from the bondage of sin, *"Therefore, there is no condemnation for those who are in Christ Jesus."* (Romans 8:1) We are no longer miserable sinners, but redeemed saints!

> *"Praise be to the God and Father of our Lord Jesus Christ, who has blessed us in the heavenly realms with every spiritual blessing in Christ. [4]For he chose us in him before the creation of the world to be holy and blameless in his sight."*
> *Ephesians 1:3*

In spite of our new position as saints, our actions fueled by the flesh, the world, and the devil, are often sinful. We should be ashamed, sorry; and then confess and repent of them. We can be sure that God is at work in us, perfecting us into the image of Christ and we are going to be like Him someday. In the meantime, let's rejoice in the fact that we are no longer miserable sinners, but saints in the eyes of God.

Father, thank you for who I am in You! By the power of Your Spirit, let me live like it. Amen

Taking it to the Lord...

How can I apply this truth?____

____

Father, I've come to worship and praise you! You are my:___________________

____

I give you all Glory, Honor, and Praise O Lord!

Father, I am sorry that I have sinned by:__________________________________

Help me to repent. Cleanse me, strengthen me, restore me.

Father, THANK YOU for all your love, grace, mercy and blessings of life that you continually shower down upon me. Thank you especially for:

1.________________________________　　2.________________________________

3.________________________________　　4.________________________________

5.________________________________　　6.________________________________

THANK YOU for answered prayers:_______________________________________

Father, I need:____

Father, I ask that YOU:____

____

____

____

Lord, bless me that I may be a blessing. Give me Your heart for loving and serving others. Keep Your hand upon me. Keep me from all evil and harm, and let me cause harm to no one. Bind Satan that he have no power over me. All this I pray in subjection to your will and in the strong name of my Lord and Savior, Jesus Christ. Amen.

Is God Fair?

"He is entirely fair and just in this present time when he declares sinners to be right in his sight because they believe in Jesus" Romans 3:26 NLT

If beauty is in the eye of the beholder, fairness is often in the eye of the self-interested. Whether criticizing referee's calls against our favorite team, or complaining about someone making more money than us, or getting promoted over us, "it's not fair" is often one of the most subjective judgments we ever make.

> *"For I was envious of the boastful, When I saw the prosperity of the wicked."*
> *Psalm 73:3*

Many books have been written about the fairness of bad things happening to good people. And many people have been estranged from God, because of their anger of what they perceive to be unfair treatment by God.

We need to remember several things before we rush to judgment about the fairness of God. First of all, we must recognize that God is sovereign and we are His to do with as He pleases. Secondly, we need to remember that God's ways are higher than our understanding. We also need to remember that often in "working all things to the good" of those who love Him, God uses discipline, chastening, and sometimes bad things in order to conform us into the image of His Son.

> *"I wish to give to this last man the same as to you. Is it not lawful for me to do what I wish with my own things?"*
> *Matthew 20:14b, 15*

Before we go down the road questioning the fairness of God, we need to remember that if God were fair, we would all be bound for hell. We have all sinned and fallen short of the glory of God, and our personal righteousness is as filthy rags.

Thank God that He is not fair, but full of grace and mercy. Do we dare bring God's fairness into question?

Father, let me never trade the assurances I have in your grace and mercy for the consequences I would suffer if you were fair. Amen

Taking it to the Lord...

How can I apply this truth?____

____

____

Father, I've come to worship and praise you! You are my:_______________________

____

I give you all Glory, Honor, and Praise O Lord!

Father, I am sorry that I have sinned by:_____________________________________

Help me to repent. Cleanse me, strengthen me, restore me.

Father, THANK YOU for all your love, grace, mercy and blessings of life that you continually shower down upon me. Thank you especially for:

1.___________________________________ 2.___________________________________

3.___________________________________ 4.___________________________________

5.___________________________________ 6.___________________________________

THANK YOU for answered prayers:____

Father, I need:____

Father, I ask that YOU:____

____

____

Lord, bless me that I may be a blessing. Give me Your heart for loving and serving others. Keep Your hand upon me. Keep me from all evil and harm, and let me cause harm to no one. Bind Satan that he have no power over me. All this I pray in subjection to your will and in the strong name of my Lord and Savior, Jesus Christ. Amen.

Wanna Dance?

"Praise his name with dancing, accompanied by tambourine and harp. For the LORD delights in his people; He crowns the humble with salvation." Psalm 149:3 NLT

Like it or not, we all are going to dance to the tune of someone. It may be with the siren of fleshly pleasure that will consume us if it can. We might be dancing to the beat of fame and fortune, or boogieing to win the approval of our peers. Lady Luck may be beckoning, or the ever-popular money grabbers' stomp may be the tune.

> *"Observe and obey all these words which I command you, that it may go well with you and your children after you forever, when you do what is good and right in the sight of the LORD your God."*
> *Deuteronomy 12:28*

The older we get, the more we are going to realize that this dance in the ballroom of life is going to end. The things we held so dear and thought so important are going to turn out to be wood, hay, and stubble from God's perspective.

It is time to remember the one who brought us to the dance, who said: *"You have seen what I did to the Egyptians, and how I bore you on eagles' wings and brought you to Myself. Now therefore, if you will indeed obey My voice and keep My covenant, then you shall be a special treasure to Me above all people; for all the earth is Mine" (Exodus 19:5)*

Outside of eternal life can you imagine any greater blessing than that which comes from obedience? Wouldn't you really rather be a "special treasure" to God and enjoy all the promises and privileges of sonship?

> *"Or do you despise the riches of His goodness, forbearance, and longsuffering, not knowing that the goodness of God leads you to repentance?"*
> *Romans 2:4*

His arms are outstretched and bidding you to come dance and enjoy the joy of the Lord and the blessings of obedience in this life and the next. When you dance with God, you don't even have to worry about paying the fiddler.

Father, I am not a very good dancer, but I know that You are a good leader. By the power of Your Spirit teach me to dance to Your tune all the days of my life. Amen

Taking it to the Lord...

How can I apply this truth?____

____

Father, I've come to worship and praise you! You are my:_____________________

____

I give you all Glory, Honor, and Praise O Lord!

Father, I am sorry that I have sinned by:____

Help me to repent. Cleanse me, strengthen me, restore me.

Father, THANK YOU for all your love, grace, mercy and blessings of life that you continually shower down upon me. Thank you especially for:

1.____________________________   2.____________________________

3.____________________________   4.____________________________

5.____________________________   6.____________________________

THANK YOU for answered prayers:___________________________________

Father, I need:____

Father, I ask that YOU:____

____

____

Lord, bless me that I may be a blessing. Give me Your heart for loving and serving others. Keep Your hand upon me. Keep me from all evil and harm, and let me cause harm to no one. Bind Satan that he have no power over me. All this I pray in subjection to your will and in the strong name of my Lord and Savior, Jesus Christ. Amen.

Going to the Dogs

"But you, Timothy, belong to God; so run from all these evil things, and follow what is right and good. Pursue a godly life, along with faith, love, perseverance, and gentleness 1 Timothy 6:11 NLT

> *"Let us pursue the knowledge of the LORD. His going forth is established as the morning; He will come to us like the rain."*
> *Hosea 6:3*

Greyhound racing is a big business in Florida and a few other states. Millions of dollars are spent each year betting on which dog will get closest to the mechanical bunny at the finish line.

Night after night for several years, the greyhounds will run like the wind in a futile pursuit of catching that bunny.

Before we consider how dumb those dogs must be, lets clean out our closets of all the vain and fruitless "bunnies" we may be or might have been pursuing. How many times have we spent a big part of our time, talents, and treasures pursuing worldly fame and fortune, love in all the wrong places, or some other trivial pursuit?

God tells us that we are to pursue the kingdom of God and His righteousness so that all of the love, peace, and joy that He wants for us may be ours. He has promised to be a *"rewarder of those who seek Him,"* to *"grant us the desires of our heart,"* and to *"work all things to the good for those who love Him and are called according to His purposes."*

> *"See that no one renders evil for evil to anyone, but always pursue what is good both for yourselves and for all."*
> *1 Thessalonians 5:15 NLT*

If God is all-powerful, and He is, if God cannot lie, and He can't; isn't He really the one we should be chasing? We don't have to run very far or very fast. Unlike those elusive bunnies He is standing at the door knocking and bidding us to come.

Father, in Your mercy, help me to give up my trivial pursuits and help me to focus on pursuing the peace and joy that can only be found in You. Amen

Taking it to the Lord...

How can I apply this truth?____

____

____

Father, I've come to worship and praise you! You are my:_____________________

____

I give you all Glory, Honor, and Praise O Lord!

Father, I am sorry that I have sinned by:__________________________________

Help me to repent. Cleanse me, strengthen me, restore me.

Father, THANK YOU for all your love, grace, mercy and blessings of life that you continually shower down upon me. Thank you especially for:

1.____________________________   2.____________________________

3.____________________________   4.____________________________

5.____________________________   6.____________________________

THANK YOU for answered prayers:____

Father, I need:____

Father, I ask that YOU:____

____

____

Lord, bless me that I may be a blessing. Give me Your heart for loving and serving others. Keep Your hand upon me. Keep me from all evil and harm, and let me cause harm to no one. Bind Satan that he have no power over me. All this I pray in subjection to your will and in the strong name of my Lord and Savior, Jesus Christ. Amen.

Get it Right the First Time!

"Don't be ornery like a horse or mule that needs bit and bridle to stay on track." God-defiers are always in trouble; GOD-affirmers find themselves loved every time they turn around." Psalm 32:9 MSG

Whether training horses, dogs, or children, manufacturing a car or other product, the importance of doing it right the first time cannot be overlooked. It is twice as hard and takes twice as long. We not only have to train but untrain. Look at the billions of dollars spent on automobile, tire and other product recalls.

> *"Train me, GOD, to walk straight; then I'll follow Your true path. Put me together, one heart and mind; then, undivided, I'll worship in joyful fear."*
> *Psalm 86:11(MSG)*

This may be why God's Word places so much emphasis on training children. *"Train up a child in the way he should go, And when he is old he will not depart from it."* (Proverbs 22:6)

What a blessing it is to be one of those who were planted in the "good soil" where we were fed and nourished early in life and have enjoyed the blessings of abiding all the days of our lives. If you are one of these, don't feel cheated that you don't have a dramatic testimony concerning your "before" and "after" life. Just praise God for His faithfulness in keeping His promises to believers and their children.

> *"With these weapons we break down every proud argument that keeps people from knowing God. With these weapons we conquer their rebellious ideas, and we teach them to obey Christ."*
> *2 Corinthians 10:5 NLT*

If you were one of those "ornery " ones like the prodigal son before receiving salvation, be thankful that God tracked you down and did whatever it took to bring you into that saving relationship with Him.

We should all try to spare our children the anguish of wandering aimlessly lost by encouraging them in God's Word and setting a good example of the joy and blessings of Christian living so that they might "get it right" from the "getgo"!

Father, now that You have claimed me as Your very own, by the power of Your Spirit, help me to "get it right" so that I can avoid the painful consequences of sin. Amen

Taking it to the Lord...

How can I apply this truth?____

____

Father, I've come to worship and praise you! You are my:___________________________

____

I give you all Glory, Honor, and Praise O Lord!

Father, I am sorry that I have sinned by:____

Help me to repent. Cleanse me, strengthen me, restore me.

Father, THANK YOU for all your love, grace, mercy and blessings of life that you continually shower down upon me. Thank you especially for:

1._________________________________   2._________________________________

3._________________________________   4._________________________________

5._________________________________   6._________________________________

THANK YOU for answered prayers:____

Father, I need:____

Father, I ask that YOU:____

____

____

Lord, bless me that I may be a blessing. Give me Your heart for loving and serving others. Keep Your hand upon me. Keep me from all evil and harm, and let me cause harm to no one. Bind Satan that he have no power over me. All this I pray in subjection to your will and in the strong name of my Lord and Savior, Jesus Christ. Amen.

Are You "Keeping the Faith"

"You are the light of the world—like a city on a mountain, glowing in the night for all to see. Don't hide your light under a basket! Instead, put it on a stand and let it shine for all." Matthew 5:14-15 NLT

There is a lot to be said for the "perseverance of the saints" who, by the power of the Holy Spirit, keep their faith throughout all of the disappointments failures and problems of life. We all need to "anchor deep" in the faith of a God who cannot lie, and a Savior who cannot fail.

> *"Everyone will share the story of Your wonderful goodness;*
> *they will sing with joy of Your righteousness."*
> *Psalm 145:7 NLT*

Unfortunately, there are too many Christians who are "keeping the faith" in the wrong way. They are "keeping the faith" to themselves and for themselves.

We have close-knit communities of believers who believe that the church exists to uphold the traditions and doctrines of their denomination and to minister to them and their families without regard for the Great Commission.

We have believing individuals who are "closet Christians" who may bring their Christianity out on Sundays, but for the most part, keep their faith as a deep dark secret.

Faith is not something that we hoard, but something that we are commanded to share! Where would you be today if someone had not shared the "good news" with you?

And how do we share our faith? By being "sermons in shoes" through living a life that reflects our love for God and for others. We are told: *"Instead, you must worship Christ as Lord of your life. And if you are asked about your Christian hope, always be ready to explain it." (1 Peter 3:15 NLT)*

> *"Always thanking the Father, who has enabled you to share the inheritance that belongs to God's holy people, who live in the light."*
> *Colossians 1:12 NLT*

May God give us all the more passion to "pass on our faith" to others than we have to share our interests in our favorite ball clubs, hobbies, cars, children, and other topics of conversation. May we never bury our wonderful gift of salvation in the ground and suffer the fate of the unfaithful steward!

Father, help me to let my light shine in the power of Your Spirit. Amen

Taking it to the Lord...

How can I apply this truth?____

____

Father, I've come to worship and praise you! You are my:___________________

____

I give you all Glory, Honor, and Praise O Lord!

Father, I am sorry that I have sinned by:_________________________________

Help me to repent. Cleanse me, strengthen me, restore me.

Father, THANK YOU for all your love, grace, mercy and blessings of life that you continually shower down upon me. Thank you especially for:

1.___________________________   2.___________________________
3.___________________________   4.___________________________
5.___________________________   6.___________________________

THANK YOU for answered prayers:_________________________________

Father, I need:____

Father, I ask that YOU:____

____

____

Lord, bless me that I may be a blessing. Give me Your heart for loving and serving others. Keep Your hand upon me. Keep me from all evil and harm, and let me cause harm to no one. Bind Satan that he have no power over me. All this I pray in subjection to your will and in the strong name of my Lord and Savior, Jesus Christ. Amen.

Do You Have A Record?

"He canceled the record that contained the charges against us. He took it and destroyed it by nailing it to Christ's cross." Colossians 2:14 NLT

Hopefully, you don't have a criminal record, but you do have a record

> *"LORD, if you kept a record of our sins, who, O Lord, could ever survive?"*
> *Psalm 130:3 NLT*

of everything else. We have traffic violation records, school records, Social Security records, credit records, dental records, medical records, and "track" records on how we have done in the race of life.

What about our sin record? When we consider that every thought, word, and deed against the clear commandments and nature of God is sin, do we dare try to count the sins on record against us?

For most of us to make it through the day with less than 5 unkind thoughts, words, or deeds of jealousy, envy, lust, anger, selfishness, pride, etc., would be a very fine day. We are told that *"if we say we have no sin, we deceive ourselves and the truth is not in us"* (1 John 1:8) So if we sin just 4 times a day that's 1460 sins per year, and by age 50 that's 73,000 sins!

Would you really like to take a chance standing before God with this kind of record, without the righteousness of Christ? As believers that Jesus Christ died on the cross for our sins so that we would not have to die in the "lake of fire", we should live out our lives giving praise and glory to God in thanksgiving for what He has done for us.

> *"And anyone whose name was not found recorded in the Book of Life was thrown into the lake of fire."*
> *Revelation 20:15 NLT*

We should wear the white robe of righteousness that He has covered us with and let our record be full of the good works for which God created us to do even before we were born. Our good works are the only works that we are going to be held accountable for at the resurrection of the just.

Lord, thank You for your amazing grace that cleanses me from all sin and makes me righteous in Your sight by the blood of Your lamb. Amen

Taking it to the Lord...

How can I apply this truth?____

____

____

Father, I've come to worship and praise you! You are my:_______________________

____

I give you all Glory, Honor, and Praise O Lord!

Father, I am sorry that I have sinned by:________________________________

Help me to repent. Cleanse me, strengthen me, restore me.

Father, THANK YOU for all your love, grace, mercy and blessings of life that you continually shower down upon me. Thank you especially for:

1.______________________________   2.______________________________

3.______________________________   4.______________________________

5.______________________________   6.______________________________

THANK YOU for answered prayers:____

Father, I need:____

Father, I ask that YOU:____

____

____

Lord, bless me that I may be a blessing. Give me Your heart for loving and serving others. Keep Your hand upon me. Keep me from all evil and harm, and let me cause harm to no one. Bind Satan that he have no power over me. All this I pray in subjection to your will and in the strong name of my Lord and Savior, Jesus Christ. Amen.

True Worship

"Now if you will fear and worship the LORD and listen to His voice, and if you do not rebel against the LORD'S commands, and if you and your king follow the LORD your God, then all will be well. " 1 Samuel 12:14 NLT

We are all worshippers! Whether it be the one true God or NFL Football, everyone has things that they give their adoration and devotion. If time, talents, and treasures are the measures of our worship, and if we are honest with ourselves, our worship of God leaves much to be desired.

> *"Happy are those who hear the joyful call to worship, for they will walk in the light of Your presence, LORD."*
> *Psalm 89:15 NLT*

We are all, at one time or another, children of a lesser god. We often put family, pleasure, fame and fortune, careers, ahead of the One who created us in His image, loves us with an everlasting love, and asks only that we worship no other gods, love Him, and love others.

It really comes down to a matter of control. Does your love of God control you and everything that you do, or do you spend more of your time and resources on other pursuits?

> *"These people honor Me with their lips, but their hearts are far away. Their worship is a farce, for they replace God's commands with their own man-made teachings."*
> *Mark 7:7 NLT*

How would you compare your time spent in corporate worship with your time spent on recreational pursuits. How would you compare your time spent in home bible study, prayer, and devotions with time spent watching TV? How about the time spent talking about some race or ball game compared to the time-sharing the love of God with others?

When it comes to money, who's in control?

Father, I am sorry to confess that I do not give You the first fruits of my time, talents, and treasures that I should. By the power of Your Spirit, help me to be a true worshipper of you in every area of my life. Amen

Taking it to the Lord...

How can I apply this truth?____

____

Father, I've come to worship and praise you! You are my:____________________________

____

I give you all Glory, Honor, and Praise O Lord!

Father, I am sorry that I have sinned by:____

Help me to repent. Cleanse me, strengthen me, restore me.

Father, THANK YOU for all your love, grace, mercy and blessings of life that you continually shower down upon me. Thank you especially for:

1.___________________________________   2.___________________________________
3.___________________________________   4.___________________________________
5.___________________________________   6.___________________________________

THANK YOU for answered prayers:____

Father, I need:____

Father, I ask that YOU:____

____

____

Lord, bless me that I may be a blessing. Give me Your heart for loving and serving others. Keep Your hand upon me. Keep me from all evil and harm, and let me cause harm to no one. Bind Satan that he have no power over me. All this I pray in subjection to your will and in the strong name of my Lord and Savior, Jesus Christ. Amen.

God's B & B

"So we, *being* many, are one body in Christ, and individually members of one another." Romans 12:5

> *"Sing to the LORD a new song. Sing His praises in the assembly of the faithful."*
>
> **Psalm 149:1b NLT**

Bed and Breakfast lodgings are increasing in popularity and usage throughout the world. Staying at one can be a wonderful experience if it is a good one.

God's B and B's are also meant to be a wonderful experience. We are talking about "Believing" and "Belonging"!. There seem to be a lot of people who don't connect the two, but God surely does. What is so hard to understand about *"And let us consider one another in order to stir up love and good works, not forsaking the assembling of ourselves together, as is the manner of some, but exhorting one another, and so much the more as you see the Day approaching." (Hebrews 10:24,25)*

Christ established His church and gave it the keys to the kingdom of God. This is the "Good News" of the gospel that we received and through which we became joint heirs with Christ. It is the chosen bride of Christ through which we receive encouragement, love, and accountability, and celebrate the presence of God in a very special way.

Christ's Church is where we share the joy of corporate worship, the opportunities for ministry and service, for growing in the Word, and for being on mission for the Great Commission.

> *"Let the word of Christ dwell in you richly in all wisdom, teaching and admonishing one another in psalms and hymns and spiritual songs, singing with grace in your hearts to the Lord."*
>
> **Colossian 3:16**

Our call to salvation is a call to membership into the priesthood of believers and communion of saints. Belonging is not an option, it is a command, and we dare not ignore it and miss out on the blessings that obedience to this command brings.

The Lone Ranger may have been a great childhood hero, but he has no standing in the family of God.

Father, thank you for providing Your church, where I can worship, grow, and be nurtured by the love and encouragement of other believers. Amen

Taking it to the Lord...

How can I apply this truth?____

____

____

Father, I've come to worship and praise you! You are my:_________________________

____

I give you all Glory, Honor, and Praise O Lord!

Father, I am sorry that I have sinned by:_____________________________________

Help me to repent. Cleanse me, strengthen me, restore me.

Father, THANK YOU for all your love, grace, mercy and blessings of life that you continually shower down upon me. Thank you especially for:

1.______________________________   2.______________________________

3.______________________________   4.______________________________

5.______________________________   6.______________________________

THANK YOU for answered prayers:____

Father, I need:____

Father, I ask that YOU:____

____

____

Lord, bless me that I may be a blessing. Give me Your heart for loving and serving others. Keep Your hand upon me. Keep me from all evil and harm, and let me cause harm to no one. Bind Satan that he have no power over me. All this I pray in subjection to your will and in the strong name of my Lord and Savior, Jesus Christ. Amen.

Swiss Cheese Religion

"Have you not seen a futile vision, and have you not spoken false divination? You say, 'The LORD says,' but I have not spoken." Ezekial 13:7

Swiss cheese makes a wonderful sandwich, especially when combined with ham, bread and all the "fixings".

> *"Through Your precepts I get understanding; therefore I hate every false way."*
> *Psalm 119:104*

But it is holey, not holy. The difference between "holey" and "holy" seems to escape millions of well-meaning but seriously misinformed misinterpreters of the Bible, whose "Swiss Cheese" religions have so many holes there's hardly any real holiness.

We have those who blame all failed healings on the sick one's lack of faith. There is the "Santa Claus" contingent that teaches God wants us all to be wealthy financially. There was the widespread teaching of a few years ago that Rock N. Roll records were satanic because if you played them backwards you would get a satanic message. (As if anyone would really play records backwards)!

At one time or another, life Insurance, dancing, boy scouts, Proctor and Gamble's trademark and automobiles have been called creations of the devil.

The really big holes that can have serious consequences are the teachings that Jesus Christ's death on the cross was not sufficient for our salvation and that we have to do something to earn it; that somehow our salvation is all about what we do instead of what Jesus did; that it's all about feelings, or that it's all about our relationship with a denomination instead of our relationship with a Savior.

> *"In this the love of God was manifested toward us, that God has sent His only begotten Son into the world, that we might live through Him."*
> *1 John 4:9*

We need our 'Swiss Cheese' covered top and bottom with the real "Bread of Life" so that we can be "anchored deep" in the saving faith of knowing Jesus Christ as our Savior and Lord and that our "hope is build on nothing less than Jesus Blood and righteousness!"

Father, help me to stay anchored deep in Your truth. Protect me from the distractions of the world, the flesh, and the evil one that take me away from Your truth. Amen

Taking it to the Lord...

How can I apply this truth?______________________________________

____

Father, I've come to worship and praise you! You are my:___________________

____

I give you all Glory, Honor, and Praise O Lord!

Father, I am sorry that I have sinned by:_______________________________

Help me to repent. Cleanse me, strengthen me, restore me.

Father, THANK YOU for all your love, grace, mercy and blessings of life that you continually shower down upon me. Thank you especially for:

1._____________________________   2._____________________________

3._____________________________   4._____________________________

5._____________________________   6._____________________________

THANK YOU for answered prayers:___________________________________

Father, I need:____

Father, I ask that YOU:____

____

____

Lord, bless me that I may be a blessing. Give me Your heart for loving and serving others. Keep Your hand upon me. Keep me from all evil and harm, and let me cause harm to no one. Bind Satan that he have no power over me. All this I pray in subjection to your will and in the strong name of my Lord and Savior, Jesus Christ. Amen.

What's Your Blood Type?

"Much more then, having now been justified by His blood, we shall be saved from wrath through Him."
Romans 5:9

Just as air, food, and water are the outside essentials of physical life, so blood is probably the key interior ingredient of sustaining life. Whether we lose it by injury or internal bleeding, a blood transfusion is all that can keep us alive. We all have one of four types of blood, and it is essential that any transfusion that we receive be of the same type.

> *"Come now, and let us reason together," says the* LORD, *"Though your sins are like scarlet, they shall be as white as snow;"*
> *Isaiah 1: 18*

There are over 350 biblical references to blood and it is significant in several ways.

First of all, we are all "blood relatives" of Adam and it has been through the blood of generation after generation that our corrupt sin nature has lived on in everyone. Secondly, the blood of circumcision signified the purifying of the child by the shedding of blood. (Hebrew 9:22)

The Passover blood of a sacrificial lamb posted on the lintels of their home caused the angel of death to "pass over" the houses of the Israelites when God struck down the first born of all the Egyptians.

Abraham's faith in being willing to sacrifice his son was accepted as righteousness by God, and God promised that *"In your seed all the nations of the earth shall be blessed."* This promise was fulfilled in Jesus Christ, by whose blood sacrifice, all who would receive Him as Savior by faith would be accepted as righteous in the eyes of God.

> *"So Christ was offered once to bear the sins of many. To those who eagerly wait for Him He will appear a second time, apart from sin, for salvation."*
> *Hebrews 9:28*

Whether your blood type is A, B, AB, or D. only a faith transfusion of the blood of Christ can purify your heart and free you from the inherited corruption of your sin nature and bondage to sin.

Father, keep me ever mindful that You made the supreme blood sacrifice on the cross by dying for my sins, so that I can live forever with You. Amen

Taking it to the Lord...

How can I apply this truth?____

____

____

Father, I've come to worship and praise you! You are my:____________________

____

I give you all Glory, Honor, and Praise O Lord!

Father, I am sorry that I have sinned by:__________________________________

Help me to repent. Cleanse me, strengthen me, restore me.

Father, THANK YOU for all your love, grace, mercy and blessings of life that you continually shower down upon me. Thank you especially for:

1.__________________________   2.__________________________
3.__________________________   4.__________________________
5.__________________________   6.__________________________

THANK YOU for answered prayers:____

Father, I need:____

Father, I ask that YOU:____

____

____

Lord, bless me that I may be a blessing. Give me Your heart for loving and serving others. Keep Your hand upon me. Keep me from all evil and harm, and let me cause harm to no one. Bind Satan that he have no power over me. All this I pray in subjection to your will and in the strong name of my Lord and Savior, Jesus Christ. Amen.

Who Says "Quitters Never Win"?

"The Lord isn't really being slow about his promise to return, as some people think. No, he is being patient for your sake. He does not want anyone to perish, so he is giving more time for everyone to repent." 2 Peter 3:9 NLT

It's all about context! While perseverance and endurance are admiral character traits for everyone, when they become pride driven, hard headedness, and stubbornness, they can easily turn anyone into a loser in the game of life now and forever. We should certainly never quit loving God and loving and forgiving others, or believing in Jesus Christ as our Savior.

> *"Depart from evil, and do good; and dwell forevermore." Psalm 37.27*

Our call to faith is a call to repentance or a call to "quitting" our old ways and taking on a new life in Christ. People who quit smoking, quit gossiping, quit being so selfish and self-centered, or who quit any of the hundreds of attitudes and activities that are not pleasing to God become winners by quitting.

In cards and stocks, knowing when to quit is a virtue. In relationships, knowing when to quit arguing, quit complaining, and quit demanding our way paves the way for a better relationship. Sometimes, we need to give up on people that are pulling us down, instead of building us up.

> *"Even if I give away all that I have and surrender my body so that I may boast but have no love, I get nothing out of it." 1 Corinthians 13:3 NIV*

We need to quit sinning or die to sin daily so that we can know the great faithfulness of God, whose compassion never fails, and whose grace and mercy are renewed every day. He is the only one who never quits!

Father, give me the wisdom and spiritual discernment to know how and when to quit. Amen

Taking it to the Lord...

How can I apply this truth?____

____

Father, I've come to worship and praise you! You are my:____________________

____

I give you all Glory, Honor, and Praise O Lord!

Father, I am sorry that I have sinned by:_________________________________

Help me to repent. Cleanse me, strengthen me, restore me.

Father, THANK YOU for all your love, grace, mercy and blessings of life that you continually shower down upon me. Thank you especially for:

1.____________________________________   2.____________________________________

3.____________________________________   4.____________________________________

5.____________________________________   6.____________________________________

THANK YOU for answered prayers:_______________________________________

Father, I need:____

Father, I ask that YOU:____

____

____

Lord, bless me that I may be a blessing. Give me Your heart for loving and serving others. Keep Your hand upon me. Keep me from all evil and harm, and let me cause harm to no one. Bind Satan that he have no power over me. All this I pray in subjection to your will and in the strong name of my Lord and Savior, Jesus Christ. Amen.

God Does Remember Some Things

"For God is not unfair. He will not forget how hard you have worked for Him and how you have shown your love to Him by caring for other Christians, as you still do." Hebrews 6:10 (NLT)

God's selective memory works just the opposite of ours. We tend to dwell on the bad things people do, and forget the good, while God, who "remembers our sins no more" remembers about everything else.

> *"He does not forget the cry of the humble."*
> *Psalm 9:12*

God remembers our names that He has written in the Book of Life. If He remembers every sparrow (Luke 12:6), He certainly will remember you!

He will not forget to help the children of Israel (Isaiah 44:21); He will not forget any promise He has ever made. *"For the LORD your God is merciful—he will not abandon you or destroy you or forget the solemn covenant he made with your ancestors." (Deuteronomy 4:31 NLT)*

We need to understand that God is always watching us and that He is greatly pleased when we do the things that reflect His character and His will for how we should live our lives. Whether it's visiting the sick or those in prison, feeding the hungry, helping the needy, or forgiving as we have been forgiven, we can be sure that He is not only pleased, but that He will remember.

> *"Can a woman forget her nursing child, And not have compassion on the son of her womb? Surely they may forget, Yet I will not forget you."*
> *Isaiah 49:15*

When *"the resurrection of the just" (Luke 14:14)* takes place and we must give account for the stewardship of our lives, how comforting it is to know that our random acts of kindness, obedience, generosity, and love will be remembered! This is what "storing up treasures in heaven" is all about.

Father, thank you for forgiving and forgetting my sins while not forgetting any good works that I have done that glorify You. Amen.

Taking it to the Lord...

How can I apply this truth?____

____

____

Father, I've come to worship and praise you! You are my:________________________

____

I give you all Glory, Honor, and Praise O Lord!

Father, I am sorry that I have sinned by:_____________________________________

Help me to repent. Cleanse me, strengthen me, restore me.

Father, THANK YOU for all your love, grace, mercy and blessings of life that you continually shower down upon me. Thank you especially for:

1.___________________________   2.___________________________

3.___________________________   4.___________________________

5.___________________________   6.___________________________

THANK YOU for answered prayers:____________________________________

Father, I need:____

Father, I ask that YOU:____

____

____

Lord, bless me that I may be a blessing. Give me Your heart for loving and serving others. Keep Your hand upon me. Keep me from all evil and harm, and let me cause harm to no one. Bind Satan that he have no power over me. All this I pray in subjection to your will and in the strong name of my Lord and Savior, Jesus Christ. Amen.

The Great Remodeler

"He lifted me out of the pit of despair, out of the mud and the mire. He set my feet on solid ground and steadied me as I walked along." Psalm 40:2 NLT

Whether houses or people, remodeling is never easy. More and more you see perfectly good buildings being torn down to make way for new ones because it costs more to remodel than to build from scratch.

> *"Is this not the fast that I have chosen: to loose the bonds of wickedness, to undo the heavy burdens, to let the oppressed go free, and that you break every yoke?"*
> Isaiah 58:6

It's interesting to note that the greatest success in curing addiction and reforming criminals has been with faith-based programs that recognize the sovereignty and power of the Great Remodeler!

While it is true that God does not make any junk, it is also true that every one is born with a sinful nature that only a heart transplant can cure. How fortunate are those who can receive this transplant before sin and darkened understanding take complete control and lead to more serious problems.

. That Saul could be "remodeled" into the Apostle Paul is living proof that *"Therefore if the Son makes you free, you shall be free indeed." (John 8:36)*

> *"But we all, with unveiled face, beholding as in a mirror the glory of the Lord, are being transformed into the same image from glory to glory, just as by the Spirit of the Lord."*
> 2 Corinthians 3:18

While we may have never been jailed for our sins, we have all been captive to them and need the "heart transplant" and transformation by the power of the Holy Spirit that remodels our conduct to conform to our new identity in Christ. This "remodeling" begins the minute we receive Jesus Christ as our Savior, and will continue until we meet our "Great Remodeler face to face in heaven."

Father, thank you for loving me enough to have the long suffering and patience to continue remodeling me into the image of Your son. Amen

Taking it to the Lord...

How can I apply this truth?____

____

Father, I've come to worship and praise you! You are my:_______________________
____

I give you all Glory, Honor, and Praise O Lord!

Father, I am sorry that I have sinned by:____

Help me to repent. Cleanse me, strengthen me, restore me.

Father, THANK YOU for all your love, grace, mercy and blessings of life that you continually shower down upon me. Thank you especially for:

1.___________________________   2.___________________________
3.___________________________   4.___________________________
5.___________________________   6.___________________________

THANK YOU for answered prayers:____

Father, I need:____

Father, I ask that YOU:____

____

____

Lord, bless me that I may be a blessing. Give me Your heart for loving and serving others. Keep Your hand upon me. Keep me from all evil and harm, and let me cause harm to no one. Bind Satan that he have no power over me. All this I pray in subjection to your will and in the strong name of my Lord and Savior, Jesus Christ. Amen.

Got any Excess Baggage?

"Cease from anger, and forsake wrath; do not fret—*it* only *causes* harm." Psalm 37:8

> *"Let us lay aside every weight, and the sin which so easily ensnares us, and let us run with endurance the race that is set before us."*
> *Hebrews 12:1b*

It is amazing to see how much baggage some people take on trips. Whether by train, plane, or on cruises one has to wonder how anyone could possibly need to pack that much.

Unfortunately the excess physical, emotional, and spiritual baggage we choose to carry, can threaten our well being and often the well being of those around us.

Excess weight can cause heart attacks, strokes, loss of self-esteem, and many other problems.

The baggage of worry, fear, guilt, rejection, or remorse can cause even more problems. Our health, our peace, our joy, and our relationships with others are all put at risk when we carry these excesses. How many marriages have failed because either the bride or groom or both have come with this excess baggage?

Satan is a master at discouraging us by letting this baggage fester in our hearts and rob us of the peace and joy that is promised every believer in Christ.

> *"Which of you by worrying can add one cubit to his stature?"*
> *Matthew 6:27*

God sent His Son, Jesus Christ into the world not only to save us, but to bear these burdens so that we wouldn't have to. *Psalm 55:2* tells us: "*Cast your burden on the* LORD, *And He shall sustain you;*" Before we let baggage come to fill up our closets, let us always remember to dump our excess baggage at the foot of the cross.

Father, let me always remember that fear, worry and despair are not the fruit of Your Spirit and give me the power of Your Spirit to live a life unencumbered with this kind of excess baggage. Amen

Taking it to the Lord...

How can I apply this truth?____

____

Father, I've come to worship and praise you! You are my:____________________

____

I give you all Glory, Honor, and Praise O Lord!

Father, I am sorry that I have sinned by:__________________________________

Help me to repent. Cleanse me, strengthen me, restore me.

Father, THANK YOU for all your love, grace, mercy and blessings of life that you continually shower down upon me. Thank you especially for:

1.____________________________   2.____________________________
3.____________________________   4.____________________________
5.____________________________   6.____________________________

THANK YOU for answered prayers:__________________________________

Father, I need:____

Father, I ask that YOU:____

____

____

Lord, bless me that I may be a blessing. Give me Your heart for loving and serving others. Keep Your hand upon me. Keep me from all evil and harm, and let me cause harm to no one. Bind Satan that he have no power over me. All this I pray in subjection to your will and in the strong name of my Lord and Savior, Jesus Christ. Amen.

How's Your Portfolio?

"For riches certainly make themselves wings: They fly away like and eagle toward heaven." Proverbs 23:5

These words of wisdom offered by Solomon centuries ago, sound as if they might have been written yesterday by one of millions of investors who have seen their 401 plans, college bound funds, and personal investment portfolios take a hit and vanish into the clear blue skies.

> *'By humility and the fear of the Lord are riches, honor and life,"*
> *Proverbs 22:4*

In both the financial and the spiritual worlds, "think long term" is good advice. The "blue chips" of our spiritual portfolios are the investments we make in using our time, talent, treasure, and passion in things that will glorify God and bless others. God says: *"With me are riches and honor, enduring riches and righteousness". (Proverbs 8:18 NIV)* Scripture is full not only of admonitions, but of ways that we are to invest our treasures in heaven.

Just as the stock market has a daily list of winners and losers, Scripture gives us a list of winning and losing investments. Starting with obedience to the Great Commandment, Great Commission, and saving faith, we can add trust in God, humility, and doing good works to our "blue chip" list.

> *"Command those who are rich in this present age not to be haughty, nor to trust in uncertain riches but in the living God, who gives us richly all things to enjoy."*
> *1 Timothy 6:17*

Our losers need to be dumped at the foot of the cross daily. A critical and unforgiving spirit, pride and arrogance, anger, envy, lust, and idolatry of any form have to got to go. The time, talents, and resources we invest in these pursuits may have some short-term appeal, but over the long haul they are going to be worthless and disastrous. Have you inventoried your spiritual portfolio lately?

Father, by the power of Your Spirit, help me to eliminate my losing investments from my spiritual portfolio. Amen

Taking it to the Lord...

How can I apply this truth?____

____

Father, I've come to worship and praise you! You are my:_______________________________

____

I give you all Glory, Honor, and Praise O Lord!

Father, I am sorry that I have sinned by:____

Help me to repent. Cleanse me, strengthen me, restore me.

Father, THANK YOU for all your love, grace, mercy and blessings of life that you continually shower down upon me. Thank you especially for:

1._________________________________   2._________________________________

3._________________________________   4._________________________________

5._________________________________   6._________________________________

THANK YOU for answered prayers:____

Father, I need:____

Father, I ask that YOU:____

____

____

Lord, bless me that I may be a blessing. Give me Your heart for loving and serving others. Keep Your hand upon me. Keep me from all evil and harm, and let me cause harm to no one. Bind Satan that he have no power over me. All this I pray in subjection to your will and in the strong name of my Lord and Savior, Jesus Christ. Amen.

Have You Ever Been Convicted?

"There is therefore now no condemnation to those who are in Christ Jesus, who do not walk according to the flesh, but according to the Spirit. For the law of the Spirit of life in Christ Jesus has made me free from the law of sin and death." Romans 8:1, 2

> *"Oh, do not hold us guilty for our former sins! Let Your tenderhearted mercies quickly meet our needs, for we are brought low to the dust."*
> *Psalm 79:8 NLT*

If you were ever arrested for being a Christian, would there be enough evidence to convict you? This often asked, but still valid question can be very convicting in itself. Too often, too many of us would have to answer no. Although we "talk the talk", we "walk the walk" of the unbeliever, and no witness could be found to the fruits of the Spirit, good works for which we were created, or fruits of righteousness that should be evidenced in the lives of all who claim the name of Christian.

The word convicted carries a double meaning, both good and bad. When it means to be found guilty (except for being a Christian) is bad; when used to mean to be convinced, it is good.

In His love, God has given us His Holy Spirit to convict us of our sinfulness that leads to saving faith in Jesus Christ, and to continually convict us of our specific sins that need daily cleansing and repentance.

> *"Yet now God in His gracious kindness declares us not guilty. He has done this through Christ Jesus, who has freed us by taking away our sins."*
> *Romans 3:24 NLT*

The Holy Spirit also convicts us that we are unconditionally loved, forever forgiven, and totally accepted with the righteousness of Christ, when we receive Him as our Savior. He convinces us through faith that His grace is sufficient for all our needs, that He works all things for our good, that nothing will be able to separate us from His love, and many other promises that we can cling to and appropriate by faith.

Oh what joy there is when we become convicted by the power of the Holy Spirit!

Father, thank you for making me a convict for Christ and saving me from the condemnation and damnation that I deserve. Amen

Taking it to the Lord...

How can I apply this truth?____

____

Father, I've come to worship and praise you! You are my:______________________

____

I give you all Glory, Honor, and Praise O Lord!

Father, I am sorry that I have sinned by:___________________________________

Help me to repent. Cleanse me, strengthen me, restore me.

Father, THANK YOU for all your love, grace, mercy and blessings of life that you continually shower down upon me. Thank you especially for:

1.____________________________ 2.____________________________

3.____________________________ 4.____________________________

5.____________________________ 6.____________________________

THANK YOU for answered prayers:____

Father, I need:____

Father, I ask that YOU:____

____

____

Lord, bless me that I may be a blessing. Give me Your heart for loving and serving others. Keep Your hand upon me. Keep me from all evil and harm, and let me cause harm to no one. Bind Satan that he have no power over me. All this I pray in subjection to your will and in the strong name of my Lord and Savior, Jesus Christ. Amen..

Panning For Gold

"And the Lord said, "Simon, Simon! Indeed, Satan has asked for you, that he may sift *you* as wheat. But I have prayed for you, that your faith should not fail; and when you have returned to *Me,* strengthen your brethren." Luke 22:31

In the daily battles of life, our faith is continually being sifted or tested.   We often fail miserably. It is through this sifting that the impurities of our lives are washed away, and we are cleansed to live lives fully pleasing to God.

> *"But He knows the way that I take; when He has tested me, I shall come forth as gold."*
> *Job 23:10*

In testimony after testimony in Scripture and in the personal witnessing of others, we find that God does indeed sift to where only our faith sustains us. The sifting of Peter is a perfect example of how God will sometimes allow us to go to the absolute pit of shame and despair, so that we can become "sermons in shoes" to the transforming and restoring grace of God

In His love, God is continually inspecting, correcting, and perfecting us into the image of Christ.

Life itself is, in a sense, an exercise in panning for gold. Our value system is continually changing as we find that all that glitters is not gold. The older we get, the more we realize that so much of the "stuff" that we prized so highly is only "stuff", offering no lasting pleasure or satisfaction.

> *"That the genuineness of your faith, being much more precious than gold that perishes, though it is tested by fire, may be found to praise, honor, and glory at the revelation of Jesus Christ."*
> *1 Peter 1:7b*

Whether it is burned in the refiner's fire, or sifted in a sieve, the "wood, hay, and stubble of our lives" is going to disappear, and only the golden nuggets produced by a life of faith lived in bearing the fruits of the Spirit, and producing the good works for which we were created will have any value in the First National Bank of Heaven!

Father, by the power of Your Spirit, help me to endure Your panning, and to find the real gold of living a life pleasing to You and fruitful in every good work. Amen

Taking it to the Lord...

How can I apply this truth?____

____

____

Father, I've come to worship and praise you! You are my:_________________________

____

I give you all Glory, Honor, and Praise O Lord!

Father, I am sorry that I have sinned by:_______________________________________

Help me to repent. Cleanse me, strengthen me, restore me.

Father, THANK YOU for all your love, grace, mercy and blessings of life that you continually shower down upon me. Thank you especially for:

1.____________________________   2.____________________________

3.____________________________   4.____________________________

5.____________________________   6.____________________________

THANK YOU for answered prayers:____

Father, I need:____

Father, I ask that YOU:____

____

____

Lord, bless me that I may be a blessing. Give me Your heart for loving and serving others. Keep Your hand upon me. Keep me from all evil and harm, and let me cause harm to no one. Bind Satan that he have no power over me. All this I pray in subjection to your will and in the strong name of my Lord and Savior, Jesus Christ. Amen.

God is Ready!

"Then the LORD said to me, "You have seen well, for I am ready to perform My word." Jeremiah 1:12

Our God is an awesome God! He is all-powerful, all knowing, ever present, and never changing. He is ever loving, and thankfully ever ready! He is ever ready to forgive, and He is ever ready to save!

> *"For You, Lord, are good, and ready to forgive, and abundant in mercy to all those who call upon You."*
> *Psalm 86:5*

The great wedding feast has been prepared and the invitations go out on a daily basis. All of the privileges and blessings of the new covenant of grace are awaiting those who come to the wedding. We have the forgiveness of our sins, the favor of God, the peace that surpasses all understanding.

We have access to the throne of grace, and the comfort of the Spirit. The preparations have been made for a heaven on earth now, and for heaven in the future. To reject this invitation into a personal love relationship with God through faith in Jesus Christ is the worst thing anyone can do other than to come to the wedding clothed in hypocrisy instead of the white robe of righteousness.

God is not only ready to forgive, He is ready to comfort, to protect, to supply all our needs, and to work all things for our good. He is ready to make us conduits of His love to others.

> *"See, I have prepared my dinner; my oxen and fatted cattle are killed, and all things are ready. Come to the wedding."*
> *Matthew 22:4b*

How about you? Have you "rsvp'd" your invitation? Are you now enjoying all of the joys and privileges of a right relationship with God through faith in Jesus Christ, or are you one of those who is not quite "ready" to go to the wedding? There is limited seating, so you best get ready while there are still seats available.

Father, thank you for including me on your guest list and giving me the power of Your Spirit so that I can accept the invitation. Amen

Taking it to the Lord...

How can I apply this truth?____

____

Father, I've come to worship and praise you! You are my:___________________________

____

I give you all Glory, Honor, and Praise O Lord!

Father, I am sorry that I have sinned by:____

Help me to repent. Cleanse me, strengthen me, restore me.

Father, THANK YOU for all your love, grace, mercy and blessings of life that you continually shower down upon me. Thank you especially for:

1.__________________________________   2.__________________________________
3.__________________________________   4.__________________________________
5.__________________________________   6.__________________________________

THANK YOU for answered prayers:____

Father, I need:____

Father, I ask that YOU:____

____

____

Lord, bless me that I may be a blessing. Give me Your heart for loving and serving others. Keep Your hand upon me. Keep me from all evil and harm, and let me cause harm to no one. Bind Satan that he have no power over me. All this I pray in subjection to your will and in the strong name of my Lord and Savior, Jesus Christ. Amen.

Beware of the Leaven

"Then they understood that He did not tell *them* to beware of the leaven of bread, but of the doctrine of the Pharisees and Sadducees" Matthew 16:12

Yeast is an amazing ingredient. Just a tiny amount can hardly be recognized in a big batch of dough, but it affects all of the dough. When added, it goes to work silently and is hard to detect. It will gradually permeate the dough and take control of the whole loaf.

> *"A true witness delivers souls, but a deceitful witness speaks lies."*
> *Proverbs 14:25*

The false teachings and hypocrisy of the Scribes and Pharisees had exactly the same effect. Puffed up with pride, self-righteousness, and hypocrisy, they corrupted practically the whole body of believers against Christ and caused Him to be rejected, ridiculed and crucified.

There is no room for this leaven in the body of Christ. We are to be sincere, humble, and without guile in the living and exercising of our faith.

Unfortunately, both the leaven of false doctrine and hypocrisy are at work in the body of Christ at every level – personal, congregational, and denominational

On one hand we have those who place upholding tradition and doctrine way above the Great Commandment and Great Commission. On the other we have those with the mistaken notion that love means condoning what God calls sin and abominations.

> *"Therefore let us keep the feast, not with old leaven, nor with the leaven of malice and wickedness, but with the unleavened bread of sincerity and truth."*
> *1 Corinthians 5:8*

Which of the two extremes is worse in the sight of God might best be left to the providence of God. Who can deal with either much better than us. *God* makes one thing very clear: *"For I say to you, that unless your righteousness exceeds the righteousness of the Scribes and Pharisees, you will by no means enter the kingdom of heaven." (Matthew 5:20)*

Father, by the power of Your Spirit, give me the spiritual wisdom and discernment to recognize and resist the leaven of hypocrisy, self righteousness, and false doctrine. Amen

Taking it to the Lord...

How can I apply this truth?____

____

____

Father, I've come to worship and praise you! You are my:_______________________

____

I give you all Glory, Honor, and Praise O Lord!

Father, I am sorry that I have sinned by:____________________________________

Help me to repent. Cleanse me, strengthen me, restore me.

Father, THANK YOU for all your love, grace, mercy and blessings of life that you continually shower down upon me. Thank you especially for:

1.____________________________ 2.____________________________

3.____________________________ 4.____________________________

5.____________________________ 6.____________________________

THANK YOU for answered prayers:____________________________________

Father, I need:____

Father, I ask that YOU:____

____

____

Lord, bless me that I may be a blessing. Give me Your heart for loving and serving others. Keep Your hand upon me. Keep me from all evil and harm, and let me cause harm to no one. Bind Satan that he have no power over me. All this I pray in subjection to your will and in the strong name of my Lord and Savior, Jesus Christ. Amen.

God is Faithful!

"Because of the LORD's great love we are not consumed, for His compassions never fail. They are new every morning; great is Your faithfulness." Lamentations 3:22,23 NIV

There are living testimonies to the faithfulness of God all around us. There are not enough sheepfolds to hold all of the lost and wandering sheep that have strayed from the flock and been found and restored by the faithfulness of the Good Shepherd.

> *"I will sing of the LORD's great love forever; with my mouth I will make Your faithfulness known through all generations." Psalm 89:1 NIV*

Scripture after Scripture speaks of the unfailing love and faithfulness of God. Because God is faithful, His promises are sure. *"The LORD is faithful to all His promises and loving toward all He has made." (Psalm 145:13)* What joy and comfort we have in knowing that God is faithful and that His promises are sure!

We can believe that He works all things for our good, that He loves us with an everlasting love, that He hears and answers our prayers, and that nothing can separate us from His love that is ours through faith in Jesus Christ.

Because of God's faithfulness and promises, we have great expectations for the future that He has prepared for us in heaven. We can live the abundant life here on earth, secure in the freedom from condemnation that Christ bought for us on the Cross of Calvary.

> *"Now it is God Who makes both us and you stand firm in Christ. He anointed us, set His seal of ownership on us, and put His Spirit in our hearts as a deposit, guaranteeing what is to come." 2 Corinthians 1:21,22 NIV*

"Since we have these promises, dear friends, let us purify ourselves from everything that contaminates body and spirit, perfecting holiness out of reverence for God." (2 Corinthians 7:1 NIV)

Father, help m to give You thanks for Your faithfulness by living life to the fullest in and for You. Amen

Taking it to the Lord...

How can I apply this truth?____

____

____

Father, I've come to worship and praise you! You are my:________________________

____

I give you all Glory, Honor, and Praise O Lord!

Father, I am sorry that I have sinned by:____

Help me to repent. Cleanse me, strengthen me, restore me.

Father, THANK YOU for all your love, grace, mercy and blessings of life that you continually shower down upon me. Thank you especially for:

1.__________________________________   2.__________________________________

3.__________________________________   4.__________________________________

5.__________________________________   6.__________________________________

THANK YOU for answered prayers:______________________________________

Father, I need:____

Father, I ask that YOU:____

____

____

Lord, bless me that I may be a blessing. Give me Your heart for loving and serving others. Keep Your hand upon me. Keep me from all evil and harm, and let me cause harm to no one. Bind Satan that he have no power over me. All this I pray in subjection to your will and in the strong name of my Lord and Savior, Jesus Christ. Amen.

Diplomatic Immunity

"*There is* therefore now no condemnation to those who are in Christ Jesus who do not walk according to the flesh, but according to the Spirit." Romans 8:1

> *"In the LORD all the descendants of Israel shall be justified, and shall glory."*
> *Isaiah 45:25*

Diplomatic immunity is in effect throughout most of the world. It gives special status to foreign diplomatic agents giving them the highest degree of privileges and immunities, including personal inviolability; which means that they may not be arrested or detained, or their work and lives hindered in any way.

As believers in and ambassadors of Jesus Christ, we also enjoy the highest degrees of privileges and immunities. We become members of a royal priesthood and joint heirs with Christ.

When Satan tries to undermine our faith by continually reminding us of our failures and shortcomings as a means of making us doubt our faith and salvation, we need to repent and invoke our "diplomatic immunity" We need always to remember that when we confess our sins they are forgiven and erased from God's memory bank, and only Satan, never God, will bring them up again as though they were not forgiven.

We need to remember that when we received Jesus Christ as our Savior we were given the Holy Spirit *"in whom also, having believed, you were sealed with the Holy Spirit of promise, who is the guarantee of our inheritance until the redemption of the purchased possession, to the praise of His glory." (Ephesians 1:13b, 14)*

> *"Who shall bring a charge against God's elect? It is God who justifies. Who is he who condemns?"*
> *Romans 8:33*

In other words, if we are <u>true</u> believers, we have been set free from condemnation and the power of sin to destroy us, and free to bear the fruits of righteousness and produce the good works for which we were created. With the power of the Holy Spirit and Christ in us, we have the immunity we need to live the abundant life that is ours in Christ.

Father, thank you for covering me with the blood of Your Son that I am immunized from eternal damnation. Amen

Taking it to the Lord...

How can I apply this truth?____

____

____

Father, I've come to worship and praise you! You are my:____________________

____

I give you all Glory, Honor, and Praise O Lord!

Father, I am sorry that I have sinned by:__________________________________

Help me to repent. Cleanse me, strengthen me, restore me.

Father, THANK YOU for all your love, grace, mercy and blessings of life that you continually shower down upon me. Thank you especially for:

1.______________________________   2.______________________________

3.______________________________   4.______________________________

5.______________________________   6.______________________________

THANK YOU for answered prayers:____

Father, I need:____

Father, I ask that YOU:____

____

____

____

Lord, bless me that I may be a blessing. Give me Your heart for loving and serving others. Keep Your hand upon me. Keep me from all evil and harm, and let me cause harm to no one. Bind Satan that he have no power over me. All this I pray in subjection to your will and in the strong name of my Lord and Savior, Jesus Christ. Amen.

Meeting Expectations

"Now to Him who is able to do exceedingly abundantly above all that we ask or think, according to the power that works in us, to Him *be* glory in the church by Christ Jesus to all generations, forever and ever. Amen." Ephesians 3:20

> *"Uphold me according to Your word, that I may live; and do not let me be ashamed of my hope."*
> *Psalm 119:116*

We sometimes feel overcome by the expectations others place on us. Our parents, our peers, our spouses, our bosses, our customers and parishioners have expectations we can't possibly meet. How great it is when some person or product exceeds our expectations. "Better than expected" is music to the ears to the research companies that are continually monitoring customer satisfaction on behalf of automobile, manufacturers, cruise lines, banks, etc.

What about our expectations of God? Do we have Him confused with Santa Claus? Do we think we will have no more problems once we become a child of God? Do we get angry with God when He allows bad things to happen to us or to our loved ones?

The better we get to know God through His Son, who came to reveal Him to us, the more realistic and more fulfilling our expectations of God will become. When we learn the secret of abiding, we will find that God's plans, promises, disciplining and pruning, and His on going presence within us are all part of His "working all things for the good of those who love Him and are called according too His purposes" for now and forever.

> *"Eye has not seen, nor ear heard, Nor have entered into the heart of man the things which God has prepared for those who love Him."*
> *1 Corinthians 2:9b*

He came fulfill the law that we couldn't keep for ourselves. He died on the cross and was raised to life on the third day by God the Father to validate that our sin debt was paid in full.

That He has ascended into heaven to prepare a place for us in an eternity with no more pain, no more tears, no more sickness, and no more sin should really excite us about our Great Expectations!

Father, thank you for Your love, grace, and mercy, which exceed all my expectations. Amen

Taking it to the Lord...

How can I apply this truth?____

____

____

Father, I've come to worship and praise you! You are my:_____________________

____

I give you all Glory, Honor, and Praise O Lord!

Father, I am sorry that I have sinned by:__________________________________

Help me to repent. Cleanse me, strengthen me, restore me.

Father, THANK YOU for all your love, grace, mercy and blessings of life that you continually shower down upon me. Thank you especially for:

1._________________________________   2._________________________________

3._________________________________   4._________________________________

5._________________________________   6._________________________________

THANK YOU for answered prayers:____

Father, I need:____

Father, I ask that YOU:____

____

____

Lord, bless me that I may be a blessing. Give me Your heart for loving and serving others. Keep Your hand upon me. Keep me from all evil and harm, and let me cause harm to no one. Bind Satan that he have no power over me. All this I pray in subjection to your will and in the strong name of my Lord and Savior, Jesus Christ. Amen.

I Know Someone Who Does

"Surely it was for my benefit that I suffered such anguish. In your love you kept me from the pit of destruction; you have put all my sins behind your back." Isaiah 38:17 NIV

> *"He is despised and rejected by men, a Man of sorrows and acquainted with grief." Isaiah 53:3*

Some times, we find ourselves trying to comfort someone who has experienced such tragedy or pain that we can't begin to know how they feel, because, by the grace of God, we have never yet had to go through such a thing.

Whether it's the death of a spouse, or a child, a devastating illness or accident, or the rejection of a spouse, we can imagine but never really know how they feel.

Sometimes, just the comfort of our presence and our silence is the best comfort. During these times, we need to remember that we know someone who does know how bad it hurts.

Jesus knew the physical pain of beating, scourging, and being nailed to a cross. He knew the emotional pain of abandonment by his friends and rejection by the world. He knew the humiliation of being paraded through the streets of Jerusalem stark naked. He was betrayed, lied about, made to suffer for the sins of the world, none of which He ever committed. He was finally crucified at the town dump.

Sometimes God puts us through some of these ordeals in order that we might be a comforter and encourager for someone else going through the same thing. Because we have "been there and done that," people will listen and take heart from what we say.

> *"For we do not have a High Priest who cannot sympathize with our weaknesses, but was in all points tempted as we are, yet without sin." Hebrews 4:14*

All the time, we have, through faith in Jesus Christ, a Savior who can empathize with our pain or sorrow and give us the comfort of the Holy Spirit Living within us and fill our hearts with peace. This is part of the really good news we believers can appropriate by faith for every situation.

Father, thank you for the comfort of Your love and the strength of Your Spirit in my times of pain and suffering. Amen

Taking it to the Lord...

How can I apply this truth?____

____

____

Father, I've come to worship and praise you! You are my:_________________________________

____

I give you all Glory, Honor, and Praise O Lord!

Father, I am sorry that I have sinned by:____

Help me to repent. Cleanse me, strengthen me, restore me.

Father, THANK YOU for all your love, grace, mercy and blessings of life that you continually shower down upon me. Thank you especially for:

1.____________________________________   2.____________________________________

3.____________________________________   4.____________________________________

5.____________________________________   6.____________________________________

THANK YOU for answered prayers:____

Father, I need:____

Father, I ask that YOU:____

____

____

____

Lord, bless me that I may be a blessing. Give me Your heart for loving and serving others. Keep Your hand upon me. Keep me from all evil and harm, and let me cause harm to no one. Bind Satan that he have no power over me. All this I pray in subjection to your will and in the strong name of my Lord and Savior, Jesus Christ. Amen.

Happy Are The Poor in Spirit?

"Blessed *are* the poor in spirit, for theirs is the kingdom of
heaven." Matthew 5:3

When we come to the realization that we are sinners who need a Savior, we receive the kingdom of heaven, under the New Covenant of grace.

> *"You shame the counsel of the poor, But the LORD is his refuge." Psalm 14:6*

As long as we continue to live in our own self-centered world and validate ourselves without acknowledging that we have a sin problem, the joys of the kingdom of heaven in this world and the next will elude us.

We are told *"But seek first the kingdom of God and His righteousness, and all these things shall be added to you." (Matthew 6:33)* Unfortunately, many of us treasure other people and things, first, and never enter into the fullness of joy that comes only from putting God first in every area of our lives.

> *"Do not lay up for yourselves treasures on earth, where moth and rust destroy and where thieves break in and steal." Matthew 6:19*

God is looking for a broken spirit and a contrite heart. As we learn from His comments about the Scribes and Pharisees, being puffed up with pride, and thinking more highly of ourselves than we ought, is not the way to approach God.

When we approach God in true repentance and with godly sorrow for our sins, we will by no means be cast out, and we receive the keys to the kingdom and all its benefits. We receive "God's riches at Christ's expense," and always realize that it is the "Gift of God, lest any man should boast."

Father, the poverty of my separation from You has turned into enjoying the blessings of a right relationship with You through faith in Jesus Christ. Keep me ever mindful and thankful of Your amazing grace. Amen

Taking it to the Lord...

How can I apply this truth?____

____

Father, I've come to worship and praise you! You are my:___________________________

____

I give you all Glory, Honor, and Praise O Lord!

Father, I am sorry that I have sinned by:____

Help me to repent. Cleanse me, strengthen me, restore me.

Father, THANK YOU for all your love, grace, mercy and blessings of life that you continually shower down upon me. Thank you especially for:

1.__________________________________   2.__________________________________

3.__________________________________   4.__________________________________

5.__________________________________   6.__________________________________

THANK YOU for answered prayers:____

Father, I need:____

Father, I ask that YOU:____

____

____

Lord, bless me that I may be a blessing. Give me Your heart for loving and serving others. Keep Your hand upon me. Keep me from all evil and harm, and let me cause harm to no one. Bind Satan that he have no power over me. All this I pray in subjection to your will and in the strong name of my Lord and Savior, Jesus Christ. Amen.

Blessed Are the Peacemakers

"Salt *is* good, but if the salt loses its flavor, how will you season it? Have salt in yourselves and have peace with one another." Mark 9:50

Sometimes, it seems that there is no peace. Conflicts between countries, within families, within churches, on the job, and within the hearts of men abound all around us.

> *"Depart from evil and do good; seek peace and pursue it."*
> *Psalm 34:14*

We can be sure that all of the hatred and strife, all of the arrogance and pride, and all of man's inhumanity to man are not from God. They are the manifestations of the evil One, who is still working overtime throughout the world and in the hearts of both believers and unbelievers.

President Jimmy Carter will be best remembered by me, as a godly man who made peace between Egypt and Israel. To me, he is a walking testimony to the truth of Proverbs 16:7: *"When a man's ways please the LORD, He makes even his enemies to be at peace with him."* Of all the qualities of a peacemaker, being a godly man who pleases the Lord ranks at the top of the list. Just as *"a soft answer turns away wrath" (Proverbs 15:1)*, so does the "humble approach" seem to be indispensable in resolving conflicts and making peace.

The saddest commentary of all is the terrible witness and offense given by professing Christians participating in intra church strife. The words and deeds that come out of many pastors and leaders, as well as lay people, is an affront to God, which severely hinders the building up of His Kingdom, and brings rejoicing only to Satan.

> *"For God is not the author of confusion, but of peace, as in all the churches of the saints."*
> *1 Corinthians 14:33*

The good news is that we have, in Jesus Christ, the ultimate peacemaker. *"For He Himself is our peace, who has made both one, and has broken down the middle wall of separation."(Ephesians 2:14)* No wonder He said that peacemakers would be called the sons of God!

Father, let the peace that I have in You carry over to being a peacemaker in every arena of my life. Amen

Taking it to the Lord...

How can I apply this truth?____

____

____

Father, I've come to worship and praise you! You are my:_______________________________

____

I give you all Glory, Honor, and Praise O Lord!

Father, I am sorry that I have sinned by:____

Help me to repent. Cleanse me, strengthen me, restore me.

Father, THANK YOU for all your love, grace, mercy and blessings of life that you continually shower down upon me. Thank you especially for:

1.________________________________ 2.________________________________

3.________________________________ 4.________________________________

5.________________________________ 6.________________________________

THANK YOU for answered prayers:____

Father, I need:____

Father, I ask that YOU:____

____

____

____

Lord, bless me that I may be a blessing. Give me Your heart for loving and serving others. Keep Your hand upon me. Keep me from all evil and harm, and let me cause harm to no one. Bind Satan that he have no power over me. All this I pray in subjection to your will and in the strong name of my Lord and Savior, Jesus Christ. Amen.

The Quality of Mercy

"Return to the LORD your God, for He *is* gracious and merciful, slow to anger, and of great kindness; and He relents from doing harm." Joel 2:13

Although most consider grace and mercy to mean the same, to me, it is helpful to make the distinction that grace means getting undeserved favor, and mercy means not getting deserved punishment or consequences.

> *"Let, I pray, Your merciful kindness be for my comfort, according to Your word to Your servant."*
> *Psalm 119:76*

Our Lord said: *"Blessed are the merciful, for they shall obtain mercy."*(Matthew *5:7*) In other words, the best way of being sure to receive mercy is to be merciful. Our Lord showed mercy to the thief on the cross. The spouse who forgives a cheating mate is showing great mercy. The parable of the unjust steward speaks clearly about the importance of being merciful and the consequences of being unmerciful.

When I think of all the whippings I deserved and didn't get because my mother showed mercy, of the many sinful and unkind things I have done and said, but did not get the consequences I deserved, I am grateful for God's mercy.

When I consider that after almost 75 years of sins and sinning, I still must plea, "Lord have mercy upon me," I am so thankful that God, in His grace, move, and mercy, has removed my sins as far as the east is from the west. He remembers them no more, and His love, grace, and mercy is from everlasting to everlasting.

> *"For He is kind to the unthankful and evil. Therefore be merciful, just as your Father also is merciful."*
> *Luke 6:35b, 36*

We receive the undeserved favor of God by faith in Jesus Christ and by believing that He died on the Cross for our sins. Salvation is a free gift that we did nothing to earn or deserve, and we have only to receive by faith. How can we possibly be unforgiving and unmerciful to anyone, when we consider what we have received, rather than what we deserved?

Father, keep me ever mindful to be merciful so that I might receive the mercy I need. Amen

Taking it to the Lord...

How can I apply this truth?____

____

Father, I've come to worship and praise you! You are my:_______________________________

____

I give you all Glory, Honor, and Praise O Lord!

Father, I am sorry that I have sinned by:____

Help me to repent. Cleanse me, strengthen me, restore me.

Father, THANK YOU for all your love, grace, mercy and blessings of life that you continually shower down upon me. Thank you especially for:

1.___________________________   2.___________________________

3.___________________________   4.___________________________

5.___________________________   6.___________________________

THANK YOU for answered prayers:____

Father, I need:____

Father, I ask that YOU:____

____

____

Lord, bless me that I may be a blessing. Give me Your heart for loving and serving others. Keep Your hand upon me. Keep me from all evil and harm, and let me cause harm to no one. Bind Satan that he have no power over me. All this I pray in subjection to your will and in the strong name of my Lord and Savior, Jesus Christ. Amen.

The Supreme Six Pack

"It is good to give thanks to the Lord, and to sing praises to Your name, O Most High." Psalm 92:1

You won't find this six-pack in the cooler at your favorite convenience store, and although it's non-alcoholic in content, it's almost 100% proof in producing a spiritual high. If you go through a six pack a day of this, you will soon become a much happier, more cheerful person.

> *"Oh, that men would give thanks to the Lord for His goodness, and for His wonderful works to the children of men!"*
> *Psalm 107:8*

Whether you pray in the morning, in the evening, or on the run, take the time to offer a six pack of praise to God for six blessings, large or small, that you have received and enjoy, and try to come up with six different ones every day. Start with all the needs God supplies on a daily basis.

No matter how bad things may seem, or how badly you may feel, there are still blessings abounding, if you think about it. How many people has God given to love you or given you to love? Thank Him for one or two a day! How many abilities and talents has God given you? Thank Him for one a day! (If you can read or write, walk and see, cook or sew, sing or dance, you have abilities and talents to be thankful for.)

How many answers to prayers have you received? Thank Him for one a day, even when He has answered "no". How many ways does God love you? Thank Him for one a day! How many other ways has God blessed you? Thank Him for one a day! Once you start really thinking about all of the blessings God has showered upon you, including the wonders of nature, the miracle inventions that

> *"Rejoice always, pray without ceasing, in everything give thanks; for this is the will of God in Christ Jesus for you."*
> *1 Thessalonians 5:16*

we take for granted, etc., at six a day, you might never get around to thanking Him for all of them.

Father, thank You for my overflowing cup of blessings. Let me never take them for granted, but be truly thankful. Amen

Taking it to the Lord...

How can I apply this truth?____

____

Father, I've come to worship and praise you! You are my:__________________________

____

I give you all Glory, Honor, and Praise O Lord!

Father, I am sorry that I have sinned by:____

Help me to repent. Cleanse me, strengthen me, restore me.

Father, THANK YOU for all your love, grace, mercy and blessings of life that you continually shower down upon me. Thank you especially for:

1.__________________________________   2.__________________________________
3.__________________________________   4.__________________________________
5.__________________________________   6.__________________________________

THANK YOU for answered prayers:____

Father, I need:____

Father, I ask that YOU:____

____

____

Lord, bless me that I may be a blessing. Give me Your heart for loving and serving others. Keep Your hand upon me. Keep me from all evil and harm, and let me cause harm to no one. Bind Satan that he have no power over me. All this I pray in subjection to your will and in the strong name of my Lord and Savior, Jesus Christ. Amen.

Happy Are Those Who Mourn

"Weeping may endure for a night, but joy *comes* in the morning." Psalm 30:5

The blessings of mourning are something we have to think about. We grieve the loss of a friend or loved one

"I cried out to God with my voice and He gave ear to me." Psalm 77:1

and are comforted by the blessed assurance that they have gone on to a better life with no more sorrow, no more tears, and no more pain. For this, we should not only be comforted, but mourn with thanksgiving and praise to God.

The mourning over the loss of a friend or loved one, who has not died in the Lord, is another matter. We are filled with a tremendous sense of loss and sometimes with the feeling that we could have and should have done more to share our faith and try to shepherd them into a saving relationship with God, through faith in Jesus Christ, and now it's too late. We can only take comfort in knowing that God judges the heart and that there had hopefully been a change of heart we didn't know about.

The most probable meaning of Jesus' words, here, are the comfort we receive when we mourn over our sins. To have a broken spirit and contrite heart over our repeated failures to measure up to God's standards of conduct and obedience is a good thing. God forbid that we let sins go unconfessed and unrepented and the hardness of heart sets in so that we no longer mourn for our sins.

God takes our godly sorrow over our sins and comforts us with His love. When we are honest with God, as we have to be since He knows our hearts, He is able to work that true repentance in our hearts and give us the peace that only the forgiveness of God can afford. When your comfort zone gets squeezed by your sins, think about the blessings of this promise that those who mourn will be comforted by the Holy Spirit living within you.

"Who comforts us in all our tribulation." 2 Corinthians 1:4

Father, give me godly sorrow to mourn over my sins. By the power of Your Holy Spirit, comfort me and work true repentance in my heart. Amen

Taking it to the Lord...

How can I apply this truth?____

____

____

Father, I've come to worship and praise you! You are my:_________________________________

____

I give you all Glory, Honor, and Praise O Lord!

Father, I am sorry that I have sinned by:____

Help me to repent. Cleanse me, strengthen me, restore me.

Father, THANK YOU for all your love, grace, mercy and blessings of life that you continually shower down upon me. Thank you especially for:

1.__________________________________   2.__________________________________

3.__________________________________   4.__________________________________

5.__________________________________   6.__________________________________

THANK YOU for answered prayers:____

Father, I need:____

Father, I ask that YOU:____

____

____

Lord, bless me that I may be a blessing. Give me Your heart for loving and serving others. Keep Your hand upon me. Keep me from all evil and harm, and let me cause harm to no one. Bind Satan that he have no power over me. All this I pray in subjection to your will and in the strong name of my Lord and Savior, Jesus Christ. Amen.

A Few of God's Favorite Things

"For God so loved the world that He gave His only begotten Son, that whoever believes in Him should not perish but have everlasting life." John 3:16

Eternal life consists of getting to know God through His Son whom He has sent. It begins the moment we receive Jesus Christ as our Savior and will continue forever. Our response to God's gift of salvation should be to love Him and to please Him by loving the things He loves.

> *"I love those who love me, and those who seek me diligently will find me."*
> *Proverbs 8:17*

God loves Jesus: *"For the Father Himself loves you, because you have loved Me."* (John 16 27)

God loves obedience: *"Jesus answered and said to him, 'If anyone loves Me, he will keep My word, and My Father will love him, and We will come to him and make our home with him.'" (John 14:23) "The steps of a good man are ordered by the LORD, and He delights in his way." (Psalm 37:3). "He loves righteousness and justice." (Psalm 34.4)*

God loves to give good gifts to His children. *"If you then, being evil, know how to give good gifts to your children, how much more will your Father who is in heaven give good things to those who ask Him!" (Matthew 7:11) "God loves a cheerful giver." (2 Corinthians 9:7)*

Although He hates sin, God loves sinners: *"But God, who is rich in mercy, because of His great love with which He loved us, even when we were dead in trespasses, made us alive together with Christ (by grace you have been saved), and raised us up together, and made us sit together in the heavenly places in Christ Jesus." (Ephesians 2:4)*

How about you? Are these some of your favorite things? Is there any reason they shouldn't be?

> *"Therefore do not be unwise, but understand what the will of the Lord is."*
> *Ephesians 5:17*

Father, help me to love the things You love, and to despise that which is evil and to grow in Your Word constantly so that I might know these things. Amen

Taking it to the Lord...

How can I apply this truth?____

____

____

Father, I've come to worship and praise you! You are my:_________________________

____

I give you all Glory, Honor, and Praise O Lord!

Father, I am sorry that I have sinned by:_______________________________________

Help me to repent. Cleanse me, strengthen me, restore me.

Father, THANK YOU for all your love, grace, mercy and blessings of life that you continually shower down upon me. Thank you especially for:

1._________________________________   2._________________________________

3._________________________________   4._________________________________

5._________________________________   6._________________________________

THANK YOU for answered prayers:____

Father, I need:____

Father, I ask that YOU:____

____

____

Lord, bless me that I may be a blessing. Give me Your heart for loving and serving others. Keep Your hand upon me. Keep me from all evil and harm, and let me cause harm to no one. Bind Satan that he have no power over me. All this I pray in subjection to your will and in the strong name of my Lord and Savior, Jesus Christ. Amen.

Follow the Directions!

"All Scripture *is* given by inspiration of God, and *is* profitable for doctrine, for reproof, for correction, for instruction in righteousness, that the man of God may be complete, thoroughly equipped for every good work." 2 Timothy 3:16

In this "assemble it yourself" age, there seems to be a new occupation for people with a sadistic streak. It's designing and writing assembly or operating instructions! Sometimes, the type is so small you can't read it. Other times, they do not make sense. Often, we just wing it and end up with too many extra nuts and bolts, and usually, have to undo everything and start from scratch.

> *"To receive the instruction of wisdom, justice, judgment, and equity,"*
> *Proverbs 1:3*

God has given us "assembly instructions" for the abundant life. His directions are very clear, but sometimes hard to follow because they often seem to get in the way of what we perceive to be the abundant life. Often, we try putting a happy life together without following the instructions and suffer a lifetime of painful consequences.

God first gave specific instructions to Adam and Eve, and their failure that followed them set off a chain reaction of consequences for which, we are still suffering. God then gave specific instructions to the children of Israel, and their failure to follow them kept them wandering around in the wilderness for forty years.

> *"Then they asked Him, saying, "Teacher, we know that You say and teach rightly, and You do not show personal favoritism, but teach the way of God in truth."*
> *Luke 20:21*

Finally, in His mercy, God came to earth in the flesh of His own Son to not only die to save us, but to live to show us how we should live and to give us written instructions on how to live.

Starting with the instructions to love God, and to love others, Jesus wrote the perfect instruction manual. It's called the "Holy Bible!"

Father, help me to better learn your instructions by spending more time in Your instruction book. Amen

Taking it to the Lord...

How can I apply this truth?____

____

____

Father, I've come to worship and praise you! You are my:_______________________

____

I give you all Glory, Honor, and Praise O Lord!

Father, I am sorry that I have sinned by:___________________________________

Help me to repent. Cleanse me, strengthen me, restore me.

Father, THANK YOU for all your love, grace, mercy and blessings of life that you continually shower down upon me. Thank you especially for:

1._________________________________   2._________________________________

3._________________________________   4._________________________________

5._________________________________   6._________________________________

THANK YOU for answered prayers:____

Father, I need:____

Father, I ask that YOU:____

____

____

Lord, bless me that I may be a blessing. Give me Your heart for loving and serving others. Keep Your hand upon me. Keep me from all evil and harm, and let me cause harm to no one. Bind Satan that he have no power over me. All this I pray in subjection to your will and in the strong name of my Lord and Savior, Jesus Christ. Amen.

Under New Management

"And you *He made alive,* who were dead in trespasses and sins, in which you once walked." Ephesians 2:1, 2a

When we become dead to sin and alive in Christ through receiving Jesus Christ as our Savior, we experience a new spiritual birth and receive a new spiritual birth right by the power of the Holy Spirit. This birthright is the indwelling presence of the Holy Spirit, who comes to take over the management of our lives.

> *"O LORD, You brought my soul up from the grave; You have kept me alive, that I should not go down to the pit."*
> *Psalm 30:4*

Under the management of the Holy Spirit, sin has no more dominion over us. We are free to be all that we can be in Christ and empowered to do what God has called us to do in producing the good works for which we were created. We are instantly restored and renewed, and we are continually being restored and renewed as God continues to conform us to the likeness of His Son.

We find ourselves giving up more and more control of the flesh and submitting more and more to the management of the Spirit, who is constantly at work guiding us into all truth, convicting us of our sins, and making intercession for us with God the Father.

> *"Likewise you also, reckon yourselves to be dead indeed to sin, but alive to God in Christ Jesus our Lord."*
> *Romans 6:11*

The transformation worked by the Spirit within the hearts of believers is why they call grace "amazing." We find that the things we wanted to do become things we no longer care about doing, as we discover the better, more satisfying, way of living in Christ. We find ourselves exercising our freedom to reject the influence of Satan and our flesh more and more and to opt for living in the peace and joy of the Lord, bearing the fruit of His Spirit.

Can those around us see that we are under new management?

Father, thank you for the gift of the Holy Spirit, and for making me a temple for His presence. Amen

Taking it to the Lord...

How can I apply this truth?____

____

____

Father, I've come to worship and praise you! You are my:___________________

____

I give you all Glory, Honor, and Praise O Lord!

Father, I am sorry that I have sinned by:________________________________

Help me to repent. Cleanse me, strengthen me, restore me.

Father, THANK YOU for all your love, grace, mercy and blessings of life that you continually shower down upon me. Thank you especially for:

1.________________________________   2.________________________________

3.________________________________   4.________________________________

5.________________________________   6.________________________________

THANK YOU for answered prayers:_______________________________________

Father, I need:____

Father, I ask that YOU:____

____

____

Lord, bless me that I may be a blessing. Give me Your heart for loving and serving others. Keep Your hand upon me. Keep me from all evil and harm, and let me cause harm to no one. Bind Satan that he have no power over me. All this I pray in subjection to your will and in the strong name of my Lord and Savior, Jesus Christ. Amen.

Class Reunion

"Not that I speak in regard to need, for I have learned in whatever state I am, to be content." Philippians 4:11

Bill was the most likely to succeed in the class of 1953, and he came to the reunion to show that he did it! Even if you didn't ask, he would remind you of his success and many "toys". Tom also attended the reunion. He was living on Social Security in a modest mobile home park.

> *"There is one who makes himself rich, yet has nothing; and one who makes himself poor, yet has great riches."*
> *Proverbs 13:7*

Tom finally had enough of Bill's bragging, and said: "you may have all these things, but I am a lot richer than you!." "How can you say that?" Bill asked. Tom replied: "because I have enough, and your are never going to have enough!"

How much is enough for you? Is "just a little bit more" your response to what it would take to make you happy?   Are you going through life thinking, "I would be happy if I only had __________(a nicer car, a bigger house, a better job, a better spouse, etc., etc.)

There is no question of who had been the most successful from the world's viewpoint. The question is who has been the most successful from God's viewpoint. Who did the "toys" own, and who owned the real treasures?

It is only when we base our happiness on who we are in Christ that we will ever have the real wealth of peace and godly contentment, and real security.

> *"Now godliness with contentment is great gain."*
> *1 Timothy 6:6*

To know that in Christ we are unconditionally loved, totally accepted, and forever forgiven; and to know that we are significant because of the relationship we have with God the Father through faith in God the Son, is to have more than enough. In knowing this, we are truly rich.

Father, give the security and contentment of Your love so that I won't have to depend on the things of this world for my happiness and validation. Amen

Taking it to the Lord...

How can I apply this truth?____

____

Father, I've come to worship and praise you! You are my:___________________________

____

I give you all Glory, Honor, and Praise O Lord!

Father, I am sorry that I have sinned by:____

Help me to repent. Cleanse me, strengthen me, restore me.

Father, THANK YOU for all your love, grace, mercy and blessings of life that you continually shower down upon me. Thank you especially for:

1.___________________________   2.___________________________

3.___________________________   4.___________________________

5.___________________________   6.___________________________

THANK YOU for answered prayers:____

Father, I need:____

Father, I ask that YOU:____

____

____

Lord, bless me that I may be a blessing. Give me Your heart for loving and serving others. Keep Your hand upon me. Keep me from all evil and harm, and let me cause harm to no one. Bind Satan that he have no power over me. All this I pray in subjection to your will and in the strong name of my Lord and Savior, Jesus Christ. Amen.

Fair Weather Friends

"God will surely do this for you, for He always does just what He says, and He is the one who invited you into this wonderful friendship with His Son, Jesus Christ, our Lord." 1 Corinthians 1:9 NLT

It's amazing how friends seem to vanish when you can't be of anymore use to them. The prodigal son had plenty of friends to play with on his way to the pigpen. Politicians out of office and purchasing agents out of jobs often find out about fair weather friends.

> *"As iron sharpens iron, a friend sharpens a friend."*
> *Proverbs 27:17*

Jesus has had and continues to have more "fair weather" friends than anyone in the history of mankind. When He provided free lunch, five thousand became His new "best friends", and would probably later be among those shouting, "Crucify Him". The disciples were nowhere to be found when trouble came.

It seems that many today base their friendship with Jesus on what He can do for them instead of what He has done for them. As long as the "free lunches" and the cup of material and physical blessings keep overflowing, "God is in His heaven and all's right with the world."

When troubles and problems arise, as they surely will and do, many respond with anger and falling away from God instead of anchoring deeper and deeper into their love relationship with Him and experiencing the strength and comfort of His promises.

> *"And here is how to measure it-the greatest love is shown when people lay down their lives for their friends."*
> *John 15:13 NLT*

Every rose garden has thorns. Until God takes us home to heavenly bliss, He promises His all-sufficient grace to handle the scratches.

When we learn the secret of abiding in God through getting to know Him through His Son, we will find out what real friendship is all about.

Father, let me be more than a "fair weather friend". By the power of Your Spirit, let me be a friend in all seasons for all the right reasons. Amen

Taking it to the Lord...

How can I apply this truth?____

____

____

Father, I've come to worship and praise you! You are my:_______________________

____

I give you all Glory, Honor, and Praise O Lord!

Father, I am sorry that I have sinned by:_______________________________________

Help me to repent. Cleanse me, strengthen me, restore me.

Father, THANK YOU for all your love, grace, mercy and blessings of life that you continually shower down upon me. Thank you especially for:

1._________________________________   2._________________________________

3._________________________________   4._________________________________

5._________________________________   6._________________________________

THANK YOU for answered prayers:____

Father, I need:____

Father, I ask that YOU:____

____

____

Lord, bless me that I may be a blessing. Give me Your heart for loving and serving others. Keep Your hand upon me. Keep me from all evil and harm, and let me cause harm to no one. Bind Satan that he have no power over me. All this I pray in subjection to your will and in the strong name of my Lord and Savior, Jesus Christ. Amen.

"God Never Wastes a Hurt"

"The suffering you sent was good for me, for it taught me to pay attention to your principles." Psalm 119:71 NLT

The "life to the fullest" that we have in Christ begins the minute we receive Him as our Savior and never ends. We receive a lot of great things in addition to eternal life.

> *"You have allowed me to suffer much hardship, but you will restore me to life again and lift me up from the depths of the earth." Psalm 71:20 NLT*

We have the presence of the Holy Spirit – Christ in us to pray for us, comfort and correct us, call all things to our remembrance, and to fill us with strength and power from on high.

We have the promise that God will work all things for our good, that He will do whatever it takes to mold us into the image of Christ. God promises to meet our every need, to provide a means of escape from temptation, to keep us in the security of His love and His forgiveness until we see him face to face.

The one thing that God does not promise is to keep us from knowing pain, suffering and sorrow in this life. That promise is reserved for heaven. In doing whatever it takes to bring us to saving faith, and then to keep us there and growing into the fullness of Christ, God often allows problems that inspect, correct, protect, and make us more like Christ.

How can we be like Christ if we went through life knowing no pain or suffering or temptation? How better can we be a comforter and blessing to others than having gone through the pain and suffering they are presently experiencing?

> *"So when we are weighed down with troubles, it is for your benefit and salvation!" 2 Corinthians 1:5 NLT*

How could we help becoming proud and self-centered without the humbling discipline of God, which keeps us Christ centered and aware of our total dependency upon Him. To what good use has God put your pain and sufferings?

I am indebted to Rick Warren, author of "The Purpose Driven Life" for the thought that "God never wastes a hurt."

Father, thank you for doing whatever it takes to conform me to the image of Christ, and to equip me to produce the fruits for which you created me. Amen

Taking it to the Lord...

How can I apply this truth?____

____

____

Father, I've come to worship and praise you! You are my:_________________________________

____

I give you all Glory, Honor, and Praise O Lord!

Father, I am sorry that I have sinned by:____

Help me to repent. Cleanse me, strengthen me, restore me.

Father, THANK YOU for all your love, grace, mercy and blessings of life that you continually shower down upon me. Thank you especially for:

1.___________________________________ 2.___________________________________

3.___________________________________ 4.___________________________________

5.___________________________________ 6.___________________________________

THANK YOU for answered prayers:____

Father, I need:____

Father, I ask that YOU:____

____

____

____

Lord, bless me that I may be a blessing. Give me Your heart for loving and serving others. Keep Your hand upon me. Keep me from all evil and harm, and let me cause harm to no one. Bind Satan that he have no power over me. All this I pray in subjection to your will and in the strong name of my Lord and Savior, Jesus Christ. Amen.

Watch Out for Side Effects!

"A prudent person foresees the danger ahead and takes precautions; the simpleton goes blindly on and suffers the consequences." Proverbs 22:3 NLT

I can't believe all the advertisements for new drugs and how they list the possible side effects of nausea, diarrhea, blurred vision, coughing, etc. It Sure doesn't make me want to rush out and buy.

> *"You will enjoy the fruit of your labor. How happy you will be! How rich your life!"*
> *Psalm 128.2 NLT*

People are still smoking worldwide in record numbers in spite of the conclusive evidence and warning that cigarettes cause a lot of health problems, including death.

It's a shame that all of the beer ads don't have to carry the same warning as drugs - that possible side effects include spouse and child abuse, car wrecks, loss of control of senses, etc.

The side effects of sexual immorality, which can include AIDS, herpes, unwanted pregnancy, broken homes and guilt, should give anyone with a weakness in this area a warning to keep their guard up.

Even a new birth in Christ can trigger some hurtful side effects. We may lose some friends and undergo some severe testing as Satan unleashes more of his darts at us. The Apostles learned all about these side effects.

Thank God that the good side effects of living in a right relationship with Him through faith in Jesus Christ far overcome any temporary pain, sadness, or discomfort!

> *"Don't be misled. Remember that you can't ignore God and get away with it. You will always reap what you sow!"*
> *Galatians 6:7 NLT*

We have peace that surpasses all understanding, the joy of the Lord, friendship with God, and the power of His Spirit living within us. We have the assurance that He will work all things for our good. We will know His unfailing love in this life and the life to come.

Father, protect me from sin and its consequences. Help me live in the freedom and joy of a right relationship with You through Your Son. Amen.

Taking it to the Lord...

How can I apply this truth?____

____

Father, I've come to worship and praise you! You are my:_______________________

____

I give you all Glory, Honor, and Praise O Lord!

Father, I am sorry that I have sinned by:____________________________________

Help me to repent. Cleanse me, strengthen me, restore me.

Father, THANK YOU for all your love, grace, mercy and blessings of life that you continually shower down upon me. Thank you especially for:

1.________________________________   2.________________________________
3.________________________________   4.________________________________
5.________________________________   6.________________________________

THANK YOU for answered prayers:____

Father, I need:____

Father, I ask that YOU:____

____

____

Lord, bless me that I may be a blessing. Give me Your heart for loving and serving others. Keep Your hand upon me. Keep me from all evil and harm, and let me cause harm to no one. Bind Satan that he have no power over me. All this I pray in subjection to your will and in the strong name of my Lord and Savior, Jesus Christ. Amen.

$5,000 Reward!

"So you, by the help of your God, return; Observe mercy and justice, and wait on your God continually."
Hosea 12:6

> *"Happy is he who has the God of Jacob for his help, Whose hope is in the LORD his God,"*
> *Psalm 146:5*

Yes, we are offering a $5,000 reward to anyone who can prove that the phrase: "God helps those who help themselves" is found in scripture. Could just as easily offer a million, because contrary to widespread belief, <u>it just isn't there!</u>

This quotation from Benjamin Franklin's "Poor Richard's Almanac" is probably the most misquoted non-scripture of them all.

As a matter of fact, God helps everyone, especially those who can't help themselves. "He makes the sun to shine on the just and the unjust". For those who believe: "He is our refuge and strength, a very present help in time of trouble."

For those who buy into the false religion of secular humanism and believe that they can make it on their own, sooner or later they are going to realize that it is just not true. As Will Rogers once said: "Whenever I see a self made man, I usually see what a bad job he has done." As scripture says: "there is a way that seems right to man, the way of which leads to destruction".

Sooner or later, we are going to realize People, possessions, and pride are most often going to disappoint. The love of God that is ours through faith in Jesus Christ will never disappoint. It is not possible for God to lie or not do what He has promised

> *"Let us therefore come boldly to the throne of grace, that we may obtain mercy and find grace to help in time of need."*
> *Hebrews 9:16*

"For I know the thoughts that I think toward you, says the LORD, thoughts of peace and not of evil, to give you a future and a hope." (Jeremiah 29:11)

Whether its spiritual, physical, financial, or relational help, *"And my God shall supply all your need according to His riches in glory by Christ Jesus." (Philippians 4:19)*

Father, thank you for being my very present help. Given my propensity for falling short, I am so thankful that I don't. Amen

Taking it to the Lord...

How can I apply this truth?____

____

Father, I've come to worship and praise you! You are my:_______________________

____

I give you all Glory, Honor, and Praise O Lord!

Father, I am sorry that I have sinned by:___________________________________

Help me to repent. Cleanse me, strengthen me, restore me.

Father, THANK YOU for all your love, grace, mercy and blessings of life that you continually shower down upon me. Thank you especially for:

1.______________________________   2.______________________________
3.______________________________   4.______________________________
5.______________________________   6.______________________________

THANK YOU for answered prayers:___________________________________

Father, I need:____

Father, I ask that YOU:____

____

____

Lord, bless me that I may be a blessing. Give me Your heart for loving and serving others. Keep Your hand upon me. Keep me from all evil and harm, and let me cause harm to no one. Bind Satan that he have no power over me. All this I pray in subjection to your will and in the strong name of my Lord and Savior, Jesus Christ. Amen.

World's Top 2 Tourist Destinations

"Eye has not seen, nor ear heard, nor have entered into the heart of man The things which God has prepared for those who love Him." *1 Corinthians 2:9*

If you are thinking Mecca and Disney World, think again! Actually, from God's perspective, there are only two tourist destinations - heaven or hell!

> *"The way of life winds upward for the wise, That he may turn away from hell below."*
> *Proverbs 15:24*

Like it or not, we are all "tourists" passing through this world on our way to eternity and we have a choice of spending eternity in heaven, where there is no more sorrow, no more sadness, no more pain, and only the perfect bliss of living in a place without the sin which causes all these things; or in hell where we will suffer the eternal torment of the damned.

God would not have that anyone should perish, but that all should be saved and spend eternity with Him in heaven. But He didn't make us robots, and gave us a free will either to receive or reject His love, His forgiveness, His mercy and grace which he extends to us when receive Jesus Christ as our Lord and Savior.

With God as our travel agent, and faith in Jesus Christ as our ticket, we are given confirmed reservations via many great "airlines" for the trip home. We have a lot of good choices including: "Air Vatican", "Spirit Air", "Baptist Air Express", and "Lutheran International Airlines", etc. There is even a big "welcome home" party when you arrive amidst a lot of joy from the Saints who have gotten there before you.

Unfortunately, there are no airlines serving the other destination, due to "the lake of fire" and submerged location. You can only get there via the "highway of unbelief" or "road of good intentions": both of which just drop off into a bottomless pit of agony and despair.

> *"And many will follow their destructive ways, because of whom the way of truth will be blasphemed."*
> *2 Peter 2:2*

When the Spirit of God calls and convicts you of your sin and your need for a Savior, don't put off receiving your "confirmed reservation" to the ultimate destination!

Father, thank you for paying for my ticket to heaven with the blood of your own dear Son, Jesus Christ. Thank you for your blessed assurance that He has gone to prepare a place for me. Amen

Taking it to the Lord...

How can I apply this truth?____

____

Father, I've come to worship and praise you! You are my:______________________

____

I give you all Glory, Honor, and Praise O Lord!

Father, I am sorry that I have sinned by:____________________________________

Help me to repent. Cleanse me, strengthen me, restore me.

Father, THANK YOU for all your love, grace, mercy and blessings of life that you continually shower down upon me. Thank you especially for:

1.__________________________________   2.__________________________________
3.__________________________________   4.__________________________________
5.__________________________________   6.__________________________________

THANK YOU for answered prayers:____

Father, I need:____

Father, I ask that YOU:____

____

____

Lord, bless me that I may be a blessing. Give me Your heart for loving and serving others. Keep Your hand upon me. Keep me from all evil and harm, and let me cause harm to no one. Bind Satan that he have no power over me. All this I pray in subjection to your will and in the strong name of my Lord and Savior, Jesus Christ. Amen.

#1 in Customer Satisfaction

"He himself gives life and breath to everything, and he satisfies every need there is." Acts 17:25 NLT

Testimonials from satisfied customers continue to be one of the most effective marketing tools in the world today.

> *"Sing praises to the LORD, who dwells in Zion! Declare His deeds among the people."*
> *Psalm 9:11*

Whether for losing weight, banking, or automobiles, companies realize that customer satisfaction should be the number 1 priority, because they know that satisfied customers will be their best advertising.

Although our relationship with God is much, much more; we are also in some ways customers who are being fought over. We have needs for love, acceptance, and significance to be met and the gospel of Jesus Christ has stiff competition from the world and the devil on how these needs might best be met.

In a vast majority of cases, the Holy Spirit works through the testimony of a "satisfied customer" witnessing to the truth of God's Word (often a parent or close friend) through which we receive the true love, acceptance, and security that comes only from receiving Jesus Christ as our Lord and Savior.

In our transient society, denominational loyalties become less and less important to many, and we go "church shopping" to find the church that best meets our needs. Many times we are so impressed with a "satisfied customer" of a particular church that we are drawn to their church.

Whether a call to salvation, or a call to fellowship, the "contagious Christianity" as spread by "satisfied customers" has always and always will be the Holy Spirit's conduit of choice for fulfilling the great commission.

> *"Moreover, brethren, I declare to you the gospel which I preached to you, which also you received and in which you stand,"*
> *Romans 15:1*

Are you known as a "satisfied customer" or contagious Christian who God is using to draw others into fellowship and a saving relationship with Jesus Christ? By the power of the Holy Spirit living within you, there is absolutely no reason why you can't or shouldn't be.

Father, let those around us see the light of your love in me and be drawn to you through my testimony in word and deed. Amen

Taking it to the Lord...

How can I apply this truth?____

____

____

Father, I've come to worship and praise you! You are my:___________________

____

I give you all Glory, Honor, and Praise O Lord!

Father, I am sorry that I have sinned by:________________________________

Help me to repent. Cleanse me, strengthen me, restore me.

Father, THANK YOU for all your love, grace, mercy and blessings of life that you continually shower down upon me. Thank you especially for:

1.___________________________   2.___________________________

3.___________________________   4.___________________________

5.___________________________   6.___________________________

THANK YOU for answered prayers:___________________________________

Father, I need:____

Father, I ask that YOU:____

____

____

Lord, bless me that I may be a blessing. Give me Your heart for loving and serving others. Keep Your hand upon me. Keep me from all evil and harm, and let me cause harm to no one. Bind Satan that he have no power over me. All this I pray in subjection to your will and in the strong name of my Lord and Savior, Jesus Christ. Amen.

Watch out for Un!

"Beware, brethren, lest there be in any of you an evil heart of unbelief in departing from the living God;" Hebrews 3:12

We are not talking about the United Nations, although it may bear watching also. We are talking about the two worst letters in the alphabet, U and N! When these 2 letters get together, absolutely terrible things happen.

> *"I said, "I will confess my transgressions to the LORD, And You forgave the iniquity of my sin."*
> *Psalm 32:5b*

Belief becomes unbelief, forgiveness unforgiveness, godly ungodly, known unknown, accountable unaccountable, etc, etc. For all the ramifications of these two letters, please check any dictionary.

As for the two worst "un's" it is a close call between unbelief and unforgiveness as both cause very serious consequences.

With unbelief in Jesus as Savior, all hope of heaven is gone. With unbelief in Jesus' promises, all power for living in the joy of the Lord is gone. "Oh ye of little faith" is actually saying "Oh ye of unbelief". As the father of the healed child said, "Lord, I believe, help my unbelief."

Scripture is full of examples of people missing out because of their unbelief. It is only by the power of the Holy Spirit that any of us can come to belief in Jesus Christ as our Savior and the power to obey His commands. 'Lord, help my unbelief" should be our constant prayer.

Next to hypocrisy, unforgiveness is probably the sin our Lord deals with the most severely. The parable of the steward who had been forgiven a million dollar debt and wouldn't forgive a hundred dollar debt, is a sober reminder that forgiveness is not an option, it is a command, and the consequences for disobedience are severe indeed. In the Lord's Prayer, Jesus made it clear that we should forgive as a condition for receiving forgiveness.

> *"But if you do not forgive, neither will your Father in heaven forgive your trespasses."*
> *Mark 11:26*

If you are harboring the cancer of unforgiveness towards someone in your heart, don't let it fester and cause you any more pain or consequences. Remember that we are all going to need all the forgiveness we can muster, and we absolutely cannot afford the luxury of an unforgiving spirit, that can make us sick and even kill us physically and spiritually.

Father, protect me from the pitfalls of unbelief and unforgiveness by the power of the Holy Spirit. Amen

Taking it to the Lord...

How can I apply this truth?____

____

Father, I've come to worship and praise you! You are my:______________________

____

I give you all Glory, Honor, and Praise O Lord!

Father, I am sorry that I have sinned by:__________________________________

Help me to repent. Cleanse me, strengthen me, restore me.

Father, THANK YOU for all your love, grace, mercy and blessings of life that you continually shower down upon me. Thank you especially for:

1.__________________________________   2.__________________________________

3.__________________________________   4.__________________________________

5.__________________________________   6.__________________________________

THANK YOU for answered prayers:____

Father, I need:____

Father, I ask that YOU:____

____

Lord, bless me that I may be a blessing. Give me Your heart for loving and serving others. Keep Your hand upon me. Keep me from all evil and harm, and let me cause harm to no one. Bind Satan that he have no power over me. All this I pray in subjection to your will and in the strong name of my Lord and Savior, Jesus Christ. Amen.

Always Forgiveness But Often Consequences

"For You, Lord, *are* good, and ready to forgive, and abundant in mercy to all those who call upon You." Psalm 86:5

> *"Have mercy upon me, O God, According to Your loving kindness; According to the multitude of Your tender mercies, Blot out my transgressions."*
> *Psalm 51:1*

What joy and what freedom we have in knowing that God has forgiven us for everything we have ever done and remembers our sins no more. To be able to dump the baggage of our sins at the foot of the cross and have the burden of guilt lifted is one of the many real blessings every believer can claim by faith.

By faith, we have been given a new life in Christ, and sin has no more dominion over us, although our flesh, the world, and the Devil temporarily take charge if we fail to put on the armor that God has provided.

We need to know that while disobedience will be forgiven, the consequences remain, sometimes for as long as we live. As a consequence of disobedience, the Children of Israel wandered in the desert for 40 years until all those who had disobeyed died off. As a consequence of David's sin with Bathsheba, the child conceived in this sin died, and David suffered many other consequences.

As a consequence of their sin in lying about how much they got for their property, Annanias and Sapphira were struck dead instantly. Today, we see   AIDS spreading all around us as a consequence of sexual sin. Many pay the consequences of abusing their bodies through over eating, smoking, or alcohol, drug, or substance abuse either with their own health or with birth defects in their children. Broken homes are often the consequences for sins that never should have happened.

Before you go down the "yellow brick road" of seeking self-centered gratification in disobedience to God and contrary to the way He would have you live your life, think about the consequences. When the Holy Spirit, sounds the alarm within you, flee the temptation. A lifetime of sorrow over the consequences of even forgiven sins is too high a price to pay.

> *"For the good that I will to do, I do not do; but the evil I will not to do, that I practice."*
> *Romans 7:19*

Father, thank you for your forever forgiveness, and the power to escape when temptation would overcome me. Amen

Taking it to the Lord...

How can I apply this truth?____

____

Father, I've come to worship and praise you! You are my:__________________________

____

I give you all Glory, Honor, and Praise O Lord!

Father, I am sorry that I have sinned by:_____________________________________

Help me to repent. Cleanse me, strengthen me, restore me.

Father, THANK YOU for all your love, grace, mercy and blessings of life that you continually shower down upon me. Thank you especially for:

1.____________________________________ 2._________________________________

3.____________________________________ 4._________________________________

5.____________________________________ 6._________________________________

THANK YOU for answered prayers:____

Father, I need:____

Father, I ask that YOU:____

____

Lord, bless me that I may be a blessing. Give me Your heart for loving and serving others. Keep Your hand upon me. Keep me from all evil and harm, and let me cause harm to no one. Bind Satan that he have no power over me. All this I pray in subjection to your will and in the strong name of my Lord and Savior, Jesus Christ. Amen.

About Unity, Liberty, and Love

"But why do you judge your brother? Or why do you show contempt for your brother? For we shall all stand before the judgment seat of Christ." Romans 14:10

Phillip Melancthon is not nearly as well known as Martin Luther, but He was Luther's influential co-worker in the Reformation and writer of the Augsburg Confession, which is still one of the great documents coming out of the Reformation. Perhaps the most profound statements written by Dr. Melancthon, was the exhortation: "On essentials, let there be Unity, on nonessentials, Liberty, and in all things Love".

> *"The LORD gives freedom to the prisoners."*
> *Psalm 146:7*

The centrality of the gospel of Jesus Christ is that "God so loved the World that He gave His only begotten Son, that whosoever believeth in Him should not perish but have everlasting life." (John 3:16) This is the essential profession of the Christian Faith about which there must be unity. Anyone who professes this faith in Jesus Christ should be considered a brother and co-heir in Christ.

In matters of "idiophoria," which means things neither commanded nor forbidden, or different understandings that do not determine our salvation, St. Paul says we should not judge our brothers and sisters in Christ.

Within the Christian family of God, there are a wide divergence of understandings, all claiming to be based on scripture, that somehow manage to get into a spiritual superiority contest over who believes and who does not believe the Bible. We Christians with different understandings about which we can disagree, should not do so disagreeably.

> *"Therefore let us pursue the things which make for peace and the things by which one may edify another."*
> *Romans 14:19*

When we find our perfect peace and fulfillment in the Love of God, and Love for others, there should be no need for arguments and fallings out over our different understandings, once we have agreed that Jesus Christ died on the Cross for our sins, and that we are saved by grace, not of works, lest anyone should boast! It is hard for some to accept, but the truth is that there will be no denominations in heaven!

Jesus, thank you for your "Church Triumphant" where faith in your Son is the only common denominator, and my membership is not determined by the label of my denomination, but that I have You in my heart. Amen

Taking it to the Lord...

How can I apply this truth?____

____

Father, I've come to worship and praise you! You are my:_______________________________

____

I give you all Glory, Honor, and Praise O Lord!

Father, I am sorry that I have sinned by:____

Help me to repent. Cleanse me, strengthen me, restore me.

Father, THANK YOU for all your love, grace, mercy and blessings of life that you continually shower down upon me. Thank you especially for:

1.______________________________   2.______________________________

3.______________________________   4.______________________________

5.______________________________   6.______________________________

THANK YOU for answered prayers:____

Father, I need:____

Father, I ask that YOU:____

____

Lord, bless me that I may be a blessing. Give me Your heart for loving and serving others. Keep Your hand upon me. Keep me from all evil and harm, and let me cause harm to no one. Bind Satan that he have no power over me. All this I pray in subjection to your will and in the strong name of my Lord and Savior, Jesus Christ. Amen.

Happy Are the Meek

"Take My yoke upon you and learn from Me, for I am gentle and lowly in heart, and you will find rest for your souls." Matthew 11:29

There are a lot of misconceptions about what "meek" means. To many, it means being "wimpy" and letting people walk all over you. To others, it means being humble and having a gentle spirit. Perhaps, the understanding to be "meek" means not to be conceited or stuck on oneself is the best understanding of all.

> *"But the meek shall inherit the earth, and shall delight themselves in the abundance of peace."*
> *Psalm 37:11*

Our Lord was the perfect example of meekness. As He said: *"I am gentle and lowly in heart."* When we in meekness submit to the yoke of Christ and to His loving discipline, we become teachable, preachable and usable. As surely as God will resist the proud, He will pour out His grace on the meek. (1 Peter 5:5, James 4:6)

> *"And a servant of the Lord must not quarrel but be gentle to all, able to teach, patient, in humility correcting those who are in opposition,"*
> *2 Timothy 2:24,25a*

The pride and self-righteousness of the Scribes and Pharisees were quite a contrast to the meekness and gentleness of Christ. As followers of Christ, we should strive to enjoy the blessedness of the meek, and to love others as Christ loves us.

There is a marked difference in the health, well being, and quality of life of the meek, who are calm, cool, and collected, when compared with the proud, self centered types who lead more turbulent, stress filled lives.

Father, help me to claim the promise of my inheritance for blessings in this life by appropriating the meekness of Christ in my life, by the power of Your Spirit. Amen

Taking it to the Lord...

How can I apply this truth?____
____
____

Father, I've come to worship and praise you! You are my:_________________________________
____

I give you all Glory, Honor, and Praise O Lord!

Father, I am sorry that I have sinned by:____

Help me to repent. Cleanse me, strengthen me, restore me.

Father, THANK YOU for all your love, grace, mercy and blessings of life that you continually shower down upon me. Thank you especially for:

1.____________________________________   2.____________________________________
3.____________________________________   4.____________________________________
5.____________________________________   6.____________________________________

THANK YOU for answered prayers:____

Father, I need:____

Father, I ask that YOU:____
____
____

Lord, bless me that I may be a blessing. Give me Your heart for loving and serving others. Keep Your hand upon me. Keep me from all evil and harm, and let me cause harm to no one. Bind Satan that he have no power over me. All this I pray in subjection to your will and in the strong name of my Lord and Savior, Jesus Christ. Amen.

The Annual Pass

"Don't be misled. Remember that you can't ignore God and get away with it. You will always reap what you sow!" Galatians 6:7

Some of the great theme parks are discovering that selling annual passes, good for one whole year, are a real bonanza for business. They know that it is not going to cost them anymore because they have to stay open anyhow, that you will probably spend money on refreshments and parking, and even bring friends who don't have passes.

> *"Because of your unfailing love, I can enter your house; with deepest awe I will worship at your Temple."*
> *Psalm 5:7 NLT*

There is cause to wonder if they might have gotten this idea from some nominal Christians who think they have an annual pass from God, which only requires meeting with him in His church on an annual basis of either Easter or Christmas.

When we rationalize and say that we don't have to go to Church to saved, we are absolutely right. When we are really saved, we will want to go to celebrate our joy in the Lord and to Love God and one another.

Our faith is a living faith that needs to flourish and grow as we become more like Christ day by day. It needs not only the nourishment of the daily manna of prayer and abiding in the Word, but also the encouragement and fellowship of other believers that only comes from being plugged into the power source of regular authentic corporate worship.

> *"But since you are like lukewarm water, I will spit you out of my mouth!"*
> *Revelation 3:16 NLT*

Although true faith can never die, it can suffer from debilitating malnutrition that no once a year pass can ever cure. Jesus Christ died to give us a lifetime pass to for this life with a pass over into eternal life in heaven. We need to start acting like "frequent flyers."

Father, let me feast not only daily, but weekly when I come to praise you and encourage and be encouraged by other Saints. Amen

Taking it to the Lord...

How can I apply this truth?____

____

____

Father, I've come to worship and praise you! You are my:_____________________

____

I give you all Glory, Honor, and Praise O Lord!

Father, I am sorry that I have sinned by:__________________________________

Help me to repent. Cleanse me, strengthen me, restore me.

Father, THANK YOU for all your love, grace, mercy and blessings of life that you continually shower down upon me. Thank you especially for:

1.__________________________________   2.__________________________________

3.__________________________________   4.__________________________________

5.__________________________________   6.__________________________________

THANK YOU for answered prayers:____

Father, I need:____

Father, I ask that YOU:____

____

____

____

Lord, bless me that I may be a blessing. Give me Your heart for loving and serving others. Keep Your hand upon me. Keep me from all evil and harm, and let me cause harm to no one. Bind Satan that he have no power over me. All this I pray in subjection to your will and in the strong name of my Lord and Savior, Jesus Christ. Amen.

Do You Know Jot Tittle?

"For assuredly, I say to you, till heaven and earth pass away, one jot or one tittle will by no means pass from the law till all is fulfilled." Matthew 5:18

If you ever asked a number of people on the street if they knew Jot Tittle, you would be amazed at the responses. "Oh Yeah, he was one of those embedded correspondents during the war in Iraq wasn't he." or maybe: "sure, he was a quarterback for the New York Giants". Very few would realize that Jot Tittle was not a person, but biblical terms for "smallest detail.

> *"Consider how I love Your precepts; Revive me, O LORD, according to Your loving kindness."*
> *Psalm 119: 59*

The Scribes and Pharisee's sure loved the "Jot and Tittles"! When Jesus went through the grain field eating grain, the Scribes and Pharisees were enraged. When Jesus healed the man with the withered hand they plotted as to how they might kill Jesus.

In Christ, we have God' fulfillment of every "jot and tittle" of the Law, and we by faith have Christ's imputed righteousness in God's sight.

Our commandments have been condensed only to "Love God" and "Love Others", and the Holy Spirit has put them into our hearts. Although the Ten Commandments are still in effect to convict us of our sinfulness, to guide us along the path's of righteousness, and as boundary markers or curbs to keep us on the path, obeying them does not earn us salvation or give us a right standing with God.

> *"Therefore it is lawful to do good on the Sabbath."*
> *Matthew 12:11b*

You don't have to look very far to see that some would have "Jot Tittle" keeping us in the grave clothes of the law and have us live as slaves to the Law as though Christ never died to bring in the New Covenant of Grace and freedom from the judgment of the law. Religious traditions and codes on how we should worship, how we should dress, and how we should conform in many other outward appearances continue to discourage the seekers, give hypocritical glory to believers, and stymie the carrying out of the both the great commission and great commandment.

Father, give me the wisdom and spiritual discernment to distinguish between tradition and truth and to know that God always judges my heart, not outward appearances. Amen

Taking it to the Lord...

How can I apply this truth?____

____

Father, I've come to worship and praise you! You are my:____________________

____

I give you all Glory, Honor, and Praise O Lord!

Father, I am sorry that I have sinned by:________________________________

Help me to repent. Cleanse me, strengthen me, restore me.

Father, THANK YOU for all your love, grace, mercy and blessings of life that you continually shower down upon me. Thank you especially for:

1.___________________________   2.___________________________
3.___________________________   4.___________________________
5.___________________________   6.___________________________

THANK YOU for answered prayers:________________________________

Father, I need:____

Father, I ask that YOU:____

____

Lord, bless me that I may be a blessing. Give me Your heart for loving and serving others. Keep Your hand upon me. Keep me from all evil and harm, and let me cause harm to no one. Bind Satan that he have no power over me. All this I pray in subjection to your will and in the strong name of my Lord and Savior, Jesus Christ. Amen.

"You Can Be Sure if it's Westinghouse"

"This hope we have as an anchor of the soul, both sure and steadfast." Hebrews 6:9a

The Westinghouse Electric Corporation is one of the biggest and best of the great companies that emerged from the industrial revolution. Although concentrating today on Nuclear Power, during the 1930's into the 1960's Westinghouse was one of the major manufacturers of home appliances and one of the first National TV advertisers. Their theme, "You can be sure if it's Westinghouse" was one of the marketing successes of the 1950's.

"For the Lord is the great God, And the great King above all gods." Psalm 95:3

Today manufacturers, financial institutions, and service companies strive to achieve this kind of credibility for their products and services.

People today get caught up in the same kind of striving to validate their credibility to themselves and the world for all the applause, power and acceptance the world has to offer.

Whether in excelling in athletics or intellect, accumulating wealth, or some other pursuit, they all turn out to be trivial in the overall picture of eternity.

The only "sure thing" is the reality that we are going to depart from this life as we know it, and that we are going to spend an eternity in heaven or hell depending on the sureness of our faith that we are saved by grace alone, through faith alone, and not of our own goodness or works lest any of us should boast.

"but these are written that you may believe that Jesus is the Christ, the Son of God, and that believing you may have life in His name." John 20:31

Since God has come in Spirit and Truth in His Word made flesh in Jesus Christ, and given us the written record of His Word in scripture, we have no excuse for not being sure of who we are and where we are going.

Father, by the power of the Holy Spirit help me always to be sure in you and in your Son Jesus Christ. Amen

Taking it to the Lord...

How can I apply this truth?____
____
____

Father, I've come to worship and praise you! You are my:_________________________
____

I give you all Glory, Honor, and Praise O Lord!

Father, I am sorry that I have sinned by:_____________________________________

Help me to repent. Cleanse me, strengthen me, restore me.

Father, THANK YOU for all your love, grace, mercy and blessings of life that you continually shower down upon me. Thank you especially for:

1.______________________________   2.______________________________
3.______________________________   4.______________________________
5.______________________________   6.______________________________

THANK YOU for answered prayers:____
Father, I need:____
Father, I ask that YOU:____
____
____

Lord, bless me that I may be a blessing. Give me Your heart for loving and serving others. Keep Your hand upon me. Keep me from all evil and harm, and let me cause harm to no one. Bind Satan that he have no power over me. All this I pray in subjection to your will and in the strong name of my Lord and Savior, Jesus Christ. Amen.

NASCAR Church

"For where your treasure is, there your heart will be also." Luke 12:34

There is a great awakening going on! Practically every Sunday, thousands of followers congregate at Charlotte, Atlanta, Talladega, Darlington, or wherever the big event is happening, and millions more join in via radio and TV. New converts by the thousands are being added every week.

> *"For all the gods of the people are idols, But the Lord made the heavens."*
> *Psalm 96:4*

The faithful live vicariously through their heroes Junior, Bobby, Rusty, Jeff, etc. who they know by their first names and with whom they seem to have a close personal relationship.

There are probably some Christians who would begrudge giving God $5.00 but I willingly fork out $50, $100, or sometimes up to several thousand dollars for the privilege of being on hand for NASCAR Church any given week.   People who complain about sitting an hour in Christ's Church will gladly arrive half a day before race time, and sit through 5 or 6 hours of NASCAR Church and drive a thousand miles to get there.

They shout praises and encouragement for their personal hero. They will seek out every story, keep track of every word uttered by their hero or his followers, and spend hours sharing this information with other fans. (We can substitute "Cowboy", "Packer", "Gator", "PGA", or any number of other pursuits that might come to possess us)

> *"You cannot serve the LORD, for He is a holy God. He is a jealous God;"*
> *Joshua 24:19*

There is nothing wrong with NASCAR racing, or most other spectator sports or recreational pursuits, unless they take over in first place that is demanded by and reserved for God.

Oh that God would give us the passion to pack His house, keep track of His every word, and be as generous to Him!

Father, give me the knowledge of your will with wisdom and spiritual discernment so that I not get my priorities mixed up. Amen

Taking it to the Lord...

How can I apply this truth?____

____

Father, I've come to worship and praise you! You are my:_______________________

____

I give you all Glory, Honor, and Praise O Lord!

Father, I am sorry that I have sinned by:_____________________________________

Help me to repent. Cleanse me, strengthen me, restore me.

Father, THANK YOU for all your love, grace, mercy and blessings of life that you continually shower down upon me. Thank you especially for:

1.___________________________ 2.___________________________

3.___________________________ 4.___________________________

5.___________________________ 6.___________________________

THANK YOU for answered prayers:____

Father, I need:____

Father, I ask that YOU:____

____

____

Lord, bless me that I may be a blessing. Give me Your heart for loving and serving others. Keep Your hand upon me. Keep me from all evil and harm, and let me cause harm to no one. Bind Satan that he have no power over me. All this I pray in subjection to your will and in the strong name of my Lord and Savior, Jesus Christ. Amen.

God's WD 40

Let no corrupt word proceed out of your mouth, but what is good for necessary edification, that it may impart grace to the hearers. Ephesians 4:29

> *"The Lord will give grace and glory' No good thing will He withhold From those who walk uprightly."*
> *Psalm 84:11b*

WD 40 is an amazing product. It is a penetrating agent that reduces friction and enables us to loosen the tightest nuts. It is a wonderful product for removing tape residue after we have removed any kind of tape.

How much more amazing is the Grace of God! It can unloosen the darkest of hearts and convict them of their need for a Savior. It continually removes the residue of our sins for which we need daily cleansing.

Even the toughest nuts have been known to loosen up by the power of God's Spirit. God loosens the grip of the flesh, the world, and the devil and brings that wonderful peace and joy that lightens every load, brightens every dark corner and oils us with the balm of Gilead.

In our daily lives, Grace can reduce the relational friction that often creeps up with our spouses, children, friends, and fellow workers.

"But where sin abounded, grace abounded much more, (Romans 5:20b)" Whatever the circumstance, whatever the provocation or conflict when we respond with the grace of God great things happen. As *"A soft answer turns away wrath" (Proverbs 15:1),* so responding with the love, joy, peace, longsuffering, kindness, goodness, faithfulness, gentleness, and self-control of the Spirit brings about amazing results.

> *"And God is able to make all grace abound toward you,"*
> *2 Corinthians 9:8*

Father, let me abound in your grace and always be ready to apply it whenever frictions arise. Amen

Taking it to the Lord...

How can I apply this truth?____
____
____

Father, I've come to worship and praise you! You are my:_________________________
____
I give you all Glory, Honor, and Praise O Lord!

Father, I am sorry that I have sinned by:____
Help me to repent. Cleanse me, strengthen me, restore me.

Father, THANK YOU for all your love, grace, mercy and blessings of life that you continually shower down upon me. Thank you especially for:

1.___________________________________   2.___________________________________
3.___________________________________   4.___________________________________
5.___________________________________   6.___________________________________

THANK YOU for answered prayers:____

Father, I need:____

Father, I ask that YOU:____
____
____

Lord, bless me that I may be a blessing. Give me Your heart for loving and serving others. Keep Your hand upon me. Keep me from all evil and harm, and let me cause harm to no one. Bind Satan that he have no power over me. All this I pray in subjection to your will and in the strong name of my Lord and Savior, Jesus Christ. Amen.

For Everything Else, There's MASTERSCARD!

"But seek the kingdom of God, and all these things shall be added to you." Luke 12:31

The simple pleasures listed as "priceless" in the very successful Mastercard advertising campaign are nothing compared to the priceless benefits enjoyed by those holding the "Master's Card"! When our names get recorded in the "book of life" as we receive the saving faith of Jesus Christ as our Savior, we enter into the world of VIPS!

> *"What shall I render to the LORD For all His benefits toward me."*
> *Psalm 116:12*

Angels rejoice in heaven over our coming to faith. We become the adopted sons and daughters of God, with Jesus as our brother. We become joint heirs of life forever with Jesus in the family of God! We get a beautiful new white robe of righteousness to wear before the King.

We experience love, joy, contentment, and friendship with God. We receive an "in house advisor" called the Holy Spirit, who guides us into all truth, picks us up and cleans us off when we fall in the dirt of our sins, and is our guarantee that God will allow nothing to separate us from His love, which is ours through Christ Jesus.

We have our own toll free number to the throne of grace, which is open 24 hours a day and 7 days a week to give grace, mercy, power, and strength if we only ask in faith.

We have a master who "delights in giving good gifts to His children" and who not only supplies all our needs, but many times even the "desires of our hearts"

> *"Life is more than food, and the body is more than clothing."*
> *Luke 12:23*

Unfortunately, this "Masterscard" was not priceless. Although given free to us by grace, it cost God the death of God's only Son as payment for our sins. We are never going to be worthy of this price, but we can certainly always be grateful by "Thanksliving to the Glory of God!"

Father, thank you for giving me all the benefits of your salvation. By the power of your Spirit, give me an "attitude of gratitude." Amen

Taking it to the Lord...

How can I apply this truth?____

____

____

Father, I've come to worship and praise you! You are my:_____________________

____

I give you all Glory, Honor, and Praise O Lord!

Father, I am sorry that I have sinned by:__________________________________

Help me to repent. Cleanse me, strengthen me, restore me.

Father, THANK YOU for all your love, grace, mercy and blessings of life that you continually shower down upon me. Thank you especially for:

1._________________________________   2._________________________________

3._________________________________   4._________________________________

5._________________________________   6._________________________________

THANK YOU for answered prayers:____

Father, I need:____

Father, I ask that YOU:____

____

____

____

Lord, bless me that I may be a blessing. Give me Your heart for loving and serving others. Keep Your hand upon me. Keep me from all evil and harm, and let me cause harm to no one. Bind Satan that he have no power over me. All this I pray in subjection to your will and in the strong name of my Lord and Savior, Jesus Christ. Amen.

Get Your Peace of the Rock

"For they drank of that spiritual Rock that followed them, and that Rock was Christ." 1 Corinthians 10:4b

For years, Prudential Life Insurance has had the rock of Gibralter as part of their logo, identifying with the strength and security that this majestic wonder conveys. For years, people have been urged to "get a piece of the rock" through buying insurance or investment services offered by this company. Chevrolet trucks are supposedly built "like a rock".

> *"The LORD is my rock and my fortress and my deliverer; My God, my strength, in whom I will trust;"*
> *Psalm 18:2*

As Christians we have the *peace* of the rock of our salvation that Peter expressed when he proclaimed: *"You are the Christ, the Son of the living God."* Matthew 16:16b. With this confession as the bedrock of our faith, we have the sure foundation of a faith that will not fail, in a Savior Who will never disappoint.

With this foundation, we receive the indwelling presence of the Holy Spirit who will guide us along the path of righteousness and continue the ongoing process of being made holy by being conformed to the image of Christ.

We are all works in progress. While we were sanctified and made holy in the sight of God when we received Jesus Christ as our Savior, we are continually being sanctified and made holy by God who loves us just the way we are, but loves us too much to lets us stay that way.

> *"Therefore whoever hears these sayings of Mine, and does them, I will liken him to a wise man who built his house on the rock:"*
> *Matthew 7:24*

Sometimes when the "road dirt" of life seems to be in control of our lives, we need the encouragement of knowing that Jesus is the Rock of our Salvation and daily die to sin and arise in the newness of life we have in Christ, through daily confession and repentance.

The Apostle Paul tells us: *"being confident of this very thing, that He who has begun a good work in you will complete it until the day of Jesus Christ;"* (Philippians 1:6) Aren't you glad you own your own peace of the rock?

Father, thank you for being the peace of my rock, and empowering me to stand on the sure foundation I have through faith in Jesus Christ. Amen

Taking it to the Lord...

How can I apply this truth?____

____

Father, I've come to worship and praise you! You are my:__________________________

I give you all Glory, Honor, and Praise O Lord!

Father, I am sorry that I have sinned by:____________________________________

Help me to repent. Cleanse me, strengthen me, restore me.

Father, THANK YOU for all your love, grace, mercy and blessings of life that you continually shower down upon me. Thank you especially for:

1.______________________________   2.______________________________

3.______________________________   4.______________________________

5.______________________________   6.______________________________

THANK YOU for answered prayers:____

Father, I need:____

Father, I ask that YOU:____

____

____

Lord, bless me that I may be a blessing. Give me Your heart for loving and serving others. Keep Your hand upon me. Keep me from all evil and harm, and let me cause harm to no one. Bind Satan that he have no power over me. All this I pray in subjection to your will and in the strong name of my Lord and Savior, Jesus Christ. Amen.

The Ultimate Security Blanket

"Be of good comfort, be of one mind, live in peace; and the God of love and peace will be with you." 2 Corinthians 13:11b

A child's need for security sometimes manifests itself with a favorite stuffed animal, doll, pillow, or blanket--becoming a constant companion, and absolutely essential need for them to go to bed and go to sleep. As a child grows older, they become secure in the love of parents, and the acceptance of their peers.

> *"I will trust in the shelter of Your wings." Psalm 61:4b*

As adults we often seek security in our material possessions, approval of peers, or own strength and abilities, and success according to the world's standards.

The need for security and acceptance is a basic need of our human condition. It is a sad thing indeed, that so many never find the only real security that comes only in a right personal relationship with God through faith in Jesus Christ. This is the sure foundation and the only one that will endure through the struggles of life and the sands of time.

People, health, wealth, and popularity may all disappoint, or fade away; but the security we have in an unchanging God, who loves us unconditionally, accepts us just as we are, and forgives us for everything we have ever done or will ever do, is the ultimate security that supplies our every need, and makes possible the peace and joy that comes from knowing our "refuge and strength", our "very present help in time of trouble", our "redeemer" our "sanctifier", and our "friend who sticketh closer than a brother".

> *"Let us therefore come boldly to the throne of grace, that we may obtain mercy and find grace to help in time of need." Hebrews 4:16*

Father, blanket me with the security of your love that is mine through your Son and my Savior and brother, Jesus Christ. Amen

Taking it to the Lord...

How can I apply this truth?____

____

____

Father, I've come to worship and praise you! You are my:___________________________

____

I give you all Glory, Honor, and Praise O Lord!

Father, I am sorry that I have sinned by:_______________________________________

Help me to repent. Cleanse me, strengthen me, restore me.

Father, THANK YOU for all your love, grace, mercy and blessings of life that you continually shower down upon me. Thank you especially for:

1._________________________________   2._________________________________
3._________________________________   4._________________________________
5._________________________________   6._________________________________

THANK YOU for answered prayers:____

Father, I need:____

Father, I ask that YOU:____

____

____

Lord, bless me that I may be a blessing. Give me Your heart for loving and serving others. Keep Your hand upon me. Keep me from all evil and harm, and let me cause harm to no one. Bind Satan that he have no power over me. All this I pray in subjection to your will and in the strong name of my Lord and Savior, Jesus Christ. Amen.

Checked Your Filter Lately?

"Therefore, having these promises, beloved, let us cleanse ourselves from all filthiness of the flesh and spirit, perfecting holiness in the fear of God." 2 Corinthians 7:1

Filters are an essential part of life. Just as our kidney's work to filter out impurities in our bodies, air, oil, and fuel

> *"Wash me, and I shall be whiter than snow."*
> *Psalm 51:7*

filters work to keep car engines running smoothly by filtering out dirt and grime and other impurities.   We have air conditioner filters, coffee filters, pool filters, and noise filters. Some filters are to be replaced regularly, others are to be cleaned and reused.

God, in His mercy, has provided sin filters for us who claim the name of Christians. He has filtered out the penalty for our sins with the blood of Christ on the cross at Calvary. He has washed away our sins in the filter of baptism.

By the power of the Holy Spirit who lives within us, He daily cleanses our sin filters by "the washing of water by the word"- i.e. by washing away our sins by daily confession, repentance, and dying to sin and becoming alive in Christ.

> *"If we confess our sins, He is faithful and just to forgive us our sins and to cleanse us from all unrighteousness."*
> *1 John 1:3*

Have you checked your sin filter lately? Are there any roots of bitterness that need to be washed away? Is there any unforgiveness festering? Have the cares of this world, the pride of the flesh, or the onslaughts of Satan taken their toll? Thanks be to God for his long suffering and patience toward us, and for His provision to Continually clean our filters by confession, repentance, and intercession.

Father, thank you for filtering out all my sin and unrighteousness with the righteousness of Christ, so that I may be acceptable in your sight. Amen

Taking it to the Lord...

How can I apply this truth?____

____

____

Father, I've come to worship and praise you! You are my:___________________________________

____

I give you all Glory, Honor, and Praise O Lord!

Father, I am sorry that I have sinned by:____

Help me to repent. Cleanse me, strengthen me, restore me.

Father, THANK YOU for all your love, grace, mercy and blessings of life that you continually shower down upon me. Thank you especially for:

1._____________________________________   2._____________________________________

3._____________________________________   4._____________________________________

5._____________________________________   6._____________________________________

THANK YOU for answered prayers:____

Father, I need:____

Father, I ask that YOU:____

____

____

____

Lord, bless me that I may be a blessing. Give me Your heart for loving and serving others. Keep Your hand upon me. Keep me from all evil and harm, and let me cause harm to no one. Bind Satan that he have no power over me. All this I pray in subjection to your will and in the strong name of my Lord and Savior, Jesus Christ. Amen.

Be Like Mike?

"Therefore be imitators of God as dear children. And walk in love, as Christ also has loved us and given Himself for us, an offering and a sacrifice to God for a sweet-smelling aroma." Ephesians 5:1

Role models are big business and big influences these days. Some are so unbelievably bad. It gives cause to wonder about the future of generations to come. Why anyone would want to be like any number of today's hero's is a mystery to most.

> *"Oh, send out Your light and Your truth! Let them lead me; Let them bring me to Your holy hill."*
> *Psalm 43:3*

Role models often become objects of hero worship. People old and young join fan clubs, follow the lead and suggestions of their hero in buying everything from tennis shoes to deodorant and collect all sorts of memorabilia connected with their hero.

Manufacturers and even Corporations spend billions of dollars securing endorsements or appearances by today's famous and infamous because they sell products or boost attendance.

And where is the perfect role model in your life? Who set the example of living the perfect life? Who healed the sick, and raised the dead. Isn't the one who thought you were worth dying for worth living for?

> *"For I have given you an example, that you should do as I have done to you."*
> *John 13:15*

Do you know as much about the life and teachings of the Lord Jesus Christ as you do about the lives and accomplishments of Michael Jordon, Rusty Wallace, or whoever your hero might be?

Father, help me to be conformed to the image of Christ by getting to know and love Him as He reveals Himself to me through His Word. Amen

Taking it to the Lord...

How can I apply this truth?____
____
____

Father, I've come to worship and praise you! You are my:_________________________________
____

I give you all Glory, Honor, and Praise O Lord!

Father, I am sorry that I have sinned by:____

Help me to repent. Cleanse me, strengthen me, restore me.

Father, THANK YOU for all your love, grace, mercy and blessings of life that you continually shower down upon me. Thank you especially for:

1._________________________________   2._________________________________
3._________________________________   4._________________________________
5._________________________________   6._________________________________

THANK YOU for answered prayers:____
Father, I need:____
Father, I ask that YOU:____
____
____
____

Lord, bless me that I may be a blessing. Give me Your heart for loving and serving others. Keep Your hand upon me. Keep me from all evil and harm, and let me cause harm to no one. Bind Satan that he have no power over me. All this I pray in subjection to your will and in the strong name of my Lord and Savior, Jesus Christ. Amen.

The Ultimate Stain Remover

"If we confess our sins, He is faithful and just to forgive us *our* sins and to cleanse us from all unrighteousness. If we say that we have not sinned, we make Him a liar, and His word is not in us." 1 John 1:9

Stain removal and cleaning is a multi billion dollar business throughout the world. People seem to have an obsession for cleanliness when it comes to their clothing, their homes, and their bodies. We daily see ads and commercials for the "new and improved" detergent, cleansing cream, shampoo, or whatever.

> *"Wash me thoroughly from my iniquity, And cleanse me from my sin."*
> *Psalm 51:2*

O that we would have such an obsession for the spiritual cleansing that comes through the blood of Jesus Christ! By faith, we have been cleansed, sanctified and made righteous in the sight of God, and given a spotless white robe of righteousness that assures our acceptance in God's sight.

The scarlet stain of every sin that we have ever committed has been washed as white as snow, by the precious blood of the Lamb of God! By faith, we have been justified and made holy (just as if we had never sinned), and given the perfect cleanliness of Christ in God's sight.

> *"Though your sins are like scarlet, They shall be as white as snow;"*
> *Isaiah 1:18*

Although the war has been won, daily battles seem to encompass all believers. The "road dirt" of the world, our flesh, and the devil seems to soil our white robes of righteousness on an almost hourly basis.

Thanks be to God that He not only cleansed us once and for all, but that he continues to cleanse and remove every stain when we come to him confessing and repenting of our sins.

Father, give me a passion to keep my robe of righteousness clean and spotless by washing my garment daily with your blood through confession and repentance. Amen

Taking it to the Lord...

How can I apply this truth?____

____

____

Father, I've come to worship and praise you! You are my:_________________________

____

I give you all Glory, Honor, and Praise O Lord!

Father, I am sorry that I have sinned by:_______________________________________

Help me to repent. Cleanse me, strengthen me, restore me.

Father, THANK YOU for all your love, grace, mercy and blessings of life that you continually shower down upon me. Thank you especially for:

1.____________________________   2.____________________________

3.____________________________   4.____________________________

5.____________________________   6.____________________________

THANK YOU for answered prayers:____

Father, I need:____

Father, I ask that YOU:____

____

____

____

Lord, bless me that I may be a blessing. Give me Your heart for loving and serving others. Keep Your hand upon me. Keep me from all evil and harm, and let me cause harm to no one. Bind Satan that he have no power over me. All this I pray in subjection to your will and in the strong name of my Lord and Savior, Jesus Christ. Amen.

November 7   **Read Matthew 14:14-29, Psalm 58**

Don't Miss Out!

"For we are His workmanship, created in Christ Jesus for good works, which God prepared beforehand that we should walk in them." Ephesians 2:10

We've professed faith in Jesus Christ. We've been baptized and attend church regularly. We know that we have eternal life through faith in Jesus Christ. We know that we can do nothing to add to the perfect sacrifice of the cross. So what else is there?

> *"Surely there is a reward for the righteous; Surely He is God who judges in the earth."*
> *Psalm 58:11b*

There is the important matter of the stewardship of the life that God has given us. What about those good works for which we were created?

The parable of the mina tells us that we will stand before God and give an account of the stewardship of our lives, and be rewarded accordingly. The exact nature of these heavenly rewards is one of the great mysteries of the faith, but Scripture makes it abundantly clear that they exist.

We are told to "store up our treasures in heaven" (Matthew 6:20), and that we will be rewarded later: "for you shall be repaid at the resurrection of the just." (Luke 14:14) There are numerous other references to heavenly rewards.

> *"His lord said to him, 'Well done, good and faithful servant; you were faithful over a few things, I will make you ruler over many things."*
> *Matthew 25:21*

Bear in mind, these rewards have nothing to do with our heavenly destination. We have confirmed reservations in heaven by virtue of our faith in Jesus Christ, and this has nothing to do with our good works, but is a result of His great work at the cross. These rewards have everything to do with receiving the sacred delight of hearing our Lord say "Well done, good and faithful servant!"

Whether it is leading someone else to Christ, or glorifying God by our love or service to others, we have all been gifted to serve and created to bear the fruit of the good works for which God has created us in Christ.

Father, help me to be about your business, and strengthen me and guide me by your Spirit, that I may do those good works for which you created me. Amen

Taking it to the Lord...

How can I apply this truth?____

____

____

Father, I've come to worship and praise you! You are my:____________________

____

I give you all Glory, Honor, and Praise O Lord!

Father, I am sorry that I have sinned by:__________________________________

Help me to repent. Cleanse me, strengthen me, restore me.

Father, THANK YOU for all your love, grace, mercy and blessings of life that you continually shower down upon me. Thank you especially for:

1.___________________________________   2.___________________________________

3.___________________________________   4.___________________________________

5.___________________________________   6.___________________________________

THANK YOU for answered prayers:____

Father, I need:____

Father, I ask that YOU:____

____

____

Lord, bless me that I may be a blessing. Give me Your heart for loving and serving others. Keep Your hand upon me. Keep me from all evil and harm, and let me cause harm to no one. Bind Satan that he have no power over me. All this I pray in subjection to your will and in the strong name of my Lord and Savior, Jesus Christ. Amen.

The Original Global Positioning System

"Your word *is* a lamp to my feet and a light to my path." Psalm 119:105

> *"As for God, His way is perfect."*
> *Psalm 18:30a*

Onboard positioning systems are one of the fastest growing options in the automobile industry. Whether in the City, or on a cross -country trip, these amazing gadgets can guide and direct you wherever you want to go, and even send your location signal in case you need assistance.

Long before automobiles were ever invented, God installed an onboard navigation system into the heart of every believer. He is called the Holy Spirit. He will guide you into all truth, and He carries a lifetime guarantee "that He who has begun a good work in you will complete it until the day of Jesus Christ;" Philippians 1:6

When it comes to your eternal destination, there is only one way, and that is Jesus Christ, Son of God, Savior of the World, who came not only to be the way, but to show us the way to reconciliation with God through faith in His death on the cross as payment in full for our sins.

> *"Jesus said to him: "I am the way, the truth, and the life. No one comes to the father except through me."*
> *John 14:6*

The Holy Spirit will guide us along the paths of righteousness, set us back on the highway to heaven when we make wrong turns, and continually make intercession for us for things that we don't even know how to pray for.

For your journey of life, don't settle for the wolves in sheep's clothing that will lead you down the paths of destruction. Ask the Holy Spirit to come live within you as honored guest to show you the way, the truth and the life!

Father, thank you for giving me the power, strength and guidance of the Holy Spirit to navigate my path on the journey of life eternal. Amen

Taking it to the Lord...

How can I apply this truth?____

____

Father, I've come to worship and praise you! You are my:_______________________

____

I give you all Glory, Honor, and Praise O Lord!

Father, I am sorry that I have sinned by:_____________________________________

Help me to repent. Cleanse me, strengthen me, restore me.

Father, THANK YOU for all your love, grace, mercy and blessings of life that you continually shower down upon me. Thank you especially for:

1.____________________________ 2.____________________________

3.____________________________ 4.____________________________

5.____________________________ 6.____________________________

THANK YOU for answered prayers:____

Father, I need:____

Father, I ask that YOU:____

____

____

Lord, bless me that I may be a blessing. Give me Your heart for loving and serving others. Keep Your hand upon me. Keep me from all evil and harm, and let me cause harm to no one. Bind Satan that he have no power over me. All this I pray in subjection to your will and in the strong name of my Lord and Savior, Jesus Christ. Amen.

Make Lemonade!

"But as for you, you meant evil against me; *but* **God meant it for good, "** **Genesis 50:20**

Pity the poor lemon. Because of the sourness of its taste it is a most inedible fruit. Its name has become synonymous with something defective or worthless. There are even "lemon laws" to protect us from defective products.

"I would have lost heart unless I had believed That I would see the goodness of the Lord."
Psalm 27:13

God also has a lemon law. By the sweetness of His grace He is able to turn even the worst of circumstances and evil into Lemonade.

The life of Joseph is probably the greatest example of God turning "lemons" into lemonade. After being sold into slavery by his brothers, He became manager over Potiphar's house. After being wrongfully accused by Potiphar's wife and imprisoned he became overseer of the entire prison. After being forgotten by the chief butler until Pharoah had a troubling dream, He became the Leader of Egypt. Finally, he tells his brothers: *"But as for you, you meant evil against me; but God meant it for good, in order to bring it about as it is this day, to save many people alive."* Genesis 50:20

We need to always be mindful that *"God works all things to the Good to those who love God, to those who are the called according to His purpose",(Romans 8:28)* We can find great strength and comfort in knowing that God can and will turn the "lemons" of our lives into lemonade. It's a promise worth remembering when we get squeezed by the lemons of life--in a sin-sick world.

"For I consider the sufferings of this present time are not worthy to be compared with the glory that will be revealed in us.
Romans 8:18

Father, thank you for loving me enough not only to die for me, but also to give me cause to rejoice in my sufferings knowing that you will work all things for my good. Amen

Taking it to the Lord...

How can I apply this truth?____

____

____

Father, I've come to worship and praise you! You are my:_________________________________

____

I give you all Glory, Honor, and Praise O Lord!

Father, I am sorry that I have sinned by:____

Help me to repent. Cleanse me, strengthen me, restore me.

Father, THANK YOU for all your love, grace, mercy and blessings of life that you continually shower down upon me. Thank you especially for:

1.___________________________________   2.___________________________________
3.___________________________________   4.___________________________________
5.___________________________________   6.___________________________________

THANK YOU for answered prayers:____

Father, I need:____

Father, I ask that YOU:____

____

____

Lord, bless me that I may be a blessing. Give me Your heart for loving and serving others. Keep Your hand upon me. Keep me from all evil and harm, and let me cause harm to no one. Bind Satan that he have no power over me. All this I pray in subjection to your will and in the strong name of my Lord and Savior, Jesus Christ. Amen.

How Do You Spell Relief?

**"Therefore, having been justified by faith, we have peace with God through our Lord Jesus Christ,"
Romans 5:1**

We find relief for headaches, toothaches, backaches, and for practically everything except heartaches over the counter at any drug store. Many have names we can't pronounce, much less spell.

> *"You have been my help;
> Do not leave me nor
> forsake me,
> O God of my salvation."
> Psalm 27:9*

Many also seek relief for emotional hurts in a bottle, pill or powder. They try to escape from reality by numbing their senses and soaking or frying their brains.

Relief from the emotional pains caused by our sins or the sins of others cannot be found in a bottle, powder, or other substance.   We often look in all these wrong places before we discover that it is only a prayer away. When we learn, by faith, to call upon the name of Jesus, we find the comfort of His love, the power of His presence, and the relief we need.

He replaces our sorrow with joy, our despair with hope, our hate with love. Only Jesus can heal the broken hearted so that they weep no more, heal the blind so that they can see, and set the prisoners free from bondage to any hurt, any addiction, or any sin.

Jesus gives us the comfort of His love through the presence of the Holy Spirit living within us. He is our refuge and strength, our very present help in time of trouble, our brother, our best friend, and our peace.

> *"Therefore if there is any
> consolation in Christ, if
> any comfort of love, if any
> fellowship of the Spirit, if
> any affection and mercy,"
> Philippians 2:1*

Jesus is "pearl of great price", the treasure that fills our hearts, calms our troubled spirit, and makes life worth living. Have you found your relief in the precious name of Jesus?

Father, thank you for giving me relief from guilt, sin, and death that I receive by calling upon the name of Jesus. Amen

Taking it to the Lord...

How can I apply this truth?____

____

Father, I've come to worship and praise you! You are my:___________________________________

____

I give you all Glory, Honor, and Praise O Lord!

Father, I am sorry that I have sinned by:____

Help me to repent. Cleanse me, strengthen me, restore me.

Father, THANK YOU for all your love, grace, mercy and blessings of life that you continually shower down upon me. Thank you especially for:

1.___________________________________   2.___________________________________
3.___________________________________   4.___________________________________
5.___________________________________   6.___________________________________

THANK YOU for answered prayers:____

Father, I need:____

Father, I ask that YOU:____

____

____

Lord, bless me that I may be a blessing. Give me Your heart for loving and serving others. Keep Your hand upon me. Keep me from all evil and harm, and let me cause harm to no one. Bind Satan that he have no power over me. All this I pray in subjection to your will and in the strong name of my Lord and Savior, Jesus Christ. Amen.

Trouble shooting Rule #1

"But you shall receive power when the Holy Spirit has come upon you;" Acts 1:8

A close examination of the trouble shooting section of most instruction manuals for household appliances,

"Blessed be the Lord, Who daily loads us with benefits, The God of our salvation!" Psalm 68:18

computers, or sound systems will reveal step #1 as "make sure the product is plugged in to a power source".

Hours of wasted effort, unnecessary service calls, and sheer stress could have been avoided by simply checking the connection to the power source.

God's instruction manual for believers also emphasizes the importance of staying "plugged in" to the power that is ours through the Holy Spirit.

We have the "power of God" unto salvation that is ours when the Holy Spirit comes to work faith into our hearts and acceptance of Jesus Christ as our Savior.

We have the "power of God" unto sanctification with which the Holy Spirit both instantly and continually conforms us to the image of Christ.

We have the power of intercession, through which the Holy Spirit is interceding on our behalf by prayer.

We have the "power of God" in the full armor with which the Holy Spirit equips us to stand firm against the powers and principalities of this world.

"Now to Him who is able to do exceedingly abundantly above all that we ask or think, according to the power that works in us, 21to Him be glory in the church by Christ Jesus to all generations, forever and ever. Amen." Ephesians 3:20

Although the war has been won, and our salvation assured, the ongoing battles against the forces of evil embodied in our flesh, the World and the devil are often lost when we get disconnected from our power source through neglect, apathy, or willful disobedience to the commands of God. Like David, we should daily pray, "create in me a clean heart O Lord, and renew a right spirit within me"

Father, help me to stay "plugged into" your power through Abiding in You and Your Word. Amen

Taking it to the Lord...

How can I apply this truth?____

____

____

Father, I've come to worship and praise you! You are my:_____________________

____

I give you all Glory, Honor, and Praise O Lord!

Father, I am sorry that I have sinned by:__________________________________

Help me to repent. Cleanse me, strengthen me, restore me.

Father, THANK YOU for all your love, grace, mercy and blessings of life that you continually shower down upon me. Thank you especially for:

1.______________________________   2.______________________________

3.______________________________   4.______________________________

5.______________________________   6.______________________________

THANK YOU for answered prayers:_______________________________________

Father, I need:____

Father, I ask that YOU:____

____

____

Lord, bless me that I may be a blessing. Give me Your heart for loving and serving others. Keep Your hand upon me. Keep me from all evil and harm, and let me cause harm to no one. Bind Satan that he have no power over me. All this I pray in subjection to your will and in the strong name of my Lord and Savior, Jesus Christ. Amen.

How Do you Like your Eggs?

"Restore to me again the joy of your salvation, and make me willing to obey you." Psalm 51:12

Nobody likes to get "egg in the face" by committing some big blunder or making a bad choice. Once the yolk is broken, and the egg whites and yolks are mixed, you surely can't have your eggs unscrambled!

> *"You have forgiven the iniquity of Your people; You have covered all their sin."*
> *Psalm 85:2*

The lives of Christians are filled with growth pills disguised as problems. God often arranges circumstances to discipline, test, humble, and confound us in the process of refining us and conforming us into the image of Christ.

Most of the time, we make the beds that we have to lie in through willful disobedience and trading God control for self-control, and we have to suffer the consequences that often will plague us for the rest of our lives.

The question is not if, but when we get egg in our face, undergo God's discipline and chastening, or slip into our flesh mode. How do we respond? We can blame others, rationalize, deny, fall into self-pity and feeling sorry for ourselves. The worst mistake we can make is to get angry at God.

That "roaring lion" is just waiting to step up when we step down to self-centered justification instead of Christ centered confession and repentance.

> *"But may the God of all grace, who called us to His eternal glory by Christ Jesus, after you have suffered a while, perfect, establish, strengthen, and settle you."*
> *1 Peter 5:10*

When we "blow it" we join an all-star lineup of Saints who did the same thing. Starting with Adam and Eve, Moses, Jonah, David, Peter and Paul, just to name a few.

When the "Master Chef: seasons our sins with forgiveness and grace, he can turn our "scrambled eggs" fit to serve the King!

Father, help me to know that you are always more ready to forgive than I am to be forgiven. Amen

Taking it to the Lord...

How can I apply this truth?____

____

____

Father, I've come to worship and praise you! You are my:____________________

____

I give you all Glory, Honor, and Praise O Lord!

Father, I am sorry that I have sinned by:__________________________________

Help me to repent. Cleanse me, strengthen me, restore me.

Father, THANK YOU for all your love, grace, mercy and blessings of life that you continually shower down upon me. Thank you especially for:

1.__________________________   2.__________________________

3.__________________________   4.__________________________

5.__________________________   6.__________________________

THANK YOU for answered prayers:________________________________

Father, I need:____

Father, I ask that YOU:____

____

____

Lord, bless me that I may be a blessing. Give me Your heart for loving and serving others. Keep Your hand upon me. Keep me from all evil and harm, and let me cause harm to no one. Bind Satan that he have no power over me. All this I pray in subjection to your will and in the strong name of my Lord and Savior, Jesus Christ. Amen.

God's Alarm System

"But the Counselor, the Holy Spirit, whom the Father will send in my name, will teach you all things and will remind you of everything I have said to you." John 14:26

> *"Be pleased, O LORD, to deliver me; O LORD, make haste to help me!"*
> *Psalm 40:13*

Burglar alarms and security systems are a multi billion dollar industry. Many are rightfully concerned about safeguarding their homes and properties from thieves, fires, and other perils.

As believers, we have one of the finest alarm systems ever devised for safeguarding our souls. The Holy Spirit first comes to us first to sound the alarm that we are sinners who need a savior. He empowers us to deal with this problem by accepting Jesus Christ as our Savior.

He takes up residence in our hearts to strengthen us and to keep us in that saving relationship with Jesus Christ through all eternity.

He speaks through our conscience, through God's Word, through prayer, and sometimes through other believers to guide us and guard us "sound the alarm" when we would stray from the paths of righteousness and holiness.

Best of all, He provides us with armor that empowers us to stand when the "roaring lion" comes to devour, or when our flesh or the cares of this World would seek to destroy us. *"Stand therefore, having girded your waist with truth, having put on the breastplate of righteousness, and having shod your feet with the preparation of the gospel of peace; above all, taking the shield of faith with which you will be able to quench all the fiery darts of the wicked one. And take the helmet of salvation, and the sword of the Spirit, which is the word of God;" (Ephesians 6:14-17)*

> *"However, when He, the Spirit of truth, has come, He will guide you into all truth;"*
> *John 16:13*

Father, thank you for providing me with my own built in security system to keep me close to you. Amen

Taking it to the Lord...

How can I apply this truth?____

____

____

Father, I've come to worship and praise you! You are my:__________________________

____

I give you all Glory, Honor, and Praise O Lord!

Father, I am sorry that I have sinned by:____

Help me to repent. Cleanse me, strengthen me, restore me.

Father, THANK YOU for all your love, grace, mercy and blessings of life that you continually shower down upon me. Thank you especially for:

1.______________________________   2.______________________________

3.______________________________   4.______________________________

5.______________________________   6.______________________________

THANK YOU for answered prayers:____

Father, I need:____

Father, I ask that YOU:____

____

____

____

Lord, bless me that I may be a blessing. Give me Your heart for loving and serving others. Keep Your hand upon me. Keep me from all evil and harm, and let me cause harm to no one. Bind Satan that he have no power over me. All this I pray in subjection to your will and in the strong name of my Lord and Savior, Jesus Christ. Amen.

Roadside Assistance

"God *is* our refuge and strength, a very present help in trouble."

> *"Happy is he who has the God of Jacob for his help,*
> *Whose hope is in the LORD his God,"*
> *Psalm 46:1*

Roadside assistance is a big business. There is a nationwide network of roadside service providers on call to bring you gas if you run out, change a tire, jump start your car, or tow you to a garage in case you break down. Most manufacturers give this service free for a few years when you buy their car, or you can get roadside assistance privileges by joining a travel club.

What do you do when you need roadside assistance on the highway of life? Who do you call when you "run out of gas"? Where do you get a "jump start"?

Today's parable of the Good Samaritan shows how God can use anyone to provide help in time of need. More importantly, God's Word is full of promises and examples of how He can and will provide "roadside assistance" to all who call upon Him.

The Journey of the Israelites to the Promised Land has more examples of God's "roadside assistance" than we can begin to list here.

We have a "Good Shepherd" who leads us beside the still waters, and restores our souls.

> *"So we may boldly say:*
> *"The LORD is my helper;*
> *I will not fear.*
> *What can man do to me?"*
> *Hebrews 13:6*

We have the promises of God's power, God's presence, and God's love in His all sufficient grace to sustain us and provide for our every need whether it be spiritual, physical, relational, or financial. The Holy Spirit living within the heart of all believers is always at work on our behalf and ready to provide the strength and encouragement we need for the journey of life.

Father, thank you for always being "on call" to give me the assistance I need on the journey of life. Amen

Taking it to the Lord...

How can I apply this truth?____

____

Father, I've come to worship and praise you! You are my:_____________________

____

I give you all Glory, Honor, and Praise O Lord!

Father, I am sorry that I have sinned by:___________________________________

Help me to repent. Cleanse me, strengthen me, restore me.

Father, THANK YOU for all your love, grace, mercy and blessings of life that you continually shower down upon me. Thank you especially for:

1.__________________________________   2.__________________________________
3.__________________________________   4.__________________________________
5.__________________________________   6.__________________________________

THANK YOU for answered prayers:____

Father, I need:____

Father, I ask that YOU:____

____

____

Lord, bless me that I may be a blessing. Give me Your heart for loving and serving others. Keep Your hand upon me. Keep me from all evil and harm, and let me cause harm to no one. Bind Satan that he have no power over me. All this I pray in subjection to your will and in the strong name of my Lord and Savior, Jesus Christ. Amen.

Don't Feed The Lion!

"Be sober, be vigilant; because your adversary the devil walks about like a roaring lion, seeking whom he may devour." 1 Peter 5:8

How can anyone look around and not see that there is a great manifestation of sin and evil all about them? In Revelation 12 we find that the devil has come down among us with great wrath because he knows that he has a short time.

> *"But You, O LORD, do not be far from Me;*
> *O My Strength, hasten to help Me!"*
> *Psalm 22:19*

Although the victory over our flesh, the world, and the devil has been won for us by Jesus Christ's death on the cross, the battles remain, and this wounded and defeated enemy of our souls is still very powerful and very dangerous.

Our adversary is a liar and a thief. He is cunning and without a conscience. He knows our every weakness and how to exploit them. In our own strength, we are fair game as he feeds on our pride, greed, anger, lust, envy, misfortunes, and especially our self pity and depression to try to keep us from receiving our salvation, and after we receive it to try to separate us from the love of God and our assurance of eternal life that we have In Christ.

> *"Likewise you also, reckon yourselves to be dead indeed to sin, but alive to God in Christ Jesus our Lord."*
> *Romans 6:11*

Our Lord himself showed us how to deal with this tyrant. In Matthew 4, every time Satan tempted our Lord, Jesus responded with the "Sword of the Spirit" which is the Word of God, "and the devil left him". In 1 John 4:4 we learn that He who is in us believers is greater than he who is in the world.

Best of all, we have the full armor of God "that we may be able to stand against the wiles of the devil". The next time he comes looking to munch on you, just tell him that Jesus says that the kitchen is closed!

Father, sometimes I feel overcome by the enemy of my soul. Help me to say "get thee behind me Satan" and stand firm in the power of Your Spirit. Amen

Taking it to the Lord...

How can I apply this truth?____

____

____

Father, I've come to worship and praise you! You are my:__________________

____

I give you all Glory, Honor, and Praise O Lord!

Father, I am sorry that I have sinned by:________________________________

Help me to repent. Cleanse me, strengthen me, restore me.

Father, THANK YOU for all your love, grace, mercy and blessings of life that you continually shower down upon me. Thank you especially for:

1._________________________________   2._________________________________

3._________________________________   4._________________________________

5._________________________________   6._________________________________

THANK YOU for answered prayers:____

Father, I need:____

Father, I ask that YOU:____

____

____

Lord, bless me that I may be a blessing. Give me Your heart for loving and serving others. Keep Your hand upon me. Keep me from all evil and harm, and let me cause harm to no one. Bind Satan that he have no power over me. All this I pray in subjection to your will and in the strong name of my Lord and Savior, Jesus Christ. Amen.

Would Anyone Want to be Like You?

"But you shall receive power when the Holy Spirit has come upon you; and you shall be witnesses to Me in Jerusalem, and in all Judea and Samaria, and to the end of the earth." Acts 1:8

The most effective witnessing tool that we believers have is the lives we lead. We are to be the shining lights of the gospel in the world that others may glorify our Father because of us. It is a sobering thought that we are all called to be sermons in shoes, that others around us may be drawn to the light of God's love through us. Unfortunately we often fall short of this calling even to the extent that others are repelled because of us. We are warned against being a stumbling block.

> *"Who cover Yourself with light as with a garment,"*
> *Psalm 104.2*

To "talk the talk" without "walking the walk" is one of the biggest deterrents to the building of the kingdom of God. As James exhorts "But be doers of the word, and not hearers only, deceiving yourselves." (*James 1:22*)

Are you witnessing the contagious joy of the Lord or are you a joyless, critical, self righteous, grumpy Christian that would be hard for anyone to love, much less want to be like?   Are you singing in the choir on Sundays, and being "one of the boys or girls" the rest of the week, going places where Christians shouldn't go, saying and doing things not becoming to one who claims the name of Christian?

> *"For you were once darkness, but now you are light in the Lord. Walk as children of light* [9]*(for the fruit of the Spirit is in all goodness, righteousness, and truth."*
> *Ephesians 5:8, 9*

We are all works in progress and are never going to be faithful to either the great commandment or the great commission all the time. The fact is that it is only by God's grace, and by the power of the Holy Spirit that we can be faithful any time at all. May God grant us all the power to live lives fully pleasing to Him and bearing the fruit of the Spirit that will make us fruitful witnesses to others.

Father, help me to be aware that I will never look anyone in the eye that you do not love, and that commandment that I love them also is not a suggestion, but a commandment. Amen

Taking it to the Lord...

How can I apply this truth?____

____

Father, I've come to worship and praise you! You are my:_____________________________

____

I give you all Glory, Honor, and Praise O Lord!

Father, I am sorry that I have sinned by:____

Help me to repent. Cleanse me, strengthen me, restore me.

Father, THANK YOU for all your love, grace, mercy and blessings of life that you continually shower down upon me. Thank you especially for:

1.___________________________________   2.___________________________________

3.___________________________________   4.___________________________________

5.___________________________________   6.___________________________________

THANK YOU for answered prayers:____

Father, I need:____

Father, I ask that YOU:____

____

____

Lord, bless me that I may be a blessing. Give me Your heart for loving and serving others. Keep Your hand upon me. Keep me from all evil and harm, and let me cause harm to no one. Bind Satan that he have no power over me. All this I pray in subjection to your will and in the strong name of my Lord and Savior, Jesus Christ. Amen.

Trash or Treasure?

"But we have this treasure in earthen vessels, that the excellence of the power may be of God and not of us." 2 Corinthians 4:7

Every weekend, millions of people go out on a treasure hunt. Garage sales just keep getting bigger and bigger.

> *"I rejoice at Your word*
> *As one who finds great treasure."*
> *Psalm 119:162*

There are hundreds of people making a good living by knowing what is a real value, and then buying them cheap and reselling them on E-Bay or to collectors for really big profits. There are many stories documenting rare art or other incredibly valuable collectors items found at garage sales. Mostly garage sales are filled with once valued items that are no longer of any value to the owner.

All of this is leading up to the question of the trash and treasure in our lives. Where are our treasures? Are we focused on the things above, or are we in the materialistic rat race of the world somehow buying into the idea that the one with the most toys wins? The old cliché that you "never see a hearse pulling a U haul trailer" is something we all need to think about.

The nearer to death we get, the more we are going to realize that so many of the things we held so dear, that we strived so hard to obtain, that we thought so important were nothing but trash.

> *"A good man out of the good treasure of his heart brings forth good; and an evil man out of the evil treasure of his heart brings forth evil."*
> *Luke 6:45*

When we start thinking about what is going to be left after all the wood, hay, and stubble of our lives has been burned away at the resurrection of the just, we begin to realize that we have not stored up as many treasures in heaven as we should and could have.

While there is still time, may we all seek those treasures that are the good works that God prepared for us beforehand and get busy storing them up for that coming day of judgment.

Father, forgive me for getting caught up in the materialism of this world, and help me to focus on the real treasures in this life and the next. Amen

Taking it to the Lord...

How can I apply this truth?____

____

Father, I've come to worship and praise you! You are my:_______________________

____

I give you all Glory, Honor, and Praise O Lord!

Father, I am sorry that I have sinned by:____

Help me to repent. Cleanse me, strengthen me, restore me.

Father, THANK YOU for all your love, grace, mercy and blessings of life that you continually shower down upon me. Thank you especially for:

1._______________________________   2._______________________________
3._______________________________   4._______________________________
5._______________________________   6._______________________________

THANK YOU for answered prayers:____

Father, I need:____

Father, I ask that YOU:____

____

____

Lord, bless me that I may be a blessing. Give me Your heart for loving and serving others. Keep Your hand upon me. Keep me from all evil and harm, and let me cause harm to no one. Bind Satan that he have no power over me. All this I pray in subjection to your will and in the strong name of my Lord and Savior, Jesus Christ. Amen.

What Are You Waiting For?

"And this is eternal life, that they may know You, the only true God, and Jesus Christ whom You have sent." John 17:3

Where did we ever get the idea that eternal life begins when we die and go to heaven? Why would anyone think that we have to wait until we die before we can enjoy all the benefits of the new life that is ours when we receive Jesus Christ as our Savior? Unfortunately, many of us have had or continue to have this wrong idea.

> *"Delight yourself also in the LORD, And He shall give you the desires of your heart." Psalm 37:4*

Eternal life is not dying and going to heaven--it is knowing God through faith in Jesus Christ. We get to know God by knowing Jesus as He reveals Himself through God's Word. Jesus actually is God's Word made flesh and dwelling among us.

Eternal life begins when we by faith enter into a personal love relationship with God, by getting to know His Son. It carries on throughout the seasons of our life in this world, and through the next forever. We will get to know him not only as our Savior, but as the Lord of our life, Who has come that we might have life and have it more abundantly.

> *"I know that nothing is better for them than to rejoice, and to do good in their lives, and also that every man should eat and drink and enjoy the good of all his labor—it is the gift of God." Ecclesiastes 3:12,13*

We will know the abundance of His love, His grace, His comfort, His provision for our every need, and many times even the desires of our heart. We will get to know Him as our best friend and brother, our refuge and strength, our very present help in time of trouble. He will be our companion and confidante.

If you are missing out on the blessings of eternal life today by thinking of them only as something that will happen in a future life, think again! He has come that you might have life and have it more abundantly, here and now!

Father, thank you for loving and setting me free, for giving your life just for me so that I can experience the fullness of your love in both this life and the next. Amen

Taking it to the Lord...

How can I apply this truth?____

____

____

Father, I've come to worship and praise you! You are my:___________________________

____

I give you all Glory, Honor, and Praise O Lord!

Father, I am sorry that I have sinned by:____

Help me to repent. Cleanse me, strengthen me, restore me.

Father, THANK YOU for all your love, grace, mercy and blessings of life that you continually shower down upon me. Thank you especially for:

1._____________________________________   2._____________________________________

3._____________________________________   4._____________________________________

5._____________________________________   6._____________________________________

THANK YOU for answered prayers:____

Father, I need:____

Father, I ask that YOU:____

____

____

Lord, bless me that I may be a blessing. Give me Your heart for loving and serving others. Keep Your hand upon me. Keep me from all evil and harm, and let me cause harm to no one. Bind Satan that he have no power over me. All this I pray in subjection to your will and in the strong name of my Lord and Savior, Jesus Christ. Amen.

How Good is Good Enough?

"For I say to you, that unless your righteousness exceeds *the righteousness* of the scribes and Pharisees, you will by no means enter the kingdom of heaven." Matthew 5:20

> *"O my soul, you have said to the LORD,*
> *"You are my Lord, My goodness is nothing apart from You."*
> *Psalm 16:2*

The Scribes and Pharisees were the brightest of the best. They had spent a lifetime studying scripture, and knew every jot and title of the law, but they were not good enough to get to heaven.

The rich young man was not good enough in spite of observing the law and being upright all his life. The disciples were certainly not good enough, because they slept when they should have stayed awake, ran away in time of trouble.

When you hear someone confess that they are not good enough to get to heaven or tell you that you are not good enough to get to heaven you are hearing truth!

It may be hard to believe, but even Billy Graham is not good enough to get to heaven. And if Billy Graham can't make it on his goodness, who in the world can? Scripture truthfully tells us that "all have sinned and fall short of the glory of God," "that all our righteousness are as filthy rags", and "If we say we have no sin" we deceive ourselves and the truth is not in us".

Praise God that He came down as man and lived the perfect, sinless life, died on the cross as a sacrifice for us so that we would be clothed in His goodness. Jesus Christ imputes his goodness to us by faith. It is His goodness, not ours that makes us acceptable to God the Father. To think that we can add anything to His perfect goodness and holiness is an insult to the Father and the Son.

> *"But the free gift is not like the offense. For if by the one man's offense many died, much more the grace of God and the gift by the grace of the one Man, Jesus Christ, abounded to many."*
> *Romans 5:15*

Father, I thank you that because Jesus was more than good enough, I do not have to be. Thank you for your marvelous free gift of heaven that I cannot earn, buy, or borrow; but only receive by faith in the blood of Jesus shed on the Cross of Calvary. Amen

Taking it to the Lord...

How can I apply this truth?____

____

Father, I've come to worship and praise you! You are my:___________________

____

I give you all Glory, Honor, and Praise O Lord!

Father, I am sorry that I have sinned by:_________________________________

Help me to repent. Cleanse me, strengthen me, restore me.

Father, THANK YOU for all your love, grace, mercy and blessings of life that you continually shower down upon me. Thank you especially for:

1.__________________________ 2.__________________________

3.__________________________ 4.__________________________

5.__________________________ 6.__________________________

THANK YOU for answered prayers:______________________________________

Father, I need:____

Father, I ask that YOU:____

____

____

Lord, bless me that I may be a blessing. Give me Your heart for loving and serving others. Keep Your hand upon me. Keep me from all evil and harm, and let me cause harm to no one. Bind Satan that he have no power over me. All this I pray in subjection to your will and in the strong name of my Lord and Savior, Jesus Christ. Amen.

WDJD?

"A new commandment I give to you, that you love one another; as I have loved you, that you also love one another." John 13:34

The "What Would Jesus Do?" bracelets have been one of the most popular phenomena in Christian circles in the past decade, if not longer. Millions of these have been sold and have been worn and are being worn as reminders that we are to be "Imitators of Christ."

> *"Depart from evil and do good;*
> *Seek peace and pursue it."*
> *Psalm 34:11*

As someone pointed out in Discipleship magazine a few years ago, we need to know what Jesus did, if we are going to have a clue as to what He would do today in any given situation.

We need to know that he did only what His Father commanded. So we can be sure that He loved and obeyed God. We can be sure that He loved others, including you and me. He healed the sick, fed the hungry, and forgave sinners. He confronted religious hypocrisy wherever he encountered it.

Jesus prayed continually, knew and quoted the scriptures regularly, as he lived the perfect life so that He could be the perfect, unblemished sacrifice for our sins. He calls each of us into a personal love relationship with Him so that we can get to know the Father through Him. He wants to not only be our Savior, but our Lord, our brother, and our best friend. He has gone to prepare a place for us in heaven, and left the Holy Spirit to live within us to comfort us, guide us, strengthen us, and keep us safely in the fold until He comes again.

> *"Let your light so shine before men, that they may see your good works and glorify your Father in heaven."*
> *Matthew 5:16*

"What Would Jesus Do?" might be a much more meaningful question if we would know "What Did Jesus Do"?

Father, fill me with the knowledge of your will with all wisdom and spiritual understanding that I may live a life fully pleasing to you and conformed to the image of Your Son. Amen

Taking it to the Lord...

How can I apply this truth?____

____

____

Father, I've come to worship and praise you! You are my:_______________________

____

I give you all Glory, Honor, and Praise O Lord!

Father, I am sorry that I have sinned by:_____________________________________

Help me to repent. Cleanse me, strengthen me, restore me.

Father, THANK YOU for all your love, grace, mercy and blessings of life that you continually shower down upon me. Thank you especially for:

1.___________________________   2.___________________________

3.___________________________   4.___________________________

5.___________________________   6.___________________________

THANK YOU for answered prayers:___________________________________

Father, I need:____

Father, I ask that YOU:____

____

____

Lord, bless me that I may be a blessing. Give me Your heart for loving and serving others. Keep Your hand upon me. Keep me from all evil and harm, and let me cause harm to no one. Bind Satan that he have no power over me. All this I pray in subjection to your will and in the strong name of my Lord and Savior, Jesus Christ. Amen.

The Smartest Man in the World

"For the wisdom of this world is foolishness with God. For it is written, *"He catches the wise in their own craftiness,"* **1 Corinthians 3:19**

There is a story about a Preacher, a Boy Scout, and a Nuclear Physicist getting ready to crash in a plane and had only one parachute. The preacher told the Boy Scout to take it, as he had

> *"So teach us to number our days, That we may gain a heart of wisdom."*
> *Psalm 90:12*

his whole life before him. The Physicist said: "No, I'm taking it, "I am the smartest man in the World! The world needs my mind!" After the physicist jumped, the preacher said: "I'm sorry, son. I tried." The Boy Scout replied: "It's OK pastor, the smartest man in the world just jumped out with my knapsack instead of the parachute!"

Jesus said in Luke 10:21: "I thank You, Father, Lord of heaven and earth, that You have hidden these things from *the* wise and prudent and revealed them to babes". There is just no room for the pride of the flesh or intellect to glory in the grace of God. It is only through the supernatural power of the Holy Spirit that anyone can receive Jesus Christ as Savior, as this faith is spiritually discerned.

Jesus said: *"Assuredly anyone who does not receive the kingdom of God as a little child will by no means enter it" Luke 18:17*. People can make intellectual pilgrimages and study all the great philosophers and even religions of the world, and be filled with head knowledge without limit; but no one can call Jesus Christ Lord except by the supernatural power of the Holy Spirit working in and through the revelation of God whether by written, preached, or given in the testimony of a believer.

> *"Professing to be wise, they became fools,"*
> *Romans 1:22*

This does not mean that one has to send his "brains out to lunch" in order to become a Christian. As we move from the milk of the word into the meat in the process of being conformed to the Image of Christ, intellect and faith will merge and we will know God intellectually and spiritually.

Father, Fill me with the knowledge of you and your will with all wisdom and spiritual understanding. Amen

Taking it to the Lord...

How can I apply this truth?____

____

____

Father, I've come to worship and praise you! You are my:_____________________________

____

I give you all Glory, Honor, and Praise O Lord!

Father, I am sorry that I have sinned by:____

Help me to repent. Cleanse me, strengthen me, restore me.

Father, THANK YOU for all your love, grace, mercy and blessings of life that you continually shower down upon me. Thank you especially for:

1._______________________________   2._______________________________

3._______________________________   4._______________________________

5._______________________________   6._______________________________

THANK YOU for answered prayers:____

Father, I need:____

Father, I ask that YOU:____

____

____

Lord, bless me that I may be a blessing. Give me Your heart for loving and serving others. Keep Your hand upon me. Keep me from all evil and harm, and let me cause harm to no one. Bind Satan that he have no power over me. All this I pray in subjection to your will and in the strong name of my Lord and Savior, Jesus Christ. Amen.

God's Big Eraser

"So then each of us shall give account of himself to God." Romans 14:12

There is a story about a man claiming to be able to talk with God. The priest who was checking out his claim, asked him to ask God what sin the priest had done in his youth that was so terrible. When the man came back, he told the priest that God had said: "I don't remember!"

> *"As far as the east is from the west, So far has He removed our transgressions from us."*
> *Psalm 103:12*

Justification by faith is one of the great truths of the Christian faith. Through our faith that Jesus Christ died on the cross as full payment for our sins, we are justified and regain right standing with God "just as if we had never sinned." We have the imputed righteousness of Christ.

When our "book of life" is opened at the "resurrection of the just", we are going to find that all of our sins have been erased, and the only thing left for us to account for are the good works "for which we were created".

This fact that we have forever forgiveness should never be considered a license to keep on sinning. Rather it should be a reminder that we should keep on forgiving others as we have been forgiven, and to live lives fully pleasing to our forgiver and being fruitful in every good work.

> *"For I will be merciful to their unrighteousness, and their sins and lawless deeds I will remember no more."*
> *Hebrews 8:12*

When we learn to accept the forgiveness of God, forgive others, and to forgive ourselves can we begin to live in the joy of the Lord and in a vital and personal relationship with Jesus Christ.

Father, Keep me ever mindful that you erased my sins with the precious blood of your only Son, and although I can never be worthy, let me always be thankful.   Amen

Taking it to the Lord...

How can I apply this truth?____

____

____

Father, I've come to worship and praise you! You are my:_________________________

____

I give you all Glory, Honor, and Praise O Lord!

Father, I am sorry that I have sinned by:____

Help me to repent. Cleanse me, strengthen me, restore me.

Father, THANK YOU for all your love, grace, mercy and blessings of life that you continually shower down upon me.

Thank you especially for:

1._________________________________   2._________________________________

3._________________________________   4._________________________________

5._________________________________   6._________________________________

THANK YOU for answered prayers:____

Father, I need:____

Father, I ask that YOU:____

____

____

Lord, bless me that I may be a blessing. Give me Your heart for loving and serving others. Keep Your hand upon me. Keep me from all evil and harm, and let me cause harm to no one. Bind Satan that he have no power over me. All this I pray in subjection to your will and in the strong name of my Lord and Savior, Jesus Christ. Amen.

Hypocritical Glory is Alive and Well

"Hypocrite! First remove the plank from your own eye, and then you will see clearly to remove the speck from your brother's eye." Matthew 7:5

The oft-told story about the gangster who offered to give the church a large sum of money if only his gangster brother could be called a saint at his funeral is a wonderful commentary on hypocritical glory. The story is that the pastor accomplished this by saying: "This man was a thief, murderer and crook, and a really bad human being, but compared to his brother sitting over there, He was a Saint!

> *"The wicked in his pride persecutes the poor"*
> *Psalm 10:2*

Our Lord reserved his harshest words and severest criticism for the scribes and Pharisees and religious leaders of the day who thought they were so much better than others. Many today promote this kind of hypocrisy by preaching about the sins and failures of other people and other churches and making us feel better because we don't have those problems, although ours may be worse..

Those who say that they don't want anything to do with church because the church is full of hypocrites are in effect practicing their own hypocrisy by implying that they are better than Christians, when they should be thinking how much better off Christians are because they have forgiveness for their sins.

It seems to be in the dark nature of our flesh, the world, and the Devil to lead us to seek to validate ourselves by comparing ourselves hypocritical glory vanish. When we see how miserably we fail to even come close to His perfection, the truth that our righteousness is as filthy rags, leaves us no room to glory over how much better we are than anyone else to others. This is the real cause of discrimination by race, religion, sex, or national origin. It is only when we compare ourselves to Jesus Christ, can the shame of hypocritical glory vanish. When we see how miserably we fail to even come close to His perfection, the truth that our righteousness is as filthy rags leaves us no room to glory about how much better we are than any one.

> *"Blind guides, who strain out a gnat and swallow a camel"*
> *Matthew 23:24*

Lord, have mercy upon me, a poor miserable sinner, saved only by your grace. Amen

Taking it to the Lord...

How can I apply this truth?____

____

Father, I've come to worship and praise you! You are my:_____________________________

____

I give you all Glory, Honor, and Praise O Lord!

Father, I am sorry that I have sinned by:____

Help me to repent. Cleanse me, strengthen me, restore me.

Father, THANK YOU for all your love, grace, mercy and blessings of life that you continually shower down upon me. Thank you especially for:

1.____________________________________   2.____________________________________
3.____________________________________   4.____________________________________
5.____________________________________   6.____________________________________

THANK YOU for answered prayers:____

Father, I need:____

Father, I ask that YOU:____

____

____

Lord, bless me that I may be a blessing. Give me Your heart for loving and serving others. Keep Your hand upon me. Keep me from all evil and harm, and let me cause harm to no one. Bind Satan that he have no power over me. All this I pray in subjection to your will and in the strong name of my Lord and Savior, Jesus Christ. Amen.

Will I See You in Heaven?

"He who believes in the Son has everlasting life; and he who does not believe the Son shall not see life, but the wrath of God abides on him." John 3:36

Do you have a spouse, a child, relative or friend who has not accepted Jesus Christ as their Savior? Are you going to a funeral filled with the sadness that you are never going to see this person again? Is your heart breaking over a loved one's rebellion against God?

> *"The fool has said in his heart,*
> *"There is no God."*
> *Psalm 14:1*

This question is one of the most compelling ways you can use to find out the spiritual condition of a loved one. When you ask out of love and real concern, and not in a "holier than thou" self righteous manner, you might well be the conduit through which the Holy Spirit calls this loved one into a love relationship with God through faith in Jesus Christ, or you might be at least planting the seed which can lead to salvation.

Before you ask, make sure that you yourself have the "confirmed reservations" for heaven that come by grace alone through faith alone. Make sure that you understand and believe that Christ was good enough, so that you don't have to base your hope on whether you are good enough.

> *"In My Father's house are many mansions; if it were not so, I would have told you. I go to prepare a place for you."*
> *John 14:2*

Make sure that you know that we all have sinned and fall short of the Glory of God. Make sure you know that God would have all to be saved and offers this wonderful gift of eternal life to all who would believe on the Lord Jesus Christ.

What joy there will be when you see this loved one at the great reunion in heaven knowing that God has called them through you and this question!!

Lord, give me godly concern for those I know who do not know you, and the boldness to ask this question in the power of Your Spirit. Amen

Taking it to the Lord...

How can I apply this truth?____
____
____
Father, I've come to worship and praise you! You are my:_____________________
____
I give you all Glory, Honor, and Praise O Lord!
Father, I am sorry that I have sinned by:__________________________________
Help me to repent. Cleanse me, strengthen me, restore me.
Father, THANK YOU for all your love, grace, mercy and blessings of life that you continually shower down upon me. Thank you especially for:

1.___________________________________   2.___________________________________
3.___________________________________   4.___________________________________
5.___________________________________   6.___________________________________

THANK YOU for answered prayers:____
Father, I need:____
Father, I ask that YOU:____
____
____
____

Lord, bless me that I may be a blessing. Give me Your heart for loving and serving others. Keep Your hand upon me. Keep me from all evil and harm, and let me cause harm to no one. Bind Satan that he have no power over me. All this I pray in subjection to your will and in the strong name of my Lord and Savior, Jesus Christ. Amen.

You Will When You Get There!

"But I will show you whom you should fear: Fear Him who, after He has killed, has power to cast into hell; yes, I say to you, fear Him!" Luke 12:5

How sad to hear someone say they do not believe in hell! What a surprise awaits them! The reality and finality of hell escapes the notice of unbelievers, or fails to penetrate the hardness of their hearts. As one answered to one who said they didn't believe in hell, "you will when you get there!"

> *"The fool has said in his heart, "There is no God."*
> *Psalm 53:1*

Can you imagine the shock and dismay of one who has deliberately and willfully chosen to reject the eternal life offered to all who would believe on the Lord Jesus Christ and be saved? As today's scripture reading explains, it will be too late.

As we too often see in the lives of those around us who are blinded there is no reasoning with them because of their darkened understanding. The heart that is hardened against God regards the word of God as foolishness and nothing to consider.

The idea that they might have to give up their freedom to live in bondage to sin in order to receive the true freedom to live in perfect peace and security with God that only a right faith relationship with Jesus Christ affords is totally beyond their understanding.

We pray that the Holy Spirit who can change hearts and work faith within hearts will come upon the unbeliever before it's too late.

> *"For I have five brothers, that he may testify to them, lest they also come to this place of torment.' Abraham said to him, 'They have Moses and the prophets; let them hear them.' And he said, 'No, father Abraham; but if one goes to them from the dead, they will repent.' But he said to them, 'If they do not hear Moses and the prophets, neither will they be persuaded though one rise from the dead.'"*
> *Luke 28:31*

Father, give me a heart for the unsaved, and help me to pray daily for their salvation. Amen

Taking it to the Lord...

How can I apply this truth?____

____

____

Father, I've come to worship and praise you! You are my:___________________

____

I give you all Glory, Honor, and Praise O Lord!

Father, I am sorry that I have sinned by:________________________________

Help me to repent. Cleanse me, strengthen me, restore me.

Father, THANK YOU for all your love, grace, mercy and blessings of life that you continually shower down upon me. Thank you especially for:

1._______________________________   2._______________________________
3._______________________________   4._______________________________
5._______________________________   6._______________________________

THANK YOU for answered prayers:_______________________________________

Father, I need:____

Father, I ask that YOU:____

____

____

____

Lord, bless me that I may be a blessing. Give me Your heart for loving and serving others. Keep Your hand upon me. Keep me from all evil and harm, and let me cause harm to no one. Bind Satan that he have no power over me. All this I pray in subjection to your will and in the strong name of my Lord and Savior, Jesus Christ. Amen.

The Stewardship of Time

"Whereas you do not know what *will happen* tomorrow. For what *is* your life? It is even a vapor that appears for a little time and then vanishes away." James 4:14

How are you spending the time God has given you? As time goes by, we become aware of the time we have wasted in pursuing the "good life" as defined by the world, instead of living the eternal life that began when we entered into a personal relationship with Jesus Christ.

> *"And in Your book they all were written,*
> *The days fashioned for me, when as yet there were none of them."*
> *Psalm 139:16b*

There always seems to be a lot of competition for our time. We've got our recreation to enjoy, our trips to take, chores to do, and "mountains to climb" Some times spouses and children are left dangling while we pursue our own selfish interests. Often wonderful friendships are left to wither and die because we won't take the time to keep them going.

When we near the end of our journey, what regrets are we going to have about how we used or abused our time?

A lot of us are "couch potato" Christians too much of the time. When we compare the hours spent in front of the TV screen, and other idle pursuits with the time spent in abiding in the Word, prayer, and ministering the love of God to others through loving and serving them, the day of accounting we are all going to give for our stewardship of the time we were given becomes a cause for concern instead of something we can anticipate with joy.

> *"And if you call on the Father, who without partiality judges according to each one's work, conduct yourselves throughout the time of your stay here in fear;"*
> *1 Peter 1:12*

Lord, let me live my life and spend my time in a manner pleasing to you and abounding in the good works for which you created me. Amen

Taking it to the Lord...

How can I apply this truth?____

____

____

Father, I've come to worship and praise you! You are my:_______________________

____

I give you all Glory, Honor, and Praise O Lord!

Father, I am sorry that I have sinned by:___________________________________

Help me to repent. Cleanse me, strengthen me, restore me.

Father, THANK YOU for all your love, grace, mercy and blessings of life that you continually shower down upon me. Thank you especially for:

1.________________________________   2.________________________________

3.________________________________   4.________________________________

5.________________________________   6.________________________________

THANK YOU for answered prayers:____

Father, I need:____

Father, I ask that YOU:____

____

____

Lord, bless me that I may be a blessing. Give me Your heart for loving and serving others. Keep Your hand upon me. Keep me from all evil and harm, and let me cause harm to no one. Bind Satan that he have no power over me. All this I pray in subjection to your will and in the strong name of my Lord and Savior, Jesus Christ. Amen.

Abiding Brings Answered Prayers

"If you abide in Me, and My words abide in you, you will ask what you desire, and it shall be done for you." (John 15:7)

When we abide in Christ and in His Word, we receive the mind of Christ which transforms us into praying with Christ centered motives and prayers that are consistent with His words which abides in us.

> *"Hear my prayer, O LORD, And give ear to my cry ;Do not be silent at my tears;"*
> *Psalm 39:12*

What a sacred delight to know that we can approach the throne of grace boldly, knowing that our prayers are answered. We can and should ask for blessings so that we can be a blessing to others. Whether it be treasures, talents, time, or love, we can not pass on to others something we have not received. So we ask God for these things with these motives, and He will surely answer.

As we gain more wisdom and spiritual discernment through abiding, we pray more in the will of God, rather than in our self-centered will, and we find more and more of our prayers being answered in the affirmative.

We can and should ask for more opportunities and more power to serve God and to be His ambassadors.

> *"That whatever you ask the Father in My name He may give you."*
> *John 15:16b*

It is only when we are fully abiding in the vine and totally surrendered to the understanding that " we know that all things work together for good to those who love God, to those who are the called according to *His* purpose."(*Romans 8:28)* that we can submit every prayer and supplication confident that it is in accordance with God's will.

What joy there is in having the confidence that comes from knowing that God has promised to answer our prayers when we abide in Him.

Lord, thank you for the blessing of answered prayers. Help me to pray more from your perspective with total confidence. Amen

Taking it to the Lord...

How can I apply this truth?____

____

____

Father, I've come to worship and praise you! You are my:_____________________________

____

I give you all Glory, Honor, and Praise O Lord!

Father, I am sorry that I have sinned by:____

Help me to repent. Cleanse me, strengthen me, restore me.

Father, THANK YOU for all your love, grace, mercy and blessings of life that you continually shower down upon me. Thank you especially for:

1.__________________________________   2.__________________________________
3.__________________________________   4.__________________________________
5.__________________________________   6.__________________________________

THANK YOU for answered prayers:____

Father, I need:____

Father, I ask that YOU:____

____

____

Lord, bless me that I may be a blessing. Give me Your heart for loving and serving others. Keep Your hand upon me. Keep me from all evil and harm, and let me cause harm to no one. Bind Satan that he have no power over me. All this I pray in subjection to your will and in the strong name of my Lord and Savior, Jesus Christ. Amen.

The Stewardship of Talents

"For to everyone who has, more will be given, and he will have abundance; but from him who does not have, even what he has will be taken away." Matthew 25:29

The difference between the parable of the mina in Luke and the parable of the talents in Matthew is very clear.

> *"Serve the LORD with gladness;" Psalm 100:2*

In the parable of the mina in Luke, we were all given one life, for which we must give an account. In the parable of the talents in Matthew, we were given differing abilities and gifts, and must give an account for making the most of the talents we have been given.

Just as we are not expected to give money we don't have, neither are we expected to give abilities we don't have. We have been *"created in Christ Jesus for good works, which God prepared beforehand that we should walk in them"(Ephesians 2:10b).* If we have been given much in the way of abilities and talents, we have been given the responsibility to use these gifts and talents to the glory of God.

> *"There are diversities of gifts, but the same Spirit. [5]There are differences of ministries, but the same Lord. And there are diversities of activities, but it is the same God who works all in all."* 1 Corinthians 12:4-6

What a shame and insult to the Grace of God to have believers squander their talents in pursuit of the fame, fortune, and pleasures of this World, and to be stingy in using them for building up the Kingdom of God!

When God calls for an accounting of the stewardship of our abilities and talents may we all be found faithful and pleasing in His sight!

Lord by the power of your Spirit, help me to be faithful in using my gifts and talents to Glorify You and to fulfill the purposes for which You made me. Amen

Taking it to the Lord...

How can I apply this truth?____

____

Father, I've come to worship and praise you! You are my:_______________________

____

I give you all Glory, Honor, and Praise O Lord!

Father, I am sorry that I have sinned by:_____________________________________

Help me to repent. Cleanse me, strengthen me, restore me.

Father, THANK YOU for all your love, grace, mercy and blessings of life that you continually shower down upon me. Thank you especially for:

1._________________________________   2._________________________________

3._________________________________   4._________________________________

5._________________________________   6._________________________________

THANK YOU for answered prayers:____

Father, I need:____

Father, I ask that YOU:____

____

____

Lord, bless me that I may be a blessing. Give me Your heart for loving and serving others. Keep Your hand upon me. Keep me from all evil and harm, and let me cause harm to no one. Bind Satan that he have no power over me. All this I pray in subjection to your will and in the strong name of my Lord and Savior, Jesus Christ. Amen.

What the Locusts Have Taken

"In his kindness God called you to his eternal glory by means of Jesus Christ. After you have suffered a little while, he will restore, support, and strengthen you, and he will place you on a firm foundation. All power is his forever and ever." 1 Peter 5:10, 11 NLT

Whether referring to swarms of locusts symbolically or literally, this prophecy in Joel paints a frightening picture.

> *"You have rejected us, O God, and broken our defenses. You have been angry with us; now restore us to your favor."*
> *Psalm 60:1 NLT*

Whether foretelling a real plague of locusts, or the destruction of Jerusalem, or to the fire that is going to test the wood, hay, and stubble of our lives on judgment day, the real message is repentance!

On a personal level, we can liken the locusts to all of the afflictions that plagued Job, or to the locusts of sin that sometimes consume and seek to destroy us.

Job was told to "curse God and die". David was consumed by guilt and had to endure the consequences of his sin with Bathsheba. The prodigal son was down to eating slop with the hogs before his plague ended.

> *"The LORD says, "I will give you back what you lost to the stripping locusts, the cutting locusts, the swarming locusts, and the hopping locusts"*
> *Joel 2:25 NIV*

When we drop our guard and the great deceiver sneaks in and overcomes us, we get so overcome by guilt and remorse that we are made to doubt our salvation and wonder whether we are really saved.

It is at these times when we get an idea of what Joel is talking about. When we bring our broken hearts to the throne of grace in true repentance; the restoration that God promises and demonstrates in the lives of Job, David, and the prodigal son will be ours.

Father, thank you for restoring what the locusts have eaten through the trials of my life, and for giving me assurance that I will be protected and covered by your righteousness on judgment day. Amen

Taking it to the Lord...

How can I apply this truth?____

____

Father, I've come to worship and praise you! You are my:_________________________________

____

I give you all Glory, Honor, and Praise O Lord!

Father, I am sorry that I have sinned by:____

Help me to repent. Cleanse me, strengthen me, restore me.

Father, THANK YOU for all your love, grace, mercy and blessings of life that you continually shower down upon me. Thank you especially for:

1.____________________________________   2.____________________________________

3.____________________________________   4.____________________________________

5.____________________________________   6.____________________________________

THANK YOU for answered prayers:____

Father, I need:____

Father, I ask that YOU:____

____

____

Lord, bless me that I may be a blessing. Give me Your heart for loving and serving others. Keep Your hand upon me. Keep me from all evil and harm, and let me cause harm to no one. Bind Satan that he have no power over me. All this I pray in subjection to your will and in the strong name of my Lord and Savior, Jesus Christ. Amen.

Abiding Brings Awareness of the Love of Others

"This is My commandment, that you love one another as I have loved you. Greater love has no one than this, than to lay down one's life for his friends." John 15:12,13

"God is all around us, His Love is everywhere".. The words from this contemporary hymn sums up one of the great truths that overwhelms believers who abide in Christ.

> *"Because of the house of the LORD our God I will seek your good."*
> *Psalm 122:9*

As we would have others see "Christ in us", we begin to see Jesus in others as they express the love of God in random acts of kindness, care and concern for us.

When others bear the fruit of the Spirit showing love, joy, peace, longsuffering, kindness, goodness, faithfulness, gentleness, or self-control to us, we are overwhelmed by the awareness of God's love all around us.

In times of sickness, grief, or tragedy, the love of others buoys our spirits and shares our burdens. In times of great blessing and joy, the love of others multiplies our joy as we share it with them.

> *"For we have great joy and consolation in your love, because the hearts of the saints have been refreshed by you, brother."*
> *Philemon 1:7*

When supported by the prayers of loved ones and fellow believers we are strengthened and encouraged through the difficulties of life.

So many times we are so preoccupied and self-centered that we miss the love that is all around us. As we become more Christ centered through abiding in Him, our sensitivity to the love that is all around us begins to overwhelm us and give us cause to praise the Lord more and more.

Lord, help me to become more aware of and be thankful for the love that is all around me. Amen

Taking it to the Lord...

How can I apply this truth?____

____

____

Father, I've come to worship and praise you! You are my:_____________________

____

I give you all Glory, Honor, and Praise O Lord!

Father, I am sorry that I have sinned by:__________________________________

Help me to repent. Cleanse me, strengthen me, restore me.

Father, THANK YOU for all your love, grace, mercy and blessings of life that you continually shower down upon me. Thank you especially for:

1._________________________________   2._________________________________

3._________________________________   4._________________________________

5._________________________________   6._________________________________

THANK YOU for answered prayers:____

Father, I need:____

Father, I ask that YOU:____

____

____

Lord, bless me that I may be a blessing. Give me Your heart for loving and serving others. Keep Your hand upon me. Keep me from all evil and harm, and let me cause harm to no one. Bind Satan that he have no power over me. All this I pray in subjection to your will and in the strong name of my Lord and Savior, Jesus Christ. Amen.

Call Waiting

"Therefore I, a prisoner for serving the Lord, beg you to lead a life worthy of your calling, for you have been called by God." Ephesians 4:1 NLT

Some times people keep God's call to salvation waiting until it's too late. We have too many wild oats to sow, too many fish to fry, and are too much in love with ourselves and the world to pick up God's phone.

> *"Happy are those who hear the joyful call to worship, for they will walk in the light of your presence LORD."*
> *Psalm 89:15 NLT*

Once we are saved, many seem to get the idea that that's all we need to do about it until we get to heaven and we choose to ignore some very important calls from God.

In addition to God's calls for obedience to the Great Commandment and Great Commission, we are called to daily repentance, not just the one time turning from our sin to receive Christ as our Savior.

We are called to sanctification or holiness, which we received in the sight of God when we confessed Christ, but which we also need to answer daily as the Spirit of God works in us and through God's Word to make us more Christ-like day by day.

Ministry and Worship are a couple more of the calls from God that He seems to have a problem getting through to us because of our preoccupation with the calls of our self-centered flesh and the world.

> *"For it pleased God in his kindness to choose me and call me, even before I was born! What undeserved mercy!"*
> *Galatians 1:15b NLT*

Scripture also speaks of God's calls to love and obedience (Deuteronomy 10:12, 13), a call to trust (Isaiah 8:12), a call to faithfulness (Malachi 2:10), a call to generous giving (2 Corinthians 8:7), and a call to perseverance. (Hebrews 10:23) Which of these calls do you still have waiting?

Father, thank you for Your forgiveness for the many times I have not answered the calls You have waiting. By the power of Your Spirit, enable me to answer all your calls. Amen

Taking it to the Lord...

How can I apply this truth?____

____

____

Father, I've come to worship and praise you! You are my:_____________________________

____

I give you all Glory, Honor, and Praise O Lord!

Father, I am sorry that I have sinned by:____

Help me to repent. Cleanse me, strengthen me, restore me.

Father, THANK YOU for all your love, grace, mercy and blessings of life that you continually shower down upon me. Thank you especially for:

1.___________________________________ 2.___________________________________

3.___________________________________ 4.___________________________________

5.___________________________________ 6.___________________________________

THANK YOU for answered prayers:____

Father, I need:____

Father, I ask that YOU:____

____

____

Lord, bless me that I may be a blessing. Give me Your heart for loving and serving others. Keep Your hand upon me. Keep me from all evil and harm, and let me cause harm to no one. Bind Satan that he have no power over me. All this I pray in subjection to your will and in the strong name of my Lord and Savior, Jesus Christ. Amen.

Abiding Brings Greater Awareness of God's Love

"As the Father loved Me, I also have loved you; abide in My love." John 15:9

When we enter into a personal relationship with God through faith in Jesus Christ, we become aware of the Love of God in providing for our salvation.

> *"And those who love His name shall dwell in it."*
> *Psalm 69:36b*

As we grow in the grace of God and getting to know Him as His Son has revealed Him through Scripture, we become more and more aware of the Amazing Love of God in every aspect of our lives.

He who has begun that good work in us by the Holy Spirit that He sends to live within the heart of every believer, will do whatever it takes to conform us to the image of His Son. He will discipline and chasten, He will convict us of our sin and our need to confess and repent.

> *"Now hope does not disappoint, because the love of God has been poured out in our hearts by the Holy Spirit who was given to us."*
> *Romans 5:5*

We will submit more and more areas of our lives to obedience and delight in God's law, and less and less to our self centered flesh and world perspective.

As we abide in Christ and His Word more, His wants become our wants and the awareness of His love leads us to be transformed by the renewing of our minds into an even deeper love relationship with God. The Awareness of His love inspires us to respond in Love to Him and to others.

Lord, as you reveal yourself to me more and more through hearing and studying your Word, Help me to abide in you more and enjoy the blessings of abiding. Amen

Taking it to the Lord...

How can I apply this truth?____

____

Father, I've come to worship and praise you! You are my:___________________

____

I give you all Glory, Honor, and Praise O Lord!

Father, I am sorry that I have sinned by:_______________________________

Help me to repent. Cleanse me, strengthen me, restore me.

Father, THANK YOU for all your love, grace, mercy and blessings of life that you continually shower down upon me. Thank you especially for:

1.___________________________ 2.___________________________

3.___________________________ 4.___________________________

5.___________________________ 6.___________________________

THANK YOU for answered prayers:________________________________

Father, I need:____

Father, I ask that YOU:____

____

____

Lord, bless me that I may be a blessing. Give me Your heart for loving and serving others. Keep Your hand upon me. Keep me from all evil and harm, and let me cause harm to no one. Bind Satan that he have no power over me. All this I pray in subjection to your will and in the strong name of my Lord and Savior, Jesus Christ. Amen.

Divine Revelation

"Jesus answered and said to him, "Blessed are you, Simon Bar-Jonah, for flesh and blood has not revealed *this* to you, but My Father who is in heaven." Matthew 16:17

Knowledge of God and belief in God are sometimes as different as night and day….as different as life and death.. Some of the most knowledgeable scholars and philosophers of all time have had more knowledge of God than anyone, and yet God has "hidden these things from *the* wise and prudent and has revealed them to babes"(Matthew 11:15b).

> *"The Lord has made known His Salvation: His righteousness He has revealed in the sight of the nations."*
> *Psalm 98:2*

God, "who desires all men to be saved and to come to the knowledge of the truth." (1 Tim 2:4), calls us into that saving relationship of faith in Jesus Christ by the power of His Spirit. When we rebel in our free will and choose to reject His call, we grieve the Holy Spirit and short circuit the power of God to overcome our spiritual blindness.

When God, through the power of the Holy Spirit, transforms our knowledge into belief that Jesus Christ died on the Cross so that we might live forever, and into faith that we have been justified and reconciled to God because of this; we can be sure that we have been called by God and have received the divine revelation that is the "power of God unto salvation" (Romans 1:16).

> *"Nor does anyone know the Father except the Son, and the one to whom the Son wills to reveal Him."*
> *Matthew 11:27b*

As we grow into spiritual maturity by growing into the fullness of Christ through Word and Sacrament, we receive more and more understanding of the "divine revelation" of the Father, through the Son that He has sent.

Father, thank you for revealing to me your wonderful gift of eternal life through faith in the life, death, and resurrection of Your dear Son, and my Lord and Savior, Jesus Christ. Amen

Taking it to the Lord...

How can I apply this truth?____

____

____

Father, I've come to worship and praise you! You are my:__________________________

____

I give you all Glory, Honor, and Praise O Lord!

Father, I am sorry that I have sinned by:______________________________________

Help me to repent. Cleanse me, strengthen me, restore me.

Father, THANK YOU for all your love, grace, mercy and blessings of life that you continually shower down upon me. Thank you especially for:

1.__________________________________   2.__________________________________

3.__________________________________   4.__________________________________

5.__________________________________   6.__________________________________

THANK YOU for answered prayers:____

Father, I need:____

Father, I ask that YOU:____

____

____

Lord, bless me that I may be a blessing. Give me Your heart for loving and serving others. Keep Your hand upon me. Keep me from all evil and harm, and let me cause harm to no one. Bind Satan that he have no power over me. All this I pray in subjection to your will and in the strong name of my Lord and Savior, Jesus Christ. Amen.

From Here to Infinity

"Great is our Lord, and mighty in power; His understanding is infinite." Psalm 147.5

There is a limit to our understanding. Try as we may, study as long and as hard as we like, we will never fully comprehend the glory, the power, and the majesty of God. We are limited by our flesh and human reasoning and by their boundaries.

> *"To Him who alone does great wonders, For His mercy endures forever." Psalm 136:4*

Our God is all knowing, ever present, all-powerful and everlasting. He is not limited by space, time, or any other factor. Best of all, He is ever loving!

This is why His grace is so amazing. It is beyond the limits of our human understanding that someone would care enough to give us His very best as a sacrifice for our sins so that we may be reconciled to Him.

> *"Be anxious for nothing, but in everything by prayer and supplication, with thanksgiving, let your requests be known to God; and the peace of God which surpasses all understanding will guard you hearts and minds through Christ Jesus." Philippians 4:6*

"Amazing Grace, how can it be" that by faith we become God's love offering to Christ, who has died to assure that none of us who God has given to Him will be lost.

To experience the "peace that surpasses all understanding" is just a foretaste of the glories that are going to be revealed to us when we meet our Savior face to face and come into a full understanding of the mysteries that we can never fully understand this side of infinity.

Lord, by the power of your Spirit, fill us with your joy and your peace until we see you face to face. Amen

Taking it to the Lord...

How can I apply this truth?____

____

Father, I've come to worship and praise you! You are my:_____________________

____

I give you all Glory, Honor, and Praise O Lord!

Father, I am sorry that I have sinned by:_________________________________

Help me to repent. Cleanse me, strengthen me, restore me.

Father, THANK YOU for all your love, grace, mercy and blessings of life that you continually shower down upon me. Thank you especially for:

1._________________________________   2._________________________________

3._________________________________   4._________________________________

5._________________________________   6._________________________________

THANK YOU for answered prayers:____

Father, I need:____

Father, I ask that YOU:____

____

____

Lord, bless me that I may be a blessing. Give me Your heart for loving and serving others. Keep Your hand upon me. Keep me from all evil and harm, and let me cause harm to no one. Bind Satan that he have no power over me. All this I pray in subjection to your will and in the strong name of my Lord and Savior, Jesus Christ. Amen.

Misunderstanding #1

"For by grace you have been saved through faith, and that not of yourselves; *it is* the gift of God, not of works, lest anyone should boast." Ephesians 2:8

If you were to stand before God today, and He should ask "Why should I let you into my heaven", what would your answer be? It might surprise you to know that among Christians and non-Christians, the answer is all too often performance based instead of faith based. "I have been a good person", "I have tried to do the right thing", "I go to church", "I have been baptized ", "I have a good heart" are among the most common answers given.

> *"Blessed is the man whose strength is in You,"*
> *Psalm 84:5*

As admirable as these qualities are, none of them ever saved anyone! No one is going to go to heaven based on conduct or performance! Our eternal life here and in heaven is not based on our performance, but on our faith in the performance of our Lord and Savior, Jesus Christ.

All of our righteousness is as filthy rags, compared to the perfect righteousness with which Jesus Christ lived the sinless life, and fulfilled the demands of the law for us by dying on the Cross of Calvary for the forgiveness of our sins.

> *"Knowing that a man is not justified by the works of the law but by faith in Jesus Christ, even we have believed in Christ Jesus, that we might be justified by faith in Christ and not by the works of the law;"*
> *Galatians 2:16a*

It is an insult to God to think that we can add anything to what He did to earn our salvation. We can only be thankful for this wonderful gift, and show our appreciation by letting our lives be a celebration of praise to Him for His goodness and mercy, and let this celebration be in doing all the things He created us to do to glorify Him as He accomplishes His purposes through us.

Father, let me never fall into the trap of misunderstanding whose performance it is by which I am saved. Amen

Taking it to the Lord...

How can I apply this truth?____

____

____

Father, I've come to worship and praise you! You are my:________________

____

I give you all Glory, Honor, and Praise O Lord!

Father, I am sorry that I have sinned by:__________________________________

Help me to repent. Cleanse me, strengthen me, restore me.

Father, THANK YOU for all your love, grace, mercy and blessings of life that you continually shower down upon me. Thank you especially for:

1.____________________________ 2.____________________________

3.____________________________ 4.____________________________

5.____________________________ 6.____________________________

THANK YOU for answered prayers:________________________________

Father, I need:____

Father, I ask that YOU:____

____

____

Lord, bless me that I may be a blessing. Give me Your heart for loving and serving others. Keep Your hand upon me. Keep me from all evil and harm, and let me cause harm to no one. Bind Satan that he have no power over me. All this I pray in subjection to your will and in the strong name of my Lord and Savior, Jesus Christ. Amen.

Godly Understanding

"Consider what I say, and may the Lord give you understanding in all things". 2 Timothy 2:2

> *"Give me understanding, and I shall keep Your law;*
> *Indeed, I shall observe it with my whole heart."*
> *Psalm 119:34*

Human understanding is a wonderful gift in many areas. With it, we have advanced remarkably in our understanding of health, wealth, and physical sciences. It is awesome to know that about 80% of today's scientific knowledge and understanding has been acquired in the last fifty years.

We can get any where in the world in a few hours. We can communicate with anyone anywhere instantly. Unfortunately, as our human knowledge and understanding have increased, godly understanding has decreased and the consequences are all around us.

A seemingly large, majority of people throughout the world have become wise in their own conceits and discarded faith in a Savior for faith in self and the world. Secular Humanism, which teaches that there is no God, that we are the captains of our fate, truth is relative and that there is no such thing as sin, has become the religion of choice in our schools and much of the World.

> *"But the wisdom that is from above is first pure, then peaceable, gentle, willing to yield, full of mercy and good fruits, without partiality and without hypocrisy."*
> *James 3:17*

We should not be surprised by this. God's Word tells us: "There is a way that seems right to a man, but its end is the way of death. (Proverbs 14:12). How much better to heed the exhortation of Proverbs 3:5: "Trust in the Lord with all your heart, and lean not on your own understanding. In all your ways acknowledge Him, and He will direct your paths."

Father, give me your Godly understanding of all that I should know and the strength of your Spirit to walk in your ways always. Amen

Taking it to the Lord...

How can I apply this truth?____

____

____

Father, I've come to worship and praise you! You are my:_________________________

____

I give you all Glory, Honor, and Praise O Lord!

Father, I am sorry that I have sinned by:____

Help me to repent. Cleanse me, strengthen me, restore me.

Father, THANK YOU for all your love, grace, mercy and blessings of life that you continually shower down upon me. Thank you especially for:

1.______________________________   2.______________________________

3.______________________________   4.______________________________

5.______________________________   6.______________________________

THANK YOU for answered prayers:_______________________________________

Father, I need:____

Father, I ask that YOU:____

____

____

Lord, bless me that I may be a blessing. Give me Your heart for loving and serving others. Keep Your hand upon me. Keep me from all evil and harm, and let me cause harm to no one. Bind Satan that he have no power over me. All this I pray in subjection to your will and in the strong name of my Lord and Savior, Jesus Christ. Amen.

Understanding of Humility

"Thus says the LORD God of the Hebrews: 'How long will you refuse to humble yourself before Me?"
Exodus 10:3

Pride is perhaps the number one sin problem affecting the human race. It is usually at the heart of our relational difficulties with God and with others.

"He does not forget the cry of the humble."
Psalm 9:12b

Our pride makes us self-centered instead of Christ Centered. We want to live our way instead of God's way. We respond to God's teaching with rebellion and willful disobedience. The Lust of the Flesh, whether it be sexual, material, or self-image related is always at work within us just waiting for the opportunity to take control.

Pride and the desire to exalt ourselves is as destructive in our relationships with others, as it is with our relationship with God.

Pride keeps us from admitting our mistakes and our share of the blame for disagreements and misunderstandings. Pride feeds our unforgiving spirit and fertilizes the seeds of bitterness that take root in unforgiveness. Pride makes us want God and others to submit to us and let us be in control.

"Therefore humble yourselves under the mighty hand of God, that He may exalt you in due time,"
1 Peter 5:6

Nothing grieves the Spirit of God more than the grace quenching unbridled pride of the children of God that fuels willful disobedience and rebellion within us.

Out Lord and Savior, Jesus Christ, gives us the antidote for pride. *"He humbled Himself and became obedient to the point of death, even the death of the cross."* (Philippians 2:8)

Father, by the power of your Spirit, help me to deal with my sinful pride and disobedience that I might grow into the fullness of Christ and abundance of your joy. Amen

Taking it to the Lord...

How can I apply this truth?____
____
____

Father, I've come to worship and praise you! You are my:____________________
____
I give you all Glory, Honor, and Praise O Lord!

Father, I am sorry that I have sinned by:________________________________
Help me to repent. Cleanse me, strengthen me, restore me.

Father, THANK YOU for all your love, grace, mercy and blessings of life that you continually shower down upon me. Thank you especially for:

1.______________________________   2.______________________________
3.______________________________   4.______________________________
5.______________________________   6.______________________________

THANK YOU for answered prayers:____
Father, I need:____
Father, I ask that YOU:____
____
____

Lord, bless me that I may be a blessing. Give me Your heart for loving and serving others. Keep Your hand upon me. Keep me from all evil and harm, and let me cause harm to no one. Bind Satan that he have no power over me. All this I pray in subjection to your will and in the strong name of my Lord and Savior, Jesus Christ. Amen.

True Treasure

**"There is desirable treasure, and oil in the dwelling of the wise, but a foolish man squanders it."
Proverbs 21:20**

What is the true treasure? For most, it's whatever we think will make us happy. I would be happy if only I had a nicer car, a nicer home, a nicer husband, a better job, a better appearance, one more drink, one more snort, etc. etc.

*"In the house of the righteous there is much treasure,"
Proverbs 15:6*

Lives are wrecked, homes are broken up, and the consequences of sin and misery multiply as we pursue the treasures of the flesh, the world, and the devil; and never experience the true treasure that comes only from a right relationship with God through faith in Jesus Christ.

It is only when we realize that we are happy because we are unconditionally loved, forever forgiven, and accepted just as we are; and that our lives have significance, meaning, and validation in Christ that we can be truly happy.

This is the living water that lets us thirst no more, that pours out an ocean of joy and overflowing cup of blessings within us which flow through us and into the lives of those around us as we become conduits of God's love.

*"Again, the kingdom of heaven is like treasure hidden in a field, which a man found and hid; and for joy over it he goes and sells all that he has and buys that field."
Matthew 13:44*

Are you living out a life of joy and peace from the true treasure of God's love in Christ? It is there for all believers who grow into the fullness of Christ and are conformed to His image.

Lord, help me to get my price tags lined up with your values. Let me not miss out on the greatest treasures of life found only in that close and personal love relationship with you. Amen

Taking it to the Lord...

How can I apply this truth?____

____

____

Father, I've come to worship and praise you! You are my:_______________________

____

I give you all Glory, Honor, and Praise O Lord!

Father, I am sorry that I have sinned by:_____________________________________

Help me to repent. Cleanse me, strengthen me, restore me.

Father, THANK YOU for all your love, grace, mercy and blessings of life that you continually shower down upon me. Thank you especially for:

1.______________________________   2.______________________________
3.______________________________   4.______________________________
5.______________________________   6.______________________________

THANK YOU for answered prayers:____

Father, I need:____

Father, I ask that YOU:____

____

____

____

Lord, bless me that I may be a blessing. Give me Your heart for loving and serving others. Keep Your hand upon me. Keep me from all evil and harm, and let me cause harm to no one. Bind Satan that he have no power over me. All this I pray in subjection to your will and in the strong name of my Lord and Savior, Jesus Christ. Amen.

Quiet Understanding

"The Lord your God in your midst, The Mighty One, will save; He will rejoice over you with gladness, He will quiet *you* with His love." Zephaniah 2:17a

Where shall we find peace in times of pressure? Where shall we find peace in times of doubt? How can we calm the storms of life?

The following passage speaks to these questions in a very real and personal way:

> *"Be still, and know that I am God; I will be exalted among the nations, I will be exalted in the earth!"*
> *Psalm 46:10*

"Then He arose and rebuked the wind, and said to the sea, "Peace, be still!" And the wind ceased and there was a great calm. But He said to them, "Why are you so fearful? How *is it* that you have no faith?" (Mark 4:39,40)

When our hope is anchored in the work of Jesus Christ on the Cross of Calvary we receive that quiet understanding that calms our troubled spirits and worried hearts.

The beloved hymn: "Be still my soul" sums up this "quiet understanding" that should be a treasure of our heart.   With the blessed assurance that God is on our side and our eternal life is secure, what need do we have to sweat or fret the cares of the world and the problems of life?

> *That you also aspire to lead a quiet life, to mind your own business, and to work with your own hands, as we commanded you,"*
> *1 Thessalonians 4:11*

With the quiet understanding giving us peace we can rejoice in our tribulations and know that they are conforming us into the image of Christ so that we can better Glorify God in the works that He has created us for in this life.

Father, by Your grace bless me with the comfort of Your Spirit that I may remain calm and secure during the storms of life. Amen

Taking it to the Lord...

How can I apply this truth?____

____

Father, I've come to worship and praise you! You are my:__________________________

____

I give you all Glory, Honor, and Praise O Lord!

Father, I am sorry that I have sinned by:_____________________________________

Help me to repent. Cleanse me, strengthen me, restore me.

Father, THANK YOU for all your love, grace, mercy and blessings of life that you continually shower down upon me. Thank you especially for:

1.______________________________   2.______________________________

3.______________________________   4.______________________________

5.______________________________   6.______________________________

THANK YOU for answered prayers:____

Father, I need:____

Father, I ask that YOU:____

____

____

Lord, bless me that I may be a blessing. Give me Your heart for loving and serving others. Keep Your hand upon me. Keep me from all evil and harm, and let me cause harm to no one. Bind Satan that he have no power over me. All this I pray in subjection to your will and in the strong name of my Lord and Savior, Jesus Christ. Amen.

Distorted Understanding

"And His mercy *is* on those who fear Him from generation to generation." Luke 1:50

Where did anyone ever get the idea that all our problems would be solved, that we would become perfect, or that we Christians are better than others when we accept Jesus Christ as our Savior?

> *"Be of good courage, And He shall strengthen your heart, All you who hope in the* LORD.*"*
> *Psalm 32:21*

While it is true that we receive forgiveness for all our sins, and the righteousness of Christ in God's sight, we should never let an unrealistic assumption that the Christian Life is a rose garden set us up for a big disappointment in times of trouble.

As long as we live in this sin sick world, in a flesh that is corrupted, and face the darts of Satan who goes around like a roaring lion seeking to destroy us, we can expect troubles. It is never a question of if, but only of when.

The good news is that when we enter into the faith relationship with Jesus Christ, we have all that we need to see us through these troubles. His all-sufficient grace will give us the strength to persevere through any difficulty. The fact that He is "our refuge and strength, a very present help in trouble" (Psalm 46.1) is not only a fact, but a promise to believers.

The fact that " we know that all things work together for good to those who love God, to those who are the called according to *His* purpose." (Romans 8:28) should empower us to rejoice through any trouble. The One who loved us enough to die for us certainly loves us enough to continue to mold us into His image and develop His character within us as he continues to sanctify us and make us more like Him every day of our life on the earth.

> *"For our light affliction, which is but for a moment, is working for us a far more exceeding and eternal weight of glory,"*
> *2 Corinthians 4:17*

We believers are not better than others, but thanks be to God we are so much better off because of who we are and what we have in Christ.

Father, thank you for the assurances of your Word, which we as believers can believe and bank on as we go through the trials of life. Amen

Taking it to the Lord...

How can I apply this truth?____

____

Father, I've come to worship and praise you! You are my:___________________________

____

I give you all Glory, Honor, and Praise O Lord!

Father, I am sorry that I have sinned by:___________________________________

Help me to repent. Cleanse me, strengthen me, restore me.

Father, THANK YOU for all your love, grace, mercy and blessings of life that you continually shower down upon me. Thank you especially for:

1.__________________________________   2._________________________________

3.__________________________________   4._________________________________

5.__________________________________   6._________________________________

THANK YOU for answered prayers:____

Father, I need:____

Father, I ask that YOU:____

____

____

Lord, bless me that I may be a blessing. Give me Your heart for loving and serving others. Keep Your hand upon me. Keep me from all evil and harm, and let me cause harm to no one. Bind Satan that he have no power over me. All this I pray in subjection to your will and in the strong name of my Lord and Savior, Jesus Christ. Amen.

Abiding Love

"But the anointing which you have received from Him abides in you, and you do not need that anyone teach you; but as the same anointing teaches you concerning all things, and is true, and is not a lie, and just as it has taught you, you will abide in Him.*"1 John 2:27**

God's love for us began before we were born and will abide or remain with us forever. As He called us into a salvation relationship with Him through the gospel; He also calls us into a day-by-day love relationship with Him where He abides in us and we abide in Him through the power of His Holy Spirit. His abiding love embraces every aspect of our being. He is *"our refuge and strength, a very present help in time of trouble."* He *"works all things for the good of those who love Him and who have been called according to his purpose."*

> *"He who dwells in the secret place of the Most High Shall abide under the shadow of the Almighty."*
> *Psalm 91.1*

We do not have to wait until we die and go to heaven to enjoy eternal life. The secret is to abide in Him through His Word and prayer so that we receive the heart of Christ and become fruitful in every good work.

From the time we are saved by faith until the time we see Him face to face in glory, He abides in us producing the fruit of His Spirit for us to bear as evidence that we are abiding in Him and submitting to the control of His Spirit in our lives.

> *"Then Jesus said to those Jews who believed Him, "If you abide in My word, you are My disciples indeed."*
> *John 8:31*

As we experience His abiding love we come to know Him not only as our forgiver, but as our *shield and defender,* the *giver of every good and perfect gift,* and our best friend and companion.

Father, thank you for your abiding love that nourishes me and sustains me daily as I abide in you. Amen

Taking it to the Lord...

How can I apply this truth?____

____

____

Father, I've come to worship and praise you! You are my:________________________________

____

I give you all Glory, Honor, and Praise O Lord!

Father, I am sorry that I have sinned by:____

Help me to repent. Cleanse me, strengthen me, restore me.

Father, THANK YOU for all your love, grace, mercy and blessings of life that you continually shower down upon me. Thank you especially for:

1._________________________________   2._________________________________
3._________________________________   4._________________________________
5._________________________________   6._________________________________

THANK YOU for answered prayers:____

Father, I need:____

Father, I ask that YOU:____

____

____

____

Lord, bless me that I may be a blessing. Give me Your heart for loving and serving others. Keep Your hand upon me. Keep me from all evil and harm, and let me cause harm to no one. Bind Satan that he have no power over me. All this I pray in subjection to your will and in the strong name of my Lord and Savior, Jesus Christ. Amen.

All Powerful Love

"Finally, be strong in the Lord and in the power of His might." Ephesians 6:10

The sovereign power of God is all around us. The heavens and earth declare His power and glory. The sun rises and sets at His pleasure. Only a fool says that there is no God.

> *"He has declared to His people the power of His works,"*
> *Psalm 111:6a*

We are all totally dependent upon God. Every breath that we take, every day that we live, is at His pleasure. There is strength and comfort in knowing that the God who was powerful enough to create the World and all that is in it is the God who is more than powerful enough to keep every promise that He has ever made to us.

There is no greater demonstration of God's powerful love than the life, death, and resurrection of Jesus Christ. The power of God to give eternal life to all who believe is also the power that gives strength to the weak, help to the helpless, hope to the hopeless, and love to the loveless.

God provides power for living and loving Him and our fellow man. He gives us the power to forgive, and to stand. He transforms us and renews us by the power of the Holy Spirit. He has given us the power to receive His wonderful gift of eternal life and the resurrection power of Jesus.

Just as there is no greater love than the love of God, there is no greater power than the power of God's love to change hearts, renew minds, and transform lives.

> *"Nor is He worshiped with men's hands, as though He needed anything, since He gives to all life, breath, and all things."*
> *Acts 17:24:25*

Father, my life is in your hands. By the power of your Spirit give me your daily outpouring of grace and mercy that I might live my life as a testimony to you. Amen

Taking it to the Lord...

How can I apply this truth?____
____
____

Father, I've come to worship and praise you! You are my:________________________________
____

I give you all Glory, Honor, and Praise O Lord!

Father, I am sorry that I have sinned by:____

Help me to repent. Cleanse me, strengthen me, restore me.

Father, THANK YOU for all your love, grace, mercy and blessings of life that you continually shower down upon me. Thank you especially for:

1.________________________________   2.________________________________
3.________________________________   4.________________________________
5.________________________________   6.________________________________

THANK YOU for answered prayers:____

Father, I need:____

Father, I ask that YOU:____
____
____

Lord, bless me that I may be a blessing. Give me Your heart for loving and serving others. Keep Your hand upon me. Keep me from all evil and harm, and let me cause harm to no one. Bind Satan that he have no power over me. All this I pray in subjection to your will and in the strong name of my Lord and Savior, Jesus Christ. Amen.

No Round Trip Tickets!

"And God will wipe away every tear from their eyes; there shall be no more death, nor sorrow, nor crying. There shall be no more pain, for the former things have passed away." Revelation 21:4

Did you ever wonder why there are no round trips, no exchanges, no refunds--on the trip to heaven or hell?

"For he remembered that they were merely mortal, gone in a moment like a breath of wind, never to return." Psalm 78:39 NLT

After God has given everyone ample opportunity to receive Him, the realization that some will never receive Him ends in the finality of death with no pardons and no reprieves.

Jesus Christ is the only one ever to get a round trip ticket, and He got 2 instead of one.

When Lazarus was told that he couldn't come back to warn his brothers, he was also told this very thing. If they wouldn't listen to the prophets, they wouldn't listen to Lazarus.

When people time after time resist the call of God and fail to open the door, the window of opportunity eventually closes and all hope is gone. People who put off the call do so at great peril. This is a limited time offer that can be withdrawn at any time either by death or by the return of Christ to claim His own. This is why we are warned time and time again to be ready.

The reason why there are no return tickets to heaven is very simple. There are no customers! The bliss and joy of heaven is going to be so great that it will blot out all sadness, heartaches, and suffering. We will not even think about wanting to go back to those we've left behind, but rather be thinking about how our great joy will be even greater when our loved ones come to join us.

"Now you have every spiritual gift you need as you eagerly wait for the return of our Lord Jesus Christ." 1 Corinthians 1:7 NLT

The important thing is that we purchase our ticket ASAP to avoid a sell out, and to get those reservations confirmed by the ticket agent Himself – the Holy Spirit, who will confirm us by sanctifying and cleansing us daily through the blood of the Lamb. Just make sure you don't take the wrong flight!

Father, I can't begin to even imagine the unspeakable joy of heaven, but I do know how to get there. Help me to share this wonderful knowledge with others. Amen

Taking it to the Lord...

How can I apply this truth?____

____

Father, I've come to worship and praise you! You are my:________________________________

____

I give you all Glory, Honor, and Praise O Lord!

Father, I am sorry that I have sinned by:____

Help me to repent. Cleanse me, strengthen me, restore me.

Father, THANK YOU for all your love, grace, mercy and blessings of life that you continually shower down upon me. Thank you especially for:

1.________________________________   2.________________________________

3.________________________________   4.________________________________

5.________________________________   6.________________________________

THANK YOU for answered prayers:____

Father, I need:____

Father, I ask that YOU:____

____

____

____

Lord, bless me that I may be a blessing. Give me Your heart for loving and serving others. Keep Your hand upon me. Keep me from all evil and harm, and let me cause harm to no one. Bind Satan that he have no power over me. All this I pray in subjection to your will and in the strong name of my Lord and Savior, Jesus Christ. Amen.

Chastening Love

And the God of all grace, who called you to his eternal glory in Christ, after you have suffered a little while, will himself restore you and make you strong, firm and steadfast. 1 Pet 5:10

Aren't you glad you have a God who loves you enough to do what ever it takes to get you back on the right track when you get "de-railed" by your flesh, the world, and Satan? Aren't you glad that "the author and perfecter" of your faith, loves you enough to discipline you when you need it?

"My son, do not despise the chastening of the LORD, Nor detest His correction;" Proverbs 3:11

Unlike some earthly fathers, God never disciplines out of anger or wrath, but always out of love. He not only knows, but He wants what's best for all of us. Unfortunately, our free will often lets us choose to walk in the flesh instead of the spirit, we allow the pride, anger, lust, jealousy, and all of the sins of the flesh to take control, and the consequences can be devastating.

We become "carnal Christians" infected with the leprosy of sin that harms not only us, but also those around us. We can be sure that God will discipline us in some manner when this happens.

How much better to enjoy the blessings of abiding in God, by submitting to His yoke of love and righteousness? We can avoid so much heartbreak and so much pain when we choose to trust and obey as an act of our free will, and to stand firm when temptation comes.

"For whom the LORD loves He chastens" Hebrews 12:6

Thanks be to God, that in his grace and mercy and in the resurrection power of His Spirit, He will do whatever it takes to bring us back into His sheepfold and restore us into that right relationship with Him

Father, thank you for loving me enough not only to die for me, but also enough to correct me and to keep me under the shelter of your wings. Amen

Taking it to the Lord...

How can I apply this truth?____
____
____

Father, I've come to worship and praise you! You are my:_________________________
____

I give you all Glory, Honor, and Praise O Lord!

Father, I am sorry that I have sinned by:_____________________________________

Help me to repent. Cleanse me, strengthen me, restore me.

Father, THANK YOU for all your love, grace, mercy and blessings of life that you continually shower down upon me. Thank you especially for:

1.___________________________________   2.___________________________________
3.___________________________________   4.___________________________________
5.___________________________________   6.___________________________________

THANK YOU for answered prayers:____
Father, I need:____
Father, I ask that YOU:____
____
____
____

Lord, bless me that I may be a blessing. Give me Your heart for loving and serving others. Keep Your hand upon me. Keep me from all evil and harm, and let me cause harm to no one. Bind Satan that he have no power over me. All this I pray in subjection to your will and in the strong name of my Lord and Savior, Jesus Christ. Amen.

Comforting Love

"For I will turn their mourning to joy, Will comfort them, and make them rejoice rather than sorrow."
Jeremiah 31:13b

The journey of life has often led us through a valley of tears. Tragedy, sorrow, and disappointment are swarming all around us, and usually sooner than later we are going to find them invading our lives and threatening to rob us of our joy and our peace.

> *"Let, I pray, Your merciful kindness be for my comfort,"*
> *Psalm 119:76*

These things do not come from God; they are the manifestation of the sinfulness of man and the sinfulness of the world in which we live. God in His Sovereignty may choose to allow what we perceive to be bad things to happen for our good and His glory, and often we are never going to fathom His ways.

What comfort there is in knowing that in Christ, we have a Savior who is well acquainted with sorrow and grief. He mourned. He was abandoned, rejected, mocked, scorned, abused, and even nailed to the Cross. In light of His experiences we can be sure that He knows exactly how we feel when we are suffering.

> *"Blessed be the God and Father of our Lord Jesus Christ, the Father of mercies and God of all comfort, [4]who comforts us in all our tribulation, that we may be able to comfort those who are in any trouble, with the comfort with which we ourselves are comforted by God."*
> *2 Corinthians 1:3. 4*

What consolation there is when, in our times of mourning and sorrow, we turn to our God's comforting love with which He comforts us, and comforts others through us.

Father, thank you for the strength of your Spirit, and the Comfort of your love in my times of tragedy, mourning, and sorrow. Help me to overcome my grief and depression with the assurance of your love and in the power of your presence. Amen

Taking it to the Lord...

How can I apply this truth?____

____

Father, I've come to worship and praise you! You are my:_______________________

____

I give you all Glory, Honor, and Praise O Lord!

Father, I am sorry that I have sinned by:____________________________________

Help me to repent. Cleanse me, strengthen me, restore me.

Father, THANK YOU for all your love, grace, mercy and blessings of life that you continually shower down upon me. Thank you especially for:

1._________________________________ 2._________________________________
3._________________________________ 4._________________________________
5._________________________________ 6._________________________________

THANK YOU for answered prayers:____

Father, I need:____

Father, I ask that YOU:____

____

____

____

Lord, bless me that I may be a blessing. Give me Your heart for loving and serving others. Keep Your hand upon me. Keep me from all evil and harm, and let me cause harm to no one. Bind Satan that he have no power over me. All this I pray in subjection to your will and in the strong name of my Lord and Savior, Jesus Christ. Amen.

Covenant Love

"Know therefore that the Lord your God is God; he is the faithful God, keeping his covenant of love to a thousand generations of those who love him and keep his commands." Deuteronomy 7:9

Since the beginning of time, God has established relationships with His people through sovereign pronouncements of purpose and intent.

> *"The covenant which He made with Abraham,*
> *And His oath to Isaac,*
> *And confirmed it to Jacob for a statute,*
> *To Israel as an everlasting covenant,"*
> *Psalm 105:9,10*

Human response has always been important in that obedience promises blessings, and disobedience promises discipline, but human failures have never been able to block the ultimate fulfillment of God's purpose and intent in making the covenant.

Jesus Christ as "*mediator of a new covenant, that those who are called may receive the promised eternal inheritance - now that he has died as a ransom to set them free from the sins committed under the first covenant*" (Heb 9:5) reflects the love of God in allowing us to enter into His presence with confidence through the perfect sacrifice of His Son.

How happy we can be in knowing that God is love, He created us in love and He has covenanted with us in Love, and fulfilled His covenant with us through Jesus Christ. For the first time since we were born under the curse of sin through the fall of Adam, through faith, we have a new life with *Christ in us, our hope of glory* (Col. 1:27). We have the enabling power of the Holy Spirit living within us to live free from the bondage of sin.

> *"And for this reason He is the Mediator of the new covenant,"*
> *Hebrews 9:15a*

Father, thank you for fulfilling your promise of a Savior so that I can be reconciled and enjoy a love relationship with You. Amen

Taking it to the Lord...

How can I apply this truth?____
____
____

Father, I've come to worship and praise you! You are my:_________________________________
____

I give you all Glory, Honor, and Praise O Lord!

Father, I am sorry that I have sinned by:____

Help me to repent. Cleanse me, strengthen me, restore me.

Father, THANK YOU for all your love, grace, mercy and blessings of life that you continually shower down upon me. Thank you especially for:

1.___________________________________   2.___________________________________
3.___________________________________   4.___________________________________
5.___________________________________   6.___________________________________

THANK YOU for answered prayers:____

Father, I need:____

Father, I ask that YOU:____
____
____

Lord, bless me that I may be a blessing. Give me Your heart for loving and serving others. Keep Your hand upon me. Keep me from all evil and harm, and let me cause harm to no one. Bind Satan that he have no power over me. All this I pray in subjection to your will and in the strong name of my Lord and Savior, Jesus Christ. Amen.

Everlasting Love

"For I am persuaded that neither death nor life, nor angels nor principalities nor powers, nor things present nor things to come, nor height nor depth, nor any other created thing, shall be able to separate us from the love of God which is in Christ Jesus our Lord." *Romans 8:37-39*

Everlasting is a long, long time! Our finite minds cannot comprehend infinity and eternity.

> *"For the LORD is good; His mercy is everlasting, and His truth endures to all generations."*
> *Psalm 100:5*

When we think of God as the Alpha and Omega, without beginning or end we begin to realize that both God and Eternity are timeless - existing from everlasting to everlasting. Isn't it comforting to know that we have an all powerful, all knowing, and ever present God who loves us with an everlasting love that transcends time and space; who promises us that He is with us always, that He will never leave nor forsake us?

We need to remember that our life on this earth is limited, and that the window of opportunity that God gives each of us to grow into the fullness of His Son is limited, and that we need to make the most of it by getting into an ever closer and growing relationship with His Son as He reveals himself through His Word.

> *"But whoever drinks of the water that I shall give him will never thirst. But the water that I shall give him will become in him a fountain of water springing up into everlasting life."*
> *John 4:14*

Eternal life does not begin when we die and go to heaven, but rather when we die to self and receive the everlasting love of God through faith in Jesus Christ.

Father, by the power of your Holy Spirit, which enabled me to confess you as Savior and Lord, let me grow in your grace and become more like you day by day. Amen

Taking it to the Lord...

How can I apply this truth?____

____

Father, I've come to worship and praise you! You are my:_________________

____

I give you all Glory, Honor, and Praise O Lord!

Father, I am sorry that I have sinned by:________________________________

Help me to repent. Cleanse me, strengthen me, restore me.

Father, THANK YOU for all your love, grace, mercy and blessings of life that you continually shower down upon me. Thank you especially for:

1.__________________________   2.__________________________

3.__________________________   4.__________________________

5.__________________________   6.__________________________

THANK YOU for answered prayers:__________________________________

Father, I need:____

Father, I ask that YOU:____

____

____

Lord, bless me that I may be a blessing. Give me Your heart for loving and serving others. Keep Your hand upon me. Keep me from all evil and harm, and let me cause harm to no one. Bind Satan that he have no power over me. All this I pray in subjection to your will and in the strong name of my Lord and Savior, Jesus Christ. Amen.

Unholy Presumption

"But those who obey God's word really do love him. That is the way to know whether or not we live in him." 1 John 2:1 NLT

The world takes its toll on all of us. Day after day, week after week, month after month, year after year we are barraged by sinful thoughts, sinful acts and sinful practices until we become callous and the power of these outrages against God to shock us becomes weaker and weaker.

"O God, you take no pleasure in wickedness; you cannot tolerate the slightest sin." Psalm 5:4 NLT

We make unholy presumptions that maybe these things are not so bad after all. We rationalize that every one's doing it. That it's only a movie…that it really doesn't matter. We appropriate low standards of conduct and morality so that we are no longer set apart as salt and light. We compromise our witness, give aid and comfort to the enemy and great sadness to God.

We always want to think about the Love, and grace and mercy of God, without thinking about the fact that God still hates sin and is angered by it. In His love, His wrath still falls, His chastening still occurs. Jesus' reaction to the moneychangers and the hypocrites shows that God's righteous indignation is real.

"And when people escape from the wicked ways of the world by learning about our Lord and Savior Jesus Christ and then get tangled up with sin and become its slave again, they are worse off than before." 2 Peter 2:16 NLT

He loves us as His dear children in whom He delights and wants to take pleasure. He gives us growth pills of prayer, Word and Sacrament that so that we grow strong in Him. He didn't make us to be willows bending and yielding with every breeze. He wants us to be mighty oaks standing firm against the storms.

When we see the stripes that were inflicted on Christ, the pain he suffered because of our sins, there is nothing trivial or casual about them. We should never fall into unholy presumption about sin.

Father, keep me ever mindful of the price Jesus had to pay for me, and let me live accordingly. Amen

Taking it to the Lord…

How can I apply this truth?____

____

____

Father, I've come to worship and praise you! You are my:____________________

____

I give you all Glory, Honor, and Praise O Lord!

Father, I am sorry that I have sinned by:__________________________________

Help me to repent. Cleanse me, strengthen me, restore me.

Father, THANK YOU for all your love, grace, mercy and blessings of life that you continually shower down upon me. Thank you especially for:

1._________________________________   2._________________________________

3._________________________________   4._________________________________

5._________________________________   6._________________________________

THANK YOU for answered prayers:____

Father, I need:____

Father, I ask that YOU:____

____

____

____

Lord, bless me that I may be a blessing. Give me Your heart for loving and serving others. Keep Your hand upon me. Keep me from all evil and harm, and let me cause harm to no one. Bind Satan that he have no power over me. All this I pray in subjection to your will and in the strong name of my Lord and Savior, Jesus Christ. Amen.

Was I Worth It?

"You see, at just the right time, when we were still powerless, Christ died for the ungodly. Very rarely will anyone die for a righteous man, though for a good man someone might possibly dare to die. But God demonstrates his own love for us in this: While we were still sinners, Christ died for us." Romans 5:6-8 NIV

"Saving Private Ryan" was one of the most brutal movies ever made before "The Passion of Christ" came to the screen. The opening showed private Ryan in the sunset of life, with his wife, children, and grand children visiting the grave of Captain who had died finding him and saving him during World War II.

> *" I will offer to You the sacrifice of thanksgiving, and will call upon the name of the LORD."*
> *Psalm 116:17 NLT*

Captain Miller often said and felt: "this guy had better be worth it" as he saw men dying all around him, and he himself in "Saving Private Ryan.

Anyone who has ever seen or will ever see "The Passion of Christ" will have the price of the pain and suffering Christ bore for us embedded in their minds as never before, and will be moved "try to be worth it" by living a life fully pleasing to God.

When we stand before God at the great white throne of judgment and give account of the stewardship of the life He died to give us, his "well done, though good and faithful servant", is the only validation that we will ever get affirming that we have lived a life pleasing to Him.

The truth is that no, we certainly were not worth dying for, and it was only by the grace of God that He loved us enough to come live in perfect righteousness and goodness so that He could die to buy us eternal life by his blood.

The question that we all need to ponder is how can we respond to this "greater love" and priceless gift of eternal life that we have received. Only one of the healed lepers came to give thanks.

> *"You do not belong to yourself, for God bought you with a high price. So you must honor God with your body."*
> *1 Corinthians 6:20 NLT*

Should we not, at the very minimum, strive to live a life fully pleasing to God that might make him at least feel that he didn't die in vain.

Father, help me to always remember what I cost Your Son, and that I can never be worthy, but should always be thankful. Amen

Taking it to the Lord...

How can I apply this truth?____

____

Father, I've come to worship and praise you! You are my:_______________________

____

I give you all Glory, Honor, and Praise O Lord!

Father, I am sorry that I have sinned by:___________________________________

Help me to repent. Cleanse me, strengthen me, restore me.

Father, THANK YOU for all your love, grace, mercy and blessings of life that you continually shower down upon me. Thank you especially for:

1.____________________________________   2.____________________________________

3.____________________________________   4.____________________________________

5.____________________________________   6.____________________________________

THANK YOU for answered prayers:____

Father, I need:____

Father, I ask that YOU:____

____

____

Lord, bless me that I may be a blessing. Give me Your heart for loving and serving others. Keep Your hand upon me. Keep me from all evil and harm, and let me cause harm to no one. Bind Satan that he have no power over me. All this I pray in subjection to your will and in the strong name of my Lord and Savior, Jesus Christ. Amen.

'Tis the Season

"I have told you this so that you will be filled with my joy. Yes, your joy will overflow!" John 15:11 NLT

Joy is never out of season for the believer. It is the inheritance and the promise of all who claim the name of Christian. All of this joy begins when God, in His love, came down to be born as a babe in Bethlehem. The glad tidings of great joy are not just an empty promise.

"Sing a new song to the LORD, for he has done wonderful deeds." Psalm 98:1 NLT

With this all being true, why is it that the joy of Christmas is missing in the lives of so many people? Why is depression so widespread and suicides so much more prevalent during the Christmas holiday season?

For many, it is the ghosts of Christmases past and loss of loved ones who shared our joy that cause our sadness. For others it is the loss of innocence that time and sins have taken away. The financial stress of trying to meet everyone's expectations for gifts and how we will pay for them takes its toll.

I personally suspect that Satan gets so upset over the coming of the one who brought real peace and joy to the world that he unleashes his distractions of doubt, guilt, discontent and depression to rob as many as he can of the joy of Christmas.

Christmas is not the end of anything, but the beginning of everything that brings abundant joy into the lives of God's children. Only when we focus on Who Christmas is all about, instead of what the world would turn it into, can we really know the joy of the season.

Jesus' joy is ours when we abide in Him. It is a joy for all seasons, and for all circumstances. It is our strength and our peace. When life seems unfair, our hearts are broken, and we have only God's promise that He works all things for our good to cling to. When we respond in the joy of the Lord, good things will happen.

"I bring you good news of great joy for everyone!" Luke 2:10

Father, fill me with your joy this Christmas and every day of my life. Amen

Taking it to the Lord...

How can I apply this truth?____

____

____

Father, I've come to worship and praise you! You are my:_________________________

____

I give you all Glory, Honor, and Praise O Lord!

Father, I am sorry that I have sinned by:_______________________________________

Help me to repent. Cleanse me, strengthen me, restore me.

Father, THANK YOU for all your love, grace, mercy and blessings of life that you continually shower down upon me. Thank you especially for:

1.____________________________________   2.____________________________________

3.____________________________________   4.____________________________________

5.____________________________________   6.____________________________________

THANK YOU for answered prayers:____

Father, I need:____

Father, I ask that YOU:____

____

____

____

Lord, bless me that I may be a blessing. Give me Your heart for loving and serving others. Keep Your hand upon me. Keep me from all evil and harm, and let me cause harm to no one. Bind Satan that he have no power over me. All this I pray in subjection to your will and in the strong name of my Lord and Savior, Jesus Christ. Amen.

When Nobody's Looking

"¹O Lord, You have searched me and known me. You know my sitting down and my rising up; you understand my thought afar off. You comprehend my path and my lying down, and are acquainted with all my ways." Psalm 139:1-3

God knows us better than we know ourselves. We can deceive others, and even deny, rationalize and deceive ourselves, but we can never deceive God.   We cannot escape from His presence. All the secret thoughts and deeds are not hidden from God. What a scary thought!

> *"God would surely have known it, for he knows the secrets of every heart." Psalm 44:21*

The most amazing thing about amazing grace is that in spite of knowing everything we have ever done and will ever do, of everything we should have done and didn't, God still loves us just as we are.

A lot of times we are so overcome with guilt and shame we cannot love ourselves, but God still loves us. We abuse the grace of God so often and so terribly it is inconceivable that through it all, God still loves us.

All we have to do is look at the prodigal son, at Peter, Paul, David, and host of other heroes of the faith and we will realize that God forgives and forgets and gives a glad welcome back to all those who have washed their sins in the blood of the lamb by receiving Jesus Christ as their personal Savior.

> *"A good man out of the good treasure of his heart brings forth good; and an evil man out of the evil treasure of his heart brings forth evil." Luke 6:45*

While God not only loves us just as we are, He loves us too much to let us stay that way. He gives us His Spirit to strengthen us, His Word to guide us. He gives us a new heart with a new desire to hate the things that He hates and to love and do the things that He loves. He even accomplishes His purposes through us, and makes us conduits of His love to others, even when we feel that nobody else is looking and that nobody else cares.

Lord, let me use the knowledge that you are looking over my shoulder give me a keen conscience and a great desire to live a life fully pleasing to you. Amen

Taking it to the Lord...

How can I apply this truth?____
____
____

Father, I've come to worship and praise you! You are my:_______________________
____

I give you all Glory, Honor, and Praise O Lord!

Father, I am sorry that I have sinned by:___________________________________

Help me to repent. Cleanse me, strengthen me, restore me.

Father, THANK YOU for all your love, grace, mercy and blessings of life that you continually shower down upon me. Thank you especially for:

1.________________________________   2.________________________________
3.________________________________   4.________________________________
5.________________________________   6.________________________________

THANK YOU for answered prayers:____
Father, I need:____
Father, I ask that YOU:____
____
____
____

Lord, bless me that I may be a blessing. Give me Your heart for loving and serving others. Keep Your hand upon me. Keep me from all evil and harm, and let me cause harm to no one. Bind Satan that he have no power over me. All this I pray in subjection to your will and in the strong name of my Lord and Savior, Jesus Christ. Amen.

Do You Love Me?

"If you want to be my follower you must love me more than your own father and mother, wife and children, brothers and sisters—yes, more than your own life." John 14:26 NLT

It's pretty easy for believers to answer the famous Evangelism Explosion questions of "If you were to die tonight are you sure you would go to heaven?", and "if you were to die tonight and God should ask you 'why should I let you into my heaven?'". Although it is amazing how many Christians who have gone to church and Sunday School all their lives answer the second question based on their performance, instead of Jesus Christ's death on the cross.

> *"For he understands how weak we are; He knows we are only dust."*
> *Psalm 103:4*

It's a little tougher to answer "if you were ever arrested for being a Christian, would there be enough evidence to convict you?" This convicting question points out the wide gap between talking the talk and walking the walk, and the truth of James assertion that "faith without works is dead." (James 2:20)

The toughest question of all is the question Jesus asked Peter three times: "Do you love me?" Before we get all bent out of shape as Peter did when Jesus asked him the question three times, we might first review what God says about loving Him. *"If you love your father or mother more than you love me, you are not worthy of being mine;" Matthew 10:37). "If you love me, obey my commandments." (John 14:15) "for the Father himself loves you dearly because you love me and believe that I came from God." (John 16:27) "But I have this complaint against you. You don't love me, or each other as you did at first! Look how far you have fallen from your first love!" (Revelation 2:4)*

> *"He said to him the third time, "Simon, son of Jonah, do you love Me?" Peter was grieved because He said to him the third time, "Do you love Me?"*
> *John 21: 17*

Jesus Himself equates loving Him with all these things plus whether we feed His sheep, or whether we follow Him. When we consider Jesus' words before we answer this question, we are humbled and ashamed that we do not, have not, and will not always love God as He says we should.

The Good News is that in spite of our failures to love and obey God as we should, He still loves us, forgives us, and accepts us just as we are as He continues to mold us into the image of His Son so that we can really love Him as we should. **Father, it is saddening to have to admit that I don't love You as I should. Forgive me and strengthen me by the power of your Spirit that I might love you more. Amen**

Taking it to the Lord...

How can I apply this truth?____

____

____

Father, I've come to worship and praise you! You are my:___________________

____

I give you all Glory, Honor, and Praise O Lord!

Father, I am sorry that I have sinned by:_________________________________

Help me to repent. Cleanse me, strengthen me, restore me.

Father, THANK YOU for all your love, grace, mercy and blessings of life that you continually shower down upon me. Thank you especially for:

1.__________________________________   2.__________________________________

3.__________________________________   4.__________________________________

5.__________________________________   6.__________________________________

THANK YOU for answered prayers:____

Father, I need:____

Father, I ask that YOU:____

____

Lord, bless me that I may be a blessing. Give me Your heart for loving and serving others. Keep Your hand upon me. Keep me from all evil and harm, and let me cause harm to no one. Bind Satan that he have no power over me. All this I pray in subjection to your will and in the strong name of my Lord and Savior, Jesus Christ. Amen.

No Vacancy

"And she brought forth her first born Son, and wrapped Him in swaddling cloths, and laid Him in a manger, because there was no room for them in the inn." Luke 2:7

It is no fun to be on the road late at night, worn out from a long trip, and no place to stay. For those of us who have been there and done that, we can better relate to Joseph's predicament in trying to find some place to spend the night.

> *"Because You have been my help, therefore in the shadow of Your wings I will rejoice."*
> *Psalm 63:7*

Most all of His life on earth and up to this very day, Jesus still has the same problem.

The religious leaders of the day were so self absorbed in religion that they had no room for God when He came calling. Jesus stands at the door and knocks today, and many will not even open the door.

Today, the preoccupation with Christmas preparations takes up so much of our time, talents, and resources, leaves little or no room for the real reason for the season.

The world seems to be doing its best to see that there is no room for Christ at Christmas. His birthday can no longer be celebrated in our schools. He has been X'd out and reduced to Xmas in many circles. He has been taken out of the equation in too many quarters.

How about you? After all the shopping till you drop, out decorating the neighbors, and partying in the wrong places, have you any room for Jesus in the Inn of your heart?

Have the "glad tidings of great joy" become the sad tidings of great debt? Is this the time to pray: "restore unto me the joy of my salvation."

> *"For out of the abundance of the heart his mouth speaks."*
> *Luke 6:45*

Is this the time for a spiritual house cleaning to make more room in our hearts for the one who came to make room in heaven for us?

Father, help me to be sure to make plenty room in my heart for you this Christmas and every day of my life. Amen

Taking it to the Lord...

How can I apply this truth?____

____

____

Father, I've come to worship and praise you! You are my:_________________________________

____

I give you all Glory, Honor, and Praise O Lord!

Father, I am sorry that I have sinned by:____

Help me to repent. Cleanse me, strengthen me, restore me.

Father, THANK YOU for all your love, grace, mercy and blessings of life that you continually shower down upon me. Thank you especially for:

1.__________________________________   2.__________________________________
3.__________________________________   4.__________________________________
5.__________________________________   6.__________________________________

THANK YOU for answered prayers:____

Father, I need:____

Father, I ask that YOU:____

____

____

____

Lord, bless me that I may be a blessing. Give me Your heart for loving and serving others. Keep Your hand upon me. Keep me from all evil and harm, and let me cause harm to no one. Bind Satan that he have no power over me. All this I pray in subjection to your will and in the strong name of my Lord and Savior, Jesus Christ. Amen.

What Can I Give the One Who Has Everything?

**"The LORD is more pleased when we do what is just and right than when we give him sacrifices."
Proverbs 21:3 NLT**

Somewhere along the way of life, the idea of gift giving has gotten out of whack. The wise men certainly knew who the recipient of Christmas gifts should be. We should know that Christmas is about God's gift to us, and our gift to God.

> *"What can I give back to GOD for the blessings he's poured out on me?"
> Psalm 116:12 MSG*

As nice as it is to shower gifts upon family and friends, and to be the recipients of these gifts, it is a lot nicer to shower gifts upon the One Who came to die so that we wouldn't have to, the one who brings us peace, joy, and the comfort of His love and the assurance of eternal life.

Since God owns it all, it's impossible to give Him what He already owns. There are, however, many things that God has given us a free will to give or withhold, and these are the things that will give God a truly Merry Christmas

First of all, we can give Him our hearts! When we give our hearts, we give Him the gift of obedience and submission to His expressed will for our lives and begin doing what brings Him pleasure.

Next we need to give the gift of forgiveness to anyone who has hurt or offended us.

> *"Then the King will say, 'I'm telling the solemn truth: Whenever you did one of these things to someone overlooked or ignored, that was me—you did it to me.'"
> Matthew 25:36 MSG*

After these are right, those little "in-as-much-as" like loving and ministering to the sick, the hungry, the lonely, and the prisoners give us the opportunity to be the only Jesus that many will ever see. These are the things that turn our thanksgiving into thanksliving.

May our joy in the Lord and our salvation be the joy of Christmas, and every day of our lives.

Father, don't let me get caught up in the glitter and tinsel and miss the real joy of Christmas. Amen

Taking it to the Lord...

How can I apply this truth?____

____

Father, I've come to worship and praise you! You are my:________________________

____

I give you all Glory, Honor, and Praise O Lord!

Father, I am sorry that I have sinned by:______________________________________

Help me to repent. Cleanse me, strengthen me, restore me.

Father, THANK YOU for all your love, grace, mercy and blessings of life that you continually shower down upon me. Thank you especially for:

1.______________________________   2.__________________________________

3.______________________________   4.__________________________________

5.______________________________   6.__________________________________

THANK YOU for answered prayers:____

Father, I need:____

Father, I ask that YOU:____

____

____

____

Lord, bless me that I may be a blessing. Give me Your heart for loving and serving others. Keep Your hand upon me. Keep me from all evil and harm, and let me cause harm to no one. Bind Satan that he have no power over me. All this I pray in subjection to your will and in the strong name of my Lord and Savior, Jesus Christ. Amen.

Good Tidings of Great Joy

"Peace I leave with you, My peace I give to you; not as the world gives do I give. Let not your heart be troubled." John 14:27

Peace is a word of many connotations. In terms of strife between countries and peoples, it is sometimes a very rare condition.

> *"GOD's about to pronounce his people well, the holy people he loves so much, so they'll never again live like fools. You have taken away all Your wrath; You have turned from the fierceness of Your anger."*
> *Psalm 85:7 MSG*

The "peace on earth good will towards men" of Christmas is the greatest gift that we have ever received. We should be celebrating it and rejoicing in it not only on December 15, but 24/7-365+!

Peace is the sense of well being and completeness that comes only from the manifestation of God and His presence in our lives. God came as the babe in the manger to reconcile us sinners back to Him and His righteousness and give us this peace with Him through the reconciliation of the Cross.

Peace is being rightly related with God and with each other. It is what the great commandment is all about!

God's peace surpasses all human understanding. It is experienced inwardly by all believers It embodies freedom from fear, worry, and even sin itself. It includes security… joy… mercy…. Grace…love….life, and righteousness. The peace of Christmas is a fruit of the Spirit – a part of the full armor of God.

> *"For He Himself is our peace, who has made both one, and has broken down the middle wall of separation, having abolished in His flesh the enmity,"*
> *Ephesians 2:14,15a*

This peace becomes a reality in our lives as we express this inward peace outwardly in the way live and the way we love others.

May you be filled to overflowing with this peace and the great joy that only having this peace can give. Merry Christmas!

Father, thank you for the blessed assurance of your love and salvation that is mine in Christ, and which gives me your peace. Amen

Taking it to the Lord…

How can I apply this truth?____

____

____

Father, I've come to worship and praise you! You are my:_______________________

____

I give you all Glory, Honor, and Praise O Lord!

Father, I am sorry that I have sinned by:_____________________________________

Help me to repent. Cleanse me, strengthen me, restore me.

Father, THANK YOU for all your love, grace, mercy and blessings of life that you continually shower down upon me. Thank you especially for:

1.___________________________________ 2.___________________________________

3.___________________________________ 4.___________________________________

5.___________________________________ 6.___________________________________

THANK YOU for answered prayers:____

Father, I need:____

Father, I ask that YOU:____

____

____

Lord, bless me that I may be a blessing. Give me Your heart for loving and serving others. Keep Your hand upon me. Keep me from all evil and harm, and let me cause harm to no one. Bind Satan that he have no power over me. All this I pray in subjection to your will and in the strong name of my Lord and Savior, Jesus Christ. Amen.

Abiding Brings Fruitfulness

"You did not choose Me, but I chose you and appointed you that you should go and bear fruit, and *that* your fruit should remain," (John 15:16a)

It is a very sobering thought to consider which, if any, of our fruits will remain after the "wood, hay, and stubble" of our lives has been burned away.

> *"They shall still bear fruit in old age; They shall be fresh and flourishing."*
> **Psalm 92:13**

To realize *"For we are His workmanship, created in Christ Jesus for good works, which God prepared beforehand that we should walk in them." Ephesians 2:10* make James statement that *"Thus also faith by itself, if it does not have works, is dead" James 2:17* very convicting.

Although salvation is a gift which we receive by faith, *("For by grace you have been saved through faith, and that not of yourselves; it is the gift of God, [9]not of works, lest anyone should boast" (Ephesians 2:8,9)*, the call to salvation is also a call to fruitfulness which we dare not ignore.

> *"If anyone's work which he has built on it endures, he will receive a reward. If anyone's work is burned, he will suffer loss; but he himself will be saved, yet so as through fire."*
> **1 Corinthians 3:13,14**

Our response to the Love of God that is ours in Christ Jesus, should always be to show our love for Him by loving others and growing into the fullness of Christ by doing the "good works" for which he created us.

Whether it is obeying the great commandment or great commission, our fruitfulness will increase as we abide in the Christ.

Lord, fill me with the knowledge of your will with all wisdom and spiritual understanding, that I might lead a life fully pleasing to you and abounding in good works. Amen

Taking it to the Lord...

How can I apply this truth?____

____

Father, I've come to worship and praise you! You are my:_______________________________

____

I give you all Glory, Honor, and Praise O Lord!

Father, I am sorry that I have sinned by:____

Help me to repent. Cleanse me, strengthen me, restore me.

Father, THANK YOU for all your love, grace, mercy and blessings of life that you continually shower down upon me. Thank you especially for:

1.____________________________________   2.____________________________________

3.____________________________________   4.____________________________________

5.____________________________________   6.____________________________________

THANK YOU for answered prayers:____

Father, I need:____

Father, I ask that YOU:____

____

____

____

Lord, bless me that I may be a blessing. Give me Your heart for loving and serving others. Keep Your hand upon me. Keep me from all evil and harm, and let me cause harm to no one. Bind Satan that he have no power over me. All this I pray in subjection to your will and in the strong name of my Lord and Savior, Jesus Christ. Amen.

Grace Abuse

"What shall we say then? Shall we continue in sin that grace may abound? Certainly not! How shall we who died to sin live any longer in it." Romans 6:1, 2

The grace of God has not only brought us salvation, but it has bought us freedom! For the first time, we have the power within us to live in freedom from not only the penalty of sin, but from the power of sin.

> *"Remember me, O Lord, with the favor You have toward Your people."*
> *Psalm 106:4*

When we experience the new birth through faith in Jesus Christ, we die to sin and become alive in Christ. Although sin still abounds in this world and in our flesh, the grace of God much more abounds in our spirit and we are free to live in the freedom of our new life in Christ.

Although our God is long suffering and patient, how can we think that our profession of faith we made years ago is all we need when there is absolutely no corroborating evidence in the way we live our lives? James tells us: *"But be doers of the word, and not hearers only, deceiving yourselves. For if anyone is a hearer of the word and not a doer, he is like a man observing his natural face in a mirror; for he observes himself, goes away, and immediately forgets what kind of man he was. But he who looks into the perfect law of liberty and continues in it, and is not a forgetful hearer but a doer of the work, this one will be blessed in what he does."* (James 1:21-25)

We sometimes, in our freedom, allow our flesh to take control and cause us to fall into sin momentarily. We deal with this by confession and repentance and by going on. But we should never abuse the grace of God by willfully choosing to sin as though we had a license. The excuse that "I am just a sinner and can't help it" will no longer cut it.

> *"And having been set free from sin, you became slaves of righteousness."*
> *Romans 6:18*

In Christ, we are saints who have been set free from bondage to sin. The sooner we start living like we believe this, the more abundant our lives will become.

Father, keep me ever mindful that Your grace is not cheap, that it cost you the life of Your own dear Son. Let me never abuse it. Amen

Taking it to the Lord...

How can I apply this truth?____

____

Father, I've come to worship and praise you! You are my:_________________________________

____

I give you all Glory, Honor, and Praise O Lord!

Father, I am sorry that I have sinned by:____

Help me to repent. Cleanse me, strengthen me, restore me.

Father, THANK YOU for all your love, grace, mercy and blessings of life that you continually shower down upon me. Thank you especially for:

1._________________________________   2._________________________________
3._________________________________   4._________________________________
5._________________________________   6._________________________________

THANK YOU for answered prayers:____

Father, I need:____

Father, I ask that YOU:____

____

____

Lord, bless me that I may be a blessing. Give me Your heart for loving and serving others. Keep Your hand upon me. Keep me from all evil and harm, and let me cause harm to no one. Bind Satan that he have no power over me. All this I pray in subjection to your will and in the strong name of my Lord and Savior, Jesus Christ. Amen.

Get to Work!

"All good athletes train hard. They do it for a gold medal that tarnishes and fades. You're after one that's gold eternally." 1 Corinthians 9:24 MSG

Whether in athletics, music, or any other area of life, people seem to rise up from nowhere to fame and fortune.

"Reverence for the LORD is the foundation of true wisdom. The rewards of wisdom come to all who obey him."
Psalm 111:10 NLT

More often than not, this "no where" has been a training ground of diligence in studying, practicing, or training. The great ones have self discipline and discipline to go with their talent and have worked hard to excel.

The ad that claimed "we will sell no wine before it's time" is a reminder that time is an essential in seasoning or perfecting. There is a saying in racehorse training circles that if you don't take your time in training, injuries and breakdowns will make you wish you had.

The Bible is full of examples of the importance of laying a good foundation for buildings and for faith. Time and time again, Scripture tells of the importance of training children in Scripture and the way that they should walk.

.   St. Paul admonished Timothy *to "Do your best to present yourself to God as one approved, a workman who does not need to be ashamed and who correctly handles the word of truth." (2 Timothy 2:15 NIV)*

"It is by our actions that we know we are living in the truth, so we will be confident when we stand before the Lord,"
1 John 3:19 NLT

While we receive the gift of salvation and do nothing to earn it, we will be held accountable for what we do with this gift.

We can bury it in the ground and wait for heaven fruitlessly, or we can respond by loving the God Who loved us enough to die for us enough to live for Him and to grow into the fullness of His Son.

Father, in the power of the Holy Spirit let me exercise due diligence, discipline, and perseverance in living for You. Amen

Taking it to the Lord...

How can I apply this truth?____
____
____

Father, I've come to worship and praise you! You are my:_________________________________
____

I give you all Glory, Honor, and Praise O Lord!

Father, I am sorry that I have sinned by:____

Help me to repent. Cleanse me, strengthen me, restore me.

Father, THANK YOU for all your love, grace, mercy and blessings of life that you continually shower down upon me. Thank you especially for:

1._____________________________________   2._____________________________________
3._____________________________________   4._____________________________________
5._____________________________________   6._____________________________________

THANK YOU for answered prayers:____

Father, I need:____

Father, I ask that YOU:____
____
____

Lord, bless me that I may be a blessing. Give me Your heart for loving and serving others. Keep Your hand upon me. Keep me from all evil and harm, and let me cause harm to no one. Bind Satan that he have no power over me. All this I pray in subjection to your will and in the strong name of my Lord and Savior, Jesus Christ. Amen.

Forgiving Love

"This is my blood of the covenant that is poured out for many for the forgiveness of sins. " Mathew 26:28

The love of God in sacrificing his only begotten Son for the forgiveness of our sins is the very heart of the "good news".

> *"Bless the LORD, O my soul, And forget not all His benefits:*
> *³Who forgives your iniquities,"*
> *Psalm 103:2*

It is really hard to accept sometimes the fact that God is more willing to forgive than we are to be forgiven. There should never be any lingering guilt over confessed and repented sins. God covered them with the blood of His very own son on the cross of Calvary, and we dare not forget that God's love is a forgiving love.

The fact that He not only forgives, but that He forgets is foreign to our human nature and understanding of the world. The world says: "get even" the Word says: "If you forgive men when they sin against you, your heavenly Father will also forgive you. But if you do not forgive men their sins, your Father will not forgive your sins." Matthew 6:14

> *"For I will be merciful to their unrighteousness, and their sins and their lawless deeds I will remember no more."*
> *Hebrews 9:12*

Just as we have freely received salvation and the forgiveness of our sins, we are admonished to freely give forgiveness to others. It is not an option, but a command.

Knowing the forgiveness that we are going to need on judgment day, how can we even think of harboring an unforgiving spirit that will be held against us when our own forgiveness is at stake. Let us never choke on the fruit of an unforgiving spirit that robs us of our joy and poisons our relationship with God.

Father forgive me for my un-forgiveness. By the power of your Spirit take away all my anger and resentment against anyone who has ever wronged me or offended me in any way so that I may be forgiven. Amen

Taking it to the Lord...

How can I apply this truth?____

____

____

Father, I've come to worship and praise you! You are my:_________________________________

____

I give you all Glory, Honor, and Praise O Lord!

Father, I am sorry that I have sinned by:____

Help me to repent. Cleanse me, strengthen me, restore me.

Father, THANK YOU for all your love, grace, mercy and blessings of life that you continually shower down upon me. Thank you especially for:

1.____________________________________   2.____________________________________

3.____________________________________   4.____________________________________

5.____________________________________   6.____________________________________

THANK YOU for answered prayers:____

Father, I need:____

Father, I ask that YOU:____

____

____

Lord, bless me that I may be a blessing. Give me Your heart for loving and serving others. Keep Your hand upon me. Keep me from all evil and harm, and let me cause harm to no one. Bind Satan that he have no power over me. All this I pray in subjection to your will and in the strong name of my Lord and Savior, Jesus Christ. Amen.

Fulfilling Love

"If you really keep the royal law found in Scripture, Love your neighbor as yourself, you are doing right." James 2:8 (NIV)

When Jesus Christ lived the perfect life and became the unblemished sacrifice, he fulfilled the requirements of the law for all who come to Him in faith.

"He will fulfill the desire of those who fear Him;" Psalm 145:19

This fulfilling love was not easy, and only God, Whose love is perfect, could ever have decided to come in the flesh to fill the righteous demands of the law and die to fulfill it, so that we would not have to.

The law still serves as a mirror for our sin, guides us on how we should live our lives, and serves as a curb to help keep us from disobeying God, but no longer are we chained to the grave clothes of the law that never saved anyone.

We are now free to live in the power of the Holy Spirit and to bear the fruit of the Spirit that He produces in us, no longer in bondage to sin and disobedience.

"Owe no one anything except to love one another, for he who loves another has fulfilled the law." Romans 13:8

As the love, grace, mercy, and forgiveness of God that is ours in Christ flows into us by the power of His Spirit, we want to pass it on to our neighbors. We will no longer have to worry about keeping the commandments of the old law toward our neighbors that says do them no harm; but we now have the God given power to love them and do good to them as opposed to simply doing them no harm. As we have freely received, we can freely give the love of God to our neighbors.

Father, let me love others as you love me, and let the New Covenant of Grace live in me and through me as I seek to fulfill your command that I love you and love others in the power of your Spirit. Amen

Taking it to the Lord...

How can I apply this truth?____

____

____

Father, I've come to worship and praise you! You are my:_____________________________

____

I give you all Glory, Honor, and Praise O Lord!

Father, I am sorry that I have sinned by:____

Help me to repent. Cleanse me, strengthen me, restore me.

Father, THANK YOU for all your love, grace, mercy and blessings of life that you continually shower down upon me. Thank you especially for:

1.__________________________________   2.__________________________________

3.__________________________________   4.__________________________________

5.__________________________________   6.__________________________________

THANK YOU for answered prayers:____

Father, I need:____

Father, I ask that YOU:____

____

____

Lord, bless me that I may be a blessing. Give me Your heart for loving and serving others. Keep Your hand upon me. Keep me from all evil and harm, and let me cause harm to no one. Bind Satan that he have no power over me. All this I pray in subjection to your will and in the strong name of my Lord and Savior, Jesus Christ. Amen.

Healing Love

"He himself bore our sins in his body on the tree, so that we might die to sins and live for righteousness; for by his wounds you have been healed." 1 Peter 2:23 (NIV)

No wonder Jesus is often referred to as the "Great Physician". During his earthly ministry, He healed the lame,

> *"O LORD my God, I cried out to You, And You healed me. Psalm 30:2*

the sick and the blind and He does the same today. Whether working through a doctor, a medication, or by supernatural intervention the miracles of physical and emotional healing are all around us.

One of the great tragedies of the Christian life are the well meaning, but misinformed believers who proclaim the "name it and claim it philosophy" not only for finances but for healing.

How many people do your know who have been prayed over and told that they were healed only to be dead a short time later. The cruelest thing of all in these situations is to then say that person wasn't healed because their faith wasn't strong enough.

We often sometimes forget that death is the ultimate healing and fail to consider that "Father knows best" when this is the kind of healing experienced. For the believer, physical death is only a door that we are all going to have to pass through whether early or late in life.

Jesus continues to heal the broken hearted. He is there through all our turmoil and trials of abusive and broken relationships, failures, and betrayals that leave us in depression and despair. Just as he heard David's cry and answered him; He will do the same for us when we go to him in prayer.

> *"The chastisement for our peace was upon Him, And by His stripes we are healed." Isaiah 53:5b*

What a privilege is ours to have the healing love of the Father through our faith relationship with the Son, and the peace and comfort of the Spirit. No matter what trial we are going through, the "Great Physician" is always at our side.

Father, thank you for all of the physical, emotional, and spiritual healing you have already given in my life, and for all that you are going to give until that final day when there will be no more sickness or sorrow, and you will wipe away every tear from my eye. Amen

Taking it to the Lord...

How can I apply this truth?____

____

____

Father, I've come to worship and praise you! You are my:__________________________

____

I give you all Glory, Honor, and Praise O Lord!

Father, I am sorry that I have sinned by:_______________________________________

Help me to repent. Cleanse me, strengthen me, restore me.

Father, THANK YOU for all your love, grace, mercy and blessings of life that you continually shower down upon me. Thank you especially for:

1.___________________________   2.___________________________

3.___________________________   4.___________________________

5.___________________________   6.___________________________

THANK YOU for answered prayers:____

Father, I need:____

Father, I ask that YOU:____

____

____

Lord, bless me that I may be a blessing. Give me Your heart for loving and serving others. Keep Your hand upon me. Keep me from all evil and harm, and let me cause harm to no one. Bind Satan that he have no power over me. All this I pray in subjection to your will and in the strong name of my Lord and Savior, Jesus Christ. Amen.